D1551728

The Handbook Of Emotion and Memory
Research and Theory

The Handbook Of Emotion and Memory
Research and Theory

Edited by

Sven-Åke Christianson
University of Stockholm
Sweden

1992

LAWRENCE ERLBAUM ASSOCIATES, PUBLISHERS
Hillsdale, New Jersey   Hove and London

WITHDRAWN

McCONNELL LIBRARY
RADFORD UNIVERSITY

Lawrence Erlbaum Associates, Inc., Publishers
365 Broadway
Hillsdale, New Jersey 07642

Library of Congress Cataloging-in-Publication Data

The Handbook of emotion and memory / edited by Sven-Åke Christianson.
        p.   cm.
    Includes bibliographical references and index.
    ISBN 0-8058-0704-7
    1. Emotions. 2. Memory. 3. Psychiatry.   I. Christianson, Sven
-Ake.
    BF311.H355 1991
    153.1'2--dc20   91-26351
                                                                           CIP

Printed in the United States of America
10 9 8 7 6 5 4 3

Contents

v

PART II
METHODOLOGICAL ISSUES

PART III
BIOLOGICAL ASPECTS

PART IV
CLINICAL OBSERVATIONS

Foreword

Extreme statements about the influence of emotion on memory are freely given. One place to find them is in reported legal cases, and here they are set in a particularly interesting context. Take the case of Commonwealth of Pennsylvania versus Anthony Gallagher (547 A.2d 355; 1988). The Gallagher case arose out of a nasty crime that occurred back in 1977. An intruder knocked on the door of the victim's home, claiming to be a police officer. Then he raped his victim and forced her into various sexual outrages.

Two weeks later, the victim saw photos, including Gallagher's, and she faced him live in a one-on-one confrontation. In neither case did she identify him. But 4 years later, she identified Gallagher from a photo display, and he was arrested and tried 5 years after the crime. The victim identified Gallagher at trial with great confidence.

At Gallagher's trial, the prosecution, wishing to bolster the victim's identification after such an extended lapse of time, called an expert witness on Rape Trauma Syndrome (RTS), Dr. B. She related her opinion of how the syndrome affects the identification process, and Gallagher was swiftly convicted.

Dr. B. had explained to the jury that a victim of rape has a flood of emotions about the rape that can readily persist over a 5-year period.

Something in the environment triggers the event and brings it back. "By bringing it all back," she was asked, "does it also bring the face back of the original assailant? Is that the kind of thing that would flash right back before you eyes?" "Oh, yes," Dr. B. answered.

In commenting on Dr. B's testimony, the majority opinion of the higher court summarized it succinctly: "the victim's failure to identify (Gallagher) two weeks after the rape is unremarkable, as she was in the acute phase of RTS . . . and the in-court identification five years later is particularly credible, as it results from a flashback, with the mind operating like a computer."

Although the court ultimately decided that the expert testimony should not have been admitted at trial (one witness should not comment on the credibility of another) and ordered a new trial for Gallagher, the published opinion provides us with one example of an extreme "theory" of emotion and memory freely offered to the public. Does scientific research support the proposition that a traumatic event leaves a memory trace that is "particularly credible," that can cause a "flashback," that works like a "computer"? As readers of this volume will learn, if the question were posed to researchers in emotion and memory, there would be considerable disagreement about the answer.

As the desire to understand the relationship between emotion and memory increases, whether it be for theoretical or applied reasons, so does the alliance increase among researchers from such diverse disciplines as cognitive psychology, neuroscience and clinical psychology. In this handbook, Sven Christianson has brought together experts in these areas of inquiry. Here, gathered in one volume, readers will learn about how cognitive, clinical, and biologically oriented scientists study emotion and memory from experiments, from field studies, and from case studies. Our understanding of the connection between emotion and memory is clearer from this vast array of work, but a number of points of disagreement remain. With the creation of a volume that so articulately provides us with both the accomplishments of the field and the points of disagreement, Christianson has given the brain, clinical, and cognitive sciences an invaluable resource that will be relied upon by 21st-century researchers as they develop their own approaches to the issues.

—Elizabeth F. Loftus

Preface

Emotion and memory is hardly a new theme in psychological research. Recently, however, interest in this subject has rapidly increased. We have to go back to Sigmund Freud's writings to find a similar interest. In fact, some of our leading researchers regard the topic of emotion and memory of key interest for psychological research during the next decade.

Today, studies on emotion and memory flourish in several diverse areas. Among the topics studied are arousal and memory, mood and memory, eyewitness memory, flashbulb memories, implicit and explicit emotional memories, traumatic amnesia, and emotional disorders and memory. The study of emotion and memory is indeed a complex enterprise.

Some of the specific issues under study include the following: What neural circuits and cellular mechanisms are critical to emotional memories? Does pronounced negative emotional arousal or a very bad mood inhibit or enhance one's ability to perceive and remember information from an emotional event? Is there a special memory mechanism or system involved when we create emotional memories; that is, do emotional memories have special characteristics that differ from those produced by "ordinary" memory mechanisms or systems? Do people with emotional disturbances remember differently than normal people? What factors play the most crucial role in traumatic amnesia?

Although extensive experimental and clinical research has been conducted on these issues over the past 20 years, it has never been compiled into a comprehensive volume. To date, the only resources are either general textbooks or edited volumes that address general aspects of emotion and cognition but do not cover in depth the current knowledge about the way memory in particular is affected by changes in our emotions. Not only is there no single volume devoted exclusively to this important area of psychological study, but there is no one volume that fully addresses the conceptual and methodological difficulties that this area presents. The chapters in this book represent the first attempt to provide a contemporary reference source on theory and research related to emotion and memory.

This volume fulfills three general objectives. First, it reviews and summarizes research findings from laboratory studies, field studies, and clinical studies concerning emotion and memory, where particular emphasis is accorded to empirical research on arousal and memory, mood and memory, implicit and explicit aspects of emotion and memory, biological aspects of emotion and memory, eyewitness memory, traumatic amnesia, and emotional disorders and memory. Second, it addresses conceptual and methodological difficulties that are associated with different paradigms and procedures currently used to study the relationship between emotion and memory. Third, the book presents broad theoretical perspectives to guide further research in the field of emotion and memory.

Content

The chapters in this volume are organized into four parts. Part I includes chapters outlining general perspectives on emotion and memory. Part II includes chapters dealing with the role of arousal and emotion in memory using different methodological approaches. The chapters in Part III present a biological–evolutionary perspective on emotion and memory. The chapters in the last section, Part IV, present research on emotion and memory from a clinical perspective.

A brief overview of the chapters ahead may be helpful at this point. In the first chapter of Part I, Bower provides a comprehensive discussion of what an emotion is—which is often neglected in studying the relationship between emotion and memory. Besides issues of emotion theory, Bower also discusses the role of motivation and emotion in controlling attention, and the learning and retrieval of memories and action plans. Bower argues that emotion directs attention to causally significant aspects of a discrepant situation, and that arousal of emotion retrieves associated thoughts, plans, and memories. He concludes that this selective retrieval underlies such phenomena as mood-congruent biases in thinking, preferences, judgment, learning, and mood–state-dependent-memory.

In chapter 2, Johnson and Multhaup discuss the role of emotion as a mediator in a long-term memory model called MEM (Multiple-Entry, Modular memory system). Looking at emotion from this framework, the chapter highlights many areas for future empirical investigation (e.g., the relation between cognitive development and emotional development; the relation between cognitive deficits and affective memory). Johnson and Multhaup also relate MEM to current knowledge about the neurobiology of emotion and cognition.

Most research on memory and emotional processes has focused on conscious, intentional recollection of some previous episodes (i.e., explicit memory). However, as noted by Tobias, Kihlstrom, and Schacter in chapter 3, there is more to memory than what an individual can bring to awareness, and that does not require conscious or intententional recollection of experiences (cf. implicit memory). This chapter focuses on implicit memory and addresses the bidirectional relation between emotional experience and implicit memory. The distinction between implicit and explicit memory has proved very useful in analyzing various memory findings and is also discussed in several other chapters in the book.

In chapter 4, Mandler presents a constructivist view of emotion and stresses the interaction of evaluative states and autonomic arousal. The way in which these two processes affect unconscious (implicit) and conscious (explicit) memories is discussed. Furthermore, recent research on the relation between stress and memory, and between mood and memory, is reviewed to illustrate the general principals of arousal and evaluative functions of emotion, and the interaction with memorial tasks.

The literature on arousal and memory produced during the last decades is extensive. The second part of the book (Part II) presents data and theory relevant to clarify the relationship between arousal, affect, and memory. Chapter 5 by Revelle and D. Loftus provides a review of the effects of global shifts of nonspecific arousal on memory. This review illustrates how an increase in arousal has systematic effects upon both immediate and delayed memory. The authors also consider how the effect of manipulations of affect and mood may be understood in terms of an intervening construct of arousal, and how individual differences in personality can clarify the relationship between arousal, emotion, and memory.

Chapter 6 by Reisberg and Heuer reviews the literature on emotion and memory with emphasis on memory for detailed information in emotionally arousing events. The authors question the claim that arousal or emotionality undermines memory accuracy for minute detail and argue that emotionality at the time of an event improves both memory for the event's core and memory for peripheral detail. As possible critical factors behind this pattern, Reisberg and Heuer discuss how subjects think about emotional events and the impact of arousal that accompanies emotion. In the following chapter Leichtman, Ceci, and Ornstein review empirical research on the role of emotion in children's memory. This specific issue is not only theoretically important; it is also one of the most controversial topics in emotion and memory research. The authors make clear that developmental memory researchers are still far from being able to offer a cohesive, integrative picture of the processes by which affect influences the unfolding memory system. However, among various views of the affect–memory linkage, the authors believe that an integrated trace explanation is the most promising in bringing a global perspective to children's memories studied in autobiographical studies and traditional laboratory settings.

Chapter 8 focuses on the role of emotions in eyewitness memory. The first half of this chapter is devoted to a critical evaluation of the experimental research dealing with the effects of emotion on eyewitness memory. Yuille and Tollestrup argue that the behavior of witnesses in laboratory research is not representative of that of witnesses to actual crimes. In the second half, the authors, advocating a field-study approach, present a model for how emotion may have an impact on so called "remarkable memories." Related questions are addressed in chapter 9 by Christianson, Goodman, and E. F. Loftus, who explore research methodology and highlight some inadequacies in research on eyewitness memory for emotional events. This chapter presents some distinctions that might be helpful in interpreting past findings and in guiding future research on eyewitness memory for stressful events. Chapter 9 also explores the ethical questions facing psychologists who are asked to provide testimony on this topic.

Part III represents the biological section of the book. Chapter 10 by McGaugh presents neurobiological evidence suggesting that memory can be influenced by treatments affecting brain systems (e.g., the amygdaloid complex) known to be activated by emotional

stimulation. According to McGaugh, an emotionally exciting experience activates the release of adrenalin and other stress-related
hormones, which play a crucial role in regulating long-term memory
storage of the experience. It is argued that the memory-modulating
effects of hormones and drugs are dose dependent, suggesting that
the strength of memories depends on the degree of emotional
activation, and that such effects might underlie long-lasting consequences as expressed in, for example, post-traumatic stress disorders.

In Chapter 11, LeDoux explores how the brain forms memories for
the emotional significance of events. In this chapter emotion is
treated as a memory process rather than as a process that simply
influences (facilitates or inhibits) memory. LeDoux argues that
different neural circuits underlie the memory for emotional significance of an event and the memory of the event itself. In discussing the
neural underpinnings for affective memories, the amygdala is considered as an "emotional computer" in the initial establishment of
these memories.

Chapter 12 by Nilsson and Archer deals with three aspects of stress
and memory from a psychobiological perspective: (a) remembering
deficits shown by persons suffering from affective disorders, (b)
stress- and separation-induced deficits in learning and memory
performance, and (c) stressful reactions causing disruptions of
electrophysiological correlates of learning and memory. In discussing different evidence from human and animal research, Nilsson and
Archer advocate the distinction between implicit and explicit memory
as a useful conceptualization of learning and memory in analyzing
clinical realities.

To round out Part III, chapter 13 by Christianson challenges a
unidimensional view of a simple relationship between emotion or
arousal and memory. In an effort to discuss potential underlying
mechanisms to various findings of traumatic memories, it is assumed that critical characteristics of emotional events may be
extracted and processed by a preattentive and automatic mechanism, which will act as an emotional prime and thus trigger attentional
selectivity and controlled memory processing mediated by more
evolved and sophisticated memory mechanisms. Some future directions of psychological–biological research on emotion and memory
are outlined.

Part IV presents research on emotion and memory from a clinical
perspective. The theoretical interpretations in this last part of the
book represent cognitive process-oriented theory, psychodynamic
theory, and personality-based explanations of the clinical observa-

tions. Chapter 14 by Horowitz and Reidbord explores aspects of memory in patients with post-traumatic stress disorders. The authors provide a description of post-traumatic experiential phenomena, with emphasis on their degree of conscious representation. In order to understand how cognitive processing can either admit or exclude memory-based emotions from consciousness, Horowitz and Reidbord present a theory of schemas (i.e., a schematic meaning structure as a form of generalized memory) that organizes complex emotional states. In a related chapter, Pennebaker and Harber explore the role of trauma-related memories in traumatic recovery. On the one hand, unwanted thoughts and memories of traumatic experiences cause post-traumatic stress; on the other hand, active inhibition of traumatic memories may compound traumatic recovery by inducing physical illness. To better understand this paradox, the authors outline a general theory of assimilation and dissociative processes in memory, where the main idea is that assimilation of thoughts and feelings surrounding traumatic events leads to positive health outcomes.

Chapter 16, by Treadway, McCloskey, Gordon, and Cohen presents two intensive case studies on functional amnesia. In contrast to typical cases of psychogenic amnesia, where the memory impairment is informationally specific and temporally general, the amnesias reported in this chapter are defined by the time at which the memories were acquired, rather than by the content of the memories. The authors introduce the idea that important life contexts might serve as landmarks around which memory is organized, and that dramatic changes in life context can cause functional dissociations among memories acquired during different time periods.

In chapter 17, Braun and Frischholz describe various memory deficits that have been observed in patients suffering from Multiple Personality Disorder (MPD). This chapter considers what MPD is and how it differs from other medical and psychiatric conditions. In this regard, the authors specifically focus on the difference between structural and functional memory deficits and how they are related to encoding, storage, and retrieval processes.

Chapters 18 and 19 are concerned primarily with emotional disorders and memory. In the former, Eysenck and Mogg focus on anxiety and memory. Although a negative recall bias has been demonstrated in depressive patients, this has proved extremely difficult to obtain in anxious patients. Eysenck and Mogg discuss possible reasons for this in the context of the theoretical distinction between explicit and implicit memory. In addition, various empirical findings are related to a general theory of anxiety, that emphasizes the effects of anxiety on the attentional system. In the concluding chapter, Williams relates memory in patients with emotional disorders (suicidal tendencies and depression) to findings from autobiographical research and findings from mood and memory. Williams discusses a deficiency in these patients in being able to be specific in their memory. It is argued that such a deficit arises out of an overgeneral encoding style that is compounded by difficulties at retrieval owing to preoccupation with recent life events. The implications of these findings for clinical work and for theories of autobiographical memory is discussed.

Taken together, the chapters in this volume show that the field of emotion and memory is a truly interdisciplinary undertaking, one of interest to clinical and experimental psychologists, neuropsychologists, neurologists, psychiatrists, psychotherapists, police departments, and lawyers. For both students and professionals interested in expanding their knowledge or conducting research in this field the book is an up-to-date and needed resource.

The planning and preparation of this volume started while the editor was a Visiting Scholar at the Department of Psychology, University of Washington, and was greatly aided by fellowship awards from the Fulbright Commission and from the Swedish Institute. I would like to thank Stuart Ostfeld and Ann Becherer for their help in correspondence and editing, and to Robert T. Croyle for valuable advice at an early stage of preparation of this book. Also, I express my appreciation to Elizabeth F. Loftus, not only for endless stimulating discussions on emotion and memory, but also for her support and encouragement. Finally, I wish to express my gratitude to the contributors for their responsiveness to suggestions and willingness to augment the quality of this book, and to Judith Amsel, Hollis Heimbouch, and their associates at Lawrence Erlbaum Associates for printing the book. It has been a great pleasure to cooperate with all of you.

—Sven-Åke Christianson

I

GENERAL PERSPECTIVES

How Might Emotions Affect Learning?

Gordon H. Bower
Stanford University

The relation of emotion to learning and memory is a vast, complex topic. In earlier writings on the topic (e.g., Bower, 1981; Bower & Cohen, 1982; Bower & Mayer, 1989), I have concentrated almost exclusively on the "memory" part of that relationship and used only an informal, layman's view of emotions. I advanced no particular conceptualization of what an emotion is, what taxonomies of emotions are plausible, what functions emotions might perform in a cognitive system, nor how they might be related to learning in general. Because several commentators have criticized my earlier neglect of these topics, I use this present opportunity to set forth my views on the broader issues of emotion theory before moving on to the more specialized topic of this handbook, namely, the relation of emotion to learning.

THE PLACE OF EMOTION IN A COGNITIVE ARCHITECTURE

One approach to theory development is to consider humans as biological machines endowed with a cognitive system (for acquiring and using knowledge), and to ask what role motives and emotions should play in such a system. This is the approach exemplified in treatments by Frijda (1986; Frijda & Swagerman, 1987), Oatley and Johnson-Laird (1987), Simon (1967), Sloman (1987; Sloman & Croucher, 1981), and Toda (1982). The following discourse borrows heavily from those writings.

Emotion is evolution's way of giving meaning to our lives. Our lives are ordered and organized by our needs, motives, and concerns. Human actions are guided and motivated, firstly, by biological needs and all the instrumental plans that developed to achieve them, and, secondly, by social-cognitive motives and goals, and plans that issue from them. Evolution has endowed most organisms with inherent nervous mechanisms for detecting and evaluating internal states and external environments as beneficial or harmful to their plans, as reinforcing or punishing. Events come to be evaluated according to the evaluations of the situations they bring about or terminate.

In order to operate successfully in its ecological niche, each goal-seeking biological system needs to have certain design characteristics:

1.   The system must have ways to detect the existence and urgency of its different needs and motive states.

2.   It must have some means for prioritizing these needs according to their importance, urgency, and delay ability.

3.   It must have some planning routines that can either construct an action plan or retrieve one from memory to pursue the satisfaction of whatever motive is accorded the foremost priority. The planner must be able to adjust its action sequence to the multiple constraints of the current situation; and it must be able to plan recursively to create subplans to deal with subgoals as they are generated. This ability requires both an *attention controller* that allocates processing resources to one among several prospective plans (and thereby inhibits competing plans), and a *working memory* that can keep track of the organism's place in its currently active plan as well as hold the stack of goals and subgoals it may generate while planning and/or executing a plan. The more adaptive, "intelligent" planners will be able to foresee and have methods to resolve conflicting plans, to schedule work on plans (e.g., allocating times of the day to work on them), and to create compromise plans that can satisfy several goals concurrently.

4.   The organism should have some sensors that monitor its internal and external environment for signals implicating its important concerns, and an ability to interrupt or suspend an ongoing plan in order to deal with an urgent crisis, whether positive or negative. This characterizes opportunistic planners that have a

collection of resident goals prepared to be triggered whenever their appropriate goal-stimulus happens by.

A system without these components will perish when confronted with an uncertain, largely hostile environment within which it must pursue satisfaction of its biological motives and concerns. A system with these components will exhibit "emotions" as a by-product of translating its concerns into goal-directed actions in such an unpredictable environment (Frijda, 1986, especially champions this view). Events appraised as achieving its concerns, or aiding plans to achieve them, lead to the positive emotions of pleasure, pride, delight, relief, and enjoyment. Events appraised as thwarting a plan, causing injury or loss of a goal-state, lead to the negative emotions of sadness, fear, and anger. The specific emotion depends on the circumstances and the cognitions surrounding the event.

The unpredictability of the environment plays a central role in the life of the emotions. Our best laid plans oft go awry because unanticipated events create new outcomes or block expected ones, leading to the largely negative emotions. Our emotional reactions are triggered by "computational demons" in the brain that monitor how our plans are faring during execution, whether they are progressing towards their anticipated conclusions, whether a given plan is taking too much time or effort, whether some goal has become unattainable, whether the outcomes match the intended goal-objects or goal-states, and so on. A given plan may fail because it was blocked or thwarted by an adversary (leading to anger); an expected goal-object may not be forthcoming (leading to disappointment or sadness); a new event may threaten us with injury, harm, or rejection (leading to fear).

In computational models of the system (e.g., Bower & Cohen, 1982; Dyer, 1987; Frijda & Swagerman, 1987), the emotional demons can be represented by a collection of production rules that specify a class of external situations that will be recognized as ones appropriate for turning on that emotion. For example, one rule for triggering an "anger demon" would recognize when someone deliberately harms us or causes us unpleasantness. Upon matching such a situation, the rule would fire, causing activation of an "anger emotion" in the system. In an earlier paper (Bower, 1981), this process was modeled as the activation of a specific emotion unit or node connected into an associative network.

Upon activation of a given emotion in a given situation, a collection of memories and a repertoire of action plans will be activated. In the classical learning theories of Hull (1943) and Estes (1958), motive (drive) states were presumed to have corresponding internal drive stimuli that entered into, and activated, stimulus–response associations. In particular, for biological motives like hunger and thirst, the responses associated to the drive stimulus would be those that in the past had been followed by reduction of the drive via successful consummation of the goal-object (the so-called "drive reduction" theory of reinforcement; see Miller, 1951).

For humans, an important kind of memory triggered by a primary emotional or motivational condition is the person's estimate (based on past experience) of his or her ability to cope with whatever threat has just arisen. Comparing a threat or danger to one's ability to cope with it is the process called *secondary appraisal* (by Lazarus, 1966), and it can either reduce or heighten the emotional activation caused by the initial threat.

The repertoire of responses made available by an emotional signal consists of several types. First, for signals of imminent injury, organisms have fast, preprogrammed reflexes for exhibiting startle (flinching, ducking, shrieking), orienting (pausing to listen intently, freezing), and possibly fleeing (running away) or fighting. These early reflexes are fast, often preemptive, difficult to inhibit, and associated with innate facial expressions. Second, as noted before, the action plans retrieved from memory are those that in the past have been generally appropriate to that motive or emotion in similar situations. The general plan is to approach and maintain contact with sources of positive emotions (e.g., good tastes, pleasant friends, beautiful scenery) and to remove or escape from sources of negative emotions. For example, fear retrieves plans for avoiding the danger, minimizing the threat, escaping the harm; anger retrieves plans for circumventing the frustration, removing or overcoming an obstacle, taking revenge upon an offending perpetrator. Many of these action plans are social and require interactions with others, to enlist aid, invite sympathy, bargain, intimidate, threaten, provide rewards (smiling), and so forth. Facial expressions of emotions often function for social communication between individuals; by appraising someone's facial expression, we pick up clues as to how to smooth or coordinate our interactions with them. We use the boss' facial expression to tell us whether it is best to ask for a raise now or to postpone the request.

Of particular interest to this chapter is the relation between the emotional or motivational state and the memories that it may call to mind. We return to this topic later after a digression on the development of emotions.

THE DEVELOPMENT OF EMOTIONS

Human emotions and emotional responses develop by a long process of acculturation acting upon an infant's biological substrate. Infant researchers agree that within the first year of life human infants display the facial expressions and gross action patterns appropriate to basic emotions such as fear, anger, sadness, affection, and joy. These emotions can be elicited by reasonably simple stimuli (e.g., a loud startling noise; confinement of movements; tickling), they have an almost reflex-like quality and tend to be cross-cultural. As time passes, infants develop a broader range of emotions and a more complex, differentiated set of emotional appraisals involving more culturally specific interpretations of situations involving emotional displays. Different observers have classified and organized these inter-related families of appraisals into hierarchies of emotional categories. For example, Shaver, Schwartz, Kirson, and O'Connor (1987) proposed a hierarchy with three layers, from superordinate (groupings of positive or negative emotions) to basic, universal emotions, thence to subordinate emotions (more differentiated and specific to different situations). Their proposed hierarchy is depicted in Fig. 1.1.

The basic emotions are presumably universal, biologically based, present from infancy, and have associated facial expressions and primitive action scripts. Their names are typically the first emotion words that children learn, and words referring to them (or close equivalents) exist in most cultures. One can dispute whether Fig. 1.1 has listed all the basic emotions (for example, Ekman, 1984, would add *disgust* to the list). However, the general layout of the emotion domain in Fig. 1.1 seems intuitively compelling.

The superordinate groupings into positive and negative emotions abstractly characterize events that either produce beneficial gains or noxious losses. In behavioristic parlance, they describe positive or negative reinforcers. Children appear to learn very early labels to apply to people, events, and situations that arouse these generic emotions: They are termed *nice, like, good* versus *bad, mean, don't like*. This positive/negative polarity exists in all cultures and seems fundamental to human cognition (see, e.g., Osgood, Suci, & Tannenbaum, 1957).

The subordinate emotions (only a few are shown in Fig. 1.1) develop in later years as differentiations and refinements within the basic-level categories. These are often more complex, socially constructed emotions such as pride, jealousy, resentment, and guilt.

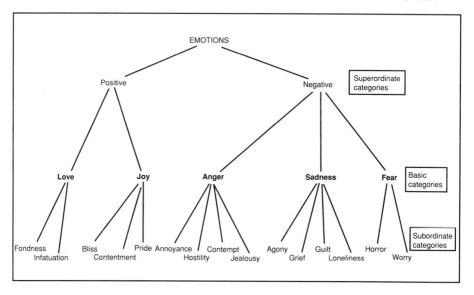

FIG. 1.1. A simplified version of the emotion hierarchy reported by Shaver et al. (1987). Only a few of the subordinate emotions are included here. (Reproduced by permission from "How emotions develop and how they organize development," by K. W. Fischer, P. R. Shaver, & P. Carnochan, in *Cognition and Emotion, 4*, 1990, 81–127.)

Children only gradually learn how to apply labels for subordinate emotions as they come to discriminate relevant features of social success versus failure, of accidental versus intentional actions, and of moral responsibility (see Stein & Levine, 1989). The subordinate emotions display considerable variation across cultures and across different historical periods within a culture. Some subordinate terms designate a constellation of basic emotions elicited in a given social relationship; for example, *jealousy* involves both fear of loss (of a loved one) and anger at the loved one for threatening to withdraw his or her affection.

Taxonomies of Emotion Terms

Attempts to classify human emotions and to analyze their subtypes inevitably encounter the vagaries of emotional language, and the imprecise way linguistic terms map onto human experience (e.g., Fehr & Russell, 1984). For all practical purposes, human experience is infinitely diverse; yet, to communicate we need some words and concepts to classify our many experiences. There are over 600 words in English alone referring to affective experiences; yet few of us would claim that there are that many distinctly different types of emotions. But how can one decide what is to serve as a label for a basic emotion in a hierarchy such as Fig. 1.1? What is to count as the name of an emotion as distinct from some alternative type of psychological state?

The classification and taxonomy of the emotion domain is a topic of currently active debate. One attractive taxonomy provided by Johnson-Laird and Oatley (1989; Oatley & Johnson-Laird, 1987), identifies five basic or primitive emotions. Each emotion corresponds to some juncture in the goal-planning process. Specifically, *happiness* arises when some goal is achieved, sadness when some major goal is lost or plan fails, anxiety when a self-preservation goal is threatened, *anger* when an active plan is frustrated, and *disgust* when a gustatory goal is violated (see Oatley & Johnson-Laird, 1987, Table 1, p. 36).

Another taxonomy, provided by Ortony, Clore, and Collins (1988; also Clore & Ortony, 1988), followed upon an earlier semantic analysis of the affective lexicon by Ortony, Clore, and Foss (1987). These authors start with the observation that the 600-plus items in the affective lexicon comprise an amalgam of poetic metaphors, slang, extensions, historical accidents, and conceptual confusions. They argue that any serious scientific investigation must begin by carefully distinguishing between what is "properly" considered to be an emotion term as opposed to the many nonemotional terms found amongst the affective lexicon of English. The taxonomy of Ortony et al. (1987) distinguishes, first, between terms referring to external conditions that may cause emotions as opposed to internal conditions. Thus, terms like *abandoned*, *neglected*, *lonely*, *guilty*, *safe*, or *quiet* refer first and foremost to objective factual descriptions of a person's situation or behavior but are not themselves emotion terms. They are judged to be not emotion terms because it is entirely sensible for them to fit in the frame "I am X even though I do not feel X." An alternative indicator is that people rate "feeling x" *(guilty, abandoned,* etc.) as more like a prototypical emotion than "being X." Thus, although "feeling abandoned" may refer to a complex of emotions (such as fear and sadness) typically associated with a given external condition, *abandoned* itself does not designate a basic emotion. It appeared to be an emotion term only because of various tricks of ellipsis in English, whereby expressions like "I'm lonely" come to serve as short-hand for "I have those feelings typically experienced by someone who believes he or she is alone and who does not like it."

A second distinction in their taxonomy is between words describing mental versus nonmental conditions. The latter include terms referring to physical and bodily states such as *sleepy, nauseous, aroused,* and *faint.* Subjects rated these either as not emotions at all or as very poor examples. In further semantic brush clearing, Ortony et al. (1987) noted distinctions between affective terms that refer to occurrent states (that might be emotions) versus traits, the latter referring to long-term dispositions or frames of mind, captured in names such as attitude, trait, or temperament. Occurrent states refer to a present feeling that "grips" someone; a trait or frame of mind refers to the disposition to experience a given occurrent state. Thus, *terror, ecstasy,* and *disgusted* are labels for occurrent states, whereas devoted, *bitchy,* and *shy* are labels for traits or frames of mind. Some terms are ambiguous and can be used to refer either to a state or a trait (e.g., "He's angry now" vs. "He's an angry person"). The emotional trait is ascribed to someone when the occurrent state in question is easily and frequently provoked. Thus, we say that a man has hostility as a trait if he is frequently and easily provoked to feel anger.

An oft-noted feature of our emotional system is that it soon *adapts* to fixed environmental conditions, much as a homeostatic mechanism corrects deviations from its equilibrium point. Emotions are primarily spasmodic reactions to changes in our fortunes or life circumstances, such as learning that we have just inherited great wealth or have a fatal disease; such "emotional events" produce massive autonomic discharge and endocrine (adrenal) secretions that pump up our heart rate, breathing rate, sweating, blood-pressure, and so on. But the physiological reactions dissipate in several minutes or hours, as our autonomic nervous system returns to baseline. Our emotional adaptation to ambient life circumstances is somewhat analogous to the adaptation of the retina of the eye to a new level of light or darkness. We adjust eventually to our new conditions, and events come to be evaluated *relative* to our new expectations, to the ambient frequencies of "good" and "bad" things as newly defined. This adaptation to prevailing life circumstances plus the relativity of what's an "improvement" may be the reason that objective measures of social-economic status often correlate very poorly with people's subjective sense of well-being or "happiness."

Following upon their semantic analysis, Ortony, Clore, and Collins (1988) classified types of emotions in terms of three broad classes, distinguished by whether the attentional focus of the affect is on events, agents, or objects. One can be pleased or displeased about desirable or undesirable events, approve or disapprove of someone, and like or dislike some object. These categories may be further subdivided by whether the focus is on oneself or another person, whether the event has occurred or is prospective, and so on. Thus, we can be *happy-for* the good fortune of a loved one, or *gloat* over the bad fortune of an enemy. We feel *satisfied* when a hoped-for gain is confirmed, *disappointed* when it is disconfirmed, and *relieved* when a feared loss is avoided. We feel *pride* (vs. *shame)* when we approve (vs. disapprove) of something we have done, *admiration* (vs. *reproach*) when we approve (vs. disapprove) of what someone else has done. The outcome of these distinctive features is a taxonomy that distinguishes 22 basic emotion types according to the constellation of their eliciting mental attributes rather than objective circumstances. Each type of emotion constellation tends to have at least a few labels in the affective lexicon (Ortony, 1987). The 22 types include *joy, distress, fear, relief, disappointment, shame, anger,* and *love,* among others.

Another distinction frequently discussed in this literature is that between emotion and mood. An emotion has many of the properties of a reaction: It often has an identifiable cause or stimulus; it is usually a brief, spasmodic, intense experience of short duration; and the person is typically much aware of it. Emotional states typically have bodily concomitants the person is well aware of. A mood tends to be more subtle, longer lasting, less intense, more in the background, a frame of mind, casting a positive or negative light over experiences. Moods tend to be relatively nonspecific (e.g., only happy/sad/anxious; or energetic/lethargic) compared to emotions that are far more specific and differentiated. People may not be aware of their mood until their attention is drawn to it. Mood variations may be caused by disturbances in biogenic amines in the brain, disturbed sleep–waking biorhythms, the weather, illness, sore muscles, an accumulation of unpleasant events, and so on (see Thayer, 1989, for a review). To compound the terminological confusions, one of the causes of a mood is the persisting after-effects of a strongly aroused emotional state. Thus, if a person has just experienced considerable sadness due to reflecting upon, say, his or her failed marriage, those somber feelings may persist for several minutes or hours as a "sad mood," especially if the person occasionally thinks again of the saddening events. This is the method by which happy or sad moods are typically induced in people serving as subjects for research on mood and memory (see Kenealy, 1986).

Scripts for Emotions?

Earlier we indicated that arousal of a given emotion activated a repertoire of responses or action plans. Fischer, Shaver, and Carnochan (1990) have suggested further that each emotion (they confine it to the "basic" emotions in Fig. 1.1) has a corresponding generic "script" associated with it in memory. Like the scripts described by Schank and Abelson (1977) for routine activities, the proposed emotion scripts would describe prototypical events and list a set of antecedent (triggering) conditions, the generic participants who have roles to play in the script, a set of attributions and responses, and (in the case of negative emotions) a set of coping or self-control procedures. For example, a typical script for anger would list "illegitimate interruption or harm" by someone as an antecedent; protest, fight, or retaliate against the perpetrator as possible responses; and suppression or counting-to-ten might serve as self-control procedures.

Such scripts supposedly develop during childhood as the child learns to recognize more conditions for elicitation of the emotion (e.g., empathic anger on behalf of a friend who's been treated unjustly) and learns a larger repertoire of appropriate actions. This script knowledge is used to understand the emotions that situations elicit in others, to predict their actions, and to guide one's own actions when the eliciting conditions arise.

My own view is that the script-construct implies far more specificity and definiteness of actions than Fischer et al. (1990) require for emotional situation-reaction pairs. And if the script is very abstract and not reasonably specific, then it loses its predictive value relative to our common-sense understanding of emotional reactions. In fact, Schank, who originally proposed the script idea, later argued against them as a means for recording individual experiences, even those with routine activities (Schank, 1982). He has argued instead for using more flexible schema (called Memory Organizing Packets, MOPs) that can be more easily assembled to describe and record in memory the diversity of human experience. Experimental evidence for MOPs in human memory has been reported by McKoon, Ratcliff, and Seifert (1989).

Memory and Attention to Anomalies

It is a commonplace that what we encode and remember from an event depends on our attention—whether we attended to it at all, how much, and to which of its aspects. The more attention paid to some aspect of an event, the more securely it is encoded into memory; this is achieved by relating it to other concepts, themes, and events in our memory. One of the major determinants of attention is the *interestingness* of the event or some aspect of the information; but an event or some information is interesting to us primarily because it is either anomalous (unexpected) or is affectively arousing. Thus we pay more attention to unpredicted anomalies, and as a consequence learn more about them.

This central idea, that encoding is driven by expectation failures and error correction, is a common theme in learning theory. Leon Kamin (1969) used it to explain the phenomena of blocking and overshadowing in classical conditioning. Rescorla and Wagner (1972) elevated it to an axiom of their learning theory, whereby conditioning was seen as reducing the discrepancy between what the organism expected and what reinforcement prevailed on a given learning trial. In the connectionist PDP models of Rumelhart and McClelland (1986), the delta rule for adjusting weights between neural units in a learning network is an error-correction method that aims to minimize the error between the actual output of the network and the desired output for a given stimulus pattern. Feigenbaum (1959; Feigenbaum & Simon, 1961) in the original EPAM model used errors to develop more finely articulated discrimination nets during learning of strings of letters or paired associates, whereas correct responses caused no revisions of the network (i.e., no learning). Schank (1982) and his colleagues (Schank & Osgood, 1990; Kolodner, 1983a, 1983b) have argued that the growing and organizing of knowledge should be centered around expectation failures and differences from norms. Schank and Osgood (1990) have proposed that, when storing memory for an event, one's emotional reaction to it could serve as a useful index that the mind uses for later locating a similar emotional memory when we need to be reminded.

The relevance of this discussion about expectation failures in a chapter on emotion and memory is that such failures and surprises are also likely to be causes of emotional reactions (see Mandler, 1984, for an interruption theory of emotion). When a plan that is normally successful becomes blocked due to some unsatisfied side condition, that interruption causes frustration that mobilizes attention and new learning that has two goals: (a) to search for some way to modify the plan to deal with the immediate blockage, and (b) to identify the unsatisfied precondition and devise means to avoid its recurrence on future occasions. For example, if after eating at a restaurant we discover we have left our wallet at home and cannot pay the bill, we (a) leave our watch with the proprietor as collateral as we return home for our wallet, and (b) devise procedures for checking for our wallet in the future before going out again to a restaurant. Another example of surprise is that an action that receives an unexpected consequence, perhaps an unusually large or small payoff relative to expectation, will cause an emotional reaction (of delight or disappointment, respectively), which will then modify the relevant outcome expectations.

Emotional Controls of Attention

In the prototypical examples cited, the emotional reaction to the discrepant outcome causes the person to focus attention on the relevant feature of the situation that might explain (or have caused) the failure, as a result of which the person learns how to refine his or her expectations and actions accordingly. This focusing is adaptive. In addition to controlling attention to selected aspects of the external environment, a strong affective reaction after an event also causes the reactivation, rehearsal, or "mulling over" in working memory of the encoded version of that event. Whereas the emotional system is fast to react mentally to some threat or upset, it also engages the autonomic nervous system and hormone system; these release hormones into the blood stream, and this creates a persistent arousal and activation of whatever thoughts are salient in the cognitive system (see Gold, 1990; McGaugh, 1983). This arousal persists for several minutes and has an effect analogous to involuntary recycling, rehearsal, and reimaging of the events leading up to the emotional reaction. Such rehearsal enhances the degree of learning of whatever has been encoded of the emotional experience.

Beyond this immediate physiological arousal that continues for several minutes, our minds have a tendency to return repeatedly and spontaneously to memories of emotionally upsetting events. Who has not replayed in imagination a particularly upsetting insult (given or received), a traumatic accident and injury, a tender scene of exchanged affections, a heart-rending parting from a lover? The repetition seems to be especially prominent with negative, aversive events. We ruminate and go over these emotionally loaded events again and again as though trying to habituate their painfulness. The rumination or replaying may continue for brief spasms distributed over many hours, even days, but with dwindling frequency and emotional impact as we habituate to the experience. The memories of these events are connected to such strong emotions that we seem barely able to suppress intrusive thoughts of them (see Horowitz, 1988). It is as though the upsetting thought lies barely submerged below consciousness as we try to occupy ourselves with the busy work of daily chores; but it lies ready to spring into consciousness the moment we disengage our attention from other chores—for example, when we try to fall asleep at night. Aberrations of this ruminative process appear to underlie emotional disturbances such as pathological grief, depression, and post-traumatic stress disorder (Horowitz, 1988).

Summarizing the foregoing, emotional reactions play three separate functional roles in directing learning of associated events. First, emotions frequently accompany failed expectations (or interruptions) and thus direct attention to the preceding or accompanying events as important items to be learned. Second, emotions mobilize attention to features of an external situation that learners judge to be significant or predictive of the failed expectation, and, in so doing, caused them to encode or learn about them. Third, the inertial persistence of the emotional arousal, and its slow decay, leads to continued recycling or rehearsal of those encoded events viewed as causally belonging to the arousal. All three of these are factors that will usually promote better learning of relevant emotional material.

Psychological Evidence for Emotional Selectivity in Memory

Considerable evidence suggests the validity of the preceding account, at least in broad outline. First, as a general principle, events associated with strong emotional reactions tend to be well learned, and usually more so (within limits) the stronger the reaction. As one example, the level of classical conditioning of emotional reactions (e.g., fear of shock) depends directly on the amplitude of the unconditioned reaction to the unconditional stimulus (see, e.g., Mackintosh, 1974). Similar findings are common in studies of human verbal learning. For example, Dutta and Kanungo (1967) had Bengali students read bogus "scientific personality surveys" that attributed to their own group some desirable and some undesirable personality traits and attributed to an adversarial ethnic group a similar collection of some positive and negative traits. The students rated the intensity of their affective reaction to each attribution (of a trait to a group) their degree of liking or disliking of each "fact." Later, when asked to free recall the trait attributions, subjects recalled far more of those adjectives that had evoked more intense affective reactions. The memory advantage for highly affective material was the same for negative as for positive reactions to the material.

Similar benefits for memory of strong emotional reactions have been often reported for autobiographical memories (e.g., Holmes, 1970). A recent example is a detailed study by Brewer (1988), whose college-student volunteers recorded and rated time-sampled daily events (cued by a random beeper) over a 13-day period, with memory tested at the end of that time, or 23, or 46 days later. Among many results, Brewer found that a strong determinant of memory for an event was how much emotion it had originally aroused; this correlation held equally well whether the experience was pleasant or unpleasant. Other strong correlates of an event's memorability were its infrequency and uniqueness or distinctiveness. Highly frequent, routine events (e.g., a student studying in his room) were rapidly forgotten. But highly distinctive events that rarely occurred (e.g., an argument with one's faculty adviser) were remembered very well. Such rare events were also often associated with strong emotional reactions. This correlation seems built into our social ecology: We arrange our world so that our goals are satisfied routinely in an expected manner, so that we avoid unpleasant surprises; therefore, by designing our own environment, strong emotional incidents are kept at low frequency. Besides being often emotional, infrequent types of events probably also gain in memorability due to the nature of indexing in most retrieval systems. In any memory-indexing scheme for locating events in storage, retrieval would always be easier for those rare events indexed by whatever unique or distinctive features set them apart from the routine cases. The previous considerations argue that rare cases would be indexed by their unusual features about which our standard expectations fail. Brewer's results are consistent with this line of argument.

We hypothesized that, compared to neutral events, emotional ones will receive higher priority in processing and will persist longer in working memory, so that they will be better remembered in standard circumstances. This hypothesis is supported by introspection as well as by considerable evidence from learning experiments. To take just one example, consider a study of free recall of names of pictures of unrelated common objects (Ellis, Detterman, Runcie, McCarver, & Craig, 1971). After studying then recalling several lists of 15 unrelated, neutral objects (to obtain a baseline), the subjects studied a final list whose eighth item was an emotionally-surprising photograph of a human nude. Free recall of this final list yielded the serial-position curve shown in Fig. 1.2.

In comparison to the serial-position curve for the baseline condition, that for the critical list revealed three effects, (a) elevated free recall of the emotional (eighth) item itself, (b) clearly lowered recall for several items that were presented just following the emotional item, and (c) slightly lowered recall of a few items just preceding the critical item. Our hypothesis predicts just these effects: The affective reaction aroused by the nude photograph gives it priority in a rehearsal buffer. Consequently, the critical event would (a) prematurely terminate rehearsal in working memory of the last few items preceding the emotional item, (b) exaggerate rehearsal of that critical item, and (c) due to its continued high priority in the rehearsal loop, the critical item would cause subsequent items to receive less than normal processing. The subsequent items would be poorly processed either because they do not enter working memory or do not receive the same amount of rehearsal as baseline items because working memory capacity has been taken up by the emotional item.

On Irrelevant Emotions. A corollary of the idea that emotional reactions soak up processing resources is that reactions to some emotionally significant event or feature A can detract from processing information about some concurrent, independent event B, with the consequence that the person stores in memory very little about event B. Such "distraction" appears to be operative in those circumstances when emotions create decrements in performances, including learning and retrieval. For example, very depressed or anxious people are usually poor learners because their working memory is so preoccupied or "filled" with ruminations associated with their emotions. Thus, students with test anxiety may be ruminating so extensively about their probable failure on a test that they have little attentional resources left over to concentrate on the retrieval cues in the test questions and sort out the relevant answers those cues should evoke.

This hypothesis is similar to the resource allocation theory of Ellis and Ashbrook (1988, 1989), who wrote (1988): "The essence of the resource allocation model, in accounting for the effects of generally disruptive mood states on memory, is to assume that emotional states regulate the amount of capacity that can be allocated to some criterion task. Most tasks involving memory of information require some allocation of capacity and thus the effect of a disruptive mood state is to reduce the amount of capacity for processing the criterion task" (p. 26). Ellis and Ashbrook review a number of findings consistent with the idea that emotional states that are *irrelevant* or unrelated to the learning material will lead to poor learning and/or retrieval. Although most decrements arise from negative emotions such as depression and anxiety, a recent report (Ellis, 1990) also found poorer memory (than controls) due to irrelevant elation as well as depression. (These mood states had been induced by the Velten procedure.) In a further study Ellis had subjects verbalize their concurrent thoughts while working on a difficult learning task.

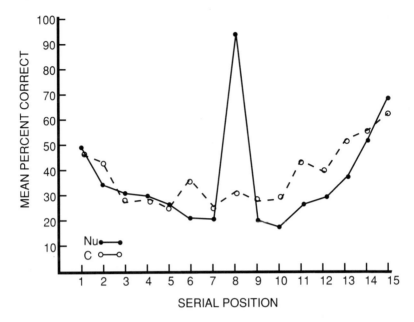

FIG. 1.2.   Percentage recall of names of pictures according to their
position in the list. The critical list (Nu, solid curve) contained a
photograph of a nude in serical position 8, whereas the noncritical list
(C, dashed curve) used only the familiar, unemotional pictures.
(Reproduced by permission from "Amnesic effects in short-term
memory," by N. R. Ellis et al., (1971) *Journal of Experimental Psychology*,
89, 357–361.)

He observed that elated as well as depressed subjects expressed
nearly twice as many task-irrelevant thoughts as did neutral-mood
control subjects. Moreover, the greater the proportion of task-
irrelevant thoughts subjects had articulated, the poorer was their
later recall of the central task (the two variables correlated –.67). Just
such a correlation is expected by the resource allocation hypothesis.

On Emotional Selectivity of Focus

To continue this review, it is important to note that what one
remembers from an emotional episode depends critically on which
features or aspects the emotion causes the person to focus on. This
selectivity of learning has been shown very clearly in research by
Christianson and his colleagues (Christianson, 1984; Christianson &
Loftus, 1987, 1991; Christianson & Nilsson, 1984). The Christianson
and Loftus (1987) study is especially clear in making the important
distinction between central versus peripheral features of an emo-

tionally arousing scene. They show that the central element of an emotional scene is better encoded and remembered than is a similarly central element in a neutral scene; however, peripheral features of the emotional scene are more poorly remembered than are comparable neutral elements. To illustrate, subjects in the first experiment by Christianson and Loftus saw a series of 15 neutral slides depicting a mother leaving home with her 7-year-old son, walking with him towards school, passing through a park, a downtown area, catching a taxi to drop him off at school, later placing a phone call and returning to her home. For half the subjects the middle five slides (hailing a taxi, etc.) were replaced by slides showing the boy being hit by a car, lying bleeding profusely upon the car's hood, being transported by ambulance to a hospital, and the mother entering and eventually leaving the hospital. These "emotional" slides were known to provoke elevated galvanic skin responses as indicators of emotional arousal. Each slide was shown for 3 seconds followed by a 7-second blank interval during which the subject recorded a word or phrase indicating the central theme or feature of the scene just viewed. For example, for the slide of the boy lying bleeding on the hood of the car, a subject might record "blood" or "head injury." Following presentation of the slides, subjects were tested either 20 minutes or 2 weeks later for recall (of their central-theme words) and then recognition of the slides. Recognition was tested by four-alternative multiple choice, pitting each presented slide against three others that were of the same thematic objects but taken from a different angle or perspective, or which showed somewhat different background details (e.g., another car passing on the road beyond the accident car).

Comparing memory in the two groups, the results were very clear. Subjects who saw the emotional slides recalled their "thematic" encodings of those slides more than control subjects recalled their encodings of the nonemotional slides in comparable serial positions. However, recognition accuracy was poorer for the exact emotional (accident) slides shown than for neutral slides, either those shown before and after the accident, or those shown to control subjects who viewed only the neutral, nonaccident sequence. This pattern of results held just as strongly at the 2-week retention test as at the 20 minute test. Moreover, a telephone interview with subjects 6 months later found that the central theme of the slide sequence could be remembered by 89% of subjects who had viewed the emotional slides compared to 52% of those who had viewed the neutral slides.

The main conclusion is that people will recall better the central idea of an emotional event but may so focus on this central feature that they fail to encode the peripheral details of that scene. Christianson and Loftus (1991) reported further demonstrations of this principle in experiments varying the nature of the background and peripheral details (see also Christianson & Nilsson, 1984).

Mood Congruity in Cognition

The idea that emotional arousal directs attention has been played out in another set of studies, those concerned with mood-congruity effects in cognition. The hypothesis is that people in a given emotional or mood state will give more attention to stimulus events, objects, or situations that are affectively congruent with their emotional state. In effect, these are stimuli whose typical effect is to maintain or preserve the person's current emotional state. Thus, happy people find pleasant stimuli—words, descriptions, pictures, people, music—more attractive, salient, and attention provoking; as a result, such stimuli receive deeper processing and are better learned. Paradoxically, sad people seem to prefer the opposite types of stimuli—serious, somber, nostalgic music, movies, or stories—and such stimuli receive deeper processing when people are in a somber mood.

A variety of these effects were extensively reviewed in an earlier paper (Bower, 1991). As one illustration, one of my students, Colleen Kelley (cited in Bower, 1983), induced college students to feel temporarily happy or sad, then had them inspect a series of photographic slides at their own pace, dwelling on each according to its interest to them. Half the slides were of pleasant scenes—people laughing, playing, or celebrating victories; half were of unpleasant scenes—slides depicting people's failures, rejections, defeats, funerals, the aftermath of disasters. Unbeknownst to subjects, Kelley recorded how much time they looked at each slide. She found that when viewers were happy they spent more time looking at happy scenes rather than unpleasant ones; when they were sad, they spent more time dwelling on the sad scenes. This is selective exposure to materials that agree with the viewer's mood. Often subjects were not aware they were biased in this manner. Perhaps as a consequence of their different exposure times, happy subjects also freely recalled more happy pictures; sad subjects recalled more sad pictures.

A similar preference was found in unpublished experiments by M. Snyder (personal communications, March 7, 1988; May 10, 1990). His subjects indicated their preferences for viewing briefly described movie film-clips to judge as part of a mock consumer survey.

Subjects made temporarily depressed (by the Velten procedure) chose to look at more serious, somber films than did subjects who were temporarily elated. In later studies, sad subjects also selected more sad nostalgic music to listen to than did happy subjects; sad subjects also indicated that in the coming weeks they intended to spend a greater percentage of their time on somber, serious, and solitary activities, whereas elated subjects intended to spend more time in light-hearted, sociable, enjoyable activities. So, here again, subjects were selecting activities and exposing themselves to situations that would tend to maintain their current mood states.

A pattern of exposure and recall results similar to Kelley's were obtained by Forgas and Bower (1987) in a study of social-impression formation. Their subjects were first made to feel happy or sad by bogus feedback about their scores on a "personality test." A few minutes later they formed an impression of a stranger by reading (self-paced line by line on a CRT) some statements describing his prosocial, desirable behaviors mixed among some statements describing some of his unattractive behaviors. We found that happy subjects spent longer dwelling on descriptions of the stranger's positive, sociable behaviors, whereas unhappy subjects dwelled longer on his negative, unattractive behaviors. A later rating of the stranger's personality showed the expected bias, with happy subjects rating him far more likable, sociable, attractive, and intelligent than did the unhappy subjects. When later asked to recall the behavioral descriptions they had read, happy subjects recalled more positive than negative attributes, whereas unhappy subjects recalled more negative than positive descriptions. The theory suggests that these results arose because people pay more attention to, and process more "deeply," mood-congruent stimuli. A possibly related consequence is that mood-congruent statements (or scenes) more often cause the perceiver to be *reminded* of similar autobiographic incidents due to mood-congruent retrieval; whereas such remindings increase processing time, they also enhance later memory for the evoking stimulus that is thus elaborated (see Anderson, 1985, for why elaboration enhances memory).

The better learning of mood-congruent material does not require greater subject-controlled exposure to such material. A similar advantage arises even when the experimenter controls the subjects' exposure time to the positive and negative material (see e.g., Bower & Mayer, 1989). Among various hypotheses offered to explain this advantage, the author favors that which attributes the effect to more elaborative processing and more plentiful associations evoked during the study of mood-congruent material.

Emotionally Congruent Biases

In addition to these preferences for mood-congruent situations, the emotion activation hypothesis also predicts a collection of emotional biases in attributions, thought patterns, inferences, and interpretations of ambiguous situations. In an earlier paper I wrote (Bower, 1983):

> When emotions are strongly aroused, concepts, words, themes, and rules of inference that are associated with that emotion will become primed and highly available for use by the emotional subject. We can thus expect the emotional person to use top-down or expectation-driven processing of his social environment. That is, his emotional state will bring into readiness certain perceptual categories, certain themes, certain ways of interpreting the world that are congruent with his emotional state; these mental sets then act as interpretive filters of reality and as biases in his judgments. (p. 395).

In that paper evidence was reported demonstrating how temporarily induced moods of happiness, sadness, or anger gave rise to mood-congruous biases in people's free associations, their imaginative fantasies, snap judgments of their acquaintances, their momentary self-concept, and their attributional style. For example, happy subjects tend to give very charitable, benevolent opinions about themselves, and their acquaintances, and they view the future with optimism. Sad subjects tend to be just the opposite, denigrating themselves, blaming failures on their incompetence, and being relatively pessimistic about the future and their efficacy in coping with various problems. Temporarily happy people attribute their successes to their ability and their failures to bad luck, whereas temporarily depressed people have the opposite attributional biases.

Mood-State Dependent Retrieval

Memory is said to be mood-state dependent in case the memories that subjects store when they are in one emotional state are more retrievable later if they re-enter that same emotional state; and their recall is worse if they attempt recall in a different emotional state from original learning. This is an example of a general "context" effect of the type that has been found when people learn and recall in different rooms, different postures or arousal states, different times of day, different drug states, and even above versus below water. Such effects are typically small (5 to 10%) but have been frequently reported (for some exceptions, see Fernandez, & Glenberg, 1985). In mood-dependent retrieval (MDR), recall is supposed to be better the greater the similarity of the retrieval mood is to that prevailing during learning.

MDR has proven to be an elusive phenomenon, appearing and disappearing in different experiments with exasperating unpredictability (at least to me). Enough solid demonstrations of MDR exist to resolve doubts about it being a spurious artifact (for recent demonstrations, see Bullington, 1990; Kuiken, 1989; Lewis & Williams, 1989). However, researchers are still trying to sort out the crucial experimental conditions for producing MDR in the laboratory.

From the current state of research on MDR, several tentative generalizations seem warranted. First, unless the moods induced are fairly intense and the two mood conditions are rather different from one another, then MDR is not likely to occur. This follows, of course, from the premise that MDR reflects a failure of items learned in one condition (mood) to *generalize* to the other, and generalization is more likely to fail the more dissimilar two conditions are. Second, MDR is rarely observed with recognition memory tests or strongly cued recall tests; it is most likely to be observed with free recall, when subjects have to generate their own "internal" retrieval cues for the target material (Eich, 1980). Third, MDR is most reliably observed when people retrieve autobiographical memories in different mood states. For example, when asked to report an "unselected" sample of incidents from their childhood, sad subjects will recall a higher proportion of unhappy incidents whereas happy subjects will recall more happy incidents. This is mood-dependent retrieval (i.e., the input and output moods match) insofar as subjects presumably felt appropriately happy or sad when the incidents occurred originally. In contrast, MDR is less reliable when subjects learn and recall artificial material in laboratory tasks in different mood states. Fourth, when the target material is learned in the laboratory, MDR has proven to be more reliable when the material is largely generated by subjects themselves from their long-term memory. Examples would include having subjects generate 10 free associates to several words or first letters (e.g., associates of *life,* or words beginning with F), or having them recall a set of autobiographic memories produced to cues on an earlier occasion (e.g., some life incident suggested by the cue *lake).* Eich (1990; Eich & Metcalfe, 1989) has reported especially strong, replicable MDR effects in experiments meeting these conditions.

The last two boundary conditions suggest a tentative hypothesis. Let us suppose that subjects associate an emotion with a stimulus or situation only if they causally relate their emotional reaction to the occurrence of that stimulus. If subjects causally attribute their emotional reaction to the material—if they perceive the two as "causally belonging" together—then we hypothesize that they will form a strong association in memory between the stimulus event and the emotion it evoked. According to this view, contiguity alone of the two events, without belongingness, will produce only weak or non-existent associations (see Thorndike, 1932). This hypothesis makes sense in terms of ecological validity. Organisms should associate their emotional reactions to those events that either evoked or removed those emotions. In this way, they are enabled to react appropriately upon recurrence of those situations.

This "causal belongingness" hypothesis of MDR (proposed in Bower & Mayer, 1989) may account for some of the generalizations noted before. First, demonstrations of reliable MDR with autobiographic memories are expected because these are memories for which the emotions causally belonged *originally* to the incidents being recalled. Thus, the incident-to-emotion association, which underlies the MDR phenomenon, would have been strongly formed initially, hence to be retrieved upon later testing when subjects re-enter a similar mood.

Second, the hypothesis suggests why standard laboratory attempts to produce MDR with arbitrary, artificial learning material often leads to either weak or nonexistent effects. One merely needs to note that in the standard MDR experiments the mood is induced several minutes before presentation of the material to be learned. The subject is supposed to experience the mood as a continuing background while the items to be learned are presented in the foreground. Thus, the onset of the emotional state is not synchronized with the item presentations so the temporal order for causally attributing the emotional reaction to the target items is violated. Moreover, subjects are typically not instructed to causally attribute their current emotion to the presented items, but rather to view the item presentations as unrelated events occurring coincidentally while they are in a certain feeling state. These conditions are exactly those of contiguity without causal belonging, which, according to the hypothesis, should produce only weak associations at best.

The same hypothesis can be used to understand the fourth generalization aforementioned, namely, the greater reliability of MDR for self-generated target material. Figure 1.3 is used to describe the explanation.

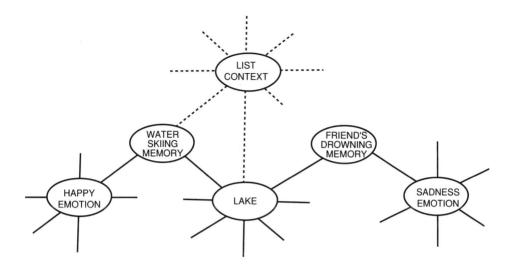

FIG. 1.3. Fragment of a hypothetical subject's associative memory surrounding the concept *lake*. Lines represent associations connecting emotion nodes to descriptions of two different events, one happy and one sad. The experimental context becomes associated to experiences that occurred in that setting.

Suppose that the experiment to be modeled is one in which a woman subject has been made to feel happy during the initial phase of one of Eich's experiments, and during the initial phase she is asked to recall an incident from her life suggested by the target word *lake*, among many others. Fig. 1.3 illustrates a hypothetical fragment of this subject's long-term associative memory (see, e.g., Anderson & Bower, 1973). The concept *lake* has a large number of associations, but among them are memories of several biographic incidents, one describing an earlier occasion on which she was made very happy by the thrill of water-skiing on a lake, another describing a different occasion on which she was saddened by hearing of the death of a friend who drowned in a lake. Through causal belongingness, the memory of the water-skiing incident had been associated to that node in the system that corresponds to feeling happy, and the memory of the drowning incident had been associated to the sadness emotion it caused (see Bower, 1981, for discussion of emotion nodes in associative networks).

When feeling happy and presented with the word *lake*, this subject is more likely to retrieve the water-skiing memory than the drowning memory. This is because the former memory receives greater activation spreading from two sources, the cue *lake* and the happy emotion node, whereas the latter memory receives lesser activation from only the one source, *lake*. Suppose then that the happy subject does in fact produce the water-skiing memory to the cue *lake* during the first phase of the experiment. We must assume that at that time the subject forms some associations between the experimental list context and the events that were just caused to transpire there, namely, having been presented with the word *lake* and being reminded of the water-skiing incident. These contextual associations are illustrated with dashed lines in Fig. 1.3.

These contextual associations are called upon later when the subject is asked to free recall the incidents (or the cue words) that she had produced earlier. (For the central role of contextual cues in free recall, see Anderson & Bower, 1972; or Raaijmakers & Shiffrin, 1981.) In free recall, the subject probes long-term memory with the context as a search cue, spreading activation from that node in the associative network. However, the context is a greatly overloaded cue because many different items have been weakly associated to it (notice the many different dashed lines emanating from the context node in Fig. 1.3). Consequently, activation arriving down any single branch may be too weak to produce recall of many items. This is the basis for the associative interference that causes normal forgetting. However, if the subject is again feeling happy at the time of free recall, then activation from that emotion node summates with that from the context node, perhaps thus to raise the activation of the water-skiing memory above the threshold for overt recall. On the other hand, if the person's mood had been switched (say, to sadness) between learning and recall, the emotion during recall would not help retrieval of the water-skiing incident and its cue word that occurred during the initial phase of the experiment. In this manner the hypothesis explains why mood matching during original learning and testing would facilitate reproduction of the original memories or their cues.

Several features of this explanation should be noted. First, the emotion prevailing during Phase I is not directly associated to the cue word *lake* in Fig. 1.3 because they have no belonging; by contrast, the associations between the emotions and the biographic incidents were established by causal belonging in the subject's past and are simply being reactivated in this experimental context.

Second, a similar explanation goes through if the experimental materials are words and the subject generates word associates as target materials (or if first letters are cues and word associates are targets). Thus, to a cue word like *life* subjects will have large numbers of associations, some linked to positive emotions (*freedom, love*), some to negative emotions *(death, struggle),* and many neutral. If the subject's mood during recall is the same as during the initial learning phase, then the mood-congruent associations likely to have been evoked during the initial phase would also receive more activation and be more likely to be retrieved during the test phase. The effect would be similar for mood-congruent word associates to first-letter cues (e.g., F suggests *Fun* vs. *Funeral).*

Third, the hypothesis expects MDR will be weaker or nonexistent in recognition memory tests wherein the subject is given the item *(lake)* and asked whether it has an association to the initial list context. Retrieval of that specific associative pairing is not influenced by mood matching or mismatching because the paired cues *(LIST-lake)* bypass the emotion nodes entirely (and is not so harmed by associative overload). This outcome is consistent with the human learning literature (e.g., Baddeley, 1990), which shows that, compared to recall tests, accuracy on recognition memory tests is far less decremented by associative interference.

We have thus seen how the causal belonging hypothesis can make some sense of the boundary conditions surrounding phenomena of mood-dependent retrieval. Direct tests of the causal belonging hypothesis are logistically difficult to arrange with human subjects because the tests require that subjects experience a collection of realistic incidents in which they causally attribute their emotional reactions to some experimentally arranged events. Such experiments raise such ethical concerns that most of us are reluctant to do them. One attempt to arrange for subjects to *imagine* that specified, hypothetical events were causing them increasingly elevated emotional reactions (of elation or depression) produced MDR in one experiment but failed in a replication (Bower & Mayer, 1989, Experiments 4 and 5). However, that manipulation lacked ecological as well as face validity, and cannot be generally recommended as an experimental method. A more promising approach used by Munakata and Bower (submitted) provided positive or negative (bogus) feedback apparently contingent on subjects' performance on each of a series of intellectual tasks. Subjects later induced to feel happy recalled more of their successful than their failed tasks, whereas subjects induced to feel sad recalled more of their failed than their successful tasks. The result shows mood-dependent retrieval because further evidence indicated that success or failure on a task attached some positive or negative affect to its memory. Other avenues for testing the hypothesis would be welcome; perhaps memory of sports fans for emotional events in sports might be a useful naturalistic arena for testing such ideas. In the meanwhile, causal belongingness provides a plausible hypothesis to account for the boundary conditions surrounding mood-dependent retrieval of memories.

In summary, I have articulated what I see as a commonly prevailing view about the role of motivation and emotion in controlling the learning and retrieval of memories and action plans. Motivation and emotion serve multiple functions in the cognitive system. Whereas motivation mobilizes resources for action, directs attention, and guides execution of plans, emotions serve largely as "commentators" reacting to the present situation, evaluating the execution of plans and their outcomes. The emotions signal to the cognitive system the important discrepancies (between actual and expected outcomes) which are to be reduced through further learning. The emotion directs attention to the causally significant aspects of the discrepant situation, serves to encode and index the unusual event in memory, and promotes persisting rehearsal of the new, more adaptive action. In this way, new learning articulates a more accurate model of the current situation to guide future expectations about similar situations. Later arousal of an emotion retrieves associated thoughts, plans, and memories. I argue that this selective retrieval underlies such phenomena as mood-congruent biases in thinking, preferences, judgment, learning, and mood–state-dependent memory.

ACKNOWLEDGMENTS

Gordon Bower's research is supported by research grant MH-47575 from the U.S. National Insitute of Mental Health, and grant 87-0282A from the U.S. Air Force Office of Scientific Research.

REFERENCES

Anderson, J. R. (1985). *Cognitive psychology and its implications.* (2nd ed.). New York: W.M.Freeman.

Anderson, J. R., & Bower, G. M. (1972). Recognition and retrieval processes in free recall. *Psychological Review, 79,* 97–123.

Anderson, J. R., & Bower, G. M. (1973). *Human associative memory.* Washington, DC: Winston.

Baddeley, A. (1990). Human memory: theory and practice. Boston: Allyn & Bacon.

Bower, G. H. (1981). Mood and memory. *American Psychologist, 36,* 129–148.

Bower, G. H. (1983). Affect and cognition. *Philosophical Transactions of the Royal Society of London* (Series B), *302,* 387–402.

Bower, G. H. (1991). Mood congruity of social judgments. In J. Forgas (Ed.), *Emotion and social judgments* (pp. 31–54). Oxford, England: Pergamon Press.

Bower, G. H. & Cohen, P. R. (1982). Emotional influences on memory and thinking: Data and theory. In S. Fiske & M. Clark (Eds.), *Affect and cognition* (pp. 291–331). Hillsdale, NJ: Lawrence Erlbaum Associates.

Bower, G. H., & Mayer, J. D. (1989). In search of mood-dependent retrieval. In D. Kuiken (Ed.), *Mood and memory: Theory, research, and applications.* Special issue of *Journal of Social Behavior and Personality, 4*(2), 121–156.

Brewer, W. F. (1988). Memory for randomly sampled autobiographical events. In U. Neisser & E. Winograd (Eds.), *Remembering reconsidered: Ecological and traditional approaches to the study of memory.* New York: Cambridge University Press.

Bullington, J. C. (1990). Mood congruent memory: A replication of symmetrical effects for both positive and negative moods. In J. W. Neuliet (Ed.), *Handbook of replication research in the behavioral and social sciences.* Special issue of the *Journal of Social Behavior and Personality, 5*(4), 123–134.

Christianson, S.-Å. (1984). The relationship between induced emotional arousal and amnesia. *Scandanavian Journal of Psychology, 25,* 147–160.

Christianson, S.-Å., & Loftus, E. F. (1987). Memory for traumatic events. *Applied Cognitive Psychology, 1,* 225–239.

Christianson, S.-Å., & Loftus, E. F. (1991). Remembering emotional events: The fate of detail information. *Cognition and Emotion, 5,* 81–108.

Christianson, S.-Å., & Nilsson, L.-G. (1984). Functional amnesia as induced by a psychological trauma. *Memory and Cognition, 12,* 142–155.

Clore, G. L., & Ortony A. F. (1988). The semantics of the affective lexicon. In B. Hamilton, G. H. Bower, & N. H. Frijda (Eds.), *Cognitive perspectives on emotion and motivation* (pp. 367–398). Dordrecht, The Netherlands: Kluwer Academic Publishers.

Dutta, S., & Kanungo, R. (1967). Retention of affective material: A further verification of the intensity hypothesis. *Journal of Personality and Social Psychology, 5,* 476–480.

Dyer, M. G. (1987). Emotions and their computations: Three computer models. *Cognition & Emotion, 1,* 323–348.

Eich, E. (1980). The cue dependent nature of state dependent retrieval. *Memory and Cognition, 8,* 157–173.

Eich, E. (1990, June). Searching for mood-dependent memory. *Speech given at Convention of American Psychological Society,* Dallas, TX.

Eich, E., & Metcalfe, J. (1989). Mood dependent memory for internal versus external events. *Journal of Experimental Psychology: Learning, Memory and Cognition, 15,* 443–456.

Ekman, P. (1984). Expression and the nature of emotions. In K. R. Scherer & P. Ekman (Eds.), *Approaches to emotion* (pp. 319–344). Hillsdale, NJ: Lawrence Erlbaum Associates.

Ellis, H. C. (1990). The role of thoughts in influencing the effects of mood states on memory. *Speech at Convention of the American Psychological Society,* Dallas, TX.

Ellis, H. C., & Ashbrook, P. W. (1988). Resource allocation model and the effects of depressed mood states on memory. In K. Fiedler & J. Forgas (Eds.), *Affect, cognition and social behavior.* Toronto, Canada: Hogreff.

Ellis, H. C., & Ashbrook, P. W. (1989). The state of mood and memory research: A selective review. In D. Kuiken (Ed.), *Mood and memory: Theory, research, and applications.* Special issue of the *Journal of Social Behavior and Personality, 4*(2), 1–22.

Ellis, N. R., Detterman, D. K., Runcie, D., McCarver R. B., & Craig, E. M. (1971). Amnesic effects in short-term memory. *Journal of Experimental Psychology, 89,* 357–361.

Estes, W. K. (1958). Stimulus–response theory of drive. In M. R. Jones (Ed.), *Nebraska Symposium on Motivation,* (Vol. 6). Lincoln: University of Nebraska Press.

Fehr, B, & Russell, J. A. (1984). Concept of emotion viewed from a prototype prospective. *Journal of Experimental Psychology: General, 113,* 464–486.

Feigenbaum, E. A. (1959). *An information processing theory of verbal learning.* RAND Corporation Paper, P-1817.

Feigenbaum, E. A., & Simon, H. A. (1961). *Performance of a reading task by an elementary perceiving and memorizing program.* RAND Corporation Paper, P-2358.

Fernandez, A., & Glenberg, A. M. (1985). Changing environmental context does not reliably affect memory. *Memory and Cognition, 13,* 333–345.

Fischer, K. W., Shaver, P. R., & Carnochan P. (1990). How emotions develop and how they organize development. *Cognition & Emotion, 4,* 81–127.

Forgas, J. P., & Bower, G. M. (1987). Mood effects on person perception. *Journal of Personality and Social Psychology, 53,* 53–60.

Frijda, N. H. (1986). *Emotions.* New York: Cambridge University Press.

Frijda, N. H., & Swagerman, J. (1987). Can computers feel? Theory and design of an emotional system. *Cognition & Emotion, 1,* 235–258.

Gold, P. E. (1990, June). Regulation of memory storage in animals and humans: Implications for aging research. *Speech given at Convention of American Psychological Society,* Dallas, TX.

Holmes, D. S. (1970). Differential change in affective intensity and the forgetting of unpleasant personal experiences. *Journal of Personality and Social Psychology, 15,* 234–239.

Horowitz, M. J. (1988). *Introduction to psychodynamics: A new synthesis.* New York: Basic Books.

Hull, C. L. (1943). *Principles of behavior.* New York: Appleton–Century–Croft.

Johnson-Laird, P. N., & Oatley, K. (1989). The language of emotions: An analysis of a semantic field. *Cognition and Emotion, 3,* 81–123.

Kamin, L. J. (1969). Predictability, surprise, attention, and conditioning. In B. A. Campbell & R. M. Church (Eds.), *Punishment.* New York: Appleton–Century–Croft.

Kenealy, P. M. (1986). The Velten mood induction procedure: A methodological review. *Motivation and Emotion, 10,* 315–335.

Kolodner, J. L. (1983a). Maintaining organization in a dynamic long term memory. *Cognitive Science, 7,* 243–280.

Kolodner, J. L. (1983b). Reconstructive memory: A computer model. *Cognitive Science, 7,* 281–328.

Kuiken, D. (1989). *Mood and memory: Theory, research and applications.* Special issue of the *Journal of Social Behavior and Personality,* 4(2).

Lazarus, R. S. (1966). *Psychological stress and the coping process.* New York: McGraw–Hill.

Lewis, V. E., & Williams, R. N. (1989). Mood congruent versus mood state dependent learning: Implications for a view of emotions. In D. Kuiken (Ed.), *Mood and memory: Theory, research, and applications.* Special issue of the *Journal of Social Behavior and Personality,* 4(2), 157–171.

MacKintosh, N. J. (1974). *The psychology of animal learning.* London: Academic Press.

Mandler, G. (1984). *Mind and body: Psychology of emotion and stress.* New York: Norton.

McGaugh, J. L. (1983). Hormonal influences on memory. *Annual Review of Psychology, 54,* 297–324.

McKoon, G., Ratcliff, R., & Seifert, C. M. (1989). Making the connection: Generalized knowledge structures in story understanding. *Journal of Memory and Language, 28,* 711–734.

Miller, N. E. (1951). Learnable drives and rewards. In S. S. Stevens (Ed.), *Handbook of Experimental psychology.* New York: Wiley.

Munakata, Y. and Bower, G. H. (submitted). Causal belonging of affects to events: An hypothesis about mood-dependent memory.

Oatley, K., & Johnson-Laird, P. N. (1987). Towards a cognitive theory of emotions. *Cognition and Emotion, 1,* 29–50.

Ortony, A. F. (1987). Is guilt an emotion? *Cognition and Emotion, 1,* 283–298.

Ortony, A. F., Clore, G. L., & Collins, A. (1988). *The cognitive structure of emotions.* New York: Cambridge University Press.

Ortony, A. F., Clore, G. L., & Foss, M. A. (1987). The referential structure of the affective lexicon. *Cognitive Science, 11,* 261–284.

Osgood, C. E., Suci, J., & Tannenbaum, P. M. (1957). *The measurement of meaning.* Urbana: University of Illinois Press.

Raaijmakers, J. G. W., & Shiffrin R. M. (1981). Search of associative memory. *Psychological Review, 88,* 83–134.

Rescorla, R. A., & Wagner, A. R. (1972). A theory of Pavlovian conditioning: variations in the effectiveness in reinforcement and non-reinforcement. In A. Black & W. A. Prokasy (Eds.), *Classical Conditioning: II. Current research and theory.* New York: Appleton–Century–Croft.

Rumelhart, D. E., & McClelland, J. (1986). *Parallel distributing processing, Vol. 1, Foundations.* Cambridge: MIT Press.

Schank, R. (1982). *Dynamic memory.* Cambridge, England: Cambridge University Press.

Schank:, R. C., & Abelson, R. (1977). *Scripts, plans, goals, and understanding.* Hillsdale, NJ: Lawrence Erlbaum Associates.

Schank, R. C., & Osgood, R. (1990). *A content theory of memory indexing (Tech. Rep. No. 2).* Institute for the Learning Sciences, Northwestern University.

Shaver, P., Schwartz, J., Kirson, D., & O'Connor, C. (1987). Emotion knowledge: Further exploration of a prototype approach. *Journal of Personality & Social Psychology, 52,* 1061–1086.

Simon, H. A. (1967). Motivational and emotional controls of cognition. *Psychological Review,* 74(1), 29–39.

Sloman, A. (1987). Motives, mechanisms and emotions. *Cognition & Emotion, 1,* 217–334.

Sloman, A., & Croucher, M. (1981). Why robots will have emotions. *The Seventh Proceedings of the International Joint Conference on Artificial Intelligence* (197–202). Vancouver, British Columbia.

Stein, N. L., & Levine, L. J. (1989). The causal organization of emotional knowledge: A developmental study. *Cognition and Emotion, 3,* 343–378.

Thayer, R. E. (1989). *The biopsychology of mood and arousal.* New York: Oxford University Press.

Thorndike, E. L. (1932). *The fundamentals of learning.* New York: Teacher's College.

Toda, M. (1982). *Man, robot and society.* The Hague: Neijhoff.

2

Emotion and MEM

Marcia K. Johnson
Kristi S. Multhaup
Princeton University

In this chapter, we outline a general cognitive architecture called MEM (a Multiple-Entry, Modular memory system, Johnson, 1983; 1990; 1991a; 1991b; Johnson & Hirst, in press), discuss the relation between emotion and cognition from the perspective of MEM, and describe results of studies of memory for affect that were motivated by this framework. We think that MEM provides a coherent way of organizing a range of empirical facts about emotion and of integrating a number of theoretical ideas that have figured prominently in analyses of emotion. In addition, considering emotion in terms of MEM highlights several issues that have received relatively little attention but that could provide useful future directions for research.

MEM

Memory serves an extraordinary range of functions, for example, remembering autobiographical events, comprehending stories, recognizing people, learning concepts, remembering telephone numbers long enough to dial them, navigating the environment, dancing, driving cars, solving geometry problems, learning how to plan and, most central to the topic of this book, developing affective responses such as preferences and fears. It is possible that a single, undifferentiated cognitive system accomplishes all this, but it seems unlikely. On the other hand, it seems even more unlikely that different specialized cognitive/memory subsystems evolved to handle each of these functions. A more likely possibility is that several subsystems evolved and work together in different combinations and degrees to flexibly meet the many cognitive demands we face. MEM is a set of working hypotheses about the minimum number of subsystems and component processes, and their configuration, that would be required for such diverse purposes.

The approach of dividing cognition into subcomponents or classes of processes in order to better understand the whole is common (e.g., Anderson, 1983; Atkinson & Shiffrin, 1968; Baddeley, 1986; Craik & Lockhart, 1972; Hasher & Zacks, 1979; Jacoby, 1983; Kosslyn, 1980; Mandler, 1980; Paivio, 1971; Posner, Petersen, Fox, & Raichle, 1988; Roediger & Blaxton, 1987; Shallice, 1988; Sherry & Schacter, 1987; Cohen & Squire, 1980; Tulving, 1983; Warrington & Weiskrantz, 1982; Waugh & Norman, 1965; Wickelgren, 1979, among others). Various proposals differ in their characterization of basic processes or subsystems. The subsystems identified in the MEM architecture express the fundamental assumption that memories reflect their origin in perceptual and reflective processes (see Johnson, 1983, 1990; Johnson & Hirst, in press; Johnson & Hirst, in preparation, for more discussion of the relation of MEM to other cognitive models).

According to MEM, memory consists of a perceptual memory system for engaging in and recording perceptual activities (seeing, hearing, etc.) and a reflective memory system for engaging in and recording selfgenerated activities (planning, comparing, speculating, imagining, etc.). As shown in Fig. 2.1, the perceptual system includes two subsystems, P–1 and P–2. P–1 and P–2 both are involved in recording perceptual aspects of experience but differ in the type of perceptual information to which they respond. As Fig. 2.2b indicates, P–1 and P–2 subsystems consist of component subprocesses. Component subprocesses of P–1 might include *resolving* stimuli (e.g., through detecting edges), *locating* stimuli, *tracking* stimuli, and *extracting* invariants from perceptual arrays (e.g., cues specifying the rapid expansion of features in the visual field). These P–1 component processes contribute to developing relations or associations involving perceptual information of which we are often unaware, such as the stimulus properties that specify that an object is moving toward one, or perceptual relations that make certain sounds seem similar (e.g., the sound of a word) even though spoken in different voices. Component processes of P–2 might include *identifying* objects, *placing* objects in spatial relation to each other, *examining* or redirecting attention to perceptually investigate stimuli, and *struc-*

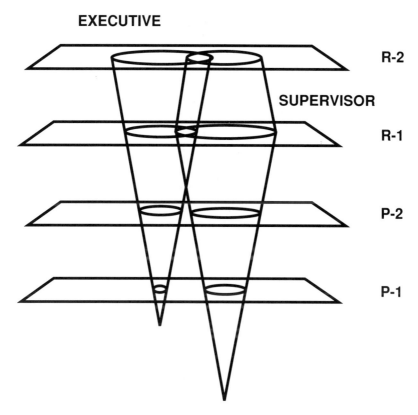

EXECUTIVE

R-2

SUPERVISOR

R-1

P-2

P-1

FIG. 2.1. A multiple-entry, modular memory system, consisting of two reflective subsystems, R–1 and R–2, and two perceptual subsystems, P-1 and P-2. One way reflective and perceptual subsystems interact is through control and monitoring processes (supervisor and executive processes of R–1 and R–2, respectively), which have relatively greater access to and control over reflective than perceptual subsystems. Adapted from Johnson (1991a) with permission.

turing or constructing a pattern of organization across temporally extended stimuli. P–2 processes identify and respond to a world of objects and events; they are responsible for activities (or "computations") that yield and maintain a record of such phenomenal experiences as eating an apple, seeing a deer, or hearing a siren (Johnson & Hirst, in preparation).

The reflective system also includes two subsystems, R–1 and R–2. Both R–1 and R–2 allow one to go beyond perception, that is, beyond the immediate consequences of ongoing perceptual stimuli. Fig. 2.2a shows important component processes of reflection. In R–1, these

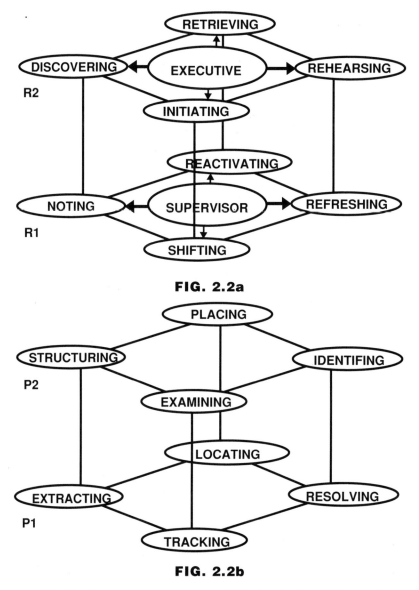

FIG. 2.2a

FIG. 2.2b

FIG. 2.2.   Component subprocesses of (a) R–1 and R–2 and (b) P–1 and P–2. Adapted from Johnson (1991b) with permission.

component processes include *noting* relations between activated concepts, *shifting* attention to new aspects of stimulii or concepts, *refreshing* information to keep potentially useful information active, and *reactivating* information that has ceased to be part of the ongoing activation pattern. R–2 processes include *discovering, initiating, rehearsing,* and *retrieving* and are more strategic and involve more embedding of subgoals than do R–1 processes (see Johnson, 1990; Johnson & Hirst, in press). For example, a record activated by a partial match between ongoing reflection and previous reflection (e.g., noting a relation between two stimuli and being reminded of having previously noted the same relation) would be an instance of reactivating (an R–1 process). A record activated by using a strategy of presenting oneself with cues in order to find a match (e.g., trying to remember the name of a restaurant by thinking of possible people who might have told you about it) would be an instance of retrieving (an R–2 process).

R–1 and R–2 also include, respectively, *supervisor* and *executive* processes. These processes hold agendas active (e.g., remember the name of a restaurant) and monitor outcomes with respect to these agendas (Miller, Galanter, & Pribram, 1960; Nelson & Narens, 1990; Stuss & Benson, 1986) and recruit reflective component processes for these purposes. Agendas arise as a consequence of stimulus conditions (e.g., hunger to be satisfied, city streets to be navigated) and as a consequence of ongoing reflective activity (e.g., a conflict to be resolved between two equally reasonable but inconsistent theoretical ideas). Agendas differ in complexity, that is, in the complexity of the cognition required to carry them out. For example, an agenda to make old/new recognition judgments may set up decision criteria that require little more than assessing familiarity of a stimulus, activities easily controlled and monitored by the R–1 supervisor (of course, recognition tasks can under some circumstances engage additional, R–2 processes as well). An agenda to recall one's life story would be more likely to involve R–2 executive processes of specifying subgoals within more general goals (e.g., divide life into three main parts, childhood, school years, work years; within parts, use major geographic locations to cue significant events, etc.), and R–2 and R–1 might operate interactively (see next paragraph) to coordinate recall to produce a cohesive, organized product.

As shown in Fig. 2.1, agendas set in R–1 and R–2 can activate information in perceptual subsystems as well as in reflective subsystems but, typically, supervisor and executive functions have greater access to reflective memory than to perceptual memory, and greater access to P–2 than to P–1. A central feature of MEM is that the supervisor and executive processes in R–1 and R–2 can recruit and monitor each other (see overlap in Fig. 2.1), providing, among other things, a mechanism for sequencing subgoals. The phenomenal experience of volition or deliberation, or what some investigators have called effort, will, or control (e.g., Hasher & Zacks, 1979; Norman & Shallice, 1986; Shiffrin & Schneider, 1977), arises in part, from this overlap in R–1 and R–2; that is, the interaction between R–1 and R–2 creates a sense of effort or awareness of one's own thought processes.

Finally, we assume that as individuals develop from infancy, subsystems increase in functional possibilities in the order P–1, P–2, R–1, and R–2 (e.g., Flavell, 1985; Perlmutter, 1984; Schacter & Moscovitch, 1984). Learning, of course, continues throughout life in all subsystems.

A number of researchers have found it useful to think in terms of distinguishable subsystems of memory (e.g., Sherry & Schacter, 1987; Squire, 1987; Tulving, 1983). Others have begun to emphasize differences between externally derived and centrally generated processes (Craik, 1986; Jacoby, 1983; Roediger & Blaxton, 1987). MEM is both similar to and different from these approaches and could be viewed as an intersect between subsystem and processing accounts. Subsystem accounts typically posit nonoverlapping structures that handle different types of content such as procedural, espisodic, or semantic memories; process accounts tend to be associated with unitary memory models and with arguments against subsystems. MEM is a subsystem account, framed in terms of processes, in which subsystems interact to yield complex thought and behavior. In this view, all subsystems may contribute to procedural, episodic, or semantic memory, depending on specific task requirements.

It remains useful to distinguish among procedural, episodic, and semantic *tasks* in order to help characterize the functional scope of the memory system and to delineate research domains. Nevertheless, we argue against identifying tasks with subsystems because it is likely that acquisition and expression of procedural, episodic, and semantic knowledge draw on some of the same processes, though they may do so to different degrees. Note also that MEM's "modularity" is not the same as that described by Fodor (1983). According to MEM, memory has a modular capability in that organized/ functional modules or groupings of processes might on some occasions operate without drawing on or being influenced by other modules (e.g., P–1 without R–2). MEM does not, however, define modules as units that are non-interacting or "impenetrable." In fact, specifying the nature of the interactions among subsystems is a major theoretical goal. An additional point of clarification is that the distinction between perceptual and reflective activity in MEM is not equivalent to "bottom-up" and "top-down" processing (e. g, Palmer,

1975) as those terms are often used. Perception is influenced by learning and by expectations based, for example, on activated perceptual schemas, and MEM's P–1 and P–2 systems include such "top-down" effects (e.g., P–2 processes help us read sloppy handwriting by interpreting letters in the context of words). Reflection involves mental activities that go beyond the phenomenal consequences of constructed perception.

Compared to what we will undoubtedly eventually need to model human memory, MEM is a relatively simple cognitive architecture. Even so, it provides a framework for considering a wide range of phenomena and issues in cognition, including relations among direct and indirect memory measures or between attention and memory (Johnson, 1983), anterograde amnesia (Johnson, 1990; Johnson & Hirst, in press), reality monitoring and confabulation (Johnson, 1988; Johnson in 1991a), and the concept of the "self" (Johnson, 1991b). In the next section we expand on some ideas about emotion and MEM suggested previously (Johnson, 1983, 1985; Johnson, Kim, & Risse, 1985).

EMOTION IN MEM

Emotions or affective responses range from conditioned avoidance to nostalgia, from mild positive and negative evaluative impressions to ecstasy and rage. Affective experiences, like other experiences, include autonomic nervous system activity and other bodily responses and sensations, including kinesthetic feedback from voluntary movements such as raising one's fist. Of course, the degree and salience of autonomic and other bodily sensations varies widely across different types of valenced experiences and for different individuals. We are assuming here that subjects' conscious perception of their own autonomic activity (or an experimenter's detection of it) is not necessary for a response to be classified as affective. Rather, in this chapter, we use the terms emotion and affect interchangeably to refer to valenced responses of any type. Nevertheless, autonomic and other bodily responses are factors that contribute to learning and memory (e.g., as energizers and motivators), and therefore they must be incorporated eventually into general cognitive models. Here, however, we are focusing on cognitive aspects of emotion, especially cognitive contributions to affect as phenomenally experienced. How emotion is expressed (e.g., on a person's face, or in action) is not addressed although, in general, the role of learning amid individual differences should be greater as we move from P–1 to R–2 involvement.

A characterization within the MEM framework of the relation between emotion and cognition is shown in Fig. 2.3a and Fig. 2.3b. Emotion arises as a consequence of processes within subsystems (along with accompanying autonomic and motor responses) and becomes part of the record of the ongoing activities of the subsystems. In Fig. 2.3a, the circular area indicated in each subsystem represents emotions that arise from processing within that subsystem. The cylinders represent the idea that some emotions have analogs in more than one subsystem. The major point to note in Fig. 2.3a is that all four subsystems, P–1, P–2, R–1, and R–2, contribute to emotion. Each subsystem is shaded differently in Fig. 2.3a to help identify the corresponding subsystem in Fig. 2.3b (a top-down view of Fig. 2.3a).

Fig. 2.3b illustrates two fundamental points. The first point, as just indicated, is that similar emotions (analogs) are associated with different subsystems. In particular, some emotions (e.g., anger, fear) are likely to be "computed" in all subsystems. Nevertheless, although we might use the same word to refer to emotions arising from processes in different subsystems, the exact character of the emotion depends on the specific processes from which it is derived. Thus in MEM there is no single "node" (e.g., Bower, 1981) corresponding to a particular emotion. The fear you experience from seeing a fist come toward you (arising primarily from P–1 activity) and the fear you experience from imagining yourself speechless at a party (arising from R–1 activity, and perhaps embellished by R–2 activity) are not exactly the same. Emotion is the consequence of certain types of activities carried out in cognitive subsystems, and phenomenally similar feelings arise from diverse activities. Feelings are a blend of cognitive and autonomic activity and other bodily sensations. Part of the similarity among feelings generated in different situations arises from similarities in the autonomic responses produced from different patterns of cognitive activity.

The second point is that the range of possible emotions expands as we move from P–1 through R–2 subsystems. Some emotions (e.g., remorse, jealousy) arise from R–1 and R–2 activity. For example, remorse often requires the reactivation or retrieval of a prior commitment, along with the knowledge that one has failed to keep it. Thus, reflective processes are important in creating the conditions for certain emotions. Furthermore, within any particular subsystem, an emotion would be more complex if more component subprocesses were involved. So, for example, an emotion resulting from the R–1 reactivation (see Fig. 2.2) of information that had dropped from consciousness (e.g., guilt induced by seeing a person and remembering you had gossiped about him the day before) would be more complex

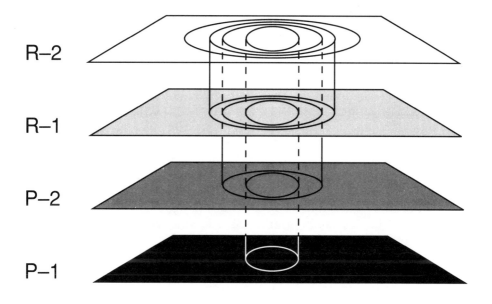

FIG. 2.3a

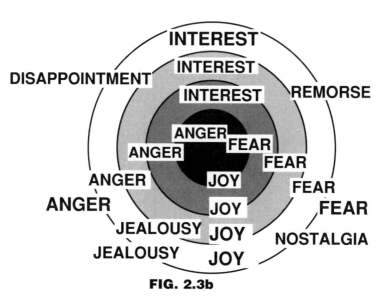

FIG. 2.3b

FIG. 2.3. (a) The range of emotions increases from P–1 to R–2;
(b) all sybsystems in MEM contribute to affect;

41

than an emotion that did not require reactivation of information (e.g., sadness at watching a sick baby bird die).

Emotions arising from P–1 or P–2 activity may correspond to what other investigators have called basic or biologically primitive emotions (e.g, Plutchik, 1980; Tomkins, 1962, 1963). These emotions are thought to be evolutionarily old (Ekman, 1984), appear early in an individual's development (Leventhal & Tomarken, 1986; Lewis, Sullivan, Stanger, & Weiss, 1989), arise quickly and "automatically" (Berkowitz, 1990; Ekman, 1977), are expressed in universally recognizable configurations of facial movements (Ekman, 1973), are correlated with differentiable autonomic system activity (Ekman, 1984; Ekman, Levenson, & Friesen, 1983), may show subcortical conditioning (LeDoux, in press), may be predisposed to certain stimuli (Öhman, Dimberg, & Öst, 1985; Seligman, 1971), and serve fundamental motivational functions within the individual and communication functions among a social group (Ellsworth & Smith, 1988; Izard, 1977; Oatley & Johnson-Laird, 1987; Plutchik, 1980; Polivy, 1990; Tomkins, 1963). As an example of their communication function, expressions of emotion regulate social interaction by encouraging approach or withdrawal, depending on the situation. The pleasure one feels at simply seeing a friend is often expressed in a smile that encourages conversation.

The more complex emotions that require R–1 and R–2 processing correspond to "secondary" or "derived" emotions. As compared with basic emotions, these would be more recent evolutionarily, appear later in development, arise relatively slowly and seem "constructed," may be difficult to read on other people's faces or from other nonverbal cues, may share autonomic patterns with other emotions, are likely to involve cortical processing, may be associated with a wide range of stimuli including abstract concepts (e.g., patriotic feelings toward the concept of one's country), may underlie complex motivation within the individual, and may contribute much of the nuance of our social environment.

MEM's processing subsystems not only contribute to the experience of affect, they determine the characteristics of the acquisition and retention of affect as well. Just as emotions are experienced as a consequence of particular activities in various subsystems, they can be reactivated only by appropriate probes (as suggested by the encoding specificity principle, Tulving; 1983). A related point is that different, and perhaps conflicting, emotional responses to the same nominal stimulus may coexist, mediated by different subsystems; which of these would be active would depend on contextual factors, such as the type of probe, that might favor one or the other. For example, a person once chased by a dog might feel interest or admiration at watching a guide dog for the blind work but experience apprehension or fear if the dog looked at them. Establishing different affective responses to objects or situations should be most successful if alternative emotional responses are established within the same subsystem that supports the old affect (Johnson, 1983). Thus therapeutic interventions directed at changing emotional responses (or any response, for that matter) should be most effective if they take into account which subsystem(s) are supporting that particular emotional response (Johnson, 1985; cf. Brewin, 1989; Jacobs & Nadel, 1985; Lang, 1969). This might determine, for example, the relative balance between in vivo exposure and more cognitive (e.g., restructuring) techniques (e.g., Beck & Emery, 1985; Meichenbaum, 1977).

To further clarify this characterization of emotion in MEM, we next consider several issues in more detail.

To What Extent Does Emotion Depend on Cognition?

Zajonc (1980) offered an especially provocative idea regarding the relation of cognition and emotion, namely, that affect may not be the result of cognitive processes at all but may accumulate from minimal perceptual and cognitive input (Seamon, Marsh, & Brody, 1984) and may be among the earliest reactions to a stimulus (but see Mandler, Nakamura, & Van Zandt, 1987, for evidence that judgments other than affective ones may be supported by minimal perceptual processing, and Mandler & Shebo, 1983, for evidence that evaluations may not be faster than recognition judgments). Zajonc also indicated that the separate emotion system he had in mind dealt only with simple, valenced reactions, not with more complex emotional experiences and recognized that a more complete understanding of emotional experience would require a more elaborated model.

Appraisal theories (Abelson, 1983; Lazarus, 1982; Leventhal & Scherer, 1987; Mandler, 1984; Oatley & Johnson-Laird, 1987; Ortony, Clore, & Collins, 1988; Roseman, 1984; Smith & Ellsworth, 1985) attempt to deal with these more complex emotions. They highlight the role of cognition in producing (or "computing") emotions by emphasizing that emotion is a consequence of how people construe situations. For example, Oatley and Johnson-Laird (1987) suggest that an "emotion may start by being quite inchoate: Only with substantial reasoning about the situation and its implications may the full complex emotion develop" (p. 47). Appraisal approaches vary in a number of ways, for example, in the extent to which evolutionary, biological, or cross-cultural considerations motivate the scheme suggested; whether emotions are described in terms of categories or dimensions; whether the focus of analysis is emotion words (e.g., Johnson-Laird & Oatley, 1988), ratings of autobiographical memories (Smith & Ellsworth, 1985), or logical relations among emotion-eliciting situations (e.g., Ortony et al., 1988). Appraisal approaches also differ in which emotions are viewed as basic or primary and which are viewed as derived or secondary. Ortony et al. attempted to do away with the idea of basic emotions entirely, although the hierarchical structure they propose, in which some emotions are more differentiated versions of others, results, in effect, in some emotions being more basic than others. In any event, one idea about which there does seem to be consensus among theorists who emphasize the role of cognition in emotion is that emotions differ in the complexity of cognition that gives rise to them (e.g., Fiske & Pavelchak, 1986; Leventhal & Scherer, 1987; Oatley & Johnson-Laird, 1987; Ortony et al., 1988; Smith & Ellsworth, 1985).

As others have pointed out, some of the debate about whether emotion involves cognition hinges on how one defines cognition (e.g., Berkowitz, 1990; Ekman, 1984; Leventhal & Scherer, 1987). Along these lines, MEM's subsystems provide a ready mechanism for the types of effects emphasized by Zajonc (1980), as well as the types of phenomena emphasized by appraisal theorists. Emotion that is associated with perceptual subsystems, especially P–1, would arise relatively automatically, without reflection, and seem to be elicited by stimulus properties, creating the impression of affect without "cognition" (i.e., cognition in such cases is P–1 and P–2 cognition; cf. Leventhal & Scherer, 1987.) In addition, emotion generated in any subsystem from the activation of well-learned schemas, categories, or concepts with which affect is already strongly associated would arise quickly, again yielding the impression of affect without cognition (Fiske & Pavelchak, 1986). In contrast, emotion that depended on retrieval of more information, discovering relations, and so forth— the type of evaluation initiated and monitored by R–1 and R–2 supervisor and executive processes—would be slower to arise (Fiske & Pavelchak, 1986) and would yield the impression that emotion follows cognition. Thus, the controversy between those emphasizing the immediacy and directness of emotion and those emphasizing the role of cognition disappears if we take into account variations in cognitive complexity underlying different emotions.

MEM suggests some specific ideas about how cognitive complexity might be defined in this context. Engaging more reflective component processes results in greater complexity than does engaging fewer (e.g., refreshing plus reactivation is more complex than refreshing alone, etc.). Because R–2 processes are more strategic and may involve more embedding of subgoals, R–2 processing is more complex than R–1 processing. Similarly, R–1 processing is typically more complex than P–2 processing, and so forth. For example, judgments monitored by R–1 supervisor processes tend to be made quickly, on the basis of qualitative characteristics of activated information, whereas judgments monitored by R–2 executive processes tend to involve more extended reasoning in which additional information is purposefully retrieved, including antecedents and consequences for a given event (Johnson, 1991a, 1991b). For example, suppose you expected a call from a colleague and the call did not come. Your quick, R–1 appraisal is that the person is being irresponsible and you become irritated. Suppose instead that you engaged in R–2 processes to consider why this person might not have called and remember that you said you would call her. Consequently, you might feel a bit foolish and somewhat friendly toward your colleague.

Emotion is Related to Activated Agendas

Goals and plans work in combination with comparison and evaluation processes to direct mental activity and behavior (e.g., Carver & Scheier, 1990; Miller, Galanter, & Pribram, 1960). An idea that appears in many theories of emotion is that emotions follow from the satisfaction or disruption of goals and plans (e.g., Mandler, 1984; Oatley & Johnson-Laird, 1987; Ortony et al., 1988). In MEM, goals and plans are the agendas that control processing in different subsystems. These can vary in complexity, and, especially, in the degree to which they are perceptually or situationally controlled as opposed to reflectively or self-controlled. Activated perceptual schemas function like agendas (e. g, they guide where to look, etc.) but do not necessarily require reflective control, whereas activated reflective scheme for solving certain problems (e. g, geometric proofs) require reflective control. One might experience surprise, for example, by having a perceptual schema disconfirmed or by encountering something inconsistent with a reflective schema. The phenomenal experience would be similar in the two cases, but not identical.

Activated reflective agendas are central to the idea of agency or control and, especially to self-control or self-regulation (e.g., Bandura, 1982; Carver & Scheier, 1990). One reason to be interested in agency in the present context is that agency, itself, might have motivational properties (e.g., Buck, 1985; White, 1959). Another is that the dimension of control or agency is critical for people's experience of certain emotions (Ellsworth & Smith, 1988; Smith & Ellsworth, 1985). For example, Smith and Ellsworth asked subjects to recall a time when they had experienced a particular emotion and then rate the situations along a number of dimensions. Shame and guilt were associated with self-agency, and anger, contempt, and disgust with other-agency. How then does such a sense of agency come about? Of course, many social and environmental factors in an individual's history are important in determining whether he or she feels in control in particular situations. One mechanism follows from the MEM architecture; a sense of agency and self-control arise, in part, from the interactive recruitment and monitoring that goes on between R–1 and R–2 subsystems (Johnson, 1991b). This is discussed more in the next section, which relates agency to a sense of self.

Although satisfaction and disruption of plans and assignment of agency or control are clearly basic mechanisms in emotion, it is important to note that not all emotion is related to activated agendas. For example, emotions could arise in MEM from P–1 or P–2 processing in the absence of any particular ongoing agenda (e.g., the fear you might feel if you woke from a nap under a tree just in time to see a tree branch falling toward you) other than, perhaps, some constant background agenda to preserve one's well-being.

The Development of Emotion

We have proposed that the range of emotions people experience grows out of the multiple processing subsystems they have available. We have also suggested that these subsystems develop in a specific order—P–1, P–2, R–1, and R–2. It follows that emotional range and nuance should develop as the various subsystems develop; that is, an infant who is functioning largely on the basis of P–1 processes would have a much narrower range of emotions than a child who has begun to use R–1 and R–2 processes. This is consistent with Lewis et al.'s (1989) argument that secondary emotions are not observed until appropriate cognitive development has taken place. Lewis et al. emphasized the development of a self-concept as a prerequisite for certain emotions, for example, embarrassment, empathy, and envy, and for the yet later development of standards and rules requisite for emotions such as pride, shame, and guilt. Similarly, Oatley and Johnson-Laird (1987) argued that only with the development of a reflective sense of self can the full set of complex emotions occur.

Elsewhere, one of us (Johnson, 1991b) has suggested that the self arises and is maintained, at least in part, as a by-product of reality monitoring (Johnson & Raye, 1981) processes that are a necessary consequence of the MEM architecture. Because we are capable of reflection as well as perception, we had to develop mechanisms for discriminating the products of reflection from those of perception. Engaging in such reality monitoring would create a sense of self even if one did not develop through other mechanisms. Furthermore, in MEM, the phenomenal experience of self-control arises in the course of the mutual recruiting and monitoring between R–1 and R–2 processes. Thus these mechanisms involved in reality monitoring and R–1/R–2 interaction could underlie development of the aspects of the self that are emphasized by Lewis et al. (1989), especially self–other differentiation and the ability to consider the self as a separate entity. (Rose Zacks wonders if this is the MEM version of "I think, therefore I am.") Even emotions that are not so clearly dependent on an articulated idea of self as are embarrassment or shame probably develop during childhood in order of their cognitive complexity; for example, sadness is less cognitively complex than is regret and thus should appear earlier in development.

How is Emotion Represented in Memory?

One of the most influential current conceptions of emotion among cognitive psychologists is that emotion is represented in memory as part of a more general associative network (Berkowitz, 1990; Bower, 1981; Clark & Isen 1982). For example, Bower (1981) proposed that emotions are represented by nodes in memory. Primary emotions (e.g., joy, anger, fear, sadness, surprise) are directly represented by nodes, and other emotions (e.g., disappointment, contempt) may be blends or mixtures of activation from these primary nodes. For example, disappointment may be sadness mixed with surprise. A node representing a particular emotion is connected to nodes representing propositional representations of episodic events during which the particular emotion was present, and to nodes that produce the pattern of arousal and expressive behavior associated with that emotion. These nodes, like other nodes, send and receive spreading activation and are connected to other nodes with varying degrees of strength. Hence if some aspect of an event is activated, through spreading activation, an emotion may be activated as well. Conversely, activation of an emotion (by, for example, the person's mood state) may activate events to which it is associated (Blaney, 1986; Eich, 1989).

In a recent review of emotion, Leventhal and Tomarken (1986, p. 601) questioned whether it is accurate to describe "verbal, perceptual, subjective experiential, autonomic, and expressive events as structurally similar nodes linked by a common type of associative bond (Bower, 1981)." They expressed here an understandable discomfort with dealing with all information as if it were equivalent. There are marked phenomenal differences in various aspects of experience, for example, in the realization that it was a Volvo that ran into your car, compared with your feelings of increased heart rate, cold sweat, and so forth. But representational inadequacy is not a problem unique to emotion (see also LeDoux, in press). When cognitive psychologists represent aspects of memories such as "blue" or "round" or "in my office" or "with her husband" in an associative or propositional format, the notation seems pale in comparison to the experience, and many subtleties are lost. Current representational schemes provide "place-holders" for the types of information that cognitive theorists know must be represented somehow in memory and propose to deal with empirically and theoretically; emotion has been added to the list of information to be represented by these place holders.

MEM is a set of hypotheses about the functional organization of cognitive processes at the level of a global architecture. Any number of representational formats (associative networks, connectionist networks, episodes, cases, production rules, propositions, schemas, mental models) could be incorporated into MEM. Of course, the value of postulating particular representational formats is that they imply more specific hypotheses about processing (e.g., Collins & Quillian, 1969; Pirolli & Anderson, 1985). But whatever the representational format (or combination of formats) we adopt, it seems reasonable to reject the idea that the memory system is undifferentiated. For example, it seems unlikely that an emotion such as fear is represented as a single node or a set of units in an undifferentiated associative network. Minimally, the idea that emotions are embedded, along with other information, in an associative network would have to be expanded to take into account multiple networks with some kind of internal cohesiveness corresponding to subsystems of memory such as those postulated in MEM. A similar argument holds for other representational formats. It is likely, in fact, that the type of representational format that is most useful for theoretical analysis depends on the subsystem in question; for example, connectionist networks may be more appropriate for characterizing perceptual processes and propositional representations more appropriate for some types of reflective activities. Without making a commitment to one or another representational format at this point, and leaving the exploration of implications of various formats for MEM for the future, we can still make progress on developing a broader view of what must be represented in memory and the functional relations among types of information and types of cognitive processes.

Neuropsychology of Emotion

The range of cognitive, motor, and autonomic system activity involved in computing, expressing, and reinstating various affective experiences suggests a correspondingly complex underlying anatomy, physiology, and biochemistry of emotion (e.g., Damasio & Van Hoesen, 1983; Heilman, Watson, & Bowers, 1982; LeDoux, 1987, this volume). For example, Heilman et al. (1982) pointed out that "emotion . . . depends on varied anatomic structures, including: cortical systems for producing the appropriate cognitive set, limbic structures for activating the brainstem and thalamic activating centers and for controlling the hypothalamic output, the hypothalamus for regulating endocrine and autonomic responses, and the brainstem and thalamic activating systems for producing cortical arousal" (p. 58). This complexity includes potential differences in the relative contributions to emotion of right and left hemispheres (e.g., Heilman et al., 1982; Kinsbourne & Bemporad, 1984; Leventhal & Tomarken, 1986). Such an intricate set of interrelations invites questions from many perspectives.

For us, a goal for the future is to integrate MEM with available information about the neurobiology of emotion and cognition. In doing so, we would assume that bodily sensations and motor activity combine with P–1, P–2, R–1, and R–2 processing as part of complex processing circuits. Across the full range of emotions, it is the intersect of bodily state and the type of perceptual and reflective processing defining the relevant circuit that gives emotion in any particular case its distinctive phenomenal qualities. Disruption of function anywhere along these circuits should have effects on emotional experience or behavior; we are particularly interested in potential selective effects on affect from selectively disrupted cognition. Because we work from a cognitive perspective, we would label such complex emotion circuits in terms of the perceptual and reflective subsystems that participate, even though all may involve some common neurological structures (e.g., the amygdala). Of course, the exact nature of these various emotion circuits remains to be specified (see LeDoux, in press, for an intriguing example of LeDoux and colleague' efforts to trace out what, in terms of MEM, would be a P–1 emotion circuit).

Emotion and Amnesia

In MEM, emotion may be influenced primarily by perceptual processes or it may be influenced primarily by reflective processes. This suggests one strategy for investigating emotion is studying affect in patient populations who have deficits in either perceptual or reflective processes. Johnson and Hirst (in press; Johnson, 1983, 1990) have described anterograde amnesia as a deficit of reflection. According to this view, amnesics have a relatively intact perceptual system and a disrupted reflective system, especially disruption of the component processes of reactivation and retrieval (see Johnson, 1990, and Johnson & Hirst, in press, for more complete discussions). According to this view of amnesia, and consistent with the characterization of emotion in terms of MEM described earlier, those affective responses that depend largely on perceptual processes should be intact in amnesics and those that depend on reflection should be disrupted. We have explored this hypothesis by studying three amnesic patient groups: Korsakoff amnesics (Johnson, Kim, & Risse, 1985) and nonalcoholic anterograde amnesics of mixed etiology, and patients diagnosed as having Alzheimer' s Disease (Multhaup, Johnson, Phelps, Hirst, Mattes, & Volpe, in preparation). Subjects were tested in two situations, one in which affective responses normally should be largely determined by perceptual aspects of the situation (the melodies study), and one in which affective responses normally should be more likely to involve reflective processes (the Good Guy/Bad Guy study).

The Melodies Study. Subjects heard tape recordings of brief (6–8 sec) excerpts of unfamiliar Korean melodies, played on a piano. Each melody was played 1, 5, or 10 times, in random order. These melodies were then mixed with new melodies from the same pool and presented to subjects in random order. Subjects rated each melody on a 5-point scale, indicating how much they liked it.Under such circumstances, normal subjects often prefer items to which they have previously been exposed, a phenomenon called the mere exposure effect (Seamon et al., 1984; Zajonc, 1980; see Bornstein, 1989, for a review). (The fact that this effect does not necessarily depend on old/new recognition of the stimuli [e.g., Seamon et al.,

1984] is one type of evidence that Zajonc used to argue that emotion can occur in the absence of cognition.) We assumed that preferences for the melodies in the present situation would largely be determined by their perceptual properties, including any changes in perceptual processing as a consequence of experience with them (e.g., increased fluency, Jacoby & Dallas, 1981; perceptual organization, etc.). Thus, we expected normal acquisition of affect in amnesics under these circumstances.

The preference scores for the three amnesic groups and their respective controls are shown in Table 2.1a (collapsed across frequency of presentation, which did not reliably affect preferences; see also Mandler & Shebo, 1983). For both the Korsakoff and the Alzheimer studies, there was a main effect for type of item (old vs. new), and type of item did not interact with group (amnesic vs. control). Subjects preferred old melodies to new ones, and this preference effect was similar in size for patients and controls. In the anterograde amnesic study, there was no overall old/new effect, but when the groups were analyzed separately, the amnesics preferred the old melodies to the new ones ($p < .05$, one-tailed) whereas the

TABLE 2.1
Mean Preference Ratings and Recognition Probabilites
for Patients and Controls

a. Mean Preference Ratings for Old and New Melodies

	Korsakoff* Patients (n = 9)	Korsakoff Controls (n = 9)	Anterograde Amnesics (n = 5)	Ant. Amn. Controls (n = 5)	Alzheimer Patients (n = 12)	Alzheimer Controls (n = 12)
Old	4.10	3.77	4.13	3.47	3.90	3.69
New	3.74	3.46	3.76	3.27	3.58	3.49

b. Probability of Correctly Recognizing Old Melodies

	Korsakoff Patients[a] (n = 9)	Korsakoff Controls[a] (n = 9)	Anterograde Amnesics[b] (n = 5)	Ant. Amn. Controls[b] (n = 5)	Alzheimer Patients[b] (n = 12)	Alzheimer Controls[b] (n = 12)
1 Exp.	.42	.64	.65	.73	.53	.65
5 Exps.	.75	.89	.55	.88	.64	.81
10 Exps.	.61	.97	.70	.93	.72	.86

*Note: Korsakoff data adopted from Johnson, M. K., Kim, J. K., & Risse, G. (1985).
[a]Subjects were given a forced-choice recognition test.
[b]Subjects were given a yes/no recognition test. Scores are the average proportion correct on target and distractor items.

controls did not, although the old/new difference was in the expected direction.

Subjects in all three studies were also tested for recognition memory on a comparable set of melodies (which melodies were tested for preference and which for recognition was counterbalanced across subjects). Recognition scores are shown in Table 2.1b. The data for Korsakoff patients and their controls is based on forced-choice recognition and the data for anterograde amnesics, Alzheimer's patients, and their respective controls, on yes/no recognition; otherwise, testing conditions were similar. It is apparent in Table 2.1b that increasing the number of exposures generally improved recognition (although not significantly so in the case of the anterograde amnesics and their controls), and all amnesic groups showed a marked disruption in recognition relative to their controls.

Recognition is a complex task that tends to draw on both reflective and perceptual processes (e.g., Mandler, 1980, in press). Impaired performance in amnesics on recognition tests is consistent with the idea that they have impaired reflective processes (Johnson, 1983; Johnson & Hirst, in press). The fact that amnesics profit from repetitions on recognition tests is consistent with other findings (Hirst, Johnson, Kim, Phelps, & Volpe, 1986; Hirst, Johnson, Phelps, & Volpe, 1988; Johnson & Kim, 1985; Weinstein & Johnson, 1990), suggesting that some of the processes involved in recognition are intact in amnesia, presumably those drawing on perceptual processes.

Because amnesics and controls were markedly different on recognition but quite similar on preference, and recognition was generally more sensitive to number of exposures than was preference, these data suggest that although both recognition and preference draw on perceptual records recognition and preference in this situation involve somewhat different information or attribution processes. In addition, our primary prediction was supported: The preserved acquisition of preferences for melodies in our three amnesic groups is consistent with the idea that affect that is the consequence of perceptual processes is preserved in amnesia. A related finding is Tranel and Damasio's (1990) report that a severe amnesic (patient Boswell) picked the person who had given him numerous treats significantly above chance when asked to "choose the person you would go to for rewards." This observation is consistent with what we would expect from the MEM framework and our findings from the melody studies, namely that for amnesics as well as normals, affect can become associated with perceptual properties of stimuli. The next study suggests, however, some limitations in the affect that is supported only by perceptual cues.

The Good Guy/Bad Guy Study. This study investigated acquisition of affect in a situation involving much more reflection than would be likely in the melody study. The same three amnesic groups were studied (except that one Alzheimer patient from the melody study was not tested in the Good Guy/Bad Guy Study and there were seven additional Alzheimer patients and six additional Alzheimer Controls). All subjects initially were shown a photograph of a young man, whom we called Bill, and asked to rate him on several personality characteristics (e.g., honesty, intelligence). Then they were shown a photograph of a young man, whom we called John, and asked to rate him on the same attributes. Subjects next heard a tape of some "biographical" information that depicted Bill as a bad guy (e.g., he stole things, broke his wife's arm) and John as a good guy (e.g., he helped his father, he got a Navy commendation for saving someone's life). We did not, of course, expect the amnesics to recall this information as well as the controls. But we were interested in the impact that the biographical information might have on an indirect measure of affective memory—subjects' subsequent impression ratings of the two men.

The exact details of the studies varied somewhat to accommodate exigencies of scheduling (these studies were conducted in the context of other studies that were not necessarily the same across amnesic populations) and, especially, the greater cognitive impairment of the Alzheimer patients. Korsakoff and anterograde amnesics and their corresponding controls rated both men on 20 attributes using a 5-point scale, listened to the biographical information once, and made their second impression rating after approximately 1–2 hours. They heard the biographical information a second time at the end of the first session, returned for a second session after 2–7 days, and rated the men again. They heard the biographical information a third and final time during the second session, and then after about an hour there was a recognition test and the subjects rated the men again. Korsakoffs and their controls returned once more after an average of 20 days and were asked to recognize the target pictures and to rate the men a final time. Alzheimer patients and controls rated each of the men on 7 characteristics on a 3-point scale, heard the biographical information 3 times and rated the men after about a 5-minute delay. They returned 1 month later and were asked to recognize the target pictures and to rate sentences from the biographies for how good or bad the actions were (the results indicated that the Alzheimer patients understood the general meaning of individual sentences of the biographical information). After this comprehension test and a 5-minute delay, they gave impression ratings again. The 5 impression ratings from the Korsakoffs and controls are shown in Fig. 2.4a, the 4 impression ratings from the anterograde amnesics and controls in Fig. 2.4b, and the 3 impression ratings from the Alzheimer patients and controls in Fig. 2.4c.

Both control and amnesic patients initially rated the good guy and the bad guy approximately equally (which is to be expected because pictures were counterbalanced with biographies). The three control groups look quite similar. After hearing the biographical information, they subsequently gave the good guy more favorable ratings and the bad guy less favorable ratings, and these effects persisted over considerable retention intervals (approximately 20 days in Fig. 2.4a, a week in Fig. 2.4b, and a month in Fig. 2.4c). All amnesic groups also showed some impact of the biographical information on impression ratings. Consider T4 in Fig 2.4a and Fig 2.4b. At this point, both Korsakoffs and anterograde amnesics had heard the biographical information three times, with the last presentation being approximately one hour earlier, and they showed more favorable impressions of the good guy than the bad guy. (Interestingly, for the Korsakoffs, impressions persisted for 20 days; see T5). Turning now to the Alzheimer's patients, at T2 they also had heard the biographical information three times (presented in a single session rather than in two sessions as in the other groups) and they also showed differential impressions for the two men when tested 5 minutes after the last presentation. Furthermore, in the Alzheimer group, larger differences on impression ratings were associated with less severe impairment on the Global Deterioration Scale (Reisberg, Ferris, deLeon, & Crook, 1982). Overall, the amnesic patients look generally similar to each other in that the biographical information affected their impression ratings, but the impact was muted compared to effects on the corresponding controls.

Subjects were also tested for recall of the biographical information. Whereas control subjects generally recalled some biographical details, amnesics from all patient groups recalled very little, although some did have the sense that Bill was bad and John was good. In contrast, recognition of the pictures of Bill and John (when each was paired with a distractor) was remarkably good. After an average delay of 20 days, the Korsakoff patients and their controls all recognized both target pictures. Similarly, the anterograde amnesics and their controls all recognized both targets after approximately an hour retention interval. After a 1-month delay all Alzheimer controls and 17 of 18 patients recognized both target pictures. In an additional session 6 months later (with no intervening exposure to the pictures) 14 of 14 Alzheimer controls recognized both target pictures,

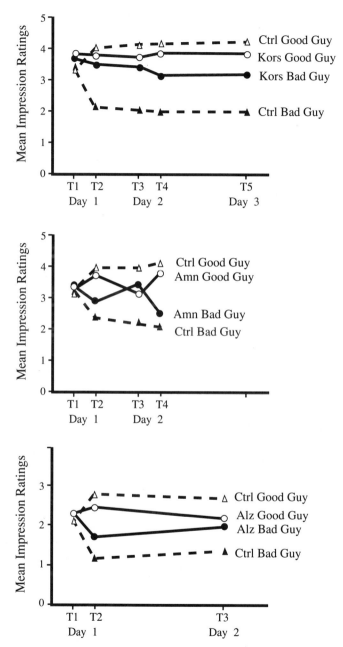

FIG. 2.4. Impression ratings of (a) Korsakoff patients (n = 9) and their controls (n = 9), (b) anterograde amnesics (n = 5) and their controls (n = 5), and (c) Alzheimer patients (n = 18) and their controls (n = 18). FIG. 2.4 Adapted from Johnson, M. K., Kim, J. K., and Risse, G. (1985).

as did 12 of 14 Alzheimer patients (4 patients and 4 controls could not be contacted after the 6-month delay).

In summary, whereas the patient groups showed normal acquisition of preferences for melodies, their acquisition and retention of evaluative impressions about Bill and John was severely disrupted. There are a number of differences in these two studies that might have influenced the results. One interpretation of the difference in outcome between the melody and the Good Guy/Bad Guy studies is that, whereas preferences for melodies depend largely on perceptual processes, evaluative impressions and preferences for people are likely to depend on reflective activity and, most importantly, on its later reactivation. For example, positive affect is likely to accumulate as one hears different positive things about a person and is reminded of earlier positive things. Similarly, negative affect is likely to accumulate as one hears different negative things and is reminded of earlier negative things. Furthermore, impressions may also be influenced by comparing a person to other people you have known, and by making comparative judgments between possible behaviors of the people being thought about. These are cognitive activities that depend on an intact reflective system (especially reactivation and retrieval processes), both for carrying them out and for reviving them later. Normal subjects would be able to engage in such activities and to retrieve them later thus reinstating affective impressions, whereas amnesics would be severely impaired.

The Happy/Sad Study. Another study we conducted with Alzheimer patients provides additional evidence that the impact of some kinds of affective information will be markedly reduced when reflection is disrupted. Patients and controls (18 of each) were shown line drawings of scenes (e.g., a man and a woman sitting at a table). For each one they were told either a "happy" story (e.g., the man and woman are enjoying great success in their restaurant business) or a "sad" story (e.g., the woman is confronting the man about stealing money). The pictures themselves were affectively neutral and whether the story that was paired with a particular picture was happy or sad was counterbalanced across subjects. Approximately 15 minutes later, subjects were shown pairs of pictures, each including one that had been paired with a happy story and one paired with a sad story, and were asked to choose the sadder of the two pictures. This test did not require subjects explicitly to recall the stories and thus, like the preferences and impression ratings in the melody and Good Guy/ Bad Guy studies, provided an indirect measure of retention of affective information.

Alzheimer patients chose the sad picture at a level above chance but were significantly below the controls. When given a new set of items 2 months later and with similar acquisition and testing procedures, the patients were somewhat more impaired than previously (the interaction between group and session was $p < .06$). In a third session 1 month after the second session, we tested subjects on the items that had been presented in sessions 1 and 2. For half the items subjects were to select the sadder of two old pictures and for the other half the familiar picture from an old/new pair. Whereas controls were able to choose the sad picture above chance both for items seen 1 month earlier and for items seen 3 months earlier, Alzheimer patients were at chance on items from both retention intervals. This was not, however, because the patients remembered nothing from the original experience. The Alzheimer patients were above chance (though below controls) for both retention intervals in their ability to discriminate old pictures from new pictures in the forced choice recognition test. Thus, as in the Good Guy/Bad Guy study, for Alzheimer patients, some affective information was initially available, but it did not persist. In contrast, in both the Good Guy/Bad Guy and the happy/sad study, the recognition performance of Alzheimer patients was surprisingly good considering the substantial retention intervals involved.

Although our control subjects did not show any decrease in their impressions of the Good Guy and the Bad Guy over the retention intervals we used, perhaps with enough time they would begin to look like amnesics. The muted affective responses associated with poor recall in amnesics may help explain such phenomena as the reinstatement of Richard Nixon to national acceptability. Those of us who lived through the Watergate hearings and Nixon's resignation from office may now have negative reactions when we read about him or see him on TV, but as it becomes more difficult to recall his specific misdeeds, and what we thought about them at the time, the original rage is gone. Perhaps we don't forgive and forget—rather, we forget and forgive. However, we should not conclude from these studies that emotion is necessarily short-lived compared to other information, although this might be true in some cases (Suengas & Johnson, 1988). Perhaps the relative durability of affective aspects of experience depends on the subsystem that gives rise to the emotion as well as the intensity of the emotion experienced. In the Richard Nixon example, affect would involve a great deal of reflection. In contrast, some investigators have emphasized the potential durability of affective responses arising from what would be P–1 and P–2 processing in MEM (Brewin, 1989; Jacobs & Nadel, 1985).

Memory for Perceived
Versus Imagined Events

Empirical studies of emotion and memory have focused on a range
of phenomena, for example, on accuracy of recall or recognition of
details of emotional events (e. g, Christianson & Loftus, 1987; Loftus
& Burns, 1982), emotion as a cue to event recall (e.g., Bower, 1981),
and effects of mood on memory (see Blaney, 1986, for a review). In
our lab, we have been primarily interested in factors that influence
the likelihood that emotion will be a qualitative part of a memory.
Our studies with amnesics suggest that recapturing affect depends
on whether it is possible to reinstate the records of the initial
processing that led to the initial affective response. Other studies
from our lab have investigated memory for various aspects, including emotion, of complex events. In one study (Suengas & Johnson,
1988, Experiment 3), subjects either imagined (guided by a script) or
actually engaged in a number of "minievents" such as wrapping a
package, having coffee and cookies, and writing a letter. Subjects
then rated their memories for half the situations using a Memory
Characteristics Questionnaire (MCQ) that included items assessing
such qualitative characteristics of their memory as visual detail,
spatial information, emotion, and so forth. The next day subjects
returned and rated their memories for the other half the items (they
also rated the first half again, but those data are not of interest here).
Comparison of Day-1 with Day-2 ratings provide us with information about the retention of various qualitative characteristics of
memories for both actual and imagined events.

   Two things seemed to us to be particularly interesting about these
data. One was that ratings decreased more for imagined than for
perceived events on questions that assessed visual and other perceptual detail. Because perceptual qualities provide highly salient information for discriminating perceived from imagined events in memory
(Johnson, Foley, Suengas, & Raye, 1988; Johnson & Raye, 1981), the
more rapid loss of perceptual information in imagined events than
in perceived events would be quite functional. The second was that
items assessing apperceptive qualities of memories (thoughts and
feelings) showed a relatively rapid loss over the retention interval for
both perceived and imagined events. Thus, relative to other information, the kind of mild affect generated by ordinary events appears to
be forgotten quickly. Again, we thought this finding was interesting
with respect to reality monitoring because results of another study
(Suengas & Johnson, 1988, Experiment 1) had suggested that thinking about apperceptive aspects of real and imagined events after the

fact might reduce their discriminability. If apperceptive qualities were forgotten rapidly, this would reduce the chances that these qualities might be thought about later and create potential difficulty in reality monitoring.

Using a similar minievents paradigm, Hashtroudi, Johnson, and Chrosniak (1990) compared young (mean age = 19.8) and older (mean age = 68.7 years) adults' memories for perceived and imagined complex events. In addition to the MCQ ratings, subjects recalled the events after rating them on Day 2. Again we found greater forgetting of visual detail for imagined than for perceived events. This time, the decrease in thoughts and feelings was not so marked; however, the initial apperceptive ratings in the younger group were somewhat lower than in the previous study, so perhaps ratings did not have so far to fall. In this study, one of the most interesting findings was that older individuals indicated in their ratings that they had better memory for thoughts and feelings than did younger subjects. Consistent with this, in recalling the events, older subjects reported thoughts and feelings and evaluative statements more often than did younger subjects. In contrast, older individuals reported fewer colors, references to nonvisual sensory information, spatial references, and actions than did younger adults. These findings are consistent with the possibility that, in remembering events, there may be a tradeoff between perceptual and affective information (Christianson & Loftus, 1987; Deffenbacher, 1983; Easterbrook, 1959; Mueller, 1979).

To explore reality monitoring, after a 3-week retention interval, subjects were phoned and asked to indicate whether each event (wrapping the package, etc.) was perceived or imagined. Older adults were significantly worse at reality monitoring than were younger adults. This result is consistent with the findings reported by Suengas and Johnson (1988), suggesting that attention to affective qualities of memories might reduce accuracy of reality monitoring. Our conclusions here are tentative because both age groups were near perfect and not all subjects were reached by phone. However, other evidence of poorer reality monitoring in older adults has been reported (Cohen & Faulkner, 1989; Rabinowitz, 1989, but see Hashtroudi, Johnson, & Chrosniak, 1989).

After these data were published, we did additional exploratory analyses and saw an intriguing pattern. The correlations between subjects' ratings of their memories on clarity (a factor largely assessing visual qualities) and the subjects' certainty in the accuracy of their memories was about the same for older (.71) and younger (.76) subjects, but the correlation between the thoughts and feelings factor and certainty in accuracy was significantly higher for older subjects (.51) than for younger subjects (.35). This pattern suggests that older subjects give greater weight to thoughts and feelings in making reality monitoring judgments. If so, it would be consistent with the idea that there are differences between younger and older adults in what is most salient (Hasher & Sacks, 1988). The potential impact on reality monitoring for any age group of differential attention to emotional aspects of experience remains to be explored.

CONCLUSIONS

Among the most central ideas in the emotion literature, and one about which there is considerable consensus, is that emotions differ in the degree of cognitive complexity that gives rise to them. A number of models have been offered to account for this (e.g., Oatley & Johnson-Laird, 1987; Ortony et al., 1988; Roseman, 1984; Smith & Ellsworth, 1985). All add to the developing picture of emotion and, perhaps more importantly, each suggests somewhat different directions for research. In this present chapter, we have tried to show how a number of current ideas about emotion fit within MEM, a general cognitive architecture that characterizes subsystems of mental processes and relations among them. Looking at emotion from this framework highlights a number of interlocking areas for future empirical investigation. These include: an analysis of the relation between emotion and cognitive complexity as indexed in terms of MEM's subsystems and component processes (e.g., retrieving, noting, shifting, rehearsal); conditions controlling a sense of agency and their associated impact on emotional experience; the relation between cognitive development as characterized in MEM and emotional development; the relation between specific cognitive deficits as characterized in MEM and emotional experience and affective memory; and a comparison of the emotional qualities of memories for real and imagined events and the impact of such memories on thought and behavior. Finally, two additional challenging issues are evaluating the usefulness of alternative representational formats for emotion and MEM, and relating MEM to what is currently known about the underlying neurobiology of emotion and cognition.

ACKNOWLEDGMENTS

We would like to thank Carol Raye, Steve Lindsay, Rose Zacks, Joseph LeDoux, Shahin Hashtroudi, and George Mandler for helpful comments on an earlier draft of this chapter.

REFERENCES

Abelson, R. P. (1983). Whatever became of consistency theory? *Personality and Social Psychology Bulletin, 9*, 37–54.

Anderson, J. R. (1983). *The architecture of cognition.* Cambridge, MA: Harvard University Press.

Atkinson, R. C., & Shiffrin, R. M. (1968). Human memory: A proposed system and its control processes. In K. W. Spence (Ed.), *The psychology of learning and motivation: Advances in research and theory* (Vol. 2, pp. 89–195). New York: Academic Press.

Baddeley, A. D. (1986). Domains of recollection. *Psychological Review, 89*, 708–729.

Bandura, A. (1982). The self and mechanisms of agency. In J. Suls (Ed.), *Psychological Perspectives on the Self* (pp. 3–39). Hillsdale, NJ: Lawrence Erlbaum Associates.

Beck, A. T., & Emery, G. (1985). *Anxiety disorders and phobias: A cognitive perspective.* New York: Basic Books.

Berkowitz, L. (1990). On the formation and regulation of anger and aggression: A cognitive-neoassociationistic analysis. *American Psychologist, 45*, 494–503.

Blaney, P. H. (1986). Affect and memory: A review. *Psychological Bulletin, 99*, 229–246.

Bornstein, R. F. (1989). Exposure and affect: Overview and meta-analysis of research, 1968-1987. *Psychological Bulletin, 106*, 265–289.

Bower, G. H. (1981). Mood and memory. *American Psychologist, 36*, 129–148.

Brewin, C. R. (1989). Cognitive change processes in psychotherapy. *Psychological Review, 96*, 379–394.

Buck, R. (1985). Prime theory: An integrated view of motivation and emotion. *Psychological Review, 92*, 389–413.

Carver, C. S., & Scheier, M. F. (1990). Principles of self-regulation: Action and emotion. In E. T. Higgins & R. M. Sorrentino (Eds.), *Handbook of motivation and cognition: Foundations of social behavior* (Vol. 2, pp. 3–52). New York: The Guilford Press.

Christianson, S-Å. & Loftus, E. F. (1987). Memory for traumatic events. *Applied Cognitive Psychology, 1*, 225–239.

Clark, M. S., & Isen, A. M. (1982). Toward understanding the relationship between feeling states and social behavior. In A. H. Hastorf & A. M. Isen (Eds.), *Cognitive social psychology* (pp. 73–108). New York: Elsevier/North Holland.

Cohen, G., & Faulkner, D. (1989). Age differences in source forgetting: Effects on reality monitoring and on eyewitness testimony. *Psychology and Aging, 4*, 10–17.

Cohen, N. J., & Squire, L. R. (1980). Preserved learning and retention of pattern analyzing skill in amnesia: Dissociation of knowing how and knowing that. *Science, 210*, 207–210.

Collins, A. M., & Quillian, M. R. (1969). Retrieval time from semantic memory. *Journal of Verbal Learning and Verbal Behavior, 8*, 240–247.

Craik, F. I. M. (1986). A functional account of age differences in memory. In F. Klix & H. Hagendorf (Eds.), *Human memory and cognitive capabilities* (pp. 409–422). Amsterdam: North Holland.

Craik, F. I. M., & Lockhart, R. S. (1972). Levels of processing: A framework for memory research. *Journal of Verbal Learning and Verbal Behavior, 11*, 671–684.

Damasio, A. R., & Van Hoesen, G. W. (1983). Emotional disturbances associated with focal lesions of the limbic frontal lobe. In K. M. Heilman, & P. Satz (Eds.), *Neuropsychology of human emotion* (pp. 85–110). New York: The Guilford Press.

Deffenbacher, K. (1983). The influence of arousal on reliability of testimony. In B. R. Clifford, & S. Lloyd-Bostock (Eds.), *Evaluating witness evidence*, (pp. 235–251). Chichester: Wiley.

Easterbrook, J. A. (1959). The effect of emotion on cue utilization and the organization of behavior. *Psychological Review, 66*, 183–201.

Eich, E. (1989). Theoretical issues in state dependent memory. In H. L. Roediger III & F. I. M. Craik (Eds.), *Varieties of memory and consciousness: Essays in honour of Endel Tulving* (pp. 331–354). Hillsdale, NJ: Lawrence Erlbaum Associates.

Ekman, P. (1973). Cross-cultural studies of facial expression. In P. Ekman (Ed.), *Darwin and facial expression: A century of research in review* (pp. 169–222). New York: Academic Press.

Ekman, P. (1977). Biological and cultural contributions to body and facial movement. In J. Blacking (Ed.), *Anthropology of the body* (pp. 39–84). London: Academic Press.

Ekman, P. (1984). Expression and the nature of emotion. In K. Scherer & P. Ekman (Eds.), *Approaches to emotion* (pp. 319–343). Hillsdale, NJ: Lawrence Erlbaum Associates.

Ekman, P., Levenson, R. W., & Friesen, W. V. (1983). Autonomic nervous system activity distinguishes between emotions. *Science, 221*, 1208–1210.

Ellsworth, P. C., & Smith, C. A. (1988). From appraisal to emotion: Differences among unpleasant feelings. *Motivation and Emotion, 12*, 271–302.

Fiske, S. T., & Pavelchak, M. A. (1986). Category-based versus piecemeal-based affective responses: Developments in schema-triggered affect. In R. M. Sorrentino & E. T. Higgins (Eds.), *Handbook of motivation and cognition: Foundations of social behavior* (pp. 167–203). New York: The Guilford Press.

Flavell, J. H. (1985). *Cognitive Development* (2nd ed.). Englewood Cliffs, NJ: Prentice-Hall.

Fodor, J. A. (1983). *The modularity of mind.* Cambridge: MIT Press.

Hasher, L., & Zacks, R. T. (1979). Automatic and effortful processes in memory. *Journal of Experimental Psychology, 108*, 356–388.

Hasher, L., & Zacks, R. T. (1988). Working memory, comprehension, and aging: A review and a new view. In G. H. Bower (Ed.), *The psychology of learning and motivation: Advances in research and theory* (Vol. 22), (pp. 193–225). New York: Academic Press.

Hashtroudi, S., Johnson, M. K., & Chrosniak, L. D. (1989). Aging and source monitoring. *Psychology and Aging, 4*, 106–112.

Hashtroudi, S., Johnson, M. K., & Chrosniak, L. D. (1990). Aging and qualitative characteristics of memories for perceived and imagined complex events. *Psychology and Aging, 5*, 119–126.

Heilman, K. M., Watson, R. T., & Bowers, D. (1982). Affective disorders associated with hemispheric disease. In K. M. Heilman, & P. Satz (Eds.), *Neuropsychology of human emotion* (pp. 45–64). New York: The Guilford Press.

Hirst, W., Johnson, M. K., Kim, J. K., Phelps, E. A., Risse, G., & Volpe, B. T. (1986). Recognition and recall in amnesics. *Journal of Experimental Psychology: Learning, Memory, and Cognition, 12*, 445–451.

Hirst, W., Johnson, M. K., Phelps, E. A, & Volpe, B. T. (1988). More on recognition and recall in amnesics. *Journal of Experimental Psychology: Learning, Memory, and Cognition, 14*, 758–762.

Izard, C. E. (1977). *Human emotions.* New York: Plenum Press.

Jacobs, W. J., & Nadel, L. (1985). Stress-induced recovery of fears and phobias. *Psychological Review, 92*, 512–531

Jacoby, L. L. (1983). Remembering the data: Analyzing interactive processes in reading. *Journal of Verbal Learning and Verbal Behavior, 22,* 485–508.

Jacoby, L. L., & Dallas, M. (1981). On the relationship between autobiographical memory and perceptual learning. *Journal of Experimental Psychology: General, 110,* 306–340.

Johnson, M. K. (1983). A multiple-entry, modular memory system. In G. H. Bower (Ed.), *The psychology of learning and motivation: Advances in research theory* (Vol. 17), (pp. 81–123). New York: Academic Press.

Johnson, M. K. (1985). The origin of memories. In P. C. Kendall (Ed.), *Advances in cognitive-behavioral research and therapy* (Vol. 4), (pp. 1–26). New York: Academic Press.

Johnson, M. K. (1988). Discriminating the origin of information. In T. F. Oltmanns, & B. A. Maher (Eds.), *Delusional beliefs: Interdisciplinary perspectives* (pp. 34–65). New York: Wiley.

Johnson, M. K. (1990). Functional forms of human memory. In J. L. McGaugh, N. M. Weinberger & G. Lynch, (Eds.), *Brain organization and memory: Cells, systems and circuits* (pp. 106–134). New York: Oxford University Press.

Johnson, M. K. (1991a). Reality monitoring: Evidence from confabulation in organic brain disease patients. In G. Prigatano & D. L. Schacter (Eds.), *Awareness of deficit after brain injury* (pp. 176–197). New York: Oxford University Press.

Johnson, M. K.(1991b). Reflection, reality monitoring, and the self. In R. Kunzendorf (Ed.), *Mental Imagery.* New York: Plenum Press.

Johnson, M. K., Foley, M. A., Suengas, A. G., & Raye, C. L. (1988). Phenomenal characteristics of memories for perceived and imagined autobiographical events. *Journal of Experimental Psychology: General, 117,* 371–376.

Johnson, M. K., & Hirst, W. (in press). Processing subsystems of memory. In R. G. Lister & H. J. Weingartner (Eds.), *Perspectives in cognitive neuroscience.* New York: Oxford University Press.

Johnson, M. K., & Hirst, W. (in preparation). *MEM: Cognitive subsystems as processes.*

Johnson, M. K., & Kim, J. K. (1985). Recognition of pictures by alcoholic Korsakoff patients. *Bulletin of the Psychonomic Society, 23,* 456–458.

Johnson, M. K., Kim, J. K., & Risse, G. (1985). Do alcoholic Korsakoff's syndrome patients acquire affective reactions? *Journal of Experimental Psychology: Learning, Memory, and Cognition, 11,* 22–36.

Johnson, M. K., & Raye, C. L. (1981). Reality monitoring. *Psychological Review, 88,* 67–85.

Johnson-Laird, P. N., & Oatley, K. (1988, September). *The language of emotions: An analysis of a semantic field,* Princeton University: Cognitive Science Laboratory. Tech. Rep. #33.

Kinsbourne, M., & Bemporad, B. (1984). Lateralization of emotion: A model and the evidence. In N. A. Fox & R. J. Davidson (Eds.), *The psychobiology of affective development* (pp. 259–291). Hillsdale, NJ: Lawrence Erlbaum Associates.

Kosslyn, S. M. (1980). *Image and mind.* Cambridge, MA: Harvard University Press.

Lang, P. J. (1969). The mechanics of desensitization and the laboratory study of fear. In C. M. Franks (Ed.), *Behavior therapy: Appraisal and status* (pp. 160–191). New York: McGraw-Hill.

Lazarus, R. S. (1982). Thoughts on the relations between emotion and cognition. *American Psychologist, 37,* 1019–1024.

LeDoux, J. E. (1987). Emotion. In F. Plum (Ed.), *Handbook of physiology: Sec. 1 The nervous system: Vol. 5. Higher functions of the brain* (pp. 419–459). Bethesda, MD: American Physiological Society.

LeDoux, J. E. (in press). Information flow from sensation to emotion: Plasticity in the neural computation of stimulus value. In M. Gabriel & J. Moore (Eds.), *Neurocomputation and learning: Foundation of adaptive networks.* Cambridge: MIT Press.

LeDoux, J. E., Romanski, L., & Xagoraris, A. (1989). Indelibility of subcortical emotional memories. *Journal of Cognitive Neuroscience, 1,* 238–243.

Leventhal, H., & Scherer, K. (1987). The relationship of emotion to cognition: A functional approach to a semantic controversy. *Cognition and Emotion, 1,* 3–28.

Leventhal, H., & Tomarken, A. J. (1986). Emotion: Today's problems. *Annual Review of Psychology, 37,* 565–610.

Lewis, M., Sullivan, M. W., Stanger, C., & Weiss, M. (1989). Self-development and self-conscious emotions. *Child Development, 60,* 146–156.

Loftus, E. F., & Burns, T. E. (1982). Mental shock can produce retrograde amnesia. *Memory and Cognition, 10,* 318–323.

Mandler, G. (1980). Recognizing: The judgment of previous occurrence. *Psychological Review, 87,* 252–271.

Mandler, G. (1984). *Mind and body: Psychology of emotion and stress.* New York: Norton.

Mandler, G. (in press). Your face looks familiar but I can't remember your name: A review of dual process theory. In W. E. Hockley & S. Lewandowsky (Eds.), *Relating theory and data: Essays on human memory in honor of Bennet B. Murdock.* Hillsdale, NJ: Lawrence Erlbaum Associates.

Mandler, G., Nakamura, Y., & Van Zandt, B. J. S. (1987). Nonspecific effects of exposure on stimuli that cannot be recognized. *Journal of Experimental Psychology: Learning, Memory, and Cognition, 13,* 646–648.

Mandler, G., & Shebo, B. J. (1983). Knowing and liking. *Motivation and Emotion, 7,* 125–144.

Meichenbaum, D. (1977). *Cognitive-behavior modification: An integrative approach.* New York: Plenum Press.

Miller, G. A., Galanter, E., & Pribram, K. A. (1960). *Plans and the structure of behavior.* New York: Holt, Rhinehart, & Winston.

Multhaup, K. S., Johnson, M. K., Phelps, E. A., Hirst, W., Mattes, J. A., & Volpe, B. T. (in preparation). *Affect and memory disorders: Anterograde amnesia and Alzheimer's disease.*

Nelson, T. O., & Narens, L. (1990). Metamemory: A theoretical framework and some new findings. In G. H. Bower (Ed.), *The psychology of learning and motivation* (Vol. 26, pp. 125–173). New York: Academic Press.

Norman, D. A., & Shallice, T. (1986). Attention to action: Willed and automatic control of behavior. In R. J. Davidson, G. E. Schartz, & D. Shapiro, (Eds.), *Consciousness and self regulation* (pp. 1–18). New York: Plenum Press.

Oatley, K., & Johnson-Laird, P. N. (1987). Towards a cognitive theory of emotions. *Cognition and Emotion, 1,* 29–50.

Öhman, A., Dimberg, U., & Öst, L. G. (1985). Animal and social phobias: Biological constraints on learned responses. In S. Reiss & R. Bootzin (Eds.), *Theoretical Issues in behavior therapy* (pp. 123–175). New York: Academic Press.

Ortony, A., Clore, G. L., & Collins, A. (1988). *The cognitive structure of emotions.* New York: Cambridge University Press.

Paivio, A. (1971). *Imagery and verbal processes.* New York: Holt.

Palmer, S. E. (1975). Visual perception and world knowledge: Notes on a model of sensory-cognitive interaction. In D. A. Norman & D. E. Rumelhart (Eds.), *Exploration in cognition* (pp. 279–307). San Francisco: Freeman.

Perlmutter, M. (1984). Continuities and discontinuities in early human memory paradigms, processes, and performance. In R. Kail & N. E. Spear (Eds.), *Comparative perspectives on the development of memory* (pp. 253–284). Hillsdale, NJ: Lawrence Erlbaum Associates.

Pirolli, P. L., & Anderson, J. R. (1985). The role of practice in fact retrieval. *Journal of Experimental Psychology: Learning, Memory, and Cognition, 11,* 136–153.

Plutchik, R. (1980). *Emotion: A psychoevolutionary synthesis.* New York: Harper & Row.

Polivy, J. (1990). Inhibition of internally cued behavior. In E. Tory Higgins & R. M. Sorrentino (Eds.), *Handbook of motivation and cognition: Foundations of social behavior* (Vol. 2, pp. 131–147). New York: The Guilford Press.

Posner, M. I., Petersen, S. E., Fox, P. T., & Raichle, M. E. (1988). Localization of cognitive operations in the human brain. *Science, 240,* 1627–1631.

Rabinowitz, J. C. (1989). Judgments of origin and generation effects: Comparisons between young and elderly adults. *Psychology and Aging, 4,* 259–268.

Reisberg, B., Ferris, S. M., deLeon, M. J., & Crook, T. (1982). The global deterioration scale for assessment of primary degenerative dementia (PDD). *American Journal of Psychiatry, 139,* 1136–1139.

Roediger, M. L., III, & Blaxton, T. A. (1987). Retrieval modes produce dissociations in memory for surface information. In D. S. Gorfein & R. R. Hoffman (Eds.), *Memory and cognitive processes: The Ebbinghaus centennial conference* (pp. 349–379). Hillsdale, NJ: Lawrence Erlbaum Associates.

Roseman, I. J. (1984). Cognitive determinants of emotion: A structural theory. In P. Shaver (Ed.), *Review of personality and social psychology* (pp. 11–36). Beverly Hills, CA: Sage.

Schacter, D. L., & Moscovitch, M. (1984). Infants, amnesics, and dissociable memory systems. In M. Moscovitch (Ed.), *Infant memory* (pp. 173–216). New York: Plenum Press.

Seamon, J. G., Marsh, R. L., & Brody, N. (1984). Critical importance of exposure duration for affective discrimination of stimuli that are not recognized. *Journal of Experimental Psychology: Learning, Memory, and Cognition, 100,* 465–469.

Seligman, M. E. P. (1971). Phobias and preparedness. *Behavioral Therapy, 2,* 307–321.

Shallice, T. (1988). *From neuropsychology to mental structure.* Cambridge: Cambridge University Press.

Sherry, D. F., & Schacter, D. L. (1987). The evolution of multiple memory systems. *Psychological Review, 94,* 439–454.

Shiffrin, R. M., & Schneider, W. (1977). Controlled and automatic human information processing: II. Perceptual learning, automatic attending, and a general theory. *Psychological Review, 84,* 127–190.

Smith, C. A., & Ellsworth, P. C. (1985). Patterns of cognitive appraisal in emotion. *Journal of Personality and Social Psychology, 48,* 813–838.

Squire, L. R. (1987). *Memory and brain.* New York: Oxford University Press.

Stuss, D. T., & Benson, D. F. (1986). *The frontal lobes.* New York: Raven Press.

Suengas, A. G., & Johnson, M. K. (1988). Qualitative effects of rehearsal on memories for perceived and imagined complex events. *Journal of Experimental Psychology: General, 117,* 377–389.

Tomkins, S. S. (1962). *Affect, imagery, consciousness. 1: The positive affects.* New York: Springer-Verlag.

Tomkins, S. S. (1963). *Affect, imagery, consciousness. 2: The negative affects.* New York: Springer-Verlag.

Tranel, D., & Damasio, A. R. (1990, February). *Covert learning of emotional valence in patient Boswell.* Paper presented at the meeting of the International Neuropsychological Society, Kissimmee, FL.

Tulving, E. (1983). *Elements of episodic memory.* New York: Oxford University Press.

Warrington, E. G., & Weiskrantz, L. (1982). Amnesia: A disconnection syndrome? *Neuropsychologia, 20,* 233–248.

Waugh, N. C., & Norman, D. A. (1965). Primary memory. *Psychological Review, 72,* 89–104.

Weinstein, A., & Johnson, M. K. (1990, February). *Recognition memory in amnesia.* Paper presented at the meeting of the International Neuropsychological Society, Kissimmee, FL.

White, R. W. (1959). Motivation reconsidered: The concept of competence. *Psychological Review, 66,* 297–333.

Wickelgren, W. A. (1979). Chunking and consolidation: A theoretical synthesis of semantic networks, configuring in conditioning, S–R versus cognitive learning, normal forgetting, the amnesic syndrome, and the hippocampal arousal system. *Psychological Review, 86,* 44–60.

Zajonc, R. B. (1980). Feeling and thinking: Preferences need no inferences. *American Psychologist, 35,* 151–175.

3

Emotion and Implicit Memory

Betsy A. Tobias
John F. Kihlstrom
Daniel L. Schacter
University of Arizona

A topic of major theoretical interest within cognitive psychology pertains to the bidirectional relations among cognitive and emotional processes. In this literature, most attention has been focused on memory phenomena of various kinds (Blaney, 1986; Bower, 1981; Ellis & Ashbrook, 1987, 1988; Johnson & Magaro, 1987). And almost without exception, this research has focused on "conscious" or explicit memory: the person's conscious, intentional recollection of some previous episode, most commonly reflected in standard tests of recall and recognition. So, for example, congruence between the the individual's mood states at encoding and retrieval appears to affect the accessibility of memories (Eich & Metcalfe, 1989). Moreover, the retrieval of emotional memories obviously can affect the individual's mood state—although this effect has not received much attention in the experimental literature. However, there is more to memory than what the individual can bring to awareness in an act of conscious, intentional, recall or recognition. The purpose of this chapter is to review findings that can be conceptualized as involving what has variously been referred to as unconscious memory (e.g., Breuer & Freud, 1893/1955; Prince, 1914), memory without awareness (e.g., Eich, 1984; Eriksen, 1960; Jacoby & Witherspoon, 1982), or implicit memory (Graf & Schacter, 1985; Schacter, 1987, 1989, in press).

DISSOCIATIONS BETWEEN IMPLICIT
AND EXPLICIT MEMORY

Defined most broadly, implicit memory is demonstrated by a change
in behavior that is attributable to some prior episode of experience,
but that cannot be accounted for by explicit memory for that event.
Typically, implicit memory is revealed by tasks that do not require
conscious or intentional recollection of those experiences (Schacter,
1987, p. 501). For example, in an experiment by Kihlstrom (1980),
hypnotized subjects memorized a list of words, followed by suggestions of posthypnotic amnesia for the learning experience. As expected, these subjects showed a dense amnesia for the wordlist, as
measured by free recall. Nevertheless, they were more likely to
produce list items as responses on a word-association task. Similar
results were obtained in a second experiment involving category
instance generation. In an experiment by Graf and Schacter (1985),
amnesic patients and normal controls studied a list of paired associates. Later, they were presented with the first word of the pair. For
some test items, the subjects were asked to recall the associated word
from the previously studied list; not surprisingly, the amnesic patients performed quite poorly. For other items, the subjects were
provided with the first three letters of the second item and gave the
first word that came to mind: On this task, amnesics and controls
were equally likely to give an item from the previous list.

In both experiments, subjects showed a facilitation in task performance that was attributable to a prior experience. Nevertheless,
these same subjects were unable to remember the experiences
themselves. Thus, these experiments illustrate the dissociation between explicit and implicit memory (for more complete reviews, see
Richardson-Klavehn & Bjork, 1988; Schacter, 1987, 1989, in press).
This dissociation is manifested in one of two ways. First, explicit
memory is impaired whereas implicit memory is (at least relatively)
spared. This situation is illustrated in the specimen experiments
described before, as well as in aging (Schacter, Kaszniak, & Kihlstrom,
in press) and surgical anesthesia (Kihlstrom & Schacter, 1990a).
Second, different variables affect performance on explicit and implicit
memory tasks. For example, some experiments find that level of
processing affects explicit but not implicit memory (Graf & Mandler,
1984), whereas others find that modality shifts between study and
test affect implicit but not explicit memory (Schacter & Graf, 1989).

It is possible that explicit and implicit memory effects reflect the
operations of several different memory systems in the brain concerned with the perceptual representation of experience, procedural

memory for skill knowledge, semantic memory for conceptual relations, and episodic memory for experiences (Tulving & Schacter,
1990). Although theoretical interpretation of relevant phenomena
remains somewhat controversial, what is clear is that explicit and
implicit memory are two different modes by which memory for some
prior event can be expressed. In this chapter, we focus on implicit
expressions of memory, in order to address two fundamental questions derived from the bidirectional relations between memory and
emotion: "Does implicit memory affect emotional experience?"; and
"Does emotional experience affect implicit memory?"

EMOTION AS IMPLICIT MEMORY

Although studies of implicit memory have most commonly employed verbal tasks such as stem and fragment completion, lexical
decision, or free association, in principle a great variety of tasks can
reveal the impact of a previous event on experience, thought, and
action. For example, Schacter, Cooper, and Delaney (1990) showed
that implicit memory facilitated subjects' decisions about whether
line drawings represented possible or impossible objects—a perceptual task far removed from conventional memory paradigms. Implicit
memory has also been revealed on tasks involving eyelid conditioning
(e.g., Weiskrantz & Warrington, 1979), identification of dot patterns
(Musen & Triesman, 1990), and judgments of auditory noise (Jacoby,
Allan, Collins, & Larwill, 1988). Accordingly, it seems possible that
implicit memory may also be expressed through emotional responses;
that is, emotional responses, as well as performance on perceptual
and semantic memory tasks, may reflect implicit memory for some
prior experience.

Consider the following illustrations of the type of phenomenon we
have in mind:

> In a classic demonstration of organic amnesia, Claparede (1911/1951)
> pricked an unsuspecting Korsakoff's syndrome patient with a pin hidden
> in his hand. Subsequently the patient refused to shake his hand, despite
> the fact that she had no explicit memory for the prior incident.

> Madame D, a case reported by Janet (1893, 1904), acquired hysterical
> somnambulism with amnesia after some men jokingly deposited her
> drunken husband on her doorstep and announced that he was dead. She
> had no conscious recollection of the event but "froze with terror" every
> time she passed that door.

> Bagby (1928) reported on a woman with a phobia for running water. She
> had no memory of the circumstances under which this reaction had been

acquired until adulthood when she was visited by an aunt who triggered memory for a childhood incident where she had strayed away from a picnic and became trapped under a waterfall.

Levinson (1967) reported on a woman who came out of surgery inexplicably weepy, depressed, and disconsolate. To his surprise the woman blurted out while under hypnosis, "the surgeon says it might be malignant"! Further investigation revealed that the doctors had discovered a possible malignancy during the surgery and had discussed it while she was anesthetized.

In each of these cases, the person shows a change in emotional response—refusing to shake hands, freezing at a doorway, fearing running water, or feeling depressed—that is directly attributable to some previous experience; yet in each case, the experience itself is not remembered. In principle, this dissociation between the person's emotional response and his or her conscious recollection is analogous to the dissociation between implicit and explicit memory observed in the laboratory. In the following pages, we expand this anecdotal evidence, reviewing four areas of research that seem to reveal experience-based changes in evaluative judgment, affective response, or emotional state that occur in the absence of explicit memory for the experiences themselves: emotional behavior in brain-damaged patients, functional amnesias observed in the dissociative disorders, hypnotic alterations in emotional state, and "mere exposure" effects in implicit perception.

Neurological Patients

Some of the most dramatic dissociations between explicit and implicit memory have been observed in patients with organic brain syndrome. For example, bilateral lesions in the medial portions of the temporal lobe (including the hippocampus) and diencephalon (including the mammillary bodies) results in a gross anterograde amnesia, such that the patients cannot remember events that occurred since the damage occurred. For example, when asked to study a list of familiar words and then recall the items, they show gross impairments of memory. However, when asked to complete a stem or fragment with a meaningful word, they show much the same priming effects as intact subjects, demonstrating intact implicit memory (e.g., Graf, Squire, & Mandler, 1984; Moscovitch, 1982; Schacter, 1985; Warrington & Weiskrantz, 1974).

Both anecdotal evidence and formal experiments indicate that emotional responses can be preserved as implicit memories in amnesic patients, in the absence of explicit memory for the experiences on which these responses are based. The observation by Claparede (1911/1951), already noted, could be construed in this manner. Even earlier, Korsakoff (1889)—who first identified the amnesic syndrome—observed that a patient who had received an electrical shock, but had no explicit memory for the experience, responded to the case that contained the shock apparatus by stating that the doctor had probably come to electrify him, again suggesting a link between emotional response and implicit memory.

Two studies by Johnson, Kim, and Risse (1985) turned these kinds of anecdotal observations into formal experiments. Their first study was based on the "mere exposure" effect documented by Zajonc (1968), who showed that repeated exposure to an object tends to increase judgments of likability, even if there is no substantive information presented that would support such attitudinal change.[1] In the experiment, Korsakoff patients and controls were presented with unfamiliar Korean melodies. As expected from the mere exposure effect, both Korsakoff patients and controls preferred old melodies over new melodies. However, the patients showed greatly impaired levels of recognition. A second study provided subjects with more substantive contact with the stimulus materials. Amnesics and controls were presented with pictures of two faces, accompanied by fictional biographical information, that depicted one individual positively and the other negatively. When asked whom they preferred, control subjects always chose the face that had been paired with the positive information; and they were always able to state that their judgment was made on the basis of the accompanying descriptive information. The patients also showed a strong preference for the "good guy"; however, they could give only vague reasons, usually the person's physical appearance, for their judgment. This preference was maintained at 1-year follow-up.

A similar experiment was performed by Damasio, Tranel, and Damasio (1985) using patient Boswell, a man who was rendered densely amnesic following a case of herpes encephalitis. Despite a profound inability to recognize people, it had been noted that Boswell would go to a particularly generous staff member if he

---

[1]Whether these kinds of preference judgments represent truly affective responses is open to debate. Preferences may be based on emotional considerations, as when one falls in love; but they may also reflect purely intellectual judgments, as when one admires a musical composition by Elliot Carter for the way the notes are strung together; in some cases, they may merely stem from a social requirement to make a choice, despite the lack of any motivation or basis for doing so. Whatever their source, it is clear that expressed preferences may have emotional consequences.

wanted something. In the experiment, Boswell had an extended series of positive, negative, and neutral encounters, respectively, with three different confederates. Upon subsequent questioning, Boswell was unable to recall anything about any of the people and never indicated that they were familiar in any way. Nonetheless, when asked on a forced-choice test whom he liked best, and would approach for rewards and favors, he strongly preferred the "good" confederate over the "bad" one, with the neutral confederate falling inbetween. These preferences were also maintained at a 4-year follow-up.

The Damasio et al. (1989) experiment is somewhat more difficult to interpret than the one by Johnson et al. (1985), because the pairing of faces and affective valence was not counterbalanced, no information regarding checks on pre-experimental preferences was given, and exposure time was confounded with valence. Nevertheless, pending confirmation with tighter controls, the study suggests that emotional responses involving relatively complex behavioral interactions can reflect implicit memory in amnesic patients. It also offers a new type of implicit measure, a social judgment (who the patient would they go to for treats), and thus broadens the areas of emotional behavior that can be said to be affected by implicit memory.

Somewhat similar findings have been observed in prosopagnosic patients who suffer a deficit in facial recognition following bilateral lesions in the mesial portions of the occipital and temporal cortex. These patients are unable to recognize previously encountered faces as familiar, but they do show differential autonomic responses to old and new faces, as measured by skin conductance or resistance (Bauer, 1984; deHaan, Young, & Newcombe, 1987; Tranel & Damasio, 1985). Of course, such responses are not necessarily emotional in nature. Nevertheless, most theorists agree that emotion is accompanied by physiological arousal. Thus, these studies raise the possibility that at least the beginnings of an emotional response to a face may be preserved, even in the absence of conscious memory for the prior experience(s) on which that response is based.

Functional Amnesia

In addition to the disorders of memory produced by lesions to specific brain structures, there are also functional amnesias—memory losses attributable to events or processes that do not result in damage or injury to the brain but that produce more forgetting than would normally occur (for reviews, see Hilgard, 1977; Kihlstrom & Schacter, in press; Kihlstrom, Tataryn, & Hoyt, 1990; Schacter & Kihlstrom,

1989). Chief among these are the dissociative syndromes of psychogenic amnesia (also known as limited amnesia), psychogenic fugue (also known as functional retrograde amnesia), and multiple personality disorder. In each case, the patient experiences a loss of autobiographical memory, often accompanied by a loss or change in personal identity as well. In most instances, the memory loss is instigated by some traumatic event, which is itself covered by the amnesia. One of the interesting features of the functional amnesias is that patients often display implicit memory for events lost to conscious recollection: Sometimes this implicit memory takes the form of an emotional response. Janet's (1893, 1904) case of Madame D., cited earlier, illustrates this point. Another case involved a woman who had no conscious recollection of the events surrounding the death of her mother but had recurring "hallucinations" regarding those events that contained specific emotionally laden memories from the days immediately preceding and following the death.

More recent case studies show the same kinds of effects. For example, Gudjonsson and Haward (1982) found that a fugue patient who had been suicidal prior to the onset of her amnesia responded to Rorschach inkblots predominantly with death-related images, even though she had no explicit memory for her suicide threats or the circumstances surrounding it. In a case reported by Kaszniak et al. (1988), a victim of attempted homosexual rape was amnesic for the incident but experienced severe distress when shown a TAT card picturing a person attacking another from behind. Similarly, Christianson and Nilsson (1989) observed that a woman who had suffered severe amnesia following assault and rape became extremely upset when taken back to the scene of the assault, even though she had no explicit memory for the event.

Amnesia between personalities has come to be known as one of the most striking features of multiple personality disorder (Schacter & Kihlstrom, 1989) although this phenomenon is unfortunately not well represented in current diagnostic criteria (Kihlstrom et al., 1990). As in other cases of functional amnesia, there is some indication that certain types of implicit memory may transfer across ego states (e.g. Nissen, Ross, Willingham, Mackenzie, & Schacter, 1988), and that implicit memory may take the form of an emotional response. Prince's (1910) Miss Beauchamp is such a case. Personality "B IV," experienced strong emotional reactions to people and places that had emotional meaning to personality "B I" and vice versa. However, neither personality had explicit memory for the emotionally arousing objects of the other, and each would be puzzled by their intense reactions to such stimuli.

An experimental study by Ludwig and his colleagues (Ludwig, Brandsma, Wilbur, Bendfeldt, & Jameson, 1972) examined transfer of acquired information between personalities in the case of patient Jonah, one of whose ego states was densely amnesic for the other three. They found evidence for the transfer of a conditioned fear response to a light or tone (previously paired with shock) and of a GSR response to words that had unique emotional significance for each of the personalities. This study was not formally conceptualized in terms of the explicit–implicit distinction, and the transfer of implicit memory between alter egos was not limited to emotional material. Nevertheless, the results show that dissociated ego states can share emotional responses to events, even if they do not share conscious access to the memories on which these responses are based. Insofar as amnesia is a diagnostic feature of multiple personality (Kihlstrom et al., 1990), further study of emotional learning in multiple personality would seem to be in order.

Amnesia and the Hypnotic Induction of Emotion

Hypnosis is a social interaction in which one person offers suggestions to another person for imaginative experiences involving alterations in perception, memory, thought, and voluntary behavior. Among the most dramatic effects is posthypnotic amnesia, in which subjects are unable to remember the events and experiences that transpired during hypnosis. Nevertheless, as indicated earlier, a wide variety of studies indicates that the effects of posthypnotic amnesia are selective, impairing explicit memory but sparing implicit memory (e.g., Kihlstrom, 1980; for reviews, see Kihlstrom, 1985; Kihlstrom & Hoyt, 1990). Hypnotic suggestions are typically intended to alter some aspect of cognitive functioning, but they can also have emotional and motivational effects; that is, subjects' emotional states can be altered, directly or indirectly, by means of hypnotic suggestion.

In a classic series of studies, Luria (1932) suggested to hypnotized subjects that they had committed a crime that was too terrible to think about; this paramnesia was then followed by a further suggestion for posthypnotic amnesia. Although the subjects did not have any conscious recollection for the paramnesia suggestion and failed to recognize the significance of words drawn from the paramnesia, they tended to respond to stimulus words relating to the paramnesia with irrelevant hand movements (a sign of emotional distress; see Wishner, 1955), despite their failure to recognize the relevance of the critical words to the suggestion. Luria's observations were essentially confirmed by Huston, Shakow, and Erickson (1934; see also Erickson, 1935, 1944). These and other early findings (for reviews, see Deckert & West, 1963; Reyher, 1962) prompted further research by a number of investigators. For example, Reyher (1967) and his colleagues, working from an avowedly psychoanalytic perspective quite different from that which guided Luria, suggested paramnesias designed to induce sexual or aggressive feelings.

Other researchers have employed alternatives to the paramnesia technique. For example, Blum (1967, 1979) and his colleagues asked hypnotized subjects to relive an actual experience from their own childhood that is of a conflictual, ego-threatening nature. The remembered event itself was then covered by an amnesia suggestion, leaving the subject in a state of free-floating emotional arousal. They have shown that arousal, manipulated in this manner, affects performance on a variety of cognitive and personality tests. Similarly, Bower (1981) devised a hypnotic mood induction technique that involves giving suggestions during hypnosis to visualize and re-experience personal emotionally valent events and experience a certain intensity of affect during this retrieval. A posthypnotic suggestion is then given that they will have no memory for the images that generated the emotions but that they will nevertheless respond to a cue (a colored piece of paper) with a particular emotion.

Levitt and his colleagues (e.g., Levitt & Chapman, 1979; Levitt, Persky, & Brady, 1964), by contrast, administered direct suggestions for anxiety, followed by suggestions for amnesia. In both cases, the subjects showed increased signs of emotional arousal on both standard psychological tests (e.g., responses on the MMPI or projective techniques) and experimental tasks (e.g., psychophysiological indices, Stroop performance), compared to controls. Reyher (1967) and his colleagues have gone even further, by showing that their procedures can produce a variety of somatic symptoms, such as nausea, headaches, and perspiration. However, by virtue of amnesia the subjects in these experiments are unaware of the source of their emotional state.

Except for Bower's (1981) work, these studies were designed and interpreted within an explicitly psychoanalytic framework, in which posthypnotic amnesia was construed as analogous to repression. Thus, the experience of emotion and other signs of conflict, in the context of a failure to consciously remember the source of the emotional state, were considered to be analogous to the "return of the repressed" in classic Freudian theory. However, there is no good evidence that posthypnotic amnesia is analogous to repression

(Kihlstrom & Hoyt, 1990). An alternative interpretation is simply in terms of the dissociation between explicit and implicit memory; that is, the amnesic subjects lack explicit memory for the suggestion (e.g., to relive a particular emotional experience); but the emotional arousal they subsequently experience can be construed as an implicit memory for that event. Thus subjects exhibit implicit memory for the images in their responses to the cue in the absence of any explicit memory for why they are experiencing the emotion.

"Mere Exposure" Effects in Implicit Perception

In the standard implicit memory experiment, subjects are aware of the event at the time it occurs but subsequently fail to consciously recollect that event. However, similar effects can be observed even in the absence of conscious awareness (Kihlstrom, 1987, 1990). For example, Zajonc and his colleagues have obtained mere exposure effects on preference ratings even when subjects are unaware of the exposure trials. Wilson (1979) found that subjects preferred tones that had been presented in the unattended channel during a dichotic listening procedure to tones that had not been previously presented, despite the fact that their recognition of these tones was significantly impaired. Similarly, Kunst-Wilson & Zajonc (1980; Zajonc, 1980) gave subjects brief tachistoscopic presentations of irregular polygons and found that rated preference was affected by prior exposure, even though the stimuli themselves were recognized at chance levels. Their "subliminal" mere exposure effect was replicated and extended by Seamon and his colleagues (Seamon, Brody, & Kauff, 1983a, l983b; Seamon, Marsh, & Brody, 1984). Mandler, Nakamura, and Van Zandt (1987) also confirmed this finding and extended it to a variety of other, nonemotional, judgments.

Subjects' expressed preferences, reflecting implicit perception and memory, may have implications for subsequent emotional judgments and behavior that would be clearly labelled as "emotional." Bargh and Pietromonaco (1982) found that subjects who had been subliminally exposed to hostile words attributed significantly more negative qualities to a pictured person than subjects who had not received this exposure. Similarly, Bornstein, Leone, and Galley (1987) found that subliminal exposures can affect not only preferences for people's faces but also subsequent interpersonal behavior towards those same people. Finally, Greenwald, Klinger, and Liu (1989) found that evaluative judgments of words were facilitated by the masked presentation of a prime with the same affective valence.

Dissociation and Desynchrony

All four of the areas just reviewed provide some evidence for changes in evaluative judgment, affective response, or emotional state in the absence of explicit memory for the experiences themselves. In some respects, the dissociation observed between emotional responses to an event on the one hand, and explicit memory for the event itself on the other, is reminiscent of the concept of desynchrony among response systems in emotion (Hodgson & Rachman, 1974; Rachman, 1978; Rachman & Hodgson, 1974). In classic research on experimental neurosis in dogs (for a review, see Mineka & Kihlstrom, 1978), Gantt (1953) had observed that separate components of a conditioned response may be acquired and extinguished at different rates and persist for different lengths of time, resulting in a state of "schizokinesis." More recently, Lang (1968, 1971) proposed a multiple-system theory of emotion, in which several components—subjective, behavioral, and physiological—were only imperfectly coupled. When all three systems act together, the person experiences intense emotional arousal. Under conditions of mild arousal, however, they may be partially independent. Later, Rachman (1978; Hodgson & Rachman, 1974; Rachman & Hodgson, 1974) explored the implications of desynchrony among emotional systems for the treatment of anxiety disorders. For example, treatments such as flooding (implosion therapy) will affect the behavioral component of fear before they affect the subjective and physiological components (see also Mineka, 1979, 1985a, 1985b).

Desynchrony is nicely illustrated by research by Miller (Miller & Marlin, 1979; Miller & Springer, 1973) on electro convulsive shock (ECS) induced amnesia in rats. In their experiment, administration of ECS immediately following a standard one-trial, step-down, passive-avoidance conditioning paradigm (rats stepped off a shelf and received footshock) produced the usual retrograde amnesia: The animal no longer made the passive-avoidance response. However, when the rats stepped off the shelf, EKC recordings showed a substantial increase in heart rate. The discrepancy between the behavioral response (passive avoidance) and the physiological response (heart rate acceleration) to a fear stimulus is what is meant by desynchrony. Of course, both responses are indices of memory (for the footshock) as well as fear (of stepping down), and it is worth noting that similar dissociations between verbal behavior and physiological responses have been documented in the studies of amnesic syndrome and hypnotic amnesia described earlier.

Although the analogy between desynchrony and dissociation is tempting, it is not exact. Thus, for example, verbal reports of recall or recognition, usually classified as evidence of explicit memory, presumably reflect the subjective experience of remembering; but they are also items of behavior. Accordingly, it is not easy to identify explicit memory with one component of emotion, and implicit memory with the others. Furthermore, it would seem that the subjective experience of emotion itself has at least three components, reflecting the person's awareness of his or her emotional state, of the eliciting stimulus, and of past emotional encounters with that stimulus. In this way, the dissociation between explicit and implicit memory offers a new perspective on the problem of desynchrony: There may be dissociations *within* emotion components, as well as between them (Hugdahl, 1981).

EMOTIONAL EFFECTS ON IMPLICIT MEMORY

We turn now to a consideration of whether mood or emotional state can affect implicit memory, as expressed on nominally nonemotional tasks. The effects of mood on memory fall into three general categories: (a) mood-dependent memory effects, where retrieval is facilitated by a match between encoding and retrieval mood states; (b) mood-congruent memory effects, where mood at time of encoding or retrieval facilitates retrieval of affectively congruent material; and (c) resource allocation effects, where extreme or negative mood states at encoding or retrieval impair processing. As noted earlier, all these effects have been documented in studies of explicit memory, employing conventional tests of recall or recognition. This raises the question of the effects of emotional state on implicit memory.

Two Hypotheses About Context and Memory

From one point of view, it might be expected that emotional state would have relatively little effect on implicit memory. Consider the phenomenon of mood-dependent retrieval. A shift in mood state between encoding and retrieval can be considered analogous to a change in the subject's internal physiological environment, as in the classic phenomenon of drug-state-dependent memory, or in the external ecology, as in the phenomenon of environment-dependent memory. In all three cases, the shift in context (internal or external, physiological or mental) appears to induce a type of amnesia. In many forms of amnesia, memory loss often is greatest in the explicit domain, with implicit memory being relatively preserved. From this fact, one might expect that implicit memory would be preserved for material that is rendered inaccessible to explicit memory because of mood shifts. That is to say, implicit memory may transfer over various mood states, even when explicit memory does not.

This hypothesis is supported by further consideration of the functional dissociations observed between explicit and implicit memory. Although explicit memory is affected by a wide variety of encoding factors, the variables that most consistently have been found to affect implicit memory are changes in the surface features of the events (e.g., Roediger & Blaxton, 1987; Roediger, Weldon, & Challis, 1989; Schacter, in press)—at least when the implicit measure is data driven or perceptually based. Because affect changes the connotative meanings of events, but not their perceptual features, mood may constitute another variable that affects explicit but not implicit memory.

On the other hand, there may be reasons to suggest that context effects, including mood effects, will be observed to a *greater* extent in implicit memory than explicit memory. For example, the psychoactive drugs that induce state-dependent memory in humans (e.g., alcohol, marijuana, barbiturates) can alter sensory-perceptual processes. In fact, Graf (1989) suggested that environmental contexts directly alter the processing of perceptual or surface features of events, producing effects analogous to modality shifts. Accordingly, Graf has found that shifts in environmental context affect implicit memory even when they do not affect explicit memory. The same argument could be made for the effects of mood contexts: Perhaps the world does look darker to sad people, and brighter to those who are happy.

Moreover, it is important to recognize that mood is not just a state, like sleep or hypnosis, that alters perception or induces a kind of amnesia. Mood is also a contextual cue, like other cues, that is processed when memories are encoded and guides the course of retrieval. In an effort to understand the apparent unreliability of context-dependent memory, Eich (1980, 1989) has argued that state-dependent memory is a cue-dependent phenomenon that critically depends on the nature of the cues available at retrieval (see also Kihlstrom, 1989; Kihlstrom, Brenneman, Pistole, & Shor, 1985). From his point of view, a primary reason for inconsistency in the results of studies on context-dependent memory findings is the tendency for other, stronger cues to overshadow the usually weak context cue. These potentially stronger cues may include experimenter-presented or subject-generated cues. So, for example, state-dependent effects on memory are greatest under conditions of free recall, as opposed to cued-recall or recognition tests (Eich, 1980, 1989). And environment-dependent memory effects are abolished when subjects are instructed to *imagine* the environment in which the items had been studied (Smith, Glenberg, & Bjork, 1978).

The foregoing analysis suggests two conditions under which chances of finding mood dependency would be increased: (a) if the link between the subject's mood and the list items is strengthened; and (b) if other potentially superceding cues are eliminated, thereby highlighting the mood cue (a similar argument can be made for context dependency; see Smith, 1987).

With respect to the mood–item link, there is no reason to think that this association is encoded automatically (Kihlstrom, 1989). Rather, it seems likely that the mood–item connection will most likely be made if subjects actively attend to their moods. Of course, one way to insure that subjects will attend to their moods is to make the moods relatively intense—a requirement that may be difficult to meet in the laboratory (Tobias, Buenaver, Hinderliter, & Kihlstrom, 1989). Moreover, Bower and Mayer (1989) have argued that the links between items and mood can be most effectively strengthened if subjects are asked to relate the items they study to the mood they are in. This procedure highlights the relevance of mood to the material and increases the likelihood that mood cues will be encoded with the memory. On the other hand, it increases the risk that mood-dependent memory will be confounded with mood-congruent memory (Teasdale & Fogarty, 1979); that is, if items are explicitly related to mood at the time of encoding, it is no longer clear if these items receive an advantage in recall because of the congruence between encoding and retrieval moods, or because of the congruence between mood and memory.

With respect to the elimination of potentially competing cues, use of free recall-tests, as opposed to cued recall or recognition, effectively reduces the amount of cue information supplied by the experimenter (Tulving, 1974). Moreover, incidental as opposed to intentional learning conditions minimizes the probability that subjects will generate cues at time of encoding that can later be used to aid their own retrieval. Indeed, Ellis (1985, 1990) has found that mood effects are more likely to emerge when encoding is impoverished and incidental. However, whereas incidental learning and free recall would seem to substantially reduce competing cues, they cannot eliminate them completely. Free-recall tests still specify the spatiotemporal context in which learning occurred, and subjects are highly likely to generate cues for themselves over the course of intentional retrieval, even if they did not generate them during incidental encoding.

We propose that use of implicit memory tests can further reduce both experimenter-supplied and subject-generated cues. By definition, implicit memory tasks eliminate all explicit references to any prior learning episode: They do not require retrieval of autobiographical memories. Thus, no cues pertaining to spatiotemporal context are supplied by the experimenter; and subjects have no incentive to deliberately generate episodic cues that might aid their performance. Therefore, the combination of incidental learning and implicit memory will reduce the salience of potentially competing cues and isolate and highlight cues pertaining to mood and other aspects of context.[2]

. . . and Some Experiments

Implicit memory has only recently emerged as a topic for formal research, and so it is perhaps not surprising that few experiments have assessed mood effects (or, indeed, any type of context effect) on implicit memory. Weingartner, Miller, and Murphy (1977) found evidence for state dependency in the generation of word associations: Subjects were more likely to generate the same associates when they were in the same mood as on a previous trial. However, this study was not explicitly designed as a test of implicit memory and did not include a comparable explicit memory task. More recently, Hertel and Hardin (1990) found that implicit memory (homophone spelling) transferred between depressed and neutral moods, whereas recognition did not.

Another recent study, by Mathews, Mogg, May, and Eysenck (1989), examined attentional biases in anxious subjects (mood-congruent encoding) using threat-related words and stem completion. The results indicated a bias in clinically anxious subjects towards retrieving threat-related words in both the implicit and explicit conditions; however, this differential tendency was significant only in the implicit memory condition. Thus, as predicted, the effects of mood were stronger on implicit than on explicit memory. Mathews et al. (1989) suggested that the relation between emotional state and memory for mood-congruent items is not straightforward, but they interpreted their data as demonstrating attentional bias. Unfortunately, the operation of mood effects at encoding or retrieval

---

[2]It should be noted that this logic applies to mood-congruent effects as well as mood-dependent effects. In studies of mood congruency, the power of mood to cue affectively related material may still be overshadowed by the effects of other experimenter-supplied and subject-generated cues.

and the contribution of explicit effects cannot be ruled out because mood was not manipulated in this experiment; nor was a clear functional dissociation shown between implicit and explicit memory. In fact, findings from our laboratory, discussed later, suggest that mood-congruent retrieval, but not mood-congruent encoding, may be found in implicit memory.

We have recently begun to study the effects of experimentally induced happiness and sadness on both explicit and implicit memory. In our first study (Tobias, Schacter, & Kihlstrom, 1989), we sought evidence of mood-dependent implicit memory using the word-stem completion paradigm. Mood was manipulated at encoding and retrieval by means of a musical mood induction. No evidence of mood dependency was found in either explicit or implicit memory. Nor was mood-congruent retrieval evident in a subsequent study that also used a stem-completion task. However, although stem completion is the paradigm of choice for many studies of implicit memory, it may not be ideal for experiments on mood and other context effects. In the first place, three-letter stems are relatively powerful cues; thus, this experimenter-supplied information may well overshadow mood cues. Another possible difficulty with stem completion is that it is primarily data driven (Roediger & Blaxton, 1987; Roediger et al., 1989): It taps into memory for the perceptual qualities of the list items (e.g., how they appear on the page, or how they sound when spoken). Although it may be argued, following Graf, that mood "colors" our perception of events, it is also clear that mood changes how they are interpreted. If emotional effects are primarily conceptual in nature, considerations of transfer-appropriate processing (Roediger et al. 1989) lead us to expect that mood would have no effect on a data-driven task such as stem completion.

Accordingly, we set out to develop a set of novel implicit memory tasks that both minimized experimenter-supplied nominal cues and were classifiable as conceptually driven, in the hope that they would prove more sensitive to context cues (Tobias, Wunderlich, & Kihlstrom, 1990). The subjects first studied a list of positive, negative, and neutral words, about which they made either structural or semantic judgments. Following this encoding activity, they listened to 15 minutes of tape-recorded mood music. Subjects in the implicit memory condition were then falsely informed that the tape was of the "subliminal perception" variety, in which a list of words had been masked by the music. In order to determine whether the words had been subliminally perceived, they were asked to perform one of four tasks:

1. One group was given a sheet with blank spaces on it, setting up the conditions for a free-recall test.
2. A second group was provided with the first letters of target words, thus creating a cued-recall test with minimal cues.
3. A third group was provided with cues representing broad conceptual categories, in the form of phrase completions: "The person felt ____ " or "The person bought the ____ "
4. A fourth group was prompted with standard three-letter stems. In all conditions, subjects were asked simply to list the first words that came to mind. A comparable set of cued recall memory tasks was also administered, in which subjects were specifically instructed to list items from the wordlist they had studied.

Data analysis revealed significant priming effects on each of the implicit memory tasks; that is, significantly more target than baseline words appeared in the subjects' lists. Whereas the strength of the experimenter-supplied cue affected the sheer number of target and baseline words generated, it had no effect on the magnitude of priming observed. Moreover, cued recall was affected by the level of processing at the time of encoding, but priming was not. These results confirmed that we had, indeed, developed implicit-memory analogues of free and minimally cued recall. In the "no cue" condition, subjects are simply presented with a blank sheet of paper and asked to write down the first words that come to mind, without any reference to the study phase. In fact, our minor deception may have actually directed subjects' attention *away* from the study phase. Obviously, this condition reduces to an absolute minimum the influence of potentially competing experimenter-supplied and subject-generated cues.

With an appropriate implicit memory task in hand, we returned to the question of mood effects (Tobias & Kihlstrom, 1990). Happy and sad mood was musically manipulated at encoding and retrieval. In order to strengthen the link between items and mood, we included in the list some words with positive and negative affective valence, as well as emotionally neutral items. Examining only those items that were affectively congruent to encoding mood (the condition where the cue value of mood should be strongest), no mood-dependent memory was observed in explicit memory—another tribute to the unreliability of mood-dependent memory effects. However, a strong mood-dependency effect was seen in the implicit conditions involving free and minimally cued recall. Subjects who were happy at both encoding and retrieval produced significantly more positive target words than those who were happy at encoding but sad at retrieval. Similarly, subjects who were sad at both encoding and retrieval produced more negative words than those who were sad at encoding but happy at retrieval. No evidence of mood dependency was found for neutral or incongruent items, raising the question of the degree to which strict mood dependency has been contaminated by mood congruence in our study.[3]

MOOD AS MEMORY,
AND MEMORY FOR MOOD

It seems that the results of these preliminary experiments need to be confirmed, and the paradigm needs to be explored in more detail. However, taken together with the study of anxiety by Mathews et al. (1989), our preliminary results indicate that mood effects on implicit memory may be greater than those on explicit memory—to the extent that implicit effects are found even when explicit effects are absent. From a theoretical point of view, this outcome is interesting for several reasons.

To begin with, our findings underscore the potential differences between mood and other aspects of context. Like physiological state and environmental surround, mood is a feature of an event that can be encoded along with other aspects of a memory and serve as a potential retrieval cue. Like the physiological states induced by psychoactive drugs, it can affect the deployment of attention towards some features of the environment as opposed to others. Unlike drug-induced states, however, it is probably not something that can alter perception or induce amnesia directly. Mood also may differ from external, environmental context, in that—unless they are exceptionally noisy or otherwise aversive—environments per se do not affect the availability of attentional resources for information processing. Moreover, mood may differ from environmental context in another way, because it can alter the connotative meaning of events, in addition to serving as some kind of passive background. These considerations suggest that moods, drug states, and environments may not have parallel effects on memory.

---

[3]Nor were any mood-congruency effects observed in the explicit memory condition. However, there was evidence of mood-congruent retrieval in implicit memory. There was a bias toward generating negative targets when retrieval mood was negative, and positive targets when it was happy—irrespective of encoding mood.

Moreover, these results may shed new and important light on the nature of the relations between these two expressions of memory. Most functional dissociations between explicit and implicit memory are asymmetrical; that is, whereas a number of variables may affect explicit but not implicit memory, relatively few variables (aside from modality shifts) affect implicit but not explicit memory. In the case of mood, the available evidence is of just this type. In the absence of double dissociations, in which a single variable exerts *opposite* effects on explicit and implicit memory (e.g., impairing one while improving the other), the accumulation of single dissociations in which implicit memory is impaired but explicit memory is spared supports the hypothesis of qualitatively different memory processes or systems, rather than mere differences in task difficulty (Schacter, in press; Tulving & Schacter, 1990). Generally, the argument is for two memory systems, one encoding a structural description of perceptual input, the other representing the event itself, in its episodic context. But if, as Leventhal (1980, 1984) and Christianson (Christianson, 1991; Christianson, Loftus, Hoffman, & Loftus, in press; see also chapter 13, this volume) have suggested, emotional memories themselves are supported by a separate memory mechanism or system, concerned exclusively with representing emotional experiences, a question must be raised as to whether two such systems are now necessary, one supporting explicit and the other implicit emotional memories.

Be that as it may, the fact that changes in evaluative judgment and other aspects of emotional response may be dissociated from explicit memory expands the boundaries of what might be considered evidence of implicit memory. The typical implicit memory task involves verbal behavior: The subject lists the first words that come to mind, for example, or makes a judgment about whether a stimulus is a word. Recently, evidence of implicit memory has been found on perceptual tasks involving spatial rather than verbal processing (Musen & Triesman, 1990; Schacter, Cooper, & Delaney, 1990). In the clinical anecdotes and formal research reviewed here, though, evidence of implicit memory comes from feelings rather than words. The patients observed by Claparede, Janet, Bagby, and Levinson are not performing anything like a perceptual-cognitive task. They *feel an emotion* because of what they have previously experienced, even though they do not remember the experience at all.

This fact reminds us that implicit memory can be revealed by a wide variety of alterations in experience, thought, or action that is attributable to some prior episode, regardless of whether the change resembles the kinds of perceptual-cognitive tasks performed under laboratory conditions. If an assault victim has frequent nightmares or panic attacks when he or she was not prone to them before the crime, this change in behavior may reflect implicit memory even if the contents of the dream do not remotely resemble any details of the incident; and even if—we might say *especially* if—he or she does not remember the event itself. It also reminds us of the insight of Breuer and Freud (1893/1955):

> Hysterics suffer mainly from reminiscences (p. 7), [but] In the great majority of cases it is not possible to establish the point of origin by a simple interrogation of the patient, however thoroughly it may be carried out . . . principally because he is genuinely unable to recollect it and often has no suspicion of the causal connection between the precipitating event and the pathological phenomenon. (p. 3)

What Breuer and Freud meant as unconscious (or repressed) memories, we can substitute implicit ones. If a wide variety of pathological symptoms, not just emotional reactions, can reflect implicit memory, we are afforded a new means of integrating psychodynamic insights with contemporary psychological theory, particularly with respect to the structure of memory. They also stimulate further questions about the relations among cognitive, emotional, and motivational processes, and about psychosomatic interactions.

ACKNOWLEDGMENTS

The point of view presented in this chapter is based on research supported in part by Grants MH-44739 and MH-35856 from the National Institute of Mental Health, and Grant AG-08441 from the National Institute on Aging. We thank Terrence M. Barnhardt, Jill Booker, Jeffrey Bowers, Barbara Church, Suzanne M. Delaney, Elizabeth L. Glisky, Martha L. Glisky, Susan Mineka, Sheila A. Mulvaney, Douglas J. Tataryn, Mindy Tharan, and Michael Valdiserri for their comments at various stages.

REFERENCES

Bagby, E. (1928). *The psychology of personality.* New York: Holt.
Bargh, J. A., & Pietromonaco, P. (1982). Automatic information processing and social perception: The influence of trait information presented outside of conscious awareness on impression formation. *Journal of Personality and Social Psychology, 43,* 437–449.

Bauer, R. M. (1984). Autonomic recognition of names and faces in prosopagnosia: A neuropsychological application of the guilty knowledge test. *Neuronpsychologia, 22,* 457–469.

Blaney, P. H. (1986). Affect and memory: A review. *Psychological Bulletin, 99,* 229–246.

Blum, G. S. (1967). Hypnosis in psychodynamic research. In J. E. Gordon (Ed.), *Handbook of clinical and experimental hypnosis* (pp. 83–109). New York: Macmillan.

Blum, G. S. (1979). Hypnotic programming techniques in psychological experiments. In E. Fromm & R. E. Shor (Eds.), *Hypnosis: Developments in research and new perspectives.* New York: Aldine.

Bornstein, R. F., Leone, D. R., & Galley, D. J. (1987). The generalizability of subliminal mere exposure effects: Influence of stimuli perceived without awareness on social behavior. *Journal of Personality and Social Psychology, 53,* 1070–1079.

Bower, G. H. (1981). Mood and memory. *American Psychologist, 36,* 129–138.

Bower, G. H., & Mayer, J. D. (1989). In search of mood-dependent retrieval. *Journal of Social Behavior and Personality, 4,* 121–156.

Breuer, J., & Freud, S. (1893/1955). On the psychical mechanism of hysterical phenomena: Preliminary communication. In J. Strachey (Ed.), *The standard edition of the complete psychological works of Sigmund Freud* (Vol. 2, pp. 3–17). London: Hogarth Press.

Christianson, S.-Å. (1991). *Emotional stress and eyewitness memory: A critical review.* Manuscript submitted for publication.

Christianson, S.-Å., Loftus, E. F., Hoffman, H., & Loftus, G. R. (1991). Eye fixations and memory for emotional events. *Journal of Experimental Psychology: Learning, Memory, and Cognition.*

Christianson, S.-Å., & Nilsson, L. G. (1989). Hysterical amnesia: A case of aversively motivated isolation of memory. In T. Archer & L. G. Nilsson (Eds.), *Aversion, avoidance, and anxiety* (pp. 289–310). Hillsdale, NJ: Lawrence Erlbaum Associates.

Claparede, E. (1951). [Recognition and 'me'ness.] In D. Rapaport (Ed.), *Organization and pathology of thought* (pp. 58–75). New York: Columbia University Press. (Reprinted from Archives de Psychologies, 1911, *11,* 79–90).

Damasio, A. R., Tranel, D., & Damasio, H. (1989). Amnesia caused by herpes simplex encephalitis, infarctions in basal forebrain, Alzheimer's disease and anoxia/ischemia. In F. Boller & J. Grafman (Eds.), *Handbook of neuropsychology* (Vol. 3). Amsterdam: Elsevier.

Deckert, G. H., & West, L. J. (1963). Hypnosis and experimental psychopathology. *American Journal of Clinical Hypnosis, 5,* 256–276.

deHaan, E. H. F., Young, A., & Newcombe, F. (1987). Face recognition without awareness. *Cognitive Neuropsychology, 4,* 385–415.

Eich, J. E. (1980). The cue-dependent nature of state-dependent retrieval. *Memory and Cognition, 6,* 156–183.

Eich, J. E. (1984). Memory for unattended events: Remembering with and without awareness. *Memory and Cognition, 12,* 105–111.

Eich, J. E. (1989). Theoretical issues in state-dependent memory. In H. L. Roediger & F. I. M. Craik (Eds.), *Varieties of memory and consciousness: Essays in honour of Endel Tulving* (pp. 331–354). Hillsdale, NJ: Lawrence Erlbaum Associates.

Eich, J. E., & Metcalfe, J. (1989). Mood dependent memory for internal versus external events. *Journal of Experimental Psychology: Learning, Memory, and Cognition, 15,* 443–455.

Ellis, H. C. (1985). On the importance of mood intensity and encoding demands in memory: Commentary on Hasher, Rose, Zacks, Sanft, and Doren. *Journal of Experimental Psychology: General, 114*, 392–395.

Ellis, H. C. (1990). Depressive deficits in memory: Processing initiative and resource allocation. *Journal of Experimental Psychology: General, 119*, 60–62.

Ellis, H. C., & Ashbrook, P. W. (1987). Resource allocation model of the effects of depressed mood states on memory. In K. Fiedler & J. Forgas (Eds.), *Affect, cognition, and social behavior.* Toronto: Hogrefe.

Ellis, H. C., & Ashbrook, P. W. (1988). The "state" of mood and memory research: A selective review. *Journal of Social Behavior and Personality.*

Erickson, M. H. (1935). A study of an experimental neurosis hypnotically induced in a case of ejaculatio praecox. *British Journal of Medical Psychology, 15*, 35–40.

Erickson, M. H. (1944). The method employed to formulate a complex story for the induction of an experimental neurosis in a hypnotic subject. *Journal of General Psychology, 31*, 67–84.

Eriksen, C. W. (1960). Discrimination and learning without awareness: A methodological survey and evaluation. *Psychological Review, 67*, 279–300.

Gantt, W. H. (1953). Principles of nervous breakdown in schizokinesis and autokinesis. *Annals of the New York Academy of Sciences, 56*, 141–165.

Graf, P. (1989, November). *Implicit and explicit remembering in same and different environments.* Paper presented at the annual meeting of the Psychonomic Society, Chicago.

Graf, P., & Mandler, G. (1984). Activation makes words more accessible, but not necessarily more retrievable. *Journal of Verbal Learning and Verbal Behavior, 23*, 553–568.

Graf, P., & Schacter, D. L. (1985). Implicit and explicit memory for new associations in normal and amnesic subjects. *Journal of Experimental Psychology: Learning, Memory, and Cognition, 11*, 501–518.

Graf, P., Squire, L. R., & Mandler, G. (1984). The information that amnesic patients do not forget. *Journal of Experimental Psychology: Learning, Memory, & Cognition, 10*, 164–178.

Greenwald, A. G., Klinger, M. R., & Liu, T. J. (1989). Unconscious processing of dichoptically masked words. *Memory & Cognition, 17*, 35–47.

Gudjonsson, G. H., & Haward, L. R. C. (1982). Case report-Hysterical amnesia as an alternative to suicide. *Medicine, Science and the Law, 22*, 68–72.

Hertel, P. T., & Hardin, T. S. (1990). Remembering with and without awareness in a depressed mood: Evidence of deficits in initiative. *Journal of Experimental Psychology: General, 119*, 45–59.

Hilgard, E. R. (1977). *Divided consciousness: Multiple controls in human thought and action.* New York: Wiley-Interscience.

Hodgson, R., & Rachman, S. (1974). II. Desynchrony in measures of fear. *Behavior Research & Therapy, 12*, 319–326.

Hugdahl, K. (1981). The three-systems-model of fear and emotion: A critical examination. *Behavior Research and Therapy, 19*, 75–86.

Huston, P. E., Shakow, D., & Erickson, M. H. (1934). A study of hypnotically induced complexes by means of the Luria technique. *Journal of General Psychology, 11*, 65–97.

Jacoby, L. L., Allan, L. G., Collins, J. C., & Larwill, L. K. (1988). Memory influences subjective experience: Noise judgments. *Journal of Experimental Psychology: Learning, Memory, & Cognition, 14*, 240–247.

Jacoby, L. L., & Witherspoon, D. (1982). Remembering without awareness. *Canadian Journal of Psychology, 36*, 300–324.

Janet, P. (1893). Continuous amnesia. *Revue Generale Des Sciences, 4*, 167–179.

Janet, P. (1904). Amnesia and the dissociation of memories by emotion. *Journal de Psychologie Normale et Pathologique, 1*, 417–453.

Johnson, M. H., & Magaro, P. A. (1987). Effects of mood and severity on memory processes in depression and mania. *Psychological Bulletin, 101*, 28–40.

Johnson, M. K., Kim, J. K., & Risse, G. (1985). Do alcoholic Korsakoff's syndrome patients acquire affective reactions? *Journal of Experimental Psychology: Learning, Memory, & Cognition, 11*, 27–36.

Kaszniak, A. W., Nussbaum, P. D., Berren, M. R., & Santiago, J. (1988). Amnesia as a consequence of male rape: A case report. *Journal of Abnormal Psychology, 97*, 100–104.

Kihlstrom, J. F. (1980). Posthypnotic amnesia for recently learned material: Interactions with "episodic" and "semantic" memory. *Cognitive Psychology, 12*, 227–251.

Kihlstrom, J. F. (1985). Posthypnotic amnesia and the dissociation of memory. In G. H. Bower (Ed.), *The psychology of learning and motivation* (Vol. 19, pp. 131–178). New York: Academic Press.

Kihlstrom, J. F. (1987). The cognitive unconscious. *Science, 237*, 1445–1452.

Kihlstrom, J. F. (1989). On what does mood-dependent memory depend? *Journal of Social Behavior and Personality, 4*, 23–32.

Kihlstrom, J. F. (1990). The psychological unconscious. In L. Pervin (Ed.), *Handbook of personality: Theory and research* (pp. 445–464). New York: Guilford.

Kihlstrom, J. F., Brenneman, H. A., Pistole, D. D., & Shor, R. E. (1985). Hypnosis as a retrieval cue in posthypnotic amnesia. *Journal of Abnormal Psychology, 94*, 264–271.

Kihlstrom, J. F., & Hoyt, I. P. (1990). Repression, dissociation, and hypnosis. In J. E. Singer (Ed.), *Repression: Defense mechanism and personality style* (pp. 181–208). Chicago: University of Chicago Press.

Kihlstrom, J. F., & Schacter, D. L. (1990a). Anaesthesia, amnesia, and the cognitive unconscious. In B. Bonke, W. Fitch, & K. Millar (Eds.), *Awareness and memory during anaesthesia* (pp. 22–44). Amsterdam: Swets & Zeitlinger.

Kihlstrom, J. F., & Schacter, D. L. (in press). Functional amnesia. In J. H. Byrne, L. Nadel, H. L. Roediger, D. L. Schacter, & R. F. Thompson, (Eds.), *Encyclopedia of learning and memory*. New York: Macmillan.

Kihlstrom, J. F., Tataryn, D. J., & Hoyt, I. P. (1990). Dissociative disorders. In P. A. Sutker & L. L. Adams (Eds.), *Comprehensive handbook of psychopathology* (2nd ed.) (in press). New York: Plenum Press.

Korsakoff, S. S. (1889). Etude medico-psychologique sur une forme des maladies do la memoire (Medical-psychological study of a form of diseases of memory). *Revue Philosophique, 28*, 501–530.

Kunst-Wilson, W. R., & Zajonc, R. B. (1980). Affective discrimination of stimuli that cannot be recognized. *Science, 207*, 557–558.

Lang, P. J. (1968). Fear reduction and fear behavior: Problems in treating a construct. In J. M. Shlein (Ed.), *Research in psychotherapy* (Vol. 3, pp. 90–103). Washington, DC: American Psychological Association.

Lang, P. J. (1971). The application of psychophysiological methods to the study of psychotherapy and behavior modification. In A. E. Bergin & S. L. Garfield (Eds.), *Handbook of psychotherapy and behavior change: An empirical analysis* (pp. 75–125). New York: Wiley.

Leventhal, H. (1980). Toward a comprehensive theory of emotion. In L. Berkowitz (Ed.), *Advances in experimental social psychology* (Vol. 13, pp. 139–207). New York: Academic Press.

Leventhal, H. (1984). A perceptual-motor theory of emotion. In K. R. Scherer & P. Ekman (Eds.), *Approaches to emotion* (pp. 271–291). Hillsdale, NJ: Lawrence Erlbaum Associates.

Levinson, B. W. (1967). States of awareness during general anesthesia. In J. Lassner (Ed.), *Hypnosis and psychosomatic medicine.* New York: Springer-Verlag.

Levitt, E. E., & Chapman, R. H. (1979). Hypnosis as a research method. In E. Fromm & R. E. Shor (Eds.), *Hypnosis: Developments in research and new perspectives.* New York: Aldine.

Levitt, E. E., Persky, H., & Brady, J. P. (1964). *Hypnotic induction of anxiety: A psychoendocrine investigation.* Springfield, IL: Thomas.

Ludwig, A. M., Brandsma, J. M., Wilbur, C. B., Bendfeldt, F., & Jameson, D. H. (1972). The objective study of multiple personality. *Archives of General Psychiatry, 26,* 298–310.

Luria, A. R. (1932). *The nature of human conflict.* New York: Liveright.

Mandler, G., Nakamura, Y., & VanZandt, B. J. S. (1987). Nonspecific effects of exposure on stimuli that cannot be recognized. *Journal of Experimental Psychology: Learning, Memory, and Cognition, 13,* 646–648.

Mathews, A., Mogg, K., May, J., & Eysenck, M. (1989). Implicit and explicit memory bias in anxiety. *Journal of Abnormal Psychology, 98,* 236–240.

Mayer, J. D. (1986). How mood influences cognition. In N. E. Sharkey (Ed.), *Advances in cognitive science* (pp. 290–314). Chichester, West Sussex: Ellis Horwook Limited.

Miller, R. R., & Marlin, N. A. (1979). Amnesia following electroconvulsive shock. In J. F. Kihlstrom & F. J. Evans (Eds.), *Functional disorders of memory* (pp. 143–178). Hillsdale, NJ: Lawrence Erlbaum Associates.

Miller, R. R., & Springer, A. D. (1973). Amnesia, consolidation, and retrieval. *Psychological Review, 80,* 69–79.

Mineka, S. (1979). The role of fear in theories of avoidance learning, flooding, and extinction. *Psychological Bulletin, 86,* 985–1011.

Mineka, S. (1985a). Animal models of anxiety-based disorders: Their usefulness and limitations. In J. Maser & A. H. Tuma (Eds.), *Anxiety and the anxiety disorders* (pp. 199–244). Hillsdale, NJ: Lawrence Erlbaum Associates.

Mineka, S. (1985b). The frightful complexity of the origins of fears. In F. R. Brush & J. B. Overmier (Eds.), *Affect, conditioning, and cognition: Essays in the determinants of behavior* (pp. 55–73). Hillsdale, NJ: Lawrence Erlbaum Associates.

Mineka, S., & Kihlstrom, J. F. (1978). Unpredictable and uncontrollable aversive events: A new perspective on experimental neurosis. *Journal of Abnormal Psychology, 87,* 256–271.

Moscovitch, M. (1982). Multiple dissociations of function in amnesia. In L. S. Cermak (Ed.), *Human memory and amnesia* (pp. 337–370). Hillsdale, NJ: Lawrence Erlbaum Associates.

Musen, C., & Triesman, A. (1990). Implicit and explicit memory for visual patterns. *Journal of Experimental Psychology: Learning, Memory, & Cognnition, 16,* 127–137.

Nissen, M. J., Ross, J. L., Willingham, D. B., Mackenzie, T. B., & Schacter, D. L. (1988). Memory and awareness in a patient with multiple personality disorder. *Brain & Cognition, 8,* 117–134.

Prince, M. (1910). *The dissociation of a personality.* New York: Longmans, Green.

Prince, M. (1914). *The unconscious.* New York: Macmillan.

Rachman, S. (1978). Human fears: A three systems analysis. *Scandinavian Journal of Behavior Therapy, 7,* 237–245.

Rachman, S., & Hodgson, R. (1974). I. Synchrony and desynchrony in fear and avoidance. *Behavior Research and Therapy, 12*, 311–318.

Reyher, J. (1962). A paradigm for determining the clinical relevance of hypnotically induced psychopathology. *Psychological Bulletin, 59*, 344–352.

Reyher, J. (1967). Hypnosis in research on psychopathology. In J. E. Gordon (Ed.), *Handbook of clinical and experimental hypnosis* (pp. 110–147). New York: Macmillan.

Richardson-Klavehn, A., & Bjork, R. A. (1988). Measures of memory. *Annual Review of Psychology, 39*, 475–543.

Roediger, H. L., & Blaxton, T. A. (1987). Retrieval modes produce dissociations in memory for surface information. In D. Gorfein & R. R. Hoffman (Eds.), *Memory and cognitive processes: The Ebbinghaus Centennial Conference* (pp. 349–379). Hillsdale, NJ: Lawrence Erlbaum Associates.

Roediger, H. L., Weldon, M. S., & Challis, B. H. (1989). Explaining dissociations between implicit and explicit measures of retention: A processing account. In H. L. Roediger & F. I. M. Craik (Eds.), *Varieties of memory and consciousness: Essays in honour of Endel Tulving* (pp. 3–41). Hillsdale, NJ: Lawrence Erlbaum Associates.

Schacter, D. L. (1985). Priming of old and new knowledge in amnesic patients and normal subjects. *Annals of the New York Academy of Sciences, 444*, 44–53.

Schacter, D. L. (1987). Implicit memory: History and current status. *Journal of Experimental Psychology: Learning, Memory, and Cognition, 13*, 501–518.

Schacter, D. L. (1989). On the relation between memory and consciousness: Dissociable interactions and conscious experience. In H. L. Roediger & F. I. M. Craik (Eds.), *Varieties of memory and consciousness: Essays in honour of Endel Tulving* (pp. 355–390). Hillsdale, NJ: Lawrence Erlbaum Associates.

Schacter, D. L. (in press). Perceptual representation systems and implicit memory: Toward a resolution of the multiple memory debate (Ed.), *Development and neural bases of higher cognitive function. Annals of the New York Academy of Sciences.*

Schacter, D. L., Cooper L. A., & Delaney, S. M. (1990). Implicit memory for unfamiliar objects depends on access to structural descriptions. *Journal of Experimental Psychology: General, 119*, 5–24.

Schacter, D. L., & Graf, P. (1989). Modality specificity of implicit memory for new associations. *Journal of Experimental Psychology: Learning, Memory, & Cognition, 15*, 3–12.

Schacter, D. L., Kaszniak, A. W., & Kihlstrom, J. F. (in press). Models of memory and the understanding of memory disorders. In T. Yanagihara & R. C. Peterson (Eds.), *Memory disorders in clinical practice.* New York: Dekker.

Schacter, D. L., & Kihlstrom, J. F. (1989). Functional amnesia. In F. Boller & J. Grafman (Eds.), *Handbook of Neuropsychology.* Amsterdam: Elsevier.

Seamon, J. G., Brody, N., & Kauff, D. (1983a). Affective discrimination of stimuli that are not recognized: Effects of shadowing, masking, and cerebral laterality. *Journal of Experimental Psychology: Learning, Memory, and Cognition, 9*, 544–555.

Seamon, J. G., Brody, N., & Kauff, D. (1983b). Affective discrimination of stimuli that are not recognized: II. Effect of delay between study and test. *Bulletin of the Psychonomic Society, 21*, 187–189.

Seamon, J. G., Marsh, R. L., & Brody, N. (1984). Critical importance of exposure duration for affective discrimination of stimuli that are not recognized. *Journal of Experimental Psychology: Learning, Memory, and Cognition, 10*, 465–469.

Smith, S. M. (1987). *Implicit and explicit measures of environmental context-dependent memory* (Tech. Rep. #CSCS-005). Texas A&M University.

Smith, S. M., Glenberg, A. M., & Bjork, R. A. (1978). Environmental context and human memory. *Memory & Cognition, 6*, 342–353.

Teasdale, J. D., & Fogarty, S. J. (1979). Differential effects of induced mood on retrieval of pleasant and unpleasant events from episodic memory. *Journal of Abnormal Psychology, 88*, 248–257.

Tobias, B. A., Buenaver, L., Hinderliter, C., & Kihlstrom, J. F. (1989, April). *Cognitive and affective consequences of laboratory mood inductions.* Paper presented at the joint annual convention of the Western Psychological Association and the Rocky Mountain Psychological Association, Reno.

Tobias, B. A., & Kihlstrom, J. F. (1990, August). *Effects of mood on implicit and explicit memory.* Paper presented at the annual meeting of the American Psychological Association, Boston.

Tobias, B. A., Schacter, D. L., & Kihlstrom, J. F. (1989, June). *Under what conditions does implicit memory transfer across moods?* Paper presented at the 1st annual convention of the American Psychological Society, Arlington, Va.

Tobias, B. A., Wunderlich, D., & Kihlstrom, J. F. (1990, April). *Minimally cued implicit memory tests: Sensitivity and utility for detecting context effects.* Paper presented at the annual meeting of the Rocky Mountain Psychological Association, Tucson.

Tranel, D., & Damasio, A. R. (1985). Knowledge without awareness: An autonomic index of facial recognition by prosopagnosics. *Science, 228*, 1453–1454.

Tulving, E. (1974). Cue-dependent forgetting. *American Scientist, 62*, 74–82.

Tulving, E., & Schacter, D. L. (1990). Priming and human memory systems. *Science, 247*, 301–306.

Warrington, E. K., & Weiskrantz, L. (1974). The effect of prior learning on subsequent retention in amnesic patients. *Neuropsychologia, 12*, 419–428.

Weingartner, H., Miller, H., & Murphy, D. L. (1977). Mood-dependent retrieval of verbal associations. *Journal of Abnormal Psychology, 86*, 276–284.

Weiskrantz, L., & Warrington, E. K. (1979). Conditioning in amnesic patients. *Neuropsychologia, 17*, 187–194.

Wilson, W. R. (1979). Feeling more than we can know: Exposure effects without learning. *Journal of Personality and Social Psychology, 37*, 811–821.

Wishner, J. (1955). The concept of efficiency in psychological health and psychopathology. *Psychological Review, 62*, 69–80.

Zajonc, R. B. (1968). Attitudinal effects of mere exposure. *Journal of Personality and Social Psychology Monogragh, 9*, 1–28.

Zajonc, R. B. (1980). Feeling and thinking: Preferences need no inferences. *American Psychologist, 35*, 151–175.

Memory, Arousal, and Mood: A Theoretical Integration

George Mandler
*University of California, San Diego
and
University College, London*

Any discussion of the relation between memory and emotion is bounded by theoretical assumptions. Thus any assertions, other than purely empirical ones that claim little or no generality, are necessarily constrained by on theoretical predilections, whether stated or implied. Having been involved and concerned with research and theory on both memory and emotion, I present theoretically motivated definitions of memory and emotion. Memory is discussed in terms of activation and elaboration processes, and the role of arousal and evaluation is developed for emotional phenomena. I then discuss phenomena that involve the interaction of memory and arousal and of memory and mood. However, before dealing with memory and emotion specifically, I need to discuss the functions of consciousness that play an important role in memorial and emotional processes as well as in their interaction.

CONSIOUSNESS, MEMORY, AND EMOTION

The Functions of Consciousness

I take a constructivist view of consciousness. Current conscious contents are constructed out of activated structures/schemas on the one hand, and the requirements of the task and situation on the other. I also invoke the concept of the schema which has served psychologists well for the last 200 years—and particularly for the past 50 years. A schema is a coherent and structured representation that organizes experience. Schemas are not carbon copies of experience, but generalized representations of experienced regularities. Schemas range from the very concrete, involving the categorization of perceptual experience, to the very abstract, representing general levels of meaning such as "love" or "justice". Abstract schemas subsume more concrete schemas; the resulting structure is hierarchical. Schemas are built up in the course of interaction with the social and physical environment. They organize and interpret experience in that current encounters are defined and interpreted in terms of the schemas laid down by past cognate experiences. Currently active schemas define what we are likely to see, hear, and remember, and also determine what we are unlikely to hear or see. Thus, we note the "time" when looking at clock in a public square, but are unlikely to see (process) the precise form of the numerals. The activation of schemas proceeds automatically from concrete to general schemas (bottom-up), and also from high-level schemas, which constrain perception and conception, to lower schemas (top-down). Expectations include those elements of schemas activated by top-down processing that are not directly supported by input evidence.

Schemas are not rigidly bounded representations but are best seen as dispositional, (i.e., they are generated from their distributed features and attributes at each occurrence). Currently available evidence and information constructs a particular representation that responds both to the immediate information and to the regularities (schemas) generated by past events. The schema is constructed out of distributed features of previously developed schemas. Once generated, a schema represents the unit of thought and perception; it is bounded and distinct. When co-occurrences in the world have been organized into a schema of the event or scene, they appear to "evoke" one another. However, organization of two or more events, other than some purely perceptual or procedural events, into a new schema requires active elaborative processing (see later). Sheer contiguity is—under this view—not sufficient for subsequent "evocation."

Of equal importance to the current discussion is a view of consciousness as a complement to an underlying representational system that is characterized by schemas represented by distributed features (cf. Rumelhart & McClelland, 1985). Such a system is relatively large (i.e., it represents the accumulated experiences of the individual), it is relatively fast in accessing information, and, finally, it operates in a parallel fashion (i.e., a large number of relevant features and schemas are accessed and activated at the same time). These characteristics would—without an additional buffer—make action and thought difficult if not impossible. The individual would be overwhelmed by information rapidly emerging in parallel fashion, and action decisions in particular and decision processes in general would be overwhelmed by the amount and speed of the information produced. Consciousness is the buffer that solves this problem. It is first of all serial (i.e., only one [small] cluster of information is accessed at any one time), and it is also relatively slow and limited in capacity to a few items or events. It is the limited capacity of consciousness in particular that is of importance in the interaction between memory and emotion (for extensive discussions of these issues see Mandler 1984, 1985, 1988, in press b).

Memory

I have previously presented an extended discussion of memory phenomena and their relation to the functions of consciousness (Mandler, 1989b). The major points of relevance to the present discussion are:

1. Underlying representations of objects and events are subject to two kinds of processes relevant to memorial phenomena: activation/ integration and elaboration. Sheer presentation of previously experienced objects and events activates the relevant representations. The activation of these representations (best considered as schemas with distributed features) leads to further mutual activation of the constituent features and results automatically in the integration of the representation and its unitization. One of the consequences of activation is the phenomenal experience of familiarity. Activation occurs automatically (i.e., it does not involve or require conscious participation). Elaboration on the other hand probably requires deliberate (conscious) activity. It is the process whereby existing mental units (representations) are related to each other, and it makes possible retrieval and search processes.

2. Recall requires elaboration at time of presentation that makes later access possible by providing appropriate connections to and relations with other mental contents. These "pathways" established by elaboration make possible the retrieval processes, which are often marked by waystations that appear in consciousness. Recall is typically achieved by higher order structures/schemas that specify the "gist" or context of the to-be-recalled information and produce veridical information as well as the typical context-related errors in recall.

3. Recognition may involve both activation and elaborative processes. The dual process theory of recognition (e.g., Mandler, 1980) distinguishes between two components of phenomenal recognition— the experience **that** an event has been encountered previously, and the identification of **what** the event is. These phenomena are in turn generated, respectively, by activation and elaboration. However, rudimentary recognition performance is possible with activation alone. Prior presentation of an item activates its representation, and the presentation of a copy of the item shortly thereafter further raises its activation. The result of such a highly activated representation is the phenomenal experience of "familiarity." The effect is similar to, but not identical with, some priming phenomena, where activation of a representation makes it (or a related representation) more accessible.

Emotion

My theoretical approach to emotion has been extensively documented in the past 15 years (Mandler, 1975, 1984, 1990). It is a constructivist theory that addresses the subjective experience of emotion. It is not a theory of emotional behavior, which may or may not be accompanied or followed by positive or negative emotional experience. This contrast avoids a confusion that has been with us at least since Charles Darwin—a confusion that equates the observation of affectively categorized behavior with emotional experience. The theory views the construction of emotion as consisting of the concatenation of a cognitive evaluative schema with visceral arousal that is perceived as emotional intensity. This conscious construction is a unitary experience, even though it may derive from separate and even independent schematic representations (Mandler, 1985; Marcel, 1983). Such a view of emotion only approximates the commonsense meaning of the term. To ask "what is an emotion?" is not—in principle—answerable. The term is a natural language expression that has all the advantages (communicative and inclusive) and disadvantages (imprecise and vague) of the common language. However, for communicative purposes one needs to approximate the common meaning as a first step.

I have focused on two dimensions out of the many available from analyses of common language "emotions": the notion that emotions express some aspect of value, and the assertion that emotions are "hot"—they imply a gut reaction, a visceral response. The cognition of values—what is good or bad, pleasant or unpleasant, noxious or desirable—provides the quality of the emotional experience, and the visceral reaction generates its quantitative aspect. An analysis of the concatenation of value and visceral arousal addresses natural language usage as well as theoretically interesting problems. Given the many different possible evaluative states, one of the consequences of such a position is that it leads to the postulation of a potentially innumerable number of different emotional states. There are of course regularities in human thought and action that produce general categories of these constructions, categories that have family resemblances and overlap in the features that are selected for analysis (whether it is the simple dichotomy of good and bad, or the appreciation of beauty, or the perception of evil). These families of occasions and meanings construct the categories of emotions found in the natural language (and psychology). The emotion categories are fuzzily defined by external and internal situations.

The source of the categories of emotion varies from case to case, and different emotional categories may be based on different experiential or environmental factors. Sometimes an emotional category is based on the similarity of external conditions (as in the case of some fears and environmental threats). Sometimes an emotional category may be based on a collection of similar behaviors (in the subjective feelings of fear related to avoidance and flight). Sometimes a common category arises from a class of incipient or intended actions (as in hostility and destructive action). Sometimes hormonal and physiological reactions provide a common basis (as in the case of lust), and sometimes purely cognitive evaluations constitute an emotional category (as in judgments of helplessness that eventuate in anxiety). Others, such as guilt and grief, depend on individual evaluations of having committed undesirable acts or trying to recover the presence/comfort of a lost person or object. All these emotional states involve evaluative cognitions, and the features common to any particular category give rise to the appearance of discrete categories of emotions.

The problem of *cognitive evaluation* is common to all emotion theories. Even advocates of a small vocabulary of basic emotions need to have an analytic mechanism whereby the individual evaluates the current scene. For the basic emotion theorist, such evaluations could then be postulated to elicit prepackaged emotions. For all theories of emotion the problem of value involves the different external and internal sources that lead us to see some person or event as good or bad, as evil or benign, as harmful or beneficent.

If evaluative cognitions provide the quality of an emotional experience, then visceral activity provides its intensity and peculiar "emotional" characteristic. As a first approximation I assume that degree of autonomic (sympathetic) arousal can be mapped into the felt intensity of an emotion. Affective judgments can obviously occur without visceral involvement. To say that something is pretty or fine or awful or even disgusting may be said quite dispassionately and unemotionally. Thus, so-called affective or evaluative judgments are experienced as such, but under this interpretation they are not full-blown "emotions." What we need to understand are the occasions when visceral activity (however slight) co-occurs with these affective judgments.

In one version of the common understanding of emotion, the occurrence of some visceral or gut reaction is assumed. Emotions are said to occur when we feel "aroused," "agitated," when our "guts are in an uproar," and so forth. The reference is almost invariably to some autonomic nervous system activity, such as increased heart rate, sweating, or gastro–intestinal upheavals. The autonomic nervous system (ANS) has been systematically implicated in quasi-emotional activity ever since Walter Cannon (e.g., 1929) delineated the function of the sympathetic and parasympathetic systems in fight/flight reactions, giving them a function over and beyond energy-expending and energy-conserving functions that keep the internal environment stable. However, if one looks at the literature on the ANS, one is faced with a lack of any principled account of the sources of ANS activation.

I have argued that a majority of occasions for visceral (sympathetic nervous system) arousal follows the occurrence of some perceptual or cognitive discrepancy, or the interruption or blocking of some ongoing action. It should be remembered, though, that discrepancies are only a sufficient, not a necessary, condition for sympathetic arousal. Other sources of sympathetic nervous system arousal can and do also play a role in emotional experience. Discrepancies and interruptions depend to a large extent on the organization of the mental representations of thought and action. Within the purview of schema theory, these discrepancies occur when the expectations generated by some schema are violated. This is the case whether the violating event is worse or better than the expected one—and accounts for visceral arousal in both unhappy and joyful occasions. Most emotions follow such discrepancies, just because the discrepancy produces visceral arousal. And it is the combination of that arousal with an ongoing evaluative cognition that is the subjective experience of an emotion. Interruption, discrepancies, blocks, frustrations, novelties, and so forth are occasions for ANS activity. Whether or not an emotional construction accompanies such arousal depends on the evaluative activity of the individual. It is the concatenation of an evaluative process and ANS arousal that produces emotion (cf. MacDowell & Mandler, 1989; Mandler, 1964).

The notion of discrepancy as the basis for much of the intensity of human emotions may at first sound out of place when one is dealing with the positive emotions. However, positive events are often unexpected, and, in addition, some reflection discloses that the complexity of human thought practically always produces ambivalences and alternative outcomes for positive as well as negative events. Fear of the loss of the loved one, anticipation of possible negative outcomes even for the most joyful occasions, and alternative constructions of negative outcomes illustrate the ambivalences that provide the discrepancies for most emotional occasions (see also Mandler, 1990).

Finally, the construction of emotions requires conscious capacity. The experience of emotion preempts the limited capacity of consciousness. Limited capacity refers to the fact that conscious contents are highly restricted and limited at any one point in time. Whenever some particular construction preempts conscious capacity, then other processes that require such capacity will be impaired. The best example is found in stress and panic reactions when emotional reactions prevent adequate problem solving activities. Emotional experiences may inhibit the full utilization of our cognitive apparatus, thoughts may become stereotyped and canalized, and we tend to revert to simpler modes of problem solving. However, the effects of emotion are not necessarily intrusive and deleterious. In part, the effects will depend on other mental contents and processes that are activated by the emotional experience and that may become available for dealing with stressful situations. For example, stress tends to focus attention on the perceived central aspects of a situation, and such focusing may be useful. The relationship of "emotions" to discrepancies and autonomic nervous system recruitment also points to their adaptive function; emotions occur at important times in the life of the organism and may serve to prepare it for more effective thought and action when focused attention is needed.

THE INTERACTION OF
MEMORY AND EMOTION

I now address the most widely investigated interactions between memory and emotion within the context of the theoretical orientations just presented (for a related discussion of affect and learning, see Mandler, 1989a). One obvious point of departure is the distinction between the two components of emotional experience—arousal and evaluation. I shall discuss arousal in the context of the relation between memory and "stress." Evaluation—the cognitive aspect of emotion—is treated under the rubric of the relation between memory and mood. There are a number of different sources of evaluative schemas, including direct experience, social predication, and schematic discrepancy (cf. Mandler, in press a). One group of evaluative schemas, relevant to the present discussion, is developed when in an emotional state. These schemas organize current memories and evaluations as well as the emotional experiences into individual schematic structures, which may then be accessed at a subsequent time. These are frequently described as situational moods and affect. My review of the respective areas is not intended to be exhaustive, but rather to discuss the phenomena by reference to illustrative examples from the literature.

Memory and Arousal

There is an older tradition—still referred to and used—that typically addresses the arousal function as a problem of the relation between memory and stress. The most frequently cited reference on the relation between memory and stress is the Yerkes–Dodson law. Yerkes and Dodson (1908) found *improvement* in performance of easy tasks with increasing stress, but with difficult tasks they found an inverted U-shaped function of better performance with medium stress and worse performance with low or high stress. The distinction between easy and difficult tasks and the fact that the "law" was developed by the use of electric shock as an implementation of "stress" is sometimes forgotten.

Two difficulties in applying the Yerkes–Dodson inverted U-shaped function to the stress/memory literature are that: (1) it is generally assumed that the task is difficult (i.e., that the inverted U-shaped function actually applies), and (2) frequently the subjective judgment by the experimenter decides what the functional stress level is in any particular study. For example, Deffenbacher (1983), in a review of the literature on arousal and eyewitness testimony, concluded that 10 studies suggested better eyewitness accuracy with high arousal, whereas another 11 studies produced lower accuracy of memory. Deffenbacher then reclassified stress levels in the various studies and concluded that the 21 studies reviewed actually revealed the inverted U-shaped function!

Given the confusion generated by the misuse and reinterpretations of the Yerkes–Dodson law, it is probably best to start with a definition of stress (or emotion). Within the confines of my theoretical approach, I am concerned only with the relation between autonomic (sympathetic) arousal and performance. Only such arousal, perceived and interacting with ongoing processes, is of *psychological* interest. The typical definition of stress describes occasions for sympathetic nervous system arousal. There are of course other concomitants of stress, such as the noxious nature of the stress stimulus and the resultant attempts to remove it. Unfortunately, definitions of stress as introduced by major investigators of the physiological stress concept such as Selye are psychologically opaque. Selye (1982) defined stress as the results of any demand on the body, using "objective indicators such as bodily and chemical changes that appear after any demand" (p. 7). Whether these changes are psychologically effective (i.e., act on receptors and influence thought and action), is irrelevant to this use of the stress concept. However, even in psychological circles it is still fashionable to invoke an "objective" approach to stress (e.g., Breznitz & Goldberger, 1982): "Somewhere between the stressor and its effects lies the subjective, phenomenological experience of stress itself. Although from the individual's point of view experiencing stress is the most germane factor in confronting stressful conditions, such experience lies outside the realm of objective inquiry" (p. 3).

I have assumed that it is exactly the phenomenal experience of stress that determines its effect on such other processes as memorial retrieval. The reason is that it is the "phenomenal" aspect that affects the limited capacity of consciousness (or, in some versions, the limited capacity of short-term memory). In general, it has been useful to use a general measure of sympathetic nervous system activity as an index of the source of experienced stress. It is the perception of such arousal as well as the preoccupation with the stressing occasion that interferes with ongoing conscious processing (Mandler 1979, 1984). Current theory about the effects of arousal was influenced by Easterbrook's (1959) hypothesis that increased arousal (emotion) reduces the number of cues utilized in a situation. The suggestion also came from psychiatric concerns (Callaway & Dembo, 1958) and was often coupled with the notion that arousal (in this case anxiety or panic) frequently produced task-irrelevant behavior (Bachrach, 1970; Mandler & Sarason, 1954). In addition, research on work in dangerous environments added the important suggestion that tasks central to the current situation will tend to improve in the presence of danger, whereas peripheral tasks will deteriorate (Baddeley, 1972).

There is a body of evidence that efficiency (and probably memory) differ for the central and for the peripheral aspects of a stressful situation. Some of the evidence for the central/peripheral distinction comes from research showing that auditory noise may differentially affect central and peripheral aspects of performance (Hockey, 1970). Other supporting evidence was found in situations that simulate danger, where peripheral stimuli apparently receive less attention (Weltman, Smith, & Egstrom, 1971). Bacon (1974) was concerned with developing an independent criterion for the distinction. He noted that responsiveness to those aspects of the situation that initially attract "a lesser degree of attentional focus" is reduced. This makes it possible to identify "peripheral" events in terms of initial attention. It appears then that arousal and noise generate similar effects, and it is useful to think of both of them as "noise" that interferes with conscious capacity. Irrelevant mentation will of course produce similar interference, but I concentrate here on the effects of arousal per se.

We can now attempt an explanation of the inverted U-shaped function of memory performance as a function of increasing arousal. I deal with the function in two parts: the increase in memorial accuracy with arousal moving from low to moderate levels, and the subsequent decrease as arousal becomes severe. For low levels of arousal the focus of attention (i.e., the current conscious content) is likely to be the main task at hand, and with moderate increases of arousal these central, important events will receive exclusive access to conscious capacity. The same is likely to be true of easy tasks that do not in themselves produce significant stress and arousal. At the lowest level of arousal (often associated with very easy tasks or situations), there will be a low level of attention to the task and haphazard accuracy. With increasing but low levels of arousal, attention will focus on central aspects of the task and will produce increasing efficiency with moderate increases in arousal. When arousal attains high levels, it is likely to be because there has been a failure to solve the task, or because external sources (e.g., arousal inducers such as shock) require additional attention to the sources of the disturbance. Under these circumstances task-irrelevant be-havior is likely to increase; attention to such behavior is by definition peripheral. In addition, the further limitation of conscious capacity makes very little of it available for attention to the central aspects, and other mental content will intrude. As a result memorial accuracy with respect to the central aspect of the situation suffers with increasing arousal. One example is found in conditions of panic where people are often seen to pursue failing solutions without being able to consider other possible responses (e.g., by rushing for the same exit in a fire, or failing to follow instructions not to open windows, etc). In general, severe limitations of conscious capacity are likely to produce a situation in which concentration on the central aspect of the situation will be lost.

What is the experimental evidence for the inverted U-shaped function in memory? I address first the effect of arousal/emotion on memory, and then some of the questions about central and peripheral memorial processing.

Apart from the clinical literature, which I do not cover, a direct demonstration of presumed emotional reaction and its effect on memory was given by Loftus and Burns (1982), who showed that inserting a disturbing element into film produced retrograde loss of detailed information. A more detailed demonstration was given by Christianson and Nilsson (1984), who demonstrated worse memory performance for verbal descriptors presented with mutilated faces than for those presented with neutral control faces. They showed effects on recall and recognition, though their forced-choice recognition data are difficult to interpret given the absence of possibly informative false alarm rates. Christianson and Nilsson also collected physiological data (skin conductance and heart rate), which showed that the experimental subjects were in fact autonomically aroused. One can assume that autonomic interference as well as preoccupation with the mutilated faces interfered with the adequate elaboration (encoding) of the tested information. Christianson and Nilsson also showed anterograde recall decrements on items following the traumatic ones, which suggests that elaboration was interfered with by the lingering effects of the emotional items. However, there was no anterograde *recognition* decrement for the neutral items following the emotional ones. It is interesting to contrast the recognition decrement for the target items with the lack of an effect on subsequent (anterograde) items. Keeping in mind the restricted information provided about recognition in these experiments, the recognition decrement of the target items could be due either to a lack of elaboration (demonstrated in recall) or to avoiding looking at the traumatic material at all (i.e., activation is absent). For the neutral items, the recall decrement on the one hand and the maintenance of recognition performance on the other hand indicates that activation of neutral items was not affected.

In contrast to this account, Christianson and Nilsson invoke a resource allocation hypothesis to account for their data. I find this kind of explanation not generally useful because it is often unclear what the resource is and what mechanism is involved in the "allocation."

It does not seem quite clear whether arousal per se is an adequate condition for the restriction of conscious capacity and the impairment of memory. The theoretical approach outlined here does, of course, predict that positive emotional events will produce autonomic arousal just as negative ones do (cf. MacDowell & Mandler, 1989), and that these should also have an interfering effect on memory (see Christianson, 1986). As far as sheer arousal is concerned, Zillmann (1978) has conducted extensive studies that showed that arousal from a prior (usually unrelated) event produced emotional reactions in a subsequent situation. He interpreted these findings of excitatory transfer in terms of an attribution model in which the prior arousal is attributed to a current affective situation in which emotional reactions are then observed. However, he noted that, when the prior induction of arousal was "immediately apparent and unambiguous," subjects did not misattribute the excitation produced by the prior event. He concluded that whenever subjects are aware of a "causal" connection between the arousal and the prior event, they will not attribute the arousal to the current situation. Christianson and Mjörndal (1985) found no difference in memorial performance between a group autonomically aroused with adrenalin and a control group who were given saline injections. In their experiment, it was likely that the subjects connected any perceived arousal with the injections (but see also Christianson, Nilsson, Mjörndal, Perris, & Tjellden, 1986, where only a few subjects attributed their arousal to the injections).

In addition, individual differences may also play a role in this effect. Overson (1989) gave subjects an addition task immediately following physical exercise (which raised heart rates by 70%). The subjects were told that the exercise should "help them think more clearly." A control group was given no exercise and informed that their performance and heart rate would be used to provide baseline data for other subjects. Under these conditions Overson found no difference in accuracy, but, when compared with control subjects, slower performance rates for high-anxiety subjects and faster performance rates for low-anxiety subjects following exercise.

Assigning the arousal to the prior event (whether activity or injection) makes it possible for the individual either to ignore the subjective arousal or to maintain attention on the "central" aspect of the task. Emotional effects apparently require a "belongingness" between the arousal and the target material, a hypothesis that I explore in greater detail in connection with the mood and memory studies that follow.

On the question of differential memory for central or peripheral aspects of emotional events, one needs first of all to disengage a research literature on memory of outstanding, unique, unusual events (such as flashbulb memories). These are not typically related to situations where arousal (i.e., "full" emotions) usually occurrs. Thus, if memory for particularly impressive events seems to be better than usual, one can assume that this is related to the special processing (e.g., attention, rehearsal, extensive elaboration) that it engenders.

The only memory studies of which I am aware that tested and confirmed the notion that central aspects of *emotional* events are better remembered than peripheral ones have been reported by Christianson and Loftus (1987, 1991). Christianson and Loftus (1987) investigated both short-term and long-term memories for traumatic and nontraumatic slide presentations. They compared traumatic and nontraumatic versions of the same event and noted that the theme of the traumatic materials was better remembered after a delay than was the theme of the nontraumatic material. Christianson and Loftus (1991) specifically showed that, when compared with neutral events, emotional events produced better memory for central details and worse memory for peripheral details.

Memory and Mood

The problem of mood and memory has in part been confounded with a definitional confusion. "Emotion" is a natural language term that suffers the usual vagaries of its kind. I have chosen to consider as emotional states those that combine arousal and cognition. However, others have often used such terms as emotion, mood, affect, preference, emotional attitudes, etc. interchangeably. I believe the best way to characterize the memory and mood literature is to say that most of the research has depended on having subjects adopt a specific cognitive evaluative attitude or attribution. Rarely, if ever, have investigators of mood effects induced emotional states with more than slight increases in autonomic arousal, and some investigators refer to mood as "little emotions." In other words, the mood and memory literature deals with the relation between memory and evaluative schemas such as being depressed, sad, or happy. Typically, the moods are considered as states of the individual, and the resulting research is concerned with such state-dependent memories.

Most of the research discussed here deals with explicit memories, involving elaborative mechanisms. However, there is evidence that affective "states" also produce implicit memory phenomena. Implicit memory may be demonstrated by showing priming of verbal productions, as for example in the stem completion test, where subjects are presented with the initial three letters of words previously seen (e.g., CHA, for CHAIR) and are asked to complete the stem with the first word that comes to mind. Priming is demonstrated when the completion CHAIR is more likely than alternative ones like CHASE, CHASTE, CHAIN, etc. Unconscious/implicit priming can be contrasted with deliberate/explicit completions in cued completion when subjects are asked to complete the stem with words that had been previously presented. Mathews, Mogg, May, and Eysenck (1989) presented anxious and nonanxious subjects with threatening and nonthreatening wordlists, followed by either cued or uncued stem completion tests of the presented words. They found no difference between the two groups in cued completion, but in uncued completion anxious subjects produced more completions of the threat words. Thus, implicit memory for the threat words suggests that these are highly activated in anxious subjects, who do not explicitly (consciously) access these words preferentially in the cued test (see also Mathews, Richards, & Eysenck, 1989, for related evidence).

Research on mood-dependent retrieval has not typically used implicit tests. An apparently robust demonstration of mood-dependent retrieval in which subjects show better recall when the mood at retrieval matches that at input was reported in 1978 by Bower, Monteiro, and Gilligan (see also Bower, 1981). The effect would be important for practical reasons in the case of memory loss following trauma and for understanding the preoccupying negative thoughts of depressive patients. After some successful replications the robustness of the effect soon withered. For example, in 1985 Bower and Mayer (1985a; published in Bower & Mayer, 1989) reported a failure to replicate the original finding of Bower et al. (1978). However, Bower and Mayer (1985b) also found that the effect could be reliably produced if subjects "attributed the cause of their emotional reaction to the material being learned." Bower (1985) generated the hypothesis of "causal belongingness" to describe these findings. Bower's invocation of causal belongingness is probably too strong a requirement. All that is needed for mood-dependent retrieval to occur is for mood-*related* structures (schemas) to be created at the time of presentation and storage. What seems to be required is an

active (probably conscious) elaboration of to-be-remembered material with the affective evaluative schema of the "mood." Thus, an
active identification of the target material with the evaluation ("This
is the list of words that made me, or where I felt, depressed") is
necessary. This elaboration results in new schemas of the situation
that provide easy access (relationship) between the affective mood
features and the attributes of the target material. Under those
circumstances, one should expect a later mood manipulation to be
useful in retrieving the target material. Such a mechanism is probably necessary for all hypotheses that relate context or background
to retrieval—sheer contiguity is not enough. Such formulations are
versions of Schachter and Singer's (1962) seminal attribution theory
relating arousal to cognitive factors.

With respect to the "belongingness" aspects of arousal mentioned
earlier (cf. Zillmann, 1978), I assume that in those experiments a
well-established schema exists that has encoded the relationship
between arousal and the original eliciting condition.

The phenomenon that mood-congruent material is retained more
easily can also be accommodated by this approach. The typical
mood-congruent demonstration shows that subjects remember sad
or happy words better if they are in a respectively sad and happy
mood at the time of presentation (cf. the work of Alice Isen and
collaborators; e.g., Isen, Shalker, Clark, & Karp, 1978). In this
situation prior experience has generated a schematic organization of
features relevant to a particular mood or affect (the evaluative
characteristics of, for example, sad/depressed states). The induction
of the sad state activates the features (including words and phrases
symptomatic of them) previously associated with it, and that activation will make later retrieval more likely. Such an interpretation
contrasts with one that postulates preformed "emotion" nodes that
are activated by appropriate emotional inductions (Bower, 1981).

In addition to these findings, there have also been consistent
reports that when depressed moods are induced subjects show
poorer recall than in a neutral control condition (e.g., Ellis, Thomas,
& Rodriguez, 1984). A variety of explanation have been offered for
this effect, but I suggest that before one assigns particular properties
to the state of depression one should consider the demand characteristics of the typical experimental situation in which mood is
induced. It is a common belief among the general population that sad
and depressed people are inefficient at intellective tasks, do not have
any "pep," and generally show "depressed" performance. Such a
belief may induce subjects to perform accordingly.

SUMMARY

I have presented a theoretical approach to memory and emotion that permits an analytic approach to the memory/emotion literature. In particular, the two factors that participate in the production of emotional experience—arousal and evaluation—are shown to interact specifically and differentially with memorial tasks. Further research interests are also generated by this approach. Thus, it would be useful to have more information about the distinction between central and peripheral aspects of memorial tasks performed under stress, as well as about the effect of positive emotional states on memory. More data about the interaction between emotional states and implicit memories (i.e., memory generated by sheer activation and involving no deliberate/conscious retrieval) would also further the theoretical integration of memory and emotion.

ACKNOWLEDGMENTS

Preparation of this chapter was supported in part by a grant from the Spencer Foundation. I am grateful to Jean Mandler for helpful critical comments.

REFERENCES

Bachrach, A. J. (1970). Diving behavior. *Human performance and scuba diving.* Chicago: Athletic Institute.

Bacon, S. J. (1974). Arousal and the range of cue utilization. *Journal of Experimental Psychology, 102,* 81–87.

Baddeley, A. D. (1972). Selective attention and performance in dangerous environments. *British Journal of Psychology, 63,* 537–546.

Bower, G. H. (1981). Mood and memory. *American Psychologist, 36,* 129–148.

Bower, G. H. (1985, September). *Review of research on mood and memory.* Paper presented at meeting of the Cognitive Psychology Section of the British Psychological Society.

Bower, G. H., & Mayer, J. D. (1985a). Failure to replicate mood-dependent retrieval. *Bulletin of the Psychonomic Society, 23,* 39–42.

Bower, G. H., & Mayer, J. D. (1985b). *In search of mood-dependent retrieval.* Unpublished manuscript.

Bower, G. H., & Mayer, J. D. (1989). In search of mood-dependent retrieval. *Journal of Social Behavior and Personality, 4,* 121–156.

Bower, G. H., Monteiro, K. P., & Gilligan, S. G. (1978). Emotional mood as a context of learning and recall. *Journal of Verbal Learning and Verbal Behavior, 17,* 573–585.

Breznitz, S. & Goldberger, L. (1982). Stress research at a crossroads. In L. Goldberger & S. Breznitz (Ed.), *Handbook of stress: Theoretical and clinical aspects*. New York: The Free Press.

Callaway, E. III, & Dembo, D. (1958). Narrowed attention: A psychological phenomenon that accompanies a certain physiological change. *AMA Archives of Neurology and Psychiatry, 79*, 74–90.

Cannon, W. B. (1929). *Bodily changes in pain, hunger, fear and rage* (2nd ed.). New York: Appleton–Century–Crofts.

Christianson, S.-Å. (1986). Effects of positive emotional events on memory. *Scandinavian Journal of Psychology, 27*, 287–299.

Christianson, S.-Å., & Loftus, E. F. (1987). Memory for traumatic events. *Applied Cognitive Psychology, 1*, 225–239.

Christianson, S.-Å., & Loftus, E. F. (1991). Remembering emotional events: The fate of detailed information. *Cognition & Emotion, 5*, 81–108.

Christianson, S.-Å., and Mjörndal, T. (1985). Adrenalin, emotional arousal and memory. *Scandinavian Journal of Psychology, 26*, 237–248.

Christianson, S.-Å., & Nilsson, L.-G. (1984). Functional amnesia as induced by psychological trauma. *Memory & Cognition, 12*, 142–155.

Christianson, S.-Å., Nilsson, L.-G., Mjörndal, T., Perris, C., & Tjellden, G. (1986). Psychological versus physiological determinants of emotional arousal and its relationship to laboratory induced amnesia. *Scandinavian Journal of Psychology, 27*, 300–310.

Deffenbacher, K. A. (1983). The influence of arousal on reliability of testimony. In S. M. A. Lloyd-Bostock & R. B. Clifford (Ed.), *Evaluating witness evidence: Recent psychological research and new perspectives*. Chichester: Wiley

Easterbrook, J. A. (1959). The effect of emotion on cue utilization and the organization of behavior. *Psychological Review, 66*, 183–201.

Ellis, H. C., Thomas, R. L., and Rodriguez, I. A. (1984). Emotional mood states and memory: Elaborative encoding, semantic processing, and cognitive effort. *Journal of Experimental Psychology: Learning, Memory, and Cognition, 10*, 470–482.

Hockey, G. R. J. (1970). Effect of loud noise on attentional selectivity. *Quarterly Journal of Experimental Psychology, 22*, 28–36.

Isen, A. M., Shalker, T., Clark, M., & Karp, L. (1978). Affect, accessibility of material in memory and behavior: A cognitive loop? *Journal of Personality and Social Psychology, 36*, 1–12.

Loftus, E. F., & Burns, T. E. (1982). Mental shock can produce retrograde amnesia. *Memory and Cognition, 10*, 318–323.

MacDowell, K. A., & Mandler, G. (1989). Constructions of emotion: Discrepancy, arousal, and mood. *Motivation and Emotion, 13*, 105–124.

Mandler, G. (1964). The interruption of behavior. In E. Levine (Ed.), *Nebraska Symposium on Motivation*. Lincoln: University of Nebraska Press.

Mandler, G. (1975). *Mind and emotion*. New York: Wiley

Mandler, G. (1979). Thought processes, consciousness, and stress. In V. Hamilton & D. M. Warburton (Ed.), *Human stress and cognition: An information processing approach*. London: Wiley.

Mandler, G. (1980). Recognizing: The judgment of previous occurrence. *Psychological Review, 87*, 252–271.

Mandler, G. (1984). *Mind and body: Psychology of emotion and stress*. New York: Norton.

Mandler, G. (1985). *Cognitive psychology: An essay in cognitive science*. Hillsdale, NJ: Lawrence Erlbaum Associates.

Mandler, G. (1988). Problems and directions in the study of consciousness. In M. Horowitz (Ed.), *Psychodynamics and cognition*. Chicago: Chicago University Press.

Mandler, G. (1989a). Affect and learning: Causes and consequences of emotional interactions. In D. B. McLeod & V. M. Adams (Ed.), *Affect and mathematical problem solving: A new perspective*. New York: Springer–Verlag.

Mandler, G. (1989b). Memory: Conscious and unconscious. In P. R. Solomon, G. R. Goethals, C. M. Kelley, & B. R. Stephens (Ed.), *Memory: Interdisciplinary approaches*. New York: Springer–Verlag.

Mandler, G. (1990). A constructivist theory of emotion. In N. S. Stein, B. L. Leventhal, & T. Trabasso (Ed.), *Psychological and biological approaches to emotion*. Hillsdale, NJ: Lawrence Erlbaum Associates.

Mandler, G. (in press a). Approaches to a psychology of value. In M. Hechter, L. Cooper, & L. Nadel (Ed.), *Towards a scientific study of value*. Palo Alto, CA: Stanford University Press.

Mandler, G. (in press b). Toward a theory of consciousness. In H. G. Geissler, S. Link, & J. G. Townsend (Ed.), *Cognition, information processing and psychophysics: Basic issues*. Hillsdale, NJ: Lawrence Erlbaum Associates.

Mandler, G., & Sarason, S. B. (1952). A study of anxiety and learning. *Journal of Abnormal and Social Psychology, 47*, 166–173.

Marcel, A. J. (1983). Conscious and unconscious perception: An approach to the relations between phenomenal experience and perceptual processes. *Cognitive Psychology, 15*, 238–300.

Mathews, A., Mogg, K., May, J., & Eysenck, M. (1989). Implicit and explicit memory bias in anxiety. *Journal of Abnormal Psychology, 98*, 236–240.

Mathews, A., Richards, A., & Eysenck, M. (1989). Interpretation of homophones related to threat in anxiety states. *Journal of Abnormal Psychology, 98*, 31–34.

Overson, C. (1989). *Stress and anxiety in mathematical problem solving*. Unpublished doctoral dissertation, University of California, San Diego.

Rumelhart, D. E., & McClelland, J. L. (1985). *Parallel distributed processing: Explorations on the microstructure of cognition* (Vol. 1 - Foundations). Cambridge: MIT Press.

Schachter, S., & Singer, J. E. (1962). Cognitive, social and physiological determinants of emotional state. *Psychological Review, 69*, 379–399.

Selye, H. (1982). History and present status of the stress concept. In L. Goldberger & S. Breznitz (Ed.), *Handbook of stress: Theoretical and clinical aspects*. New York: The Free Press.

Weltman, G. , Smith, J. E., & Enström, G. H. (1971). Perceptual narrowing during simulated pressure-chamber exposure. *Human Factors, 13*, 99–107.

Yerkes, R. M., & Dodson, J. D. (1980). The relation of strength of stimulus to rapidity of habit-formation. *Journal of Comparative and Neurological Psychology, 18*, 459–482.

Zillmann, D. (1978). Attribution and misattribution of excitatory reactions. In J. H. Harvey, W. Ickes, & R. F. Kidd (Ed.), *New directions in attribution research* (Vol. 2). Hillsdale, NJ: Lawrence Erlbaum Associates.

II

METHODOLOGICAL ISSUES

5

The Implications of Arousal Effects for the Study of Affect and Memory

William Revelle
Debra A. Loftus
Northwestern University

INTRODUCTION

Humans as well as honey bees need to remember important events to survive. Given limitations of cognitive capacity, however, they also need to forget those moments that are least important. For it is essential in a competitive environment to allocate scarce attentional and memory resources to critical events rather than to the mundane. To be successful when threatened by hungry carnivores, our early mammalian ancestors could not be lost in thought considering the pleasures of the last meal. Similarly, for insects with brains the size of that of a honey bee, not too much memory can be allocated to remembering beautiful sunsets (McGaugh, 1990). The way that motivational and affective reactions to environmental stimuli and outcomes modulate memory seems to be one solution to the problem of remembering critical life events and forgetting the trivial. In the following pages we consider evidence from the personality and motivational literature that suggests that arousal, an intensity component of motivation, has a critical role in modulating the processes involved in the storage and retrieval of information. We propose that high levels of arousal facilitate the detection and long term retention of information but at a seeming cost of inhibiting immediate access to that information. We suggest that because many manipulations of affect and mood are also manipulations of arousal that supposed mood effects upon memory may be accounted for partly by the effect of arousal upon memory. We conclude that some of the controversy surrounding the effects of mood upon memory can be resolved by a proper appreciation of the effects of arousal upon memory.

Although our emphasis upon the arousal or intensity aspect of motivation is common in the individual differences and motivational literature, we suspect that our arousal-oriented approach to the problem of how affect or emotion relates to memory differs from those with a more cognitive interpretation of affect (e.g., Ortony, Clore, & Collins, 1990). Our orientation is quite different from those who view affect as just another memory code, the effects of which can be modeled in the same way as the type face or the color of the stimuli. We prefer to emphasize the important role that motivational and affective intensity play upon the very way in which information is detected, processed, and stored for later retrieval.

We have previously suggested that the motivational construct of arousal has a critical impact upon memory, and that any study of the relationships between affect, mood, and memory needs to take individual differences and situational sources of arousal into account (Revelle & Loftus, 1990). In the following pages we first review arousal as a useful psychological construct, discuss some of the controversy in its measurement and manipulation, consider how the construct of arousal has proven to be helpful in discriminating among competing models of personality, and then propose four different ways in which arousal affects cognitive performance. We then summarize some of the findings relating affect to memory and suggest that many of the manipulations used to change affect are in fact manipulations of arousal as well. We propose that some of the confusion relating affective state to memory performance is due to a lack of concern for the direct effects of arousal upon memory. Based upon our review we propose a model of how arousal and affect modulate memory. Finally we suggest what steps need to be taken in the study of mood and memory if the implications of the effect of arousal on memory are to be taken seriously.

In all of our discussion we emphasize that individual differences in arousal need to be taken into account if particular effects are expected to replicate across various situational manipulations. This partly reflects our own biases but also reflects a good deal of prior research (reviewed in Anderson, 1989; Revelle, 1987, 1989) that has shown that what seems at first to be a morass of conflicting findings relating arousal manipulations to performance is actually much more orderly when the effects of several personality variables are taken into account.

AROUSAL AS A PSYCHOLOGICAL CONSTRUCT

In everyday terms, to be aroused means to be wide awake, alert, vigorous, excited, and full of pep (Thayer, 1989). To be unaroused means to be sleepy, sluggish, tired, and relaxed. More formally, Duffy (1962) stated that arousal or activation "describes a condition conceived to vary in a continuum from a low point in sleep to a high point in extreme effort or intense excitement" (p. 5). Moderate levels of arousal can be equated with feelings of peppiness and vigor, although extremely high levels are felt as tense and unpleasant (Thayer, 1989). Arousal as a general construct may also be conceived of as the negative probability of falling asleep (Corcoran, 1965, 1972, 1981). It has been referred to as the non specific component of motivation that reflects the intensity rather than the direction of motivation (Humphreys & Revelle, 1984) as well as the intensity rather than the evaluational quality of affect (Whissel, Fournier, Pelland, Weir, & Makarec, 1986).

It is difficult to find an area of psychology where the construct of arousal has not played an important role. For instance, in real time theories of conditioning, arousal is necessary for some neural associations to form (Grossberg, 1987). In psychophysiology, arousal is the cause of desynchronization of the electroencephalogram (EEC), is a nonspecific response to orienting stimuli (O'Gorman, 1977), and is a response to increases in task complexity (Berlyne, 1960). In some personality theories arousal level is thought to be maintained at an intermediate value as part of a homeostatic mechanism believed to cause differences in stimulation seeking and hyperactivity (H. J. Eysenck, 1967, 1981; Zuckerman, 1979). In theories of human performance, arousal has been discussed as a determinant of sustained performance in vigilance situations (cf. Davies & Parasuraman, 1982; Mackie, 1977) and has been used as a way of relating individual differences in personality to the effects of stimulant drugs and time of day on cognitive performance (Revelle, Humphreys, Simon, & Gilliland, 1980).

Theories of generalized arousal are not without their critics (e.g., Hockey, 1979, 1984; Neiss, 1988; Venables, 1984) or, more accurately, the supporters of theories of generalized arousal are sometimes hard to find (but see Anderson, 1990; Gale, 1986, 1987; Humphreys & Revelle, 1984; Revelle, 1987, 1989; Revelle, Anderson, & Humphreys, 1987). Although many theorists recognize the appeal of a unified construct of intensity, the experimental evidence for the dissassociation of various arousal manipulations seems to some to be quite compelling[1]. Indeed, some disillusioned arousal theorists now refer to the study of the intensity aspects of performance with the less theory-laden term of *energetics*, (Hockey, Gaillard, & Coles, 1986).

Although the evidence is quite clear that there are many different biological responses to increased demands for energy expenditure it is less clear that functionally these responses are not serving a similar purpose. Following Corcoran's (1965, 1981) very compelling definition of arousal as the inverse probability of falling asleep, or the related hypothesis that arousal level is a positive function of energetic requirements, we propose that the low levels of energy expenditure associated with sleeping are a means of conserving physiological resources for more demanding activities. Conversely, high levels of arousal are associated with higher rates of metabolic response to task demands; that is, variations in arousal may be seen as serving the function of varying the resources available for information processing. Jennings, Nebes, and Brock (1988) asserted: "cardiovascular changes during information processing reflect the regulation of the organism's energetic economy in support of the specific processes required by the task at hand" (p. 641).

Compelling demonstrations of how separate arousal systems can serve the same function are the studies by McGaugh and his colleagues, who have examined how various stimulants, depressants, and neurotransmitters have similar effects upon memory modulation (McGaugh, 1990). The peripheral stimulant epinepherine, the central stimulant, norepinepherine, and the opiate antagonist, naloxone, all can be shown to modulate memory by their effect on the amygdala. Similarly, arousal changes associated with such widely disparate sources as stable personality traits (introversion/extraversion), time of day, stimulant drugs, white noise, evaluation by others, and exercise have resulted in highly similar effects on memory (Revelle & Loftus, 1990).

---

[1]It is useful to compare the arguments for unified versus multiple state theories of arousal with those arguments among memory theorists as to the multiplicity of memory systems (Hintzman, 1990). The apparent dissassociations of memory found in studies of special populations can be taken as evidence for multiple systems of memory (Schacter, 1987; Tulving, 1983) or merely an incomplete analysis of the complexity of the tasks involved (Humphreys, Bain, & Pike, 1989).

Even if all variations in arousal might be serving the same purpose, it is not necessary that they are caused by similar mechanisms; that is, for primates accustomed to gathering fruits and seeds in the daytime while looking out for predators, conserving energy by sleeping at night is a very useful adaptation to lowered visual acuity and associated higher risk of predation at night. It is functionally more efficient to reduce one's rate of metabolic activity at times when demands are low than it is to keep a constant rate. Consequently, a diurnal variation in arousal is a useful means of coping with the diurnal variation in task demands from the environment. An organism with a very strong diurnal metabolic system, however, will be particularly sensitive to predation at low points in its metabolic cycle. (Monkey's that fail to wake up when attacked by pythons late at night will have a lower reproductive fitness than those that do wake up and are able to flee.) Thus, there is a need to have a separate system that can override or compensate for the normally low nocturnal levels of arousal—a system more capable of responding in an acute sense to immediate demands within the environment. It is possible to argue for a cascade of such control systems, each of which may have evolved separately to compensate for under or over control of the previous level of energy allocation. The function of all these systems, however, may be seen as controlling the current level of energy expenditure. It is the functioning of this complex of systems that we choose to describe in terms of arousal.[2]

MEASUREMENT OF AROUSAL

Given the long history of arousal in psychological theory, it would seem that the measurement of arousal would be straightforward. Unfortunately, this is not the case. Rather, the failure of different measures of arousal to agree with each other is perhaps the greatest source of dissatisfaction with the use of arousal as a unifying theoretical construct. Some of the sources of the controversy surrounding the use of arousal as a psychological construct include debates about broad issues in measurement, the importance of individual differences, the level of inference between the measure and the construct, and the effect of various situational manipulations.

---

[2]As is true of much of the work reported here, the preceding paragraph owes much to many discussions with Michael Humphreys whose contribution is gratefully acknowledged.

Problems of Measurement

At least four different issues need to be considered when discussing
the measurement of arousal. Three of these involve the timing and
the temporal resolution of the measures: The first considers how
arousal measures vary across the psychological spectrum of temporal resolution; the second concerns the time course of various
arousal measures; and the third involves the problem of relating
measures based upon different sampling frames and latencies. A
fourth issue is the problem of between-versus-within subject measures of arousal.

Arousal and the Psychological Spectrum. Psychological phenomena range across a temporal spectrum of at least 12 orders of
magnitude: from the milliseconds used to index firing rates of
neurons, to the seconds of a verbal learning study, to the hours of a
vigilance experiment, and finally to the decades that make up a
lifetime. Different psychological phenomena typically are measured
at different temporal frequencies (or durations) across the spectrum.
For example, Event Related Potentials (ERPs) have durations of
100–600 ms, priming effects for reaction time persist over only a few
seconds, changes in affect takes tens of seconds to occur, stimulants
such as caffeine have effects only after 30–40 minutes ($\approx 2 \times 10^3$sec),
and cognitive performance changes can range over the day ($\approx 10^5$
sec), the menstrual cycle ($\approx 10^6$ sec), a year of schooling ($\approx 3 \times 10^7$
sec), and over the life-span ($\approx 3 \times 10^9$ sec).

Measures of arousal may be classified in terms of this psychological spectrum. At the shortest intervals are measures that include
indices of cortical activity such as the EEG, both event related and
resting frequency. At somewhat longer intervals are the autonomic
measures of Skin Conductance (SC) and Heart Rate (HR). At even
longer levels are endrocrine measures such as the level of Mono-
Amine Oxidase (MAO) and general metabolic measures such as core
Body Temperature (BT). Other measures with fine temporal resolution
include psychophysical sensitivities to light and sound. At a less fine
resolution are measures of activity level. In addition to the direct
physiological measures are measures of self report of arousal. By
asking subjects how peppy, active, and vigorous they feel, it is
possible to show general effects with durations from a few minutes
to a few hours. In fact, as Robert Thayer (1986, 1989) has shown, self-
report measures seem to reflect the general factor of many of the
finer grain physiological measures (see also Clements, Hafer, &
Vermillion, 1976 and Matthews, 1987, 1989).

Time Course of Arousal Measures: Growth, Level, and Decay of Arousal. Arousal changes over time. Therefore, we need to be concerned with the rates of growth and decay, as well as the average level of arousal. Variables that affect one rate of change need not affect the others. Consider the various patterns of arousal that can occur as a result of different patterns of stimulation duration (both the on and off times) if change in arousal (dA) is represented as a function of excitatory sensitivity (e) to stimulation (S) and habituation, which is a function of arousal level and some decay parameter (c): dA = eS - cA. Average arousal level is a function of e, c, and the length of time the stimulation is on or off. When measuring arousal level, it is important to remember that these parameters of arousal are logically, and frequently empirically, independent.[3]

Latency and Sampling Frame. A classic problem in the measurement of arousal is how to relate measures with different onset latencies after the stimulus. Each index of arousal has different temporal parameters, with different delays and sampling rates, so that different indices reflect arousal averaged over different lengths of time and with different delays (e.g., EEG activation will occur within milliseconds of a stimulus onset, skin conductance changes after several seconds, self-reports of activity and energy reflect arousal sampled over a longer period than either EEG or SC, and body temperature seems to indicate average activity over a period of minutes to hours). Depending on the fineness of the temporal resolution of the stimulus, these different measures will respond differently. A missing stimulus in the P300 oddball paradigm that elicits a change in EEG evoked potentials, and perhaps an Orienting Response as indexed by a change in SC or HR, should not be expected, however, to affect ratings of alertness or core body temperature. These broader measures reflect changes in the system that are so slow as to be undetectable or are discarded by those who record ERPs or GSRs.

Within - Versus Between - Subject Measures. Several different questions arise with respect to the problem of measurements taken within subjects versus between subjects. Arousal is normally thought of as something that varies within subject—a stimulus induces an orienting response, we become excited while giving a talk, exercise increases heart rate. Although some measures (such as self-report)

[3]Readers familiar with the the work of Atkinson and Birch (1970) will no doubt recognize that this emphasis upon rates of change is adapted from the their theory of the dynamics of action. (See also Revelle, 1986).

are very useful indicators of arousal changes within subjects, they are of questionable validity between subjects.[4] For instance, it is difficult to know what different people mean by the term low arousal. What person A reports as being calm, person B might well report as excited and peppy. When one of us feels exhausted and thinks that he is talking very slowly, students report that his rate of talking in a lecture is finally at a normal level. This problem of calibration between subjects is not just for self-report; for example, skin conductance differences can reflect skin thickness between subjects as well as differences in excitement within and between subjects.

Finally, it is important to note that when indices covary within individuals, they do not necessarily covary between individuals. Some individuals will respond to stimuli with greater changes in heart rate than in skin conductance, whereas others will have large increases in skin conductance but only small increases in heart rate. Within subjects, changes in SC and HR can correlate positively even though there is zero or a negative correlation between subjects. The question of how to aggregate data across subjects is particularly important for any consideration of the effect of arousal upon performance.

Individual Differences

That there are individual differences in measures of arousal at all levels of the psychological spectrum is not an issue. If there were no individual differences, then we would need no more than one subject per cell of our experimental designs. But because not all subjects within an experimental condition are the same, the question becomes whether the within-experimental condition differences are predictable by extra–experimental means; that is, are there characteristics of subjects that allow us to predict how they will respond (behaviorally or physiologically) in a particular situation. The purpose of searching for individual differences is not to demonstrate that people differ but rather to find ways of predicting behavior across situations. What is important is that differences at long temporal intervals are able to predict differences on tasks with short durations and vice versa. We discuss such evidence later when relating personality to arousal.

---

[4]Venables (1984) elaborates on the difficulties of taking a within-subjects construct and making inferences between subjects.

Range of Environmental Conditions

A consistent issue when searching for an arousal effect of any type is to specify the appropriate range of environmental conditions. There are very few interesting arousal effects or individual differences when subjects are dead or in a deep coma. Although an oversimplification, it is useful to consider person operating curves (POCs) plotting hypothetical levels of arousal (or any other outcome measure) as a function of environmental demand (Fig. 5.1). Arousal is shown as a monotonically increasing function of the environment for three hypothetical subjects. At very high and very low levels of environmental stimulation, there are no meaningful differences. It is

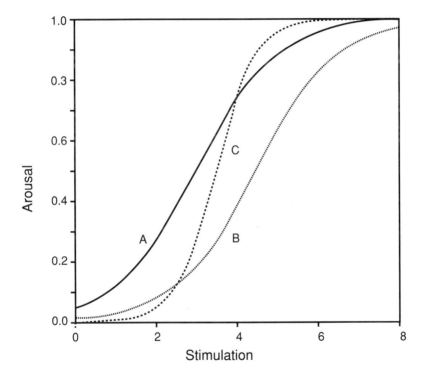

FIG. 5.1. Hypothetical levels of arousal as a function of environmental stimuli for individuals differing in base line arousal and in sensitivity to stimulation. Individual differences are less at very low and very high levels than at intermediate levels. Note that for all levels of stimulation A > B, but that at low levels of stimulation A > B > C, at medium levels A > C > B and at high levels, C > A > B. Stimulation represents the sum of external (e.g., noise, light) and internal (e.g., caffeine) stimulants.

only at intermediate values that differences can be detected. In addition, note that one POC reflects a subject who is more sensitive to the changes in environmental demand than the others; that is, for individual C, the POC is steeper at the middle level of stimulation. For this person, low levels of environmental demand lead to very low levels of arousal and high levels of demand lead to very high levels; that is, at low stimulation levels, this person is less aroused than the others, but at high stimulation values, is actually more aroused. Although making the search for reliable arousal effects as a function of individual differences more difficult, it is possible to organize the literature reporting the effects of extraversion on basal frequency of EEG in just such a manner (e.g., Gale, 1981). Reliable differences in EEG frequency between introverts and extraverts only occur at moderate levels of environmental demand.

Direct Versus Indirect Measures of Arousal

Most studies concerned with the measurement of arousal can be divided into those with an emphasis upon peripheral measures of autonomic activity such as skin conductance or heart rate, and the more central measures of cortical activity associated with variations in scalp potential as detected by the EEG. Unfortunately, these measures of the hand, the heart, and the head do not produce evidence for a unified arousal system (Lacey, 1967; Venables, 1984) From a functional point of view, the independence of the separate physiological measures is not evidence against the validity of the arousal construct. Rather it suggests that separate control processes have developed to modulate energy availability, and that it is this sum of available energy that people report as arousal.

An alternative to physiological measures is to assess the *subjective* feeling of alertness and vigor by self-report. As Thayer (1967, 1978, 1989) and Clements et al. (1976) have shown convincingly, when measures are taken within subjects, self-reports of arousal correlate more highly with each of the separate physiological measures than the measures do with each other. This is, of course, just the pattern that would be expected if the self-report measures represented either the common factor of arousal, or the sum of activity in each of several independent systems.

Situational Manipulations of Arousal

There are many ways to manipulate arousal. Manipulations used to decrease arousal level include sleep deprivation, time on task, and depressant drugs (e.g., alcohol or barbiturates). Manipulations used to increase arousal include increases in stimulation (e.g., increases in noise, light, or somatasensory input), the use of stimulant drugs (e.g., caffeine, amphetamine, or nicotine), and light to moderate exercise. Variations in arousal also occur naturally throughout the day (diurnal rhythms) with most people reaching a peak of alertness in the late morning to mid afternoon and reaching a low point between 3 and 6 am.

Each manipulation of arousal has specific effects as well as a general effect. It is important when examining the relationships between various manipulations and measures to take into account the irrelevancies of each manipulation as well as the common effects (Anderson, 1990). For instance, the behavioral consequences of lowering arousal through sleep deprivation or sustained performance are quite different than those associated with the effects of alcohol. Similarly, noise and caffeine both increase arousal, but their effects on performance differ, at least partly because high levels of noise are distracting and can mask inner speech whereas high levels of caffeine can cause muscle tremor. Much of the argument over the utility of the arousal construct centers on the relative importance of the specific versus common effects of arousal manipulations (Anderson, 1990).

The Covariation of Manipulations of Arousal and Affect

That affect and emotion have both a directional and intensity component is well known. A great deal of research and debate has been concerned with the interplay between these two components and, more specifically, the question of which is primary in one's experience of an emotion—the intensity (arousal) or the directional (evaluative) component (Schachter & Singer, 1962). The question of primacy aside, it is clear that whereas emotions such as fear and happiness are easily categorized into separate evaluational or affective dimensions (positive vs. negative), other emotional terms such as nervous and afraid must rely on an intensity factor (high vs. low in its most simplistic form) for differentiation. Whissell et al. (1986) found that a two-dimensional space (Evaluation by Activation) represented the most parsimonious categorization system for emotion words. An alternative solution to the dimensions of affective space can be found in Watson and colleagues' two orthogonal factors of positive and negative affect (PA and NA; Watson, Clark, & Tellegen, 1988; Watson & Tellegen, 1985).

Within the arousal domain, Thayer (1967, 1978, 1986, 1989) has explicated two orthogonal factors that can be related to dimensions of affect: energetic arousal and tense arousal. Energetic arousal and positive affect covary strongly as do tense arousal and negative affect. Thayer (1989) found that energetic arousal varies diurnally along with positive affect. Loftus (1990) found that an exercise induction (as compared to a relaxation induction) tended to increase positive affect whereas negative affect remained unaffected. Both energetic and tense arousal increased as a result of the exercise induction also. This result was in contrast to an earlier study performed by Thayer that suggested exercise increased energetic arousal and decreased tense arousal (Thayer, 1989).

Although the exact nature of the relationship between positive/negative affect and low/high or energetic/tense arousal has yet to be clearly delineated, it is clear that many manipulations of affect also are manipulations of arousal. The negative affect experienced while watching a horror movie is accompanied by an increase in tense arousal. The positive affect associated with a lively party is also associated with an increase in energetic arousal. It is this confounding of affective manipulations with arousal manipulations that we believe may account for at least part of the inconsistent findings (discussed later) within the study of mood–state dependent effects. In addition, it is likely that the so-called mood intensity effects are more attributable to the effects of the arousal levels present in the experiments than the affect.

PERSONALITY AND AROUSAL

As we suggested earlier, when relating arousal to cognitive performance an important source of variation is individual differences in tonic as well as phasic arousal. Although it is possible to ignore such individual differences by random assignment of subjects to affective manipulations, a more powerful design attempts to take these individual differences into account. Not only does so doing increase statistical power, it also leads to a clearer explication of the relationships between affect, arousal, and memory. In this section we discuss alternative strategies for identifying individual differences associated with arousal and then review some of the most relevant prior research.

There are two very different ways to examine these individual differences: One is to search for behavioral correlates of psychophysiological variation; the other is to search for psychophysiological correlates of variations in personality traits known to be behaviorally important. Given our orientation towards developing and testing theories of personality, it is not surprising that we prefer the latter orientation.

Bottom-Up Versus Top-Down Searches for Individual Differences. A typical finding in the psychophysiological literature is that although there are large individual differences on each measure, the separate measures do not tend to correlate very highly. This has been taken, in fact, as evidence of the separability of various types of arousal; that is, it is the low correlation between measures that makes one doubt the utility of a general factor of arousal. To anyone familiar with scale construction, such a pattern of results is not surprising. Individual items in an ability test show very low average correlations with other items (of the order of .1 to .2), even in a test that has a very high reliability (.95); that is, although the general factor in such a test might account for no more than 10% or 20% of the reliable variance in any particular item, 95% of the total test variance is due to the general factor. When using such a test to predict an important criterion, it is difficult to find high validity coefficients for any particular item (given the low saturation of the general factor in each item) even though the test as a whole has a strikingly high validity.

Those who search for reliable individual differences in arousal should consider this example carefully, for it suggests that the appropriate strategy of searching for useful individual differences is not in searching for high validity coefficients at the item level (separate measures of physiological response) but rather at a higher, test level (composite measures representing a greater sampling frame or a greater number of measures); that is, an alternative strategy to looking for correlates of specific physiological measures is to reverse the search and look for physiological correlates of personality dimensions that are known to be important. As we show next, perhaps the most important of these is the dimension of introversion–extraversion and its component, impulsivity.

Dimensions of Personality Related to Arousal. Rather than try to summarize all studies of arousal that have shown individual differences (which would be all studies with more than one subject), we have found it useful to take a top-down approach and discuss how certain broad, stable dimensions of individual differences can be related to arousal. To help the uninitiated, this means considering the relevant personality literature to suggest dimensions that on theoretical grounds should be related to arousal. For a much more thorough review, see Gale and Edwards (1986).

Several important conclusions have come out of the last 50 years of personality research. One is that there are a limited number of dimensions (between four and seven) of personality that can be used to describe individual differences in cognitive, affective, and social behavior. The second is that individual differences in these trait dimensions have remarkable stability across years and even decades. A third is that these traits have important relationships to meaningful behavioral outcomes. Lastly, some of these dimensions have been shown to have consistent relationships with various physiological measures.

That there is a limited set of dimensions that can usefully describe individual differences in social behavior has been shown by both the American steps toward an "adequate taxonomy" of folk psychological descriptions of personality (e.g., Allport & Odbert, 1936; Cattell, 1957; Digman, 1990; Goldberg, 1982; McCrae & Costa, 1987; Norman, 1963, 1969), as well as the European studies on the biological bases of personality (H. J. Eysenck 1947, 1952, 1967, 1981, 1987; H. J. Eysenck & M. W. Eysenck, 1985; Gray, 1972, 1981, 1982, 1987; Strelau, 1983, 1985). The American taxonomy project of natural language or folk psychology has suggested that five dimensions of describing others (e.g., the five factors discussed by Tupes & Christal, 1961, and Norman, 1963, 1969: surgency, agreeableness, conscientiousness, emotional stability, and culture) are the beginnings of an adequate taxonomy. The British and other Western Europeans have intensively studied three–four dimensions (introversion–extraversion, neuroticism–stability, psychoticism, and intelligence), whereas the Eastern Europeans have concentrated on three dimensions derived from Pavlovian theory (strength of the excitory and inhibitory processes, and balance between these process; Strelau, 1983).[5]

---

[5] For those who find their favorite personality trait not listed in the three–seven dimensions of the taxonomists, it is necessary to remember that the dimensional space defined by these primary dimensions can include any number of combinations of the primaries. (In fact, a major difference between the American and European taxonomists is the emphasis in Europe of searching for causal bases of the dimensions as a way of resolving the indeterminacy of rotation problem that besets the American taxonomies. Consider, for example, the debate between Eysenck (1981, 1987) and Gray (1981, 1987) as to the biological significance of introversion–extraversion and neuroticism–stability versus impulsivity and anxiety.) Whereas perhaps not appealing to all, such a dimensional framework does provide more coherence to theory development than does the alphabetical arrangement of traits favored by some (e.g., London & Exner, 1978) or the historical arrangement favored by most undergraduate texts.

Recent reviews of longitudinal studies involving this limited set of dimensions have shown quite high consistencies across periods of up to 40 years (Conley, 1984). For example, although there are clear changes across the life-span, measures of introversion in early adulthood predict social behavior 30–40 years later. Similarly, young adults high in neuroticism are more at risk for psychiatric difficulties over the life-span than are those with low neuroticism scores.

Most important for a discussion of personality and arousal, the trait of introversion–extraversion, or at least its component, impulsivity, has a striking relationship to measures of arousal. Several physiological factors appear to differ between these groups. These include differences in basal arousal level (introverts are claimed to be more aroused than extraverts), differences in speed of habituation of arousal (extraverts and high impulsives seem to habituate faster), and differences in phase of the diurnal arousal rhythm (low impulsives seem to lead high impulsives by at least several hours). These differences have been reported using a variety of diverse measures.

In several summaries of the EEG-personality relationship, Gale (1981, 1983) has suggested that, although there are reliable differences between introverts and extraverts, they are only to be found in certain, well-defined circumstances. Gale has commented that the demands of experimental conditions used in studying personality–EEG correlates vary greatly, ranging from instructing subjects to lie back in a dark room and try not to fall asleep, to having them count tones of moderate intensity, to trying to learn which extremely loud tones are associated with shock. In a post hoc classification of experimental situations, Gale found evidence for Eysenck's hypothesis of greater arousal for introverts for those studies with moderate levels of stimulation.

Other cortical measures suggesting higher arousal for introverts can be found from studies using Evoked Potentials (ERP; Stelmack & Wilson, 1982), Contingent Negative Variation (CNV; O'Conner, 1980, 1982; Werre, 1986, 1987), Photic Driving (Robinson, 1982), and the Sedation Threshold (Shagass & Jones, 1958; Shagass & Kerenyi, 1958).

Introversion–extraversion and impulsivity also relate to individual differences in arousal as assessed by autonomic measures of Skin Conductance (Fowles, Roberts, & Nagel, 1977; Smith, Rypma, & Wilson, 1981; Wilson, 1990), Spontaneous GSRs (Crider & Lunn, 1971), Orienting Response Habituation (O'Gorman, 1977; Stelmack, Bourgeois, Chian, & Pickard, 1979), and Pupil Size (Stelmack & Mandelzyz, 1975); phase differences in the basic metabolic measures of diurnal variation in Body Temperature (Blake, 1967); and differences in self-reported arousal (Thayer, 1989).[6]

Individual Differences in Arousal as Measured by Self-Report

Two Dimensions of Self-Reported Arousal. Although much simpler than measuring EEG, SC, or OR, a powerful device for assessing arousal state is self-report. Subjects will report being more lively, active, full of pep, or energetic as a function of time of day, prior exercise, or stimulant drugs. Thayer (1967, 1978, 1989) has shown that his Activation–Deactivation Adjective Check List (AD–ACL) correlates with the appropriate physiological measures and is quite sensitive to arousal manipulations (see also Clements et al., 1976). Although Thayer originally reported four factors to his AD–ACL, later analyses suggested that two factors were quite adequate: activation–deactivation (energetic arousal) and tension–relaxation (tense arousal). The former dimension shows a marked diurnal rhythm whereas the latter one does not. In addition, it is commonly found that the energetic arousal factor is a more reliable predictor of performance (Loftus, 1990; Matthews, Davies, & Lees, 1990; Thayer, 1978).

Individual Differences in Diurnal Variations of Self-Reported Arousal. It is well known that some people claim they function best in the morning and need to retire early, whereas others believe that they cannot function at all until late in the day. Individual differences in this lark versus owl tendency are reflected in body temperature differences as well as in such simple measures as time of awakening. Although in general, owls are more likely to be highly impulsive, the correlations are not particularly strong. Matthews (1989) has made use of this fact to study the performance of introverts and extraverts (and low and high impulsives) as a function of time of day and self-reported arousal. His results parallel those found with direct manipulations of arousal; that is, low impulsives who report being aroused in the morning perform less well than those who report not being aroused, whereas high impulsives who report being aroused do better in the morning than those who do not.

---

[6] The interested reader should see the very thorough review by Stelmack (1990) of basal and phasic arousal differences as they relate to introversion.

Individual Differences in
Self-Reported Arousal and Affect

We have emphasized that there are stable individual differences in tonic and phasic arousal not just because such differences are an extraneous source of variability when studying affect, but because the same dimensions of personality that relate to arousal relate to sensitivity to positive and negative affect. Recent work has shown that positive and negative affect are independent of each other (Watson & Tellegen, 1985). In addition, it is thought that susceptibility to positive affect is related to impulsivity and extraversion and that susceptibility to negative affect is related to anxiety and neuroticism (Meyer & Shack, 1989). This suggests that most manipulations of mood or affect are likely to have different effects depending on individual differences in impulsivity and anxiety.

AROUSAL AND MEMORY

We started this chapter with the claim that the study of arousal is important when studying the effect of affect upon memory. We have reviewed the reasons suggesting that arousal is a useful theoretical construct, discussed some of the problems in the measurement of arousal, and summarized the striking and reliable individual differences in either phasic or tonic arousal level. We have suggested that various manipulations of affect probably are also manipulations of arousal. We now consider evidence that arousal has at least four different effects upon the detection, storage, and utilization of information (Table 5.1). Two of these effects are beneficial: High arousal facilitates the detection and encoding for long-term retention of information. However the third effect does not seem as beneficial: High arousal at input may be associated with an inability to retrieve information for a short period of time (up to about 30 minutes) following the original encoding. Finally, the fourth effect of arousal on information processing exists in those situations where the task demands combine beneficial and detrimental effects. On such (complex) tasks, increases of arousal from low to moderate are associated with improved performance, increases from moderate to high are associated with decrements in performance. This inverted-U relationship between arousal and performance is a function of the relative task demands of detection versus immediate versus delayed memory. We also raise the question of a fifth potential effect of arousal upon information processing: arousal effects upon retrieval.

TABLE 5.1
Studies Investigating the Effect of Arousal Upon Immediate or Delayed Retention

Study — Arousal manipulation/ Individual difference	Measure of Arousal	ID	arousal within or between	memory within or between	Design — Immediate	Delay	Materials	N	Results — Immediate	Delayed	Form
Stimulus Materials											
Walker & Tarte (1963)	GSR		b	b	2 min	1 week	word–digit	72	–	+	r
Kleinsmith & Kaplan (1963)	GSR		w	b	2 min	1 week	word–digit	48	–	+	r
Kleinsmith & Kaplan (1964)	GSR		w	b	2 min	1 week	CVC–digit	36	–	+	r
Maltzman, Kantor & Langdon (1966)	GSR		b	b	immediate	30 min	words	80	+	+	0
Kaplan, Kaplan & Sampson (1968)	GSR		w	w	immediate	30 min	words–pictures		–	+	r
Levonian (1966)	GSR		w	w	30 secs	1 week	film	61	–	+	r
Corteen (1969)	GSR		w	b	immediate	2 weeks	words	60	+	+	d
Kaplan & Kaplan (1969)	GSR		w	b	2 min	2 days	word–digit	189	–	+	d
Butter (1970) exp 1	GSR		w	b	2 min	2 days	word–digit	16	–	+	r
Butter (1970) exp 2	GSR		w	b	2 min	2 days	word–digit	48	–	+	r
Schmitt & Forrester (1973)	GSR		w	b	2 min	2 days	word–digit	32	0	0	0
Saufley & LaCava (1977)	GSR		w	w	2 min	1 week	CVC–digit	96	0	0	0
White Noise											
Berlyne et al. (1965) expt. 3			w	w	short	1 day	names	90	–	+	d
McLean (1969) expt. 1	GSR		w	b	2 min	1 day	CVC–digit	160	–	–	r
McLean (1969) expt. 2	GSR		w	b	2 min	1 day	CVC–digit	40	–	+	r
Figure complexity											
Berlyne et al. (1965) expt. 1			w	w	immediate	1 day	figures–names	40	–	0	0
Diurnal variation											
Folkard, Monk, Bradbury, & Rosenthal (1977)			b	b	15 min	1 week	story	130	–	+	d
Jones, Gale, Smallbone (1979)	EEG		w	–	3 secs	–	digits	32	–	–	d

(Continued)

TABLE 5.1
Studies Investigating the Effect of Arousal Upon Immediate or Delayed Retention

Study					Immediate	Delayed	Material	N	Imm	Del	Pattern
Diurnal variation											
Jones et al. (1979) study 2	EEG		w	−	12 sec	−	digits	26	+		
Jones et al. (1979) study 3	EEG		w	−	12 secs	−	digits	20	−		
Folkard & Monk (1980)	BT		w	−	3 min	−	article	36	−		
Folkard & Monk (1980) exp 2	BT		w	w	10 min	28 days	film	50	0	+	d
Oakhill (1986)			b	b	immediate	1 week	story	64	0	+	d
Diurnal variation + Impulsivity											
Puchalski (1988)	Imp		b	b	immediate	1 week	story	164	−	+	r
Caffeine											
Terry & Phifer (1986)			b	w	immediate	5-7 minutes	words	32	−		
Exercise											
Loftus (1990) exp 1	ADACL		b	b/w	2.5 min	1 hour	word-word	28	−	+	d
Loftus (1990) expt 2.	ADACL		b	b	2.5 min	1 hour	word	63	+	0	
Observation											
Geen (1973)			b	b	2 min	45 min	CVC-digit	160	−	+	r
Deffenbacher, Platt & Williams (1974)			b	b	2 min	45 min	CVC-digit	32	−	+	r
Observation-evaluation											
Geen (1974)			b	b	2 min	45 min	CVC-digit	240	−	+	r
Introversion-Extraversion											
Howarth & Eysenck (1968)		I/E	b	b	Immediate	24 hour	CVC-CVC	110	−	+	r
Berlyne & Carey (1968)		I/E	b	−	−	1 day	word-word	64		−	
McLaughlin (1968)		I/E +S/N	b	b	Immediate	2-7 days	word-word	75	0	0	0
Eysenck, M. W (1975)	ADACL	I/E	b	b	1.5 secs	1 day	word-word	52	+	0	
Fuller (1978)		I/E	b	b	2 min	1 day	CVC-digit	314	0	0	0

Note: Arousal increased (+), had no effect (0), or hindered (−) memory performance, or two arousal variables interacted so as to have a possible curvilinear relationship (x) with memory. Delayed memory showed a reminiscence effect (r) or a decrease (d) at the longer delay.

That arousal facilitates detection and long-term retrieval is not particularly surprising, for most scientific and folk models of memory would suggest that being more alert is a good thing for most cognitive tasks. What is surprising, however, is that increased arousal at storage seems to inhibit immediate retrieval processes. (That it must be a retrieval effect can be understood when the beneficial effects of arousal on long term retrieval are considered.) Finally, most theories of cognitive performance find it difficult to explain the inverted-U relationship between arousal and performance (Hebb, 1955; Humphreys and Revelle, 1984).

Beneficial Effects of Arousal Upon Detection

High levels of arousal facilitate the sustained detection of and rapid responding to simple stimuli (Hamilton, Fowler, & Porlier, 1989). Although ignored by most memory researchers, from the subject's point of view many memory studies are rather dull. Being exposed to one or more lists of words and then eventually being asked to recall words from the list is not a particularly exciting task. Indeed, Bowyer, Humphreys, and Revelle (1983) found that the performance of subjects thought to be susceptible to decrements in arousal (high impulsives) deteriorated rapidly over four blocks of a forced choice recognition study. This was not true for low impulsives. Increased arousal as induced by moderate doses of caffeine (4 mg/kg body weight) inhibited this decay in performance. Bowyer et al. interpreted this result as consistent with the general decrement in vigilance performance for extraverts (Bakan, Belton, & Toth, 1963; Keister & McLaughlin, 1972) or other subjects thought to be in a low aroused state (cf. Mackie, 1977).

Detrimental Effects On Shorter Term Retention

Perhaps the most intriguing effect of arousal lies in the finding of a deficit in immediate or shorter term recall. Walker and Tarte (1963) and Kleinsmith and Kaplan (1963, 1964) reported evidence that high arousal led to deficits for shorter term recall but facilitated longer term recall. Their studies served to instigate numerous attempts to replicate such an effect. These early studies relied on GSR responses to arousing and nonarousing word–number pairs (Kleinsmith & Kaplan, 1963; Walker & Tarte, 1963) or to nonsense syllable–number pairs (Kleinsmith & Kaplan, 1964) as indicators of the arousal present for implicit learning. Moreover, the deficits were found anywhere from immediate recall (2 minutes postlearning; Kleinsmith & Kaplan, 1963; Walker & Tarte, 1963) to some 20 minutes later (Kleinsmith & Kaplan, 1964). Kaplan and Kaplan (1969) and Butter (1970, Expt. 1) later replicated these detriments upon shorter term recall using the arousing and nonarousing word–number pairs and GSR responses in implicit learning designs. Butter (1970, Expt. 2) also replicated the effect using word–number pairs in which the words differed in concreteness–imagery. The effect was found both when analyzed from the perspective of CSRs to the paired associates upon learning and concreteness–imagery of the stimulus word (low concreteness–imagery was associated with a shorter term detriment) as the independent variable.

In further extensions of this work using stimulus materials to induce differential arousal and GSR as a reflection of the arousal, Kaplan, Kaplan, and Sampson (1968) replicated the shorter term recall deficit using two alterations in the design: explicit learning instructions and word–picture pairs as learning materials. Levonian (1966) employed GSR during the screening of a traffic safety film to derive the same type of effect. Jones and colleagues found inferior recall of nine digit strings for those subjects who evidenced higher baseline EEG activation and higher EEG activation during the first part of the explicit learning trials (Jones, Gale, & Smallbone, 1979, Expt. 1).

In an interesting varation of this work, Geen (1973) found that the presence of an observing experimenter led to short-term decrements in recall of nonsense syllable–number pairs learned under explicit instructions. Deffenbacher and colleagues also found that the presence of an observer was sufficiently arousing to produce a highly significant deficit in recall 2 minutes after explicit learning (Deffenbacher, Platt, & Williams, 1974). In a later refinement of this work, Geen (1974) found that the presence of an evaluating observer led to a short-term decrement rather than simply an observer per se. Other novel manipulations of arousal that led to successful replication of shorter term deficits include white noise (Berlyne, Borsa, Craw, Gelman & Mandell, 1965, Expt. 3; McLean, 1969, Expt. 1 & Expt. 2); caffeine in humans (Terry & Phifer, 1986) and rats (Terry & Anthony, 1980); exercise (Loftus, 1990, Expt. 1); time of day (Gates, 1916; Folkard & Monk, 1980, Expt. 1; Folkard, Monk, Bradbury, & Rosenthal, 1977; Jones et al., 1979, Expt. 3); individual differences (Howarth & Eysenck, 1968; McLaughlin, 1968); and the interaction between time of day and individual differences (Puchalski, 1988).

Attempts to replicate this effect are not without failure, however. Saufley and LaCava's (1977) attempt to replicate using 3-letter trigram-number paired associates and explicit learning instructions failed to find any significant arousal-based effects on memory. Schmitt and Forrester (1973) utilized the same experimental materials and paradigm as Butter (1970, Expt. 2). They found a similar decrement in the shorter term recall of low concreteness–imagery words but garnered no evidence of a matching decrement as a result of GSR to the paired associates. Other failed attempts include Fuller's (1978) use of differences in introversion/extraversion and Oakhill (1986, 1988) using time of day.

Beneficial Effects On Long-Term Retention

Many of the studies that found shorter term deficits in retention evidenced a reminiscence effect. Arousal at learning led to enhancement of longer term recall such that the high-arousal subjects remembered better after some kind of longer term delay than they had shortly after learning. This pattern of results exhibits a crossover interaction between arousal at learning and retention interval. For instance, Kleinsmith and Kaplan (1963, 1964) and Walker and Tarte (1963) both found that arousing words were better remembered after 1 week than they had been 2 minutes after learning. Those studies that evidenced this dramatic pattern of results are classified as having shown a reminiscence effect in Table 5.1.

Still other studies that evidenced shorter term deficits in retention exhibited enhancement of longer term recall such that the high-arousal conditions led to a lesser degree of forgetting than the low-arousal conditions. Thus, although Loftus (1990, Expt. 1) found that high self-rated arousal produced by exercise led to inferior shorter term recall, it also led to a greater retention of the initially recalled word pairs as compared to the low-arousal group.

A few researchers have found that high arousal led to benefits both in shorter and longer term retention. Corteen (1969) garnered results that suggested high-arousal learning (as measured by GSR) of aurally presented words led to superior shorter and longer term recall across testings at immediate, 20-minute, and 2-week delays. Similarly, Maltzman, Kantor, and Langdon (1966) found that high-arousal learning led to better recall immediately and 30 minutes after learning (this finding represents more of a shorter term finding given that many studies find the reversal occurs somewhere between 20 and 40 minutes postlearning). Noteworthy here is that these materials were also presented aurally and the materials were once again single words of arousing and nonarousing quality.

Arousal Effects On Retrieval

The potential confounding of differential effects of a variable upon learning and retrieval processes often represents an inevitable aspect of memory research. Research of arousal effects upon memory is no different. The presence of state- and/or trait-based arousal differences in shorter term learning is invariably confounded with the question of the influence of that same arousal on the recall that occurs. When a retrieval task follows closely upon learning, however, it seems likely that the state of arousal would be the same for both processes. Millar, Styles, and Wastall (1980) stated: "Potentially, therefore, the changes in immediate memory performance . . may be due as much to the influence of arousal upon retrieval as upon learning or, indeed, a subtle interaction between the two processes" (p. 408).

Obviously, paradigms involving Sustained Information Transfer (SIT) resource tasks only, such as discrimination of degraded digits (Matthews et al., 1990), are less vulnerable to such confounding. In addition, studies that focus on more short-lived state manipulations of arousal and recall intervals that take place safely beyond the range of such a manipulation are also less vulnerable. When the strong influence of individual differences and circadian aspects of arousal on memory are considered, however, it would seem that even longer term retrieval paradigms are placed at risk for this type of confounding.

Some researchers have combined arousal manipulations at learning with arousal manipulations at recall in order to assess potential arousal effects on retrieval probability. Folkard and colleagues (Folkard et al., 1977; Folkard & Monk, 1980) have consistently failed to find any effect of circadian arousal at retrieval upon both longer term recall and recognition tasks. Still others have examined the more direct effect of arousal on retrieval latency and/or probability unconfounded by learning state. M. W. Eysenck (1975a) found that high levels of arousal (a measurement of energetic arousal) as measured before retrieval increased the number of words recalled by extraverts and decreased the number of words recalled by introverts. Moreover, Pascal (1949) found superior recall performance when a relaxation manipulation was given immediately prior to recall. M. W. Eysenck (1975b) also found that moderate levels of arousal (high-state arousal extraverts and low-state arousal introverts) increased the speed of retrieval when contrasted to low levels (low-state arousal extraverts) and high levels (high-state arousal introverts) of arousal.

Millar et al. (1980) found that retrieval efficiency as measured by retrieval latencies increased during the afternoon when compared to both morning and evening.

A recent study within our own lab (Loftus, 1990, Expt 2) crossed state and trait arousal at learning and immediate recall with that at longer term recall (1 week later). A highly similar pattern was found in both the shorter and longer term recall performances: High-state arousal (measured either by self-report or exercise/relaxation manipulation) tended to increase recall for the high-impulsive subjects (low-trait arousal) and decrease recall for the low-impulsive subjects (high-trait arousal). The arousal present at learning was not found to affect recall 1 week later. The similarity between the two patterns of results is striking and raises the possibility that some kind of retrieval effect was operating at both recall sessions. This pattern of results is reminiscent of an inverted-U relationship (Hebb, 1955) between arousal at retrieval and recall performance.

Theoretical Explanations

Several different theoretical explanations of the effect of arousal on memory have been reviewed by M. W. Eysenck (1976, 1977, 1981, 1983). These include Walker's (1958) theory of the action decrement, Easterbrook's (1959) hypothesis that arousal narrows the range of cue utilization, and Schwartz' (1975) arousal-based generalization of Craik and Lockhart's (1972) level of processing theory. Walker (1958) proposed that arousal increases temporary inhibition of retrieval during the formation of long-term memory traces. Easterbrook's (1959) cue utilization theory provides a partial account of the arousal effects if it is assumed that immediate memory relies more on peripheral cues (and thus is hindered by an arousal-induced narrowing of cue utilization), but that delayed memory relies more on central cues (which thus become more prominent if arousal narrows the range of cues utilized). Applying arousal to a levels of processing explanation (Craik & Lockhart, 1972) follows if low arousal is associated with less elaborative encoding than is high arousal; that is, less aroused subjects would use shallow, maintenance rehearsal, whereas more aroused subjects would tend to use more elaborative encoding. Although this explanation can predict the cross-over interaction of arousal and delay interval, it does not predict the reminiscence effect observed in some studies.

Another explanation for the effects of arousal on memory is the "tick rate hypothesis" (Humphreys & Revelle, 1984; Revelle, 1989; Revelle & Loftus, 1990), which proposes that arousal increases the rate at which the environment is sampled. In direct analogy to the clock speed of a computer, this hypothesis predicts that increased arousal should lead to a faster rate of response to environmental cues, but to a decrement in availability in immediate memory due to the increased interference associated with a more rapid sampling rate. Finally, by increasing the rate at which the to-be-learned material is associated with the internal and external context, the model also predicts that high arousal should facilitate long-term retrieval.[7]

IMPLICATIONS OF AROUSAL EFFECTS
FOR AFFECT AND MEMORY PARADIGMS

The various issues in the conceptualization, measurement, and analysis of arousal effects on memory have been outlined. In addition, substantive effects of arousal (induced a variety of ways) on information processing and memory have been summarized and discussed. In this section, a consideration of the overlap between the study of arousal and memory and that of affect and memory is developed and suggestions for a classification system to aid in the further exploration of the often confusing relationship between affect and memory are given.

Affect and Memory Research:
Why All the Confusion?

The fact that affect influences memory is borne out in one's everyday life as well as in the laboratory. One need only experience a "black mood" once to know that a prevailing mood state can serve to bias the filtering of incoming information and the accessibility of already stored information. Likewise, our everyday vernacular is full of allusions to the ways in which affective states can affect our functioning such as "seeing the world through rose-colored glasses" and "getting up on the wrong side of the bed."

Perhaps due to the pervasiveness of affect in everyday functioning, the study of the relationship between affect and memory is an intriguing one. A quick reading of the chapters available in this book

---

[7] In a personal communication, Robert Crowder has pointed out that this hypothesis may be understood in terms of the stimulus sampling theory of Estes (1959) as it is applied to the problem of spacing repetition effects. (See Crowder, 1976, pp. 277-300).

provides only a brief sampling of the wide variety of issues that exist in the more general area of affect and memory. For instance, one might choose to focus on the effects of pathological affective states (i.e., depressive or manic disorders) or alternatively on the effects of more naturally occurring affect such as the shifts in emotional state that occur as one goes about the activities of a normal day.

Given the vast number of phenomena encompassed by the study of affect and memory, perhaps it is not surprising that some areas of research have been plagued by inconsistencies in attempts to replicate promising early findings. Seminal attempts to study systematically the changes in information encoding and retrieval that occur under affectively valenced conditions garnered evidence of two effects—affect state dependent and affect congruent effects—that offered exciting possibilities for theories of both naturally occurring and pathological shifts in affective states (Bartlett & Santrock, 1977; Bower, 1981; Bower, Monteiro, & Gilligan, 1978, Study 3). Much of this work was based on Bower's influential Network Theory of Affect (Bower, 1981; Gilligan & Bower, 1984). The original theory detailed a cue-based model of information processing in which affective information can serve to both cue retrieval of previously stored information and filter the nature of incoming information through spreading activation within the memory system.

Affect-state dependent recall refers to a tendency exhibited by subjects in either a positive or negative affective state to remember information that had been learned under the same affective state (congruent conditions) better than that learned under a different affective state (incongruent conditions). Affect congruent (or mood congruency) effects are reflected in a tendency to encode or retrieve information of the same hedonic quality as the current affective state (i.e., happy or sad). Singer and Salovey (1988) further differentiate between encoding congruent and recall congruent effects within affect congruency to reflect the stage at which the mood condition is of interest. A less well researched but related prediction made by the Network Theory of Affect is that of mood intensity effects. This effect predicts that learning is positively correlated with the intensity of a mood (Gilligan & Bower, 1984; Singer & Salovey, 1988).

Although affect congruency effects have stood up fairly well to the passage of time and further study, affect-state dependent recall effects have not (see Blaney, 1986 and Singer & Salovey, 1988 for more thorough reviews). Research of this latter effect has led to a confusing "now you see it, now you don't" pattern of results. Several further strong demonstrations of affect-state dependent recall

(Bartlett, Burleson, & Santrock, 1982, Study 2; Mecklenbrauker & Hager, 1984) stand in stark contrast to frustrating failures to replicate even the original study itself (Bower & Mayer, 1985; Wetzler, 1985). Although there are doubtless several factors that might be at play in this confusing pattern of results, we have suggested (Revelle & Loftus, 1990) that one of the most straightforward explanations exists in the uncontrolled and unmeasured effects of the arousal present in the experimental conditions.

An Arousal-Based Interpretation of Affect and Memory Phenomena

Although affect may undoubtedly sometimes serve as an effective cue for the retrieval of stored information, most of the experimental paradigms utilized in the study of affect-state dependent memory inevitably confound the affect-dependent effects with possible arousal-dependent effects. Given the natural covariation between affect and arousal, it is highly likely that arousal information may also serve as an effective cue for the retrieval of stored information. Clark, Milberg, and Ross (1983) garnered evidence supportive of this hypothesis. Arousal induced by both physical exertion and arousing films resulted in state-dependent recall (see also Clark, 1982).

However, this finding does little to explain the inconsistencies in this area of research. It is interesting to note that arousal may also result in state-dependent recall but hardly surprising. Rather, the focus here is on the process-based differences that may occur as a result of the uncontrolled and unmeasured presence of arousal within the experimental situation. The likelihood that arousal-based information-processing effects are present is based on confounds seen most clearly in several aspects of these experimental paradigms: the affect inductions, the intervals between learning and recall, and the analyses performed.

More specifically, the affect or mood inductions employed in mood and memory studies vary widely. Different studies regularly employ different mood induction techniques (i.e., hypnosis, reading valenced statements, listening to music, false feedback) to achieve what are considered comparable levels of "positive" and "negative" or "happy" and "sad" mood states. Although this strategy enhances the generalizability of the results, it invites confounding of differential levels of arousal within similar classes of affect. For instance, it seems likely that listening to uplifting, bubbly music might induce a higher arousal state than hypnosis (which involves deep relaxation)—although both have been used to derive "happy" mood conditions. There has also been some suggestion that a commonly used mood induction, the Velten procedure (Velten, 1968), differs significantly in the percentages of arousing and nonarousing words that are used in each of the mood conditions (depression, elation, and neutrality) (Whissell & Levesque, 1988).

This problem is further complicated by the tendency for many researchers in this area to fail to perform sufficient manipulation checks for the inductions used—and when manipulation checks are performed, arousal is rarely measured. Eich and Metcalfe (1989) represent one exception in that arousal as well as affective levels were measured after a musical mood induction. It is interesting to note that the subjects in the happy-mood condition rated themselves as being not only happier but also significantly more aroused than the sad-mood condition subjects across seven points in time.

A second factor related to the suspected presence of arousal-type effects within these experimental paradigms is that of the recall intervals employed between initial learning and recall trials. Some studies do not even report the intervals used; others have used intervals than range anywhere from immediate recall to recall some 20 minutes (Schare, Lisman & Spear, 1984), 40 minutes (Bower & Mayer, 1985), 5 hours (Bower, Gilligan, & Monteiro, 1981), 24 hours (Wetzler, 1985), and 4 days later (Weingartner, Miller, & Murphy, 1977). Moreover, most studies employ a multiple-list learning and recall paradigm that involves a variety of intervals for each study. Once again, although such a variety of intervals might enhance the eventual generalizability of results, this mixture of shorter and longer term retrieval effects has likely served to significantly increase the inconsistency inherent in the mood-state dependent research. In addition, perhaps the most significant point to be made here is that in light of the interaction of arousal and recall interval discussed earlier, it seems highly probable that the recall performed in such studies is influenced by both cue-based affect and arousal processes as well as the processing changes due to the interaction of arousal and retention interval.

The exploration of this literature for these predictions might seem to be the most reasonable tack. However, the paucity of arousal and recall interval information available within these studies makes reanalysis impossible (Loftus, 1990). Moreover, much of the research is analyzed in terms of "congruent" (mood state same at learning and recall) and "disparate" (mood state different at learning and recall) mood groups. Thus, positive and negative mood states are often collapsed in favor of this contrast. If the positive and negative mood states were associated with different levels of arousal due to type of induction used and/or natural covariation, this practice effectively wipes out evidence for arousal effects.

A more clear-cut reinterpretation of affect-dependent effects on memory lies in the research related to the mood intensity hypothesis. The mood intensity hypothesis predicts that affectively intense memories should be better recalled and over longer periods of time. This prediction and the classical evidence in support of it found this tendency to be independent of the affective nature of the material (Dutta & Kanungo, 1967, 1975; Singer & Salovey, 1988). More recent research, however, has suggested that this is particularly true of positive affective states, whereas negative affective states interfere with the encoding of material (Ellis, Thomas, McFarland, & Lane, 1985; Ellis, Thomas, & Rodriquez, 1984). An arousal interpretation of these results would suggest that, as the positive emotional states induced in these studies are most likely highly correlated with significant levels of arousal, the tendency for these materials to be better retained over time is most likely an arousal-based enhancement of longer term retention.

CONCLUSIONS

As this brief review of some of the weaknesses in the mood and memory literature has suggested, it seems highly likely that the inconsistencies in the research of at least mood–state dependent effects would be potentially explainable by some kind of interaction between the cue-related effects of both affect and arousal information and the more complex process-related effects due to arousal. The mixture of mood inductions commonly employed, retention intervals utilized, and analytic oversights appear to make the experimental situations ripe for such process-related effects of arousal to occur unnoticed.

It is our suspicion that both arousal and affect have substantive and some qualitatively different effects on information processing. As such, the importance of considering both dimensions of emotion in experiments that seek to change either arousal or affective state should not be minimized. As the earlier summary of the arousal literature suggested, arousal tends to enhance information transfer, decrease short-term retrieval capacity, and increase long term retention; most likely, it also has some kind of inverted-U relationship with retrieval processes in general. Affect, on the other hand, appears to have a significant tendency to bias the encoding and retrieval of hedonically laden materials and, to some degree, affect the retrieval

of neutral information also. Given the natural interrelatedness of
affect and arousal, it would seem that the most reasonable tack
would lie in experimental paradigms that overtly cross both dimensions or, at least, study one dimension while trying to hold the other
constant. In both paradigms, accurate measurement of the affective
and arousal states that are induced and appropriate analyses based
on each are essential. Given the "capricious" nature of mood-state
dependent effects, it may very well turn out that the existence of such
effects is, to some degree, dependent on an interaction with arousal-
based effects on information processing.

ACKNOWLEDGMENTS

Supported in part by contract MDA903-90-C-0108 from the U. S.
Army Research Institute to William Revelle and Kristen Anderson.
Parts of this chapter were prepared for a tutorial on individual
differences in arousal presented by William Revelle at the Tenth
Annual Carmel Conference: Meta Control Processes in Human
Information Processing, Carmel, California, 1989. We would like to
thank Nestor Schmajuk for his very helpful comments.

REFERENCES

Allport, G., & Odbert, H. S. (1936). Trait names: A psycholexical study. *Psychological Monographs, 47*(211), 1–171.
Anderson, K. J. (1990). Arousal and the inverted-u hypothesis - a critique of Neiss's reconceptualizing arousal. *Psychological Bulletin, 107*(1), 96–100.
Atkinson, J. W., & Birch, D. (1970). *The dynamics of action.* New York: Wiley.
Bakan, P., Belton, J., & Toth, J. (1963). Extraversion–introversion and decrement in an auditory vigilance task. In D. N. Buckner & J. J. McGrath (Eds.), *Vigilance: A symposium* (pp. 22–33). New York: McGraw–Hill.
Bartlett, J. C., & Santrock, J. W. (1977). Affect-dependent episodic memory in young children. *Child Development, 50*, 513–518.
Bartlett, J. C., Burleson, G., & Santrock, T. W. (1982). Emotional mood and memory in young children. *Journal of Experimental Child Psychology, 34*, 59-76.
Berlyne, D. E. (1960). *Conflict, arousal, and curiosity.* New York: McGraw–Hill.
Berlyne, D., Borsa, D., Craw, R., Gelman, R., & Mandell, E. (1965). Effects of stimulus complexity and induced arousal on paired-associate learning. *Journal of Verbal Learning and Verbal Behavior, 4*, 291–299.
Berlyne, D. E., & Carey, S. T. (1968). Incidental learning and the timing of arousal. *Psychonomic Science, 13*, 103–104.
Blake, M. J. F. (1967). Relationship between circadian rhythm of body temperature and introversion–extraversion. *Nature, 215*, 896–897.
Blaney, P. (1986). Affect and memory: A review. *Psychological Bulletin, 99*, 229–246.

Bower, G., & Mayer, J. (1985). Failure to replicate mood-dependent retrieval. *Bulletin of the Psychonomic Society, 23,* 39–42.

Bower, G. H. (1981). Mood and memory. *American Psychologist, 36,* 129–148.

Bower, G. H., & Gilligan, S. G. (1979). Remembering information relating to oneself. *Journal of Research in Personality, 13,* 404–419.

Bower, G. H., Gilligan, S. G., & Monteiro, K. P. (1981). Selectivity of learning caused by affective states. *Journal of Experimental Psychology: General, 110,* 451–473.

Bower, G. H., Montiero, K. P., & Gilligan, S. G. (1978). Emotional mood as a context for learning and recall. *Journal of Verbal Learning and Verbal Behavior, 17,* 573–585.

Bowyer, P., Humphreys, M. S., & Revelle, W. (1983). Arousal and recognition memory: The effects of impulsivity, caffeine, and time on task. *Personality and Individual Differences, 4,* 41–49.

Butter, H. J. (1970). Differential recall of paired associates as a function of arousal and concreteness–imagery levels. *Journal of Experimental Psychology, 84,* 252–256.

Cattell, R. B. (1957). *Personality and motivation: Structure and measurement.* Yonkers, NY: World Book.

Claridge, G. (1981). Psychoticism as a dimension of personality. In R. Lynn (Ed.), *Dimensions of Personality.* Oxford: Pergamon.

Clark, M. (1982). A role for arousal in the link between feeling states, judgments, and behaviors. In M. Clark & S. Fiske (Eds.), *Affect and cognition.* Hillsdale, NJ: Lawrence Erlbaum Associates.

Clark, M., Milberg, S., & Ross, J. (1983). Arousal cues arousal-related material in memory: Implications for understanding effects of mood on memory. *Journal of Verbal Learning and Verbal Behavior, 22,* 633–649.

Clements, P. R., Hafer, M. D., & Vermillion, M. E. (1976). Psychometric, diurnal, and electrophysiological correlates of activation. *Journal of Personality and Social Psychology, 33,* 387–394.

Conley, J. J. (1984). Longitudinal consistency of adult personality—self-reported psychological characteristics across 45 years. *Journal of Personality and Social Psychology, 47,* 1325–1333.

Corcoran, D. W. J. (1965). Personality and the inverted-U relation. *British Journal of Psychology, 56,* 267–273.

Corcoran, D. W. J. (1972). Studies of individual differences at the applied psychology unit. In V. D. Nebylitsyn & J. A. Gray (Eds.), *Biological bases of individual behavior* (pp. 269–290). New York: Academic Press.

Corcoran, D. W. J. (1981). Introversion–extraversion, stress and arousal. In M. J. Eysenck (Ed.), *A model for personality* (pp. 111–127). Berlin: Springer-Verlag.

Corteen, R. S. (1969). Skin conductance changes and word recall. *British Journal of Psychology, 60,* 81–84.

Craik, F. I. M., & Lockhart, R. S. (1972). Levels of processing: A framework for memory research. *Journal of Verbal Learning and Verbal Behavior, 11,* 671–684.

Crider, A., & Lunn, R. (1971). Electrodermal lability as a personality dimension. *Psychophysiology, 5,* 145–150.

Crowder, R. (1976). *Principles of learning and memory.* Hillsdale, NJ: Lawrence Erlbaum Associates.

Davies, D. R., & Parasuraman, R. (1982). *The psychology of vigilance.* London: Academic Press.

Deffenbacher, K., Platt, G., & Williams, M. (1974). Differential recall as a function of socially induced arousal and retention interval. *Journal of Experimental Psychology, 103,* 809–811.

Digman, J. M. (1990). Personality structure: Emergence of the five-factor model. *Annual Review of Psychology, 41*, 417–440.

Duffy, E. (1962). *Activation and behavior.* New York: Wiley.

Duffy, E. (1972). Activation. In N. S. Greenfield & R. A. Sternbach (Eds.), *Handbook of psychophysiology* (pp. 577–622). New York: Holt, Reinhart, & Winston.

Dutta, S., & Kanungo, R. N. (1967). Retention of affective material: A further verification of the intensity hypothesis. *Journal of Personality and Social Psychology, 5*, 476–481.

Dutta, S., & Kanungo, R. N. (1975). *Affect and memory: A reformulation.* Oxford: Pergamon.

Easterbrook, J. A. (1959). The effect of emotion on cue utilization and the organization of behavior. *Psychological Review, 66*, 183–201.

Eich, E., & Metcalfe, J. (1989). Mood dependent memory for internal versus external events. *Journal of Experimental Psychology: Learning, Memory and Cognition, 15*, 443–455.

Ellis, H., Thomas, R., & Rodriguez, I. (1984). Emotional mood states and memory: Elaborative encoding, semantic processing, and cognitive effort. *Journal of Experimental Psychology: Learning, Memory, and Cognition, 10*, 470–482.

Ellis, H., Thomas, R., McFarland, A., & Lane, J. (1985). Emotional mood states and retrieval in episodic memory. *Journal of Experimental Psychology: Learning, Memory, and Cognition, 11*, 363–370.

Estes, W. K. (1959). The statistical approach to learning theory. In S. Koch (Ed.), *Psychology: A study of a science* (Vol II, pp. 380–491). New York: McGraw–Hill.

Eysenck, H. J. (1947). *Dimensions of personality.* New York: Praeger.

Eysenck, H. J. (1952). *The scientific study of personality.* London: Routledge & Kegan Paul.

Eysenck, H. J. (1967). *The biological basis of personality.* Springfield, IL: Thomas.

Eysenck, H. J. (Ed.). (1981). *A model for personality.* New York: Springer-Verlag.

Eysenck, H. J. (1987). The place of anxiety and impulsivity in a dimensional framework. *Journal of Research in Personality, 21*, 489–493.

Eysenck, H. J., & Eysenck, M. W. (1985). *Personality and individual differences: A natural science approach.* New York: Plenum Press.

Eysenck, M. W. (1975a). Arousal and speed of recall. *British Journal of Social and Clinical Psychology, 14*, 269–277.

Eysenck, M. W. (1975b). Extraversion, arousal and speed of retrieval from secondary storage. *Journal of Personality, 43*, 390–401.

Eysenck, M. W. (1976). Arousal, learning, and memory. *Psychological Bulletin, 83*, 389–404.

Eysenck, M. W. (1977). *Human memory: Theory, research, and individual differences.* Oxford: Pergamon.

Eysenck, M. W. (1981). Learning, memory and personality. In H. J. Eysenck (Ed.), *A model for personality* (pp. 169–209). Berlin: Springer-Verlag.

Eysenck, M. W. (1983). Memory and arousal. In A. Gale & J. A. Edwards (Eds.), *Physiological correlates of human behavior. Vol II: Attention and performance* (pp. 187–202). London: Academic Press.

Folkard, S., & Monk, T. H. (1980). Circadian rhythms in human memory. *British Journal of Psychology, 71*, 295–307.

Folkard, S., Monk, T. H., Bradbury, R., & Rosenthal, J. (1977). Time of day effects in school children's immediate and delayed recall of meaningful material. *British Journal of Psychology, 58*, 45–50.

Fowles, D. C., Roberts, R., & Nagel, K. E. (1977). The influence of introversion/ extraversion on the skin conductance response to stress and stimulus intensity. *Journal of Research in Personality, 11*, 129–146.

Fuller, A. R. (1978). Personality and paired-associate learning. *International Journal of Psychology, 13*, 123–128.

Gale, A. (1981). EEG studies of extraversion–introversion: What's the next step? In R. Lynn (Ed), *Dimensions of personality: Essays in honour of H. J. Eysenck.* Oxford: Pergamon.

Gale, A. (1983). Electroencephalographic correlates of extraversion–introversion: A case study in the psychophysiology of individual differences. *Personality and Individual Differences, 4*, 371–380.

Gale, A. (1986). Extraversion–introversion and spontaneous rhythms of the brain: Retrospect and prospect. In J. Strelau, F. H. Farley, & A. Gale (Eds), *The biological bases of personality and behavior: Psychophysiology, performance, and application* (Vol. 2, pp. 25–42). Washington, DC: Hemisphere.

Gale, A. (1987). Arousal, control, energetics and values—an attempt at review and appraisal. In J. Strelau & H. J. Eysenck (Eds.), *Personality dimensions and arousal* (pp. 287–316). London: Plenum Press.

Gale, A., & Edwards, J. A. (1986). Individual differences. In M.G.H. Coles, E. Donchin, & S. W. Porges (Eds.), *Psychophysiology: Systems processes, and applications* (pp. 431–507).

Gates, A. (1916). Variations in efficiency during the day. *University of California Publications 2*, 1–156.

Geen, R. (1973). Effects of being observed on short- and long-term recall. *Journal of Experimental Psychology, 100*, 395–398.

Geen, R. (1974). Effects of evaluation apprehension on memory over intervals of varying length. *Journal of Experimental Psychology, 102*, 908–910.

Gilligan, S. G., & Bower, G. H. (1984). Cognitive consequence of emotional arousal. In C. Izard, J. Kagan, & R. Zajonc (Eds.), *Emotions, Cognition and behavior.* New York: Cambridge University Press.

Goldberg, L. R. (1982). From ace to zombie: Some explorations in the language of personality. In C. D. Spielberger & J. N. Butcher (Eds.), *Advances in personality assessment* (Vol. 1, pp. 203–234). Hillsdale, NJ: Lawrence Erlbaum Associates.

Gray, J. A. (1972). The psychophysiological basis of introversion–extraversion: A modification of Eysenck's theory. In V. D. Nebylitsyn & J. A. Gray (Eds.), *The biological basis of individual behavior* (pp. 182–205). New York: Academic Press.

Gray, J. A. (1981). A critique of Eysenck's theory of personality. In H. J. Eysenck (Ed.), *A model for personality* (pp. 246–276). Berlin: Springer-Verlag.

Gray, J. A. (1982). *Neuropsychological theory of anxiety: An investigation of the septalhippocampal system.* Cambridge: Cambridge University Press.

Gray, J. A. (1987). Perspectives on anxiety and impulsivity: A commentary. *Journal of Research in Personality, 21*, 493–510.

Grossberg, S. (1987). *The adaptive brain 1: Cognition, learning, reinforcement, rhythm.* Amsterdam: Elsevier.

Hamilton, K., Fowler, B., & Porlier, G. (1989). The effects of hyperbaric air in combination with ethyl alcohol and dextroamphetamine on serial choice-reaction time. *Ergonomics, 32*, 409–422.

Hebb, D. O. (1955). Drives and the C.N.S. (conceptual nervous system). *Psychological Review, 62*, 243–254.

Hintzman, D. L. (1990). Human learning and memory: Connections and dissociations. *Annual Review of Psychology, 41,* 109–139.

Hockey, G. R. J (1979). Stress and cognitive components of skilled performance. In V. Hamilton & P. M. Warburton (Eds.), *Human stress and cognition* (pp. 141–178). Chichester: Wiley.

Hockey, G. R. J. (1984). Varieties of attentional state: The effects of environment. In R. Parasuraman & D. R. Davies (Eds.), *Varieties of attention.* New York: Academic Press.

Hockey, G. R. J., Gaillard, A. W. K., & Coles, M. G. H. (1986). *Energetics and human information processing.* Dordrect: Marinus Nijhoff.

Howarth, E., & Eysenck, H. J. (1968). Extraversion, arousal, and paired-associate recall. *Journal of Experimental Research in Personality, 3,* 114–116.

Humphreys, M. S., Bain, J. D., & Pike, R. (1989). Different ways to cue a coherent memory system: A theory for episodic, semantic, and procedural tasks. *Psychological Review, 96,* 208–233.

Humphreys, M. S., & Revelle, W. (1984). Personality, motivation, and performance: A theory of the relationship between individual differences and information processing. *Psychological Review, 91,* 153–184.

Jennings, J. R., Nebes, R., & Brock, K. (1988). Memory retrieval in noise and psychophysiological response in young and old. *Phychophysiology, 25,* 633–644.

Jones, D., Gale, A., & Smallbone, A. (1979). Short-term recall of nine-digit strings and the EEG. *British Journal of Psychology, 70,* 97–119.

Kaplan, R., & Kaplan, S. (1969). The arousal-retention interval interaction revisited: The effects of some procedural changes. *Psychonomic Science, 15,* 84–85.

Kaplan, S., Kaplan, R., & Sampson, J. R. (1968). Encoding and arousal factors in free recall of verbal and visual material. *Psychonomic Science, 12,* 73–74.

Keister, M. E., & McLaughlin, R. I. (1972). Vigilance performance related to extraversion–introversion and caffeine. *Journal of Experimental Research in Personality, 6,* 5–11.

Kleinsmith, L. J., & Kaplan, S. (1963). Paired associate learning as a function of arousal and interpolated interval. *Journal of Experimental Psychology, 65,* 190–193.

Kleinsmith, L. J., & Kaplan, S. (1964). Interaction of arousal and recall interval in nonsense syllable paired-associate learning. *Journal of Experimental Psychology, 67,* 124–126.

Lacey, J. (1967). Somatic response patterning and stress: Some revisions of activation theory. In M. H. Appley & R. Trumbell (Eds.), *Psychological stress.* New York: Appleton-Century-Crofts.

Levonian, E. (1966). Attention and consolidation as factors in retention. *Psychonomic Science, 6,* 275–276.

Loftus, D. A. (1990). *Affect and arousal in the study of mood and memory.* Unpublished doctoral dissertation, Northwestern University, Evanston, IL.

London, H., & Exner, J. (Ed.). (1978). *Dimensions of personality.* London: Wiley.

Mackie, R. R. (Ed.) (1977). *Vigilance.* New York: Plenum Press.

Maltzman, I., Kantor, W., & Langdon, B. (1966). Immediate and delayed retention, arousal and the orienting and defensive reflexes. *Psychonomic Sciences, 6,* 445–446

Matthews, G. (1987). Personality and multidimensional arousal: A study of two dimensions of extraversion. *Personality and Individual Differences, 8,* 9–16.

Matthews, G. (1989). Extraversion and levels of control of sustained attention. *Acta Psychologica, 70,* 129–146.

Matthews, G., Davies, D. R., & Lees, J. L. (1990). Arousal, extraversion, and individual differences in resource availability. *Journal of Personality and Social Psychology, 59,* 150–168.

McCrae, R. R., & Costa, P. T. (1987). Validation of the 5-factor model of personality across instruments and observers. *Journal of Personality and Social Psychology*, *52*, 81–90.

McLaughlin, R. J. (1968) Retention in paired-associate learning related to extroversion and neuroticism. *Psychonomic Science*, *13*, 333–334.

McGaugh, J. L. (1990). Significance and rememberance: The role of neuromodulatory systems. *Psychological Science*, *1*, 15–25.

McLean, P. D. (1969). Induced arousal and time of recall as determinants of paired-associate recall. *British Journal of Psychology*, *60*, 57–62.

Mecklenbräuker, S., & Hager, W. (1984). Effects of mood on memory: experimental tests of a mood-state dependent retrieval hypothesis and of a mood congruity hypothesis. *Psychological Research*, *46*, 355–376.

Mewaldt, S. P., Hinrichs, J. V., & Ghoneim, M. M. (1984). Diazepam and memory: Support for a duplex model of memory. *Memory & Cognition*, *11*, 557–564.

Meyer, G. J., & Shack, J. R. (1989). Structural convergence of mood and personality: Evidence for old and new directions. *Journal of Personality and Social Psychology*, *57*, 691–706.

Millar, K., Styles, B. C., & Wastell, O. G. (1980). Time of day and retrieval from long-term memory. *British Journal of Psychology*, *71*, 407–414.

Neiss, R. (1988). Reconceptualizing arousal: Psychobiological states in motor performance. *Psychological Bulletin*, *103*, 345–366.

Norman, W. T. (1963). Toward an adequate taxonomy of personality attributes: Replicated factor structure in peer nomination personality ratings. *Journal of Abnormal and Social Psychology*, *66*, 574–583.

Norman, W. T. (1969). "To see oursels as ithers see us!" Relations among self-perceptions, peer perceptions, and expected peer-perceptions of personality attributes. *Multivariate Behavorial Research*, *4*, 417–443.

O'Gorman, J. G. (1977). Individual differences in habituation of human physiological responses: A review of theory, method, and findings in the study of personality correlates in non-clinical populations. *Biological Psychology*, *5*, 257–318.

Oakhill, J. (1986). Effects of time of day and information importance on adults memory for a short story. *Quarterly Journal of Experimental Psychology Section A-Human Experimental Psychology*, *38*, 419–430.

Oakhill, J. (1988) Text memory and integration at different times of day. *Applied Cognitive Psychology*, *2*, 203–212.

O'Conner, K. (1980). The contingent negative variation and individual differences in smoking behavior. *Personality and Individual Differences*, *1*, 57–72.

O'Conner, K. (1982). Individual differences in the effect of smoking on frontal-central distribution of the CNV: Some observations on smokers' control of attentional behavior. *Personality and Individual Differences*, *3*, 271–285.

Ortony, A., Clore, G., & Collins A. (1990). *The cognitive structure of emotions*. Cambridge: Cambridge University Press.

Pascal, G. R. (1949). The effect of relaxation upon recall. *American Journal of Psychology*, *62*, 33–47.

Puchalski, M. (1988). *Impulsivity, time of day, and retention interval: the effect on cognitive performance*. Unpublished doctoral dissertation, Northwestern University.

Revelle, W. (1986). Motivation and efficiency of cognitive performance. In D. R. Brown & J. Veroff (Eds.), *Frontiers of motivational psychology: Essays in honor of John W. Atkinson* (pp. 107–131). Berlin: Springer.

Revelle, W. (1987). Personality and motivation: Sources of inefficiency in cognitive performance. *Journal of Research in Personality*, *21*, 436–452.

Revelle, W. (1989). Personality, motivation, and cognitive performance. In P. Ackerman, R. Kanfer, & R. Cudeck (Eds.), *Learning and individual differences: Abilities, motivation, and methodology* (pp. 297–341). Hillsdale, NJ: Lawrence Erlbaum Associates.

Revelle, W., Anderson, K. J., & Humphreys, M. S. (1987). Empirical tests and theoretical extensions of arousal based theories of personality. In J. Strelau & H. J. Eysenck (Eds.), *Personality dimensions and arousal* (pp. 17–36). London: Plenum Press.

Revelle, W., Humphreys, M. S ., Simon, L., & Gilliland, K. (1980). The interactive effect of personality, time of day, and caffeine: A test of the arousal model. *Journal of Experimental Psychology: General, 109,* 1–31.

Revelle, W., & Loftus, D. A. (1990). Individual differences and arousal: Implications for the study of mood and memory. *Cognition and emotion, 4,* 209–237.

Robinson, D. L. (1982). Properties of the diffuse thalamocortical system and human personality: A direct test of Pavlovian/Eysenckian theory. *Personality and Individual Differences, 3,* 1–16.

Saufley, W. H, & LaCava, S. C. (1977). Reminiscence and arousal: Replications and the matter of establishing a phenomenon. *Bulletin of the Psychonomic Society, 9,* 155–158.

Schacter, D. L. (1987). Implicit memory: History and current status. *Journal of Experimental Psychology: Learning, Memory and Cogniton, 13,* 501–518.

Schachter, S., & Singer, J. E. (1962). Cognitive, social, and physiological determinants of emotional state. *Psychological Review, 69,* 379–399.

Schare, M., Lisman, S., & Spear, N. (1984). The effects of mood variation on state-dependent retention. *Cognitive Therapy and Research, 8,* 387–408.

Schwartz, S. (1975) Individual differences in cognition: Some relationships between personality and memory. *Journal of Research in Personality, 9,* 217–225.

Schmitt, J. S., & Forrester, W. E. (1973). Effects of stimulus concreteness–imagery and arousal on immediate and delayed recall. *Bulletin of the Psychonomic Society, 2,* 25–26.

Singer, J. A., & Salovey, P. (1988). Mood and memory: Evaluating the network theory of affect. *Clinical Psychology Review, 8,* 211–251.

Shagass, C., & Jones, A. L. (1958). Neurophysiological test for psychiatric diagnosis. Results in 750 patients. *American Journal of Psychiatry, 114,* 1002–1010.

Shagass, C., & Kerenyi, A. B. (1958). Neurophysiological studies of personality. *Journal of Nervous and Mental Disease, 126,* 141–147.

Smith, B. D., Rypma, C. B., & Wilson, R. J. (1981). Dishabituation and spontaneous recovery of the electrodermal orienting response: Effects of extraversion, impulsivity, sociability, and caffeine. *Journal of Research in Personality, 15,* 233–240.

Stelmack, R. M. (1990). Biological bases of extraversion. *Journal of Personality, 58,* 293–312.

Stelmack, R. M., & Mandelzys, N. (1975). Extraversion and pupillary response to affective and taboo words. *Psychophysiology, 12,* 536–540.

Stelmack, R. M., Bourgeois, R. P., Chian, J. Y. C., & Pickard, C. W. (1979). Extraversion and the orienting reaction habituation rate to visual stimuli. *Journal of Research in Personality, 13,* 49–58.

Stelmack, R. M., & Wilson, K. W. (1982). Extraversion and effect of frequency and intensity on the auditory brainstem evoked response. *Personality and Individual Differences, 3,* 373–380.

Strelau, J. (1983). *Temperament–personality–activity.* London: Academic Press.

Strelau, J. (1985). Temperament and personality: Pavlov and beyond. In J. Strelau, F. H. Farley, & A. Gale (Eds.), *The biological bases of personality and behavior:*

Psychophysiology, performance, and application (Vol. 1, pp. 25–43). Washington, DC: Hemisphere.

Terry, W. S., & Anthony, S. G. (1980). Arousal and short-term memory: Effects of caffeine and trial spacing on delayed-alternation performance. *Animal Learning & Behavior, 8*, 368–374.

Terry, W. S., & Phifer, B. (1986). Caffeine and memory performance on the AVLT. *Journal of Clinical Psychology, 42*, 860–863.

Thayer, R. E. (1967). Measurement of activation through self-report. *Psychological Reports, 20*, 663–678.

Thayer, R. E. (1978). Toward a psychological theory of multidimensional activation (arousal), *Motivation and Emotion, 2*, 1–34.

Thayer, R. E. (1986). Activation–deactivation Adjective Check List: Current overview and structural analysis. *Psychological Reports, 58*, 607–614.

Thayer, R. E. (1989). *The biopsychology of mood and arousal.* New York. Oxford.

Tulving, E. (1983). *Elements of episodic memory.* New York: Oxford.

Tupes, E. C., & Christal, R. E. (1961). Recurrent personality factors based on trait ratings, USAF ASD Technical Report, No. 61–97.

Venables, P. H. (1984). Arousal: An examination of its status as a concept. In M. G. H. Coles, J. R. Jennings & J. P. Stern (Eds.), *Psychophysiological perspectives.* New York: Van Nostrand. .

Velten, E. (1968). A laboratory task for the induction of mood states. *Behavior Research and Therapy, 6*, 473–482.

Walker, E. L. (1958). Action decrement and its relation to learning. *Psychological Review, 65*, 129–142.

Walker, E. L., & Tarte, R. D. (1963). Memory storage as a function of arousal and time with homogeneous and heterogeneous lists. *Journal of Verbal Learning and Verbal Behavior, 2*, 113–119.

Watson, D., & Tellegen, A. (1985). Toward a consensual structure of mood. *Psychological Bulletin, 98*, 219–235.

Watson, D., Clark, L. A., & Tellegen, A. (1988). Development and validation of brief measures of positive and negative affect: The PANAS scales. *Journal of Personality and Social Psychology, 54*, 1063–1070.

Weingartner, H., Miller, H., & Murphy, D. (1977). Mood-state-dependent retrieval of verbal associations. *Journal of Abnormal Psychology, 86*, 276–284.

Werre, P. F. (1986). Contingent negative variation: Relation to personality, and modification by stimulation and sedation. In J. Strelau, F. H. Farley, & A. Gale (Eds), *The biological bases of personality and behavior: Psychophysiology, performance, and application* (Vol. 2, pp. 77–90). Washington, DC: Hemisphere.

Werre, P. F. (1987). Extraversion–introversion, contingent negative variation and arousal. In J. Strelau & H. J. Eysenck (Eds.), *Personality dimensions and arousal* (pp. 59–76). London: Plenum Press.

Wetzler, S. (1985). Mood state-dependent retrieval: A failure to replicate. *Psychological Reports, 56*, 759–765.

Whissell, C., & Levesque, B. (1988). The affective tone of words in Velten's mood-induction statements. *Perceptual and Motor Skills, 67*, 515–521.

Whissell, C., Fournier, M., Pelland, R., Weir, D., & Makarec, K. (1986). A dictionary of affect in language: IV. Reliability, validity, and applications. *Perceptual and Motor Skills, 62*, 875–888.

Wilson, G. D. (1990). Personality, time of day, and arousal. *Personality and individual differences, 11*, 153–168.

Zuckerman, M. (1979). *Sensation seeking: Beyond the optimal level of arousal.* London: Wiley.

6

Emotion, Arousal, and Memory for Detail

Friderike Heuer
Daniel Reisberg
Reed College

Many studies have documented the strong relation between how *vividly* an event is recalled, and the emotionality of that event. For example, researchers have questioned subjects about specific target events (e.g., when one first learned about the explosion of the American space-shuttle, Columbia) and asked the subjects to assess both how vivid their memory for this event is, and also how emotional the event was at the time of its occurrence. Across a range of target events, researchers have found a strong positive relation between these two measures—the greater the emotionality, the greater the vividness (Bohannon, 1988; Brown & Kulik, 1977; Christianson & Loftus, 1990a; Pillemer, 1984; Rubin & Kozin, 1984). In fact, this pattern is consistent across *species* of emotion, with strong correlations between emotionality and vividness for fearful events, for sad events, for happy or angry events (Reisberg, Heuer, McLean, & O'Shaughnessy, 1988; Robinson, 1980; White, 1989).

What this evidence tells us is that emotional events are remembered with great detail. What this does *not* tell us is whether emotional events are remembered with great *and accurate* detail. In fact, researchers have documented many cases of vivid but inaccurate recall, often recall involving emotional events (Christianson, 1989; Linton, 1975; McCloskey, Wible, & Cohen, 1988; Neisser, 1982; Neisser & Harsch, 1990; Wagenaar & Groeneweg, 1990). Thus we still need to ask what the relationship might be between emotionality and accurate remembering.

As it turns out, the literature provides reason to believe that memories for emotional events will be filled with inaccuracies.

151

According to the "Easterbrook claim," physiological arousal leads to a "narrowing" of attention (i.e., to a narrowing of the range of cues in the environment to which an organism will be sensitive; Bruner, Matter, & Papanek, 1955; Easterbrook, 1959; Eysenck, 1982; Mandler, 1975). Given that physiological arousal typically accompanies emotion, this implies that emotion will also be accompanied by this narrowing of attention. Thus little information about emotional events will be encoded, and so little information will be available in memory for subsequent recall. If, therefore, subjects appear to recall much information later on, this must be based largely on reconstruction and so will be prone to errors of various kinds.

This seems to lead to a remarkable conclusion: The events from our lives that are most vividly recalled turn out to be the emotional events. According to the Easterbrook claim, the events from our lives from which we encoded least information also turn out to be the emotional events. Putting these claims together, we would conclude that it is our most detailed, seemingly most complete, memories that are the memories most likely to contain fallacies, most likely to stray from historical accuracy. Many psychologists would endorse this striking claim, and, more specifically, the claim that emotionality does indeed undermine memory accuracy (cf. Kassin, Ellsworth, & Smith, 1989; Yarmey & Jones, 1983). In this chapter, we examine the warrant for these claims.

WHY CARE ABOUT MEMORY FOR MINUTIA?

Our emphasis in this review is in some ways a peculiar one: Our primary concern is with memory for minute detail, detail seemingly irrelevant to how an event unfolded, detail, one might suppose, that is just as well forgotten. Such information is almost certain to be inconsequential for most purposes. So why should we care whether a story's protagonist wore a striped tie, or a solid one? Why should we care if a subject remembers the color of the curtains in a room, or a thousand other minute details of the same picayune type?

There are several reasons why memory for trivial details is in fact of considerable interest. These details are crucial for tests of the Easterbrook claim, because it is presumably the minor details of an episode that would be excluded by the hypothesized narrowing of attention. In addition, psychologists have long been interested in the contrast between remembering the gist of an event and remembering details of how the event unfolded. Gist, it is argued, can readily be reconstructed from more schematic knowledge, whereas detailed information cannot. This by itself makes memory for detail of theoretical interest, because it is the details that allow us to discriminate between accurate recollection and plausible reconstruction.

At a very different level, memory for minute details can also be of great practical importance. Psychologists have become increasingly concerned about the role of memory in eyewitness testimony. Eyewitnesses are likely to be called on after a crime to recall many small details. In addition, the eyewitness is certain to be emotionally aroused by the crime he or she has witnessed. Therefore it is of interest to ask how accurately one can remember details of these emotional events.

Finally, the details of a remembered episode seem to be of considerable importance for the rememberer himself or herself. Recent discussions of "reality monitoring" make it plain that the subjective presentation of a memory plays a central part in determining how the rememberer treats the memory (Johnson & Raye, 1981). A memory that is detailed, and rich with "sensory" information about the event, is more likely to be accepted by the rememberer as veridical, indeed, is more likely to be accepted by the rememberer as a *memory*, as opposed to, say, being discounted as a passing fantasy.

Moreover, and still from the perspective of the rememberer, it is striking that one's memories of one's life are so richly detailed, are so laden with seeming irrelevancies about how events unfolded. At the very least, this subjective aspect of memory needs explanation. More strongly, we suggest that these details play an important part in "personalizing" one's memories, in saturating one's memories with a sense that these are indeed one's own memories, and not someone else's. Given the importance of memory in defining, say, one's sense of who one is, it seems of considerable interest to understand these "personalizing" details—to know what leads to their inclusion, and whether they are in fact faithful to history.

DEFINING DETAIL

What exactly is "detail"? Where is the boundary between the "center" of an event, and the event's "periphery"? The problem in defining these terms arises from the fact that one can describe an event at many different levels of analysis; which of these levels is "preferred" depends on one's goals. (Our discussion of this issue is influenced by earlier discussions by Brewer, 1986; Christianson & Loftus, 1991; Neisser, 1986b.) For example, one sees a house; one also sees a three-story house with a red roof; one also sees a well-maintained colonial with a large lawn. If one is looking for the hardware store, the first description is enough to know that one is in the wrong place; mention of the size of the lawn is an unnecessary detail. If describing the house to a potential buyer, then even the last description is too sketchy, and the size of the lawn may be of keen interest.

These concerns rule out several ways one might try to define detail. For example, one might claim that any information that is unimportant or inconsequential should be considered "peripheral." The problem with this, however, is that importance or consequentiality, as just seen, are clearly relative to one's purposes. Likewise, it will not serve to define "details" as those aspects of an event that can be changed without fundamentally changing the identity or nature of the event. Once again, this is relative to one's purposes.

Given these concerns, we suggest that the periphery or details of an event cannot be defined in a manner appropriate for all contexts, for all purposes. Our approach to this issue, therefore, is a pragmatic one: Although many descriptions of a scene or event are possible, one of these descriptions is "privileged" in the sense of seeming appropriate or natural to most subjects; that is, we appeal here to Rosch's notion of a "basic level" of description (Rosch 1978; also Morris & Murphy, 1990; Rifkin, 1985; Vallacher & Wegner, 1987). In reviewing the available evidence, we adopt this basic-level description of the to-be-remembered (TBR) materials and define detail relative to this description; that is, details will be those aspects of the event that can be altered without changing the event's identity at this basic level. For example, the particular clothing worn by a participant in an event seems a clear candidate for detail (insofar as the clothing's color had no bearing on how the event unfolded). Likewise, whether a particular scene was originally viewed from one camera angle or a slightly different one also seems, by this criterion, detail.

Having taken this pragmatic stance, we note that these operationalizations are not uniformly straightforward. As one concern, some types of remembered material do not fit neatly into this classification. For example, consider memory for *faces*. One could argue that this judgment involves information central to an event— contained within the canonical list of who, what, when, and where often used to describe events. At the same time, it is clear that a face might be identified based on some specific feature (e.g., a particular mole, or some such). On this view, face memory might depend on detail information, not central.

For present purposes, we regard this latter possibility (face recognition via detail) as the exception, rather than the rule. It seems to us that memory for faces is at worst an ambiguous case, and, more likely a case of central information. Interestingly, Cutler, Penrod, and Martens (1987) reported a negative correlation, in subjects' memory performance, between facial memory and memory for detail (color of someone's sweater, whether someone carried a gun in his left hand or right). We take this as confirmation of our claim that facial memory is distinct from (what we here call) memory for detail, and thus we do not consider studies of face memory in the present review. (To examine these studies, the reader might consult Deffenbacher, 1983.)

As a second, and broader, concern, our definitions lead us to consider as detail a peculiarly diverse set of to-be-remembered (TBR) details—colors of backgrounds, photographic layouts of slides, details of clothing, and so on. It is not self-evident that this set is in any way homogeneous, nor, correspondingly, that our definitions "carve nature at the joints." We regard this as entirely an empirical issue, and thus we offer these definitions essentially as working hypotheses about how the data should be organized. If this categorization scheme introduces order into the pattern of results, this will reassure us that we have divided the TBR material sensibly. To anticipate the argument to come, the data will fit reasonably well within this scheme, but, before we are through, both theory and data will lead us back to these definitional issues and will, in fact, lead us to refine these definitions somewhat. For now, however, we proceed with the working definitions just sketched.

EMOTION UNDERMINES
MEMORY FOR DETAILS

What is the evidence for emotion's effects on the accuracy of remembered detail? Closely related, what is the empirical status of the Easterbrook claim? In this section, we first consider the relevant laboratory evidence, and then turn to the evidence from more naturalistic studies.

Laboratory Evidence
for Emotion's Deleterious Effects

Loftus and Burns (1982) presented their subjects with a brief film clip depicting a bank robbery. For half the subjects, the film showed the robber run out of the bank with two men pursuing him. The robber then turned and shot a small boy in the face. For the remaining subjects, the film was the same up until the shooting, but then it cuts back to the inside of the bank where the manager is telling everyone to remain calm. Immediately after viewing the films, subjects' memories were tested for the *early* part of the film (i.e., for the portion of the film identical for the two groups). Subjects who had seen the neutral version remembered more of the details, a finding that emerged with both recognition and recall testing.

Similar findings were reported by Clifford and Hollin (1981; Clifford & Scott, 1978). Half their subjects viewed a videotaped violent event (a thief grabs a woman's purse and flees); the other half viewed a neutral event (a man approaches a woman and asks her for directions). Immediately after viewing this videotape, subjects were questioned about the event, including such details as the height, weight, and clothing of the perpetrator. The results showed poorer performance from subjects who had seen the violent event, and this effect became more pronounced with a greater number of perpetrators involved in the event. This latter point is consistent with the Easterbrook claim: If arousal narrows attention, then arousal's impact should be most visible with complex events, as these would be particularly difficult to encode under circumstances of a narrow attentional focus.

All these findings apply to only part of the Easterbrook claim. According to this claim, emotion should undermine memory for detail at an event's periphery but should not work against more central information. A few studies have examined this more specific prediction and yield findings consistent with the Easterbrook claim. For example, Kebeck and Lohaus (1986) showed subjects a film depicting an argument between a teacher and a student. In one version of the film, the argument escalated; in the other, the argument stayed calm. Subjects' memories were tested immediately after the film, and then again 2 weeks later. In addition, subjects were tested for information central to the gist of the film, and for details. Consistent with the Easterbrook claim, emotion had no impact on memory for central information. However, subjects who had seen the arousing version of the film had poorer memory for details, in both the immediate and delayed test.

Related data were reported by Christianson and Loftus (1987; Christianson & Loftus, 1991). In their study, one group of subjects saw a series of slides depicting a traumatic story; other subjects viewed an emotionally neutral story. Subjects in both groups were required to write down a word or phrase describing the most distinctive feature of each slide. This description presumably identifies information central to the slide, and so a subsequent test of memory for these (subject-generated) words tells us how well subjects remember the center, or gist, of the episode. In addition, subjects were also tested for memory for detail. Specifically, subjects were given a 4AFC recognition test, with the distractors differing from the original slide only in camera angle.

For details identified by the subjects as central, subjects who viewed the traumatic sequence showed better memory than those who viewed the neutral sequence. This was true whether memory was tested 20 minutes or 2 weeks alter the slide presentation. The reverse pattern appeared for memory of detail (i.e., camera angle). In the recognition procedure, subjects who had viewed the traumatic sequence showed appreciably poorer performance.

In sum, the evidence indicates that emotion does undermine memory for detail but has little (or inconsistent) effect on memory for more central materials. This is consistent with the Easterbrook claim that emotion, and the accompanying arousal, narrows subjects' attention, leading them to attend only to the center of an event, and to exclude more peripheral materials.

The Phenomenon of Weapon Focus

The Easterbrook claim was initially proposed as an account of laboratory evidence, but a closely analogous claim appears in discussions of law enforcement and police investigation. According to the notion of "weapon focus," witnesses to crime (particularly violent crimes) show an effect reminiscent of the Easterbrook pattern. Loftus (1979) stated: "The weapon appears to capture a good deal of the victim's attention, resulting in, among other things, a reduced ability to recall other details from the environment, to recall details about the assailant, and to recognize the assailant at a later time" (p. 35).

A number of early studies seemed to document the reality of the weapon-focus phenomenon, but the evidence was of uncertain quality. For example, Kuehn (1974) surveyed a number of police reports and found that victims of robberies provided much fuller descriptions of their assailant than did victims of rapes or assaults. This is consistent with the claim that stress or arousal lead to a narrower focus of attention, and thus to less full descriptions. However, this result is difficult to interpret, both because the various crimes differ in many regards beyond level of stress or arousal, and because it is difficult to tell if these reports reflect memory completeness, or some pattern of response bias. In addition, there is no way to assess the accuracy of these reports.

Likewise, Johnson and Scott (1976) reported that subjects who witnessed an episode containing a weapon (a bloody letter-opener) remembered less about the episode than did subjects who witnessed a control episode. However, a number of authors have expressed concerns about the interpretation of this study (e.g., Loftus, 1979; Loftus, Loftus, & Messo, 1987; McCloskey & Egeth, 1983). Among other concerns, it is unclear whether the two episodes in this study were truly comparable, because the episodes differed in several ways beyond the presence or absence of the weapon.

More recent studies, however, are more persuasive. For example, Loftus et al. (1987) had subjects view one of two sequences. In one, an individual hands a check to a cashier and receives some cash; in the other, an individual points a weapon at the cashier and receives some cash. Loftus et al. monitored subjects' eye movements during presentation of these sequences, and found that subjects looked more at the gun than they did at the comparison item (the check); this was evident in both number and duration of eye fixations. In addition, and critically for our purposes, subjects in the weapon condition showed a slight but statistically reliable disadvantage in a subsequent memory test.

Comparable data were reported by Maass and Köhnken (1989). Subjects in their study were seated in the experimental room, taking various tests, when an assistant entered the room carrying a hypodermic syringe. In the control group, no syringe was visible. The Maass and Köhnken study has the advantage that subjects were participants in the TBR event, and not merely passive viewers of a video sequence. This advantage carries with it certain ethical constraints, namely, that the assistant not march in brandishing a gun. Hence the syringe was used in place of an actual weapon. Maass and Köhnken reported that subjects who were confronted with the syringe showed poorer accuracy in subsequently identifying the assistant from a line-up. In addition, and consistent with the weapon-focus idea, these subjects also showed superior memory for various details about the syringe itself (e.g., its color).

Further confirmation for the weapon-focus claim comes from Kramer, Buckhout and Eugenio (1990). In their studies, subjects either viewed a slide sequence in which a weapon was in view, or a comparable one without a weapon. Subjects who saw the weapon sequence had poorer memory for details about the person carrying the weapon (e.g., height, weight, jewelry). Strikingly, this effect was most pronounced in those subjects who reported themselves as having been made anxious by the sequence.

These studies make it clear that subjects do pay differential attention to a weapon if one is present in a scene. This creates a memory advantage for the weapon itself, but a memory disadvantage for other aspects of the scene (see also Cutler et al., 1987; Tooley, Brigham, Maass, & Bothwell, 1987). However, it is not clear what mechanism underlies this effect. Both Kramer et al. and Loftus et al. note that they obtain these results even though subjects are not particularly aroused by these sequences; hence we must be cautious about treating these data as confirmation of the Easterbrook claim described earlier. As alternative accounts, subjects may look at, and remember, the weapon because it is unexpected or unusual, or because information about the weapon is of key importance in understanding the scene overall (e.g., where is the weapon being pointed?). We return to these issues later.

WHEN DOES EMOTION IMPROVE MEMORY FOR DETAIL?

It is possible to quibble with many of the studies just cited. For example, one might wonder, in some of these studies, whether the emotional and unemotional TBR events are matched in all regards except emotion. Likewise, it is not clear whether all these studies apply to the specific role of emotion, given reservations just mentioned about the weapon-focus evidence. For our purposes, though, the data are remarkably consistent: In study after study, subjects show poorer memory for the details of emotional materials. However, the literature does contain exceptions to this pattern. For example, Heuer and Reisberg (1990) showed subjects a series of slides depicting a story. Half the subjects were shown a neutral story; half, an emotional story. Subjects were given no additional task beyond the requirement to watch the slide sequence; memory was assessed, in a surprise test (4AFC), 2 weeks later. (The design also included two other groups, with slightly different instructions; we return to these later.)

Subjects who saw the emotional version of the story remembered more of central information and of the details than did subjects who saw the neutral version. This advantage was specific to the latter half of the story; the groups did not differ in their memory for the story's beginning (i.e., the portion of the sequence that was identical in both versions).

Related findings were obtained by Dorman (1989), Snyder (1989), and Andrews (1990). For example, Andrews took as her TBR materials scenes in commercially successful films. Andrews examined memory for pairs of scenes within each film, with the scenes varying in their emotional charge but matched for duration, placement within the film, relevance to plot, and so on. (These judgments had been determined previously by a panel of raters.) Subjects had seen these films 6–18 months prior to the test; memory was tested for both central items and details. Consistent with the other findings in this section, Andrews found better memory for the emotional scenes. This effect was actually stronger for detail memory than for central materials; this is probably due to a ceiling effect in memory for central materials.

Emotion, Retention Interval, and Memory for Word Lists

Why is it that the studies just mentioned yield an arousal *advantage* in remembering detail, while so many other studies show an arousal *disadvantage* in remembering detail? This is a difficult question to address, simply because these various studies differ in many ways (e.g., using different stimulus materials, and probing memory for different kinds of detail). In fact, one might try to explain the seeming data conflict by appealing to these differences in to-be-remembered materials. Perhaps arousal improves memory for some species of detail, but has the opposite effect on other species. If these various studies happened to include more of one species or the other in their memory tests, this could explain the data pattern.

An alternative account of the data pattern hinges on retention interval. In the studies showing that emotionality aids memory for detail, subjects were tested at least 2 weeks after viewing the TBR materials (Andrews, 1990, Study 1 and Study 2; Christianson, 1984; Dorman, 1989; Heuer & Reisberg, 1990; Snyder, 1989). In contrast, studies that showed emotionality impairs detail memory have generally employed much shorter retention intervals—typically, an hour or less (Christianson, 1984; Christianson & Loftus, 1991; Clifford & Hollin, 1981; Clifford & Scott, 1978; Deffenbacher, 1983; Kebeck & Lohaus, 1986; Loftus & Burns, 1982; Siegel & Loftus, 1978). Is this crucial? Does retention interval moderate (or even reverse) emotion's effects on memory?

Kleinsmith and Kaplan (1963, 1964) had subjects learn to associate words and numbers, using a paired-associate procedure. Some of the words were neutral ones; others had strong emotional impact (e.g., "rape", or "vomit"). Whereas memory for word lists is clearly not our main concern in this review, the Kleinsmith and Kaplan data provided an early indication that retention interval does interact with emotion's memory effects. In their study, memory was tested after various intervals. At short intervals, memory was poorer for emotional words. At longer intervals (1 week), this pattern reversed: Retention was better for emotional materials.

The Kleinsmith and Kaplan data have been replicated many times (Baddeley, 1982; Butter, 1970; Farley, 1973; Kaplan & Kaplan, 1969; McLean, 1969; Osborne, 1972; Walker & Tarte, 1963; for critical reviews, see Craik & Blankstein, 1975; Eysenck, 1976; Hockey, 1978). These studies have consistently shown a beneficial effect of arousal on memory, *provided that* memory is tested at longer retention intervals. But all these studies have employed word lists, or nonsense syllables, or numbers, as the TBR materials. One study in this literature did employ richer materials (a 10-minute film; Levonian, 1967), but memory was only globally assessed (via a brief yes–no questionnaire). Thus none of these studies can address the question of emotion's impact on memory for more peripheral information.

Emotion, Retention Interval, and Memory for Detail

A small number of studies have examined the relation between emotion, retention interval, and memory for detail. For example, Christianson (1984) showed subjects either a neutral or an arousing slide sequence; memory was tested either 12 minutes after the presentation, or after 2 weeks. With a short retention interval, subjects' performance was better in the recognition test if they had seen the neutral version of the story. With a long retention interval, this pattern reverses for the first and second phases of the slide presentation. A similar interaction (but without the crossover) was present for a separate group of subjects, tested via recall.

It is worth noting that the slides, recognition test, and retention interval employed in this study were the same as those employed in the Christianson and Loftus (1987) study mentioned earlier. However, Christianson and Loftus found a different pattern: In their data, subjects who had seen the arousing slides performed more poorly with *both* long and short retention intervals. There is, however, a conspicuous difference between the Christianson (1984) and Christianson and Loftus (1987) procedures: In the former study, subjects were simply urged to "concentrate carefully" on the slides. In the latter study, subjects were asked to write down, for each slide, a word or phrase summarizing the slide's most distinguishing feature.

This change in instructions provides a plausible source for the data contrast between these two studies. Unfortunately, though, we have no way of confirming this suggestion, and so caution seems appropriate in interpreting either of these two studies.

Closer Examination of the Effects of Retention Interval

The evidence reviewed so far leaves us uncertain about retention interval's role in moderating emotion's impact on memory. Retention interval clearly does matter for word lists, but we cannot extrapolate from this to questions of memory for detail. A small number of studies have looked directly at emotion, retention interval, and detail memory, but the crucial findings have not been replicated. The fact remains, however, that there is a consistent pattern in the literature: Studies employing shorter retention intervals (less than an hour) find that emotionality impairs memory for detail; studies employing longer retention intervals (2 weeks or more) find that emotionality improves memory for detail. But we need to be cautious about this comparison across studies, since these studies differed in many ways, including the specific items used to test memory.

Thus, retention interval may be the key to understanding this data pattern, but this claim is far from well established. As an alternative, it remains possible that the data contrast should be understood in terms of the type of TBR material used in these various studies. It is of course also possible that both retention interval and type of material play a role in moderating emotion's memory effects.

In clarifying these issues, what seems needed is a study that looks simultaneously at emotion, retention interval, and type of remembered material. Such a study was recently completed by Burke, Heuer, and Reisberg (1991). Burke et al. repeated the Heuer and Reisberg procedure described earlier, but with four groups of subjects. Half the subjects saw the neutral story; half saw the emotional story. Within each group, some subjects were tested immediately after the presentation, and the remaining subjects were tested after a delay (1 or 2 weeks in their first experiment, 1 week in their second experiment).

The Burke et al. study also examined how emotion's memory effects interact with type of TBR material, and this draws our attention back to the definitional issues sketched earlier in this chapter. Emotion may have different effects on different types of information; this is predicted both by the Easterbrook hypothesis and by claims about weapon focus. These effects will go undetected unless we partition the to-be-remembered material appropriately. The problem, though, is that we do not know which partition is the correct one (e.g., we do not know exactly how to categorize the TBR material). Burke et al. therefore proposed that we are best off, at least for now, treating this partition (and the corresponding definitions) as an empirical matter. In concrete terms, this means treating type of TBR material as a parameter to be systematically varied.

Burke et al. thus designed their study to allow a closer look at exactly what subjects do, and do not, remember. To this end, the memory test items (all 4AFC) were divided into four categories: The first two categories subdivided what Heuer and Reisberg had called "central" materials. The first category contained items pertaining to the gist or plot of the TBR material; no questions about the specific visual presentation of the materials were included in this category. The second category included all the memory-test items pertaining to a basic-level description of the slides shown to the subjects (e.g., that a slide showed mother locking the door, as opposed to walking away from the house).

Two more categories subdivided what we have so far been calling "detail" information. (The contrast here was modeled after the categorization scheme used by Christianson & Loftus, 1991). Specifically, the third category of test items included questions probing detail associated with the central characters in each slide. For example, if a slide centrally showed mother, a question about her clothing would be in this category. Finally, the fourth category included details concerned with items in the background of the slides (e.g., whether a slide centrally showing a damaged car also showed any other vehicles in the background).

The Burke et al. data were mixed with regard to retention interval: Their first experiment yielded no reliable interactions between interval and emotionality; their second experiment showed the predicted interactions only in some measures. This is reminiscent of the contrast between the Christianson (1984) and Christianson and Loftus (1987) studies, with the former showing an effect of interval, but not the latter. Thus, we can only offer tentative conclusions about retention interval. The results do imply a role for this variable, but the effects are certainly not robust. When emotion's effects interact with interval, they do so in a reliable way, and we return to this point later in the chapter. However, further data are needed to determine why retention interval seems to play a role in some studies, and not in others.

The Burke et al. data speak more strongly, though, to a different point, namely, the interaction between emotionality and type of TBR material. As we have already discussed, previous studies had indicated that emotionality had one effect on central materials, and a different effect on peripheral details. The Burke et al. findings suggest that this categorization may need further refinement: Consider first plot-irrelevant details that happen to be associated with central characters in the story. For these materials, both Burke et al. experiments showed that emotion *improved* memory in the middle phase of the presentation (the phase in which the arousing materials themselves were presented), but worked *against* memory for materials in the third (final) phase of the story. The pattern was quite different for plot-irrelevant details that happened to concern 'background.' For these, emotion undermined memory accuracy, with this effect most visible in the story's middle phase.

Broadly put, the pattern of these data is that emotion aided memory for materials tied to the "action" in the event. This included information about the plot itself (gist and basic-level visual information), but also included detail information that was spatially and temporally linked to the arousal event. Details about the background are, by definition, spatially removed from the action, and memory for these was hurt by emotion. Likewise, emotion also worked against memory for details that were associated with central characters but temporally removed from the arousing materials.

Finally, the Burke et al. procedure also examined one further issue. Subjects who were tested immediately after viewing the TBR materials were also retested 1-week later, allowing us to examine the effects of repeated testing. Overall, the immediate test seemed to act as a rehearsal, and, as a result, subjects retested after a week performed better than those tested for the first time after the same delay. At the same time, this rehearsal seems to have frozen a memory pattern in place; that is, the effects of arousal in the 1-week second test clearly resemble those in the *immediate* test and do not resemble those in the 1-week *first* test.

Thus, the Burke et al. study clearly indicates an influence on later memory tests by earlier ones. Whatever emotion's effects with longer retention intervals, these effects may not be detected if subjects' memories had also been tested at shorter intervals. To put it differently, the immediate test is a strong source of memory interference; memory tested for a second time at a delay looks quite different from memory tested for the first time at the same delay (cf. Belbin, 1950). This makes several studies in the literature, using repeated testing, very difficult to interpret (e.g., Buckhout, Alper, Chern, Silverberg, &

Slomovits, 1974; Cutler, Penrod, & Martens, 1987; Kebeck & Lohaus, 1986).

Most importantly, these data imply a reassuring conclusion: We noted at the very beginning of this chapter that emotional events seem to be remembered in vivid detail; the results just cited imply that these events may be remembered in vivid and *accurate* detail, at least for details somehow attached to the event's center. However, this claim obviously represents an extrapolation from various laboratory studies into the autobiographical domain. And that invites an important question: Can we extrapolate in this manner? Is the pattern of results the same if we consider memory outside the laboratory?

Memory Accuracy at Very Long Delays

To address the questions just raised, all we need do is assess the veracity of autobiographical memories for emotional events—one's memory of High School graduation, one's memory of a romantic weekend, and so on. As it turns out, this test is difficult to carry out. An adequate test requires that we identify events (a) that were emotional at the time they occurred, and (b) that are at some distance in the past (so that we are looking at delayed, not immediate, testing). We also need events (c) for which we can check the veracity of the recollection. Hand in hand with this, we need events, (d) which can be clearly identified at some future point—that is, we need to make certain, at the time of the memory test, that subjects understand which prior event is being probed. (We need to avoid a situation in which the researcher probes memory for one event, and the subject offers a correct account of some other event!) Then, if possible, we also want (e) to find comparison events that were not emotional, but that were otherwise comparable to the emotional events.

Finding events that fill criteria a and b is a straightforward matter. However, in the autobiographical domain, it is often difficult to find events for which the other criteria hold. A few studies have sought to finesse this problem (particularly criterion c) by examining memory *stability*, rather than veracity; that is, subjects' memories are tested shortly after an event, and then again some months later. If we find disagreements between these recollections, we can be sure that (at least) one of the recollections is in error. If, on the other hand, emotion promotes memory for detail over the long run, then we would expect that recollections of emotional events should be stable across time. (This is of course a weak test of our claim, given the possibility that subjects' memories may be *inaccurate* but nonetheless stable over time!)

Both Pillemer (1984) and Bohannon (1990) have reported that emotional memories are, in fact, relatively consistent over time. In Pillemer's study, subjects were asked about their recollections of the 1981 assassination attempt on President Reagan, 1 month and 7 months after the event. Stronger emotional reactions were associated with greater consistency of memory across these two tests. Bohannon (1990) reported similar data, with the target event being the 1986 explosion of the space-shuttle Challenger.

Broadly similar data were reported by McCloskey, Wible, and Cohen (1988). Their subjects were questioned about where they were when they first learned of the explosion of the space shuttle. Subjects were first questioned 3 days after the explosion, and then again 9 months later. Despite this long delay, subjects' memories were impressively consistent: 81% of the subjects either reported the same information, or more specific information, about where they were when they heard the news, compared to their immediate responses; 70% of the subjects reported the same or more specific information about who had told them the news. Summing across categories of information, 67% of subjects' responses at 9 months matched (or were more specific than) their responses immediately after the explosion.

As McCloskey et al. noted, however, their subjects' recollections are far from perfect. We have pointed to the 67% correct, seemingly impressive after a 9-month delay, but one can equally well point to the 33% error. However, this is not particularly problematic for the view we are developing here. Whatever else emotion does to memories, it surely does not guarantee blemishless recall! In addition, we know from Bohannon and from Pillemer that degree of affect is predictive of memory stability, but we have no information from McCloskey et al. about their subjects' degree of affect. Hence it is possible that these recollections mix together the stable recollections of subjects particularly moved by the space-shuttle tragedy, and the less stable recollections of subjects less involved with the event.

Similar remarks apply to a report offered by Neisser (1982), in which one of his own very vivid memories contained a (late-discovered) conspicuous error (see also Neisser, 1986a; Thompson & Cowan, 1986). This case again shows that vivid and emotional memories may not be 100% accurate, but it is also striking how many details Neisser does seem to remember.

The data reported by Bohannon, McCloskey et al., and Pillemer are thus consistent with the claim that emotionality does promote accurate (and therefore stable) recollection. However, contrasting data have been reported by Neisser and Harsch (1990). They interviewed subjects the morning after the space-shuttle disaster, and again 3 years later. Their data document massive inconsistencies between these two reports, with agreement between the reports being near "floor" levels at the same time that subjects' confidence in the reports is near ceiling!

This result seems inconsistent with our claims of beneficial effects of emotion on memory. However, there are several ways to resolve this inconsistency. At the simplest, all we need argue is that emotion slows, but does not eliminate, forgetting. Thus, at a suitably long delay, even emotional events are forgotten. On this view, the Neisser and Harsch data simply tell us that 3 years is enough time for subjects to forget this particular emotional event. Our suggestion, though, is that unemotional events are forgotten even more quickly.

This account of the Neisser and Harsch data is undeniably ad hoc, but our confidence in it is increased by a study by Yuille and Cutshall (1986). These researchers interviewed 13 eyewitnesses to an actual crime 4 to 5 months after the event. The crime took place in full daylight and was clearly an emotional one, inasmuch as subjects witnessed a shooting in which one person was killed and another seriously wounded. Yuille and Cutshall had available to them the police interviews, taken within 48 hours of the episode; they also had available various forensic evidence, useful in judging the accuracy of the eyewitness accounts. In addition, it is noteworthy that Yuille and Cutshall interviewed the witnesses about many details not relevant to the police investigation (e.g., the color of the blanket used to cover the dead body); this allows us to escape the repeated-testings concern described earlier.

Yuille and Cutshall report impressive accuracy in their subjects' reports. Accuracy was assessed with reasonably strict criteria (e.g., reported ages had to be within 2 years to be counted as correct, reported weights within 5 pounds). No leeway was given for the estimation of the number of shots fired in the incident. With these criteria, subjects were correct after a 4–5 month delay in 83% of the details reported about the action itself within the episode, 76% correct about descriptions of people, 90% in their descriptions of objects on the scene. This seems impressive performance and certainly consistent with the claim that emotion promotes accuracy of remembered detail.

It is interesting to contrast these findings with those of Brigham, Maass, Snyder, and Spaulding (1982). Brigham et al. studied memory for a real life unemotional event (a patron's making a purchase at a convenience store). Unfortunately, their TBR event is in many ways different from that studied by Yuille and Cutshall, making strong comparisons impossible. Nonetheless, Brigham et al.'s subjects recalled far less than Yuille and Cutshall's, despite a number of manipulations designed to make their TBR event unusual and memorable (e.g., the patron made the purchase with pennies).

Before leaving this section, we note that none of these studies will support strong conclusions. The Bohannon and Pillemer studies involve memory reliability rather than memory accuracy. We have no data in the McCloskey et al. study with which to ask about the impact of emotion. The Neisser and Harsch data are open to multiple interpretations. The Yuille and Cutshall study involves a small number of subjects, and a single TBR episode. Nonetheless, we regard the evidence in this section as broadly consistent with the theme we have been developing, namely, that emotion does promote memory for some species of detail.

MECHANISMS BEHIND EMOTION'S EFFECTS

How shall we think about all these findings? As we see it, two principles seem required to account for the evidence reviewed so far. First, emotion seems to lead to slower forgetting; second, emotion leads to narrow, but enhanced attention. Each of these principles, however, turns out to be the consequence of multiple mechanisms. We discuss each of the principles in turn.

Emotion Slows Forgetting

The suggestion that arousal slows forgetting has been anticipated by a number of authors (e..g, Cohen, 1989; Craik & Blankstein, 1975; Farley, 1973; Holmes, 1970; Maltzman, Kantor, & Langon, 1966; Menzies, 1936; Waters & Leeper, 1936). This claim implies that the advantages of arousal, when these occur, should increase over time. At the same time, the disadvantages of arousal, when these occur, should shrink over time, because an initial advantage for neutral subjects would be offset by their disadvantage for retention.

When emotion x interval interactions are observed, they match exactly the pattern just described. The beneficial memory effects of emotion are much more readily observed with delayed memory testing; memory disadvantages caused by emotion are more often observed with immediate testing. In addition, emotion seems to be associated with memories that are stable across time, again consistent with this claim of slowed forgetting.

As we have seen, though, these interactions between emotion and retention interval are not reliably observed. Perhaps this is not surprising if arousal serves to retard forgetting. As forgetting progresses, memories become more and more difficult to retrieve; this will be manifest as poor memory performance with delayed testing. However, this effect will be eliminated from the data if suitable retrieval cues are provided. When effective cues are on the scene, then subjects will be able to remember despite the forgetting. In this case, emotion's impact on forgetting will not be visible.

Whatever the fate of this conjecture, we believe that three separate factors contribute to this slowed forgetting: physiological arousal itself, the distinctiveness of emotional events, and the extra attention and rehearsal that one devotes to emotional events. For each of these factors, though, two things should be said: (a) that each does contribute to slowed forgetting, (b) that each, by itself, seems insufficient to account for emotion's overall effects. Hence, all three factors must be included in our theorizing about emotion's impact on memory.

Let us first consider the contribution of physiological arousal. Arousal may delay forgetting for several reasons. First, there is evidence that physiological arousal leads to stronger memory encoding, via its effects on glucose metabolism (Gold, 1987; Hall, Gonder-Frederick, Chewning, Silveira, & Gold, 1989; Manning, Hall, & Gold, 1990). Thus the arousal that accompanies emotionality may literally lead to more enduring memories. (This proposal is a descendant of Brown and Kulik's (1977) hypothesis, that emotional arousal triggers a biologically based memory mechanism.) In addition, aroused subjects may also have more attention (capacity, resources) to deploy, aiding performance overall (cf. Kahneman, 1973).

We note, however, that the construct of arousal itself is not straightforward, and therefore any account in terms of arousal is likely to need further specification and test (see, for example, Anderson, 1990; Neiss, 1990). In addition, and critical for our purposes, several studies have found somewhat different memory effects when arousal is exogenously induced (e.g., via injection of stimulants) and when arousal is endogenously induced by the TBR materials themselves (Christianson & Mjörndal, 1985; Christianson, Nilsson, Mjörndal, Perris, & Tjellden, 1986; Dorman, 1989). These studies indicate that physiological arousal will be part of our account of emotion's effects, but only part.

Moreover, the arousal effects just described should uniformly improve subjects' memories. Yet, as we have seen, emotion's effects are anything but uniform. Emotion undermines memory for background details, and promotes memory for central details if these are temporally associated with the arousing event. These effects are unexplained by the arousal mechanisms just sketched.

Finally, evidence indicates that arousal may not be critical for the weapon-focus effect. In the Maass and Köhnken (1989) study, subjects' memories were influenced by the sight of the weapon itself (a hypodermic syringe) quite independently of whether an injection was actually threatened (that is, sight of the syringe and the threat simply had separate effects on the data). Likewise, Kramer et al. (1990) found weapon-focus effects even with stimuli specifically designed not to be emotionally arousing. Thus, whatever does cause the weapon-focus effect, arousal may not be critical.

Similar considerations apply to the distinctiveness of emotional events. It does seem likely that emotional events are more distinctive than neutral events, and this by itself may promote memory (cf. Hunt & Elliott, 1980; McDaniel & Einstein, 1986). In particular, the distinctiveness may create a retrieval advantage, which would be particularly evident with the passage of time and so would be manifest as slowed forgetting.

Investigators have specifically entertained distinctiveness hypotheses as accounts of the weapon-focus evidence; that is, researchers have proposed that data similar to the weapon-focus effect would be obtained if subjects were simply confronted with surprising or unusual objects. Loftus et al. (1987), for example, speculate that the effects in their study would have been similar if the key character in the depicted episode pulled a banana out of his pocket, rather than a gun (see also Kramer et al., 1990).

Once again, though, distinctiveness, by itself, cannot account for all of emotion's memory effects. First, note that most of the experiments reported here have sought to match the emotional and neutral events as much as possible; this seems to make appeals to the distinctiveness of one of these events less plausible. Second, Christianson and Loftus (1991) sought to test the distinctiveness claim directly. Their subjects were shown a neutral story (in which a woman rode a bicycle), an emotional story (the woman was the victim of an accident), or a distinctive story (the woman carried the bicycle upside-down on her shoulder). Christianson and Loftus reported that the emotional slide led to improved memory for details; the distinctiveness slide did not. Thus, once again, it seems that distinctiveness cannot provide a full account of emotion's effects.

A final contribution to the slowed forgetting of emotional events comes from the extra attention and rehearsal that these events receive. Emotional materials are, by their nature, often worth thinking about. Emotional events often have consequences for one's life and the lives of others, and these also are worth contemplation. For these reasons, emotionality may lead subjects to rehearse the material more than they otherwise might, once again leading to slower forgetting.

Not only are emotional events worth thinking about *after* an event; they are also likely to seize our attention during the episode itself. To see how this matters, consider a study by Leippe, Wells, and Ostrom (1978). Subjects' memories were tested for a (staged) episode in which a theft takes place. For half the subjects, the theft was not serious (a package of cigarettes was taken); for half, the theft was more damaging (an expensive calculator). Within each group, half the subjects were told the identity of the stolen item only after the fact; half knew its identity while the event was ongoing. Leippe et al. reported an effect of crime seriousness (memory was better for subjects who witnessed the calculator theft), but only for those subjects who knew the seriousness of the crime during the theft itself. This suggests that the effect of crime seriousness (and, we assume, emotion) is not entirely mediated by events after the episode but is also influenced by events during the episode.

As with arousal and distinctiveness, however, we suggest that the effects of closer attention and fuller rehearsal contribute to emotion's impact but cannot, by themselves, provide a full account of this impact. Evidence for this claim comes from the fact that emotion's effects on memory are not mimicked by other manipulations leading to close attention and rehearsal. For example, as we have already seen, Christianson and Loftus (1987) found that an explicit "focus" task actually seemed to reverse the effects of emotion seen in other studies. Likewise, Heuer and Reisberg's (1990) study contained two additional groups, specifically designed to compare the effects of emotion with those of close attention and rehearsal. One group, the "problem-solving" group, watched emotionally neutral materials but were told that the materials were designed to mimic some recent event in the news or a popular movie. The subjects' task was to discern what event was being mimicked. This group allows us to examine the effects of close attention and engagement in an event. Another group, the "memorizing" group, also watched the neutral material, but they were told at the outset that their memories would be tested, and that they should remember as much of the story and as many of its details as they could.

Both the memorizing and problem-solving instructions influenced memory, but in a manner distinct from the emotion manipulation. These groups did well in remembering the gist of the story, relative to subjects who had merely been told to watch the materials carefully. However, neither the memorizing nor the problem-solving subjects showed an advantage in remembering detail, in contrast to subjects who had watched the emotional materials.

Emotion Biases Attention

The previous section indicated that arousal, distinctiveness, and rehearsal all contribute to the slowed forgetting of emotional events. This still leaves unexplained, however, emotion's *selective* impact on memory (i.e., a positive effect on memory for some kinds of material, but negative effects for other types of material). This selectivity, we believe, like the slowed forgetting, arises from several sources.

Part of this selectivity may be created by something like the Easterbrook mechanism, described earlier, or the related "weapon-focus" mechanism. The Easterbrook and weapon-focus claims are obviously similar—both posit a narrowing of attention in emotional situations. However, the Easterbrook claim is explicitly a claim about physiological arousal, whereas the weapon-focus effects may derive from other mechanisms (e.g., informativeness or distinctiveness of the weapon). We regard it as plausible that both these effects—one from arousal, one from informational priority—contribute to emotion's effects.

Second, and critically, one not only thinks *more* about emotional events than neutral events; one also thinks about them in a different way, in more personal, more psychological terms, and less in schematic or abstract ways. (Our suggestions here follow the lead of Hockey, 1978, who suggested a dozen years ago that emotional arousal may serve to shift attention from "semantic" to "episodic" particulars of the TBR material.) For example, having seen a story about a boy watching a car repair (the neutral stimulus in the Heuer & Reisberg study), subjects are likely not to be engaged by the particulars of this event. If they subsequently think about the event at all, they will think about it in abstract terms, focusing on the event's gist, and the gist of related events. In contrast, having seen a story about a boy watching gruesome surgery (Heuer & Reisberg's emotional stimulus), subjects are likely to be engaged by the particulars, and likely to think subsequently about these specific details.

Indirect evidence for this claim comes from the eye-movement data reported by Loftus et al. (1987). In their study, subjects' visual exploration of an emotional event was different from that for a neutral event. We note in passing that eye movements cannot by themselves explain the effects of emotionality reviewed in this chapter. Christianson, Loftus, Hoffman and Loftus (1991) took steps to match the fixations made to emotional and neutral materials. Nonetheless, they obtained emotion effects similar to those elsewhere in the literature.

More direct evidence for how subjects attend, and think about, emotional events is provided by Christianson and Loftus (1991). In this procedure, subjects watched one of three versions of a slide series, with the emotional series depicting, in its eighth slide, a woman lying on the street bleeding. Immediately after presentation of the critical slide in each series, the subjects were asked to write down their first thoughts about the content of the slide they had just seen. Subjects' thoughts, immediately after the emotional slide, were quite different from those of subjects in the other groups. The emotional and neutral groups both tended to refer to the slide's central character (the woman), but the emotional group's descriptions were both more specific, and also more likely to contain an expression of affect. The emotional group's descriptions were also more likely to refer to the slide's central action, and less likely to refer to the surroundings, than the neutral group's.

We are hesitant to draw conclusions from a single study, especially one in which the data are sparse enough to preclude statistical treatment (see Christianson & Loftus, 1991, p. 22). Nonetheless, these are certainly suggestive data (and, to our view, worth further exploration). These data, together with the eye-movement evidence, begin to build a case that subjects do indeed attend differently to emotional materials than they do to neutral materials, or, said differently, that emotionality does guide attention.

Interestingly enough, the pattern of how subjects attend and rehearse emotional events will also show up in one further way, namely, in the pattern of intrusion errors subjects make when recalling emotional events. Heuer and Reisberg (1990) reported that subjects who had watched the neutral story made many more errors about plot (whether the mother brought the child to school or to the garage; whether the mother went grocery shopping after she left the garage, and so on). In general, these subjects seemed to be constructing sensible but false aspects of the tale, as if to fill gaps in the remembered sequence. In contrast, arousal subjects made very few plot errors but tended instead to confabulate about the story's protagonists' motives or reactions. Subjects often exaggerated what the story had said about these, sometimes falsified what the story had said. For example, subjects reported vivid recollections of hearing that the mother was upset that the child saw the medical procedure, or that the mother was angry that the father allowed his son to view the surgery. (Neither of these was mentioned in the story.) In these cases, subjects seem to have projected their own emotions into their memories. Or, in Bartlettian terms, the subjects seem to have remembered an attitude that they then struggled in their recollections to justify.

These intrusion errors carry a number of implications. Among them, it appears that we may get a different view of emotion's effects with recall testing (open to these intrusions) than with recognition testing. More important for present purposes, these intrusions are wholly consistent with our claim that subjects think about emotional events quite differently from how they think about neutral events, and this will be reflected in the recollection of these events.

An Account of Emotion's Effects

We are now ready to put the pieces together. We propose, first, that subjects do attend differently to emotional materials and do, in particular, pay close attention to the central aspects of an emotional scene, at the cost of attention to the aspects in the periphery. In some sense, this seems inevitable: When engaged in an emotional event, one has neither the leisure nor the inclination to admire the scenery; one instead pays attention to the emotional matter at hand. This pattern is then reflected in the results of memory testing—emotion leads to better memory for central materials, poorer memory for peripheral materials.

In addition, we suspect that the emotionality may distract subjects during the memory test itself; that is, subjects are likely still to be emotional shortly after witnessing an emotional episode, and, with immediate testing, this may disrupt subjects' performance. In this way, emotionality may impair retrieval and so contribute to emotion's other effects on short-term testing. (This factor is not relevant to long-term testing, as subjects would have calmed down by the time of the memory test.)

Finally, at least for short-term testing, it seems that emotion's effects can be mimicked in various other ways. As we have seen, weapon-focus effects can be documented even in the absence of emotion or arousal. We believe that these effects are attributable to biased-attention mechanisms similar to the ones already described.

What about long-term testing? Thanks to arousal, and distinctiveness, and increased rehearsal, emotional events will be forgotten more slowly than neutral events. In addition, the passage of time may sharpen the selectivity of subjects' memories of emotional events; that is, the postevent elaboration is itself likely to be selective, as subjects continue to think about the specifics of the emotional episode, rather than the episode's more general features.

Given all this, the effects of emotion will shift with the passage of time. As we have seen, emotion provides a memory advantage for some kinds of information in short-term testing; this effect will grow in time, as the neutral material is gradually forgotten. For other kinds of information, emotion provides a disadvantage in short-term testing, and this effect will gradually erode (or be reversed), for the same reason. Even with these changes, however, the longer term testing should still reveal the selectivity of subjects' encoding; that is, at the time of an event, emotion leads subjects to pay attention to the event's center, at the cost of attention to background details. This pattern will be preserved in what subjects remember: an emotion advantage in remembering central materials, and also details associated with these central materials, and an emotion disadvantage in remembering details of the background. In addition, given the selectivity of rehearsal, this pattern of what is and what is not remembered may actually grow sharper with longer term testing. Finally, this selectivity will also emerge in the intrusion errors that subjects make when trying to recall emotional episodes.

CONCLUSIONS

We have offered a complex account, nowhere near the parsimonious theory one might hope for. Worse still, we have set to the side a number of complications that must enter into our ultimate conception of how emotion influences memory. For example, we have said very little about the emotional state of the subject at the time of the memory test itself, but the literature on state-dependency effects suggests that this factor will also interact with the concerns discussed so far (Blaney, 1986; Ellis & Ashbrook, 1989). Likewise, we have discussed emotion's effects as though emotion were a single thing, always existing in the same form, at the same intensity. Clearly, neither of these latter claims is correct, and we flag this as an issue in need of exploration, likely eventually to complicate our conception of emotion's memory effects. Finally, it also seems plain that individuals differ enormously in their emotional makeup, and how they react to emotional events. Although psychologists are sanguine about generalizing from college-student samples with regard to many memory issues, it seems perilous in this domain to ignore individual differences variables.

We wish to close, though, by briefly revisiting the issue with which we began this chapter. Highly vivid, detailed memories of emotional events seem ubiquitous; how accurate are those memories? Clearly emotion's effects on memory will be mixed. Emotion leads to the exclusion from memory of some information; emotion seems to lead to intrusion errors of a particular kind. What *is* remembered about emotional events, however, seems to be remembered fully and well. As we have argued, emotion leads to enhanced encoding (of some aspects of an event), and then slower forgetting. Emotion provides no guarantee of permanent or perfectly accurate recall—emotional memories will contain errors and will eventually be lost. Nonetheless, we believe it likely that we can largely trust our vivid memories of emotional events.

REFERENCES

Anderson, K. J. (1990). Arousal and the inverted-U hypothesis: A critique of Neiss's "Reconceptuatizing arousal." *Psychological Bulletin 107*, 96–100.
Andrews, K. (1990). *The Effects of emotion on memory accuracy*. Unpublished bachelor's thesis, Reed College, Portland, OR.
Baddeley, A. (1982). *Your memory: A user's guide*. New York: MacMillan.
Belbin, E. (1950). The influence of interpolated recall upon recognition. *Quarterly Journal of Experimental Psychology, 2*, 163–169.
Blaney, P. H. (1986). Affect and memory: A review. *Psychological Bulletin, 99*, 229–246.
Bohannon, J. N. (1988). Flashbulb memories of the space shuttle disaster: A tale of two theories. *Cognition, 29*, 179–196.
Bohannon, J. N. (1990, February). *Arousal and memory: Quantity and consistency over the years*. Paper presented at the Conference on Affect and Flashbulb Memories, Emory University.
Brewer, W. (1986). What is autobiographical memory? In D. C. Rubin (Ed.), *Autobiographical memory* (pp. 25–49). Cambridge, MA: Cambridge University Press.
Brigham, J., Maass, A., Snyder, L., & Spaulding, K. (1982). Accuracy of eyewitness identifications in a field setting. *Journal of Personality and Social Psychology, 42*, 673–681.
Brown, R., & Kulik, J. (1977). Flashbulb memories. *Cognition, 5*, 73–99.
Bruner, J. S., Matter, J., & Papanek, M. L. (1955). Breadth of learning as a function of drive level and mechanization. *Psychological Review, 42*, 1–10.
Buckhout, R., Alper, A., Chern, S., Silverberg, G., & Slomovits, M. (1974). Determinants of eyewitness performance on a lineup. *Bulletin of the Psychonomic Society, 4*, 191–192.

Burke, A., Heuer, F., & Reisberg, D. (in press). Remembering emotional events. *Memory & Cognition.*

Butter, M. J. (1970). Differential recall of paired associates as a function of arousal and concreteness–imagery levels. *Journal of Experimental Psychology, 84,* 252–256.

Christianson, S.-Å. (1984). The relationship between induced emotional arousal and amnesia. *Scandinavian Journal of Psychology, 25,* 147–160.

Christianson, S.-Å. (1989). Flashbulb memories: Special, but not so special. *Memory & Cognition, 17,* 435–443.

Christianson, S.-Å., & Loftus, E. (1987). Memory for traumatic events. *Applied Cognitive Psychology, 1,* 225–239.

Christianson, S.-Å., & Loftus, E. (1990a). Some characteristics of people's traumatic memories. *Bulletin of the Psychonomic Society, 28,* 195–198.

Christianson, S.-Å., & Loftus, E. (1991). Remembering emotional events: The fate of detailed information. *Cognition & Emotion, 5,* 81–108.

Christianson, S.-Å., Loftus, E., Hoffman, H., & Loftus, G. R. (1991). Eye fixations and accuracy in detail memory of emotional versus neutral events. *Journal of Experimental Psychology: Learning, Memory, and Cognition, 17,* 693–701.

Christianson, S.-Å., & Mjörndal, T. (1985). Adrenalin, emotional arousal, and memory. *Scandinavian Journal of Psychology, 26,* 237–248.

Christianson, S.-Å., Nilsson, L.-G., Mjörndal, T., Perris, C., & Tjellden, G. (1986). Psychological versus physiological determinants of emotional arousal and its relation to laboratory induced amnesia. *Scandinavian Journal of Psychology, 27,* 300–310.

Clifford, B., & Hollin, C. (1981). Effects of the type of incident and the number of perpetrators on eyewitness memory. *Journal of Applied Psychology, 66,* 364–370.

Clifford, B., & Scott, J. (1978). Individual and situational factors in eyewitness testimony. *Journal of Applied Psychology, 63,* 352–359.

Cohen, G. (1989). *Memory in the real world.* Hillsdale, NJ: Lawrence Erlbaum Associates.

Craik, F., & Blankstein, K. (1975). Psychophysiology and human memory. In P. H. Venables & M. J. Christie (Ed.), *Research in psychophysiology* (pp. 389–417). London: Wiley.

Cutler, B., Penrod, S., & Martens, T. (1987). The reliability of eyewitness identification. *Law and Human Behavior, 11,* 233–258.

Deffenbacher, K. (1983). The influence of arousal on reliability of testimony. In S. Lloyd-Bostock & B. Clifford (Ed.), *Evaluating witness evidence* (pp. 235–252). New York: Wiley.

Dorman, C. (1989). *The effects of emotional arousal on memory.* Unpublished bachelor's thesis, Reed College, Portland, OR.

Easterbrook, J. A. (1959). The effect of emotion on cue utilization and the organization of behavior. *Psychological Review, 66,* 183–201.

Ellis, H. C., & Ashbrook, P. W. (1989). The "state" of mood and memory research: A selective review. *Journal of Social Behavior and Personality, 4,* 1-21.

Eysenck, M. (1976). Arousal, learning and memory. *Psychological Bulletin, 83,* 389–404.

Eysenck, M. W. (1982). *Attention and arousal.* Berlin: Springer-Verlag.

Farley, F. (1973). Memory storage in free recall learning as a function of arousal and time with homogeneous and heterogeneous lists. *Bulletin of the Psychonomic Society, 1,* 187–189.

Gold, P. (1987). Sweet memories. *American Scientist, 75,* 151–155.

Hall, J., Gonder-Frederick, L., Chewning, W., Silveira, J., & Gold, P. (1989). Glucose enhancement of memory in young and aged humans. *Neuropsychologia, 27*, 1129–1138.

Heuer, F., & Reisberg, D. (1990). Vivid memories of emotional events: The accuracy of remembered minutiae. *Memory & Cognition, 18*, 496–506.

Hockey, G. (1978). Arousal and stress in human memory: Some methodological and theoretical considerations. In M. Gruneberg, P. Morris, & R. Sykes (Ed.), *Practical aspects of memory* (pp. 295–302.). New York: Academic Press.

Holmes, D. (1970). Differential change in affective intensity and the forgetting of unpleasant personal experiences. *Journal of Personality and Social Psychology, 15*, 234–239.

Hunt, R., & Elliott, J. (1980). The role of nonsemantic information in memory: Orthographic distinctiveness effects on retention. *Journal of Experimental Psychology: General, 109*, 49–74.

Johnson, C., & Scott, B. (1976, August). *Eyewitness testimony and suspect identification as a function of arousal, sex of witness, and scheduling of interrogation.* Paper presented at the meeting of the American Psychological Association, Washington, DC.

Johnson, M., & Raye, C. L. (1981). Reality monitoring. *Psychological Review, 88*, 67–85.

Kahneman, D. (1973). *Attention and effort.* Englewood Cliffs, NJ: Prentice-Hall.

Kaplan, R., & Kaplan, S. (1969). The arousal-retention interval interaction revisited: The effects of some procedural changes. *Psychonomic Science, 15*, 84–85.

Kassin, S., Ellsworth, P., & Smith, V. (1989). The "general acceptance" of psychological research on eyewitness testimony: A survey of the experts. *American Psychologist, 44*, 1089–1098.

Kebeck, G., & Lohaus, A. (1986). Effect of emotional arousal on free recall of complex material. *Perceptual and Motor Skills, 63*, 461–462.

Kleinsmith, L., & Kaplan, S. (1963). Paired-associate learning as a function of arousal and interpolated interval. *Journal of Experimental Psychology, 65*, 190–193.

Kleinsmith, L., & Kaplan, S. (1964). The interaction of arousal and recall interval in nonsense syllable paired-associate learning. *Journal of Experimental Psychology, 67*, 124–126.

Kramer, T., Buckhout, R., & Eugenio, P. (1990). Weapon focus, arousal and eyewitness memory: Attention must be paid. *Law and Human Behavior, 14*, 167–184.

Kuehn, L. (1974). Looking down a gun barrel: Person perception and violent crime. *Perceptual and Motor Skills, 39*, 1159–1164.

Leippe, M., Wells, G., & Ostrom, T. (1978). Crime seriousness as a determinant of accuracy in eyewitness identification. *Journal of Applied Psychology, 63*, 345–351.

Levonian, E. (1967). Retention of information in relation to arousal during continuously presented material. *American Educational Research Journal, 4*, 103–116.

Linton, M. (1975). Memory for real-world events. In D. A. Norman & D. E. Rumelhart (Ed.), *Explorations in cognition* (pp. 376–404). San Francisco: W. H. Freeman.

Loftus, E. (1979). *Eyewitness testimony.* Cambridge, MA: Harvard University Press.

Loftus, E., & Burns, T. (1982). Mental shock can reproduce retrograde amnesia. *Memory & Cognition, 10*, 318–323.

Loftus, E., Loftus, G., & Messo, J. (1987). Some facts about "weapon focus." *Law and Human Behavior, 11*, 55–62.

Maass, A., & Köhnken, G. (1989). Eyewitness identification. *Law and Human Behavior, 11*, 397–408.

Maltzman, I., Kantor, W., & Langdon, B. (1966). Immediate and delayed retention, arousal, and the orienting and defensive reflexes. *Psychonomic Science, 6*, 445–446.

Mandler, G. (1975). *Mind and emotion.* New York: Wiley.

Manning, C., Hall, J., & Gold, P. (1990). Glucose effects on memory and other neuropsychological tests in elderly humans. *Psychological Science, 1*, 307–311.

McCloskey, M., & Egeth, H. (1983). Eyewitness identification: What can a psychologist tell a jury? *American Psychologist, 38*, 550–563.

McCloskey, M., Wible, C. G., & Cohen, N. J. (1988). Is there a special flashbulb-memory mechanism? *Journal of Experimental Psychology: General, 117*, 171–181.

McDaniel, M., & Einstein, G. (1986). Bizarre imagery as an effective mnemonic aid: The importance of distinctiveness. *Journal of Experimental Psychology: Learning, Memory, and Cognition, 12*, 54–65.

McLean, P. D. (1969). Induced arousal and time of recall as determinants of paired-associate recall. *British Journal of Psychology, 60*, 57–62.

Menzies, R. (1936). The comparative memory value of pleasant, unpleasant and indifferent experiences. *Journal of Experimental Psychology, 18*, 267–279.

Morris, M., & Murphy, G. (1990). Converging operations on a basic level in event taxonomies. *Memory & Cognition, 18*, 407–418.

Neiss, R. (1990). Ending arousal's reign of error: A reply to Anderson. *Psychological Bulletin, 107*, 101–105.

Neisser, U. (1982). *Memory observed.* San Francisco: W. H. Freeman.

Neisser, U. (1986a). Remembering Pearl Harbor: Reply to Thompson and Cowan. *Cognition, 23*, 285–286.

Neisser, U. (1986b). Nested structure in autobiographical memory. In D. C. Rubin (Ed.), *Autobiographical memory* (pp. 71–81). New York: Cambridge University Press.

Neisser, U., & Harsch, N. (1990, February). *Phantom flashbulbs: False recollections of hearing the news about Challenger.* Paper presented at the Conference on Affect and Flashbulb Memories, Emory University.

Osborne, J. (1972). Short- and long-term memory as a function of individual differences in arousal. *Perceptual and Motor Skills, 34*, 587–593.

Pillemer, D. B. (1984). Flashbulb memories of the assassination attempt on President Reagan. *Cognition, 16*, 63–80.

Reisberg, D., Heuer, F., McLean, J., & O'Shaughnessy, M. (1988). The quantity, not the quality, of affect predicts memory vividness. *Bulletin of the Psychonomic Society, 26*, 100–103.

Rifkin, A. (1985). Evidence for a basic level in event taxonomies. *Memory & Cognition, 13*, 538–556.

Robinson, J. (1980). Affect and retrieval of personal memories. *Motivation and Emotion, 4*, 149–174.

Rosch, E. H. (1978). Principles of categorization. In E. Rosch & B. B. Lloyd (Ed.), *Cognition and categorization* (pp. 27–48). Hillsdale, NJ: Lawrence Erlbaum Associates.

Rubin, D. C., & Kozin, M. (1984). Vivid memories. *Cognition, 16*, 81–95.

Siegel, J., & Loftus, E. (1978). Impact of anxiety and life stress upon eyewitness testimony. *Bulletin of the Psychonomic Society, 12*, 479–480.

Snyder, N. (1989). *An empirical approach to answer what emotion might be doing for memory.* Unpublished bachelor's thesis, Reed College, Portland, OR.

Thompson, C. P., & Cowan, T. (1986). Flashbulb memories: A nicer interpretation of a Neisser recollection. *Cognition, 22*, 199–200.

Tooley, V., Brigham, J., Maass, A., & Bothwell, R. (1987). Facial recognition: Weapon effect and attentional focus. *Journal of Applied Social Psychology, 17*, 845–859.

Vallacher, R., & Wegner, D. (1987). What do people think they're doing? Action identification and human behavior. *Psychological Review, 94,* 3–15.

Wagenaar, W. A., & Groeneweg, J. (1990). The memory of concentration camp survivors. *Applied Cognitive Psychology, 4,* 77–88.

Walker, E., & Tarte, R. (1963). Memory storage as a function of arousal and time with homogeneous and heterogeneous lists. *Journal of Verbal Learning and Verbal Behavior, 2,* 113–119.

Waters, R., & Leeper, R. (1936). The relation of affective tone to the retention of experiences in everyday life. *Journal of Experimental Psychology, 19,* 203–215.

White, R. T. (1989). Recall of autobiographical events. *Applied Cognitive Psychology, 3,* 127–136.

Yarmey, A., & Jones, H. (1983). Is the psychology of eyewitness identification a matter of common sense? In S. Lloyd-Bostock & B. Clifford (Eds.), *Evaluating witness evidence: Recent psychological research and new perspectives* (pp. 13–40). New York: Wiley.

Yuille, J. C., & Cutshall, J. L. (1986). A case study of eyewitness memory of a crime. *Journal of Applied Psychology, 71,* 291–301.

The Influence of Affect on Memory: Mechanism and Development

Michelle D. Leichtman
Stephen J. Ceci
Cornell University

Peter A. Ornstein
University of North Carolina-Chapel Hill

INTRODUCTION

Traditionally, emotion and memory have come under the auspices of separate fields of psychological inquiry. Affective processes have been examined by social psychologists, whereas exploration of the functioning and development of the human memory system has been the province of cognitivists. Recently, enormous progress has been made independently in these two areas of psychology. After virtually abandoning the topic for 30 years, over the past decade researchers have shown a resurgence of interest in emotion (Campos, 1984), and this has fortified our knowledge base concerning emotional processes and their development. At the same time, our understanding of memory, an area of consistent interest, has benefitted from new theoretical insights and methodological tools (e.g., Brainerd, Reyna, Howe, & Kingma, 1990; Kail, 1990; Schneider & Weinert, 1990). Concomitant with the strides made in studying both affect and memory, researchers in the 1980s began a departure from the century-old tradition of treating them as independent psychological matters. Indeed, over the past decade investigators have shown an enhanced interest in combining our knowledge of cognition in general with that of socioemotional processes. This return in spirit to the early days of psychology, when the human

181

organism as a whole was the subject of inquiry, has been reflected in a number of edited volumes and special issues of journals devoted to the interplay between emotion and cognition (e.g., Clark & Fiske, 1982; Izard, 1989). Memory, in particular, has been studied in terms of its relationship to affect by a number of researchers (e.g., Bower, 1983; Hertel, in press; Isen, 1987).

Keeping in mind the larger backdrop of this exploration into cognitive-emotional links, our present focus is on the process by which affect influences the memory system. We have deliberately chosen to use the term affect broadly in this chapter, in order to include within our discussion the wide range of phenomena that are encompassed by this term in the literature. Phenomena that have been studied as markers of affect include general mood states, mental stress levels, and emotional reactions to specific stimuli. Whereas experimental work has demonstrated a variety of effects of this range of emotional phenomena on cognitive processing, and on memory in particular, their causal mechanism has not yet been adequately described in the literature. In this chapter, we organize a variety of research perspectives on this mechanism into what we view as five separate categories of explanation. Clearly, little continuity exists between categories in the foci of authors we include; that is, each theoretical perspective has been derived from consideration of only particular aspects of the body of data on affect and memory. Each reflects a different characterization of the memory system, as well as a different interpretation of the role of affect. In our view, the result is that these explanations do not compete directly with each other but instead serve as partial models of a complex and multichanneled process. As Leventhal and Thomarken (1986) have remarked in referring to various theories of emotion, "the diversity of theoretical perspectives virtually insures views that are neither exclusive nor complementary" (p. 366).

We fully believe that the relationship between affect and memory is a reciprocal one, in which the character and development of affect is as much influenced by memory processes as these processes are influenced by affect. In addition, in our thinking synergism between various aspects of the emotional and cognitive systems has profound implications for behavior and development. In this chapter, however, we limit our discussion primarily to the effects of affect on memory, even while acknowledging that this represents only part of a mutually important relationship. Our goal is to consider each of five explanations for the way that affect influences memory that we have distinguished in the literature. We have coined these various views of the link from emotion to memory as *network, attentional, energy, motivational, and integrated trace* explanations. Although we find this division of explanations useful in thinking about the work we treat, we do not view any of the categories as wholly self-contained. Data that we have included in one explanatory category may also be possible to interpret from the perspective of another. We have based our categorization of the studies simply on our interpretation of the theoretical gist of the various authors.

Most of the data relevant to these explanations have been gleaned from studies using adult subjects, and in each case we first briefly review these. However, given the considerable changes in the memory system across the life course that have long been recognized in the literature (Kail, 1990), we believe that any truly adequate resolution of the problem of affect's role in the memory system will also include a developmental perspective. In the case of each explanation, we thus turn to the very limited developmental work that exists to shed light on how a life-span view of the problem might eventually look. We believe that the integrated trace explanation of affect's role in the memory system is the most promising in terms of bringing a global perspective to the data described in this chapter. For this reason, after reviewing the first four explanations, we describe some of our own work in terms of this view. We emphasize, however, that this perspective does not negate the value of earlier explanations, which account for effects evidenced at the local level of the particular studies that we describe.

Network Explanation

The model of memory in which information is stored in a network of related representations has been highly influential since its inception (see Klatzky, 1980). In this conceptualization, the memory system is made up of nodes representing information that, when activated, excites pathways leading from them to concepts that are associated with them (Collins & Loftus, 1975). Within such a system, a particular affective state can be viewed as a node in the memory network, similar in character to pieces of information originating from cognitive sources. As such, affect is in a position to act as the retrieval cue for concepts located on connected pathways. In this sense, we can conceive of various "emotional addresses" in a network model, corresponding with different valences, which serve as points at which cognitions may begin to unfold. Significant effects of affective state on the memory system are then accounted for by differential chains of nodes stemming from points representing positive and negative emotion, for example. In this sense, the emotional addresses may serve as central organizational points in the network.

In a sizeable set of experiments, Isen and her colleagues have provided support for an explanation of the effects of emotion on memory that is largely based on the network concept. Isen, Shalker, Clark, and Karp (1978) first demonstrated the presence of what was termed a *cognitive loop* that resulted from the presence of positive affect. Subjects in a shopping mall whose moods were elevated by the receipt of an unexpected gift were subsequently found to give more positive ratings to products they owned, in a survey of product performance and service. In a separate laboratory study, subjects who were in a positive affective state after winning a computer game were found to have better access to positive material in memory than those who had lost the game. These findings are interpreted as evidence that affective state acts as a retrieval cue for information stored in memory. Because it is generally thought that the efficacy of a retrieval cue is contingent upon the extent to which it overlaps information that was originally encoded (Tulving & Thomson, 1973), the authors conclude that positive affect may often serve as a category within which information is organized in memory.

In two separate tasks, Isen and Daubman (1984) have further studied the influence of positive affect on categorization. Their findings show that in rating items on a scale in terms of how well they belong in a particular object category, subjects in whom positive affect had been induced gave higher ratings to fringe members of categories; that is, happy subjects tended to view the categories they were provided as more inclusive than those who were not exposed to positive affect. Similarly, in a study where subjects were instructed to group color chips, those subjects who had seen a funny film, or received a gift, organized the colors into more inclusive groups than other subjects, who had either seen a boring or depressing film. Isen and Daubman explained their findings in a manner consistent with the network-based concept of a cognitive loop: They suggested that positive affect facilitates the ability to see relations between objects or ideas because it allows access to a particularly broad range of related concepts.

Further evidence in favor of a network view comes from research on affect and processes related to creativity. Isen, Daubman, and Nowicki (1987) reported that, on moderately difficult problems requiring people to find remote word associates, subjects in a positive emotional state performed better than a control group. Likewise, positive affect was shown to improve performance on Dunker's candle task, the solution of which requires the ability to perceive unusual alternative uses for several objects. In this set of experiments, negative affect and simple physical arousal did not have a facilitative effect on the creative process. Apparently, positive affect allowed the subjects to retrieve information from memory that would otherwise have been inaccessible.

According to the few developmental studies on the topic, the process of categorizing in memory in terms of affect appears at an early age (Isen, 1990). In one study, Grade 1 students were instructed to sort 24 stimuli that varied on several salient dimensions, including color, shape, and design; the stimuli were either decorated with just a line, or with the image of a smiling face. Children in whom elation had been induced (by a gift of stickers) were shown to be significantly more likely than controls to sort first on the affective dimension. In addition, these children produced a greater number of "atypical" sorts, dividing stimuli into unexpected subcategories, for example. These findings mirror those reported in adults, in that they suggest a tendency of happy subjects to categorize on the dimension of affect, and, additionally, to see more possible relationships between stimuli.

Convergent evidence for this last result was found in a study of 3- and 4-year-olds carried out by Williams and Isen (reported in Isen, 1990). Children in whom positive affect had been induced were able to fit together significantly more nesting cups during play than children in a control group. Because the task of nesting with this type of toy is primarily dependent on the ability to see how the cups fit together, positive-affect children were demonstrating a superior ability to see relations among a larger set of stimuli. Thus, in children as well as adults, positive affect has been shown to provide a cognitive context that promotes the ability to see connections among diverse stimuli.

One aspect of the data on the affect-memory link that is somewhat perplexing for the network explanation is the fact that negative affect has rarely been shown to have effects opposite but symmetrical to those obtained using positive-affect inductions. Repeatedly, experiments in which pretesting has indicated that negative-affect inductions are equivalent in degree to positive ones have nevertheless failed to show equivalent results in these two conditions. As Isen (1990) reported, negative affect either fails to facilitate the recall of negative material or acts as a less effective retrieval cue than a positive mood-state induction. For example, when Velten mood induction procedures are used to induce both positive and negative mood states, subjects in the positive condition show increased memorial performance, whereas those in the negative condition perform at the level of controls (Isen, 1985). This phenomenon may be attributed to the looser manner in which positive affective structures are represented in memory, leading to greater spreading activation throughout a semantic network when they are excited. If information is indeed categorized in terms of the affect with which it is associated, then it follows from the network perspective that in normal individuals the category of positive affect is particularly richly furnished. Social psychological literature may be viewed as supportive of this point, insofar as it attests to a tendency toward positive thinking on the part of normal individuals, including the overestimation of success, self-enhancement, and a general push to maintain positive affect (Nisbett & Ross, 1980). Isen and Daubman have suggested that positive affect may prime material not normally perceived as having an affective component, consequently including material normally considered to be neutral in the broader category of positive affect. Thus, the primary function of positive affect is to broaden the context in which stimuli are interpreted, by acting as a cue for a large variety of material.

A study by Ikegami (1986) from the domain of person memory is also interpreted in a manner that is consistent with the network explanation. Ikegami biased the affective reactions of subjects toward an imaginary person by giving them positive or negative trait information about that person. He then provided the subjects with a list of descriptions of behaviors carried out by the imaginary person and asked them to study it. Subjects were later given a memory test in which they were asked to recognize the behavioral traits on the list. Ikegami's work shows asymmetric effects of positive and negative affective bias. Positive affective bias increased the chance that friendly behaviors would be falsely recognized as having been included in the original list, whereas negative bias had no effect on the false recognition rate. The researcher's interpretation of these results is that positive affective bias prior to presentation of the original list primed more related semantic concepts (or caused a more integrative schema to be activated) than did negative bias. Such an interpretation presumes, again, that positive affect is a richer category than negative affect and is therefore connected to a more elaborate memorial network.

Despite the evidence presented in its favor, the network explanation is not wholly satisfying. If affective state is used primarily as a retrieval cue in a network, then it is surprising that negative affect would not trigger the retrieval of associated material in the same manner as positive affect. Although, as we have just conceded, the category of information associated with negative affect may well be narrower than that of positive affect, negative affect should still make some negative information more easily retrievable from memory than positive information. This is because, when fewer routes in a network model extend outward from a particular node, access to information along these routes should be more directly recoverable from memory than in a case where a wider array of connections exists. So, although remote associates and creative options may be less available under conditions calling up the narrower category of negative affect, it is unclear why an increased supply of negative information would not be readily available.

In addition, the network interpretation does not explain results indicating that under some conditions, namely when affective arousal is more extreme than in typical experiments, both positive and negative emotional arousal can induce amnesic effects. This finding has been addressed by researchers adhering to the attentional explanation we consider next.

Attentional Explanation

A less direct route by which affect may play a role in the memory system has been described by Christianson and his colleagues. In their model, the level of arousal of an emotional response is the critical component in determining its effects on memory (Christianson & Nilsson, 1984). According to this explanation, attentional capacity is a limited resource at any given moment. High levels of arousal caused by excessive emotion demand an unusual amount of attentional capacity, thereby impinging on the attentional resources usually available to handle the encoding of information. As a result, this perspective highlights the fact that high levels of emotional arousal tend to cause amnesic effects regarding the details of events, stemming from an impoverished attentional capacity at encoding.

The original evidence leading to this attentional view came from observations under conditions of negative affect. Loftus and Burns (1982), for example, showed subjects in three experiments a disturbing film in which a young boy is shot. These subjects demonstrated poorer memory on both recognition and recall tasks than others who were shown a nonviolent version of the same film. In addition, the researchers found that the memory impairment effect was not achieved in conditions where the event in focus was unexpected, but not upsetting. On this basis, they suggest that extremely upsetting or shocking events may interfere with the normal occurrence of lingering processing that insures a solid memory trace.

When Christianson and Nilsson (1984) presented subjects with photographs of very disfigured faces in the middle of a series of normal faces, they were also able to demonstrate negative effects of trauma on memory. Compared with control subjects who witnessed only nondisfigured faces in a slide series, these subjects showed significantly worse memories for verbal descriptors accompanying and following the upsetting photographs. In contrast, the experimental subjects did not show deficits in memories associated with pictures shown before the disfigured faces, indicating that attention to these pictures was at normal levels. Such results are to be expected if the effects of trauma operate through attentional channels.

Supporting this conceptualization, Christianson (1986) reported that positive emotional arousal, induced by exposure to erotic pictures, also inhibited the performance of subjects on subsequent recall and recognition tests for verbal descriptors. Subjects presented with only neutral pictures achieved higher scores on the memory tests than those presented with a series of erotic ones.

As far as we know, no work to date has explored the developmental implications of an attentional explanation of the affect–memory relationship. However, based on a parallel that can be drawn with work on the fundamentals of memory development, there is some reason to suppose that the effects of attention-grabbing emotional arousal may be even more exaggerated for children than they are for adults. Case (1982) has resolved a contradiction between data pointing to an expanding short-term memory span with age, and other data indicating that such a capacity is invariant across the life-span. Case found that, when tasks were altered so that no difference in storage space was required for subjects in different age groups to process information, younger subjects performed as well as adults. As in Case's model, where children require more operating space to carry out mental operations, children may also require more of their total attentional resources to process high amounts of emotional arousal than do adults, even if those resources are ontogenetically stable. Although bordering on obvious circularity, it may be the case that highly arousing events sap more of the young child's limited capacity resources, thus leaving less net attentional capacity to encode, store, and retrieve.

Energy Explanations

As an alternative to attentional explanations, some researchers have treated the issue of affect's influence on memory from the perspective of what we term *energy* explanations. In this view, affective arousal has a more direct effect on the memory system than is specified by attentional theories and also works upon the system without the complexity assumed by network models. The central question from this perspective is what role the ambient level of stress and arousal at the time of encoding plays in determining whether a particular memory is permitted to enter long-term memory for storage. According to some theorists, instead of taking up critical storage space, the fundamental function of high levels of emotion is to empower the memory system.

Researchers who espouse the view that "flashbulb" memories have a qualitatively distinct character are examples of adherents to this perspective on energy. As originally presented by Brown and Kulik (1977), flashbulb memories are memories for personal circumstances during the moments when one receives an important or shocking piece of information. Unlike everyday memories, flashbulb memories are posited to enter a special type of "permastore" reservoir in the long-term memory system. In its strongest form, flashbulb memory theory holds that these privileged recollections are structurally different from other memories and, as a result, are more resistant to disintegration and decay. Affect is seen as energizing the system, and the result is a series of physiological processes that ultimately lead to superior retention of affectively driven memories (Bohannon, 1988).

On the other hand, energy explanations have also been used to account for inferior memory under some conditions. For many years, a substantial literature has existed that demonstrates how negative affect may sap energy. The low energy level of depressive subjects thus explains their poor performance on tasks that require high levels of effortful processing, relative to their performance on tasks that require less (see Ellis, Thomas, McFarland, & Lane, 1985; Hertel, in press).

Wagenaar and Groeneweg (1990) provided some evidence that is contrary to the flashbulb view. They have shown that prisoners in a brutally run Dutch prison camp in the early 1940s often forgot the names and identities of those who had tortured and maltreated them there over the course of subsequent years. In addition, when interviewed 40 years after their stay in the camp, almost a third of those who had interacted with a particularly brutal guard were unable to remember ever having seen him before (this estimate of forgetting is reported to be low, because some of the witnesses had seen the guard's picture on television just prior to being interviewed about him). These results are surprising from a flashbulb perspective, given the highly emotional nature of the experiences.

Some developmental data relevant to the energy explanation emerges in the literature on children's eyewitness memory. Like research on flashbulb memory, this work has been concerned with stressful and personally relevant circumstances. In aiming to assess the accuracy of children's eyewitness memory as a function of their ambient arousal level (e.g., Goodman, Hirschman, Hepps, & Rudy, 1991; Goodman, Rudy, Bottoms, & Aman, 1990; Peters, in press), the research has produced conflicting findings.

Goodman et al. (1990, 1991) have described results of four experiments that indicate excellent memory for highly stressful and personally relevant experiences among children. In one study, for instance, their preschool-aged subjects received either a painful venipuncture procedure or had a painless tattoo rubbed on their arms (the control group). She reported that the most highly stressed group who had the painful blood work were superior at remembering the details of the nurse and setting than were the less stressed children. The same result was found for children who were the most distressed after receiving an inoculation at a medical clinic, leading Goodman and her colleagues to conclude (1990):

> Our general finding was that stress had a facilitative effect on the children's reports. . .children at the highest stress levels recalled more information than the other children and were less suggestible. Interestingly, the children had to reach a level of great distress before beneficial effects on memory were evidenced. . . . (their) reports were completely accurate. Not a single error in free recall was made by the highly stressed children. (p. 274)

Recent work by Vandermaas has reported a mixed relationship between stress and memory among children (Vandermaas, 1990). Like Goodman et al.'s studies, this work also looked at the effects of stress level on children's memorial performance. Four- and 8-year-old children's level of emotional anxiety during a dental visit was assessed, and their memory for central as well as peripheral details related to the event was subsequently probed. Vandermaas reported that there was no deleterious effect of high anxiety on memory for either type of event-related information (though several correlations between anxiety measures did appear to be negatively correlated with accurate recall of peripheral and central information). It deserves to be noted, however, that her results also did not find that stress had a facilitative effect on memory. However, Ornstein and his colleagues have investigated children's memory for the potentially emotionally salient event of visiting the doctor. In this work, 3- and 6-year-old children were shown to have excellent memories for the details of their checkups in an immediate memory test. Furthermore, the memory performance in both age groups remained fairly good over delay intervals of up to 3 weeks, although the performance of the younger children did decline more substantially than that of the older children (Ornstein, Gordon, & Larus, in press). Although the researchers did not manipulate the variable of emotional anxiety level, their work demonstrates that potentially stressful events may be remembered well by children.

In contrast with the preceding studies, Peters (1991) conducted four studies of children's recollections of different arousing events, demonstrating the conflicting result that anxiety usually undermines the accuracy of recall. The four studies utilize both natural and contrived stressful events: One study took advantage of naturally occurring stress during a child's dental visit, another study was conducted at an inoculation clinic, a third was carried out during a nursery school visit by a strange man (who vigorously rubbed some of the children's heads while taking their pulse), and a fourth was conducted in a strange building (a psychology laboratory) when a very loud fire alarm sounded. In all of Peter's studies, anxiety ratings (e.g., pulse, blood pressure, observational measures) were administered to assess both the control and the experimental children.

The children in Peters' studies, ranging in age from 5 through 9 years, are questioned about the events they have witnessed at intervals ranging between 1 and 30 days. Thus far, he has not found that the length of the retention interval has had any influence on children's reporting accuracy. In all his studies, children are given tests of voice and face recognition for the adults in the scripts (e.g., the dentists, nurses, strangers). He usually manipulates the lineups that children are presented, insuring that half of them contain the actual adult perpetrator whereas the other half do not. Like some others who work in this field, Peters generally finds that children are far less accurate in identifying adults in the blank lineups than in the lineups that actually contain the perpetrators. However, even in the perpetrator-present lineups, children exposed to high levels of stress commit a greater number of identification errors (false identifications) than do children who are not stressed. Based on Peter's work, it appears that emotional stress can detrimentally affect children's performance, although flashbulb theory and other work on the eyewitness issue indicate that it may not always do so.

There is a controversy raging in the adult experimental literature over the privileged role of affect-laden memories, such as those associated with the space shuttle disaster (Bohannon, 1988). Because others in this volume discuss adult flashbulb memories, we say no more about this important area here. Taken together with the other studies we have mentioned, this controversy reflects the complex role that emotional arousal may play in the memory process.

Motivational Explanations

In our discussion of network models, we focused on the robust finding that the induction of a positive mood state can improve performance on memory and memory related tasks. Some of these findings
can alternatively be accounted for by simpler motivational explanations. Unlike network explanations, these explanations do not
posit spreading activation throughout a complex memorial network.
Instead, they imply that the causal mechanism for affect's influence
is a social one; when subjects are in a positive, relaxed frame of mind,
they are more willing than otherwise to take chances, and to expend
effort in ways that benefit their performance on various tasks,
including those that index memory.

Bartlett and Santrock (1979) offer an example of a developmental
study that could be interpreted in this vein. In findings mirroring
those in the adult literature (Eich, Weingartner, Stillman, & Gillin,
1975), their research demonstrates that when children are provided
with positive affect conditions throughout a memory task their
performance exceeds that obtained under negative affect conditions.
In their study, Bartlett and Santrock had 5-year-olds listen to a story,
and subsequently they administered a variety of recall and recognition tests for critical words that were in it. Children's emotional
states were manipulated by the manner in which researchers interacted with them during initial encoding and at the time of retrieval,
as well as by the emotional tone of stimulus materials presented (a
positive story about a boy who played with his friends and was given
cake vs. a negative story about an injury incident to the same boy).
The results show that when children were provided positive encoding
and retrieval conditions, they recalled 4.3 words, on average. In
contrast, when faced with negative encoding *and* retrieval conditions, they recalled, on average, only 2.3 out of 6 critical words from
the story. Clearly, then, under conditions where affective conditions
were consistent from encoding to retrieval, positive affect was
associated with superior performance. Notably, children given
positive encoding and negative retrieval conditions recalled only .5
words, and those given negative encoding and positive retrieval
recalled only 1.5 words. Thus, when the encoding and retrieval
contexts were different, children performed reliably worse than
when these contexts were the same no matter what their valence.
This finding suggests an encoding specificity mechanism.

Despite these performance differences on free-recall tests, on
recognition tests no significant effects of affective context were
reflected in parameters representing the accuracy of discrimination

between targets and lures (d'). Based on these findings, it is reasonable to conclude that affective state sometimes has an impact on children's recall through motivational and attentional channels, rather than through actual mnemonic structure. This follows from the fact that whereas vast differences were observed in free-recall performances across affect conditions, the subjects *recognized* comparable numbers of words in each of them. The affect manipulations seem to have affected performance not by altering the organizational structure of memory, but by altering the child's view of the world. Under negative affective conditions, the tasks appeared less pleasant to the children, rendering them less forthcoming, and less risk taking, and more inhibited. Similarly, the positive affect manipulation not only resulted in a greater number of correct recognitions but also in a greater number of false positives, suggesting that it is encouraging children to take more time and greater risks in generating free recall.

Results of some other studies may also be interpreted within the framework of motivational explanations. In playing concept formation games or in generating word associates, as in the studies by Isen reported earlier, positive affect conditions may convey to subjects a sense that it is acceptable to be "loose" and at ease. As one example of this, consider the finding from Isen (1990) that "positive affect promotes the tendency to see more potential relationships among stimuli and concepts and to make multiple comparisons among them" (p. 19). In their study of children's class-inclusion performance, Nevin, Isen, and Winer (1988) found that all children were better able to see the part–whole relationship among the stimuli when a positive affect induction had occurred. If a control group were added to this design that entailed instructing children to be as creative as possible, and to take chances in generating relationships, it is possible that subjects in this group would perform at the same level as those in the positive affect condition. This speculation infers that it is not positive affect per se that leads to creative problem solving, but rather the subtle assurance that it is acceptable to take chances.

Integrated Trace Explanations

Wundt (1907) was among the first theorists to conceive of a memory system in which the affective and the cognitive or perceptual elements of a particular event represented in memory were inextricably connected. It was through this conception of the character of affect that Wundt concluded that emotional components of a particular memory could rise to the surface of consciousness before associated cognitive elements. According to this view, identifiable semantic constructs, or tags, could then be retrieved from memory through their association with feelings.

An integrated trace perspective follows along the lines of Wundt's construction insofar as it considers the affect–memory relationship to be an inherent feature of the human information-processing system. In contrast to other models, this explanation posits that individuals perform interpretive analyses of stimuli concomitantly with pattern recognition analysis. As a part of this process, persons confronted with stimuli will often process not only the usual pattern recognition attributes associated with them (size, shape, contrast) but also emotional responses to the stimuli. Both cognitive-perceptual and affective features are then integrated into a single trace, which stays intact throughout the encoding process. Just as Wundt envisioned, it is then possible to cue one type of attribute with the other; for instance, calling up tags to identify emotions that have already been retrieved.

As we have already described, some researchers have conceptualized the affect–memory relationship in terms of an emotional address model, in which affect tends to empower memory through activation of concepts throughout a semantic network. However, another way to conceive of this relationship is to imagine that the phenomenon of affectively induced remembering results from the operation of an integrated memory trace that contains components of both cognitive (including perceptual) and emotional experience. To illustrate, when we study for a test we store not only the facts at hand but also the ruminations and feelings associated with them. If a memory trace contains both types of components, then it should be possible to find evidence for an integrated trace view by cuing each type of component, and showing that their respective retrievals are not independent (see Ceci, Lea, & Howe, 1980, for the details of this assumption and ways to test it). Little work has been undertaken to support this view, but one developmental study is of some relevance.

DeSimone (1991) presented identical 6-minute-long photographic slide shows, accompanied by narratives in two conditions, to 5- and 7-year-olds. In each of the conditions, the narrative was the same except with respect to nine target characters, who were described in terms evoking either positive or negative emotion. The emotional context in which each of the target characters was presented was reversed in the two conditions. Each target character was presented for a period between 5 and 15 seconds, in a photograph that gave a full facial view at close range, as well as some information about the proximal environment. One week after the slide show presentation, two memory tests were administered to each child. In the first (affect) test, the subjects gave their affective evaluations of people shown in close-up, neutral photographs resembling lineup shots. Nine photographs of the target characters were randomly interspersed with 9 photographs of people not previously seen. Children used a three-point "smiley" scale to indicate their affective reactions to the people in the 18 slides. In the second (cognitive) test, immediately following the first, children viewed the same set of 18 photographs in the same order. Before doing so, they were instructed that some of the people in the photographs had been in the slide show presented previously and were ask to make a determination of whether or not this was true for the individual in each photograph. When children identified a face as that of a character in the slide show, they were given both free and prompted recall tasks regarding that character.

The results of this study lend partial support to the notion that affective reactions to people in the photographs were closely bundled in memory with the cognitive and perceptual elements of the same trace. After the 7-day storage interval, the data indicated that children's conscious memories of the people in the slide show had faded to a very weak level. At this point, the ability to identify whether the people in the photographs had been seen before was barely above chance level, and performance on both free and prompted recall tasks aimed at eliciting perceptual details was poor. In spite of this, photographs of those individuals who had been viewed before in both positive and negative affect conditions were rated significantly more positively than those who had not been seen before. Although, as expected, the mean affective rating of negative photographs was lower than that of positive photographs, this difference was not significant. The dominantly positive context in which all the photographs were originally presented thus appears to have overwritten the subtler distinction between the two affect groups. Nonetheless, these findings suggest that some affective component associated with the faces upon initial exposure was cued by the perceptual stimulus at retrieval. If replicated and extended to include a wider range of affect at exposure, such results would lead to the conclusion that cognitive and affective details are stored in a single trace.

CONCLUSIONS

As we indicated at the outset, the viewpoints presented within our loosely organized framework emerge from the treatment of a broad range of phenomena bearing on the issue of affect's influence on memory. It is clear that developmental memory researchers are still far from being able to offer a cohesive, integrative picture of the processes by which affect influences the unfolding memory system. However, some lessons have already emerged from the research carried out to date that may shape the steps taken toward providing this fuller understanding in the future.

As developmentalists have ventured outside traditional laboratory settings, more affectively loaded experiences are serving as the stimulus materials for their experiments. The result has been a growing awareness of the important role that affect plays in remembering, both at the time of encoding and during retrieval. Beyond this, the literature amassed to date provides every reason to believe that the extent to which positive and negative affective states enhance or debilitate memorial processes is determined by a variety of factors. These include the level of arousal (e.g., high versus extremely high), the nature of the stimulus or event being remembered (central versus peripheral), and the larger context within which the encoding experience occurs. To get past the complications posed by these factors for drawing general conclusions about the affect–memory link, researchers will need to develop methods of indexing emotional state that go beyond the gross dichotomous measures widely used at present. Beyond the main effects of these important internal and external factors, their interactions with each other and with the multiple complex changes occurring in the memory system over time also must be taken into account. At present, we have very little understanding of their interaction.

Although much progress has been made at the "local" level of affective cuing, little attention has been given to the potentially fruitful "global" level of the nature of the affective schemas in remembering. It is our expectation that this is the direction in which future exploration of an integrated trace view of the memory system will lead. From work based in part on this perspective, we know that cognitive schemas possess certain characteristic properties and prototypical developmental trajectories. Affect may have similar properties and may follow some of the same rules that govern purely cognitive structures. Cognitive schemas display pronounced developmental trends in increasing differentiation and integration. If this also is true of affective schemas, then children's affective structures will become more and more differentiated over the middle childhood years (Ceci, Caves, & Howe, 1981), permitting greater balkanization of components from a unitary experience that contains disparate affective ingredients. To discover whether this is in fact the case will require research that is significantly more sensitive to the subtleties of developmental and external parameters affecting memory performance than any that has yet been carried out.

As we develop a better sense of how the separate ontogenies of affect and memory work together to influence performance throughout childhood, we will also be able to consider the role of macrolevel environmental influences in this process. Stein and Trabasso (1991), for example, have already done work along these lines, looking at the conditions of agreement and disagreement between children's memories and those of their parents. In their study with children between 3 and 7 years of age, they found that when children's memories of the affect they had experienced during past events disagreed with that ascribed to them in their parents' memories, they were unlikely to adjust their memories to conform with their parents'. In contrast, when children's memories of their own emotions agreed in general with parents' memories of how their youngsters had felt, the children were likely to incorporate details of events that the parent's suggested into their own memories. Thus, social influences interacted with affective and memorial processes to determine how autobiographical events were eventually perceived.

Evidently, the influence of affect on memorial processes throughout development can operate at a variety of levels. Those interested in developmental issues ought to be in a good position to provide some insights into the validity of the various accounts of the affect–memory linkage.

REFERENCES

Bartlett, J. C., & Santrock, J. W. (1979). Affect-dependent episodic memory in young children. *Child Development, 50*, 513–518.

Bohannon, J. N. III. (1988). Flashbulb memories for the space shuttle disaster: A tale of two theories. *Cognition, 29*, 179–196.

Bower, G. H. (1983). Affect and cognition. *Philosophical Transactions of the Royal Society of London, B302*, 387–402.

Brainerd, C. J., Reyna, V. F., Howe, M. L., & Kingma, J. (1990). The development of forgetting and reminiscence. *Monographs of the Society for Research in Child Development, 55*.

Brown, R., & Kulik, J. (1977). Flashbulb memories. *Cognition, 5*, 73–99.

Campos, J. J. (1984). A new perspective on emotions. *Child Abuse and Neglect, 8*; 147–156.

Case, R. (1982). Operational efficiency and the growth of short-term memory span. *Journal of Experimental Child Psychology, 33*, 386–404.

Ceci, S. J., Caves, R., & Howe, M. J. A. (1981). Children's long-term memory for information incongruous with their knowledge. *British Journal of Psychology, 72*, 443–450.

Ceci, S. J., Lea, S. E. G., & Howe, M. J. A. (1980). A developmental analysis of the structure of memory traces between the ages of four and ten. *Developmental Psychology, 16,* 203–212.

Christianson, S.-Å. (1986). Effects of positive emotional events on memory. *Scandinavian Journal of Psychology, 27,* 287–299.

Christianson, S.-Å. & Nilsson, L. G. (1984). Functional amnesia as induced by a psychological trauma. *Memory and Cognition, 12,* 142–155.

Clark, M. S., & Fiske, S. T. (Eds.), (1982). *Affect and cognition: The 17th Annual Carnegie Symposium on Cognition.* Hillsdale, NJ: Lawrence Erlbaum Associates.

Collins, A. M. & Loftus, E. F. (1975). A spreading activation theory of semantic processing. *Psychological Bulletin, 82,* 407–428.

DeSimone, M. D. (1991, April). *Children's unconscious memory of positive and negative affect.* Paper presented at The Biennial Meeting of the Society for Research in Child Development, Seattle.

Eich, J. E., Weingartner, H., Stillman, R. C. & Gillin, J. C. (1975). State-dependent accessibility of retrieval cues in the retention of a categorized list. *Journal of Verbal Learning and Verbal Behavior, 14,* 408–417.

Ellis, H. C., Thomas, R., McFarland, A., & Lane, W. (1985). Emotional mood states and retrieval in episodic memory. *Journal of Experimental Psychology: LMC, 11,* 363–370.

Goodman, G. S., Hirschman, J. E., Hepps, D., & Rudy, L. (1991). Children's memory for stressful events. *Merrill Palmer Quarterly, 37,* 109–158.

Goodman, G. S., Rudy, L., Bottoms, B., & Aman, C. (1990). Children's concerns and memory: Issues of ecological validity in the study of children's eyewitness testimony. In R. Fivush & J. Hudson (Eds.), *Knowing and remembering in young children* (pp. 249–284). New York: Cambridge University Press.

Hertel, P. (in press). Improving memory and mood through automatic and controlled procedures of mind. In D. Herrmann, H. Weingartner, A. Searleman, & C. McEvoy (Eds.), *Memory improvement: Implications for memory theory.* New York: Springer–Verlag.

Ikegami, T. (1986). The role of affect in person memory: The influence of positive and negative affect upon recognition memory. *Japanese Psychological Research, 28, (3),* 154–159.

Isen, A. M. (1985). The asymmetry of happiness and sadness in effects on memory in normal college students. *Journal of Experimental Psychology: General, 114,* 388–391.

Isen, A. M. (1987). Positive affect, cognitive processes, and social behavior. *Advances in Experimental Social Psychology, 20,* 203–253.

Isen, A. M. (1990). The influence of positive and negative affect on cognitive organization: Some implications for development. In N. Stein, B. Leventhal, & T. Trabasso (Eds.), *Psychological and biological approaches to emotion.* Hillsdale, NJ: Lawrence Erlbaum Associates.

Isen, A. M., & Daubman, K. (1984). The influence of affect on categorization. *Journal of Personality and Social Psychology, 47* (6), 1206–1217.

Isen, A. M., Daubman, K., & Nowicki, G. (1987). Positive affect facilitates creative problem solving. *Journal of Personality and Social Psychology, 52* (6), 1122–1131.

Isen, A. M., & Levin, P. F. (1972). Effect of feeling good on helping: Cookies and kindness. *Journal of Personality and Social Psychology, 21* (3), 384–388.

Isen, A. M., Means, B., Patrick, R., & Nowicki, G. (1982). Some factors influencing decision-making strategy and risk-taking. In M. S. Clark & S. T. Fiske (Eds.), *Affect and cognition: The 17th Annual Carnegie Symposium on Cognition* (pp. 243–261). Hillsdale, NJ: Lawrence Erlbaum Associates.

Isen, A. M., Shalker, T., Clark, M., & Karp, L. (1978). Affect, accessibility of in memory, and behavior: A cognitive loop? *Journal of Personality and Social Psychology, 36 (1),* 1–12.

Izard, C. E. (Ed.), (1989). The development of emotion-cognition relations. *Special Issue of Cognition and Emotion, 3,* 44–57.

Kail, R. (1990). *The development of memory in children.* San Francisco: W. H. Freeman.

Klatzky, R. (1980). *Human memory: Structures and processes.* San Francisco: W.H. Freeman.

Leventhal, H., & Tomarken, A. J. (1986). Emotion: Today's problems. *Annual Review of Psychology, 37,* 565–610.

Loftus, E. F., & Burns, T. (1982). Mental shock can produce reterograde amnesia. *Memory and Cognition, 10,* 318–323.

Nevin, P., Isen, A., & Winer, G. (1988). *The influence of positive affect on classification responses in children.* Unpublished manuscript. Cornell University.

Nisbett, R., & Ross, L. (1980). *Human inference; Strategies and shortcomings in social judgement.* Englewood Cliffs, NJ: Prentice-Hall.

Ornstein, P. A., Gordon, B. N., & Larus, D. M. (in press). Children's memory for a personally experienced event: Implications for testimony. *Applied Cognitive Psychology.*

Peters, D. (1991). The influence of stress and arousal on the child witness. In J. Doris (Ed.), *The suggestibility of children's recollections.* Washington, DC: American Psychological Association.

Posner, M. I., & Snyder, C. R. R. (1975). Attention and cognitive control. In R.L. Solso (Ed.), *Information processing and cognition: The Loyola Symposium.* Hillsdale, NJ: Lawrence Erlbaum Associates.

Schneider, W., & Weinert, F. E. (Eds.) (1990). *Interactions among aptitudes, strategies, and knowledge in cognitive performance.* New York: Springer–Verlag.

Stein, N., and Trabasso, T. (1991, April). *Children's and parent's memory for emotional events: Conditions for convergence or polarization.* Paper presented at The Biennial Meeting of the Society for Research in Child Development, Seattle.

Strongman, K. T., & Russell, P. N. (1986). Salience of emotion in recall. *Bulletin of the Psychonomic Society, 24,* 25–27.

Tulving, E., & Thomson, D. M. (1973). Encoding specificity and retrieval processes in episodic memory. *Psychological Review, 80,* 352–373.

Vandermaas, M. O. (1990). *The effects of anxiety on children's memory for dental procedures.* Unpublished doctoral dissertation, North Carolina State University, Raleigh.

Wagenaar, W. A., & Groeneweg, I. (1990). The memory of concentration camp survivors. *Applied Cognitive Psychology, 4,* 77–88.

Wundt, W. (1907). *Outlines of psychology.* Leipzig: Englemann.

8

A Model of the Diverse Effects of Emotion on Eyewitness Memory

John C. Yuille
Patricia A. Tollestrup
University of British Columbia

Eyewitness memory has been the principal research focus in forensic psychology (e.g., Saks, 1986). This interest in memory for witnessed events was manifest when psychology was still a new academic discipline. Several of the first generation of experimental psychologists published studies on the topic (e.g., Binet, 1900; Munsterberg, 1908; Stern, 1910). This early work had a characteristic tone of skepticism about the ability of witnesses to provide extensive and accurate accounts. Following swiftly upon the publication of the early studies, some psychologists claimed an important courtroom role for eyewitness research results (e.g., Munsterberg, 1908). They felt that the triers of fact should be alerted to the poor performance of witnesses in psychological studies. This initiated a debate about the applied value of psychological research that has continued to the present (e.g., Loftus, 1979; McCloskey & Egeth, 1983; Wigmore, 1909; Yuille & Wells, in press). This debate has had many facets, but a basic and contentious issue has been the extent to which research findings can be generalized to forensic contexts.

The primary reason for disagreement about generalizability resides in the nature of eyewitness research. For the last century most of the studies have had a typical form. Subject volunteers (or, less commonly, individuals who are not aware that they are participating in a study) witness a complex event. The event may be a theft or a violent act or a motor vehicle accident. The event is often presented via a recording (e.g., a set of slides, a film or video tape), or it may involve actors and be staged live. Whatever the medium, for obvious ethical reasons, the event is generally innocuous and has little ability to generate in witnesses much of any kind of physical involvement or strong emotional reaction. Thus, witnesses in laboratory research are essentially in the role of the uninvolved bystander; they are rarely direct participants in the to-be-remembered event, and they will not feel personal threat of the magnitude that a victim or witness to an actual crime such as a robbery is likely to feel. Here is the core of the issue of generalizability: To what extent is the memorial behavior of such aforementioned uninvolved bystanders representative of that of witnesses to actual crimes?

Many contemporary writers have provided an implicit or explicit answer to this question through their assertion that the research results are readily generalizable to a variety of forensic contexts. For example, Loftus (1979), in the most widely cited text in the field, argued persuasively that research findings provide a foundation for the understanding of eyewitnesses to all types of crimes (see also, Lloyd-Bostock & Clifford, 1983; Yarmey, 1979). The argument, put simply, is that memory for the complex events many real witnesses experience has the same basic characteristics as the memory of uninvolved witnesses in laboratory studies.

In this chapter we take issue with that argument and assert that the involvement and emotional response of a witness to an event is a central determinant of the subsequent memory for the event. Further, we suggest that the memorial consequences of an event that elicits a strong emotional response are complex and that this complexity can help us to resolve some of the apparent discrepancies in the literature concerning emotion and eyewitness memory.

THE IMPACT OF AN EVENT

Our focus in this chapter is on the role of emotions in eyewitness memory. However, we believe that the emotional response of a witness can best be understood in the context of the impact or consequences of the event for the person. We have chosen to use the term *impact of the event* to capture the breadth of our concern. By impact we mean the immediate consequences for the witness. Event impact is best conceptualized as a continuum such that the involvement of the threat of injury or death would place an event on the high end of the continuum and an event that involves no threat will be on the low end. Most laboratory studies fall at the low end of the impact continuum. A few (e.g., Christianson & Nilsson, 1984), while still relatively low threat, have succeeded in manipulating emotional response in the laboratory.

Typically, the intensity of the emotional response increases concurrently with the strength of the impact of an event. A threat of personal injury is likely to produce a strong emotion in the person threatened. However, the nature of the emotional response will vary from person to person. The same threat may produce anger in one person and fear in another. Indeed, a range of these different emotions may be produced successively in the same person such that anger follows fright. Also, a strong emotional response is not necessarily an immediate and inevitable consequence of an event of great impact. We explore the variety of responses to an event of impact in more detail later in this chapter.

The major consequence of an event of impact is increased arousal or stress. Generally, the stress response will mobilize physical and psychological resources to deal with the cause of the stress (i.e., flight or fight responses). We emphasize that most of the literature on arousal and eyewitness memory is not germane to this argument. Much of that research (e.g., Deffenbacher, 1983) has employed a source of stress such as white noise or electric shock, which is independent of what is to be remembered by the subject. This type of research is not an analogue of events of impact. The white noise is disassociated from what the laboratory witness must remember, whereas the source of stress in the event of impact is exactly what the witness will later be asked to recall. Other paradigms to examine the effects of stress on eyewitness testimony such as testing subjects memory for a film containing violence (e.g., Clifford & Hollin, 1981; Clifford & Scott, 1978) or live staged events (e.g., Leippe, Wells, & Ostrom, 1978) generally do not contain the dimension of event impact. If the impact of an event is of little consequence in terms of memory for that event, then the results from studies employing these paradigms are readily generalizable to real witnesses. If however, as we believe, the impact of an event does have an effect on memory, then we must be cautious in applying these findings to real witnesses.

Before we elaborate on the memorial consequences of events of impact, we evaluate the role of most of the existing eyewitness research in assisting the understanding of the relationship between emotion and memory.

HOW TYPICAL IS THE
UNAFFECTED BYSTANDER?

As noted earlier, psychologists have devoted most of their research efforts to the study of uninvolved bystanders. There are two components of the typical laboratory witness: being on the low end of the impact dimension and being a passive observer of the event. Obviously, the first part implies witnessing events that have low impact. Apart from witnessing minor traffic accidents, or incidents of fraud, most crimes are quite likely to have an impact on anyone who is either directly involved or who sees them being committed. Thus it is relatively easy to say that most actual witnesses are not unaffected and in this sense are different from laboratory witnesses. It is slightly more complicated to determine if the second component, being a bystander, applies to actual witnesses of crime.

The archival research reported by Yuille (1986) and the field study reported by Yuille and Cutshall (1986) bring evidence to demonstrate that real witnesses are typically not unaffected and generally are not bystanders. Briefly, the archival study (Yuille, 1986) involved assessing base rates for various crimes of violence such as homicide, robbery, and sexual and nonsexual assaults. The files of the Burnaby British Columbia Royal Canadian Mounted Police detachment were used as the data source. All reported crimes for 1 year were examined in this suburb of Vancouver. A representative sample of cases within each crime type was examined in detail to determine characteristics, such as the involvement of witnesses and various demographic aspects of both witnesses and suspects.

Table 8.1 presents an overview of the incidence rates determined from the representative sample of cases for different types of of-

TABLE 8.1
Nature of Witnesses per Crime Type

	Number of cases examined	Victim as only witness	Number of Nonvictim Witnesses		
			1	2 to 4	5
Homicide	6	--	1	--	1
Att. Murder	8	4	--	4	--
N-S Assault	368	247	57	56	8
Sex. Assault	95	92	1	2	--
Robbery	149	97	19	26	7
Totals	626	440	78	88	16

*Four out of the 6 homicide cases had no witnesses, 1 case had a single witness, and 1 case had 16 witnesses.

fences. Note that for crimes directly witnessed (robbery, sexual, and nonsexual assaults) 71% of the cases involved the victim as the only witness. Thus, the modal witness to a crime of violence is not a passive observer but rather a victim of that crime.

Table 8.2 presents data on the relationships amongst the accused, the victim, and other witnesses. When other witnesses are present they usually are acquaintances of either the offender or the victim or both. Robbery is the only type of crime which occurs with any regularity that involves witnesses who are not directly victimized and are not known to the participants. Of course, even in the case of a robbery the bystander witness may feel that the event was one of impact especially if a weapon or some other form of threat was used.

TABLE 8.2
Relationships of Witnesses

| | Victims | | | Witnesses | | | | | |
| | Victim Acquainted with Accussed | | | Nonvictim Acquainted with Victim | | | Nonvictim Acquainted with Accused | | |
	Yes	No	N/A	Yes	No	N/A	Yes	No	N/A
Homocide	1	--	--	20	--	--	17	--	--
Att. Murder	4	4	--	9	1	1	2	9	--
N-S Assualt	263	134	6	150	63	20	107	103	23
Sex. Assault	57	42	--	7	2	--	3	6	--
Robbery	5	167	--	74	54	--	3	125	--
Totals	330	347	6	257	120	21	132	243	23

These patterns of reported crimes demonstrate that the uninvolved bystander is a relatively rare type of witness in the forensic context. As noted earlier, the one exception to this may be those who witness minor automobile accidents. However, writers who have readily generalized research findings to the real world have never restricted themselves to that context. Thus the issue of generalizability from psychological research to witnesses of actual crimes is not trivial. Psychologists have focused on the study of a type of witness who is relatively uncommon. If the unaffected bystander is unusual, does his or her memory differ from the more typical victim or other affected witness? This returns us to the issue of the effect of event impact.

EVENT IMPACT AND FLASHBULB MEMORIES

For over a decade, psychologists have reported a variety of studies of flashbulb memories. The term was coined by Brown and Kulik (1977) to label events that are emotionally arousing or surprising or consequential for the individual. Initially, it was believed that flashbulb events led to detailed and vivid memories. However, more recent reports have raised doubts about the accuracy of flashbulb memories (e.g., Christianson, 1990; McCloskey, Wible, & Cohen, 1988). However, this debate is not of direct relevance to the current argument. The research on flashbulb memories has concentrated on individual memory for what a person was doing when he/she first learned of some historic event. For example, the studies have looked at people's memories on hearing of the assassinations of Lincoln (Colegrove, 1899), of Kennedy (Brown & Kulik, 1977), of Swedish Prime Minister Olof Palme (Christianson, 1989), and of the attempted assassination of Reagan (Pillemer, 1984). These events were important in the lives of those who learned about them. However, the researchers were studying people's memories for what they were doing when they learned about the event. The relationship between the memory and the event is indirect: The event served as a marker. Our concern here is the memories of individuals for the event of impact itself, not something that the event simply marks. Thus, we are not concerned here with flashbulb memories or the controversies surrounding them. We are concerned with the ability of people to remember the details of an event that they directly witnessed and that had immediate and direct impact upon them.

RESEARCH ON MEMORY
FOR EVENTS OF IMPACT

Reflecting the preoccupation of researchers with the unaffected bystander, it is not surprising that only a handful of studies on events of impact have been reported. The major reason for the lack of studies may be the difficulty involved in designing an experimental event that is sufficient to induce emotional impact and also obtain ethical approval. A researcher cannot stage an event that will threaten a subject's property or physical and mental well-being. Thus, analogue studies are ethically precluded. The only way to study memory for events of impact is to study such events as they naturally occur. However, such research is afflicted with a number of inherent obstacles and problems. Obtaining the cooperation of police forces (for access to such cases) and from the witnesses themselves is time consuming and problematic (see Yuille & Cutshall, 1986). Also, it is often difficult or impossible to verify the accuracy of eyewitness accounts.

We wish to emphasize that we are not precluding the value of laboratory research. Rather we are emphasizing that the generalizability of findings from one context to another is an empirical question. We can only know if laboratory results are generalizable if we have field study results to which we can compare them. There is no substitute, for comparison purposes, except the study of the events of impact themselves. What is required is the use of multiple methods (field studies, archival studies, experimental studies, etc.) to assure a comprehensive examination of any particular issue (e.g., Davies, 1990). Our prime concern in the present context is the degree to which the need for archival and field studies has been ignored.

The field studies that have been reported fall into two general areas: (a) studies of the memory of witnesses to major crimes (usually through police file access); and (b) individual case studies of the memory of a victim or perpetrator.

FIELD RESEARCH FROM POLICE FILES

This type of work was initiated in 1983. The general procedure that was first employed involved the examination of police files for cases involving multiple witnesses. The first case studied involved a shooting incident between a thief and the owner of the gun store the thief had robbed. Both men shot each other, and 23 witnesses observed various parts of the event. Each witness was interviewed by the police within 1 hour of the event. The researchers (Yuille & Cutshall, 1986) were able to contact and secure cooperation from 13 of the witnesses. Each witness was interviewed by the researchers 5 or 6 months after the event. The detail and accuracy of the witnesses was determined for both the police interview and the interview several months later. In some respects the memory of the witnesses showed characteristics similar to those displayed by the uninvolved bystander usually studied in research. However, in several important respects there were differences. The "real" witnesses showed little loss of detail or accuracy over the 5- to 6-month retention interval. This contrasts with the usual claim that witnesses show the typical Ebbinghaus forgetting curve, with a relatively rapid loss of information with time (e.g., Loftus, 1979). In addition, and more germane to the present topic, those witnesses who appeared to have been more stressed by the event did not show any less accurate or detailed memory. This contrasted with the frequent assertion that stress interferes with eyewitness memory (e.g., Yarmey, 1979).

This type of field study has been conducted with several actual witnesses to criminal events. The witnesses were sometimes only bystanders but were never unaffected by the event. They often felt threatened and traumatized. The results of five additional case studies with multiple witnesses (Cutshall & Yuille, 1989) showed the same pattern as the original Yuille and Cutshall (1986) study. A study of 10 additional police cases in which forensic hypnosis was used (Yuille & Kim, 1987) provided additional support.

More recently, Fisher, Geiselman, and Amador (1989) reported a similar type of field study conducted with the Miami, Dade County Police Department. They found the same type of performance in real witnesses as Yuille and his colleagues, and they concluded that: "If this difference between laboratory and field studies continues to appear, one may question the validity of describing in court the accuracy rates found in the laboratory as evidence of the general unreliability of eyewitness testimony in field cases" (p. 725).

Although the number of field studies are still few, relative to the number of laboratory studies, the pattern of their results is consistent. There do appear to be reliable differences between the uninvolved bystander witness of the laboratory and the real witness to an event of impact. The differences include the fact that the real witnesses appear to often recall more details, often have a high level of accuracy, and often show little loss of either detail or accuracy with the passage of time. Thus, in terms of our initial question, concerning the representativeness of the behavior of the uninvolved bystander, the answer appears to be negative. The uninvolved bystander is not a common witness of real crimes and his or her memorial behavior is not the same as the affected witness of a real crime.

Not only does this field research raise doubts about the representativeness of the witness that psychologists have devoted so much time and effort to study. The results of these field studies bear, at least indirectly, on the issue of the relationship between emotion and memory. It is reasonable to assume that, in general, many more real witnesses have experienced some emotional impact in observing the event than the subjects of most laboratory-style research. If emotional responses simply had a negative impact on eyewitness memory, the field research should have revealed poorer performance of real witnesses compared to the laboratory subjects. If anything, the pattern of results has been the reverse, the real witnesses have performed at least as well and often better than the psychological literature would lead one to expect. The field research indicates that an emotional response to an event probably does not simply reduce memory for the event.

INDIVIDUAL CASE STUDIES

The few case studies of real memory for crimes complicate the conclusion drawn from the field studies. The case studies have involved the study of an individual's memory for a crime. A few of these studies have examined the memory of a victim, others have looked at the memory of the perpetrator.

The case study of a victim's memory for a traumatic crime is represented by an examination of a woman's recall of a sexual assault by Christianson and Nilsson (1989). The victim showed an inability to recall any details of the event for a period of months after the attack. Eventually she recovered most of the details, especially of the core of the event. This pattern of lack of recall reflects one possible consequence of an event of personal impact: a temporary loss of memory. However, some victims never regain their memory for a traumatic event.

The study of the memory of criminals for their crimes also contributes to our understanding of the complexity of the effect of event impact on memory. First, murderers report a high rate of amnesia for their crime. Schacter (1986) indicated that 40% of murderers said that they could not remember the murder. Although some of this amnesia may be self-serving and malingered, some circumstances suggest that such amnesia can be real. For example, after completing her jail sentence and in spite of repeated efforts to recall the stabbings, a woman who murdered two successive husbands was unable to recall the murders, although her memory for the events before and after the incidents was intact (MacDonald & Gould, 1987).

In contrast to the preceding, memory for the act of murder can sometimes be vivid and detailed. For example, many serial murderers have detailed memories for their acts (e.g., Michaud & Aynesworth, 1989). It is not the nature of the act itself that affects the memory of the perpetrator as much as the meaning of the act (this points again to the complexity of defining the impact of an event). For the serial murderer the act may be an attempt to fulfill a fantasy. The act must be remembered so that it can be compared to the fantasy and serve the offender's need to act out his pathology. In this instance, even if the offender is stressed, his memory for the crime may be excellent.

In summary, field studies and individual case studies indicate that the characteristics of memories of real witnesses to events of impact can range from accurate, detailed memories that show little loss over time to virtually no memory at all for the event. In the next section we outline an explanation for the variety of effects of events of impact.

EVENT IMPACT AND
REMARKABLE MEMORIES

How can the various memorial responses to the events of impact described in the field and individual case studies be reconciled? In turn, what is the relationship between memory for those events and the memory of the uninvolved bystander? Figure 8.1 illustrates a model that we propose to account for the various memory patterns of eyewitnesses. The model focuses on the effects of event impact on the storage, maintenance, and retrieval phases of memory.

An event may or may not have a perceived impact on the witness but, as outlined earlier, most real-world criminal events are events of impact. The stress inherent in witnessing an event of impact such as a violent crime will result in witnesses focusing their attention more narrowly (Easterbrook, 1959). This narrowing of focus can be directed in one of two general directions, each of which has very different memorial consequences.

Should the witness direct their focus internally, he/she will likely not store many core details of the incident. Internal focus can be of two types. The witness might be preoccupied with his or her own emotional response to the event such as fear, hatred, or rage. Such a witness will have little memory for the event and instead will claim to have been "too scared" or "too angry," and that this is what they recall about the event. Alternatively, the witness could focus on some psychological response to threat such as mentally projecting or imaging oneself elsewhere. Whatever the form, an internally focused individual would be expected to store very limited information about the event they witnessed and rather have more prominent memories of their internal response to the event.

If the witness focuses externally, on the event itself, he/she will likely store core details at the expense of peripheral details. We refer to core details as those that represent the witness's central thematic elements. In the case of multiple witnesses, unanimity as to the core details is not expected. Further, we do not expect any necessary correlation between what police consider to be relevant information

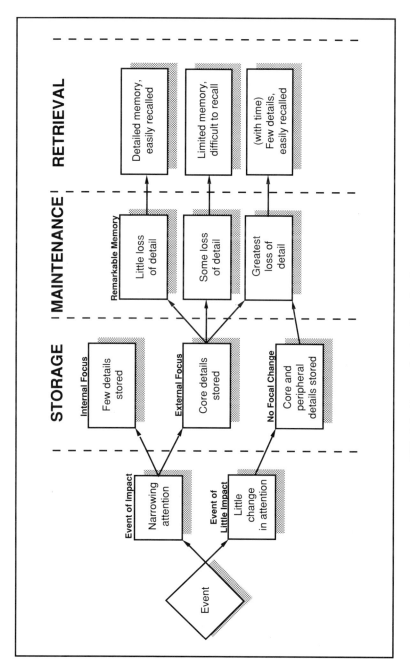

FIG. 8.1   Remembering Details of an Event.

211

to the solution of a crime and what any individual witness attends to during the course of witnessing that crime. Fortunately, there will likely be considerable overlap within those core details on which witnesses focus and those details that aid in the investigation of the event.

This narrowing of attentional focus is not expected during events of little or no impact. In this case, reflecting the less narrow focus of attention, both core and peripheral details should be stored. Thus far, we have suggested that there can be varying amounts of core and peripheral information stored as a function of event impact. Note that real witnesses will store either few details (internal focus) or core details (external focus), whereas uninvolved bystanders will store both core and peripheral details.

Cutshall and Yuille (1989) proposed the concept of a remarkable memory as one that the witness frequently repeats either to him/herself and to others. Most, but not all, events of impact will be remarkable. Consider a witness who observes a distinct event of impact such as a robbery or assault. The memory for such an event will be maintained by rehearsal as the witness thinks about it and remarks about the experience to significant others. The consequence of such retrieval practice will be the maintenance of the stored information. There will be little or no loss of information over time.

If an event such as that in the typical lab experiment is not remarkable, the stored information will not be rehearsed. This will result in loss of information over time (i.e., Ebbinghaus forgetting curve). Thus the maintenance and subsequent availability of such a memory will be poorer than that of a remarkable memory. In other words, without the enhancing features present in a remarkable event of impact, eyewitness memory will be much like everyday memory and follow a pattern of "normal" forgetting.

Of course, there is the possibility that despite adequate storage of core details the event was so traumatic and painful to recall that the witness shows psychogenic amnesia for a limited period of time after the event as in the case of rape reported by Christianson and Nilsson (1989). The inability of witnesses to recall the event should have a negative impact on the maintenance of detail. Thus there should be a loss of some detail with the passage of time.

The model summarizes four possible outcomes to the retrieval of an event. First, the witness whose focus was internalized during the course of the event will have few if any details available in memory and will only recall her or his internal state. Thus, for this type of witness, the figure does not detail the flow of information about the event in the maintenance and retrieval stages. Second, the witness who saw an event of impact and remarked on it will have a detailed and easily accessible memory for the core details. These details will vary as a function of the thematic interpretation given to the event by the witness. Third, the traumatized victim will recall few if any details. If the trauma can be relieved, access to the memory of the event would become possible. The delay of the removal of the trauma will decrease the available details. Finally, the uninvolved bystander will show progressive loss of information with the passage of time. It is possible that this memorial outcome could also be demonstrated by a witness to an event of impact whose attention was externally focused because of a failure to maintain the details of the event by rehearsal.

There are two other possible retrieval outcomes that the model does not detail. First, an experimenter could induce a remarkable event of no impact by repeatedly asking uninvolved bystanders to recall an event. This should lead to detailed recall of both core and peripheral aspects of the event with little loss of information over time. We have not included this possibility in Fig. 8.1 because the focus of this chapter is on emotion and its effects on memory. The final factor that could affect retrieval is state-dependent processes (Eich, 1980). Some murderers may be in such a different psychological state at the time of the murder that they are unable to recall the details of the crime. For example, murder committed as an act of passion, in a family dispute for example, may not fit with the normal psychological pattern of the attacker. Recall becomes more difficult as the disparity between the states at the time of the event and at the time of recall increases. State-dependency effects are probably not limited to perpetrators of crime; they may also be a factor in some victim's inability to recall.

CONCLUDING REMARKS

How does emotion affect eyewitness memory? Our conclusion is that it depends on the nature of the event, the response of the witness to the event, and the subsequent factors affecting memory maintenance and retrieval. Generally, an emotional response will occur to an event of impact. Some witnesses will internalize their attention in the presence of a strong emotion, others will direct their attention externally. The type of attentional response determines what is stored. Regardless of the contents in storage, the maintenance of the information will be affected by how often the witness retrieves the event. The nature of events of impact is such that witnesses to them are likely to remark on their experience to themselves and others, which leads to a durable memory. Events that are low on the impact dimension are not likely to be maintained by being remarked upon. Thus, memories for these kinds of events will not be as durable as those for remarkable events of impact. Highly emotional events, especially those causing trauma, will also be less likely to form remarkable experiences, and this will negatively affect maintenance. Both what is stored and how it is maintained affect retrieval. Finally, state dependency may affect retrieval.

Unfortunately, although real witnesses typically observe events of impact, researchers have devoted little attention or concern to them. Instead the uninvolved bystander, who is not typical of real witnesses and whose memory follows a different pattern, has been the main focus of psychological research. We hope this changes.

ACKNOWLEDGMENTS

The preparation of this chapter was supported by a grant to the first author from the National Science and Engineering Research Council of Canada. The authors wish to thank the editor and Elizabeth Loftus for their useful comments.

REFERENCES

Binet, A. (1900). *La suggestibilite*. Paris: Schleicher Freres.

Brown, R., & Kulik, J. (1977). Flashbulb memories. *Cognition*, *5*, 73–99.

Christianson, S.-Å. (l989). Flashbulb memories: Special, but not so special. *Memory and Cognition*, *17*, 435–443.

Christianson, S.-Å., & Nilsson, L.-G. (1984). Functional amnesia as induced by a psychological trauma. *Memory & Cognition*, *12*, 142–155.

Christianson, S.-Å., & Nilsson, L.-G. (1989). Hysterical Amnesia: A case of aversively motivated isolation of memory. In T. Archer & L.-G. Nilsson (Eds.), *Aversion, avoidance and anxiety* (pp. 289–310). Hillsdale, NJ: Lawrence Erlbaum Associates.

Clifford, B. R., & Hollin, C. (1981). Effects of type of incident and the number of perpetrators on eyewitness memory. *Journal of Applied Psychology*, *66*, 364–370.

Clifford, B. R., & Scott, J. (1978). Individual and situational factors in eyewitness testimony. *Journal of Applied Psychology*, *63*, 352–359.

Colegrove, F. W. (1899). Individual memories. *American Journal of Psychology*, *10*, 228–255.

Cutshall, J. L., & Yuille, J. C. (1989). Field studies of eyewitness memory of actual crimes. In D. C. Raskin (Ed.), *Psychological methods in criminal investigation and evidence* (pp. 97–124). New York: Springer.

Davies, G. (1990, Sept). *Influencing public policy on eyewitnessing: Problems and possibilities.* Paper presented at the 2nd European Conference on Law and Psychology, Nurenburg, Germany.

Deffenbacher, K. A. (1983). The influence of arousal on reliability of testimony. In S. M. A. Lloyd-Bostock & B. R. Clifford (Eds.), *Evaluating witness evidence* (pp. 235–251). New York: Wiley.

Easterbrook, J. A. (1959). The effect of emotion on cue utilization and the organization of behavior. *Psychological Review, 66,* 183–201.

Eich, J. E., (1980). The cue-dependent nature of state-dependent retrieval. *Memory & Cognition, 8,* 157–173.

Fisher, R. P., Geiselman, R. E., & Amador, M. (1989). Field test of the cognitive interview: Enhancing the recollection of actual victims and witnesses of crime. *Journal of Applied Psychology, 74*(5), 722–727.

Leippe, M. R., Wells, G. L., & Ostrom, T. M. (1978). Crime seriousness as a determinant of accuracy in eyewitness identification. *Journal of Applied Psychology, 63,* 345–351.

Lloyd-Bostock, S. M., & Clifford, B. R. (Eds.). (1983). *Evaluating witness evidence.* New York: Wiley.

Loftus, E. F. (1979). *Eyewitness testimony.* Cambridge, MA: Harvard University Press.

MacDonald, M., & Gould, A. (1987). *The violent years of Maggie MacDonald.* Scarborough, Ontario: Prentice–Hall.

McCloskey, M., & Egeth, H. E. (1983). Eyewitness identification: What can a psychologist tell a jury? *American Psychologist, 38,* 550–577.

McCloskey, M., Wible, C. G., & Cohen, N. J. (1988). Is there a special flashbulb-memory mechanism? *Journal of Experimental Psychology: General, 117*(2), 171–181.

Michaud, S. G., & Aynesworth, H. (1989). *Ted Bundy: Conversations with a killer.* New York: Signet.

Munsterberg, H. (1908). *On the witness stand: Essays on psychology and crime.* New York: Clark, Boardman, Doubleday.

Pillemer, D. B. (1984). Flashbulb memories of the assassination attempt on President Reagan. *Cognition, 16,* 63–80.

Saks, M. J. (1986). The law does not live by eyewitness testimony alone. *Law and Human Behavior, 10*(4), 279–280.

Schacter, D. L. (1986). Amnesia and crime: How much do we really know? *American Psychologist, 41*(3), 286–295.

Stern, L. W. (1910). Abstracts of lectures in the psychology of testimony and on the study of individuality. *American Journal of Psychology, 21,* 270–282.

Wigmore, J. (1909). The psychology of testimony. *Illinois Law Review, 3,* 399–445.

Yarmey, A. D., (1979). *The psychology of eyewitness testimony.* New York: The Free Press.

Yuille, J. C. (1986). Meaningful research in the police context. In J. C. Yuille (Ed.), *Police selection and training* (pp. 225–243). Dordrecht, The Netherlands: Martinus Nijhoff.

Yuille, J. C., & Cutshall, J. L. (1986). A case study of eyewitness memory of a crime. *Journal of Applied Psychology, 71*(2), 291–301.

Yuille, J. C., & Kim, C. K. (1987). A field study of the forensic use of hypnosis. *Canadian Journal of Behavioral Sciences Review, 19*(4), 418–429.

Yuille, J. C., & Wells, G. L. (in press). Concerns about the application of research findings: The issue of ecological validity. In J. L. Doris (Ed.), *The suggestibility of children's memory.*

9

Eyewitness Memory for Stressful Events: Methodological Quandaries and Ethical Dilemmas

Sven-Åke Christianson
University of Stockholm, Sweden

Jane Goodman
Elizabeth F. Loftus
University of Washington, Seattle

This chapter explores research methodology and ethical issues related to eyewitness memory for stressful events. Past and current approaches to the study of emotion and memory are summarized and inadequacies in past research are highlighted. Because of the diversity of research methods used, and the lack of uniformity of the phenomena studied, we present some distinctions that we hope are helpful in interpreting past findings and in guiding future research on memory for stressful events.

Our point of departure is the assassination of the Swedish Prime Minister, Olof Palme, and the subsequent trial against the accused murderer, Christer Pettersson, who was positively identified by Mrs. Palme 2 years after the assassination. Two psychologists testified as expert witnesses at the trial, offering their views on perception and memory to help the jury evaluate Mrs. Palme's testimony. We use this case and the content of the expert psychological testimonies as a springboard to discuss the use of research findings on emotion and memory in a legal context. In addition, we discuss ethical issues facing psychologists who are asked to provide this type of expert testimony.

THE MURDER OF OLOF PALME

Prime Minister Palme was gunned down on the evening of February 28, 1986, as he and his wife, Lisbeth Palme, began walking home from a movie theater in downtown Stockholm. In the course of an initial police interview the day after the murder, Mrs. Palme stated that she and her husband left their home at 8:40 p.m. to meet their son and his girlfriend at the "Grand" movie theater on Sveavägen, to see a movie starting at 9:00 p.m. After the movie, the four of them walked south on Sveavägen. They paused in front of a well-lit store window, so Prime Minister Palme could check on something noted in the movie program. After a few minutes of discussion, the son and his girlfriend left, and the Palmes decided to go window shopping on the other side of the street. They walked arm-in-arm, with Mrs. Palme on the curb side. Mrs. Palme stated that she did not recognize anyone who passed by as they walked, nor did she notice anyone following them. She admitted that she usually narrows her visual field when out walking with her husband to avoid the curious gazes from passers-by.

When Mr. and Mrs. Palme reached the corner of Tunnelgatan-Sveavägen, a few hundred meters away, Mrs. Palme heard some sudden "bangs," probably two. The noise seemed to originate close by. She thought some youngsters must be playing with fireworks and turned to her husband to remark on this. At this moment, Prime Minister Palme faltered and collapsed to the sidewalk, bleeding heavily from his chest and mouth. Mrs. Palme heard a final bang and felt her back burning. Diagonally, from the rear, she saw a man standing at the corner start running down Tunnelgatan. He stopped, turned around, then started running again. She did not see anyone else. Mrs. Palme screamed for help, and within moments several people came to her aid.

Mrs. Palme described the gunman as a man in his 40s, about 180 cm tall, with a compact body. His complexion was dark, but not clearly south European—"his hair was more brownish." He was dressed in a blue somewhat heavy quilted jacket, which reached just below his waist. He wore dark trousers, probably grey. In response to questions during the first police interview, Mrs. Palme noted nothing further about his clothing or appearance. According to the police file, Mrs. Palme was in a state of profound shock after the murder and had difficulties answering questions.

In a second police interview about 1 month later (March 25, 1986), Mrs. Palme reported that after her husband fell to the ground she looked up and saw a man standing 10–15 meters away at the corner of Tunnelgatan (interestingly, in a subsequent interview in 1989, this distance was recalled by Mrs. Palme as 5–7 meters away). She described the man as being in his 40s, about 180 cm. tall, with intense staring eyes, thin, light lips, a flat upper lip, a flat forehead and straight eyebrows, a square face with a prominent jaw and pock-marked cheeks. She described his build as broad with somewhat lifted shoulders, although he was not "big," and said he had a short neck. When she saw him running, he gave a vigorous impression. She did not notice whether he was carrying anything. The man did not say anything in the course of the event. She claimed that she was very observant at that time because she was looking for help from someone.

Two years and 10 months after the assassination (December 14, 1988), Mrs. Palme saw a videotaped lineup, consisting of 12 men, including the man accused of murdering the Prime Minister Palme. As the lineup tape began to play, Mrs. Palme picked out the suspect (Christer Pettersson) without any hesitation, saying: "It is easy to see who is an alcoholic, it's number 8, but it's not only that . . ." After reviewing the entire lineup tape, which included sequential individual presentations of the participants, she stated that number 8 fit her description with respect to ". . . the shape of his face, the eyes, and his nasty appearance." Mrs. Palme also commented that she did not recall that the murderer had a mustache. Number 8 had no mustache at the time of the crime.

The Trial

The trial of Pettersson began in June, 1989, before a jury composed of both laypeople and legal experts. Mrs. Palme was the major prosecution witness, and she positively identified Petterson as the murderer. The defense called a psychologist to testify about factors that affect the reliability of eyewitness accounts. The defendant was convicted despite this testimony, and he appealed. A higher court heard the case de novo. This time, both the defense and the prosecution called psychological experts.

The defense expert provided a nine-page written position statement plus oral testimony in which she explained that she applied "formal structure analysis," a method of analyzing a witness' verbal statements of past events. According to the defense expert, the use of statistically confirmed generalizations alone cannot help us reveal the facts of individual cases; rather it is the verbal statements that are of conclusive importance and that should be evaluated by a person well trained and experienced in applying the methodology of "Formal Structure Analysis" (see Trankell, 1963). Because there were no actual recordings (audio or video) of Mrs. Palme's initial statements, the expert could not fully apply her usual method of analysis. She could only comment on the increasingly detailed nature of the subsequent descriptions provided, which seemed to the expert to incorporate new information from the media and other sources.

The defense expert emphasized circumstances inherent in the case that could negatively affect the accuracy of the witness account. Among these were the poor lighting conditions, the brief duration of the incident, the traumatic nature of the incident, the fact that the assailant was a stranger, the extraordinary long lapse of time before any identification, the structure of the lineup, and the potential impact of media information on recollections.

The defense expert pointed out that at the lineup Mrs. Palme stated that it was easy to see who was "the alcoholic"—and picked Pettersson, suggesting that Mrs. Palme was relying upon information gained from other sources than her own memory. The expert was also concerned that Mrs. Palme had been shown the sequence in the videotape depicting the major suspect several times in succession, potentially increasing her confidence in her identification by the time of trial. Little in the way of scientific information was explicitly provided as a basis for the expert's opinions. The expert seemed to rely most heavily on the Devlin Report (extracted in her statement from a secondary source; Loftus, 1979).[1] In conclusion, the defense expert outlined the steps by which Mrs. Palme created in her mind a memory for the face of Pettersson, and how she arrived at the conviction that he was the murderer.

In rebuttal, the prosecution called an expert to respond to 10 specific questions on memory in general and on factors affecting the accuracy of eyewitness memory. He did so in a 16-page written reply and orally. The prosecution witness made clear that he had no intention to comment on Mrs. Palme's statements and identifications. He saw as his task to answer those questions he was asked on the basis of findings available in published research. He also made clear that the defense expert based her conclusions about the case on ill-founded speculations. On some topics, the opinions of the experts

---

[1]The Devlin Report was a product of a British committee convened during the 1970s to examine cases of wrongful conviction. The committee expressed reservations about the accuracy of convictions based upon eyewitness testimony alone and recommended that a statute be devised to direct the trier of fact that it is not reliable to convict upon eyewitness testimony evidence unless the circumstances are exceptional or the evidence is corroborated by information from another source.

differed. Contrary to the defense expert's view that stressful events reduce accuracy, the prosecution expert's view was that central details of stressful events are generally well retained, and typically not susceptible to postevent suggestion. Although he acknowledged that exposure time is critical for memory, his view was that the negative effect of short exposures can be mitigated by repeated exposures and short "pauses" following each exposure. The prosecution expert also acknowledged that, although exposure to postevent information (e.g., media coverage) can affect recollection, the right retrieval cues can often lead to successful recoveries of memory because of mechanisms such as "state-dependent learning" and "encoding specificity." The prosecution expert, in response to specific questions, claimed that empirical evidence in memory research certainly supports a notion that central information can be maintained in memory over long periods even if exposure times have been short and the situation has been stressful or traumatic.

At the second trial, although there were other witnesses who identified the defendant as the murderer, the prosecution's case depended primarily on Mrs. Palme's identification of the suspect. Apparently, the Devlin report was accorded considerable weight relative to other kinds of evidence and research findings, and the jury determined that Mrs. Palme might have been mistaken or perjured in her identification of the defendant. Thus the second jury acquitted Pettersson on the basis that no technical evidence had been presented that could relate him to the crime. The reaction in the Swedish community to the participation of psychologists in the trial was negative. "Let's forget the memory psychologists," the media blared. Many people believed that the "battle of the experts" was not helpful.

Is the Palme case typical? In many ways it is not. The victim was a highly public popular figure, and the case received massive publicity and attention. Nevertheless, the case provides the perfect springboard for discussing a variety of questions. One important question is the type of research that can legitimately inform us about memory for stressful events.

RESEARCH ON MEMORY FOR TRAUMATIC EVENTS

For someone who has never witnessed a traumatic event such as a murder, it is difficult to imagine such an experience, let alone what it might be like to remember that experience later on. What is the nature of highly stressful or traumatic memories? Which aspects do we focus on, and which do we retain? Mrs Palme presumably focused on her bleeding husband and perhaps on the man running from the scene of crime. Real-world recollections such as these are hard to verify, so they present a challenge to psychological researchers to devise systematic ways to study memory for traumatic events.

Clinical Assessments

The study of memory for traumatic events has been approached in a variety of ways. Freud's psychoanalytical approach assumed that people banish unacceptable and anxiety-provoking memories from consciousness to avoid emotional confrontation. Based upon his clinical work with hysterical patients, Freud proposed that patients are occasionally confronted with thoughts that, for a variety of moral and other reasons, are very painful. Accordingly, these thoughts are simply repressed (e.g., Breuer & Freud, 1895; Erdelyi & Goldberg, 1979; Freud, 1915; Nemiah, 1979). This approach is not particularly satisfying for a number of reasons. First, Freud's "data" included in-depth analyses with a collection of patients whose actual life experiences can never be precisely known. Thus, we can never know what memories, if any, are or are not being repressed. Nor can we know the accuracy of what is recalled. Second, invoking the concept of repression provides no explanation for the fact that some details from traumatic events are retained quite well.

Field Studies

A second method to the study of memory for highly emotional or traumatic events is to study victims of traumatic events. Kuehn (1974) took this approach when he analyzed data from police reports, concentrating specifically on the capability of victims of violent crimes to provide descriptions of those crimes to the police. Based upon the reports of victims of 2 homicides (the victims lived long enough to provide some information), 22 rapes, 15 assaults, and 61 robberies, Kuehn reached several conclusions. He found that victims of robberies provided fuller descriptions than did victims of rape or assault. Injured victims, no matter what the type of crime, provided less information than did noninjured victims. Thus, if anything, more information was retained in the case of the less serious crimes. With respect to the assailant, most victims could identify the gender of their assailant (93%). Only rarely could they describe the assailant's eye color (23% did so). Other traits of the assailant that were described in more than 70% of the cases, in this order of frequency, were: age, height, build, race, weight, complexion. Kuehn concluded that gross physical characteristics like gender, build, or height were more frequently identified than hair color or eye color. Kuehn (1974) cautioned his readers about the meaning of these findings in clear language: "The reader should note that completeness of description may indicate perceptual recall but this may not be accurate" (p. 1161).

A variation of this approach was adopted by Yuille and Cutshall (1986), who interviewed 13 out of 22 actual witnesses to a murder about 4–5 months after the event occurred. All witnesses had provided information to the police within 2 days of the murder. The authors reported that these witnesses had a high degree of accurate recall, with little apparent decline over the retention interval. However, some aspects of color memory and estimates of age, height, and weight were erroneous. The authors postulated that stress level at the time of the event did not appear to affect memory negatively, although stress was not measured objectively, and self-reported stress was confounded with variables such as physical distance of the observer from the crime. This study provides some useful information but has obvious limitations. Accurate recall for some details cannot be assessed because we do not know what actually happened. Given what we know about commitment effects and social pressure, consistency among witnesses, or between two versions from the same witness is no adequate guarantee of accuracy. For some details (e.g., colors of clothing), some assessments of recall accuracy can be made based on photographs taken at the scene. These data might permit some determination of the effects of emotional stress on accuracy. However, in this case we have only a single stressful event, and no "neutral" event with which to compare it. Even when witnesses are grouped based on self-reports as to who was more or less emotionally aroused by this evocative event, level of emotional stress remains confounded with other variables, such as vantage point, motivations for cooperation, etc. Thus, no full interpretation of the findings is possible (Goodman & Loftus, 1989).

A further variation on the witness interview approach is the study of so-called *flashbulb memories* (Brown & Kulik, 1977). The term refers to the hypothesis that a person who experiences a traumatic newsworthy event (e.g., hearing about an assassination of one's national leader) often "remembers" in great detail the exact circumstances in which that unpleasant news was acquired. Whereas it is clear that people remember these kinds of events better than they do ordinary events that occurred equally long ago, by no means are these flashbulb memories completely accurate (e.g., Christianson, 1989; McCloskey, Wible, & Cohen, 1988; Neisser, 1982, see also Winograde & Neisser, 1992). One problem that pervades this line of research is validation. Usually we do not know for sure what the original circumstances were, but only what the individual claims them to be.

Laboratory Studies

To circumvent the difficulties associated with field/interview studies of highly emotional memories, some researchers have used a simulation approach (see Christianson, 1992; Deffenbacher, 1983, for reviews). Commonly, laboratory studies on memory for emotional events include two conditions: a neutral condition and an emotional condition. For example, in studies by Clifford and Scott (1978) and Loftus and Burns (1982), subjects viewed a film of either a violent or a nonviolent event and were subsequently tested for memory of specific details. Both studies showed that recall of details was significantly worse among subjects who saw the violent version of the event. This was true for recall of both actions and physical descriptions of the people involved (Clifford & Scott, 1978), and recall of details acquired prior to the violent event (Loftus & Burns, 1982).

Further evidence that recall accuracy is reduced under elevated levels of stress comes from a recent study by Kramer, Buckhout, Fox, Widman, and Tusche (1985). Color slides of travel scenes were presented to subjects. One traumatic autopsy slide was embedded in the series shown the experimental group, whereas the control subjects saw a neutral slide in that position. In a subsequent recall test on the images presented, the performance of the experimental group was worse than that of the control group. Other studies have demonstrated similar detrimental effects on recall for information associated with emotional events versus neutral events (see, e.g., Christianson & Nilsson, 1984; Christianson, Nilsson, Mjörndal, Perris, & Tjelldén, 1986; Clifford & Hollin, 1981; see also Christianson, 1992; Deffenbacher, 1983, for reviews).

From these simulations, can we conclude that all details about a highly emotional event will be less well remembered than details about a neutral event? Not necessarily. Common sense seems to tell us that when something life threatening occurs—say a large black truck swerved dangerously towards our car while we were driving on the freeway—we might remember certain details such as the color of the truck better than we would have if the truck simply passed by safely. Experimentally, we know that isolating an item by making it more vivid than surrounding items positively influences memory for the isolated item (cf. the von Restorff effect, see Wallace, 1965, for a review). Moreover, the phenomenon of "weapon focus" (Cutler, Penrod, & Martens, 1987; Loftus, Loftus, & Messo, 1987; Maass & Kohnken, 1989) demonstrates that certain stress-provoking items such as a weapon used in the commission of a crime can capture a witness' attention, resulting in a fairly complete description of the weapon, presumably a central detail, at the expense of recall for other, more peripheral, details.

Research that has specifically compared memory for central and peripheral details in emotionally arousing versus neutral events (e.g., Christianson, 1984; Christianson & Loftus, 1987, 1990, 1991; Christianson, Loftus, Hoffman, & Loftus, 1991) has demonstrated that central details of emotional events are better retained than corresponding details in neutral events (see also Heuer & Reisberg, this volume). The reverse pattern emerges for recall of information about peripheral details. A common interpretation of this finding is that the attentional resources are allocated to central features of an emotional event, leaving limited resources to encode surrounding, peripheral information (cf. Easterbrook, 1959; see also Christianson, in press, and Heuer & Reisberg, this volume).

On the surface, it appears as if the witness interview studies lead to different conclusions from the laboratory simulations. Some researchers (Yuille & Cutshall, 1989) claim that witnessing real traumas leads to "qualitatively different memories than the innocuous laboratory events" (p.178; see also Yuille & Tollestrup, this volume). Certainly some laboratory simulations seem pallid in comparison with assassinations and accidents. Does this mean we cannot learn about emotional memories from laboratory simulations of them? Or, are memories in these two settings qualitatively different? There is no question that field research is important as a source to identify variables for empirical investigation. To become fully informed, convergent methods of investigation are helpful, and we advocate the use of multiple methods, including interviews, simulations, staged events, and field research. However, the descriptive, anecdotal nature of findings in naturalistic studies limits meaningful interpretation and generalizability, primarily because of confounded variables (Goodman & Loftus, 1989). Our position is that laboratory studies can and do provide useful and also comparable information. After all, in some instances people are genuinely aroused, and even frightened, when they view simulated events. Horror film makers have known this for decades. Thus, the simulation studies can succeed in elevating arousal, permitting a researcher to examine its consequences. A notable reflection by Endel Tulving on the issue of laboratory-based versus naturalistic study of memory may conclude this section: "Memory, like countless other objects of scientific curiosity, can be studied and described at many different levels, from many different perspectives, using many different approaches and methods. There need not to be, and there usually is not, any conflict between these different approaches and different levels. Normally they are complementary" (Tulving, 1991, p. 41–42).

Ethics in Inducing Emotional Stress in Laboratory Situations

Of course, one obstacle to laboratory simulation studies of memories for traumatic events is that researchers are ethically constrained from inducing trauma or emotional stress by deceiving research subjects simply to test their performance. For example, in the United States the American Psychological Association (APA) has issued ethical guidelines for studies involving human subjects (APA, 1990). These guidelines prohibit researchers from using procedures that cause psychological harm. If an experiment could induce mental discomfort, subjects must be informed of this fact and their consent must be secured beforehand. Putting subjects in an experimental situation where they are likely to be frightened or distressed must obviously be done with great caution.

Most experimental studies must be approved by review committees to ensure compliance with these professional and ethical guidelines. This limitation does not mean that realistic simulations within the guidelines cannot be devised. For example, Loftus (1979) tested the performances of subjects known to be afraid of snakes by placing a stuffed snake in the room. (Snake phobics are often afraid of stuffed snakes, even when they know there is no chance of being bitten). The frightened snake phobics performed less well on a test of memory for a previously seen incident than did nonphobics. Thus, this study showed an effect of high stress in a manner that was ethically approved.

Other examples of research on the impact of stress on memory were described by Dr. Michael McCloskey, a psychologist who has done research on eyewitness memory, in his testimony in a criminal trial (United States v. Schubert, Jr., 1985) in Federal Court in the United States. He pointed out that approved studies on the relation of stress and memory have "involved a variety of different types of procedures from things like exposing people to loud noise and testing them under these conditions, to giving people electric shock, to staging crimes of a fairly innocuous nature, to having people view films of bloody industrial accidents . . . a variety of different sorts of procedures have been used to induce moderate or high levels of stress" (p. 18).

Despite his appreciation of the variety of ways that stress can be studied in the laboratory, McCloskey still maintained that the results of the research cannot be properly applied to actual eyewitnesses, because "there are very difficult problems in extending research from the circumstances under which it was conducted to other circumstances, especially circumstances involving actual crimes and actual witnesses which most of the time we can't study directly" (p. 16). He went on to say again that "in many cases, the techniques we apply regardless of how much research we do, cannot be properly extended to actual witnesses. We cannot do a study where we can stick a gun in someone's face, and also for practical limitations in that we cannot study what may be needed in thousands of subjects at times to understand things fully that we cannot draw conclusions at this time" (p. 59).

By comparison, when a Congressional inquiry was conducted on factors that contributed to the 1988 shooting down of an Iranian air bus by the USS Vincennes, a panel of psychologists who testified before the Defense Policy Panel of the House of Armed Services Committee expressed different views. The panel of experts included Dr. Richard E. Nisbett, Dr. Robert L. Heimreich, Dr. Richard W. Pew, Dr. Paul Slovic, and Dr. Baruch Fischhoff. These experts testified that failings in human judgment under stressful conditions contributed to the accidental shooting. In this case, generalization from a series of studies, such as those involving expectations of card players, to a real-world situation was accepted (Bower, 1988; New dangers in high-tech ships, planes, 1988). So, it seems ironic that in one domain experts are arguing against the generalizability of laboratory studies to real-world phenomena but, in other domains, experts seem untroubled by issues of generalizability. The contributions of psychological experts—based largely on laboratory stories—were welcomed in the case of the U.S.S. Vincennes.

What then do we make of the apparent contradictions between results from interview studies and simulation studies? Scrutiny of the studies shows that the contradiction has to do with what particular researchers focus upon. In many witness interview studies, the researchers focus upon the accuracy of memory and its persistence over time, tending to ignore or explain away the data on errors and inconsistencies. In many simulations, the researchers focus upon errors in memory and the decline of memory over time. Early researchers of flashbulb memories focused on accuracy of recall. Then, other researchers drew attention to the errors associated with these types of memories (e.g., Christianson, 1989; McCloskey, Wible, & Cohen, 1988; Nessier, 1982, see also Winograde & Neisser, 1992). New researchers (e.g., Christianson, 1984; Heuer & Reisberg, 1990) using the simulation paradigm have drawn attention to the persistence of emotional memories. Overall, these approaches are not as inconsistent or incompatible as they appear at first blush: The data in both interview and simulation studies show both good and poor recall.

Admittedly, the literature on memory for stressful emotional events paints a somewhat complicated picture. It is natural, then, to ask whether this research has any place in court? A controversy has been brewing for years over whether psychologists ought to testify in legal cases on the reliability of eyewitness memory. The controversy is not limited to memory for stressful events but encompasses a broad range of topics (i.e., effects of lighting, the cross-racial identification problem, time estimation, confidence and accuracy, etc.). In the next section, we briefly review this controversy. However, because the focus of this volume is on emotion and memory, we emphasize expert testimony about the effects of stress or violence on memory.

EXPERT TESTIMONY IN COURT

Is Expert Testimony Helpful?

A major threshold issue determining whether psychological expert testimony ought to be presented in court is whether it will assist the jury in evaluating the evidence in a particular case. There are at least two schools of thought. Many psychologists believe the testimony is helpful (Loftus, 1983a, 1983b; Loftus, 1986; Loftus & Doyle, 1987; Goodman & Loftus, 1988; Kassin, Ellsworth, & Smith, 1989). Their belief is based in part on empirical findings demonstrating that people in general, and jurors in particular, lack knowledge about eyewitness testimony that could assist them in deciding cases (Goodman & Loftus, 1990).

Other psychologists disagree (e.g., McCloskey & Egeth, 1983a, 1983b; Pachella, 1986, 1988). Consider some of the bases of their opposition to this testimony. McCloskey and Egeth first disavowed the idea that jurors tend to give more credence to eyewitness testimony that they ought to on grounds that there was no evidence of overbelief by jurors in eyewitness testimony. This question has been addressed by a number of researchers. Studies have shown that a number of popular misconceptions about memory processes abound and may influence jury deliberations concerning the credibility of eyewitness testimony (Brigham & Bothwell, 1983; Hosch, Beck, & McIntyre, 1980; Rahaim & Brodsky, 1982; Wells, Lindsay, & Tousignant, 1980). Faced with these studies, McCloskey, in his court testimony (*United States v. Schubert, Jr.*, 1985), discounted the findings, claiming that "all of these studies have various flaws, so I wouldn't put a great deal of weight on them" (p. 49). However, when the findings of those studies provided a basis to support a proposition that McCloskey wanted to support, he freely used them. For example, to support his argument to exclude expert testimony, one finding that "approximately 75% of the persons tested feel stress impairs performance" was cited to argue that the findings were *not* counterintuitive (p. 49).

Second, McCloskey and Egeth acknowledged that jurors were not able to discriminate accurate from inaccurate eyewitness report, but questioned whether expert psychological testimony would facilitate their ability to make this distinction. Once again, this point has been addressed empirically. Early research by Hosch (1980) revealed that jurors scrutinized the evidence more when an expert was permitted to testify than when no expert testified. This finding was confirmed in a recent study by Cutler, Penrod, and Dexter (1989), showing that mock jurors exposed to expert testimony evaluated the eyewitness evidence in a qualitatively different manner from the evaluations in the absence of expert testimony.

Another argument that McCloskey made in his testimony in Federal Court was that, despite his vast knowledge of the literature and the research publications in this field, he would not be better than the average person in deciding whether or not to believe a particular witness (*United States v. Schubert, Jr.*, 1985, p. 46). By implication, he suggested, therefore, that approximately 1 hour's worth of expert testimony cannot assist the jury in deciding how much weight to accord an eyewitness. To us, this is simply a subjective conviction on McCloskey's part that ignores the available research data on the potential impact of expert testimony.

Another issue raised by critics is that the expert testimony does not provide the jurors with new information that is beyond their common knowledge (Goodman & Loftus, 1990). Note that even McCloskey and Egeth conceded that there were some issues about which laypersons might not anticipate or comprehend the impact on memory accuracy. The relation between stress and identification was one such issue. However, with respect to those issues regarding which impact on memory was not obvious, McCloskey and Egeth claimed that the research data were inadequate to support the contention that psychologists had any useful information to impart to jurors. Among the other factors included in this category were the cross-racial identification effect, the relationship between confidence and accuracy, and the impact of post-event information.

Other opponents of expert evidence on eyewitness testimony have argued that principles counter to general intuition do not achieve the necessary consensus among practitioners to qualify as expert knowledge (Berliner, 1988). These opinions, although they may be true of some psychological phenomena, mis-state the picture regarding research on eyewitness memory and do it a disservice. Evidence that opinions of this nature are not shared by the majority of the scientific community informed on this topic was gathered by Kassin et al. (1989). He and his colleagues surveyed 63 experts on 21 factors that influence the accuracy of eyewitness memory. The purpose of this survey was to determine whether there was any consensus in the professional community concerning these counterintuitive findings. They determined that there was considerable consensus as to the effects of most of these factors. The list of factors about which there was considerable consensus and about which these experts believed the research was adequate to convey to a jury included most of the factors enumerated by Egeth and McCloskey.

One survey question in particular concerned the factor of stress. Experts were asked whether they agreed with the statement "Very high levels of stress impair the accuracy of eyewitness testimony." A strong majority of experts agreed that the available evidence tends to support this statement.[2] Moreover, 71% of experts said the statement was sufficiently reliable to offer it in court. When asked whether the experts thought the statement was generally known by laypersons as a matter of common sense and experience, only 24% said "yes." Thus, the expert consensus is that the stress factor is reasonably supported

---

[2]Obviously the statement presented to the experts in the Kassin et al. study was a very general one; that is, it referred to accuracy in general, and did not ask about accuracy for different types of details. Had the question been worded differently, for example, asked about accuracy for central details, the expert consensus might have been different. Furthermore, had the group of experts who were sampled included only contributors to this volume (instead of the 63 individuals who were sampled), the group consensus might have been different.

by existing data, at least with respect to memory for peripheral detail information or information associated with emotional events, and yet it is not within the common knowledge of laypeople, making it a suitable topic for expert testimony.

Battle of the Experts

An intriguing point made by McCloskey and Egeth (1983a) was that expert testimony on both sides of a case would probably lead to an unpleasant battle of the experts. Indeed a battle ensued in the Palme case. Consider the testimony over the exposure to potentially biasing postevent information. The defense expert argued that because the identification occurred 3 years after the crime, Mrs. Palme had probably modified her memory image to conform with information presented in media. The prosecution expert emphasized that exposure to postevent information does not necessarily change the initial memory representation, particularly memory for central information; that is, details that have been focused upon in the course of emotional events. Even if the experts did not resolve the issue of the postevent information for the jury, at least they provided the background necessary for the jury to begin to evaluate the potential impact of the media and other sources of new information. This brings us to the more general point about seemingly conflicting expert testimony. Surely, two experts can disagree on a subject without rendering the educational value of the exchange null. Perhaps the educational quotient of the testimony is enhanced by the differing viewpoints.

Consider that even if the two experts were to adopt opposing viewpoints, derived from essentially the same data on an issue, this is not necessarily a reason to advocate that such testimony never be presented in court. Little is known about the ways in which jurors resolve questions of fact when two experts on a subject disagree. However, this cannot be too different from the situation faced by jurors when contradictory evidence is presented by two fact witnesses or two eyewitnesses. Absent further data, there is little sound basis to exclude expert testimony simply because there is a possibility that an opposing expert may be called who will disagree with or shed different light on certain points made by the first expert. The argument that expert testimony should be excluded from trials has more foundation in the long-standing antipathy between the law and expert witnesses in general than in any particular conduct of experts on eyewitness memory (Saks, 1990). Note that, whereas McCloskey and Egeth originally foresaw a battle of the experts on eyewitness memory as damaging to the reputation of psychology, at least one of them no longer views this outcome as the inevitable consequence of disagreement in court among qualified experts in the field (Egeth, 1990).

Impact on Conviction

Before leaving the topic of the expert testimony controversy, we mention one last recurrent concern, namely the impact this may have on the conviction rate of criminals (Loh, 1984; McCloskey & Egeth, 1983a, 1983b). For example, McCloskey, in his court testimony (*United States v. Schubert, Jr.*, 1985), stated that he and Egeth focused on the question whether jury evaluation of eyewitness testimony results in an acceptable ratio of number of innocent defendants convicted to number of guilty defendants convicted. Yet, when questioned as to what his opinion was as to an acceptable ratio of innocent defendants convicted as opposed to guilty defendants convicted, this expert stated that he "had no opinion on that, because that was a policy question" (p. 72).

This issue, too, has been the subject of some investigation. Contrary to the fears expressed about the impact of such testimony on conviction rates, Cutler, Penrod, and Dexter (1989) found that the expert testimony did not cause jurors to be more skeptical of the eyewitness evidence and to overwhelmingly refuse to convict. Rather, the presence of an expert directed jurors' attention to relevant factors, such as witnessing and identification conditions, and led them to place less emphasis on misleading factors such as the confidence level of the eyewitness. Findings of this kind require that opinions on the usefulness of expert testimony be reevaluated. Opinions that the accomplishments of psychologists would not be particularly helpful to a jury in a trial in determining the effects that events would have on an actual eyewitness must be revised.

Other researchers have examined the weight jurors give to eyewitness testimony versus scientific evidence presented by an expert. A frequent concern expressed by opponents of expert testimony is that jurors will overbelieve the experts and ignore the other evidence, including eyewitness testimony (Broeder, 1954). In a jury simulation study of a homicide case, to determine whether jurors overbelieve expert witnesses who present scientific evidence, 233 mock jurors were presented with both eyewitness testimony and scientific evidence about the frequency of certain matching blood types. Jurors rated the reliability of eyewitness testimony and scientific evidence. The mean reliability rating of eyewitness testimony was 56%; the mean reliability rating of the scientific evidence was 60%, not statistically different (Goodman, 1986). The hypothesis that jurors tend to overbelieve expert scientific evidence and to undervalue the weight of eyewitness testimony was not supported.

In another jury simulation study in which a psychiatrist testified that a criminal defendant would be dangerous in the future, jurors were presented with a science expert who testified about the validity of such predictions (Morier, 1987). The science expert was either court-appointed or appointed by the defense. In a third condition, jurors heard no science expert testimony. Results showed that the scientific expert testimony was effective in persuading jurors that psychiatrists were not accurate in predicting dangerous behavior. Contrary to expectations, the defense expert was more influential than a "neutral" court-appointed expert. Thus, once again, jurors were sensitive to the scientific information provided by the expert, but they did not accord more weight to this information merely because the expert was presented as a more neutral, and less partisan, figure.

Lineups

One special area that experts are sometimes asked to testify about is the fairness of the identification test. In the Palme case this involved a video lineup. At trial, only the defense expert commented on the video lineup, but her testimony was not about its composition or construction, only about the extent to which postevent information may have influenced the witness' choice. The prosecution expert was never asked to comment on the lineup.

Was the lineup fair? In thinking about the fairness of a lineup test, a major concern is the selection of foils or distractors. Distractors should provide plausible choices for any witness who does not clearly remember the person he or she saw. In practice, however, there are a number of ways in which witnesses who have a poor memory to begin with can figure out who the suspect is. One way this can happen is if the distractors do not fit the general description of the perpetrator provided by the witness.

Selecting distractors is a tricky aspect of lineup construction. If there are doubts about the suggestiveness of a lineup, one can use a procedure originally proposed by Doob and Kirschenbaum (1973). In their technique the lineup is presented to mock witnesses who have never seen the perpetrator or the suspect. Usually these subjects receive a general description of the crime and the witness' description of the criminal. Then they examine the lineup and try to select the participant who is most likely to be the culprit. When the suspect attracts an excess of votes, the lineup selection is said to be unfair. variations of this method have been proposed by Malpass and Devine (1981, 1983).

The experts in the Palme case did not report having conducted any such tests. However, Christianson conducted a test after the trial was over. The rationale for Christianson's test was that it is not only the witness' initial description that must be kept in mind in constructing a lineup, but also that media information could influence a witness' memory (see Loftus & Banaji, 1989, for a discussion of how media can affect memory). The murder of Olof Palme was, of course, a devastating event to the Swedish people. The assassination was covered in the media almost daily. Descriptions and witness re-constructions were published numerous times. In particular, the media published two different witness reconstruction pictures (identikit pictures), mentioned that the murderer had a strange way of walking and mentioned that the suspect had alcohol and drug problems. Thus, at the time Mrs. Palme was confronted with the lineup containing the suspect, she not only had available her own initial descriptions of the murderer but also those from the media. The Christianson test of the lineup was designed to capture these features.

In Christianson's test, 133 students at the University of Washington viewed the police videotape with the lineup. None of the subjects had read about the trial, or seen any pictures, or read any descriptions of the accused murderer. The subjects were tested in groups of 5–10 and informed that one man in the lineup was accused of murdering Prime Minister Palme. The lineup tape included 12 men, who were first presented all together, and then walking one by one, and finally by a individual close-up picture. The subjects' task was to decide which one among the 12 participants in the lineup was the accused murderer. They were asked to make a first pick, a second pick, and a third pick. Before viewing the tape, subjects in different groups were given certain prior information. In Condition 1, subjects were presented with the two identikit pictures that had been published in media. In Condition 2, subjects were shown the pictures and in-formed that the suspect had a strange way of walking/running. In Condition 3, subjects were given the pictures and the information about the suspect's gait but were also informed that the suspect was an alcoholic and a drug addict. In Condition 4, no information was given before the presentation of the videotape. The videotape was shown twice consecutively to the subjects.

TABLE 9.1
Percentage of Subjects in Four Conditions Who Selected the
Accused of the Murderer of Prime Minister Palme. Values in
Parentheses are Percentages Whose First, Second, or Third
Choice was the Accussed.

Cond. 1 (n = 23) Identikit Pictures	Cond. 2 (n = 24) Identikit Pictures & Gait	Cond. 3 (n = 23) Identikit Pictures, Gait, & Addict	Cond. 4 (n = 29) No Information
1st (1-3)	1st (1-3)	1st (1-3)	1st (1-3)
26% (61%)	33% (67%)	74% (83%)	10% (48%)

The results are presented in Table 9.1. Without any prior information (Condition 4), the suspect Petterson was chosen only 10% of the
time—not more often than the other participants in the lineup.
However, when the subjects were given all the media information
before viewing the videotape (Condition 3), three out four students
selected the suspect.

The results indicate that information presented in media, for
example, that the suspect had a strange way of walking, biased the
lineup. The fact that this information affected people who never
witnessed the crime implies that it could possibly have affected
someone who did witness the crime.

The Influence of Emotion and Victimization on Eyewitness Testimony

Are the consequences of emotion special in a legal context? For one
thing, crimes are emotional events. It is therefore common to ask
how stress or emotion affects witnesses' memory in criminal trials.
In trials in which the identification of the defendant is an issue,
eyewitness testimony may be provided by both bystander nonvictims
as well as by victims. A common line of cross-examination in
criminal trials in which an eyewitness expert is permitted to testify
concerns the fact that most research is not conducted with actual
victims of crimes, but with nonvictim bystanders. The implication of
these questions is generally that research on the memory of bystanders does not generalize to actual victims. A frequent speculation is
that the more personal, emotional involvement of a victim witness
will serve to promote attentiveness and thus, greater accuracy of
recall. A less widespread and countervailing hypothesis is that more
emotional or stressful events, including victimization in a crime, will
cause a narrowing of attention and, thus, less accurate recall.

In fact, a few researchers have examined the effect of victimization on eyewitness testimony. For example, Hosch and Cooper (1982) examined the first issue: whether a theft victim was more attentive than a nonvictim witness to a theft. They hypothesized that victim witnesses would recall more details about the thief than bystander witnesses, and that as a consequence their accuracy of recall and confidence in the identification made would exceed those of bystander witnesses. They found no significant differences in accuracy or confidence of victims versus bystanders. They reasoned that perhaps the anxiety and greater physical arousal of the victim counteracted any benefits of increased attentiveness that a victim might have in comparison with a bystander.

This second hypothesis was tested in a subsequent study by Hosch, Lieppe, Marchioni, and Cooper (1984) in which a theft was staged. Subjects were either nonvictim witnesses or victim witnesses of the theft. After the theft, all witnesses were required to provide statements to campus detectives and to make an identification of the thief from a photo montage. In this study, once again, there were no statistically significant differences between the accuracy rate of victims versus bystanders, although the mean accuracy of victims was less than that of bystanders (37% vs. 52%). Victims who were led to believe that the suspect's picture was included in the photospread and who were under stronger social pressure to make a choice from the photomontage were accurate least often and were significantly less accurate than bystander witnesses who were given the same biasing instruction.

These findings were confirmed in a recent study by Hosch and Bothwell (1990), in which the arousal level of victims and bystanders were measured, in addition to their respective descriptions of the perpetrator and identification accuracy. Victims were not differentially aroused, nor more accurate than bystanders. These empirical data cannot be readily reconciled with Yuille and Tollestrup's (this volume) position, based on field study interviews, that the unaffected bystander's memory patterns differ from those of real victims/ witnesses.

CONCLUDING COMMENTS

This chapter has discussed research methodology and ethical issues related to eyewitness memory for emotional events by referring to the trial of the accused murderer of Olof Palme. There is a body of literature applicable to this trial, and there are special purpose studies that can be conducted in court cases like this. The jury in the second Palme trial relied, in part, on representations about the Devlin Report in arriving at its verdict. The expert testimony was instrumental in bringing that report to their attention. But was it a good basis for deciding to acquit the accused? In our opinion, it would be better if the jury were aware of more informative empirical studies on which to base their conclusions, for example, the results of the lineup study on evaluating the weight to accord to Mrs. Palme's selection of Pettersson from the lineup.

It is sometimes claimed in the literature that emotional memories from laboratory simulations are qualitatively different than those of real-life events. Our position is that laboratory studies, despite ethical constraints, can and do provide useful and also comparable information about highly stressful events. Results from interview and simulation studies are not as inconsistent or incompatible as they sometimes appear. Depending on what researchers focus upon (errors or accuracy in memory, or persistence or decline in memory over time), both interview and simulation studies show both good and poor recall. Furthermore, we also believe that two experts can disagree on a subject, without rendering the educational value of the exchange null. Even if the experts do not resolve issues such as the impact of postevent information or of stress on memory for the jury, at least they provided the background necessary for the jury to begin to evaluate the potential impact of these factors on eyewitness memory.

What form should future research on emotion and eyewitness memory take? Simulation studies, field studies, and autobiographical memory studies all contribute to further our knowledge of emotion and memory, and we do see points of comparison across these methodological approaches. We also believe that special purpose studies can be helpful in court cases, such as in the Palme trial.

ACKNOWLEDGMENTS

The preparation of this chapter was a collaborative effort and was supported in part by Grant F. 158/89 from the Swedish Council for Research in the Humanities and Social Sciences to Sven-Åke Christianson, and in part by grants to Jane Goodman and Elizabeth F. Loftus from the National Science Foundation. Many thanks to John Baccus and Kyle Stephenson for their assistance in collecting the data for the lineup study.

REFERENCES

American Psychological Association. (1990). Ethical principles of psychologists (Amended June 2, 1989). *American Psychologist, 45,* 390–395.

Berliner, L. (1988). Commentary: Expert evidence and eyewitness testimony. *Journal of Interpersonal Violence, 3*(1), 108–114.

Bower, B. (1988, October 5). "Human factors" and military decisions. *Science New Magazine.*

Breuer, J., & Freud, S. (1955). Studies on hysteria. In J. Strachey (Ed.), *The standard edition of the complete psychological works of Sigmund Freud* (Vol. 2). London: Hogarth Press. (Original work published in 1895)

Brigham, J. C., & Bothwell, R. (1983). Prospective jurors' ability to predict eyewitness identification accuracy. *Law and Human Behavior, 17,* 9–30.

Broeder, D. W. (1954). The function of the jury: Facts or fictions. *University of Chicago Law Review 21,* 386–424.

Brown, R., & Kulik, J. (1977). Flashbulb memories. *Cognition, 5,* 73–99.

Christianson, S.-Å. (1984). The relationship between induced emotional arousal and amnesia. *Scandinavian Journal of Psychology, 25,* 147–160.

Christianson, S.-Å. (1989). Flashbulb memories: Special, but not so special. *Memory & Cognition, 17,* 435–443.

Christianson, S.-Å. (1992). Emotional stress and eyewitness memory: A critical review. *Psychological Bulletin.*

Christianson, S.-Å., & Loftus, E. F. (1987). Memory for traumatic events. *Applied Cognitive Psychology, 1,* 225–239.

Christianson, S.-Å., & Loftus, E. F. (1990). Some characteristics of people's traumatic memories. *Bulletin of the Psychonomic Society, 28,* 195–198.

Christianson, S.-Å., & Loftus, E. F. (1991). Remembering emotional events: The fate of detailed information. *Cognition & Emotion, 5,* 81–108.

Christianson, S.-Å., Loftus, E. F., Hoffman, H., & Loftus, G. R. (1991). Eye fixations and memory for emotional events. *Journal of Experimental Psychology: Learning, Memory, and Cognition, 17,* 693–701.

Christianson, S.-Å., & Nilsson, L.-G. (1984). Functional amnesia as induced by a psychological trauma. *Memory & Cognition, 12,* 142–155.

Christianson, S.-Å., & Nilsson, L.-G., Mjörndal, T., Perris, C., & Tjelldén, G. (1986). Psychological versus physiological determinants of emotional arousal and its relationship to laboratory amnesia. *Scandinavian Journal of Psychology, 27,* 302–312.

Clifford, B. R., & Hollin, C. R. (1981). Effects of the type of incident and the number of perpetrators on eyewitness memory. *Journal of Applied Psychology, 66,* 364–370.

Clifford, B. R., & Scott, J. (1978). Individual and situational factors in eyewitness testimony testimony. *Journal of Applied Psychology, 63,* 352–359.

Cutler, B. L., Penrod, S. D., & Dexter, H. R. (1989). The eyewitness, the expert psychologists, and the jury. *Law and Human Behavior, 13*(3), 311–332.

Cutler, B. L., Penrod, S. D., & Martens, T. K. (1987). The reliability of eyewitness identification. *Law and Human Behavior, 11*(3), 233–258.

Deffenbacher, K. A. (1983). The influence of arousal on reliability of testimony. In S. M. A. Lloyd-Bostock & B. R. Clifford (Eds.), *Evaluating witness evidence* (pp. 235–251). Chichester: Wiley.

Doob, A. N., & Kirschenbaum, H. M. (1973). Bias in police lineups—partial remembering. *Journal of Police Science and Administration, 1,* 287–293.

Easterbrook, J. A. (1959). The effect of emotion on cue utilization and the organization of behavior. *Psychological Review, 66,* 183–201.

Egeth, H. E. (1990). *Expect testimony.* Paper presented at the Annual meeting of American Psychological Society, Dallas.

Erdelyi, M. H., & Goldberg, B. (1979). Let's not sweep repression under the rug: Toward a cognitive psychology of repression. In J. F. Kihlstrom & F. J. Evans (Eds.), *Functional disorders of memory* (pp. 355–402). Hillsdale, NJ: Lawrence Erlbaum Associates.

Freud, S. (1915). Repression. In Strachey (Ed.), *The standard edition of the complete psychological works of Sigmund Freud* (Vol. 14, pp. 146–158). London: Hogarth Press (1957).

Goodman, J. (1986). *Probabilistic scientific evidence: Jurors' inferences.* Unpublished doctoral dissertation, University of Washington, Seattle.

Goodman, J., & Loftus, E. F. (1988). The relevance of expert testimony on eyewitness memory. *Journal of Interpersonal Violence, 3*(1), 115–121.

Goodman, J., & Loftus, E. F. (1989). Implications of facial memory Research for investigative and administrative criminal procedures. In A. Young & H. D. Ellis (Eds.), *Handbook of information on facial processing.* Amsterdam: Elsevier.

Goodman, J., & Loftus, E. F. (1990). Judgment and memory: The role of expert psychological testimony on eyewitness accuracy. In P. Suedfeld (Ed.), *Psychology and social policy.* Washington, DC: Hemisphere

Heuer, F., & Reisberg, D. (1990). Vivid memories of emotional events: The accuracy of remembered minutiae. *Memory & Cognition, 18,* 496–506.

Hosch, H. M. (1980). A comparison of three studies of the influence of expert testimony on jurors. *Law and Human Behavior, 4,* 297–302.

Hosch, H. M., Beck, E. L., & McIntyre, P. (1980). Influence of expert eyewitness testimony regarding eyewitness accuracy on jury decisions. *Law and Human Behavior,* 229–240.

Hosch, H. M., & Bothwell, R. K. (1990). Arousal, description and identification accuracy of victims and bystanders. *Journal of Social Behavior and Personality, 5,* 481–488.

Hosch, H. M., & Cooper, D. S. (1982). Victimization as a determinant of eyewitness accuracy. *Journal of Applied Psychology, 67,* 649–652.

Hosch, H. M., Leippe, M. R., Marchioni, P. M., & Cooper, D. S. (1984). Victimization, self-monitoring, and eyewitness identification. *Journal of Applied Psychology, 69,* 280–288.

Kassin, S. M., Ellsworth, P. C., & Smith, V. L. (1989). The "general acceptance" of psychological research on eyewitness testimony: A survey of the experts. *American Psychologist, 44*(3), 1089–1098.

Kramer, T. H., Buckhout, R., Fox, P., Widman, E., & Tusche, B. (1990). Effects of stress on recall. *Applied Cognitive Psychology, 4.*

Kuehn, L. L. (1974). Looking down a gun barrel: Person perception and violent crime. *Perceptual and Motor Skills, 39,* 1159–1164.

Loftus, E. F. (1979). *Eyewitness testimony.* London: Harvard University Press.

Loftus, E. F. (1980). Impact of expert psychological testimony on the unreliability of eyewitness identification. *Applied Psychology, 65,* 9–15.

Loftus, E. F. (1983a). Silence is not golden. *American Psychologist, 38,* 564–572.

Loftus, E. F. (1983b). Whose shadow is crooked? *American Psychologist, 38,* 576–577.

Loftus, E. F. (1986). Ten years in the life of an expert witness. *Law and Human Behavior, 10,* 241–263.

Loftus, E. F., & Banaji, M. R. (1989). Memory modification and the role of the media. In V. A. Gheorghiu, P. Netter, H. J. Eysenck, & R. Rosenthal (Eds.), *Suggestion and suggestibility* (pp. 279–293). Berlin: Springer-Verlag.

Loftus, E. F., & Burns, T. (1982). Mental shock can produce retrograde amnesia. *Memory & Cognition, 10*, 318–323.

Loftus, E. F., & Doyle, J. M. (1987). *Eyewitness testimony: Civil and criminal.* New York: Kluwer Law Book Publishers.

Loftus, E. F., Loftus, G. R., & Messo, J. (1987). Some facts about "weapon focus." *Law and Human Behavior, 11*, 55–62.

Loh, W. D. (1984). *Social research in the judicial process.* New York: Russell Sage.

Maass, A., & Kohnken, G. (1989). Eyewitness identification: Simulating the "weapon effect." *Law and Human Behavior, 13*, 397–408.

Malpass, R. S., & Devine, P. (1981). Eyewitness identification: Lineup instructions and the absence of the offender. *Journal of Applied Psychology, 66*, 482–489.

Malpass, R. S., & Devine, P. (1983). Measuring the fairness of eyewitness identification lineups. In S. Lloyd-Bostock & B. R. Clifford (Eds.), *Evaluating witness evidence.* Chichester: Wiley.

McCloskey, M., & Egeth, H. E. (1983a). Eyewitness identification: What can a psychologist tell a jury? *American Psychologist, 38*, 550–563.

McCloskey, M., & Egeth, H. E. (1983b). A time to speak, or a time to keep silent? *American Psychologist, 38*, 573–575.

McCloskey, M., Wible, C. G., & Cohen, N. J. (1988). Is there a special flashbulb-memory mechanism? *Journal of Experimental Psychology: General, 117*, 171–181.

Morier, D. M. (1987). *The role of expert psychiatric predictions of dangerousness in a capital murder trial: A multi-method investigation.* Unpublished doctoral dissertation. University of Minnesota, Minneapolis.

Neisser, U. (1982). Snapshots or benchmarks? In U. Neisser (Ed.), *Memory observed* (pp. 43–48). San Francisco: W. H. Freeman.

Nemiah, J. C. (1979). Dissociative amnesia: A clinical and theoretical reconsideration. In J. F. Kihlstrom & F. J. Evans (Eds.), *Functional disorders of memory* (pp. 355–402). Hillsdale, NJ: Lawrence Erlbaum Associates.

New dangers in high-tech ships, planes. (1988, October). *San Francisco Daily Chronicle.*

Pachella, R. G. (1986). Personal values and the value of expert testimony. *Law and Human Behavior, 10*, 145–150.

Pachella, R. G. (1988). On the admissibility of psychological testimony in criminal justice proceedings. *Journal of Interpersonal Violence, 3*(1), 111–114.

Rahaim, G. L., & Brodsky, S. L. (1982). Empirical evidence versus common sense: Juror and lawer knowledge of eyewitness accuracy. *Law and Psychology Review, 7*(1), 1–15.

Saks, M. J., (1990). Expert witnesses, nonexpert witnesses, and nonwitness experts. *Law and Human Behavior, 14*(4), 291–313.

Trankell, A. (1963). *Vittnespsykologins arbetsmetoder.* Stockholm: Liber. (in Swedish)

Tulving, E. (1991). Memory research is not a zero-sum game. *American Psychologist, 46*, 41–42.

United States v. Schubert. Jr. (1985, March 4). *Criminal Case, No. 84–224, U.S. District Court for the District Court of New Jersey.* Transcript of testimony of Michael McCloskey.

Wallace, W. P. (1965). Review of the historical, empirical, and theoretical status of the von Restorff phenomenon. *Psychological Bulletin, 63*, 410–424.

Wells. G. L., Lindsay, R. C. L., & Tousignant, J. P. (1980). Effects of expert psychological advice on human performance in judging the validity of eyewitness testimony. *Law and Human Behavior, 4,* 275–285.

Winograd, E., & Neisser, U. (Eds.). (in press). *Affect and accuracy in recall: The problem of "Flashbulb" Memories.* New York: Cambridge University Press.

Yuille, J. C., & Cutshall, J. L. (1986). A case study of eyewitness memory of a crime. *Journal of Applied Psychology, 71,* 291–301.

Yuille, J. C., & Cutshall, J. L. (1989). Analysis of the statements of victims, witnesses and suspects. In J. C. Yuille (Ed.), *Credibility assessment.* Dordrecht: Kluwer Academic Publishers.

III

BIOLOGICAL ASPECTS

10

Affect, Neuromodulatory Systems, and Memory Storage

James L. McGaugh
University of California, Irvine

INTRODUCTION

> ... it is a notorious fact that what interests us most vividly at the time is
> ... what we remember best. An experience may be so exciting emotion-
> ally as almost to leave a scar on the cerebral tissues. (James, 1890, p. 670)

Most of us would probably agree with William James' observation that emotionally exciting experiences tend to be well remembered. A writer (Lantos, 1990) commenting on memories of childhood schoolroom experiences recently came to a remarkably similar conclusion: "Traumatic events leave a deep imprint in our minds. There must be some cerebral circuit that sizzles with current when we face danger, risk or the unknown. (p. B7)" Although over a century has passed since James first suggested that emotional arousal influences memory, it is only recently that this hypothesis has been subjected to intensive experimental inquiry.

The general hypothesis expressed in the preceding quotations consists of two assumptions. The first is that arousal at the time of learning influences memory strength. The second assumption is that emotional excitement affects brain processes involved in learning. Acceptance of the first hypothesis does not, of course, require acceptance of the second. It could be, for example, that we remember exciting events simply because we pay more attention to them and thus learn more about them. We may also think about the events later and, thus, strengthen the memories through rehearsal. However, it is also possible, as the second assumption suggests, that the emotional responses induced by exciting events may affect memory by influencing brain processes underlying the storage of memory.

EMOTIONAL ACTIVATION
AND MEMORY STORAGE

The evidence considered in several other chapters in this volume leaves little doubt that events that are characterized as arousing, emotionally exciting, or stressful are generally well remembered (Revelle & Loftus, this volume; Reisberg & Heuer, this volume; McCloskey, Cohen & Treadway, this volume). Furthermore, much of the evidence is generally consistent with the view that emotional responses influence memory by affecting memory storage processes. The findings of the initial study of "flashbulb memories" (Brown & Kulik, 1977) suggested that unexpected and highly arousing events create highly vivid and detailed memories of unusual endurance. Although subsequent findings have seriously questioned Brown and Kulik's claims that flashbulb memories are based on a special memory mechanism, they have provided additional evidence supporting William James' conclusion that emotion-arousing events tend to be memorable (Heuer & Reisberg, 1990; McCloskey, Wible & Cohen, 1988; Neisser, 1982, 1986; Schmidt & Bohannon, 1988). However, in studies of learning and retention in human subjects, it is difficult to disentangle the effects of emotional excitement on attention and rehearsal from those on memory storage; that is, although we may all remember where we were and what we were doing when we learned about the assassination of President Kennedy, the explosion of the space shuttle Challenger, or the onset of the bombing of Baghdad, there is no clear way of knowing whether or to what degree our emotional responses to the news of the events influenced the storage of our memories of those events. Clearly, determination of the influence of emotional processes on memory storage requires investigation of the effects of emotional activation under conditions that exclude, or at least minimize, the possible influences of attention and rehearsal. As is discussed later, experiments using laboratory animals have addressed this issue by examining the effects, on memory, of treatments affecting neuromodulatory systems known to be activated by emotionally arousing stimulation.

As Brown and Kulik (1977) noted, Livingston had (1967) proposed a neurobiological mechanism that could provide a basis for the selective strengthening of the memory of important experiences. Livingston suggested that novel experiences activate the limbic system, which, in turn, stimulates the reticular activation system that projects diffusely to the cortex. The activation of this system would result in the storage of all recently activated brain events (Livingston, 1967): "Following 'Now print!' order, everything that has been ongoing in the recent past will receive a 'Now print!' contribution in the form of a growth stimulus or a neurohormonal influence that will favor future repetitions of the same neural activities" (p. 576). As Kety (1990) subsequently pointed out: ". . . there is obvious adaptive advantage in a mechanism that consolidates not all experience equally, but only those experiences that are significant for survival" (p. 330).

Postlearning Modulation of
Memory Storage Processes

The hypothesis that emotional responses evoked by experiences play a role in influencing memory requires the assumption that the processes underlying memory storage must be susceptible to such influences for a period of time after the initial learning (Mueller & Pilzecker, 1900). Although such postlearning storage processes do not necessarily need to be assumed in order to account for emotional influences on memories of an emotionally exciting event, such as a wedding, the birth of a child, or a graduation ceremony that occurs over a period of many minutes or hours, postlearning memory storage processes must be assumed if emotional responses are to influence the memory of a briefly experienced event, such as an automobile accident, for, in the latter case, the event may well be over by the time that the emotional reaction is expressed.

There is considerable experimental as well as clinical evidence indicating that postlearning memory storage processes are susceptible to influences affecting brain functioning. Retrograde amnesia is readily produced by a variety of treatments, including electrical stimulation of the brain, and drugs (McGaugh, 1966; McGaugh & Herz, 1972). Furthermore, there is also extensive evidence indicating that retention can be enhanced by posttraining electrical stimulation of specific brain regions as well as by drugs affecting neuromodulatory systems activated by training experiences (Bloch, 1970; Bloch, Denti,

& Schmaltz, 1966; Denti, McGaugh, Landfield, & Shinkman, 1970; McGaugh, 1973; McGaugh & Gold, 1976). In the earliest experiments investigating the memory-enhancing effects of posttraining treatments, stimulant drugs, including strychnine, picrotoxin, and pentylenetetrazol, were administered systemically to rats or mice after they were trained on appetitively motivated training tasks (mazes and discrimination tasks; Breen & McGaugh, 1961; McGaugh, Thomson, Westbrook, & Hudspeth, 1962). Low doses of the drugs enhanced retention if administered shortly after training but had no effect if administered an hour or longer after the training. Comparable effects have been obtained in many subsequent studies using a wide variety of training tasks and procedures (Dawson & McGaugh, 1973; McGaugh, 1968, 1973, 1989b; McGaugh & Petrinovich, 1965).

The findings indicating that the memory-enhancing effects of the posttraining treatments are time-dependent strongly support the view that the drugs affect retention processes underlying memory consolidation (McGaugh, 1966; McGaugh & Herz, 1972). Consequently, such findings provide a basis for the assumption that postlearning memory storage processes are susceptible to the modulating influences of emotional responses induced by training. Two other important conclusions have emerged from studies of the memory-enhancing effects of posttraining treatments. First, memory-enhancing effects of such treatments are readily obtained in experiments using learning tasks that do not evoke extensive emotional arousal. Memory-enhancing effects have been obtained in experiments using appetitively motivated learning tasks as well as latent learning (Tolman, 1932) tasks in which rewards or punishments are not used during training (Humphrey, 1968; Westbrook & McGaugh, 1964). The second conclusion of importance that has emerged from studies of posttraining memory-enhancing treatments is that such treatments do not work by acting as rewards or punishments. For example, Bloch (1970) reported that the retention-enhancing effects of posttraining electrical stimulation of the mesencephalic reticular formation were obtained at stimulus intensities below those required for inducing rewarding or arousing effects. Further, although there is evidence that rewards such as brain stimulation, food, or sugar can have memory-enhancing effects (Gold, 1991; Huston, Mondadori, & Wasser, 1974; White, 1991), studies examining the effects of posttraining administration of drugs have shown that memory enhancement is readily produced by doses that have no rewarding or punishing effects (Brioni & McGaugh, 1988; Westbrook & McGaugh, 1964). There is also clear evidence that rewards can effect performance independently of their effects on memory storage. Messier and White (1984) have reported, for example, that, although the sweet-tasting but non-nutritive substance saccharine can serve as an effective reward, it lacks memory-enhancing effects.

HORMONAL INFLUENCES ON MEMORY STORAGE

There is, no doubt, general agreement with the observation that experiences that activate emotional responses are likely to be ones that should be remembered. If our behavior is to be appropriate for the situations we encounter, our remembrance of events should be well correlated with their significance (McGaugh, 1990). Postlearning time-dependent processes appear to provide a mechanism capable of producing this critical correlation (Gold & McGaugh, 1975). Extensive evidence from studies of the effects of hormones on memory strongly supports the view that emotionally activated physiological systems regulate memory storage (de Wied, 1984, 1991; Koob, Lebrun, Bluthe, Dantzer, Dorsa, & Le Moal, 1991; McGaugh, 1983; McGaugh & Gold, 1989; Morley & Flood, 1991). Research in my laboratory has focused on the effects of adrenergic and opioid peptidergic systems. It is well documented that the adrenergic hormone epinephrine is released from the adrenal medulla during and immediately after stressful stimulation of the kinds typically used in training rats and mice. Gold and van Buskirk (1975) were the first to report that, in rats trained in an inhibitory (passive) avoidance task retention is enhanced by posttraining systemic injections of low doses of epinephrine. The epinephrine effects on retention, like those previously found with stimulant drugs, were dose dependent and time dependent: Retention was enhanced at low doses and impaired at high doses; the degree of enhancement was greatest when the injections were administered shortly after training.

Comparable effects have been obtained in subsequent experiments that have used different types of training tasks including inhibitory avoidance, active avoidance, discrimination learning and appetitively motivated tasks (Borrell, de Kloet, Versteeg, & Bohus, 1983; Gold, van Buskirk, & Haycock, 1977; Introini-Collison & McGaugh, 1986; Izquierdo & Dias, 1983; Liang, Bennett, & McGaugh, 1985; Sternberg, Isaacs, Gold, & McGaugh, 1985). In most experiments retention of the training is tested within a few days after training. However, as is shown in Fig. 10.1, memory-enhancing effects of posttraining systemic injections of epinephrine are also found with retention tests given at intervals of up to a month following training

(Introini-Collison & McGaugh, 1986). All this evidence provides strong support for the view that epinephrine influences long-term retention by acting on posttraining processes underlying memory storage. It is also important to note that Gold and McCarty (1981) have shown that the plasma levels of epinephrine measured following the administration of memory-enhancing doses of epinephrine are comparable to those found in untreated animals given training that produces good retention. Such findings are consistent with the view that endogenously released epinephrine plays a role in modulating memory storage.

The findings indicating that posttraining administration of epinephrine enhances the retention of appetitively motivated learning (Sternberg, Isaacs, Gold, & McGaugh, 1985) suggested that it is not essential that the training induce high levels of emotionality in order

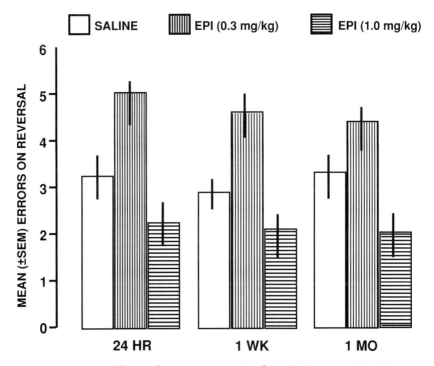

FIG. 10.1. Effects of posttraining epinephine (ip) on retention, in mice, of Y-maze discrimination training. The animals were trained to escape into one arm of the Y-maze. On the retention tests, 1 day, 1 week, or 1 month following training, the position of the correct arm was reversed and the number of errors made on six reversal training trials were used as the index of the original training. (Means ± SEM). (From Introini-Collison & McGaugh, 1986.)

for epinephrine to modulate the retention. This latter finding is of importance in that it provides evidence bearing on the issue of whether the effects of emotional experiences on learning can be dissociated from their influences on memory storage. The findings clearly show that strength of memory for a training experience can be influenced by a hormone known to be released by aversive stimulation even though the learning was not based on aversive stimulation. Highly similar effects have been obtained with vaso-pressin, another hormone known to be released by stimulation of the kinds typically used in learning experiments (Ettenberg, Le Moal, Koob, & Bloom, 1983; Ettenberg, van der Kooy, Le Moal, Koob, & Bloom, 1983).

Peripheral and Central Adrenergic Influences on Memory Storage

Because it is known that epinephrine passes the blood-brain barrier poorly, if at all (Weil-Malherbe, Axelrod, & Tomchick, 1959), it seems unlikely that the memory-modulating effects of epinephrine are due to direct influences on brain activity. Evidence from several ex-periments indicates that epinephrine influences on memory are initiated by selective activation of peripheral β-adrenergic receptors. In experiments using an inhibitory avoidance task as well as a Y-maze discrimination task (Introini-Collison, Saghafi, Novack, & McGaugh, in press), we found that the retention-enhancing effects of epinephrine are blocked by the peripherally acting β-adrenergic antagonist sotalol but are not blocked by the α-antagonists. As is shown in Fig. 10.2, we found that retention was also enhanced by posttraining systemic injections of DPE (dipivalyl epinephrine), which is less polar than epinephrine and thus probably enters the brain more readily. DPE effects on memory, unlike those of epineph-rine, were not blocked by sotalol. They were, however, blocked by propranolol, which readily enters the brain when administered systemically. These findings are consistent with other evidence (Introini-Collison & Baratti, unpublished findings), indicating that retention is enhanced by posttraining injections of clenbuterol, a β-adrenergic agonist that readily enters the brain when administered systemically. Further, as we found with DPE, propranolol, but not sotalol, blocked the memory-enhancing effects of clenbuterol.

These findings, considered together, suggest that epinephrine, as well as DPE and clenbuterol, enhance memory through effects involving the activation of central norepinephrine (NE) receptors. The DPE and clenbuterol effects appear to be due to direct activation

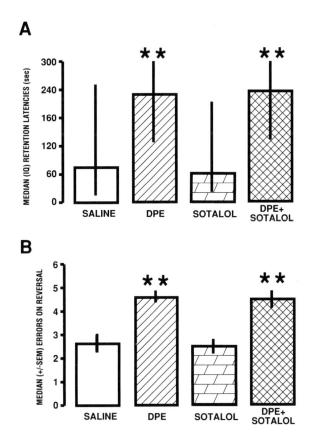

FIG. 10.2.   Effects of posttraining i.p. injections of DPE (dipivalyl
epinephrine) on retention in (A) inhibitory avoidance (median and
interquartile range) and (B) Y-maze discrimination (mean ± SEM)
tasks. The peripherally acting β-adrenergic antagonist sotalol did not
block the retention-enhancing effects of DPE. **$P < 0.01$ compared with
saline controls and group given only sotalol (unpublished findings).

of central NE receptors, because both drugs readily enter the brain
and the memory-enhancing effects of these drugs are not attenuated
by blockade of peripheral adrenergic receptors. The epinephrine
effects seem likely to be due to activation of a central noradrenergic
system, perhaps the locus coeruleus (Abercrombie & Jacobs, 1987;
Jacobs, 1986), by stimulation of peripheral adrenergic receptors on
visceral afferents projecting to the brain. This suggestion is consistent with the evidence indicating that systemic injections of epinephrine induce the release of brain NE (Gold & van Buskirk, 1978a,
1978b).

INVOLVEMENT OF THE AMYGDALA

Several lines of evidence suggest that epinephrine affects memory storage through influences involving the amygdala. It is well known that posttraining electrical stimulation of the amygdala can produce enhancement as well as impairment of memory—depending on the experimental conditions (Gold, Hankins, Edwards, Chester, & McGaugh, 1975; Gold, Macri, & McGaugh, 1973; Kesner & Wilburn, 1974; McGaugh & Gold, 1976). It is also well documented that lesions of the amygdala impair learning of tasks using emotionally arousing training conditions (Cahill & McGaugh, 1990; Hitchcock & Davis, 1987; Kesner, Walser, & Winzenried, 1989; LeDoux, this volume; LeDoux, Iwata, Cicchitti, & Reis, 1988; Weiskrantz, 1956). Such findings suggest the possibility that epinephrine released in response to arousing stimulation might influence learning by activating the amygdala.

The findings of experiments examining the memory-modulating effects of electrical stimulation of the amygdala in adrenalectomized rats were the first to provide evidence bearing on this hypothesis. Posttraining stimulation of the amygdala that impaired memory in intact rats was found to enhance memory in adrenal-demedullated rats (Bennett, Liang, & McGaugh, 1985). However, retrograde amnesia was induced in adrenal-demedullated rats if systemic injections of epinephrine were administered immediately before the brain stimulation (Liang, Bennett, & McGaugh, 1985). Thus, effects initiated by peripheral epinephrine appear to modulate amygdala sensitivity to stimulation. These findings fit well with those of Sternberg and Gold's (1981), indicating that systemically administered adrenergic antagonists block the retrograde amnesia induced by amygdala stimulation.

The evidence indicating that peripheral epinephrine influences amygdala responses to brain stimulation suggests that epinephrine may have a more general influence on amygdala functioning in memory. According to this hypothesis, lesions of the amygdala should alter the effects of epinephrine on memory. The evidence provided by several experiments is consistent with this implication. Lesions of the amygdala induced by the excitotoxin NMDA block the memory-enhancing effects of posttraining systemic injections of epinephrine (Cahill & McGaugh, 1991). Furthermore, lesions of the stria terminalis (ST), a major amygdala afferent–efferent pathway block the memory-enhancing effects of epinephrine as well as clenbuterol (Introini-Collison, Miyazaki, & McGaugh,1991; Liang & McGaugh, 1983). It is clear from these experiments that epinephrine effects on memory are obtained only in animals with an intact amygdala. Thus, the findings provide strong support for the view that epinephrine affects memory by activating the amygdala. However, these findings do not exclude the possibility that epinephrine effects of memory may be due to activation of brain systems other than the amygdala, and that such effects require concurrent input from the amygdala.

Involvement of NE Within the Amygdala

Experiments examining the effects of intra-amygdala injections of NE agonists and antagonists have provided evidence supporting the hypothesis that epinephrine influences on memory are due to activation of the amygdala rather than to influences elsewhere in the brain that require concurrent influences from the amygdala. Furthermore, the findings also strongly suggest that the effects involve activation of NE receptors within the amygdala. Gallagher and her colleagues reported posttraining intra-amygdala injections of the β-adrenergic antagonists propranolol and alprenolol impaired retention and that the impairment was blocked by NE administered concurrently (Gallagher, Kapp, Pascoe, & Rapp, 1981). If, as the evidence just summarized suggests, epinephrine influences on memory involve NE within the amygdala, intra-amygdala injections of propranolol should block the memory enhancing effects of epinephrine. The findings of an experiment examining this implication are shown in Fig. 10.3 (Liang, Juler, & McGaugh, 1986). As is shown, propranolol administered to rats intra-amygdally immediately after training in an inhibitory avoidance task attenuated the memory-enhancing effect of systemically administered epinephrine.

A major implication of the hypothesis that epinephrine enhancement of memory results from the release of NE within the amygdala is that direct intra-amygdala administration of noradrenergic agonists should enhance retention. Several experiments have provided evidence strongly supporting this implication. Retention of inhibitory avoidance training is enhanced by posttraining intra-amygdala injections of NE as well as clenbuterol (Introini-Collison, Miyazaki, & McGaugh, 1991; Liang, Juler, & McGaugh, 1986; Liang, McGaugh, & Yao, 1990). The findings shown in Fig. 10.4 indicate that the memory-modulating effects of intra-amygdala injections of NE are blocked by lesions of the ST. These findings, considered together with earlier findings indicating that ST lesions block the effects of systemically administered epinephrine (Liang & McGaugh, 1983),

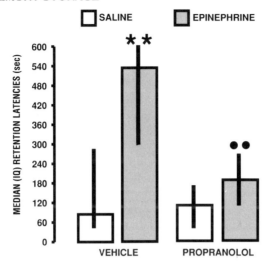

FIG. 10.3. Effects of posttraining intra-amygdala injections of propranolol (0.2 μg) on epinephrine-induced enhancement of retention of an inhibitory avoidance response. Epinephrine (0.1 mg) was administered s.c. Retention was tested 24 hours after training. **P < 0.01 as compared with the vehicle-injected control group. ••P < 0.001 as compared with the epinephrine-injected control group. (From Liang, Juler, & McGaugh, 1986.)

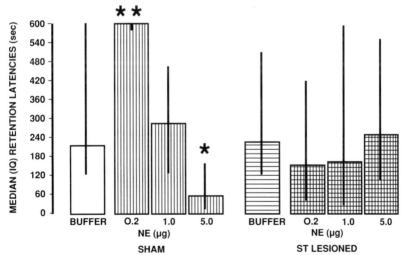

FIG. 10.4. Effects of stria terminalis (ST) lesions on the effects of intra-amygdala injections of norepinephrine (NE) on memory. ST lesions blocked NE-induced enhancement and impairment of memory. Retention was tested 24 hours after training. **P < 0.05 and *P < 0.01 compared with the buffer-injected control group. (From Liang, McGaugh, & Yao, 1990.)

suggest that the amygdala is involved in regulating memory storage in brain regions activated via the ST.

It seems clear from the findings summarized above that memory can be strengthened by drug and hormone treatments whose effects mimic, at least in part, those induced by emotionally exciting experiences. In these experiments the memory-modulating treatments were administered after the completion of the training experiences. Consequently, the evidence provides strong support for the general hypothesis that the emotional consequences of experiences play an important role in influencing memory storage (Gold & McGaugh, 1975); that is, although emotional responses may well influence learning by influencing attention at the time of learning, it seems clear that they have effects on memory storage that are independent of any influence on attention. Furthermore, the findings are consistent with other evidence suggesting that the amygdala is involved in the storage of emotionally influenced memories (LeDoux, this volume).

OPIOID PEPTIDERGIC AND GABAERGIC
INFLUENCES ON MEMORY STORAGE

Stressful stimulation is known to activate other neuromodulatory systems, including opioid peptidergic and GABAergic systems in addition to adrenergic systems. Experiments examining the memory-modulating effects of treatments affecting these systems have provided extensive evidence suggesting that the effects of these treatments, like those produced by epinephrine, involve the activation of NE receptors within the amygdala (Castellano, Brioni, & McGaugh, 1990; McGaugh, 1989a).

It is well established that posttraining systemic as well as intra-amygdala injections of opiate antagonists such as naloxone and naltrexone enhance retention (Gallagher & Kapp, 1978; Introini-Collison & McGaugh, 1987; Introini-Collison, Nagahara, & McGaugh, 1989; Izquierdo, 1979; Messing, Jensen, Martinez, Spiehler, Vasquez, Soumireu-Mourat, Liang, & McGaugh, 1979). When administered in low doses, the memory-enhancing effects of posttraining systemic injections of naloxone and epinephrine are additive (Introini-Collison & McGaugh, 1987). Further, the effects of naloxone, like those of epinephrine, are blocked by lesions of the ST (McGaugh, Introini-Collison, Juler, & Izquierdo, 1986). The findings indicating that the effects of opiate antagonists on memory are highly similar to those of epinephrine suggest that adrenergic and opiate influences on memory may work through a common mechanism. Several lines of evidence suggest that the common effect may involve influences on the release of brain NE. Abercrombie and Jacobs (1988) reported that, in animals subjected to stressful stimulation, systemic injections of naloxone potentiated the activity of noradrenergic neurons in the locus coeruleus. It is also well documented that opioid peptides inhibit the release of NE (Arbilla & Langer, 1978; Montel, Starke, & Weber, 1974; Nakamura, Tepper, Young, Ling, & Groves, 1982; Werling, Brown, & Cox, 1987; Werling, McMahon, Portoghese, Takemori, & Cox, 1989). Such evidence suggests that naloxone effects on memory may be due to antagonism of opioid inhibition of NE release. If this is the case, naloxone effects on memory, like those of epinephrine (Liang, Juler, & McGaugh, 1986), should be blocked by treatments that impair NE release or block NE receptors. There is extensive evidence consistent with this implication. The memory-enhancing effects of naloxone are blocked in animals treated with the β-adrenergic antagonist propranolol (Izquierdo & Graudenz, 1980) or DSP4, an adrenergic neurotoxin (Introini-Collison & Baratti, 1986). Furthermore, because α-antagonists or the peripherally acting β-adrenergic antagonist sotalol do not block the memory-enhancing effects of systemically injected naloxone, the naloxone effects appear to result from selective activation of central β-adrenergic receptors (Introini-Collison & Baratti, 1986).

The memory-modulating effects of opioid peptides, like those of epinephrine, appear to be mediated, at least in part, by activation of the amygdala. The effects obtained with intra-amygdala injections of opiate agonists and antagonists are comparable to those found with systemic injections: Retention is enhanced by opiate antagonists and impaired by opiate agonists (Gallagher, 1982, 1985; Gallagher & Kapp, 1978; Gallagher et al., 1981). Further, the effects appear to be mediated by influences involving NE, as the memory-enhancing effects of peripheral as well as intra-amygdala injections of naloxone are blocked in animals with neurotoxic-induced (6-OHDA) lesions of the dorsal noradrenergic pathway (Fanelli, Rosenberg, & Gallagher, 1985; Gallagher, Rapp, & Fanelli, 1985). Other recent findings indicate that the naloxone effects involve NE within the amygdala. As is shown in Fig. 10.5, posttraining intra-amygdala injections of β-adrenergic antagonists block the memory-enhancing effects of systemically administered naloxone (McGaugh, Introini-Collison, & Nagahara, 1988). In this experiment rats were trained in an inhibitory avoidance task and β-antagonists (propranolol, atenolol, or zinterol) or a buffer solution were injected intra-amygdally via implanted cannulae immediately after training. Saline or naloxone were administered i.p. immediately after the amygdala injections

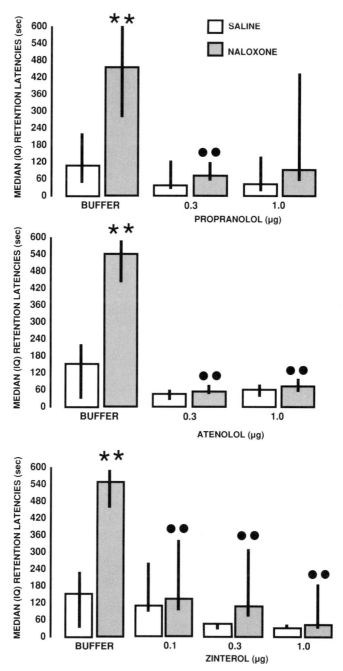

FIG. 10.5. Effects of posttraining intra-amygdala injections of β-adrenoceptor antagonists on naloxone-induced enhancement of retention of an inhibitory avoidance response (median and interquartile range). Naloxone (3.0 mg/kg) was administered i.p. Retention was tested 1 week after training. (From McGaugh, Introini-Collison, & Nagahara, 1988.)

and retention was tested 1 week later. The β-antagonists blocked the effects of systemically administered naloxone only when injected into the amygdala: Injections administered into either the caudate-putamen or cortex dorsal to the amygdala were ineffective. Also, intra-amygdala injections of α-adrenergic antagonists failed to block the effects of naloxone. The results of these experiments are consistent with the view that peripherally administered naloxone influences memory through effects involving NE within the amygdala. Other recent experiments have provided additional evidence supporting this conclusion. Fig. 10.6 shows that the retention-enhancing effects of intra-amygdala injections of naloxone are blocked by propranolol injected concurrently with naloxone (Introini-Collison, Nagahara, & McGaugh, 1989).

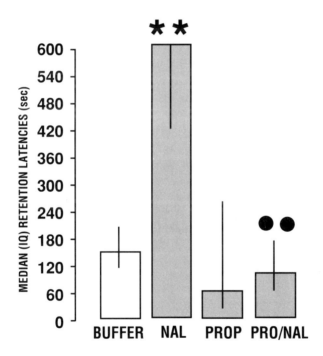

FIG. 10.6.   Effects of posttraining intra-amygdala injections of naloxone (0.1 μg) and propranolol (0.3 μg) on retention of an inhibitory avoidance response (median and interquartile range). Retention was tested 1 week after training. Propranolol blocked naloxone-induced enhancement of memory when the drugs were injected concurrently into the amygdala. **$P < 0.01$ as compared with the buffer group. ••$P < 0.01$ as compared with the naloxone-injected group. (From Introini-Collison, Nagahara, & McGaugh, 1989.)

The findings summarized above suggest that adrenergic as well as opioid peptidergic influences on memory storage are mediated by the activation of β-noradrenergic receptors within the amygdala. There is also extensive evidence indicating that retention can be modulated by GABAergic drugs (Castellano, Brioni, & McGaugh, 1990). Further, GABAergic effects on memory, like adrenergic and opiate effects, appear to involve NE receptors within the amygdala.

The findings of an early experiment (Breen & McGaugh, 1961) indicated that posttraining injections of the GABAergic antagonist picrotoxin enhanced maze learning in rats. Comparable effects have since been obtained in experiments using a variety of training tasks (Bovet, McGaugh, & Oliverio, 1966; Brioni & McGaugh, 1988; McGaugh, Castellano, & Brioni, 1990). There is now extensive evidence indicating that GABAergic antagonists (picrotoxin and bicuculline) enhance retention and that GABAergic agonists (muscimol and baclofen) impair retention (Brioni & McGaugh, 1988; Castellano, Brioni, Nagahara, & McGaugh, 1989; Castellano & McGaugh, 1989; Swartzwelder, Tilson, McLamb, & Wilson, 1987). It is of particular interest that low doses of GABAergic antagonists and opiate antagonists injected together after training are additive in their memory-enhancing effects (Castellano, Introini-Collison, Pavone, & McGaugh, 1989). Such findings suggest that drugs affecting these two systems may influence memory storage through a common mechanism. If this is the case, lesions of the amygdala should block the effects of GABAergic drugs and intra-amygdala injections of GABAergic agonists, and antagonists should produce effects on memory comparable to those induced by opiate agonists and antagonists. Recent findings are consistent with this implication. Bicuculline and muscimol do not affect retention in mice with amygdala lesions (Ammassari-Teule, Pavone, Castellano, & McGaugh, 1991). Further, as is shown in Fig. 10.7, posttraining injections of bicuculline produce dose-dependent enhancement of retention when administered directly into the amygdala. Intra-amygdala injections of baclofen and muscimol impair memory (Brioni, Nagahara, & McGaugh, 1989; Castellano, Brioni, Nagahara, & McGaugh, 1989). Other recent findings (unpublished findings) suggest that GABAergic influences on memory involve, at a subsequent step, the activation of NE receptors. When administered either systemically or intra-amygdally, propranolol blocks the retention-enhancing effects of bicuculline. Further, muscimol does not block the retention-enhancing effects of the β-adrenergic agonist clenbuterol. Thus, GABAergic effects appear to occur prior, in sequence, to noradrenergic effects and may be involved in regulating the release of NE.

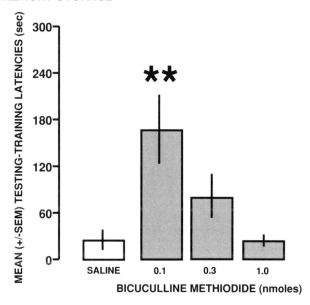

FIG. 10.7. Effects of posttraining intra-amygdala injections of bicuculline methiodide (BMI) on retention of an inhibitory avoidance task (mean ± SEM). Retention was tested 48 hours after training. **$P < 0.01$ as compared with the saline-injected control group. (From Brioni, Nagahara, & McGaugh, 1989.)

CONCLUDING COMMENTS

Figure 10.8 summarizes the interactions of adrenergic, opioid peptidergic, and GABAergic influences on memory storage suggested by the experimental evidence considered in this chapter. The model assumes that epinephrine activates a central NE system projecting to the amygdala and that GABAergic and opioid peptidergic influences regulate the release of NE. Thus, the evidence suggests the possibility that the influences of several neuromodulatory systems on memory may be integrated by interactions occurring within the amygdala. The evidence also suggests that the amygdala regulates storage in brain regions activated by the amygdala. The memory-modulating effects appear to be mediated, at least in part, by efferent projections carried by ST.

These findings quite clearly indicate that memory can be influenced by treatments affecting brain systems known to be activated by emotionally activating stimulation. The evidence thus strongly supports the general hypothesis that endogenous neuromodulatory systems activated by experiences play a role in regulating memory

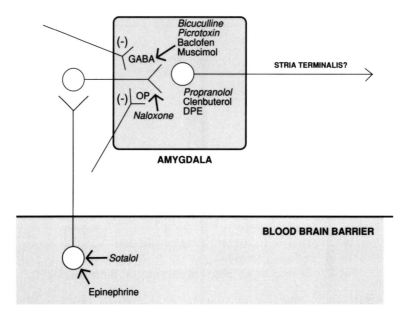

FIG. 10.8.   Interactions of hormones and neurotransmitter systems in regulating memory storage suggested by experimental findings.

storage. According to this view, emotionally exciting stimulation activates the release of adrenal epinephrine (as well as other stress-related hormones) that, in turn, causes "sizzling circuits" (Lantos, 1990) in the amygdala and sites activated by the amygdala. Such effects serve to regulate the storage of long-term memory of the experience. The extensive evidence indicating that the memory modulating effects of hormones and drugs are dose-dependent suggests that the strength of memories depends on the degree of emotional activation induced by learning. It has been suggested that such effects might underlie the long-lasting consequences of emotional experiences as expressed in the posttraumatic stress disorder (van der Kolk, Greenberg, Orr, & Pitman, 1989). Highly emotional stimulation may well, as William James (1890) suggested, "almost . . . leave a scar on the cerebral tissue" in the form of lasting changes in synaptic connectivity. The evidence indicating that long-term potentiation (LTP) is enhanced by posttraining treatments, including adrenergic drugs (Gold, Delanoy, & Merrin, 1984) and electrical stimulation of the brain (Laroche & Bloch, 1982), that produce enhancement of memory is clearly consistent with James' prescient observation.

ACKNOWLEDGMENTS

Supported by USPHS Research Grant MH12526 from NIMH and NIDA and ONR Contract N00014-90-J-1626. I thank Jorge Brioni, Larry Cahill, Claudio Castellano, Ines Introini-Collison, K. C. Liang, Munsoo Kim, and Alan Nagahara for their contributions to the experimental findings summarized in this paper and Nancy Collett for assistance in the preparation of the manuscript.

REFERENCES

Abercrombie, E. D., & Jacobs, J. L. (1987). Single-unit response of noradrenergic neurons in the locus coeruleus of freely moving cats. 1. Acutely presented stressful and nonstressful stimuli. *Journal of Neuroscience, 7*, 2837–2843.

Abercrombie, E. D., & Jacobs, J. L. (1988). Systemic naloxone administration potentiates locus coeruleus noradrenergic neuronal activity under stressful but not non-stressful conditions. *Brain research, 441*, 362–366.

Ammassari-Teule, M., Pavone, F., Castellano, C., & McGaugh, J. L. (1991). Amygdala and dorsal hippocampus lesions block the effects of GABAergic drugs on memory storage. *Brain Research, 551*, 104–109.

Arbilla, S., & Langer, S. Z. (1978) Morphine and beta-endorphin inhibit release of noradrenaline from cerebral cortex but not of dopamine from rat striatum. *Nature, 271*, 559–561.

Bennett, C., Liang, K. C., & McGaugh, J. L. (1985). Depletion of adrenal catecholamines alters the amnestic effect of amygdala stimulation. *Behavioural Brain Research, 15*, 83–91.

Bloch, V. (1970). Facts and hypotheses concerning memory consolidation. *Brain Research, 24*, 561–575.

Bloch, V., Denti, A., & Schmaltz, G. (1966). Effets de la stimulation reticulaire sur la phase de consolidation de la trace amnesique. *Journal of Physiology, 58*, 469–470.

Borrell, J., de Kloet, E. R., Versteeg, D. H. G., & Bohus, B. (1983). Inhibitory avoidance deficit following short-term adrenalectomy in the rat: The role of adrenal catecholamines. *Behavioral and Neural Biology, 39*, 241–258.

Bovet, D., McGaugh, J. L., & Oliverio, A. (1966). Effects of posttrial administration of drugs on avoidance learning of mice. *Life Sciences, 5*, 1309–1315.

Breen, R. A., & McGaugh, J. L. (1961). Facilitation of maze learning with posttrial injections of picrotoxin. *Journal of Comparative and Physiological Psychology, 54*, 498–501.

Brioni, J. D., & McGaugh, J. L. (1988). Posttraining administration of GABAergic antagonists enhance retention of aversively motivated tasks. *Psychopharmacology, 26*, 505–510.

Brioni, J. D., Nagahara, A. H., & McGaugh, J. L. (1989). Involvement of the amygdala GABAergic system in the modulation of memory storage. *Brain Research, 487*, 105–112.

Brown, R., & Kulik, J. (1977). Flashbulb memories. *Cognition, 5*, 73–99.

Cahill, L., & McGaugh, J. L. (1991). NMDA-induced lesions of the amygdaloid complex block the retention enhancing effect of posttraining epinephrine. *Psychobiology, 19*, 206–210.

Cahill, L., & McGaugh, J. L. (1990). Amygdaloid complex lesions differentially affect retention of tasks using appetitive and aversive reinforcement. *Behavioral Neuroscience, 104*, 523–543.

Castellano, C., Brioni, J. D., & McGaugh, J. L. (1990). GABAergic modulation of memory. In L. Squire & E. Lindenlaub (Eds.), *Biology of memory* (pp. 361–378). Schattauer: Verlag.

Castellano, C., Brioni, J. D., Nagahara, A. H., & McGaugh, J. L. (1989). Posttraining systemic and intra-amygdala administration of the gaba-b agonist baclofen impair retention. *Behavioral and Neural Biology, 52*, 170–179.

Castellano, C., Introini-Collison, I. B., Pavone, F., & McGaugh, J. L. (1989). Effects of naloxone and naltrexone on memory consolidation in CD1 mice: Involvement of GABAergic mechanisms. *Pharmacology, Biochemistry and Behavior, 32*, 563–567.

Castellano, C., & McGaugh, J. L. (1989). Retention enhancement with posttraining picrotoxin: Lack of state dependency. *Behavioral and Neural Biology, 51*, 165–170.

Dawson, R. G., & McGaugh, J. L. (1973). Drug facilitation of learning and memory. In J. A. Deutsch (Ed.), *The physiological basis of memory* (pp. 77–111). New York: Academic Press.

Denti, A., McGaugh, J. L., Landfield, P. W., & Shinkman, P. (1970). Effects of posttrial electrical stimulation of the mesencephalic reticular formation on avoidance learning in rats. *Physiology and Behavior, 5*, 659–662.

de Wied, D. (1984). Neurohypophyseal hormone influences on learning and memory processes. In G. Lynch, J. L. McGaugh, & N. M. Weinberger (Eds.), *Neurobiology of learning and memory* (pp. 289–312). New York: Academic Press.

de Wied, D. (1991). The effects of neurohypophyseal hormones and related peptides on learning and memory processes. In R. C A. Frederickson, J. L. McGaugh, & D. L. Felten (Eds.), *Peripheral signaling of the brain: Role in neural-immune interactions, learning and memory*, (pp. 335–350). Toronto: Hogrefe & Huber.

Ettenberg, A., Le Moal, M., Koob, G. F., & Bloom, F. E. (1983). Vasopressin potentiation in the performance of a learned appetitive task: Reversal by a pressor antagonist analog of vasopressin. *Pharmacology, Biochemistry and Behavior, 18*, 645–647.

Ettenberg, A., van der Kooy, D., Le Moal, M., Koob, G. F., & Bloom, F. E. (1983). Can aversive properties of (peripherally injected) vasopressin account for its putative role in memory? *Behavioural Brain Research, 7*, 331–350.

Fanelli, R. J., Rosenberg, R. A., & Gallagher, M. (1985). Role of noradrenergic function in the opiate antagonist facilitation of spatial memory. *Behavioral Neuroscience, 99*(4), 751–755.

Gallagher, M. (1982). Naloxone enhancement of memory processes: Effects of other opiate antagonists. *Behavioral and Neural Biology, 35*, 375.

Gallagher, M. (1985). Re-viewing modulation of learning and memory. In N. M. Weinberger, J. L. McGaugh, & G. Lynch (Eds.), *Memory systems of the brain: Animal and human cognitive processes* (pp. 311–334). New York: Guilford Press.

Gallagher, M. and Kapp, B. S. (1978). Manipulation of opiate activity in the amygdala alters memory processes. *Life Sciences, 23*, 1973–1978.

Gallagher, M., Kapp, B. S., Pascoe, J. P., & Rapp, P. R. (1981). A neuropharmacology of amygdaloid systems which contribute to learning and memory. In Y. Ben-Ari (Ed.), *The amygdaloid complex* (pp. 343–354). Amsterdam: Elsevier/North Holland.

Gallagher, M., Rapp, P. R., & Fanelli, R. J. (1985). Opiate antagonist facilitation of time-dependent memory processes: Dependence upon intact norepinephrine function. *Brain Research, 347*, 284–290.

Gold, P. E. (1991). An integrated memory regulation system: From blood to brain. In R. C. A. Frederickson, J. L. McGaugh, & D. L. Felten (Eds.): *Peripheral signaling of the brain: Role in neural immune interactions, learning and memory* (pp. 391–420). Toronto: Hogrefe & Huber.

Gold, P. E., Delanoy, R. L., & Merrin, J. (1984). Modulation of long-term potentiation by peripherally administered amphetamine and epinephrine. *Brain Research, 305,* 103–107.

Gold, P. E., Hankins, L., Edwards, R. M., Chester, J., & McGaugh, J. L. (1975). Memory interference and facilitation with posttrial amygdala stimulation: Effect on memory varies with footshock level. *Brain Research, 86,* 509–513.

Gold, P. E., Macri, J., & McGaugh, J. L. (1973). Retrograde amnesia produced by subseizure amygdala stimulation. *Behavioral Biology, 9,* 671–680.

Gold, P. E., & McCarty, R. (1981). Plasma catecholamines: Changes after footshock and seizure-producing frontal cortex stimulation. *Behavioral and Neural Biology, 31,* 247–260.

Gold, P. E., & McGaugh, J. L. (1975). A single-trace, two process view of memory storage processes. In D. Deutsch & J. A. Deutsch (Eds.), *Short-term memory* (pp. 355–378). New York: Academic Press.

Gold, P. E., & van Buskirk, R. (1975). Facilitation of time-dependent memory processes with posttrial amygdala stimulation: Effect on memory varies with footshock level. *Brain Research, 86,* 509–513.

Gold, P. E., & van Buskirk, R. (1978a). Posttraining brain norepinephrine concentrations: Correlation with retention performance of avoidance training with peripheral epinephrine modulation of memory processing. *Behavioral Biology, 23,* 509–520.

Gold, P. E., & van Buskirk, R. (1978b). Effects of alpha and beta adrenergic receptor antagonists on post-trial epinephrine modulation of memory: Relationship to posttraining brain norepinephrine concentrations. *Behavioral Biology, 24,* 168–184.

Gold, P. E., van Buskirk, R., & Haycock, J. (1977). Effects of posttraining epinephrine injections on retention of avoidance training in mice. *Behavioral Biology, 20,* 197–207.

Heuer, F., & Reisberg, D. (1990). Vivid memories of emotional events: The accuracy of remembered minute. *Memory and Cognition, 18,* 496–506.

Hitchcock, J. M., & Davis, M. (1987). Fear-potentiated startle using an auditory conditioned stimulus: Effect of lesions of the amygdala. *Physiology and Behavior, 39,* 403–408.

Humphrey, G. L. (1968). *Effects of post-training strychnine on memory of stage I and stage II of sensory preconditioning in rats.* Ann Arbor: University Microfilms.

Huston, J. P., Mondadori, C., & Waser, P. G. (1974). Facilitation of learning by reward of post-trial memory processes. *Experientia, 30,* 1038–1040.

Introini-Collison, I. B., & Baratti, C. M. (1986). Opioid peptidergic systems modulate the activity of beta-adrenergic mechanisms during memory consolidation processes. *Behavioral and Neural Biology, 46,* 227–241.

Introini-Collison, I. B., & McGaugh, J. L. (1986). Epinephrine modulates long-term retention of an aversively-motivated discrimination task. *Behavioral and Neural Biology, 45,* 358–365.

Introini-Collison, I. B., & McGaugh, J. L. (1987). Naloxone and beta-endorphin alter the effects of posttraining epinephrine on retention of an inhibitory avoidance response. *Psychopharmacology, 92,* 229–235.

Introini-Collison, I. B., Miyazaki, B., & McGaugh, J. L. (1991). Involvement of the amygdala in the memory-enhancing effects of clenbuterol. *Psychopharmacology, 104,* 541–544.

Introini-Collison, I. B., Nagahara, A. H., & McGaugh, J. L. (1989). Memory-enhancement with intra-amygdala posttraining naloxone is blocked by concurrent administration of propranolol. *Brain Research, 476*, 94–101.

Introini-Collison, I. B., Saghafi, D., Novack, G., & McGaugh, J. L. (in press). Memory-enhancing effect of posttraining dipivefrin and epinephrine: Involvement of peripheral and central adrenergic receptors. *Brain Research*.

Izquierdo, I. (1979). Effect of naloxone and morphine on various forms of memory in the rat: Possible role of endogenous opiate mechanisms in memory consolidation. *Psychopharmacology, 66*, 199–203.

Izquierdo, I., & Dias, R. D. (1983). Effect of ACTH, epinephrine, B-endorphin, naloxone, and of the combination of naloxone or B-endorphin with ACTH or epinephrine on memory consolidation. *Psychoneuroendocrinology, 8*, 81–87.

Izquierdo, I., & Graudenz, M. (1980). Memory facilitation by naloxone is due to release of dopaminergic and beta-adrenergic systems from tonic inhibition. *Psychopharmacology, 67*, 265–268.

Jacobs, B. L. (1986). Single unit activity of locus coeruleus neurons in behaving animals. *Progress in Neurobiology, 27*, 183–194.

James, W. (1890). *The principles of psychology*. New York: Henry Holt.

Kesner, R. P., Walser, R. D., & Winzenried, G. (1989). Central but not basolateral amygdala mediates memory for positive affective experiences. *Behavioural Brain Research, 33*, 189–195.

Kesner, R. P., & Wilburn, M. W. (1974). A review of electrical stimulation of the brain in context of learning and retention. *Behavioral Biology, 10*, 259–293.

Kety, S. S. (1970). The biogenic amines in the central nervous system: Their possible roles in arousal, emotion and learning. In F. O. Schmitt (Ed.), *The neurosciences*. Rockefeller University Press.

Koob, G. F., Lebrun, C., Bluthe, R.-M., Dantzer, R., Dorsa, D. M., & Le Moal, M. (1991). Vasopressin and learning: Peripheral and central mechanisms. In R. C. A. Frederickson, J. L. McGaugh, & D. L. Felten (Eds.), *Peripheral signaling of the brain: Role in neural-immune interactions, learning and memory* (pp. 351–363). Toronto: Hogrefe & Huber.

Lantos, J. (Sept 11, 1990). *The first day of school: A primal terror returns*, (p. B7). Los Angeles Times

Laroche, S., & Bloch, V. (1982). Conditioning of hippocampal cells and long-term potentiation: An approach to mechanisms of posttrial memory facilitation. In C. Ajmone Marsan & H. Matthies (Eds.), *Neural plasticity and memory formation* (pp. 575–587). New York: Raven Press.

LeDoux, J. E., Iwata, J., Cicchetti, P., & Reis, D. J. (1988). Different projections of the central amygdaloid nucleus mediate autonomic and behavioral correlates of conditioned fear. *Journal of Neuroscience, 8*, 2517–2529.

Liang, K. C., Bennett, C., & McGaugh, J. L. (1985). Peripheral epinephrine modulates the effects of posttraining amygdala stimulation on memory. *Behavioural Brain Research, 15*, 93–100.

Liang, K. C., Juler, R., & McGaugh, J. L. (1986). Modulating effects of posttraining epinephrine on memory: Involvement of the amygdala noradrenergic system. *Brain Research, 368*, 125–133.

Liang, K. C., & McGaugh, J. L. (1983). Lesions of the stria terminalis attenuate the enhancing effect of posttraining epinephrine on retention of an inhibitory avoidance response. *Behavioural Brain Research, 9*, 49–58.

Liang, K. C., McGaugh, J. L, & Yao, H. Y. (1990). Involvement of amygdala pathways in the influence of posttraining amygdala norepinephrine and peripheral epinephrine on memory storage. *Brain Research, 508*, 225–233.

Livingston, R. B. (1967). Reinforcement. In G. C. Quarton, T. Melnechuk, & F. O. Schmitt (Eds.), *The neurosciences*. New York: Rockefeller University Press.

McCloskey, M., Wible, C. G., & Cohen, N. J. (1988). Is there a special flashbulb-memory mechanism? *Journal of Experimental Psychology, General, 117*, 171–181.

McGaugh, J. L. (1966). Time-dependent processes in memory storage. *Science, 153*, 1351–1358.

McGaugh, J. L. (1968). Drug facilitation of memory and learning. In *Psychopharmacology: A review of progress* (PHS Publication 1836, pp. 891–904). Washington, DC: U. S. Government Printing Office.

McGaugh, J. L. (1973). Drug facilitation of learning and memory. *Annual Review of Pharmacology, 13*, 229–241.

McGaugh, J. L. (1983). Hormonal influences on memory. *Annual Review of Psychology, 34*, 297–323.

McGaugh, J. L. (1989a). Involvement of hormonal and neuromodulatory systems in the regulation of memory storage. *Annual Review of Neuroscience, 12*, 255–287.

McGaugh, J. L. (1989b). Dissociating learning and performance: Drug and hormone enhancement of memory storage. *Brain Research Bulletin, 23*, 339–345.

McGaugh, J. L. (1990). Significance and remembrance: The role of neuromodulatory systems. *Psychological Science, 1*, 15–25.

McGaugh, J. L., Castellano, C., & Brioni, J. D. (1990). Picrotoxin enhances latent extinction of conditioned fear. *Behavioral Neuroscience, 104*, 262–265.

McGaugh, J. L., & Gold, P. E. (1976). Modulation of memory by electrical stimulation of the brain. In M. R. Rosenzweig & E. L. Bennett (Eds.), *Neural mechanisms of learning and memory*, (pp. 549–560). Cambridge: MIT Press.

McGaugh, J. L, & Gold, P.E. (1989). Hormonal modulation of memory. In R. B. Brush & S. Levine (Eds.), *Psychoendocrinology* (pp. 305–339). New York: Academic Press.

McGaugh, J. L., & Herz, M. J. (1972). *Memory consolidation*. San Francisco: Albion.

McGaugh, J. L., Introini-Collison, I. B., Juler, R. G., & Izquierdo, I. (1986). Stria terminalis lesions attenuate the effects of posttraining naloxone and b-endorphin on retention. *Behavioral Neuroscience, 100*, 839–844.

McGaugh, J. L., Introini-Collison, I. B., & Nagahara, A. H. (1988). Memory-enhancing effects of posttraining naloxone: Involvement of B-noradrenergic influences in the amygdaloid complex. *Brain Research, 446*, 37–49.

McGaugh, J. L., & Petrinovich, L. F. (1965). Effects of drugs on learning and memory. *International Review of Neurobiology, 8*, 139–196.

McGaugh, J. L., Thomson, C. W., Westbrook, W. H., & Hudspeth, W. J. (1962). A further study of learning facilitation with strychnine sulphate. *Psychopharmacologia, 3*, 352–360.

Messier, C., & White, N. M. (1984). Contingent and non-contingent actions of sucrose and saccharin reinforcers: Effects on taste preference and memory. *Physiology and Behavior, 32*, 195–203.

Messing, R. B., Jensen, R. A., Martinez Jr., J. L., Spiehler, V. R., Vasquez, B. J., Soumireu-Mourat, B., Liang, K. C., & McGaugh, J. L. (1979). Naloxone enhancement of memory. *Behavioral and Neural Biology, 27*, 266–275.

Montel, H., Starke, K., & Weber, F. (1974). Influence of morphine and naloxone on the release of noradrenaline from rat brain cortex slices. *Naunyn-Schmiedeberg's Archives of Pharmacology, 283*, 283–369.

Morley, J. E., & Flood, J. F. (1991). Gut peptides as modulators of memory. In R. C. A. Frederickson, J. L. McGaugh, & D. L. Felten (Eds.). *Peripheral signaling of the brain: Role in neural interactions, learning and memory* (pp. 379–390). Toronto: Hogrefe & Huber.

268   McGAUGH

Mueller, G. E., & Pilzecker, A. (1900). Experimentelle beitrage zur lehre vom gedachtniss. *Zeitschrift fuer Psychologie, 1*, 1–288.
Nakamura, S., Tepper, J. M., Young, S. J., Ling, N., & Groves, P. M. (1982). Noradrenergic terminal excitability: Effects of opioids. *Neuroscience Letters, 30*, 57–62.
Neisser, U. (1982). Snapshots or benchmarks. In U. Neisser (Ed.), *Memory observed: Remembering in natural contexts* (pp. 43–48). San Francisco: W. H. Freeman.
Neisser, U. (1986). Remembering Pearl Harbor: Reply to Thompson and Cowan. *Cognition, 23*, 285–286.
Schmidt, S. R., & Bohannon, J. N. (1988). In defense of the flashbulb-memory hypothesis: A comment on McCloskey, Wible and Cohen. *Journal of Experimental Psychology, General, 117*, 332–335.
Sternberg, D. B., & Gold, P. (1981). Retrograde amnesia produced by electrical stimulation of the amygdala: Attenuation with adrenergic antagonists. *Brain Research, 211*, 59–65.
Sternberg, D. B., Isaacs, K., Gold, P. E., & McGaugh, J. L. (1985). Epinephrine facilitation of appetitive learning: Attenuation with adrenergic receptor antagonists. *Behavioral and Neural Biology, 44*, 447–453.
Swartzwelder, H. S., Tilson, H. A., McLamb, R. L., & Wilson, W. A. (1987). Baclofen disrupts passive avoidance retention in rats. *Psychopharmacology, 92*, 398–401.
Tolman, E. C. (1932). *Purposive behavior in animals and men*. New York: Appleton-Century-Crofts.
van der Kolk, B. A., Greenberg, M. S., Orr, S. P., & Pitman, R. K. (1989). Endogenous opioids, stress induced analgesia, and posttraumatic stress disorder. *Psychopharmacology Bulletin, 25*, 417–421.
Weil-Malherbe, H., Axelrod, J., & Tomchick, R. (1959). Blood-brain barrier for adrenaline. *Science, 129*, 1226–1228.
Weiskrantz, L. (1956). Behavioral changes associated with ablation of the amygdaloid complex in monkeys. *Journal of Comparative and Physiological Psychology, 49*, 381–391.
Werling, L. L., Brown, S. R., & Cox, B. M. (1987). Opioid receptor regulation of the release of norepinephrine in brain. *Neuropharmacology, 26*, 987–996.
Werling, L. L., McMahon, P. N., Portoghese, P. S., Takemori, A. E., & Cox, B. M. (1989). Selective opioid antagonist effects on opioid-induced inhibition of release of norepinephrine in guinea pig cortex. *Neuropharmacology, 28*, 103–107.
Westbrook, W. H., & McGaugh, J. L. (1964). Drug facilitation of latent learning. *Psychopharmacologia, 5*, 440–446.
White, N. M. (1991). Peripheral and central memory enhancing actions of glucose. In R. C. A. Frederickson, J. L. McGaugh, & D. L. Felten (Eds.), *Peripheral signaling of the brain: Role in neural-immune interactions, learning and memory* (pp. 421–442). Toronto: Hogrefe & Huber.

Emotion As Memory: Anatomical Systems Underlying Indelible Neural Traces

Joseph E. LeDoux
New York University

EMOTION AS MEMORY

Once as a young boy I was walking on a path just above a stream. Suddenly, I noticed that the bank of the stream below was covered with more snakes than I ever care to see again. Had I not seen those snakes, my memory of that experience would surely be much less vivid than it is. I am unable to recall the more mundane events occurring before or after encountering the snakes, but I remember the image of the snakes slithering in the mud and the appearance of the surrounding countryside as if this experience had just happened yesterday. The arousal of emotion, fear in this case, presumably made me remember for more than 30 years the details of this excursion with such clarity.

This example illustrates an important feature of the relationship between memory and emotion. The arousal of emotion can facilitate the rememberance of events occurring during the aroused state. This is the essence of the flashbulb memory' hypothesis, which suggests that events occurring during intense emotional arousal are preserved in memory with special clarity and accuracy (Brown & Kulik 1977; Christianson, 1989). However, the effect of emotion on memory may be more general than is implied by the flashbulb hypothesis. Classic learning theory argues that learning occurs (i.e., memories are established) when stimuli and/or behaviors are followed by biologically significant (i.e., reinforcing) stimuli (e.g., Dollard & Miller, 1950; Hull, 1943; Konorski, 1948; Morwer, 1960; Pavlov, 1927; Skinner, 1938; Thorndike, 1913; Watson, 1930). Most stimuli that have reinforcing properties have emotional or hedonic properties and many (though certainly not all) learning theorists assume that the capacity of a stimulus to serve as a reinforcer is directly related to its hedonic properties. In this sense, memories that are dependent on reinforcement mechansims may also be dependent on the arousal of emotion. But this is not the relationship between emotion and memory that will be discussed here.

It has also been proposed that emotion can suppress memory, as in the psychoanalytic concept of repression (Erdelyi, 1985; Freud, 1915; Rapaport, 1942). According to this view, the recall of events associated with the arousal of emotion produces anxiety. In order to protect or defend against anxiety, the memory of those events is prevented from reaching awareness. There is an extensive and controversial experimental literature related to repression that falls under the rubrics of perceptual defense and subliminal processing (see Erdelyi, 1985; Eriksen, 1962; Dixon, 1971, 1981). But this is not the relationship between emotion and memory that is discussed either.

In addition to facilitating and inhibiting the rememberance of the events we experience in life, emotion itself can be a memory. This point is graphically illustrated by a classic case from the human amnesia literature (Claparede, 1911). The patient in question had a profound memory disturbance such that she was unable to con- sciously recall events that had occurred only moments before. On one occasion, the patient was stuck by a pin held in the examiner's hand. Shortly after being stuck, she was queried about what had just happened. She had no conscious memory of the event, but she refused to shake the examiner's hand again. This observation sug- gests that the brain system that stored the memory for the unpleasant experience (painful pin prick) and allowed the patient to react adaptively on the basis of the stored information (by avoiding the examiner's hand) was undisturbed by the brain damage that greatly impaired the patient's ability to consciously recollect the details of the experience. Memories for the affective significance of experiences are mediated by different brain circuits than conscious memories, sometimes called declarative memories (Squire, 1987), for the ex- perience itself.

Affective memories can be but are not necessarily memories in the sense of conscious recollections. However, they are memories in the sense that they represent information storage in the nervous system and in the sense that they can have powerful influences on future information processing and behavior. It is this kind of memory, memory for the emotional significance of experiences and its neural underpinnings, that is the subject of this chapter. Thus, emotion is to be treated as a memory process rather than as a process that simply influences (i.e., facilitates or inhibits) memory.

EMOTION AS COMPUTATION

To the man on the street, "emotion" most typcially means a subjective feeling state, such as feeling fearful, angry, happy, or in love. Subjective feeling states (i.e., emotional experiences) are indeed an important subset of the class of events referred to by emotion. Unfortunately, we have little understanding of the brain mechanisms of emotional experience (or of any other form of conscious experience for that matter). However, *conscious* emotional experiences are the end products of more basic *unconscious* emotional mechanisms that process the emotional significance of the stimuli we encounter, and considerable progress has been made in elucidating these more basic mechanisms. Much of this chapter is devoted to an examination of these more basic mechanisms.

What does it mean when we say that conscious emotional experiences are dependent on unconscious emotional processing mechanisms? This relationship is clarified by considering three influential classes of theories about emotional experience: central, cognitive, and facial feedback theories.

According to central theories, such as those proposed earlier in this century by Cannon (1927) and Papez (1937), emotional experience is the result of neural activity in brain circuits. Sensory stimuli are transmitted through the brain to the thalamus. From there, they are relayed to the cortex, where they are elaborated into perceptions and thoughts. Thalamic sensory inputs are also relayed to the hypothalamus, where their emotional significance is determined. The hypothalamus also receives inputs from the cortex, allowing it to evaluate the sigificance of perceptions and thoughts, as well as to evaluate more primitive sensory information derived from the sensory thalamus. In these central theories, emotional experiences are initiated by way of ascending connnections from the hypothalamus to the cerebral cortex. The quality of emotional experience is thus determined solely by the information transmitted to the cortex from the hypothalamus after it evaluates the significance of inputs from the thalamus or cortex. The basic conception of these older theories has withstood the test of time amazingly well. Recent studies, described later, strongly suggest that sensory information is transmitted from both thalamus and cortex to subcortical areas that evaluate the emotional significance of the stimuli. The critical subcortical area receiving the inputs, though, appears to be the amygdala rather than the hypothalamus. Further in line with these older theories is the suggestion that transmission from the amygdala to the cortex underlies emotional experiences (LeDoux, 1987, 1989).

In its classic form, cognitive theory (e.g., Schachter, 1975; Schachter and Singer, 1962) proposed that emotional experiences result when the brain becomes aware that the body is in a state of physiological arousal. Thus, stimuli from the environment are transmitted to the brain where they initiate emotionally ambiguous peripheral emotional responses, particularly autonomic/humoral responses. Information about this state of nonspecific peripheral arousal is transmitted back to the brain, and this elicits "evaluative needs." As a result, the organism (brain) interprets the emotionally ambiguous state of arousal on the basis of situational cues from the physical and social environment. This interpretation is the condition of emotional experience in cognitive theory.

Schachter and Singer's cognitive theory of emotional experience represented an attempt to overcome what they saw as a flaw in William James' theory of emotion. James (1890) had proposed that peripheral physiological feedback completely determines the nature of emotional experience. Cannon (1929) later argued that peripheral autonomic feedback lacked the specificity necessary to determine the nature of experience. Schachter and Singer's solution was to interpose "cognition" in the chain between nonspecific arousal and experience. However, James' theory did not rely entirely on autonomic feedback. He proposed that feedback during behavior, involving the somatic musculature, also contributed significantly to emotional experience. This point is amplified in a contemporary feedback theory, the facial feedback theory. According to facial feedback theory, emotional feelings result when the state of the facial muscles during emotional expression is communicated to the brain (e.g., Izard, 1977; Tomkins, 1962). In contrast to the cognitive theory, which requires that the brain interpret nonspecific peripheral feedback on the basis of external events in the environment, the feedback to the brain from the face is specific to the emotion expressed and is the condition that determines the emotion experienced.

All three classes of emotion theory reviewed require that some emotional coding take place before the generation of an emotional experience. Cognitive theory requires that the brain be able to distinguish emotional from nonemotional situations and thereby generate nonspecific physiological responses. Central theories require that subcortical brain areas identify the exact emotional implications of the stimulus so that the cortex can be properly informed and thereby produce an emotional experience appropriate to the stimulus. Facial feedback theory requires that the brain must determine the emotional significance of the stimulus so that the facial muscles can be appropriately contracted and provide emotionally specific, emotional experience-inducing feedback to the brain. These are competing theories. If one is a correct explanation of how emotional experience arises in a given situation, the others cannot be correct for that situation. Nevertheless, it is possible that each is correct for some subset of emotional experiences, and that a theory of emotional experience will ultimately have to incorporate all three positions. The key point is that these very different theories of emotional experience do agree on one thing: that emotional processing precedes conscious emotional experience. Emotional processing that precedes conscious emotional experience must by definition be unconscious.

Recent work in cognitive psychology has shown that much of human mental functioning takes place outside of conscious awareness (Erdelyi, 1985; Jackendoff, 1987; Kihlstrom, 1987; Marcel, 1983). The end-products of unconscious processes can be represented as conscious content, but the processes themselves, often referred to as computations, are inaccessible to conscious awareness (Jackendoff, 1987; Lashley, 1956). For the sake of the following discussion, unconsious processes that determine the affective significance of sensory stimuli are referred to as emotional computations.

A prime example of unconscious affective computations is provided by studies performed by Zajonc and colleagues (see Zajonc, 1980). They made use of the "mere exposure effect." The mere exposure effect involves the presentation of a series of pictures to subjects. At some later point, the subjects are asked to rate their preferences for a series of items, some of which were included in the first series. Typically, items included in the original series are preferred to a greater extent than new items, presumably reflecting some general tendency to prefer the familiar over the unfamiliar (Harrison, 1977). Zajonc and colleagues used nonsense shapes as stimuli and modified the presentation procedure so that the inital exposure to the items was very brief (1 ms). In subsequent tests the subjects were asked to either state whether they had seen a given stimulus before or to rate their preference for the item on a forced choice scale. Whereas recognition scores for previously exposed items were at chance, the subjects showed clear preferences for the old over the new items. The brief exposure time was insufficient to support stimulus recognition but was sufficient for the formation of preferences.

Zajonc's work shows that affective reactions (preference formation) can occur prior to and independent of conscious recognition of the eliciting stimulus. The affective computations controlled behavior but were not consciously processed. The brain can thus compute the emotional significance of the stimuli we encounter independent of its mechanism for recognizing what the stimulus is.

The demonstration that affective processing can occur unconsciously does not mean that it always occurs unconsciously. As conscious beings, we would like to believe that we are aware of (if not in charge of) the forces that control our mental life and behavior. However, the introduction of a conscious homunculus into the causal chain of mentation has always been problematic for psychological theory. Emotion theory is no exception. Zajonc's work, suggesting that significant aspects of emotional processing occur as unconscious computations, gives us a way out of the homunculus problem in emotion. Unconscious computations can account for much of the behavioral and autonomic expression of emotion but may also underlie the representation of emotion in consciousness. Thus, although we cannot dismiss a possible role of consciousness in the generation of emotion, we no longer need to depend on consciousness to explain emotional behavior and memory.

THE AMYGDALA AS
AN EMOTIONAL COMPUTER

The amygdala, a small region buried in the depths of the temporal lobe, is a critical structure in the brain's emotional network. The contribution of the amygdala to emotion was first discovered through studies of the Kluver–Bucy syndrome, a complex collection of behaviors produced by lesions of the primate temporal lobe (Kluver & Bucy, 1937). Monkeys with such lesions lose their fear of previously feared stimuli, attempt to copulate with members of the same sex or with members of different species, and try to eat inappropriate objects (such as their feces). Much (though not all) of the syndrome can be explained as a disconnection between the sensory and affective or motivational properties of stimuli (Geschwind, 1965; Jones & Mishkin, 1972; Weiskrantz, 1956). For example, visual stimuli are still perceived as visual objects, but the animal no longer responds in biologically and socially appropriate ways to the objects.

The initial studies of the Kluver–Bucy syndrome involved large lesions of the temporal lobe. Subsequent work showed that lesions of the amygdala alone would produce the same emotional changes (Weiskrantz, 1956). Since then, the amygdala has been repeatedly implicated in the neural processing of emotion using a number of different experimental approaches and procedures in a variety of species (e.g., Aggleton & Mishkin, 1986; Blanchard & Blanchard, 1972; Cohen, 1984; Davis & Hitchcock, & Rosen, 1987; Downer, 1961; Gloor, 1960; Hilton & Zbrozyna, 1963; Horel & Keating, 1969; Jones & Mishkin, 1972; Kapp, Pascoe, & Bixler, 1984; LeDoux, 1987; Nishijo, Ono, & Nichino, 1988; Ono et al., 1983; Rolls, 1981, 1986).

The amygdala's contribution to emotional processing is made possible as a result of its anatomical connectivity. The amygdala receives inputs from sensory processing areas in the neocortex (e.g., Amaral, 1987; Turner et al., 1980) and thalamus (LeDoux, 1986, 1987) and projects to areas in the brainstem that control behavioral, autonomic, and humoral response systems. These connections allow the amygdala to transform sensory stimuli into emotional signals and to initiate and control emotional responses.

The fact that the amygdala is a primary output of sensory processing areas in the thalamus and cortex allows us to view amygdala processing and, by implication, emotional processing, as a direct extension of primary sensory processing. For emotional processing, the amygdala thus takes over at the point where sensory information exits the sensory system. In the case of cortico–amygdala projections, emotional processing begins late in the sensory processing sequence; the amygdala thus evaluates the significance of complex information, such as fully perceived objects and events, by way of cortico–amygdala connections. However, in the case of thalmao–amygdala projections emotional processing is initiated very early in the sensory processing sequence, long before the system has had the opportunity to construct real-world objects and events out of the available sensory cues. The stimulus representation transmitted to the amygdala from the thalamus is relatively crude. It is perhaps more appropriately conceived of in terms of features and fragments rather than as images or perceptions. The activation of the amygdala by inputs from the neocortex is thus consistent with the classic notion that emotional processing is postcognitive, whereas the activation of the amygdala by thalamic inputs is consistent with the hypothesis, advanced by Zajonc (1980), that emotional processing can be preconscious and precognitive.

The thalamo–amygdala system is shorter by several synaptic links than the thalamo–cortico–amygdala projection route and is thus faster in its transmission time to the amygdala. The thalamo–amygdala system might be especially useful as a processing channel under conditions where rapid responses are required to threatening stimuli. In such situations it may be more important to respond quickly than to be certain that the stimulus merits a response. The extra time taken for the cortical sensory system to determine exactly what the stimulus is could be life threatening to an animal in the wild faced with a rapidly approaching loud sound. The nervous system does not need to know what the stimulus is. It simply needs to have programmed into it the fact that rapidly approaching visual or auditory stimuli are likely to be dangerous. This is a relatively simple determination that is probably within the processing capacity of the thalamic neurons that project to the amaygdala. The animal can thus begin to prepare to defend itself or escape, and, if additional information about the object properties of the stimulus reaching the amygdala from the cortex allows the amygdala to determine that the stimulus is not in fact threatening, the defense reaction can be aborted.

All animals have, in varying degrees, certain genetically specified emotional programs that are triggered by relatively invariant stimuli. Although these "hard-wired" reactions are important survival mechanisms, they are limited in their applicability in rapidly changing physical and social environments such as those faced by modern man. It is thus significant that the amygdala is capable of using sensory information as a basis for learning (forming associations through Pavlovian conditioning) about the emotional significance of sensory stimuli. This greatly expands the range of environmental stimulus features that may activate the emotional system.

In real-time processing, the amygdala receives inputs from both the thalamus and cortex, and either or both of these systems can be the basis of emotional learning. However, because sensory information reaches the amygdala from the thalamus before it does by way of the cortex, thalamic inputs have the opportunity to directly influence the amygdala's response to cortical inputs. On the one hand, the early arrival of sensory inputs from the thalamus may "prepare" the amygdala to process the later arriving information from the cortex by selecting and tuning appropriate neuronal ensembles in the amygdala. In this way, thalamo–amygdala processing may aid cortico–amygdala processing. However, it is also possible that the early arrival of inputs from the thalamus might allow the amygdala to inhibit descending inputs from the cortex, thereby allowing the thalamo–amygdala system to control emotional responses and establish emotional memories unchecked by descending influences from the neocortex. In such a situation, the amygdala would be generating emotional responses and memories on the basis of features and fragments rather than full-blown perceptions of objects and events. The emotional responses and memories established would therefore not necessarily correspond to the the ongoing conscious perceptions of the individual.

Although the foregoing has used the thalamo–amygdala circuit as an example of an unconscious processing circuit, this should not imply that cortico–amygdala circuits are involved in conscious emotional processing. The difference between thalamo–amygdala and cortico–amygdala circuits is best conceived as a difference in the trigger requirements of emotion than a difference between conscious and unconscious processing of emotion. Thus, emotion is triggered by low-level sensory processing in the case of thalamo–amygdala pathways and by higher level cognitive processing (of varying degrees, including modality-specific perceptual processes as well as modality-independent thought processes) in the case of cortico–amygdala pathways. As described earlier, cognitive processing is itself most appropriately viewed as unconscious processing. Although cognitive processing may ultimately contribute to the production of conscious content, the processing itself is not available to consciousness. Sensory processing in the cortex is part of the processing channel that leads to the conscious awareness of ongoing perceptions, but sensory inputs reaching the amygdala from the thalamus have exited this channel early on and are unlikely to become the raw material of consciousness. Emotional processing triggered by thalamic sensory inputs thus does not necessarily correspond to conscious perceptions, but emotional processing triggered by cortical inputs to the amygdala is likely to correspond to conscious perceptions.

It is easy to imagine that individual's vary, as a result of constitutional (genetic) differences, in the extent to which the thalamic or cortical pathways predominate in the initiation of emotional processing through the amygdala. If so, this could influence the extent to which an individual has control and feels in control of his or her emotional life.

So far the discussion has focused on the role of the amygdala in emotional processing without much attention to its role in emotional memory per se. However, except for instances of hard-wired responses to invariant stimuli, the amygdala must draw upon stored information in order to evaluate the significance of the stimuli it receives. Animals with lesions of the amygdala no longer respond to emotional properties that have been assigned to stimuli through associative learning and are unable to learn new emotional associations (Davis et al., 1987; Kapp et al., 1984; LeDoux, 1987; McGaugh, 1989). It is not clear whether the amygdala itself stores the learned associations or whether it is simply necessary in order to access associations stored elsewhere. One study suggests that the second hypothesis may be correct (Liang et al., 1982), but the study has not been replicated (McGaugh, personal communication). This is an important area for future research.

The amygdala thus fills the role proposed for the hypothalamus in the early central theories of emotion (see earlier). It receives and evaluates the significance of inputs from sensory processing areas of the thalamus and cortex. The amygdala also sends projections back to the cortex (see Amaral, 1987). The amygdalo–cortical projections terminate in both sensory processing areas as well as in higher order association areas of the temporal and frontal lobes. It is possible that projections to these areas from the amygdala fulfill the function suggested by early central theorists for projections from the hypothalamus to the cortex—the mediation of subjective emotional experiences. However, the neural mechanisms of subjective experiences of the emotional or unemotional kind remain as mysterious today as ever.

Although most of the evidence implicating the amygdala in emotional processes has been obtained from experimental animals, observations from human neurological patients are consistent with the animal work. For example, electrical stimulation of the amygdala in humans evokes affectively charged experiences (Gloor et al., 1982; Halgren, 1981) and unit activity in the human amygdala is modified during emotional arousal (Halgren, 1981). Moreover, bilateral damage to areas of the temporal lobe, including the amygdala, has been reported to produce the Kluver–Bucy syndrome in humans (Marlowe, Mancall, & Thomas, 1975; Pilleri, 1966; Sawa, Ueki, Arita, & Harada, 1954) and stereotaxic lesions of the amygdala have been used to reduce agressive and other affective response tendencies in humans (Valenstein, 1980).

The amygdala's contribution to emotional processes is incontrovertible. However, this conclusion should not be overextended to the point of suggesting that this is the only function of the amygdala. Though relatively small in size, the amygdala is extremely complex and its diverse input and output connections could easily sustain many different functions. Thus, claims that the amygdala contributes to cognitive processes (e.g., Mishkin, 1982; Murray & Mishkin, 1986) are not necessarily competitive with the role of the amygdala in emotion.

At the same time, the conclusion that the amygdala is involved in emotional processing should not be overextended to the point of suggesting that it is the only brain area involved in emotional processing. There are two aspects of this caveat. First, many regions that project to the amygdala are capable of modulating its activity even though they do not figure into the through processing circuitry. For example, several monoamine cell groups in the brainstem project to the amygdala and could very well play a role in controlling the transmission of sensory information through the amygdala and the conversion of sensory signals into motor response commands. Second, the brain circuits described in this chapter have mainly (though not exclusively) been identified through studies of fear and and fear conditioning (Pavlovian defensive conditioning). The through processing circuitry of other emotions, including nonaversive emotions as well as other aversive emotions, could involve other circuits. Nevertheless, there is evidence that the amygdala is essential to the processing of the reward value of appetitive stimuli (Gaffan & Harrison 1987; Jones & Mishkin, 1972; Nishijo et al., 1989; Rolls, 1986), suggesting that some aspects of appetitive emotion, though perhaps not all (Cahill & McGaugh, 1990), involve the amygdala.

In sum, the amygdala has been implicated in emotional processing in a variety of situtations. It is certainly not the only brain area involved in emotional processing, but it appears to be a critical one for many aspects of emotion.

INDELIBILITY OF EMOTIONAL MEMORY

Classically conditioned emotional memories are rapidly acquired, being present after one or two training trails, and are long lasting, persisting over months or even years if not extinguished by nonreinforced presentations of the tone without the shock. Once extinguished, the responses can recur spontaneously or can be reinstated by some irrelevant event, such as an unrelated exposure to a stressful stimulus (see Jacobs & Nadel, 1985). Extinction, obviously, does not erase the memory, it simply suppresses it. Conditioned emotional memories are, in other words, indelible. This phenomenon extends beyond the laboratory. For example, a phobic patient can be treated and live without his fear for many years. An unrelated traumatic event can then be the occasion for the reinstatement of the phobia. In such instances, the phobic memory is not lost but is simply held in check by other forces.

Recent experiments shed some light on this phenomenon. Lesions of cortical sensory processing areas do not prevent with the conditioning of emotional responses to a CS presented through the sensory modality that corresponds to the area of cortex lesioned (LeDoux, Sakaguchi, & Reis, 1984; LeDoux, Xagoraris, & Romanski 1989). However, such lesions dramatically interfere with extinction. Following repeated exposure to the CS in the absence of the US, the conditioned emotional responses persist in rats with cortical lesions long after the responses have extinguished in controls (LeDoux et al., 1989; McCabe et al., 1989). Lesions of sensory processing areas of the cortex probably prevent extinction because sensory cortex is the only channel through which sensory inputs can reach areas like the hippocampus or frontal cortex, which have been implicated in extinction processes (see Gray, 1982). Lesions of the amygdala or its sensory input pathways, as we have seen, prevent the initial establishment of the memories.

These findings suggest that emotional memories are indelible and normally maintained by subcortical circuits involving the amygdala. The behavioral expression of the stored information is under the control of additional memory systems. Extinction appears to operate on the memory circuits that control the expression of conditioned emotional behavior and not on the amygdaloid circuits that form and maintain the emotional memory per se.

CELLULAR MECHANISMS
OF EMOTIONAL PLASTICITY

The identification of circuits that are necessary for the establishment of emotional memories leaves open two important questions about how those circuits actually accomplish their mnemonic task. First, where in the circuit do the essential neural changes underlying the memory take place? Second, what are the cellular mechanisms that underlie the essential changes?

It is generally believed that the critical neural changes underlying memory take place at the level of synapses (Hebb, 1949; Kandel & Spencer, 1968; Lynch & Baudry, 1984; Thompson, 1986). For emotional memories of the type described here, the critical synapses most likely involve the amygdala. This conclusion is suggested by the fact that structures afferent to the amygdala are involved in the processing of sensory specific inputs (i.e., auditory or visual inputs), and structures efferent to the amygdala are involved in the control of specific motoric response modalities (i.e., autonomic or behavioral responses). The amygdala is the only brain area involved in the circuit regardless of the sensory modality of the conditioned stimulus or the motor modality of the conditioned response. The universal, integrative processing that underlies conditioned emotional memory formation is thus likely to take place in the amygdala. Said differently, the amygdala is likely to be a site of essential synaptic plasticity in the formation of emotional memories.

Synaptic plasticity has in fact been demonstrated in the amygdala. High-frequency stimulation of thalamo–amygdala (Clugnet & LeDoux, 1990) or cortico–amygdala (Chapman et al., 1988) projections produces long-term potentiation (LTP), a form of synaptic plasticity that has been proposed as a candidate cellular mechanism for learning and memory (Bliss & Lynch, 1988; Eccles, 1987; Brown, Chapman, Kairiss, & Keenan, 1988; Teyler & DiScenna, 1987). LTP is rapidly established and long lasting and has the property of "associativity." The associative nature of LTP means that plasticity only occurs when the postsynaptic cell receives two inputs that overlap in time. The second input must come while the postsynaptic cell is still depolarized from the first input. Associativity makes LTP particularly suitable as a candidate mechanism for associative memories, such as associative emotional memories established through classical conditioning.

LTP has been most extensively studied in the hippocampus. Hippocampal LTP has been discussed as a model of the rapid, initial learning that underlies long-term storage in declarative memory (e.g., Squire, Shimamura, & Aamaral, 1989). LTP can be produced in several hippocampal circuits, and in some of these the changes in synaptic efficacy are induced by glutamate acting at NMDA receptors (see Brown et al., 1989). NMDA receptor mechanisms are of particular interest because they seem to also function "associatively." Input A releases glutamate, which binds postsynaptically to non-NMDA receptors and depolarizes the cell. Depolarization results in the release of a magnesium block on NMDA receptors. If input B arrives during depolarization, NMDA receptors are thus activated. A missing piece in the puzzle is whether the memory functions of the hippocampus are best accounted for by this NMDA dependent or other cellular models of LTP (Brown et al., 1989). Nevertheless, NMDA-dependent LTP is an exciting phenomenon that seems to offer great promise, if not as a cellular explanation of memory, then at least as an experimental tool for studying how memories might be formed.

The thalamo–amygdala pathway contains glutamate (Farb, LeDoux, & Milner, 1989) and appears to utilize glutamate in synaptic tansmsission (Clugnet et al., 1988). Moreover, NMDA receptors are located in that part of the amygdala that receives the thalamic input (Monaghan & Cotman, 1985). Although it has not yet been shown that glutamate and NMDA receptors mediate amygdala LTP, recent studies have shown that blockade of NMDA receptors in the amygdala prevents the establishment of conditioned emotional memories (Miserendino et al., 1990). NMDA receptors have also been implicated in the plasticity observed in sensory cortex during development when sensory systems are either damaged or deprived of normal inputs at critical stages (Artola & Singer, 1989).

If further work continues to support the view that synaptic plasticity (particularly LTP-like synaptic plasticity) underlies memory and that emotional memories are established through excitatory amino acid-mediated synaptic plasticity in the amygdala, we would be drawn to the hypothesis that the brain has a fairly universal learning mechanism (experience dependent, excitatory amino acid-mediated synaptic plasticity) that is used in different brain areas to accomplish very different learning tasks (declarative memory in the hippoampus, developmental plasticity in cortex, and emotional memory in amygdala). Although much work remains to be done before this hypothesis can be taken too seriously, the initial data are very suggestive.

CONCLUSION

We are now at the threshold for understanding, at the level of cells and synpases, how the brain forms memories for the emotional signficance of events. These memories, mediated by sensory inputs to the amygdala, are indelible and are different from the memory of the event itself. Although different neural circuits underlie the memory for the emotional significance of the event and the memory of the event itself, the same cellular mechanisms may make these different memories possible.

ACKNOWLEDGMENTS

This chapter was supported by research grants from the National Health Institute of Mental Health (R37MH38774), and the New York Affiliate of the American Heart Association, and by an Established Investigator Award from the American Heart Association.

REFERENCES

Abrahams, V. C., Hilton, S. M., & Zbrozyna, A. (1960). Active muscle vasodilation produced by stimulation of the brain stem: Its significance in the defence reaction. *Journal of Physiology, 154,* 491–513.

Aggleton, J . P., & Mishkin, M. (1986). The amygdala: Sensory gateway to the emotions. In R. Plutchik & H. Kellerman (Eds.), *Emotion: Theory, research and experience* (Vol. 3, pp. 281–299). Orlando: Academic Press.

Alkon, D. L. (1984). Calcium-mediated reduction of ionic currents: A biophysical memory trace. *Science, 226,* 1037–1045.

Amaral, D. C. (1987). Memory: Anatomical organization of candidate brain regions. In F. Plum (Ed.), *Handbook of physiology. Section 1: The nervous system. Vol. V, Higher functions of the brain* (pp. 211–294). Bethesda, MD: American Physiological Society.

Artola, A., & Singer, W. (1989). NMDA receptors and developmental plasticity in visual neocortex. In J. C. Watkins and C. L. Collingridge, (Eds), *The NMDA Receptor* (pp. 153–166). Oxford: IRL Press.

Ben-Ari, Y. (1972). Plasticity at unitary level. I. An experimental design. *Electroencephalography and Clinical Neurophysiology, 32,* 655–665.

Blanchard, D. C., & Blanchard, R. J. (1972). Innate and conditioned reactions to threat in rats with amygdaloid lesions. *Journal of Comparative and Physiological Psychology, 81,* 281–290.

Bliss, T. V. P., & Lynch, M.A. (1988). In P. W. Landfield & S. Deadwyler, (Eds.), *Long-term potentiation: From biophysics to behavior* (pp. 3–72). New York: Alan R. Liss.

Brown, R., & Kulik, J. (1977). Flashbulb memories. *Cognition, 5,* 73–99.

Brown, T. H., Chapman, P. F., Kairiss, E. W., & Keenan, C.L. (1988). Long-term synaptic potentiation. *Science, 242,* 724–728.

Brown, T. H., Ganong, A. H., Kairiss, E. W., Keenan, C. L., & Kelso, S. R. (1989). Long-term potentiation in two synaptic systems of the hippocampal brain slice. In J. H. Byrne & W. O. Berry (Eds.), *Neural models of plasticity* (pp. 266–306). San Diego: Academic Press.

Cahill, L., & McGaugh, J. L. (1990). Amygdaloid complex lesions differentially affect retention of tasks using appetitive and aversive reinforcement. *Behavioral Neuroscience, 104,* 532–543.

Cain, D. P., Desborough, K. A., & Mckitrick, D. J. (1988). Retardation of amygdala kindling by antagonism of NMD-aspartate and muscarinic cholinergic receptors: Evidence for the summation of excitatory mechanisms in kindling. *Experimental Neurology, 100,* 179–187.

Cannon, W. B. (1927). The James-Lange theory of emotions: A critical examination and an alternative theory. *American Journal of Psychology, 39,* 106–124.

Cannon, W. B. (1929). *Bodily changes in pain, hunger, fear, and rage.* New York: Appleton

Chapman, P. F., & Brown, T. H. (1988). Long-term potentiation in amygdala brain slices. *Society for Neuroscience Abstracts, 14,* 566–566.

Christianson, S.-Å. (1989). Flashbulb memories: Special, but not so special. *Memory and Cognition, 17*(4), 435–443.

Claparede, E. (1911). Recognition and "me-ness". In D. Rapaport (Ed.), *Organization and pathology of thought* (1951) (pp. 58–75). New York: Columbia University Press.

Clugnet, M. C., & LeDoux, J. E. (1990). Synaptic plasticity in fear conditioning circuits: Induction of LTP in the lateral nucleus of the amygdala by stimulation of the medial geniculate body. *Journal of Neuroscience, 10,* 1055–1061.

Clugnet, M. C., LeDoux, J. E., & Morrison, S. F. (1990). Unit responses evoked in the amygdala and striatum by electrical stimulation of the medial geniculate body. *Journal of Neuroscience, 10,* 1055–1061.

Clugnet, M. C., LeDoux, J. E., Morrison, S. F., & Reis, D. J. (1988). Short latency orthodromic action potentials evoked in the amygdala and caudate-putamen by stimulation of the medial geniculate body. *Society For Neuroscience Abstract, 14,* 1227–1227.

Cohen, D. H. (1984). Identification of vertebrate neurons modified during learning: Analysis of sensory pathways. In D. L. Alkon & J. Farley (Eds.), *Primary Neural Substrates of Learning and Behavioral Change.* Cambridge: Cambridge Press.

Creutzfeldt, O. D., Bell, F. R., & Ross Adey, W. (1963). The activity of neurons in the amygdala of the cat following afferent stimulation. *Progress Brain Research, 3,* 31–49.

Davis, M., Hitchcock, J. M., & Rosen J. B. (1987). Anxiety and the amygdala: Pharmacological and anatomical analysis of the fear-potentiated startle paradigm. In G. H. Bower (Ed.), *The Psychology of learning and motivation.* San Diego: Academic Press.

Dixon, N. F. (1971). *Subliminal perception: The nature of controversy.* London: McGraw-Hill

Dixon, N. F. (1981). *Preconscious processing.* New York: Wiley.

Dollard, J. C., & Miller, N. E. (1950). *Personality and psychotherapy.* New York: McGraw-Hill

Downer, J. D. C. (1961). Changes in visual gnostic function and emotional behavior following unilateral temporal lobe damage in the "split-brain" monkey. *Nature, 191,* 50–51.

Eccles, J. C. (1987). Mechanisms of learning in complex neural systems. In F. Plum (Ed.), *Handbook of Physiology, Section I: The nervous system: Vol. 5. Higher functions of the brain* (pp. 137–167). Bethesda: American Physiological Society.

Erdelyi, M. H. (1985). *Psychoanalysis: Freud's cognitive psychology.* New York: Freeman.

Eriksen, C. W. (1962). *Behavior and awareness.* Durham, NC: Duke University Press.

Farb, C. F., LeDoux, J. E., & Milner, T. A.(1989). Glutamate is present in medial geniculate body neurons that project to lateral amygdala and in lateral amygdala presynaptic terminals. *Society Neuroscience Abstract* (p. 890).

Freud, S. (1915). In J. Strachey (Ed.), *The standard edition of the complete psychological works of Sigmund Freud.* London: Hogarth.

Gaffan, D., & Harrison, S. (1987). Amygdalectomy and disconnection in visual learning for auditory secondary reinforcement by monkeys. *Journal of Neuroscience, 7,* 2285–2292.

Geschwind, N. (1965). The disconnexion syndromes in animals and man. Part I. *Brain, 88,* 237-294.

Gibbs, C. M., Cohen, D. H., & Broyles, J. L. (1986). Modification of the discharge of lateral geniculate neurons during visual learning. *Journal of Neuroscience, 6,* 627–636.

Gloor, P. (1960). Amygdala. *Handbook of Physiology, 2,* 1395–1420.

Gloor, P. (1986). Role of the human limbic system in perception, memory, and affect: Lessons from temporal lobe epilepsy. In B. H. Doane & K. E. Livingston, (Eds.), *The limbic system: Functional organization and clinical disorders* (pp. 159–169). New York: Raven Press.

Halgren, E. (1981). The amygdala contribution to emotion and memory: Current studies in humans. In Y. Ben-Ari (Ed.), *The amygdaloid complex* (pp. 395–408). Amsterdam: Elsevier.

Harrison, A. A. (1977). Mere exposure. In L. Berkowitz (Ed.), *Advances in experimental social psychology.* New York: Academic Press.

Hebb, D. O. (1949). *The organization of behavior.* New York: Wiey.

Hilton, S. M., & Zbrozyna, A. W. (1963). Amydaloid region for defense reactions and its efferent pathway to the brainstem. *Journal of Physiology, 165,* 160–173.

Horel, J. A., & Keating, E.G. (1969). Partial Kluver–Bucy syndrome produced by cortical disconnection. *Brain Research, 16,* 281–284.

Izard, C. E. (1977). *Human Emotions.* New York: Plenum.

Jackendoff, R. (1987). *Consciousness and the computational mind.* Cambridge: MIT Press.

Jacobs, W. J., & Nadel, L. (1985). Stress-induced recovery of fears and phobias. *Psychological Review, 92,* 512–531.

James, W. (1890). *Principles of Psychology.* New York: Holt.

Jones, B., & Mishkin, M. (1972). Limbic lesions and the problem of stimulus-reinforcement associations. *Experimental Neurology, 36,* 362–377.

Kandel, E. R., & Spencer, W. A. (1968). Cellular neurophysiological approaches to the study of learning. Physiology Review, 48, 65–134.

Kapp, B. S., Frysinger, R. C., Gallagher, M., & Haselton J. (1979). Amygdala central nucleus lesions: Effect on heart rate conditioning in the rabbit. *Physiology and Behavior, 23,* 1109–1117.

Kapp, B. S., Pascoe, J. P., & Bixler, M. A. (1984). The amygdala: A neuroanatomical systems approach to its contributions to aversive conditioning. In N. Buttlers & L. R. Squire (Eds.), *Neuropsychology of Memory.* New York: Guilford.

Kihlstrom, J. F. (1987). The cognitive unconscious. *Science, 237,* 1445–1452.

Kluver, H., & Bucy, P. C. (1937). "Psychic blindness" and other symptoms following bilateral temporal lobectomy in rhesus monkeys. *American Journal of Physiology, 119,* 352–353.

Lashley, H. (1956). Cerebral organization and behavior. In H. Solomon, S. Cobb, & W. Penfield (Eds.), *The Brain and Human Behavior* (pp. 1–18). Baltimore: Williams & Wilkins.

LeDoux, J. E. (1986). Sensory systems and emotion. *Integrative Psychiatry, 4,* 237–248.

LeDoux, J. E. (1987). Emotion. In F. Plum (Ed.), *Handbook of physiology. 1: The nervous system. Vol. V, Higher Functions of the Brain* (pp. 419-460). Bethesda, MD: American Physiological Society.

LeDoux, J. E. (1989b). Cognitive-emotional interactions in the brain. *Cognition and Emotion, 3,* 267–289.

LeDoux, J. E., Cicchetti, P., Xagoraris, A., & Romanski, L. R. (1990a). The lateral amygdaloid nucleus: Sensory interface of the amygdala in fear conditioning. *Journal of Neuroscience, 10,* 1062–1069.

LeDoux, J. E., Farb, C. F., & Ruggiero, D. A. (1990c). Topographic organization of neurons in the acoustic thalamus that project to the amygdala. *Journal of Neuroscience, 10,* 1043–1054.

LeDoux, J. E., Iwata, J., Cicchetti, P., & Reis, D. J. (1988). Different projections of the central amygdaloid nucleus mediate autonomic and behavioral correlates of conditioned fear. *Journal of Neuroscience, 8,* 2517–2529.

LeDoux, J. E., Romanski, L. M., & Xagoraris, A. E. (1989a). Indelibility of subcortical emotional memories. *Journal of Cognitive Neuroscience, 1,* 238–243.

LeDoux, J. E., Ruggiero, D. A., Forest, R., Stornetta, R., & Reis, D. J. (1987). Topographic organization of convergent projections to the thalamus from the inferior colliculus and spinal cord in the rat. *Journal of Comparative Neurology, 264*, 123–146.

LeDoux, J. E., Sakaguchi, J., Iwata, J., & Reis, D. J. (1986). Destruction of intrinsic neurons in the lateral hypothalamus disrupts the associative conditioning of autonomic but not behavioral emotional responses in the rat. *Brain Research, 368*, 161–166.

LeDoux, J. E., Sakaguchi, A., & Reis, D. J. (1984). Subcortical efferent projections of the medial geniculate nucleus mediate emotonal responses conditioned to acoustic stimuli. *Journal of Neuroscience, 4*, 683–698.

LeDoux, J. E., Xagoraris, A., & Romanski, L. M. (1989). Indelibility of subcortical emotional memories. *Journal of Cognitive Neuroscience, 1*, 238–243.

Liang, K. C., McGaugh, J. L., Martinez, J. L., Jensen, R. A., Vasquez, B. J., & Messing, R. B. (1982). Post-training amygdaloid lesions impair retention of an inhibitory avoidance response. *Behaviorial Brain Research, 4*, 237–249.

Lynch, G., & Baudry, M. (1984). The biochemistry of memory: A new and specific hypothesis. *Science, 224*, 1057–1063.

Marcel, A. (1983). Conscious and unconscious perception: Experiments on visual masking and word recognition. *Cognitive Psychology, 15*, 238–300.

Marlowe, W. B., Mancall, E. L., & Thomas, J .J. (1975). Complete Kluver–Bucy syndrome in man. *Cortex, 11*, 53–59.

McGaugh, J. L. (1989). Involvement of hormonal and neuromodulatory systems in the regulation of memory storage. *Annual Review of Psychology, 34*, 297–323.

Miserendino, M. J. D., Sananes, C. B., Melia, K. R., & Davis, M. (1990). Blocking of acquisition but not expression of conditioned fear-potentiated startle by NMDA antagonists in the amygdala. *Nature, 345*, 716–718.

Mishkin, M. (1978). Memory in monkeys severely impaired by combined but not separate removal amygdala and hippocampus. *Nature, 273*, 297–298.

Mishkin, M. (1982). A memory system in the monkey. Philosophical Transactions of the Royal Society of London, B, *Bilogical Science, 289*, 85–95.

Monaghan, D. T., & Cotman, C. W. (1985). Distribution of N-Methyl-D-aspartate-sensitive L-(3H)Glutamate-binding sites in rat brain. *Journal of Neuroscience, 5*, 2909–2919.

Morwer, O. H. (1960). *Learning theory and behavior.* New York: Wiley.

Murphy, J. T., Dreifuss, J. J., & Gloor, P. (1968). Responses of hypothalamic neurons to repetitive amygdaloid stimulation. *Brain Research, 8*, 153–166.

Murray, E. A., & Mishkin, M. (1985). Amygdalectomy impairs crossmodal association in monkeys. *Science, 228*, 604–606.

Murray, E. A., & Mishkin, M. (1986). Visual recognition in monkeys following rhinal cortical ablations combined with either amygdalectomy or hippocampectomy. *Journal of Neuroscience, 6*(7), 1991–2003.

Nakada, T., Lee, H., Kwee, I. L., & Lerner, A. M. (1984). Epileptic Kluver–Bucy syndrome: Case report. *Journal of Clinical Psychiatry, 45*, 87–88.

Nishijo, H., Ono, T., & Nishino, H. (1988). Single neuron responses in amygdala of alert monkey during complex sensory stimulation with affective significance. *Journal of Neuroscience, 8*, 3570–3583.

Ono, T., Fukuda, M., Nishino, H., Sasaki, K., & Muramoto, K. (1983). Amygdaloid neuronal responses to complex visual stimuli in an operant feeding situation in the monkey. *Brain Research Bulletin, 11*, 515–518.

Papez, J. W. (1937). A proposed mechanism of emotion. *Archives of Neurology and Psychiatry, 79*, 217–224.

Pavlov, I. P. (1927). *Conditioned reflexes.* New York: Dover.

Pilleri, G. (1966). The Kluver–Bucy syndrome in man. *Psychiatry and Neurology, 152*, 65–103.

Rapaport, D. (1950). *Emotions and memory.* New York: International Universities Press.

Riolobos, A. S., & Garcia, A. I. M. (1987). Open field activity and passive avoidance responses in rats after lesion of the central amygdaloid nucleus by electrocoagulation and ibotenic acid. *Physiology Behavior, 39*, 715–720.

Rolls, E. T. (1981). Responses of amygdala neurons in the primate. In Y. Ben-Ari, (Ed.) *The Amygdaloid Complex* (pp. 383–393). Elsevier, Amsterdam.

Rolls, E. T. (1986) A theory of emotion, and its application to understanding the neural basis of emotion. In Y. Oomur, (Ed.), *Emotions: Neural and Chemical Control* (pp. 325–344). Tokyo: Japan Scientific Societies Press.

Russchen, F. T. (1982). Amygdalopetal projections in the cat. I. Cortical afferent connections. A study with retrograde and anterograde tracing techniques. *Journal of Comparative Neurology, 206*, 159–179.

Sawa, M., Ueki, Y., Arita, M., & Harada, T. (1954). Preliminary report on the effects of amygdalotomy on the psychotic patient with interpretation of oral–emotional manifestation in schizophrenics. *Folia Psychiat. Neurol. Jap., 7*, 309-329.

Schachter, S., & Singer, J. E. (1962). Cognitive, social, and physiological determinants of emotional state. *Psychological Review, 69*, 379–399.

Schachter, S. (1975). *Cognition and centralist-peripheralist controversies in motivation* (pp. 529–564). New York: Academic Press.

Skinner, B. F. (1938). *The behavior of organisms: An experimental analysis.* New York: Appleton-Century-Crofts.

Squire, L. R. (1987). Memory: Neural organization and behavior. In F. Plum (Ed.), *Handbook of Physiology, Section 1: The nervous system: Vol. V. Higher functions of the brain* (pp. 295–371). Bethesda: American Physiological Society.

Squire, L. R., Shimamura, A. P., & Amaral, D. C. (1989). Memory and the hippocampus. In J. H. Byrne & W. O. Berry (Eds), *Neural Models of Plasticity* (pp. 208–239). San Diego: Academic Press.

Teich, A. H., McCabe, P. M., Gentile, C. C., Schneiderman, L. S., Winters, R. W., Liskowsky, D. R., & Schneiderman, N. (1989). Auditory cortex lesions prevent the extinction of Pavlovian differential heart rate conditioning to tonal stimuli in rabbits. *Brain Research, 480*, 210–218.

Teyler, T. J., & DiScenna, P. (1987). Long-term potentiation. *Annual Review of Neuroscience, 10*, 131–161.

Thompson, R. F. (1986). The neurobiology of learning and memory. *Science, 233*, 941–947.

Thorndike, E. L. (1913). *The psychology of learning.* New York: Teachers College.

Tomkins, S. S. (1962). *Affect, Imagery, Consciousness.* New York: Springer.

Turner, B. H., Mishkin, M., & Knapp, M. (1980). Organization of the amygdalopetal projections from modality-specific cortical association areas in the monkey. *Journal of Comparative Neurology, 191*, 515–543.

Turner, B. H. (1981). The cortical sequence and terminal distribution of sensory related afferents to the amygdaloid complex of the rat and monkey. In Y. Ben-Ari (Ed.), *The Amygdaloid Complex* (pp. 51–62). New York: Elsevier/North-Holland Biomedical Press.

Valenstein, E. S. (1980). *The psychosurgery debate: Scientific, legal, and ethical perspectives* (edited volume). San Francisco: Freeman.

Watson, J. B. (1930). *Behaviorism.* Chicago: University of Chicago Press.

Weiskrantz, L. (1956). Behavioral changes associated with ablation of the amygdaloid complex in monkeys. *Journal of Comparative Physiological Psychology, 49*, 381–391.

Zajonc, R. (1980). Feeling and thinking: Preferences need no inferences. *American Psychology, 35*, 151–175.

12

Biological Aspects of Memory and Emotion: Affect and Cognition

Lars-Göran Nilsson
University of Umeå

Trevor Archer
University of Götenborg

The relationship between emotion and memory has been of a long-standing interest in psychological theory. Although this relation appears to be a rather complex one, its understanding has no doubt been regarded as being within reach—especially so if the disciplines per se (emotion and memory) could be conceived of as relatively unitary concepts.

However, neither emotion nor memory can usefully be seen as unitary in nature. With respect to emotion, the essentially unitary requirement was first implied within the James-Lange and Descartian approaches. However, with the emerging research of Cannon (1929), physiological psychological discoveries demonstrated interactions between higher cortical mechanisms and emotional systems; in the face of these developments it appeared futile to maintain the view of an unitary concept. The basic assumption was that information about perceived stimuli reaches the cortex via subcortical systems, and that this stimulus input acquires an emotional flavor at the subcortical level. Simultaneously with, and independently of, the input to cortex from subcortex, the information about this stimulus input is sent to the peripheral system. Thus, the historical lesson to be learnt from such accumulated physiological and neuroana-tomical evidence was that emotion should not be regarded as a unitary concept. There are at least three effective processes that may be specified and that would have to be accounted for by any theory of emotion. These processes involve: first, an evaluation of the stimulus; second, the kind of bodily expression (by which we are assuming the brain and central nervous system to be orchestrating the rest of body functioning) that occurs: and, third, the conscious experience or awareness of any given emotion.

Memory, too, was first conceived of as a unitary entity, but soon other views began to emerge (for an historical and conceptual account of these, see Crowder, 1985; Tulving, 1985). For example, Cohen and Squire (1980) assumed two subsystems: declarative and procedural memory. Tulving (1983) classified three memory systems: episodic memory, semantic memory, and procedural memory. Recently, Tulving and Schacter (1990) have added a fourth system to this classification, the perceptual representation system. For both these two types of classification, each memory system is regarded as being ontologically realistic. Advantages and disadvantages with each of these and other classificatory systems are currently being debated.

A theoretically more neutral classificatory system was recently proposed by Graf and Schacter (1985) in terms of explicit and implicit memory. This classification can be regarded as orthogonal to all other classifications proposed. Rather than being assumed to be ontologically real, the terms by Graf and Schacter should be seen as descriptive only. Explicit memory is described as being involved whenever a conscious recollection of the study episode is required. Implicit memory does not require such a conscious recollection. The concept of awareness in memory may eventually prove to be of central importance despite possible indications to the contrary (see Brewer, 1974; Dawson & Schell, 1987). Recently, Boakes (1989) suggested that brain functioning utilizes a preattentive system that is directed towards temporal relationships. He suggested that this system could operate in parallel with a variety of other mental processes. An "awareness response" is registered when two events in excess of threshold strength provide a relationship that allows interruption of the central, serial processor. In the example provided by Boakes (1989), the *episodic* significance of the relationship was necessary for the construction of an explicit memory, a more simple, *semantic*, association would classify the relationship in implicit memory.

This chapter takes initially a tentative approach to relate different aspects of emotion to different forms of memory. The concepts explicit and implicit memory do appear to be theoretically neutral and therefore may provide a suitable framework for this initial endeavour (i.e., to relate the emotional causality aspect to certain forms of memory). Moreover, a series of interesting dissociations have been observed in relation to these terms—dissociations that might prove valuable for the understanding of the relationship between emotional states and memorial processes. More specifically, it has been demonstrated that amnesic patients show severe memory deficits in explicit memory tasks requiring a conscious recollection of the study episode, whereas in implicit memory tasks their performance is largely the same as that of normal control subjects. We propose as a working hypothesis that affective pathology might affect not only explicit memory but the performance in implicit memory tasks as well. Indeed, within certain types of depressive illness it may be necessary to provide analyses of implicit memory function in order to aid diagnosis and therapy.

In this chapter of some influences of *affect* on cognition, it is indicated at the outset that only a rudimentary concept of memory is employed, without reference to the intricate classifications extant. In doing so, the purpose is to suggest some striking commonalities between the evidence from various psychobiological sources on the relationships among stress, affective states, and cognitive performance.

Generally, in the laboratory setting, the measurements of memory functions following mild or traumatic stress treatment have not been applied to an analysis of memory and emotions. One recent exception is the effect of stress/separation upon social learning by rats (see following). The present treatise will deal with three aspects of stress and memory, as seen from a psychobiological perspective: (a) the evidence for deficits in remembering by depressed persons suffering affective disorders; (b) the evidence for deficits in learning performance by laboratory rats submitted to stress and/or separation anxiety; (c) some evidence for electrophysiological correlates of altered cognitive performances following treatments leading to stressful reactions.

REMEMBERING DEFICITS BY PERSONS SUFFERING FROM AFFECTIVE DISORDERS

The problem of emotional disorders following traumatic experiences was tragically illustrated many years ago by Arnold Auerbach (1947). Among other behavioral disorders noted was the inability among otherwise fully capable GIs of the United States army to go back to their academic pursuits with the same successful academic performances. Typically, a surprisingly large number of soldiers, many of whom were decorated for bravery in action, showed severe and long-lasting bouts of mood disturbance that prove an impediment to normal and effective functioning in ordinary work life. Certainly, Auerbach's (conducted over several years) interviews indicated that the emotional instability did, in many cases, affect cognitive performances.

It appears that several studies indicate that the severity of depressive illness may be an important factor determining the performance of remembering tasks (e.g., Harness, Bental, & Carmon, 1977; Sternberg & Jarvik, 1976). However, there is some doubt as to whether depressed patients do, indeed, show memory impairments or whether the evidence represents a performance deficit due to lack of effort and/or concentration (cf. Cohen, Weingartner, Smallberg, Pickar, & Murphy, 1982c; Henry, Weingartner, & Murphy, 1973; Stromgren, 1977). Certainly, one potentially complicating factor is the characteristic "loss of interest" and "lack of pleasurable experience" shown by depressed persons (e.g., Eastman, 1976; Nelson & Charney, 1981). This factor may be of some consequence, because depressed persons tended to rate videotape recordings of their own behaviors in tests of "social intelligence" more negatively (Roth & Rehm, 1980). Thus, Derry and Kuiper (1981) have shown that persons suffering from depressive illness remember significantly more words related to depression, whereas the control subjects remembered more neutral words. Other studies have shown that depressed persons remember negative events better and faster and with a higher frequency than pleasant or neutral events (cf. Clark & Teasdale, 1982; Fogarty & Hemsley, 1983; Lishman, 1972; Lloyd & Lishman, 1975). This influence of affective state upon memory appears to be quite a general finding although, even in the case of anxiety disorders, the issue is complicated. Anxious students (O'Banion & Arkowitz, 1977; Mueller & Curtois, 1980) and agoraphobics (Bradley & Mathews, 1983) show recall bias for negative or self-descriptive traits but patients suffering from generalized anxiety disorder show no bias (Mogg, Mathews, & Weinman, 1987). It may well be that anxiety- and depression-induced biases in memory are essentially different, but there appears to be some manner of overlap between these disorders (i.e., depression and anxiety) in the cognitive output (Clark & Hemsley, 1985; Hollon & Kendall, 1980). The problems inherent to interpreting these data and even more recent evidence by Eysenck, Mogg, May, Richards, and Mathews (in press) are succinctly outlined in the chapter by Eysenck and Mogg (this volume), who suggest that anxious persons may simply be more likely than nonanxious persons to emit threat-related responses although not differing in memory-processing capability. Eysenck and Mogg (ibid) consider also the likelihood of an *interpretative bias*, based on evidence from the remembering of ambiguous words by agoraphobics (Nunn, Stevenson, & Whalan, 1984). However, the chapter by Eysenck and Mogg (ibid) also lists much evidence inconsistent with a negative memory bias explanation. In order to address the essential problem of negative bias, Eysenck suggests that the tactic of studying implicit memory may be a fruitful approach and describes results by Richards demonstrating negative bias in implicit, but not in explicit, memory (see also Mathews, Mogg, & Eysenck, 1989). For present purposes it is interesting to note that some evidence may suggest that substantial emotional processing may be of an unconscious nature, as discussed in the chapter by LeDoux (this volume).

The evidence, therefore, suggests two main constraints of an altered emotional condition (as produced, for example, in an affective disorder) upon cognitive performance. First, the performance of memory/remembering tasks may be disrupted, possibly due to lack of sufficient effort. Second, there may be an "affective bias" in the recall, recognition, and/or information processing of word lists whereby only words with negative meaning are primarily recalled. In the latter case, the role of contextual variables has been discussed (Bower, 1981), whereby a depressed mood, the context, facilitates the selective recall of negative items. It is important to note that the depressive cognitive style in severely depressed patients can become normal following appropriate treatment (Hamilton & Abramson, 1983). Consensus of the information available appears to be that the depressive style of cognition does not develop prior to the onset of the disorder but rather during the illness.

A different type of emotional problem that may be observed clinically pertains to the stress or trauma resulting from menopause. It has been found that among the somatic and behavioral changes that occur with menopause, some disruptions of cognitive functioning may be prominent (Kopera, 1973; Malleson, 1953). Because menopause generally occurs around 50 years of age, it is possible that the degenerative effects of middle age on certain cognitive tasks (e.g., Botwinick, 1977; Denny, 1979) may be due to mild, generalized changes in central nervous system functioning related to the aging process. On the other hand, it is also possible that the neuroendocrine alterations characterizing menopause are the direct causes of the memory deficits (for an exhaustive review of the effects of the gonadal hormones on learning and memory performance, see Van Haaren, Van Hest, & Heinsbroek, 1990). Certainly, there is evidence that estrogen replacement to postmenopausal women may improve "cognitive detriments" (Campbell & Whitehead, 1977; Fedor-Freybergh, 1977; Hackman & Galbraith, 1977; Schneider, Brotherton, & Hailes, 1977). Nonetheless, there are also discrepant reports of a lack of differences between estrogen-treated and untreated women (e.g., Rauramo, Lagerspetz, Engblom, & Punnonen, 1975; Vanhulle & Demol, 1976). Some measure of the cognitive performance of surgically menopausal women (total hysterectomy and bilateral salpingo-oophorectomy) appears to offer one solution to the problem of menopause and memory deficits. Sherwin (1988) studied the effects of estrogen and/or androgen replacement therapy to surgically menopausal women with regard to cognitive performance in different tasks. Their ages ranged from a mean of 30.6 (hysterectomized) to 45.4 years (bilateral oophorectomized), and they were matched academically for occupational status and on personality inventories. Cognitive tests included tests for short-term memory, long-term memory, and logical reasoning. The results of this investigation appear quite clear. Combined estrogen–androgen administration led to a performance on all three types of tasks during the postoperative period that was no worse than during the preoperative period, whereas oophorectomized women receiving placebo showed lower scores on all the measures correlated with significantly lower concentrations of plasma estradiol and testosterone. Hysterectomized patients whose ovaries were retained showed stability in the memory tasks and in levels of circulating gonadal hormones. Other studies have indicated the important relationship between surgically induced menopause and mood changes with or without hormone replacements (Sherwin & Gelfand, 1984, 1985a, 1985b; Utian, 1972). These results may imply that hormonal changes have both a fundamental and a modulatory influence on mood and cognition independent of somatic changes, and that some memory defects may occur independent of affective changes.

Taken together, the clinical evidence for affective alterations leading to worsened performance on memory and learning tasks ought to be regarded with some care, although there is reason to accept some relationship. The evidence in favor of a detrimental effect of mood and cognition may be apparent rather than real, because the relationship may be correlational rather than causal. For example, in dementia, depression represented only 20% of the sample of cognitively impaired geriatric patients (Reifler, Larson, & Hanley, 1982). Niederehe (1987) compared age-matched depressed and nondepressed persons on tests of episodic, visual, semantic, and constructive memory but obtained no differences.

STRESS/SEPARATION INDUCED DEFICITS IN
LEARNING AND MEMORY PERFORMANCE

In the laboratory, an enormous body of research has demonstrated the detrimental effects of stressful and aversive events—particularly, if of an uncontrollable nature—upon cognitive performance. Hiroto (1974) studied the effect of controllable, uncontrollable, and no noise on the performance of student volunteers in a finger shuttlebox, by which noise was terminated by moving a finger backwards and forwards in an appropriate fashion. Students who had experienced the uncontrollable stress failed to solve this or other problems, as, for example, anagram solving (Abramson, Garber, & Seligman, 1980; Garber, Miller, & Seaman, 1979). Here it should be noted that the experimental induction of a "depressed" mood following uncontrollable stress treatment to otherwise normal subjects, generally, provides a similar outcome to clinical investigations of persons with altered moods (Goodwin & Williams, 1983). The effects of uncontrollable stress and/or separation on learning performance in animals have been consistently shown in a vast number of studies with rats (Seligman & Beagley, 1975), dogs (Seligman, Maier, & Geer, 1968), and primates (Mineka & Tomarken, 1989). Several neurochemical substrates appear to be involved, including dopamine, noradrenaline, serotonin, and acetylcholine; but evidence exists even for the inhibitory neurotransmitter gamma-aminobutyric acid, the endogenous opiates, histamine, nonopioid peptides, and, perhaps, even the excitatory aminoacids.

Certainly, much evidence points to different types of neurotransmitter interactions and these have been reviewed at various instances (e.g., Janowsky & Risch, 1984; Kostowski, Plaznik, & Archer, 1989; Plaznik, Kostowski, & Archer, 1989). Even brain regional—neurotransmitter interactions in the performance of tasks (e.g. avoidance learning) involving varying levels of stress must be considered. For example, olfactory bulbectomized rats and rats subjected to noradrenergic lesions (using the neurotoxin, DSP4) were studied in three different avoidance tasks: two-way active avoidance, step-down passive avoidance and fear conditioning and retention (Archer, Söderberg, Ross, & Jonsson, 1984). Noradrenaline depleted, but not bulbectomized, rats were impaired in acquiring the two-way avoidance task. Olfactory bulbectomized, but not noradrenaline-lesioned, rats demonstrated clear deficits in passive avoidance and fear retention. Combining the olfactory bulbectomy operation with noradrenaline depletion abolished the two-way avoidance deficit of noradrenaline-depleted rats as well as the passive-avoidance and fear-retention deficits of bulbectomized rats. These results confirmed the effects of noradrenaline in adaptive responses to stressful situations in which instrumental responses were used as the index of performance (Archer, 1982a, 1982b). Olfactory bulbectomy also results in maladaptive behavior but in this case it is the withholding of responding (i.e., passive avoidance) that is disrupted (e.g., Cairncross, Cox, Forster & Wren, 1978). Here, an altered emotional response is assumed from changes in basal circulating hormonal levels (Cairncross, Wren, Cox, & Schneider, 1977). It is interesting to note that the assumed effects of emotional changes in steady state that modulate learning performance are often reversed by antidepressant compounds (e.g., Broekkamp, Garrigan, & Lloyd, 1980; Cairncross, Cox, Forster, & Wren, 1978, 1979; Gorka, Earley, & Leonard, 1985), most especially those affecting serotonergic neurotransmission in the brain (O'Connor & Leonard, 1986, 1988).

For the purpose of this discussion, the implication of the studies of the involvement of the olfactory bulbs and ascending noradrenergic systems in the brain is that it is therefore necessary to consider the important neurotransmitter–endocrine interactions in the modulation of memory by emotional state involving, for example, thyroid stimulating hormone releasing factor (Loosen & Prange, 1980), the gonadal hormones, the glucocorticoids, and melanocyte stimulating hormones (e.g., Ehrensing & Kastin, 1974, 1978). Recent theorizing (e.g., Willner, 1989; Willner, & Muscat, in press) appears to suggest a dopaminergic involvement in the motivational processes modulating performance (i.e., the anhedonia resulting from traumatic experience), whereas there is some likelihood of a serotonergic modulation of performance itself (Willner, Sampson, Phillips, Fichera, Foxlow, & Muscat, 1989). Given the intimate coexistence of serotonin and various neuropeptides (e.g., substance P, thyrotropin releasing hormone, the tachkinins, etc.) in the chronic effects of antidepressant drug treatment (Kitayama et al., 1987, 1988) understand that the neuroendocrine axis underlying memory–emotion interactions is an extremely complex one (Archer, in press).

STRESSFUL REACTIONS CAUSING DISRUPTIONS OF ELECTROPHYSIOLOGICAL CORRELATES OF LEARNING

The long-term potentiation (LTP) phenomenon in the hippocampus involves a stimulation-dependent synaptic process implicating electrophysiological events in learning and memory (e.g., Bliss & Lømo, 1973; Lynch & Baudry, 1984; Teyler & DiScenna, 1984). Long-term potentiation has been described as a transient increase in synaptic efficiency that may be induced by a titanic stimulation of afferent fibers. Although the cellular mechanisms underlying LTP await clarification, both presynaptic (Dolphin, Errington, & Bliss, 1982) and postsynaptic (Lynch, Larson, Kelso, Barrionuevo, & Schottler, 1983) changes have been shown to be related to LTP. Extracellular calcium and intact synaptic transmission (Dunwiddie & Lynch, 1979) are required for the induction of LTP. The conjunction between presynaptic and postsynaptic activity utilizes N-methyl-D-aspartate (NMDA) receptor channels, which are activated by simultaneous transmitter activation and postsynaptic depolarization, to trigger LTP (but see the chapter by LeDoux, this volume). The role of NMDA receptors in LTP has been discussed comprehensively by Brown et al. (Brown, Chapman, Kairiss, & Keenan, 1988; Brown, Ganong, Kairiss, Keenan, & Kelso, 1989). The induction of LTP, offering as it does a mnemonic preparation that follows Hebb's principle of synaptic modification (Wigström, Gustafsson, Huang, & Abraham, 1986), can be made both in vivo and in vitro.

Long-term potentiation has been found to be altered by experimental conditions generally shown to affect behavior, for example, exposure to complex and novel environments (Green & Greenough, 1986; Sharp, McNaughton, & Barnes, 1985; but see also Bramham & Srebro, 1989). If LTP, indeed, represents a procedure by which the cellular mechanisms of memory may be investigated, then it is important to note that Foy, Stanton, Levine, and Thompson (1987) demonstrated that stress treatment disrupted LTP in rats. The stressors employed included both restraint and electrical shock presentation to the tail (Foy et al., 1987). This study proved innovative, especially in the context of the earlier references to cognitive performance in depressed individuals (see earlier), and Shors, Seib, Levine, and Thompson (1989) designed a procedure by which LTP could be studied in rats that had been subjected to either inescapable or escapable shocks. To do so, they employed a yoked control procedure by which the escape of the *yoked control* group, from one side of a shuttlebox to the other, terminated the shock presented to the *inescapable shock* group. A third group of rats received no shock at all. This procedure was maintained for 6 days, and, on Day 7, the rats were sacrificed and hippocampal slices prepared for an in vitro measurement of LTP. The naive control groups demonstrated more LTP than either of the two groups subjected to shock but, most important, the *yoked control* group showed considerably more LTP than the *inescapable shock* group (see Shors et al., 1989). Further investigations with adrenalectomized and demedullated rats indicated that corticosterone, itself, was probably only one factor in the detrimental effects of stress upon LTP (Shors et al., 1989). Thus, it appears that the utilization of preparations, like that of LTP, may provide methodologically stringent procedures for assessing the effects of affective states upon cognitive performance in the laboratory.

This treatise on the possible interactions of memory and emotion has, almost exclusively, dealt with cases where cognitive performance has been affected detrimentally due to various factors having in common a stressful or traumatic component. In all these cases the dependent variable has been indices of memory or learning in different test situations (employing either humans or animals) where some affective state, generally defined by some heightened emotional arousal or stress reaction, has been the independent variable. Some evidence, taken from human psychobiological research, of how poor cognitive performance, whether *real* or *perceived*, may modulate the affective state, or mood, ought to be considered. Eriksson-Mangold and her co-workers (e.g., Eriksson-Mangold & Erlandsson, 1984; Eriksson-Mangold, in prep.) have developed earlier observations by Mahapatra (1974) and Thomas (1981) that hearing handicapped adults could have quite drastic disturbances in mood, certainly occurring more often than in unhandicapped populations. Eriksson-Mangold and Erlandsson (1984) drew two conclusions from their observations: Reduction/distortion of hearing (a) decreased the individual's perception of being secure or in control; (b) increased the individual's perception of being isolated. In a current study, Mangold (in preparation) has observed both hearing-impaired and tinnitus-suffering individuals on several symptom dimensions including: somatization (e.g., weakness and faintness, dizziness, nausea, and numbness), obsessive–compulsive behavior, interpersonal sensitivity, depression, anxiety, hostility, phobic anxiety, paranoid ideation, and psychoticism. One observation was that the *perceived* hearing handicap did not consistently correlate with the degree of *actual* hearing impairment. Her analysis suggests the disruptions of speech discrimination as a consequence of the hearing disability induced psychological and somatic distress. Further, an impaired ability to discriminate speech may have produced a stronger effect on affective state (e.g., mood) than the mere loss of hearing at different frequencies, (i.e., understandability rather than audibility was disrupted). Without disregarding the undoubted relationships between personality traits and hearing loss (see Stephens, 1980), it seems reasonable to indicate that this pursuit of handicap profiles will produce a broader characterization of problems associated with emotion and cognition.

Summarizing the diversity of evidence just described, it appears that there are substantial grounds for suggesting that memory and cognition are, to a great extent, dependent on affective states and mood, and some of these effects may certainly be more than just performance changes. It may be possible to draw together evidence from the different research areas. From our perspective an overriding concern in learning and memory research has been the deep gulf between human and animal research (Nilsson & Archer, 1985), but it may be possible to draw some useful parallel by applying the implicit/explicit memory concepts. Future research could be directed towards techniques for measuring implicit and explicit memory in the animal laboratory by applying the analysis of procedural and declarative memory, as for example described by Squire (1987). Thus, one may examine possible changes in implicit or explicit memory in rats that had undergone treatments to induce depressing anxious states (e.g., separation or immobilization stress). One notable conclusion that may be drawn from this review is the failure of many analyses performed in the laboratory to perform investigations, both sufficient and necessary, designed to elucidate the clinical realities. Put another way, we have, to some extent, failed in the derivation of our animal models. A deeper understanding of the laboratory procedures may only be corrected by a broader enterprise, that not only provides a more lateral approach (cf. Bevan, Lorens, & Archer, 1989) but also a clearer insight of the human situation in disease states.

ACKNOWLEDGMENTS

We are grateful to Tracey Shors and to Maud Eriksson-Mangold for giving us preprints of their most recent work and for helpful comments. This work was supported by grants from the Swedish Council for Research in the Humanities and Social Sciences (Dnr F252/87; F1081/88; F301/90)

REFERENCES

Abramson, L. Y., Garber, J., & Seligman, M. E. P. (1980). Learned helplessness in humans: An attributional analysis. In J. Garber & M. E. P. Seligrnan (Eds.), *Human helplessness: Theory and applications* (pp. 3–34). New York: Academic Press.

Archer, T. (1982a). DSP4-(N-2-chloroethyl-N-ethyl-2-bromobenzylamine), a new noradrenaline neurotoxin, and the stimulus conditions affecting acquisition of two-way active avoidance. *Journal of Comparative, Physiological Psychology, 96,* 476–490.

Archer, T. (1982b). Signalled and unsignalled avoidance impairments following noradrenaline depletion with DSP4: An hypothesis incorporating an associative and a nonassociative factor. *Scandinavian Journal of Psychology, 24,* 75–87.

Archer, T. (1991). Animal models and drug screens for depression: Pragmaticism and the validity requirement. In B. Olivier, J. Slangen, & J. Mos (Eds), *Animal models in psychopharmacology.* Basel: Birkhäuser Verlag.

Archer, T., Söderberg, U., Ross, B., & Jonsson, G. (1984). Role of olfactory bulbectomy and DSP4 treatment in avoidance learning in the rat. *Behavioral Neuroscience, 98,* 496–505.

Auerbach, A. (1947, January). Delayed battle fatigue. *Salute* (pp. 15 & 64).

Bevan, P., Lorens, S., & Archer, T. (1989). Behavioral pharmacology of 5-HT: Possible progress in the laterality of concepts. In P. Bevan, A. Cools, & T. Archer (Eds.), *Behavioral pharmacology of 5-HT* (pp. 459–474). Hillsdale, NJ: Lawrence Erlbaum Associates.

Bliss, T. V. P., & Lømo, T. (1973). Long-lasting potentiation of synaptic transmission in the dentate area of the anaesthetized rabbit following stimulation of the perforant path. *Journal of Physiology (Lond.), 232,* 331–356.

Boakes, R. A. (1984). *From Darwin to behaviourism.* Cambridge: Cambridge University Press.

Boakes, R. A. (1989). How one might find evidence for conditioning in adult humans. In T. Archer & L-G. Nilsson (Eds.), *Aversion, avoidance, and anxiety: Perspectives on aversively motivated behavior* (pp. 381–402). Hillsdale, NJ: Lawrence Erbaum Associates.

Botwinick, J. (1977). Intellectual abilities. In J. E. Birren & K. W. Schaie (Eds.), *Handbook of the psychology of aging* (pp. 580–605). New York: Von Nostrand Reinhold.

Bower, G. H. (1981). Mood and memory. *American Psychologist, 36,* 129–148.

Bradley, B., & Mathews, A. (1983). Negative self-schemata in clinical depression. *Br. Journal of Clinical Psychology, 22,* 173–181.

Brewer, W. F. (1974). There is no convincing evidence for operant and classical conditioning in human being. In W. B. Weimer & D. J. Palermo (Eds.), *Cognition and the symbolic processes* (pp. 1–42). Hillsdale, NJ: Lawrence Erlbaum Associates.

Broekkamp, C. L., Garrigon, D., & Lloyd, K. G. (1980). Serotonin-mimetic and antidepressant drugs on passive avoidance learning by olfactory bulbectomized rats. *Pharmacology, Biochemistry and Behavior, 13,* 643–646.

Brown, T. H., Chapman, P. F., Kairiss, E. W., & Keenan, C. L. (1988). Long-term synaptic potentiation. *Science, 242,* 724–728.

Brown, T. H., Ganong, A. H., Kairiss, E. W., Keenan, C. L., & Kelso, S. R. (1989). Long-term potentiation in two synaptic systems of the hippocampal brain slice. In J. H. Byme & W. O. Berry (Eds.), *Neural models of plasticity* (pp. 266–306). San Diego: Academic Press.

Bramham, C. R., & Srebro, B. (1989). Synaptic plasticity in the hippocampus is modulated by behavioral state. *Brain Research, 493,* 74–86.

Cairncross, K. D., Cox, B., Forster, C., & Wren, A. F. (1978). A new model for the detection of antidepressant drugs: Olfactory bulbectomy compared with existing models. *Journal of Pharmacological Methods, 1,* 131–143.

Cairncross, K. D., Cox, B., Forster, C., & Wren, A. F. (1979). Olfactory projection systems, drugs and behavior: A review. *Psychoneuroendocrinology, 4,* 253–272.

Cairncross, K. D., Wren, A. F., Cox, B., & Schneider, H. (1977). Effects of olfactory bulbectomy and domicile on stress induced corticosterone release in the rat. *Physiological Behavior, 19*, 485–487.

Campbell, S., & Whitehead, M. (1977). Oestrogen therapy and menopausal syndrome. *Clinical Obstetrics and Gynaecology, 4*, 31–47.

Cannon, W. B. (1929). *Bodily changes in pain, hunger, fear and rage.* New York: Appleton.

Clark, D. M., & Hemsley, D. R. (1985). Individual differences in the experience of depressive and anxious intrusive thoughts. *Behavior Research Therapy, 23*, 625–633.

Clark, D. M., & Teasdale, J. D. (1982). Diurnal variation in clinical depression and accessibility of memories of positive and negative experiences. *Journal of Abnormal Psychology, 91*, 87–95.

Cohen, N., & Squire, L. R. (1980). Preserved learning and retention of patterning analyzing skills in amnesia: Dissociation of knowing how and knowing that. *Science, 210*, 207–210.

Cohen, B. M., Weingartner, H., Smallberg, S. A., Pickar, D., & Murphy, D. L. (1982c). Effort and cognition in depression. *Archives of General Psychiatry, 39*, 593–597.

Crohder, R. G. (1985). Basic theoretical concepts in human learning and cognition. In L-G. Nilsson & T. Archer (Eds.), *Perspectives in learning and memory* (pp. 19–37). Hillsdale, NJ: Lawrence Erlbaum Associates.

Dawson, M. E., & Schell, A. M. (1987). Information processing and human autonomic classical conditioning. In P. K. Ackles, J. R. Jennings, & M. G. H. Coles (Eds.), *Advances in psychophysiology* (Vol. I, pp. 89–165). Greenwich, CT: JAI Press.

Denny, N. W. (1979). Problem solving in later adulthood: Intervention research. In P. B. Baltes & O. G. Brim, Jr. (Eds.), *Life-span development and behavior 2* (pp. 121–133). New York: Academic Press.

Derry, P. A., & Kuiper, N. A. (1981). Schematic processing and self-reference in clinical depression. *Journal of Abnormal Psychology, 90*, 286–297.

Dolphin, A. C., Errington, M. L., & Bliss, T. V. P. (1982). Long-term potentiation of the perforant path *in vivo* is associated with increased glutamate release. *Nature, 297*, 496–498.

Dunwiddie, T. V., & Lynch, G. (1979). The relationship between extracellular calcium concentrations and the induction of hippocampal long-term potentiation. *Brain Research, 169*, 103–110.

Eastman, C. (1976). Behavioral formulations of depression. *Psychological Review, 83*, 277–291.

Ehrensing, R. H., & Kastin, A. J. (1974). Melanocyte-stimulating hormone releasing inhibiting hormone as an antidepressant. *Archives of General Psychiatry, 30*, 63–65.

Ehrensing, R. H., & Kastin, A. J. (1978). Dose-related biphasic effect of prolyl-leucyl-glycinamide (MIF-I) in depression. *American Journal of Psychiatry, 135*, 562–566.

Eriksson-Mangold, M. M. (in preparation). *Psychological and somatic distress in relation to perceived hearing handicap and audiological measurements.*

Eriksson-Mangold, M. M., & Erlandsson, S. I. (1984). The psychological importance of nonverbal sounds: An experiment with induced hearing deficiency. *Scandinavian Audiology, 13*, 243–249.

Eysenck, M. W., Mogg, K., May, J., Richards, A., & Mathews, A. (in press). Bias in interpretation of ambiguous sentences related to threat in anxiety. *Journal of Abnormal Psychology.*

Fedor-Freybergh, P. (1977). The influence of oestrogen on the well-being and mental performance in climacteric and postmenopausal women. *Acta Obstetrica Gynaecologica Scandinavica, 64*, 5–69.

Fogarty, S. J., & Hemsley, D. R. (1983). Depression and the accessibility of memories: A longitudinal study. *Br. Journal Psychiatry, 142*, 232–237.

Foy, M. R., Stanton, M. E., Levine, S., & Thompson, R. F. (1987). Behavioral stress impairs long-term potentiation in rodent hippocampus. *Behavioral and Neural Biology, 48*, 138–149.

Garber, J., Miller, W. R., & Seaman, S. F. (1979). Learned helplessness, stress and the depressive disorders. In R. A. Depue (Ed.), *The psychobiology of the depressive disorders: Implications for the effects of stress* (pp. 335–363). New York: Academic.

Goodwin, A. M., & Williams, J. M. G. (1983). Mood-induction research: Its implications for clinical depression. *Behavioral Research and Therapy, 20*, 373–382.

Gorka, Z., Earley, B., & Leonard, B. E. (1985). Effect of bilateral olfactory bulbectomy in the rat, alone or in combination with antidepressants, on the learned immobility model of depression. *Neuropsychobiology, 13*, 26–30.

Graf, P., & Schacter, D. L. (1985). Implicit and explicit memory for new associations in normal and amnesic subjects. *Journal of Experimental Psychology: Learning, Memory, and Cognition, 11*, 501–518.

Green, E. J., & Greenough, W. T. (1986). Altered synaptic transmission in detate gyrus of rats reared in complex environments: Evidence from hippocampus slices maintained in vitro. *Journal of Neurophysiology, 55*, 739–750.

Hackman, B. W., & Galbraith, D. (1977). Six month study of oestrogen therapy with piperazine oestrone sulphate and the effects on memory. *Current Medical Research and Opinion, 4*, 21–27.

Hamilton, W. H., & Abramson, L. Y. (1983). Cognitive patterns and major depressive disorder: A longitudinal study in a hospital setting. *Journal of Abnormal Psychology, 92*, 173–184.

Harness, B., Bental, E., & Carmon, A. (1977). Comparison of cognition and performance in patients with organic brain damage and psychiatric patients. *Acta Psychiatrica Belgica, 73*, 339–347

Henry, G. M., Weingartner, H., & Murphy, D. L (1973). Influence of affective states and psychoactive drugs on verbal learning and memory. *American Journal of Psychiatry, 130*, 966–971.

Hiroto, D. S. (1974). Locus of control and learned helplessness. *Journal of Experimental Psychology, 102*, 187–193.

Hollon, S., & Kendall, P. (1980). Cognitive self-statements in depression: Development of the Automatic Thoughts Questionnaire. *Cognitive Therapy and Research, 4*, 383–395.

Janowsky, D. S., & Risch, S. C. (1984). Cholinomimetic and anticholinergic drugs used to investigate an acetylcholine hypothesis of affective disorders and stress. *Drug Development Research, 4*, 125–142.

Kitayama, I., Janson, A. M., Fuxe, K., Agnati, L. F., Cintra, A., Ögren, S. O., Härfstrand, A., Eneroth, P., Tsutsumi, T., Jonsson, G., Steinbusch, H. W. M., & Visser, T. J. (1987). Effects of acute and chronic treatment with imipramine on 5-hydroxytryptamine nerve cell groups and on bulbospinal 5-hydroxytryptamine/substance P/thyrotropin releasing hormone immunoreactive neurons in the rat. A morphometric and microdensitometric analysis. *Journal of Neural Transmission, 70*, 251–285.

Kitayama, I., Janson, A. M., Cintra, A., Fuxe, K., Agnati, L. F., Ögren, S. L., Härfstrand, A., Eneroth, P., & Gustafsson, J. Å. (1988). Effects of chronic imipramine treatment on glucocorticoid receptor immunoreactivity in various regions of the rat brain. Evidence for selective increases of glucocorticoid receptor immunoreactivity in the locus coeruleus and in 5-hydroxy-tryptamine nerve cell groups of the rostral ventro medial medulla. *Journal of Neural Transmission, 73,* 191–203.

Kopera, H. (1973). Estrogens and psychic functions. *Frontiers of Hormone Research, 2,* 118–133.

Kostowski, W., Plaznik, A., & Archer, T. (1989). Possible implications of 5-HT function for the etiology and treatment of depression. *New Trends in Experimental and Clinical Psychiatry, 5,* 91–116.

Lishman, W. A. (1972). Selective factors in memory. *Psychological Medicine, 2,* 248–253.

Lloyd, G. G., & Lishman, W. A. (1975). The effect of depression on the speed of recall of pleasant and unpleasant experiences. *Psychological Medicine, 5,* 173–180.

Loosen, P. T., & Prange, A. J. (1980). Thyrotropin releasing hormone (TRH): A useful tool for psychoneuroendocrine investigation. *Psychoneuroendocrinology, 5,* 63–80.

Lynch, G., & Baudry, M. D. (1984). The biochemistry of memory: A new and specific hypothesis. *Science, 224,* 1057–1063.

Lynch, G., Larson, J., Kelso, S., Barrionuevo, G., & Schottler, F. (1983). Intracellular injections of EGTA block induction of hippocampal long-term potentiation. *Nature, 305,* 719–721.

Mahapatra, S. B. (1974). Deafness and mental health: Psychiatric and psychosomatic illness in the deaf. *Acta Psychiatrica Scandinavica, 50,* 596–611.

Malleson, J. (1953). An endocrine factor in certain affective disorders. *Lancet, ii,* 158–164.

Mathews, A., Mogg, K., May, J., & Eysenck, M. W. (1989). Implicit and explicit memory biases in anxiety. *Journal of Abnormal Psychology, 98,* 31–34.

Mineka, S., & Tomarken, A. J. (1989). The role of cognitive biases in the origins and maintenance of fear and anxiety disorders. In T. Archer & L-G. Nilsson (Eds.), *Aversion, avoidance, and anxiety: Perspectives on aversively motivated behavior* (pp. 195–221). Hillsdale, NJ: Lawrence Erlbaum Associates.

Mogg, K, Mathews, A., & Weinman, J. (1987). Memory bias in clinical anxiety. *Journal of Abnormal Psychology, 96,* 94–98.

Mueller, J. H., & Curtois, M. (1980). Retention of self-descriptive and nondescriptive words as a function of test anxiety level. *Motivation and Emotion, 4,* 229–237.

Nelson, J. C., & Charney, D. S. (1981). The symptoms of major depression. *American Journal of Psychiatry, 138,* 1–13.

Niederehe, G. (1987). Depression and memory impairment in the aged. In L. W. Poon (Ed.), *Clinical memory assessment of older adults* (pp. 226–237). Hyattsville, MD: American Psychological Association.

Nilsson, L.-G., & Archer, T. (1985). Perspective on animal learning and human memory. In L.-G. Nilsson & T. Archer (Eds.), *Perspectives on learning and memory* (pp. 3–14). Hillsdale, N.J.: Lawrence Erlbaum Associates.

Nunn, J. D., Stevenson, R. J., & Whalan, G. (1984). Selective memory effects in agoraphobic patients. *British Journal of Clinical Psychology, 23,* 195–201.

O'Banion, K., & Arkowitz, H. (1977). Social anxiety and selective memory for affective information about the self. *Social Behavior and Personality, 5,* 321–328.

O'Connor, W. T., & Leonard, B. E. (1986). Effects of chronic administration of the 6 aza analogue of mianserin (Oug 3770) and its enantiomers on behaviour and changes in noradrenaline metabolism of olfactory bulbectomized rats in the "open field" apparatus. *Neuropharmacology, 25,* 267–270.

O'Connor, W. T., & Leonard, B. E. (1988). Behavioural and neuropharmacological properties of the dibenzazepines desipramine and lofepramine: Studies on the olfactory bulbectomized rat model of depression. *Progress in Neuropsychopharmacology and Biological Psychiatry, 12,* 41–51.

Plaznik, A., Kostowski, W., & Archer, T. (1989). Serotonin and depression: Old problems and new data. *Progress in Neuropsychopharmacology and Biological Psychiatry, 13,* 623–633.

Rauramo, L, Langerspetz, K, Engblom, P., & Punnonen, R. (1975). The effect of castration and peroral estrogen therapy on some psychological functions. *Frontiers of Hormone Research, 8,* 133–151.

Reifler, B. V., Larson, E., & Hanley, R. (1982). Coexistence of cognitive impairment and depression in geriatric outpatients. *American Journal of Psychiatry, 139,* 623–626.

Roth, D., & Rehm, L. P. (1980). Relationships among self-monitoring processes, memory and depression. *Cognitive Therapy Research, 4,* 149–158.

Schneider, M. A., Brotherton, P. L., & Hailes, J. (1977). The effect of exogenous oestrogens on depression in menopausal women. *Medical Journal of Australia, 2,* 162–253.

Seligman, M. E. P., & Beagley, G. (1975). Learned helplessness in the rat. *Journal of Comparative Physiological Psychology, 88,* 534–541.

Seligman, M. E. P., Maier, S. F., & Geer, J. (1968). The alleviation of learned helplessness in the dog. *Journal of Abnormal Social Psychology, 73,* 256–262.

Sharp, P., McNaughton, B. L., & Barnes, C. A. (1985). Enhancement of hippocampal field potentials in rats exposed to a novel, complex environment. *Brain Research, 339,* 361–365.

Sherwin, B. B. (1988). Estrogen and/or androgen replacement therapy and cognitive functioning in surgically menopausal women. *Psychoneuroendocrinology, 13,* 345–357.

Sherwin, B. B., & Gelfand, M. (1984). Effects of parenteral administration of estrogen and androgen on plasma hormone levels and hot flushes in the surgical menopause. *American Journal of Obstetrics and Gynaecology, 148,* 552–557.

Sherwin, B. B., & Gelfand, M. (1985a). Sex steroids and affect in the surgical menopause: A double-blind, cross-over study. *Psychoneuroendocrinology, 10,* 325–335.

Sherwin, B. B., & Gelfand, M. (1985b). Differential symptom response to parenteral estrogen and/or androgen administration in the surgical menopause. *American Journal of Obstetrics and Gynaecology, 151,* 153–160.

Shors, T. J., Seib, T. B., Levine, S., & Thompson, R. F. (1989). Inescapable versus escapable shock modulates long-term potentiation (LTP) in the rat hippocampus. *Science, 244,* 224–226.

Stephens, S. D. G. (1980). Evaluating the problems of the hearing impaired. *Audiology, 19,* 205–220.

Stenberg, D. E., & Jarvik, M. E. (1976). Memory functions in depression. *Archives of General Psychiatry, 32,* 219–224.

Stromgren, L. S. (1977). The influence of depression on memory. *Acta Psychiatrica Scandinavica, 56,* 108–128.

Squire, L. (1987). *Memory and brain.* New York: Oxford University Press.

Teyler, T. J., & Discenna, P. (1984). Long-term potentiation as a candidate mnemonic device. *Annual Review of Neuroscience, 10,* 131–161.

Thomas, A. J. (1981). Acquired deafness and mental health. *British Journal of Medical Psychology, 54,* 219–227.

Tulving, E. (1983). *Elements of episodic memory.* New York: Oxford University Press.

Tulving, E. (1985) How many memory systems are there? *American Psychology, 40,* 385–398.

Tulving, E., & Schacter, D. L. (1990). Priming and human memory systems. *Science, 247,* 301–305.

Utian, W. H. (1972). The mental tonic effect of oestrogens administered to oophorectomized females. *S. Afr. Med. J., 46*, 1079–1082.

Van Haaren, F., Van Hest, A., & Heinsbroek, R. P. W. (1990). Behavioral differences between male and female rats: Effects of gonadal hormones on learning and memory. *Neuroscience and Biobehavioral Reviews, 14*, 23–33.

Vanhulle, G., & Demol, R. (1976). A double-blind study into the influence of estriol on a number of psychological tests in post-menopausal women. In P. A. van Keep, R. B. Greenblatt, & M. Albeaux-Fernet (Eds.), *Consensus on menopausal research* (pp. 94–99). London: MTP Press.

Wigström, H., Gustafsson, B., Huang, Y-Y., & Abraham, W. C. (1986). Hippocampal long-term potentiation is induced by paring single afferent volleys with intracellularly injected depolarizing current pulses. *Acta Physiologica Scandinavica, 126*, 317–319.

Willner, P. (1989). Towards a theory of serotonergic dysfunction in depression. In P. Bevan, A. R. Cools, & T. Archer (Eds.), *Behavioural pharmacology of 5-HT* (pp. 157–177). Hillsdale, NJ: Lawrence Erlbaum Associates.

Willner, P., & Muscat, R. (1991). Animal models for investigating the symptoms of depression and the mechanisms of action of antidepressant drugs. In B. Olivier, J. Slangen, & J. Mos (Eds.), *Animal models in psychopharmacology*. Basel: Birkhäuser Verlag.

Willner, P., Sampson, D., Phillips, G., Fichera, R., Foxlow, P., & Muscat, R. (1989). Effects of isolated housing and chronic antidepressant treatment on cooperative social behaviour in rats. *Behavioural Pharmacology, 1*, 85–90.

13

Remembering Emotional Events: Potential Mechanisms

Sven-Åke Christianson
University of Stockholm, Sweden

The purpose of this chapter is to review some of the empirical findings in the study of memory for emotional events, focusing on memory for negative emotional or traumatic events. Two claims are contrasted: that negative emotional events are remembered in exceptional detail, and that emotional stress leads to a general impairment in memory. Some recent research is presented that may bridge the gap between these apparently contradictory conclusions. This chapter also discusses the possibility that emotion influences *early perceptual processing* (e.g., factors related to arousal and affect, the distinctiveness or unusualness of a certain event, attentional or preattentive factors), and *late conceptual processing* (e.g., post-stimulus elaboration). This latter discussion is admittedly speculative, but the intention here is to stimulate new theoretical and empirical efforts rather than to provide a complete understanding of the impact of negative emotions on memory.

ARE NEGATIVE EMOTIONAL EVENTS POORLY OR WELL RETAINED?

From the literature on emotion and memory, it is evident that we retain negative emotional events differently than neutral or everyday events. This has been shown in studies using a variety of research methods, including laboratory simulations and staged events (e.g.,

Christianson, 1984; Clifford & Scott, 1978; Heuer & Reisberg, 1990, Hosch, Leippe, Marchioni, & Cooper, 1984; Loftus & Burns, 1982), field studies (e.g., Brown & Kulik, 1977; Christianson, 1989; Christianson & Loftus, 1990; Kuehn, 1974; Larsen, in press; Wagenaar & Groeneweg, 1990; Yuille & Cutshall, 1986), and clinical studies (e.g., Breuer & Freud, 1985; Christianson & Nilsson, 1989; Nemiah, 1979; Schacter, Wang, Tulving, & Freedman, 1982). Whereas it is clear that emotional events are remembered differently than ordinary events, there is a conflict in research findings concerning the direction of emotional stress on memory, that is, whether negative emotional events are well retained or poorly retained in memory. Some studies purport to show that highly emotional events promote retention of a broad spectrum of details (e.g., Bohannon, 1990; Brown & Kulik, 1977; Heuer & Reisberg, 1990; Reisberg, Heuer, McLean, & O'Shaughnessy, 1988; Yuille & Cutshall, 1986, 1989). Other studies have shown that negative emotional events are retained poorly compared to neutral or everyday events (e.g., Clifford & Hollin, 1981; Clifford & Scott, 1978; Loftus & Burns, 1982). Still other studies have demonstrated striking interactions between type of event (emotional/neutral) and (a) type of detail information (central/peripheral; e.g., Burke, Heuer, & Reisberg, 1990; Christianson & Loftus, 1987, 1991; Christianson, Loftus, Hoffman, & Loftus, 1991); (b) type of test (recall, cued recall, recognition; e.g., Christianson & Nilsson, 1984; Christianson & Larsson, 1991; Davis, 1987; 1990; Wagenaar, 1986; word-completion, Christianson & Larsson, 1991; or repeated testing; Davis, 1970, Erdelyi, 1970; Scrivner & Safer, 1988); and (c) time of test (immediate/delayed; e.g., Burke et al., 1990; Christianson, 1984, Levonian, 1967). Thus, it may be that inconsistencies in empirical findings reflect differences in the to-be-remembered (TBR) detail information and testing circumstances. In the next section, various field studies and simulation studies are reviewed in an effort to delineate some points of commonality in research findings across studies using different methodological approaches.

Studies of Real-Life Events

Many studies of real-life events suggest that negative or traumatic events are remembered quite well (see e.g., Bohannon, 1988, 1990; Brown & Kulik, 1977; Reisberg et al., 1988; Rubin & Kozin, 1984; Yuille & Cutshall, 1986). Yuille and Cutshall (1989) characterized emotional memories of traumatic events as being "detailed, accurate, and persistent" (p. 181). For example, in a study by Yuille and Cutshall (1986), witnesses to a shooting incident in which a person was killed were interviewed soon after the crime by the investigating police and again in a research interview 4–5 months later. An analysis of the eyewitness accounts provided in the police and research interviews showed a high degree of consistency of recall over 5 months. Similar claims about extremely vivid and detailed memories of emotional events have been made by Reisberg et al. (1988) and in studies of "flashbulb memories" (see Brown & Kulik, 1977).

In a survey of peoples' autobiographical memories, Reisberg et al. (1988) found that the more intense the emotional event the higher confidence in memory. In a similar interview study where subjects were asked to report their "most traumatic memory," Christianson and Loftus (1990) found a significant relationship between rated degree of emotion and the number of 'central' details, but not 'peripheral' details, the subjects believed that they remembered. Thus, according to these two interview studies, there seems to be a significant correlation between affect strength and rated memory vividness, at least for central and critical details of the emotional events.

One way to verify the consistency of real-life memories is to compare the similarity between the recollections reported on two occasions: that is, people may be asked a series of questions about details and circumstances in which they first experienced the emotional event and then asked the same questions again later on. For example, in a study of extremely emotional experiences, such as being a victim of a Nazi concentration camp, Wagenaar and Groeneweg (1990) compared testimonies from 78 former prisoners of "Camp Erika," collected in the periods of 1943–1947 and 1984–1987. A comparison between testimonies from these two periods revealed that almost all victims remembered the concentration camp experiences in great detail even after 40 years. Although errors did occur, Wagenaar and Groeneweg state that recall of the conditions in the camp and smaller details were remarkably consistent and accurate.

A domain of studies that also supports the view of persistence of detail in highly emotional events is research of so-called *"flashbulb memories."* A number of studies have shown an impressive concordance in subjects' remembering of shocking national events, such as assassinations, etc. (see e.g., Bohannon, 1988, 1990; Brown & Kulik, 1977; Christianson, 1989; Colgrove, 1899; Pillemer, 1984; Rubin & Kozin, 1984; Winograd & Killinger, 1983). Not only does such a newsworthy event itself seem to be well preserved (e.g., being told about the assassination of one's president), but so too do the subjects' memories of the specific circumstances under which they heard the news: the informant, the location, the time, any ongoing activity, the subject's own clothing, the subject's own affect, etc). Although it is clear that people remember these kinds of public negative emotional events better than ordinary events that occurred equally long ago, by no means do these flashbulb memories seem to be completely accurate (see e.g., Christianson, 1989; McCloskey, Wible, & Cohen, 1988; Neisser, 1982; Neisser & Harsch, 1990).

One problem in "flashbulb" studies, as in other studies of real-life events, is that these studies do not include a baseline measure, for example, a comparable salient everyday control event. Another problem with the real-life studies is that we cannot tell how accurate people really are in their initial descriptions of the emotion-provoking event and its concomitant circumstances. Unlike laboratory studies, there is often no way of knowing what subjects were actually doing, feeling, etc., when they first were exposed to the shocking event. The initial recalls may not have been truthful or accurate observations of the original situation but may very well be reconstructive and presumably contain some erroneous information, as most other types of memories.

Overall, however, the results from studies using a double-assessment technique in flashbulb studies (Bohannon, 1990; Christianson, 1989; McCloskey et al., 1988; Pillemer, 1984) and other studies of real-life events (e.g., Christianson & Hübinette, 1991; Wagenaar & Groeneweg, 1990; Yuille & Cutshall, 1986) indicate a fairly good consistency in recollections over longer retention intervals. Thus, the loss of clarity and detail over time seems to be far less in memories of real-life events than can be expected from the forgetting curve typically found in basic memory research (cf. Murdock, 1974).

Laboratory Studies

Whereas research on real-life events suggests that traumatic events are well preserved in memory, laboratory simulation studies show more mixed results. In various studies using a simulation approach, subjects have witnessed via slides, videotapes, films, or live stage scenarios, an emotional or a neutral event, and their memory for details has been assessed either immediately or after a delay. Several of these simulation studies (see e.g., Barton & Warren, 1988; Clifford & Hollin, 1981; Clifford & Scott, 1978; Loftus & Burns, 1982) purport to show that details of emotionally arousing events are not remembered as well as details of neutral events. Thus, it is claimed that negative emotion leads to worse memory. This view has been maintained especially within the eyewitness literature (see e.g.,

Deffenbacher, 1983; Kassin, Ellsworth, & Smith, 1989; Loftus, 1979; Loftus & Doyle, 1987).

In a survey of 63 experts on eyewitness testimony made by Kassin et al. (1989), a strong consensus was found about the negative impact of stress or event violence on memory. The experts were asked whether they agreed with the statement: "Very high levels of stress impair the accuracy of eyewitness testimony." In response to this question, the majority of the experts agreed that the available evidence tends to favor this statement, and 71% of the experts postulated that the statement was sufficiently reliable to offer in court. Thus, the "expert" consensus seems to be that emotional stress is bad for memory.

Furthermore, in a review by Deffenbacher (1983) across 21 simulation studies on arousal and eyewitness memory, 10 studies showed that high arousal levels increased eyewitness accuracy, whereas 11 studies showed a lower accuracy at high arousal levels. Deffenbacher concluded that most of the studies supported the inverted U-form relationship between arousal and memory, known as the Yerkes–Dodson law (1908)[1], with the highest levels of arousal producing a very poor memory performance.

In an often-cited study, Clifford and Scott (1978) compared memory of a videotaped event depicting either a violent event (physical assault on a bystander by a policeman) or a nonviolent event (verbal exchange between the bystander and the policeman). Subjects who had viewed the violent version performed worse in answering a 40-item questionnaire covering both actions and physical descriptions. These results are ambiguous, however, because it is unclear whether the subjects in the two conditions were tested on identical details associated with the bystander, or if the detrimental effects were found for all details presented.

A subsequent study by Clifford and Hollin (1981) examined subjects' memories immediately after they had witnessed, on videotape, either a violent incident (a mugging) or a nonviolent incident (direction seeking) in which a woman and one, three, or five perpetrators could be observed. The results revealed that the description of the principal man was more accurate in the nonviolent condition, and that the accuracy of recall for the violent condition decreased with an increase in the number of perpetrators simultaneously

---

[1]It should be noted that in the original study by Yerkes and Dodson (1908) the data provided was based on animal learning studies, and the curve described the relationship between arousal and performance. Other researchers (e.g., Deffenbacher, 1983; Loftus, 1980) have later modified this curve to even encompass emotion/arousal and memory.

present. On the other hand, photographic identification of the principal man was not found to be significantly different between conditions. Moreover, scores for memory of the woman—who should be regarded as an equally central character as the perpetrators—revealed that accuracy was unaffected either by violence or by the number of additional persons involved in the incident.

Another simulation study commonly referred to that supports the view that memory accuracy is impaired for emotional events is that of Loftus and Burns (1982). In their study, subjects were presented with either a violent or a nonviolent 2.25-min videotape of a simulated bank robbery. In the violent version, the film ended with a 15-sec sequence in which a boy was shot in the head by the robber. In the nonviolent version the shooting episode was replaced with a neutral episode depicting a conversation in the bank. The results showed that subjects who saw the violent version remembered the critical item presented prior to the emotional eliciting event (the number on the boy's football jersey) less accurately than the subjects who saw the nonviolent version. However, there were nonsignificant differences between the subjects in the two conditions in memory for date and time, physical characteristics of the robber, actions of the teller, details associated with the bank, etc; that is, there were no differences seen between the two conditions with respect to the details associated with the critical emotional or the neutral episode itself.

In considering the results of the Loftus and Burns study, we do see an interesting *retrograde* detrimental effect; that is, there was a memory impairment for detail information presented prior to the emotional event. Similar retrograde and/or anterograde detrimental effects on memory have been shown in several other laboratory studies (see e.g., Bond & Kirkpatrick, 1982; Christianson & Nilsson, 1984; Detterman, 1976; Detterman & Ellis, 1972; Erdelyi & Blumenthal, 1973; Kramer, Buckhout, Fox, Widman, & Tusche, 1985; Runcie & O'Bannon, 1977; Saufley & Winograd, 1970; Tulving, 1969). It is important to note, though, that in most of these studies demonstrating laboratory induced retrograde or anterograde "amnesia" effects, the critical emotion-eliciting event (i.e., the amnesic agent) is remembered very well and typically shows a von Restorff effect (see Wallace, 1965; see also Bower, this volume). Furthermore, similar to clinical observations of retrograde and anterograde amnesia of functional origins (see Abse, 1987; Breuer & Freud, 1895; Horowitz, 1986; Kihlstrom & Evans, 1979) or organic origins (see e.g., Cermak, 1982; Talland & Waugh, 1969; Whitty & Zangwill, 1977), "recovery" effects have been demonstrated for laboratory-induced amnesia (Christianson & Nilsson, 1984; Detterman, 1976; Detterman & Ellis, 1972; see also Eysenck, 1982, for a review of research on arousal and memory, and Singer, 1990, for a review of the literature on repression).[2]

Can we then conclude on the basis of the simulation studies that details about emotional or violent events are retained less well than details about neutral or nonviolent events? Not uniformly. A reinterpretation of the studies by Collin and colleagues suggests that peripheral, but not central information, is less well retained in emotional events. This interaction between type of event (emotional vs. neutral) and type of detail information (central vs. peripheral) has been found to be critical in a series of recent studies; that is, it seems that central details are well retained, whereas peripheral details are less well retained from emotional events compared with neutral counterparts.

Central Versus Peripheral Details. In a study by Christianson (1984), subjects were presented with a slide sequence depicting an emotional or a neutral version of the same type of event. Subjects who had watched an emotional version (a boy hit by a car) were better than those who had watched the neutral version (a boy walking beside a car) at recalling the main features, or theme, of the event. However, when the subjects were tested by means of a recognition test, in which the main features of each stimulus slide were held constant, and only the peripheral, surrounding information was manipulated, no difference was found between groups.

In a subsequent study by Christianson and Loftus (1987) using the same type of stimulus material, the subjects were instructed to select and write down the most distinguishing (central) detail of each slide and were then tested for recall of these details, as well as recognition of the pictures themselves. In line with Christianson (1984), it was found that subjects were better able to recall the details selected from emotional pictures (i.e., the central features); however, they were less able to recognize the specific slides that they had seen.

In a simulation study by Kebeck and Lohaus (1986), subjects were presented either an emotional or a nonemotional version of a film depicting an argument between a teacher and a student. Subjects in

---

[2]It should be noted that clinical observations of retrograde and anterograde amnesia indicate actual recovery effects, whereas the recovery or reminiscence effects in laboratory simulations usually refer to interactions between type of events and time or type of test; that is, simulation studies commonly indicate that high arousal events are better retained than low arousal events at delayed test intervals, or as a function of test, but they seldom show recovery of initially forgotten material.

the two conditions were equal in recall of central details of the film; however, subjects who had seen the emotional version were less able to remember peripheral information.

Also using a simulation approach, Heuer and Reisberg (1990) presented subjects with a series of slides depicting either a neutral or an emotional version of a story where a mother and her son visit the father at his workplace. The subjects were tested after a 2-week interval via a recognition test that included questions about information pertaining to the basic story or about specific details in a particular slide. Subjects presented with the emotional version of the story remembered more detail information than subjects who saw the neutral version. In a follow-up study, Burke et al. (1990) found that detail information that was spatially and temporally associated with the central characters in the slides (also the gist of the event) was better retained in the emotional condition than in the neutral condition. It was also found that the beneficial effects for central details obtained at immediate testing increased as compared with the neutral condition at delayed testing (i.e., after 1 week). Furthermore, the disadvantage found for the peripheral details in the emotional condition at immediate testing decreased at delayed testing (see also Heuer & Reisberg, this volume).

Consistent with these findings of enhanced memory for central details of emotional events is research on the phenomenon of "weapon focusing" (see e.g., Cutler, Penrod, & Martens, 1987; Kramer, Buckhout, & Eugenio, 1990; Loftus, Loftus, & Messo, 1987; Maass & Kohnken, 1989). Studies on weapon focusing typically demonstrate that certain stressful objects, like a gun or a knife being used in a crime, can capture peoples' attention and thus promote memory for the central weapon, but at the expense of other details in memory.

It could be argued, however, that people remember details from emotional events differently than details from neutral events because of inadequate equating of the detail information of the emotional and the neutral event. For example, slides depicting emotional events often differs from that of neutral events in more than the presumed elements (e.g., the complexity of the scene, the centrality of the TBR information, the background information, etc.). This issue was addressed in a study by Christianson and Loftus (1991) in which subjects viewed a thematic series of slides where the emotional valence of one critical slide in the series was varied, although the TBR details (central and peripheral) of this critical slide were identical in the emotional and the neutral versions of this critical slide. In the neutral version, the critical slide showed a woman riding a bicycle. In the emotional version, the same woman was seen lying injured on the street near the bicycle. In both versions, a peripheral car was seen in the distant background. The results from a series of experiments with this material demonstrated that the central detail information (information associated with the critical woman) was retained better in the emotional condition, but that the peripheral detail information (the car in the background) was retained better from the neutral event.

Can these findings be generalized to real-life traumatic events? Even if one should be cautious in applying laboratory results to real-life events (see Christianson, Goodman, & Loftus and Yuille & Tollestrup, this volume for a discussion of this issue), we do see indications of selective focusing in real-life situations. An example of a real-life trauma which showed selective memory for certain critical details was seen in a case study by Christianson and Nilsson (1989). This study describes a rape victim, C.M., who showed a memory loss of the traumatic episode, but who also preserved some isolated details ("bricks along a path") without being able to explain why these isolated memories came to her mind. It may be that excessive emotional stress evoked in an extremely traumatic situation may lead to a redistribution of attentional resources, such that only a limited amount of external information will be processed. This restriction of attentional resources probably made the victim in the Christianson and Nilsson's study focus on details in the environmental context that were most central and critical to her in that specific situation. Christianson and Nilsson argued that in order to avoid extreme psychological "pain," the individual may isolate some critical, but in themself neutral, details of the traumatic event from its original context. These critical neutral details could constitute a "mental bridge" to the more emotional loaded details, such as those of the actual rape situation (cf. Erdelyi & Goldberg, 1979). Thus, this phenomenon of isolation of details might be an extension of selective remembering of central details that has been observed in laboratory studies with emotional events (see studies discussed earlier, see also Baddeley, 1972; Easterbrook, 1959; Korchin, 1964).

It is, of course, difficult to determine what is central and what is peripheral information of a specific event in advance, especially outside the laboratory. For example, few would have predicted that the rape victim described by Christianson and Nilsson (1989) would preserve some isolated memories of "bricks along a path" when the victim was questioned shortly after the incident, yet a post-hoc analysis readily generated reasons why these details might be critical (critical to the possibility of escape, etc.). Laboratory studies have, however, an advantage over real-life situations because normative data can be collected to assist in the definition of centrality of detail. It must be that "centrality," as well as "associated," information (i.e., preceding and succeeding events) is defined by a continuum, and not by absolute categories. In this chapter, central and peripheral details are distinguished as differentially remembered detail information within an emotional scenario. However, whereas central details most often are emotionally valenced material, it is not justified to assume that peripheral or noncentral details are always emotional material just because they occurred within an emotional scenario (this issue is further discussed by Heuer & Reisberg in this volume).

What to Conclude from the Empirical Findings?

The pattern of results obtained from various studies using different methodological approaches suggests that some information, such as central aspects or the essence of an emotional event is well retained in memory, whereas memory is impaired for many other details, and, especially, the peripheral ones. Memory for information occurring preceding and succeeding emotional events seems to be impaired, at least temporarily. These memory effects tend to recede, however, as a function of retrieval support; if delayed testing is employed; or after repeated memory testing. These interactive effects indicate that there is no simple relationship between intense emotion and memory (i.e., that highly emotional events are poorly retained or the opposite, that intense emotional events are accurately retained). Furthermore, the Yerkes–Dodson law (1908)—proposing an inverted U-form relation between arousal/emotion and performance—does not constitute an appropriate description of the relationship between emotion and memory performance (see also McCloskey & Egeth, 1983; Näätänen, 1973; Neiss, 1988, 1990 for a discussion of the inadequacy of the Yerkes–Dodson law in this context).

Basically, it seems that those who claim that emotional stress enhances memory have focused on the accuracy of memory for the central details or the gist of emotional events (e.g., Yuille & Cutshall, 1986), whereas those who claim that emotional stress leads to an impairment in memory have focused on the errors in memory for peripheral details or information preceding or succeeding emotional events (e.g., Loftus & Burns, 1982). Considering recent research findings showing that central detail information is well retained, whereas peripheral detail information is less well retained from emotional events compared with neutral counterparts, the findings in earlier studies are not as inconsistent or incompatible as they may appear.

Why, then, are emotional events remembered in this way? In the next section, I discuss some possible mechanisms that might be critical in remembering emotional events.

POSSIBLE MECHANISMS

As yet, no one has a complete explanation to why we retain emotional events differently than ordinary, or even unusual, events. The interpretations at hand vary: Some advocate biological–evolutional factors (e.g., Bohannon, 1988,1990; Brown & Kulik, 1977; Gold, 1986; Zajonc, 1980), some emphasize psychological mechanisms, such as attentional factors (e.g., Easterbrook, 1959), reconstructive processes (e.g., Neisser, 1982), or unconscious motivational processes (e.g., Erdelyi & Goldberg, 1979; Freud, 1915). Among those advocating biological mechanisms, Brown and Kulik (1977), Bohannon (1990), and other proponents for flashbulb memories (see also Winograd & Neisser, in press, for a review) maintain the position that we have an inherent special mechanism that is triggered when an event is highly emotionally arousing, surprising, and consequential. This mechanism is considered to be of great importance for our survival and has been referred to in the flashbulb literature as a neuropsychological "Now Print!" mechanism (see Livingston, 1967), which is supposed to preserve a photographic image of the critical event in our brain.

Although it seems clear that we do not preserve emotional events in exceptional "flashbulb" detail as expressed in the idea of a "Now Print!" mechanism, it may still be the case that emotional events receive some special or preferential processing; that is, that emotion influences memory either at *early perceptual processing* (e.g., factors such as arousal, the distinctiveness or unusualness of a certain event, and attentional or preattentive factors), or *late conceptual processing* (e.g., poststimulus elaboration). Consider first factors at early perceptual processing.

Intensity and Arousal

Of specific interest in flashbulb studies is the issue of level of affect as a predictor for detailed and vivid memories. It has been claimed that the more intense the emotional reaction to the discovery of the shocking event, the better retention of attendant circumstances over

time (see e.g., Bohannon, 1988, 1990; Pillemer, 1984); that is, high
levels of emotional arousal are supposed to be associated with
persistence of a broad spectrum of detail information, both central
and peripheral. Similar claims have been made by Yuille and Cutshall
(1989) using a field-study approach, and by Heuer and Reisberg
(1990) using a laboratory-simulation approach.

McGaugh and collegues (McGaugh, 1983; this volume; McGaugh
& Gold, in press) have presented extensive research indicating that
memory is modulated by a variety of hormones that are released by
emotionally arousing experiences. McGaugh's findings indicate that
the memory-modulating effects of hormones and drugs are dose
dependent, for example, that a low dose of epinephrine (adrenalin)
enhances retention, whereas a high dose of epinephrine impairs
retention.

Being more specific, but at the same time somewhat more
speculative, about an arousal explanation, Gold (1986, in press) has
proposed a biological system that promotes the formation of memories
for individually based important events, such as emotional experiences. In short, the neurobiological mechanism suggested by Gold is
that stressors will release epinephrine, which in turn increases
circulating glucose levels. The increase in blood glucose levels has
been found by Gold and others (Gold, 1986; Manning, Hall, & Gold,
1990; Messier & Destrade, 1988) to enhance memory-storage processing in animals and humans in an inverted-U dose-response
curve. By way of extrapolation, Gold's research suggests that emotional events are well retained because of increased levels of blood
glucose.

This relationship between arousal and memory is, however, not
consistently supported. For example, in the thorough study by
Bohannon (1990) on peoples' recollection of the Challenger explosion, there was no main effect of self-reported affect on memory. A
significant interaction was only seen for subjects who had been told
about the shocking news from another person and not for those who
were told via media (it should be noted that there was a nonsignificant
difference between levels of self-rated affect between groups of
subjects). A lack of significant effect of affect on memory was also
seen in a similar study by Christianson (1989) on peoples' recollection of the murder of the Swedish Prime Minister Olof Palme.

However, even if there is a tendency in various field studies for
high levels of affect to be associated with higher levels of overall
recall, this is far from a well-established fact, and it is not justified
to assume that all details are well retained because they occurred
within an emotional scenario. As discussed earlier in this chapter,

several recent laboratory studies have shown that peripheral details tend to not persist in emotional memories. Furthermore, arguing against the notion of a *general* benefit of affect on detail memory are results from a survey study of peoples' most traumatic memories by Christianson and Loftus (1990). In this study, subjects were asked to report their most traumatic memory and to answer questions about their chosen memory. A major result was a significant relationship between rated degree of emotion and the number of central details, but not peripheral details, the subjects believed that they remembered. Similarly, Larsen (in press) collected news events and everyday personal experiences in a diary over 9 months, where both extremely upsetting and ordinary public events as well as personal events were included. In an evaluation of the impact of emotion in remembering these events, Larsen found no appreciable effect of arousal on memory of the ordinary news contexts. However, the probability of recalling *central* information ("What" and "Where" questions about news events) was consistently predicted by factors related to emotional arousal, such as perceived excitement and activity.

Moreover, results from a series of studies by Christianson and colleagues (see Christianson & Nilsson, 1984; Christianson & Mjörndal, 1985; Christianson et al., 1986) indicated that a general increase in emotional arousal is significant as an intervening variable only when the source of emotional arousal is directly associated with the TBR event—that is, when the emotional reaction is an inherent property of the TBR event (cf. the "causal belongingness" hypothesis of mood-state-dependent retrieval discussed by Bower, 1987 and in this volume).

In sum, there are several findings in the emotion and memory literature that challenge the view that intensity of affect, or a general increase in arousal, promotes memory for a broad spectrum of details. At the same time there is no case for the view that memory is generally impaired during states of high affect (see also chapters by Heuer & Reisberg, Mandler, and Revelle & Loftus for a further discussion of the role of arousal in memory).

Unusualness and Distinctiveness

It could be argued that emotional events are more distinctive than neutral events. For example, experiments in which subjects' eye movements have been monitored while they view complex scenes (e.g., Loftus, Loftus, & Messo, 1987; G.L. Loftus & Mackworth, 1978) have shown that people fixate faster, more often, and for longer durations on unusual objects. Furthermore, from weapon-focus studies (Kramer et al., 1990 a; Loftus et al., 1987; Maass & Kohnken, 1989), it seems that the weapon-focus effect may also appear with nonemotional items, such as surprising or unusual objects instead of weapons. Is then the unusualness of emotional details the critical factor that explains why emotional events are remembered differently than ordinary, neutral events? This question was partly investigated in studies by Christianson and Loftus (1991) and Christianson et al. (1991), where memory for TBR information associated with a central object in an emotional version of an event (a woman lying wounded beside a bicycle) was compared with memory for the same information presented in an unusual version (a woman carrying a bicycle on her shoulder) or a neutral version (a woman riding a bicycle) of the same event. It was found that peripheral detail information (a car seen in the distant background in all versions) was remembered equally well (or poorly) in both the emotional and the unusual conditions. However, with respect to detail information associated with the central woman (the color of the woman's clothes), memory performance for the emotional event was superior to that for the unusual event. A counterargument would be that the central information in the unusual condition was less distinctive and less attention catching than the corresponding central information in the emotional condition and therefore less well retained. Results showed, however, that the unusual event was far more distinctive and attention catching than the neutral event, yet there was no accompanying differences between these conditions in memory for the central detail information. In considering these tentative findings, it seems unlikely that the unusualness of emotional details explains the difference in memory obtained for emotional and neutral events.

Eye-Fixations and Attention

It may be that differential distribution of attention at the time of stimulus processing promotes memory for central details of emotional events but impairs processing of peripheral details. In an effort to more closely investigate the role of attention in memory for emotional versus neutral events, Christianson et al. (1991) conducted an experiment in which subjects were presented with an emotional or a neutral event, and in which the number of eye fixations was limited to only one per slide. This was accomplished by presenting the slides for 180 ms/slide and by having each slide preceded by a fixation point that was directed to the critical TBR detail information. This procedure assured that all subjects at the time of exposure paid attention to the same critical information and for the same amount of time.[3] Despite the fact that subjects in both the emotional and the neutral conditions were equated with respect to the detail information attended to during stimulus presentation, the central detail information of the emotional condition was retained better than the corresponding detail information of the neutral condition. This pattern of results was also found in a second experiment using the same procedure but different stimulus material.

In a third experiment of the same study, subjects were allowed to fixate normally on an emotional or a neutral critical slide while their eye movements were monitored. Subjects in the emotional condition fixated more often on the central detail information compared with subjects in the other two conditions, yet they fixated on this detail information for shorter durations. Subjects who fixated an equal number of times on the central detail information in the two conditions were then compared with respect to memory accuracy. The results showed that even when subjects were equated with respect to number of eye fixations, subjects in the emotional condition remembered the detail information associated with the central part of the picture better than subjects in the neutral condition. Thus, whereas number of eye fixations and attention may matter, it does not fully explain why we retain certain detail information better from emotional than from neutral events.

Preattentive and Nonconscious Processing

An intriguing finding of the Christianson et al. (1991) study, was that the level of memory performance for subjects presented with emotional stimuli at very short exposures (180 ms) was almost the same as that found for subjects presented with the same emotional stimuli at long exposures (cf. Christianson & Loftus, 1991). Pertinent to this observation is a study by Christianson and Fällman (1990), where it was found that very unpleasant scenic pictures (pictures of victims of traffic accidents, war, malady, famine, etc.) shown for very brief durations (50 msec followed by a mask slide) were better recognized

---

[3]Although attention and fixation location can, under some circumstances, be dissociated, research by Posner (see e.g., Posner, 1980; Posner, Cohen, Choate, Hockey, & Maylor, 1984) indicates that in real-world situations, attention usually reorients to the fovea with eye movements, thus keeping coordinated the direction of attention with the center of acute vision.

than neutral scenic pictures (pictures of people in everyday situations), or very positive scenic pictures (e.g., sexual pictures of nudes or very sensual summer scenes). This congruence in memory effects obtained at short and long exposure conditions may indicate that processing of emotional information does not necessarily require consciously controlled memory processes either at acquisition or retrieval, and also, it may not be necessary to reaccess specific event information for retention of affect.

There are several indications in the literature that affective components of an emotional event sometimes are encoded and retained beyond the specific details of the event itself (see e.g., Christianson & Nilsson, 1989; Greenberg, Pearlman, Schwartz, & Grossman, 1983; Johnson, 1985, 1990; Johnson, Kim, & Risse, 1985; Johnson & Multhaup, this volume; Lewecki, 1986; Leventhal, 1984; Tobias, Kihlstrom, Schacter, this volume; Zajonc, 1980, 1981, 1984): that is, sometimes people seem to remember the emotional component of an event without having access to specific event information, or, remember specific event information without having access to the emotional component of the event. These findings suggest an interesting double dissociation between memory for emotional information and memory for specific event information and could indicate that several memory mechanisms at different levels of consciousness are involved when we remember unpleasant or traumatic events. For example, it may be that the emotional valence of information is processed partly by mechanisms mediated by phylogenetically and ontogenetically more sophisticated memory systems (cf. episodic and semantic memory, see Tulving, 1972; or explicit memory, see Graf & Schacter, 1985; or reflective memory, see Johnson & Multhaup, this volume) and partly by preattentive mechanisms (cf. Neisser, 1967), which do not involve consciously controlled processes (cf. perceptual representation system, see Tulving & Schacter, 1990; or evolutionary early perceptual subsystems, see Johnson & Multhaup, this volume).

Perhaps we are predisposed to retain certain characteristics of emotional information (cf. Hansen & Hansen, 1988; Öhman & Dimberg, 1984), a kind of preattentive information processing or "emotional priming," reflecting some survival value from earlier stages in human evolution. For example, data suggesting preattentive, automatic processing of emotionally loaded information was presented by Hansen and Hansen (1988). They presented subjects with matrices of faces and found faster detection of angry faces in happy or neutral "crowds" than vice versa. They also reported that the size of the crowd had no effect on response latencies for search of angry faces, whereas size of crowd had marked effect on search for happy faces in angry crowds (see also Treisman, 1982).

Similar to Öhman (1979, 1991), it is assumed that an emotion-eliciting stimulus is processed from an automatic or preattentive level to a controlled conceptional level of processing. The preattentive or automatic information processing would be fast, nonconscious, context independent, independent of processing resources, and able to carry out parallel processing of different inputs. In contrast, controlled conceptual processing requires effort, is governed by intention, and is dependent on limited processing resources.

It may be that in a situation where an individual is exposed to an emotional event, certain stimulus features will be extracted and evaluated as emotionally significant. For example, a blood stain could be regarded as emotionally significant in the sense that it represents an emotional stimulus derived from behavior systems likely to have been shaped by evolution (cf. Öhman & Dimberg, 1984; Panksepp, 1982). In terms of Öhman's (1979) model, this automatic and nonconscious evaluation activates an orienting response[4] and the stimulus event enters the focus of attention. Due to attention-demanding stimulus characteristics and personal involvement, controlled conceptual resources are then allocated for further stimulus analysis of the emotional event (cf. "poststimulus elaboration" discussed later). Thus, in an emotionally relevant event, critical emotional details will be extracted by a preattentive mechanism, which triggers attention automatically (cf. emotional priming), and controlled selection resources will subsequently be allocated to the emotionally relevant information. This mode of processing would thus promote memory for central detail information, that is, details of the gist of the emotional event, but impair memory for peripheral details, that is, details that are irrelevant and/or spatially peripheral to the emotion-eliciting event or the source of the emotional arousal.

Emotional organization, may as well as, for example, spatial, temporal, or semantic organization, be critical for remembering emotional events. Perhaps we encode events along an emotional dimension in the same way we organize information along a time perspective. It may be that, when we remember a specific point of time an event occurred, this process of temporal organization is most likely to be mediated by conscious processing mediated by higher integrative levels in the brain (e.g., functions of the frontal lobes). Organization of emotional information, on the other hand, is pre-

---

[4]A detailed discussion of the specific signal routes to such an orienting response, as well as a discussion of preattentive processing in general, is provided by Öhman (1991).

sumably automatic and nonconscious—for one thing, emotional characteristics are difficult to describe verbally—and processing of affective components of emotional events may be mediated by subcortical structures. Thus, we might not be aware of the way we perceive and retain information through emotional organization (cf. Lewecki, 1986; Öhman, 1991; Zajonc, 1980).

Retrieval of emotional information does not necessarily require the subject to specifically remember the emotional episode itself. Sometimes, in cases with strong emotional memories, the emotional component of the memory is dissociated and accessed implicity by unconscious retrieval mechanisms (cf. Tobias, Kihlstrom, Schacter, this volume).There is some empirical evidence, and some causal evidence from case studies and personal reports, that suggests that people sometimes remember emotional information without having access to specific event information, that is, there is a dissociation between memory for affective components of an event and memory for the specific event itself. A most fascinating study that supports the idea of unconscious remembering of emotional information was presented by Johnson, Kim, and Risse (1985). In that study, it was shown that emotional information can be retained even though memory for the specific event is disrupted, that is, a dissociation between memory of emotional components and memory of event information. Johnson et al. (1985) presented Korsakoff amnesics with two pictures of faces and fictional biographical information depicting the person of the picture as either a "good guy" or a "bad guy." After a 20-day interval, the amnesics were unable to recall the biographical information. However, in emotional-evaluative ratings made by the amnesics, 78% of the patients showed a preference for the good guy over the bad guy. These preference ratings were made even though the amnesics did not have voluntary access to the biographical information on which the preferences were based. This observation suggests that we do not necessarily have to depend on conscious or reflective memories (see Johnson & Multhaup, this volume) to access emotionally related information.

This line of thinking is, to some extent, consistent with the ideas advocated by Zajonc (1980, 1981, 1984), who argues that emotion or affect is mediated by a special system that works independent of systems that are responsible for higher levels of memory processing. According to Zajonc, the former system, which is responsible for emotional responses, works in an unconscious way. It should be noted though that the empirical evidence presented by Zajonc in support for a special system or mechanism has been criticized and challenged (see e.g., Lazarus, 1982, 1984, and Zajonc, 1984, for a debate on the role of cognition in a primitive emotional-evaluative memory mechanism; see also Mandler, Nakamura, & Zandt, 1987). In contrast to the special system proposed by Zajonc (1980), the preattentive processes suggested here are supposed to interact with more recently evolved memory processes (e.g., poststimulus elaboration, see later).

Some ancillary support for automatic and nonconscious memory processing of an emotional event was demonstrated by Christianson and Nilsson (1989) in a case of functional amnesia. This case study describes a woman, C.M., who was raped while she was jogging in Stockholm and who developed total amnesia for the assault and her previous life. When she was found, she could not explain what had happened to her or identify herself. Later, when C.M. was escorted through the area of the assault, she felt very uncomfortable at specific places and she only recalled two things—bricks and path—but was not able to explain why these details crossed her mind. When she passed some crumbled bricks on a small path, she expressed an unbearable anxiety and claimed that she associated the unpleasant feelings with the pieces of bricks on the track she was walking on. She strongly felt that something must have happened to her at this place. From a confession by the rapist a few days earlier, the policemen knew that this was the place where she had been attacked and from which she was forced out onto a small meadow where the rape occurred.

C.M.'s amnesia lasted for 16 weeks, until she went running for the first time after the assault. At this time, the same internal context that she experienced the moment just preceding the attack was reinstated (estimated at the time for assault and now, 16 weeks later: increased motor activity, heightened body temperature, hyperventilation, increased cardiac activity). She was also exposed to external cues that strongly reminded her of the place of the attack (a country environment with brush, a gravel track with pieces of bricks, and a pile of bricks). It seems, then, that C.M.'s earlier memory of bricks and path, isolated from its initial context, was the external information that she focused on during the attack and, hence, was a strong cue to the specific traumatic event.

Christianson and Nilsson's case study of functional amnesia exemplifies dissociative remembering between an nonconscious memory mechanism and a conscious episodic memory system; that is, it looks like we can remember emotional information without conscious awareness of how and where we acquired this information. In terms of the explicit–implicit memory distinction (see Tobias, Kihlstrom, & Schacter, this volume), we can assume that C. M. demonstrates implicit remembering of emotional information in the memory responses for the aversive event that she showed when exposed to the place where she had been attacked. Or, in terms of the MEM framework (Johnson & Multhaup, this volume), C. M. illustrates that emotion may be attached to certain perceptual cues that may not, alone, give rise to memory for the traumatic event itself. This type of memory response looks very similar to the aversive learning response demonstrated in animal studies, a kind of conditioned emotional response (see Estes & Skinner, 1941, see also Archer & Nilsson, 1989; Bolles, 1970), and we know that this behavior in animals is mediated by early evolved brain structures, such as the cortical and subcortical limbic structures (see e.g., LeDoux, this volume; McGaugh, this volume; McGaugh, Introini-Collison, Naghara, & Cahill, 1989; Thomas, Hostetter, & Barker, 1968). Furthermore, Öhman and colleagues (see Öhman, 1991, for a review) have shown that subjects seem to be able to learn to associate fear-relevant stimuli with aversive events at an automatic or preattentive level. It seems likely, then, that similar emotional conditioned or reflex memory responses in humans and animals are mediated by a primitive emotion-evaluative memory mechanism, which animals and humans may have in common.

We also know that other limbic connections such as the olfactory system plays an important role in memory and emotional behavior (e.g., Cain, 1974; Sieck, 1972). It is conceivable that memory for taste and smell sensations associated with emotional experiences is mediated by automatic, nonconscious processing in the human memory system. For example, the first memory to return to the rape victim C. M. discussed earlier in this chapter (see Christianson & Nilsson, 1989) appeared to be the smell of beer from the attacker, which the victim immediately connected with a memory of a sexual assault she experienced as a 9-year-old girl and where the assaulter also smelled heavily of beer. It may be that the association between smell sensations in these two traumatic experiences was made nonconsciously by C. M. when she was raped, and that the memory representation of smell sensations was not accessible until probed by details that were consciously processed at the time of the assault.

The significance of smell in emotional memories was also noted in the story told by the American actress Kelly McGillis, who was savagely raped by two men in New York (McMurran, 1988). McGillis showed a detailed recollection of the terrifying ordeal she went through; among the most salient details she remembered was the smell. McGillis recalled: "I'll never forget the way they smelled—like alcohol and sweat" (McMurran, 1988, p. 155). "I couldn't go down into the subway without getting nauseous and gagging because the smell reminded me of the men who had raped me." (McMurran, 1988, p. 159). The significance of memories mediated by the olfactory system in these two cases of traumatic experience provides further indications that emotional memories are affected by subconscious memory mechanisms mediated by limbic structures in the brain. However, without a more careful study, it is important to be cautious in interpreting the role of the olfactory system in emotional memories—it may be that these olfactory cues are specific to sexual situations.

There are other examples that show a dissociation between memory for emotional information and specific event information. For example, research by Greenberg et al. (1983) on emotion, memory, and REM sleep has shown that access to emotional information connected with specific event information decreases with REM deprivation. Subjects were presented with a series of tests, including tests of immediate memory, past personal and nonpersonal memory, and past emotional memories after baseline, control-awakening, and REM-deprivation nights. The results indicated that only past emotionally important memories were affected by REM deprivation and that access to the emotion connected with the memories was decreased. This study suggests a disconnection between event memory and the emotionally meaningful parts of a person's event memory.

Although the idea of an automatic, nonconscious memory mechanism at early perceptual processing is somewhat speculative, the aforementioned examples suggest an interesting double dissociation between memory for emotional information and memory for specific event information: that is, sometimes people seem to remember the emotional component of an event without having access to specific event information, or, remember specific event information without having access to the emotional component of the event. These dissociations show to some extent that several different memory systems or mechanisms might be involved when we remember unpleasant or traumatic events. What we need to know much more about is how these various mechanisms interact, that is, to look for a cognition-emotion interface. (For further discussions of memory dissociations and implicit or unconscious memory of emotional experiences, see the chapters by Bower, Johnson & Multhaup, LeDoux, Mandler, and Tobias, Kihlstrom, & Schacter in this volume).

Poststimulus Elaboration

In combination with whatever preattentive process that may be operating, there also may be later, conceptual processes that determine how we retain emotional information (e.g., rehearsal and elaboration). According to the level of processing theory by Craik and Lockhart (1972), maintenance rehearsal does not improve long-term memory, whereas elaboration does (cf. Craik & Tulving, 1975). There are several indications in studies of unpleasant or traumatic events that the degree of self-reported frequency of maintenance rehearsal does not correlate with degree of memory performance (e.g., Bohannon, 1988; Christianson & Loftus, 1990; Larsen, in press; Rubin & Kozin, 1984). It may be, however, that differential post-stimulus elaboration (i.e., elaboration just after encoding) occurs when subjects are exposed to emotional events as compared with neutral events, and that this aspect mediates differences in memory of emotional versus neutral events. For example, compared to a neutral event, subjects presented with emotion-provoking content, such as an accident or a crime, might be more concerned with what they have just seen—about the injuries of the victim—which will lead to increased poststimulus elaboration. In terms of the level-of-processing approach (Craik & Lockhart, 1972; Craik & Tulving, 1975), and as discussed by Craik and Blankstein (1975), it can be assumed that neutral or low arousal events would be associated with maintenace rehearsal, whereas highly emotionally arousing events would lead to a deeper level or more elaborative processing that enhances memory (see also Robinson,1980).

Similar ideas about the importance of elaborative processing of emotional events have been presented by Heuer (1987), who argues that the recall pattern for emotional events and associated details is different from that of neutral events. According to Heuer, emotional memories center around the causes of the emotions—the thoughts, feelings, and reactions of the subject—and thus causes the subject to personalize a narrative account around the central elements of the emotional experience. It is then implied from Heuer's arguing that this "personalization" at states of high emotional arousal enhances memory both for the 'gist' of an event and for detail information peripheral to the event.

Heuer and Reisberg (1990) presented results indicating that subjects think more and in a different way about emotional events compared with neutral events; that is, they think of the emotional events in more personal, more psychological, and less schematic or abstract ways. For example, subjects presented with emotional slides are likely to be engaged by certain critical details in the slides and are likely to think about these specific details. Heuer and Reisberg also found that the pattern of how subjects attend to and rehearse emotional events shows up in the pattern of intrusion errors made by the subjects when recalling the emotional events: They made fewer errors about the emotional event itself but tended to confabulate about information associated with motives or reactions in the story.

Other evidence indicating differences in elaboration of emotional versus neutral events has been presented by Christianson and Loftus (1991). In this study, one experiment was conducted to gather thoughts that were evoked in the minds of the subjects while viewing a critical emotional, unusual, or neutral picture in a series of slides. Analyses of these thoughts revealed that subjects' descriptions in the emotional condition were more likely to contain expressions of affect and also more likely to make reference to the central character and the central action of the event. On the other hand, descriptions given by subjects in the neutral condition were more likely to make reference to the environment or peripheral details. Subjects in the unusual condition produced descriptions that were similar to those of the emotional subjects; that is, they were concerned about the main action and were less likely to refer to the environment. However, in comparison with the emotional group, the subjects in the unusual condition were less explicit about the central detail information of the event.

The poststimulus elaboration hypothesis is consistent with Easterbrook's (1959) theory in the sense that there is increased cue selectivity and restriction of attentional span in emotionally arousing situations. However, at the same time, we can assume that attentional narrowing during processing of emotional events is associated with more elaborative processing of the information attended to; that is, fewer aspects of the total event are attended to, which enhances processing for central details but is detrimental to processing of peripheral or surrounding information of the emotional event.

The result of the Christianson et al. (1991) study, showing that subjects remember central detail information better from emotional events than from neutral events even when the detail information is shown only for 180 msec, suggests that an elaboration mechanism may interact with preattentive mechanisms, which do not involve consciously controlled processing. Thus, the specific pattern of better central and poorer peripheral detail may result from the interaction between preattentive processes that alert people to orient to emotional information and more controlled processes (e.g., poststimulus elaboration) that causes them to preferentially process central versus peripheral details. It is, however, for future research to show whether we retain emotional events partly by preattentive memory mechanisms and partly by more evolved and consciously controlled memory mechanisms such as poststimulus elaboration.

FUTURE RESEARCH:
A PSYCHOLOGICAL–BIOLOGICAL ENTERPRISE

If we wish to reach a deeper understanding of how emotion and memory interact, it is necessary to integrate both psychological and biological knowledge. Such an analysis comprises research on, for example, how memory and emotional functions have developed to their current level; how human memory behaves in different emotional situations; and which neuroanatomical structures and neurochemical processes are involved when we experience and remember an emotional event. We know that certain brain structures have been identified as highly critical for emotional behavior and memory functions, for example, the amygdala, the hippocampus, and the olfactory bulbs (see e.g., Buck, 1976; Gainotti, 1983; LeDoux, 1986, this volume; MacLean, 1970; Malmo, 1975; McGaugh, this volume; Papez, 1937). We also know that these structures are closely located in one of the oldest areas of the brain in the human organism. This local integration strongly suggests that retention of emotional event information is probably one of the earliest characteristics developed in human memory functions.

Whereas the hippocampus is critical for learning and memory in both humans and other species, the role of the amygdala, which has been found to be critical in animal learning and emotional behavior (see e.g., LeDoux, this volume; Mishkin, 1978; McGaugh, this volume; McGaugh et al., 1989), is much less clear in human behavior. Interestingly, resections of the amygdala in connection with epilepsy surgery seldom produces postoperative changes in memory or emotional behavior (Ojemann, personal communication). Does this mean that the amygdala serves a different role in humans? Perhaps the role of an emotion-evaluative memory mechanism is normally disguised by more recently evolved memory systems? Or, it may be that current measures for studying amygdala-related behavioral changes in humans are simply not sensitive enough.

In addition to the distinction made here between neocortical and subcortical structures in the organization of emotional memories, there is also some evidence of intra and interhemispheric differences with respect to processing of emotional information (see Gainotti, 1983; LeDoux, 1986; Tucker, 1981). Numerous studies suggest that the right (nondominant) hemisphere is more important for emotional behavior than the left, speech-dominant, hemisphere (see Buck, 1986; Kolb & Whishaw, 1985; Perceman, 1983; Safer, 1981; Young, 1983, for reviews), and some studies suggest that the frontal lobe of the nondominant hemisphere is more critical for processing of emotional information than other neocortical areas of the brain (e.g., Kolb & Milner, 1981). The evidence for such a functional brain organization is, however, far from conclusive in this respect. To gain further knowledge about the relationship between emotion and memory, we definitively need to combine different measures from psychological and neurobiological research. For example, one promising technique for differential analyses of which regions in the brain are involved during behavioral activation, such as processing of emotional information, is the measurement of cerebral blood flow. It is now widely accepted that there is a close regional coupling between blood flow and tissue metabolism rate in the normal brain (see e.g., Fox, Mintun, Raichle, Miezin, Allman, & Van Essen, 1986); that is, local modulations in neural electrical activity are thought to induce similar modulations in local metabolism that in turn alter blood flow. Blood flow can therefore be used as an indirect index of brain work. Positron emission tomography (PET) is one technique that can be used to measure blood flow (see e.g., Posner, Petersen, Fox, Raichle, 1988; Reiman, Fusselman, Fox, & Raichle, 1989) and thus may provide further information about whether certain subcortical structures such as the amygdala, the hippocampus, or certain neocortical areas in the right or the left hemisphere are differently activated during processing of emotional versus neutral events.

SUMMARY AND CONCLUSIONS

This chapter reviews some empirical findings in the field of memory for negative emotional events. The literature indicates that negative emotional events are very well retained both with respect to the emotional event itself and critical, central detail information of the emotion-eliciting event, whereas peripheral, more irrelevant information, is less accurately retained. We also see that emotional events and the information associated with these events are better retained than neutral events over time. This pattern indicates that there is no simple, unidimensional relationship between intense emotion and memory; highly emotional events are not necessarily poorly retained, nor necessarily accurately retained. In fact, current research in this field, independent of the approach used, shows that the way emotion and memory interact is a very complex matter. For example, we see interactions between type of event (emotional/nonemotional) and (a) type of detail information (central/peripheral), (b) type of test (recall, recognition), and (c) time of test (immediate/delayed). These interactive effects challenge a unidimensional view of a simple relationship between emotion and memory. Hence the Yerkes–Dodson law, which is commonly referred to as an interpretation of findings in studies of emotion and memory, does not constitute an appropriate description of the relationship between emotion/stress and memory performance.

To account for the findings, this chapter discusses the possibility that emotion may affect memory at early perceptual processing and at late conceptual processing. It is suggested that attentional focusing along with an increased elaboration of those aspects attended is a plausible explanation to why central detail information is better retained, whereas peripheral detail information is less well retained from emotional events compared with neutral counterparts. It is also assumed that critical characteristics of emotional events may be extracted and processed by a preattentive and automatic mechanism, which will act as an emotional prime and thus trigger attentional selectivity and controlled memory processing. This type of automatic, nonconscious memory processing of affective components of emotional events may also be responsible for dissociations between memory for emotional information and memory for specific event information. Thus, the specific way emotional information is processed by a preattentive and automatic memory mechanism on one hand, and more evolved memory mechanisms on the other, may be of importance for the differences seen between memory for emotional events and memory for ordinary, neutral events. A word of caution, though: The empirical evidence for preattentive, unconscious identification of emotionally significant information is yet limited; thus, the main purpose here is to entertain this idea in order to stimulate new studies along the same line of thinking.

Finally, in recent years, there have been an increased number of interesting psychological and neurobiological observations that are pertinent to the topic of emotion and memory, and that increase the interest in and pose new questions about emotion and memory. Hopefully, the rapidly growing field of functional brain mapping, neurochemical analyses, and other neurobiological techniques in conjunction with growing psychological interest in field and laboratory studies on emotion and memory will lead to a more complete understanding of why emotional events are remembered differently than neutral or ordinary events.[5]

ACKNOWLEDGMENTS

This research was supported by Grant F. 158/88 from the Swedish Council for Research in the Humanities and Social Sciences and by Grant 84/253:3 from the Bank of Sweden Tercentenary Foundation. I am indebted to Trevor Archer, Robert C. Bolles, Earl Hunt, and Marcia K. Johnson for their valuable discussion and comments.

REFERENCES

Abse, D. W. (1987). *Hysteria and related mental disorders* (2nd ed.). Bristol: Wright.

Archer, T., & Nilsson, L.-G. (Eds.) (1989). *Aversion, avoidance, and anxiety: Perspectives on aversively motivated behavior.* Hillsdale, NJ: Lawrence Erlbaum Associates.

Baddeley, A. D. (1972). Selective attention and performance in dangerous environments. *British Journal of Psychology, 63,* 537–546.

Barton, S. D., & Warren, L. R. (1988, November). *Effects of an emotionally arousing incident on memory for adjacent events.* Paper presented at 29th Annual Meeting of the Psychonomic Society, Chicago.

Bohannon, J. N. (1988). Flashbulb memories for the space shuttle disaster: A tale of two stories. *Cognition, 29,* 179–196.

Bohannon, J. N. (1990, February). *Arousal and memory: Quantity and consistency over the years.* Paper presented at the Emory Cognition Project Conference on Affect and Flashbulb Memories, Atlanta, GA.

Bolles, R. C. (1970). Species-specific defense reactions and avoidance learning. *Psychological Review, 77,* 32–48.

Bond, C. F. Jr., & Kirkpatrick, K. C. (1982). Distraction, amnesia, and the next-in-line effect. *Journal of Experimental Social Psychology, 18,* 307–323.

Bower, G. H. (1987). Invited essay: Commentary on mood and memory. *Behavioral Research and Therapy, 25,* 443–455.

Breuer, J., & Freud, S. (1895). Studies on hysteria. In J. Strachey (Ed.), *The standard edition of the complete psychological works of Sigmund Freud* (Vol. 2). London: Hogarth Press, 1955.

Brown, R., & Kulik, J. (1977). Flashbulb memories. *Cognition, 5,* 73–99.

Buck, R. (1976). *Human motivation and emotion.* New York: Wiley.

---

[5]This chapter exclusively focuses on memory for negative or traumatic emotional events. Memory for negative emotional events is of considerable importance since so many crimes and accidents involve emotional stress to the victims and witnesses. But just as surely we do remember positively valanced events as well. To draw conclusions about memory for emotional events in a broader perspective, it is, of course, important to investigate the consequences of positive emotions for memory.

Buck, R. (1986). The psychology of emotion. In J. E. Ledoux & W. Hirst (Eds.), *Mind and brain* (pp. 275–300). Cambridge: Cambridge University Press.

Burke, A., Heuer, F., & Reisberg, D. (1990). *Remembering emotional events.* Manuscript submitted for publication.

Cain, D. P. (1974). The role of the olfactory bulb in limbic mechanisms. *Psychological Bulletin, 81,* 654–671.

Cermak, L. S. (Ed.). (1982). *Human memory and amnesia.* Hillsdale, NJ: Lawrence Erlbaum Associates.

Christianson, S.-Å. (1984). The relationship between induced emotional arousal and amnesia. *Scandinavian Journal of Psychology, 25,* 147–160.

Christianson, S.-Å. (1989). Flashbulb memories: Special, but not so special. *Memory & Cognition, 17,* 435–443.

Christianson, S.-Å., & Fällman, L. (1990). The role of age on reactivity and memory for emotional pictures. *Scandinavian Journal of Psychology, 31,* 291–301.

Christianson, S.-Å., & Hübinette, B. (1991). *Peoples' emotional reactions and memory associated with post office robberies.* Paper presented at the Third Annual Convention of American Psychological Society.

Christianson, S.-Å., & Larsson, M. (1990). *Implicit and explicit memory of laboratory-induced emotional events.* Unpublished manuscript.

Christianson, S.-Å., & Loftus, E. F. (1987). Memory for traumatic events. *Applied Cognitive Psychology, 1,* 225–239.

Christianson, S.-Å., & Loftus, E. F. (1990). Some characteristics of people's traumatic memories. *Bulletin of the Psychonomic Society, 28,* 195–198.

Christianson, S.-Å., & Loftus, E. F. (1991). Remembering emotional events: The fate of detailed information. *Cognition & Emotion, 5,* 81–108.

Christianson, S.-Å., Loftus, E. F., Hoffman, H., & Loftus, G. R. (1991). Eye fixations and memory for emotional events. *Journal of Experimental Psychology: Learning, Memory, and Cognition, 17,* 693–701.

Christianson, S.-Å., & Mjörndal, T. (1985). Adrenalin, emotional arousal, and memory. *Scandinavian Journal of Psychology, 26,* 237–248.

Christianson, S.-Å., & Nilsson, L.-G. (1984). Functional amnesia as induced by a psychological trauma. *Memory & Cognition, 12,* 142–155.

Christianson, S.-Å., & Nilsson, L.-G. (1989). Hysterical amnesia: A case of aversively motivated isolation of memory. In T. Archer & L.-G. Nilsson (Eds.), *Aversion, avoidance, and anxiety: Perspectives on aversively motivated behavior* (pp. 289–310). Hillsdale, NJ: Lawrence Erlbaum Associates.

Christianson, S.-Å., Nilsson, L.-G., Mjörndal, T., Perris, C., & Tjelldén, G. (1986). Psychological versus physiological determinants of emotional arousal and its relationship to laboratory amnesia. *Scandinavian Journal of Psychology, 27,* 302–312.

Clifford, B. R., & Hollin, C. R. (1981). Effects of the type of incident and the number of perpetrators on eyewitness memory. *Journal of Applied Psychology, 66,* 364–370.

Clifford, B. R., & Scott, J. (1978). Individual and situational factors in eyewitness testimony testimony. *Journal of Applied Psychology, 63,* 352–359.

Colegrove, F. W. (1899). Individual memories. *American Journal of Psychology, 10,* 228–255.

Craik, F. I. M., & Blankstein, K. (1975). Psychophysiology and human memory. In P. H. Venables & M. J. christie (Eds.), *Research in psychophysiology* (pp. 389–417). London: Wiley.

Craik, F. I. M., & Lockhart, R. S. (1972). Levels of processing: A framework for memory research. *Journal of Verbal Learning and Verbal Behavior, 11,* 671–684.

Craik, F. I. M., & Tulving, E. (1975). Depth of processing and the retention of words in episodic memory. *Journal of Experimental Psychology: General, 104,* 268–294.

Cutler, B., Penrod, S., & Martens, T. (1987). The reliability of eyewitness identification. *Law and Human Behavior, 11,* 233–258.

Davis, P. J. (1987). Repression and the inaccessibility of affective memories. *Journal of Personality and Social Psychology, 53,* 585–593.

Davis, P. J. (1990). Repression and the inaccessibility of emotional memories. In J. L. Singer (Ed.), *Repression and dissociation: Implications for personality theory, psychopathology, and health* (pp. 387–403). Chicago: The University of Chicago Press.

Deffenbacher, K. A. (1983). The influence of arousal on reliability of testimony. In S. M. A. Lloyd-Bostock & B. R. Clifford (Eds.), *Evaluating witness evidence* (pp. 235–251). Chichester: Wiley.

Detterman, D. K. (1976). The retrieval hypothesis as an explanation of induced retrograde amnesia. *Quarterly Journal of Experimental Psychology, 28,* 623–632.

Detterman, D. K., & Ellis, N. R. (1972). Determinants of induced amnesia in short-term memory. *Journal of Experimental Psychology, 95,* 308–316.

Easterbrook, J. A. (1959). The effect of emotion on cue utilization and the organization of behavior. *Psychological Review, 66,* 183–201.

Erdelyi, M. H. (1970). Recovery of unavailable perceptual input. *Cognitive Psychology, 1,* 99–113.

Erdelyi, M. H. (1990). Repression, reconstruction, and defense: History and integration of the psychoanalytic and experimental frameworks. In J. L. Singer (Ed.), *Repression and dissociation: Implications for personality theory, psychopathology, and health* (pp. 1–31). Chicago: The University of Chicago Press.

Erdelyi, M. H., & Blumenthal, D. G. (1973). Cognitive masking in rapid sequential processing: The effect of an emotional picture on preceding and succeeding pictures. *Memory and Cognition, 1,* 201–204.

Erdelyi, M. H., & Goldberg. B. (1979). Let's not sweep repression under the rug: Toward a cognitive psychology of repression. In J. F. Kihlstrom & F. J. Evans (Eds.), *Functional disorders of memory* (pp. 355–402). Hillsdale, NJ: Lawrence Erlbaum Associates.

Estes, W. K., & Skinner, B. F. (1941). Some quantitative properties of anxiety. *Journal of Experimental Psychology, 29,* 390–400.

Eysenck, M. W. (1982). *Attention and arousal: Cognition and performance.* Berlin: Springer-Verlag.

Fox, P. T., Mintun, M. A., Raichle, M. E., Miezin, F. M., Allman, J. M., & Van Essen, D. C. (1986). Mapping human visual cortex with positron emission tomography. *Nature, 323,* 806–809.

Freud, S. (1915). Repression. In J. Strachey (Ed.), *The standard edition of the complete psychological works of Sigmund Freud* (Vol. 14, pp. 146–158). London: Hogarth Press, 1957.

Gainotti, G. (1983). Laterality and affect: The emotional behavior of right and left-brain-damaged patients. In M. S. Myslobodsky (Ed.), *Hemisyndromes.* London: Academic Press.

Gold, P. E. (1986). Glucose modulation of memory storage processing. *Behavioral and Neural Biology, 45,* 342–349.

Gold, P. (in press). A proposed neurobiological basis for regulating memory storage for significant events. In E. Winograd & U. Neisser (Eds.), *Affect and accuracy in recall: The problem of "flashbulb" memories.* New York: Cambridge University Press.

Graf, P., & Schacter, D. L. (1985). Implicit and explicit memory for new associations in normal and amnesic subjects. *Journal of Experimental Psychology: Learning, Memory, and Cognition, 11,* 501–518.

Greenberg, R., Pearlman, C., Schwartz, W. R., & Grossman, H. Y. (1983). Memory, emotion, and REM sleep. *Journal of Abnormal Psychology, 3,* 378–381.

Hansen, C. H., & Hansen, R. D. (1988). Finding the face in the crowd: An anger superiority effect. *Journal of Personality and Social Psychology, 54,* 917–924.

Heuer, F. (1987). *Remembering detail: The role of emotion in long-term memory.* Unpublished dissertation. New School for Social Research, New York.

Heuer, F., & Reisberg, D. (1990) Vivid memories of emotional events: The accuracy of remembered minutiae. *Memory & Cognition, 18,* 496–506.

Horowitz, M. J. (1986). *Stress response syndromes* (2nd ed.). Northvale, NJ: Aronson.

Hosch, H. M., Leippe, M. R., Marchioni, P. M., & Cooper, S. (1984). Victimization, self-monitoring, and eyewitness identification. *Journal of Applied Psychology, 69,* 280–288.

Johnson, M. K. (1985). The origins of memories. In P. C. Kendall (Ed.), *Advances in cognitive-behavioral research and therapy* (Vol 4, pp. 1–27). New York: Academic Press.

Johnson, M. K. (1990). Reality monitoring: Evidence from confabulation in organic brain disease patients. In G. Prigatano & D. L. Schacter (Eds.), *Awareness of deficit after brain injury.* New York: Oxford University Press.

Johnson, M. K., Kim, J. K., & Risse, G. (1985). Do alcoholic Korsakoff's syndrome patients acquire affective reactions? *Journal of Experimental Psychology: Learning, Memory, and Cognition, 11,* 22–36.

Kassin, S. M., Ellsworth, P. C., & Smith, V. L. (1989). The "general acceptance" of psychological research on eyewitness testimony: A survey of the experts. *American Psychologist, 44,*1089–1098.

Kebeck, G., & Lohaus, A. (1986). Effects of emotional arousal on free recall of complex material. *Perceptual and Motor Skills, 63,* 461–462.

Kihlstrom, J. F., & Evans, F. J. (Eds.). (1979). *Functional disorders of memory.* Hillsdale, NJ: Lawrence Erlbaum Associates.

Kolb, B., & Milner, B. (1981). Performance of complex arm and facial movements after focal brain lesions. *Neuropsychologia, 19,* 491–503.

Kolb, B., & Whishaw, I. Q. (1985). *Fundamentals of human neuropsychology* (2nd ed.). New York: W. H. Freeman.

Korchin, S. J. (1964). Anxiety and cognition. In C. Scheerer (Ed.), *Cognition: Theory, research, promise* (pp. 58–78). New York: Harper & Row.

Kramer, T. H., Buckhout, R., & Eugenio, P. (1990). Weapon focus, arousal, and eyewitness memory: Attention must be paid. *Law and Human Behavior, 14,* 167–184.

Kramer, T. H., Buckhout, R., Fox, P., Widman, E., & Tusche, B. (1985, March). *Effects of emotional arousal on free recall: anterograde amnesia.* Paper presented at the Eastern Psychological Association Convention, Boston, MA.

Kuehn, L. L. (1974). Looking down a gun barrel: Person perception and violent crime. *Perceptual and Motor Skills, 39,* 1159–1164.

Larsen, S. F. (in press). Potential flashbulbs: Memories of ordinary news as a baseline. In E. Winograd & U. Neisser (Eds.), *Affect and accuracy in recall: The problem of "flashbulb" memories.* New York: Cambridge University Press.

Lazarus, R. S. (1982). Thoughts on the relations between emotion and cognition. *American Psychologist, 37,* 1019–1024.

Lazarus, R. S. (1984). On the primacy of cognition. *American Psychologist, 39,* 124–129.

LeDoux, J. E. (1986). The neurobiology of emotion. In J. E. LeDoux & W. Hirst (Eds.), *Mind and brain*. Cambridge: Cambridge University Press.

Leventhal, H. (1984). A perceptual-motor theory of emotion. In K. R. Scherer & P. Ekman (Eds.), *Approaches to emotion* (pp. 271–291). Hillsdale, N J: Lawrence Erlbaum Associates.

Levonian, E. (1967). Retention of information in relation to arousal during continuously-presented material. *American Educational Research Journal, 4*, 103–116.

Lewecki, P. (1986). *Nonconscious social information processing*. Orlando: Academic Press.

Livingston, R. B. (1967). Reinforcement. In G. C. Quarton, T. Melnechuck, & F. O. Schmitt (Eds.), *The neurosciences: A study program* (pp. 568–576). New York: Rockefeller University Press.

Loftus, E. F. (1979). *Eyewitness testimony*. London: Harvard University Press.

Loftus, E. F. (1980). *Memory*. Addison–Wesley.

Loftus, E. F., & Burns, T. (1982). Mental shock can produce retrograde amnesia. *Memory & Cognition, 10*, 318–323.

Loftus, E. F., & Doyle, J. M. (1987). *Eyewitness testimony: Civil and criminal*. New York: Kluwer.

Loftus, E. F., Loftus, G. R., Messo, J. (1987). Some facts about "weapon focus." *Law and Human Behavior, 11*, 55–62.

Loftus, G. R., & Mackworth, N. H. (1978). Cognitive determinants of fixation location during picture viewing. *Journal of Experimental Psychology: Human Perception and Performance, 4*, 565–572.

Maass, A., & Kohnken, G. (1989). Eyewitness identification: Simulating the "weapon effect." *Law and Human Behavior, 13*, 397–408.

MacLean, P. D. (1970). The limbic brain in relation to the psychoses. In P. M. Black (Ed.), *Physiological correlates of emotion*. New York: Academic Press.

Malmo, R. B. (1975). *On emotions, needs, and our archaic brain*. New York: Holt, Rinehart, & Winston.

Mandler, G., Nakamura, Y., & Van Zandt, B. J. S. (1987). Nonspecific effects of exposure on stimuli that cannot be recognized. *Journal of Experimental Psychology: Learning, Memory, and Cognition, 13*, 646–648.

Manning, C., Hall, J., & Gold, P. (1990). Glucose effects on memory and other neuropsychological tests in elderly humans. *Psychological Science, 1*, 307–311.

McCloskey, M., & Egeth, H. E. (1983). Eyewitness identification: What can a psychologist tell a jury? *American Psychologist, 38*, 550–563.

McCloskey, M., Wible, C. G., & Cohen, N. J. (1988). Is there a special flashbulb-memory mechanism? *Journal of Experimental Psychology: General, 117*, 171–181.

McGaugh, J. L. (1983). Hormonal influences on memory. *Annual Review of Psychology, 34*, 297–323

McGaugh, J. L., & Gold, P. E. (in press). Hormonal modulation of memory. In R. B. Brush & S. Levine (Eds.), *Psychoendocrinology*. New York: Academic Press.

McGaugh, J. L., Introini-Collison, I. B., Naghara, A. H., & Cahill, L. (1989). Involvement of the amygdala in hormonal and neurotransmitter interactions in the modulation of memory. In T. Archer & L.-G. Nilsson (Eds.), *Aversion, avoidance, and anxiety: Perspectives on aversively motivated behavior* (pp. 231–249). Hillsdale, NJ: Lawrence Erlbaum Associates.

McMurran, K. (1988). Memoir of a brief time in hell. *People Weekly, November 14*, 154–160.

Messier, C., & Destrade, C. (1988). Improvement of memory for an operant response by post-training glucose in mice. *Behavioural Brain Research, 31*,185.

Mishkin, M. (1978). Memory in monkeys severely impaired by combined but not by separate removal of amygdala and hippocampus. *Nature, 273,* 297–298.

Murdock, B. B. (1974). *Human memory: Theory and data.* Potomac, MD: Lawrence Erlbaum Associates.

Näätänen, R. (1973). The inverted-U relationship between activation and performance: A critical review. In S. Kornblum (Ed.), *Attention and performance* (Vol. 4, pp. 155–174). New York: Academic Press.

Neiss, R. (1988). Reconceptualizing arousal: Psychological states in motor performance. *Psychological Bulletin, 103,* 345–366.

Neiss, R. (1990). Ending arousal's reign of error: A reply to Anderson. *Psychological Bulletin, 107,* 101–105.

Neisser, U. (1967). *Cognitive psychology.* New York: Appleton.

Neisser, U. (1978). Memory: What are the important questions? In M. M. Gruneberg, P. E. Morris, & R. N. Sykes (Eds.), *Practical aspects of memory* (pp. 3–24). London: Academic Press.

Neisser, U. (1982). Snapshots or benchmarks? In U. Neisser (Ed.), *Memory observed* (pp. 43–48). San Francisco: W. H. Freeman.

Neisser, U., & Harsch, N. (1990, February). *Phantom flashbulbs: False recollections of hearing the news about Challenger.* Paper presented at the Emory Cognition Project Conference on Affect and Flashbulb Memories, Atlanta.

Nemiah, J. C. (1979). Dissociative amnesia: A clinical and theoretical reconsideration. In J. F. Kihlstrom & F. J. Evans (Eds.), *Functional disorders of memory* (pp. 355–402). Hillsdale, NJ: Lawrence Erlbaum Associates.

Öhman, A. (1979). The orienting response, attention, and learning: An information processing perspective. In H. D. Kimmel, E. H. van Olst, & J. F. Orlebeke (Eds.), *The orienting reflex in humans* (pp. 443–472). Hillsdale, NJ: Lawrence Erlbaum Associates.

Öhman, A. (1991). Orienting and attention: Preferred preattentive processing of potentially phobic stimuli. In B. A. Campell, R. Richardson, & H. Hayne, (Eds.), *Attention and information processing in infants and adults: Perspectives from human and animal research* (pp. 263–295). Hillsdale, NJ: Lawrence Erlbaum Associates.

Öhman, A., & Dimberg, U. (1984). An evolutionary perspective on human social behavior. In W. M. Waid (Ed.), *Sociophysiology* (pp. 47–86). New York: Springer-Verlag.

Panksepp, J. (1982). Toward a general psychobiological theory of emotions. *The Behavioral and Brain Sciences, 5,* 407–467.

Papez, J. W. (1937). A proposed mechanism of emotion. *Archives of Neurology and Psychiatry, 38,* 725–743.

Perceman, E. (Ed.). (1983). *Cognitive processing in the right hemisphere.* New York: Academic Press.

Pillemer, D. B. (1984). Flashbulb memories of the assassination attempt on President Reagan. *Cognition, 16,* 63–80.

Posner, M. I. (1980). Orienting of attention. The VII the Sir Frederic Bartlett Lecture. *Quarterly Journal of Experimental Psychology, 32,* 3–25.

Posner, M. I., Cohen, Y., Choate, L., Hockey, G. R. I., & Maylor, E. (1984). Sustained concentration: Passive filtering or active orienting? In S. Kornblum & J. Requin (Eds.), *Preparatory states and processes* (pp. 49–65). Hillsdale, NJ: Lawrence Erlbaum Associates .

Posner, M. I., Petersen, S. E., Fox, P. T., & Raichle, M. E. (1988). Localization of cognitive operations in the human brain. *Science, 240,* 1627–1631.

Reiman, E. M., Fusselman, M. J., Fox, P. T., & Raichle, M. E. (1989). Neuroanatomical correlates of anticipatory anxiety. *Science, 243*,1071–1074.

Reisberg, D., Heuer, F., McLean, J., & O'Shaughnessy, M. (1988). The quantity, not the quality, of affect predicts memory vividness. *Bulletin of the Psychonomic Society, 26,* 100–103.

Robinson, J. A. (1980). Affect and retrieval of personal memories. *Motivation and Emotion, 4,* 149–173.

Rubin, D. C., & Kozin, M. (1984). Vivid memories. *Cognition, 16,* 81–95.

Runcie, D., & O'Bannon, R. M. (1977). An independence of induced amnesia and emotional response. *American Journal of Psychology, 90,* 55–61.

Safer, M. A. (1981). Sex and hemisphere differences in access to codes for processing emotional expressions and faces. *Journal of Experimental Psychology: General, 110,* 86–100.

Saufley, W. H., Jr., & Winograd, E. (1970). Retrograde amnesia and priority instructions in free recall. *Journal of Experimental Psychology, 85,* 150–152.

Schacter, D. L., Wang, P. L., Tulving, E., & Freedman, M. (1982). Functional retrograde amnesia: A quantitative case study. *Neuropsychologia, 20,* 523–532.

Scrivner, E., & Safer, M. A. (1988). Eyewitnesses show hypermnesia for details about a violent event. *Journal of Applied Psychology, 73,* 371–377.

Sieck, M. H. (1972). The role of olfactory system in avoidance learning and activity. *Physiology and Behavior, 8,* 705–710.

Singer, J. L. (Ed.). (1990). *Repression and dissociation: Implications for personality theory, psychopathology, and health.* Chicago: The University of Chicago Press.

Talland, G. A., & Waugh, N. C. (Eds.). (1969). *The pathology of memory.* New York: Academic Press.

Thomas, G. T., Hostetter, G., & Barker, D. J. (1968). Behavioral functions of the limbic system. In E. Stellar & J. M. Sprague (Eds.), *Progress in physiological psychology,* (Vol 2, pp. 230–311). New York: Academic Press.

Tucker, D. M. (1981). Lateral brain function, emotion, and conceptualization. *Psychological Bulletin, 89,* 19–46.

Treisman, A. M. (1982). Perceptual grouping and attention in visual search for features and objects. *Journal of Experimental Psychology: Human Perception and Performance, 8,* 194–214.

Tulving, E. (1969). Retrograde amnesia in free recall. *Science, 164,* 88–90.

Tulving, E. (1972). Episodic and semantic memory. In E. Tulving & W. Donaldson (Eds.), *Organization of memory* (pp. 381–403). New York: Academic Press.

Tulving, E. (1987). Multiple memory systems and consciousness. *Human Neurobiology, 6,* 67–80.

Tulving, E., & Schacter, D. L. (1990). Priming and human memory systems. *Science, 247,* 301–306.

Wagenaar, W. A. (1986). My memory: A study of autobiographical memory over six years. *Cognitive Psychology, 18,* 225–252.

Wagenaar, W. A., & Groeneweg, J. (1990). The memory of concentration camp survivors. *Applied Cognitive Psychology, 4,* 77–87.

Wallace, W. P. (1965). Review of the historical, empirical, and the theoretical status of the von Restorff phenomenon. *Psychological Bulletin, 63,* 410–424.

Whitty, C. W. M., & Zangwill, O. L. (Eds.). (1977). *Amnesia.* (2nd ed.). London: Butterworth.

Winograd, E., & Killinger, W. A., Jr. (1983). Relating age at encoding in early childhood to adult recall: Development of flashbulb memories. *Journal of Experimental Psychology: General, 112,* 413–422.

Winograd, E., & Neisser (Eds.). (in press). *Affect and accuracy in recall: The problem of "flashbulb" memories.* New York: Cambridge University Press.

Yerkes, R. M., & Dodson, J. D. (1908). The relation of strength of stimulus to rapidity of habit-information. *Journal of Comparative Neurology of Psychology, 18,* 459–482.

Young, A. W. (Ed.). (1983). Functions of the right cerebral hemisphere. New York: Academic Press.

Yuille, J. C., & Cutshall, J. L. (1986). A case study of eyewitness memory of a crime. *Journal of Applied Psychology, 71,* 291–301.

Yuille, J. C., & Cutshall, J. L. (1989). Analysis of the statements of victims, witnesses and suspects. In J. C. Yuille (Ed.), *Credibility assessment.* Dordrecht: Kluwer.

Zajonc, R. B. (1980). Feeling and thinking: Preferences need no inferences. *American Psychologist, 35,* 151–175.

Zajonc, R. B. (1981). A one-factor mind about mind and emotion. *American Psychologist, 36,* 102–103.

Zajonc, R. B. (1984). On the primacy of affect. *American Psychologist, 39,* 117–123.

IV

CLINICAL OBSERVATIONS

14

Memory, Emotion, and Response to Trauma

Mardi J. Horowitz
Steven P. Reidbord
University of California, San Francisco

The experience of memory typically includes both cognitive and emotional components. How, then, can a memory at some times be consciously represented and experienced with little felt emotion, whereas at other times the same memory may evoke pangs of searing feeling? A prolonged intense mood can occur following a percept, yet the individual can be unaware that the memory of a past trauma has been nonconsciously activated. In contrast, persons during denial phases of stress response syndromes, in particular the post-traumatic stress disorders, may have conscious recollection of the fright, injury, or loss while remaining emotionally flat or numb. Traumatic events may be recalled with unusual dissociation or discordance between ideas and feelings.

Although memories and emotions are closely interdependent, variation in their degree of conscious representation requires explanation. Specifically, a theory of schemas may be needed to understand how cognitive processing can either admit or exclude memory-based emotions from consciousness. This chapter seeks to explore such theory.

The approach we take begins with a description of post-traumatic experiential *phenomena*. The formation of these phenomena is then explained at successively deeper levels of inference about conscious

343

and unconscious mental processes. These deepening levels of inference are discussed under the headings of *states of mind, schemas, and
control processes.*

TABLE 14.1
Stress Response Rating Scale: Signs and Symptoms
Reportedby Clinicians for 66 Subjects

	%*	Group Means†	SD
Intrusion Items			
Pangs of emotion	95	3.1	1.3
Ruminaton or preoccupation	90	2.9	1.4
Fear of losing bodily control or hyperactivity in any bodily system	82	2.6	1.5
Intrusive ideas (in word form)	77	2.3	1.5
Difficulty in dispelling ideas	74	2.1	1.6
Hypervigilance	69	1.6	1.4
Bad dreams	54	1.6	1.7
Intrusive thoughts or images when trying to sleep	51	1.6	1.8
Re-enactments	57	1.5	1.5
Intrusive images	51	1.4	1.6
Startle reactions	34	0.6	1.0
Illusions	26	0.6	1.1
Hallucinations, pseudohallucinations	8	0.2	0.8
Denial Items			
Numbness	69	1.8	1.5
Avoidance of associational connections	69	1.7	1.4
Reduced level of feeling responses to outer stimuli	67	1.7	1.5
Rigidly role-adherent or stereotyped	62	1.5	1.5
Loss of reality appropriacy of thought by switching attitudes	64	1.4	1.2
Unrealistic narrowing of attention, vagueness, or disavowal of stimuli	52	1.2	1.3
Inattention, daze	48	1.2	1.5
Inflexibility or constriction of thought	46	1.0	1.2
Loss of train of thoughts	44	0.9	1.2
Loss of reality appropriacy of thought by sliding meanings	41	0.8	1.2
Memory Failure	34	0.8	1.2
Loss of reality appropriacy of thought by use of disavowal	25	0.6	1.2
Warding off trains of reality-oriented thought by use of fantasy	15	0.3	0.8

*Percent positive endorsement.

† On a scale of intensity where 5 is major; 3, moderate; 1, minor; 0, not present
   (within the past seven days). From Horowitz, Wilner, Kaltreider, & Alvarez (1980).

PHENOMENA

Experiences of many persons with post-traumatic stress disorders are tabulated in Table 14.1 (Horowitz, Wilner, Kaltreider, & Alvarez, 1980).

The diagnosis of post-traumatic stress disorder requires the various caveats stipulated in the DSM III-R statement reproduced in Table 14.2 because, to an extent, the signs and symptoms that constitute the syndrome known as post-traumatic stress disorder are present also in normal responses to life stressors.

TABLE 14.2
PTSD Criteria According to DSM-III-R

Diagnostic Criteria for 309.89 Post-traumatic Stress Disorder

A. The person has experienced an event that is outside the range of usual human experience and that would be markedly distressing to almost anyone, e.g., serious threat to one's life or physical integrity; serious threat or harm to one's children, spouse, or other close relatives and friends; sudden destruction of one's home or community; or seeing another person who has recently been, or is being, seriously injured or killed as the result of an accident or physical violence.

B. The traumatic event is persistently reexperienced in at least one of the following ways:

 (1) recurrent and intrusive distressing recollections of the event (in young children, repetitive play in which themes or aspects of the trauma are expressed)
 (2) recurrent distressing dreams of the event
 (3) sudden acting or feeling as if the traumatic event were recurring (includes a sense of reliving the experience, illusions, hallucinations, and dissociative [flashback] episodes, even those that occur upon awakening or when intoxicated)
 (4) intense psychological distress at exposure to events that symbolize or resemble an aspect of the traumatic event, including anniversaries of the trauma

C. Persistent avoidance of stimuli associated with the trauma or numbing of general responsiveness (not present before the trauma), as indicated by at least three of the following:

 (1) efforts to avoid thoughts or feelings associated with the trauma
 (2) efforts to avoid activities or situations that arouse recollections of the trauma
 (3) inability to recall an important aspect of the trauma (psychogenic amnesia)
 (4) markedly diminished interest in significant activities (in young children, loss of recently acquired developmental skills such as toilet training or language skills)

(Continued)

TABLE 14.2
(Continued)

Diagnostic Criteria for 309.89 Post-traumatic Stress Disorder

---

(5) feeling of detachment or estrangement from others
(6) restricted range of affect, e.g., unable to have loving feelings
(7) sense of of foreshortened future, e.g., does not expect to have a career, marriage, or children, or a long life

D. Persistent symptoms of increased arousal (not present before the trauma), as indicated by at least two of the following:

(1) difficulty falling or staying asleep
(2) irritability or outbursts of anger
(3) hypervigilance
(5) exaggerated startle response
(6) physiologic reactivity upon exposure to events that symbolize or resemble an aspect of the traumatic event (e.g., a woman who was raped in an elevator breaks out in a sweat when entering any elevator)

E. Duration of the disturbance (symptoms in B, C, and D) of at least one month.

Specify delayed onset if the onset of symptoms was at least six months after the trauma.

Source: *Diagnostic and statistical manual of mental disorders, Vol. III - Revised.*

It is the *intensification, prolongation,* or *irrational elaboration* of memories and emotions that leads to a diagnosis of disorder rather than normal distress. The simple presence or absence of an isolated sign or symptom usually cannot differentiate a normal from pathological reaction.

This is nowhere more clear than in careful studies of grief reactions. At an earlier time it was believed that certain types of emotional reactions such as intense periods of anger and guilt were signs of a pathological grief reaction, and that a normal grief reaction would be characterized by sadness and fear for the future of the self without the benefits of the relationship. Research summarized elsewhere (Horowitz, 1986) suggests this is not the case, that phases of preoccupation with anger and guilt can be a part of normal grief. The clinical differentiation of normal from pathological grief is usually a judgment based on observing how a person progresses through phases of response; it does not hinge on the signs and symptoms experienced at a given time.

Pathological grief reactions tend to be of three types. One reaction is to be overwhelmed by severely intense, intrusive emotions and memories. A second type involves being overwhelmed not by the searing pain of intrusive ideas and feelings at any one time, but by persistent, seemingly unending experiences without a sense of progression or resolution. A third reaction is avoidance of grief, leading to what has been called *frozen grief* (Lindemann, 1944). In addition there are other disorders precipitated by loss, such as major depressive disorders, and bizarre responses such as transient psychoses.

States of Mind

In order to understand the progression through stress response syndromes, it is helpful to have a general prototype of phasic tendencies. Figure 14.1 (Horowitz, 1986) provides this prototype in terms of different states of mind, especially those that may be characterized by under or overmodulated emotionality. The outcry and intrusive phases contain undermodulated experiences; the denial phase is characterized by overmodulation, by avoidance of ideas and feelings.

A person with a normal stress response may have intensified emotion and memory in the outcry and intrusion phases of a stress response syndrome, diminution of emotion and ideation related to the traumatic events during the denial phase, and intermittent bouts of both of these extremes during the working through phase. A relative completion is marked by a reduction in the vividness of memory images as well as by a reduction of the sudden, jarring activation of emotion on recollection or confrontation with reminders of the trauma. A reminder, after completion, may elicit sad or startle reactions; one may feel some fear where, previously, during intrusive phases, one had felt raw terror or panic.

In general, the more the person experiences stages of extreme terror during an event, the more likely the imagery of that event will be inscribed in the same sensory modalities of memory as the perceptions. These memory inscriptions tend to return to conscious representation in that same modality and, because of their vividness, to re-evoke the same emotions as the original experience. On the other hand, the more the images evoke dreaded states of mind, the more there may be inhibitory efforts aimed at preventing the repetition of such memories. It is the interaction of the inhibitory efforts and the tendency towards active and repeated representation that may lead to the experience of intrusiveness. In empirical studies it was found that the persons most emotionally aroused by stressful films were those who also tended to have the most intrusive and repetitive imagery derived from those films in subsequent periods (Horowitz, 1975).

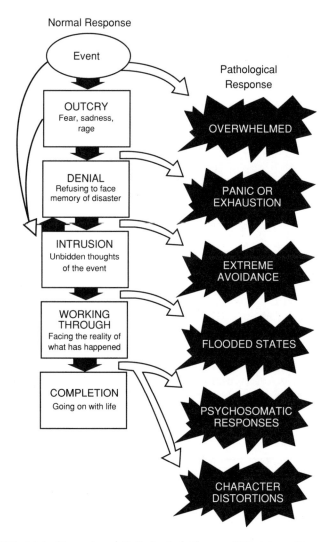

FIG. 14.1   Normal and Pathological Phases of Poststress Response
(from Horowitz, M. J. 1986). *Stress response syndromes, 2nd ed.*
Northvale, NJ: Aronson.

The great deal of data now available on bereavement reactions
allows us to summarize the phenomena that may differentiate
normal from pathological grief as organized by phases of experience.
Such a view is presented in Table 14.3.

Empirical data from such instruments as the Impact of Event
Scale (Horowitz 1986; Horowitz, Wilner, & Alvarez, 1979; Zilberg,
Weiss, & Horowitz, 1982) support the phasic nature of response, and

TABLE 14.3
Common Experiences During Grief
and Their Pathological Intensification

Phase	Normal Response	Pathological Intensification
Dying	Emotional expression and immediate coping with the dying process	Avoidant; overwhelmed, dazed, confused; self-punitive; inappropriately hostile
Death and Outcry	Outcry of emotions with news of the death and turning for help to others or isolating self with self-succoring	Panic; dissociative reactions; reactive psychoses
Warding Off (Denial)	Avoidance of reminders, social withdrawal, focusing elsewhere, emotional numbing, not thinking of implications to self or certain themes	Maladaptive avoidances of confronting the implications of the death; drug or alcohol abuse, counter phobic frenzy, promiscuity, fugue states, phobic avoidance, feeling dead or unreal
Re-Experience (Intrusion)	Intrusive experiences including recollections of negative relationship experiences with the deceased, bad dreams, reduced concentration, compulsive enactments	Flooding with negative images and emotions, uncontrolled ideation, self-impairing compulsive reenactments, night terrors, recurrent nightmares, distraught from intrusion of anger, anxiety, despair, shame or guilt themes, physiological exhaustion from hyperarousal
Working Through	Recollections of the deceased and contemplations of self with reduced intrusiveness of memories and fantasies, increased rational acceptance, reduced numbness and avoidance, more "dosing" of recollections and a sense of working it through	Sense that one cannot integrate the death with a sense of self and continued life; persistent warded-off themes may manifest as anxious, depressed, enraged, shame-filled or guilty moods, and psychophysiological syndromes
Completion	Reduction in emotional swings with a sense of self-coherence and readiness for new relationships; able to experience positive states of mind	Failure to complete mourning may be associated with inability to work, create, to feel emotion or positive states of mind

From Horowitz, M. J. (1990).

the general prototype shown in Fig. 14.1. Persons may experience particular states of mind during the intrusive phase and the denial phase that characterize these situations. What constitutes an abnormal reaction may not be the amount of distressing memory present in states of mind with intrusive ideas and emotions, but that the phase predominated by such states of mind is *prolonged*. People so affected often sense intuitively that some kind of unconscious processing to bring about resolution is not occurring, and they therefore become secondarily frightened, seek professional help, obtain a diagnosis, and, hopefully, beneficial treatment.

The phasic nature of many stress response syndromes suggests the need to develop theory to explain phasic phenomena such as the following: Sometimes during a denial phase the person can relate memories of the event to another person so that the *other person feels quite upset or frightened* at hearing the story, and yet the storyteller seems unemotional and may report feeling as though wrapped in cotton, buffered, or insulated from emotional experience. Strong emotions are implicit in the memory; not only are they activated in most others who hear the memory, but during the intrusive phase the narrator may be choked with emotion, feel flooded, and have to interrupt a recollection that he or she related calmly earlier, during a denial phase.

Secondly, on the anniversary of a traumatic event the person may not recall that the event occurred on this date. Nonetheless, the person may consciously experience, and even note as mysterious, a prevailing negative mood with emotional qualities that connect it rather clearly to the earlier traumatic event. This type of *anniversary reaction* may be more apparent to observers; if such observers explicitly note the anniversary date, the subject of the experience may react with startle.

Such varied effects in varied states of mind call for an explanatory system with multiple levels of control, and multiple schemas that can be controlled. We turn to the topic of such schemas first.

Schemas

Schemas theory describes why when the same state occurs it has a similar form. The schema is seen as the intrinsic organizer of mental states (Horowitz, 1991; Mandler 1988).

Stress response syndromes, especially those resulting from threats of injury to the self, as in death frights, and threats of or actual loss of others important to the self, are modeled well using person schemas theory (Horowitz, 1988a, 1988b, 1991; Horowitz,

Fridhandler, & Stinson, in press). A *person schema* is one that organizes information about self or another. A special and important type of person schema is a *role–relationship model*, as shown in Fig. 14.2, which organizes information about traits and interpersonal scripts expected out of wishes or fears. The relationship of role–relationship models to actual social situations, and indeed to memories of traumatic events occurring in such situations, is shown in Fig. 14.3.

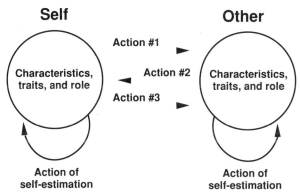

FIG 14.2   A role-relationship model (from Horowitz, Merluzzi, Ewert, Ghannam, Hartley, & Stinson, 1991). The actions and traits depicted are a mental schema of what form real events *might* take. The patterned expected sequence of the events is labled with the successive numbers. Actions include emotional expressions and conscious experiences. Self-estimation may include pride, guilt, bolstering of self, attacks on self.

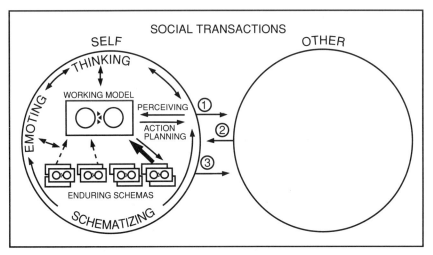

FIG. 14.3   Social transactions and person schemas, (from Horowitz, 1991).

As suggested in Fig. 14.3 there may be several person schemas, particularly role–relationship models, that could be used to derive the personal meaning of a traumatic perception and, later, the traumatic memory it becomes. The perception and eventual memory are traumatic in part because they cannot be integrated with enduring attitudes, that is, with the existing repertoire of schemas. There is no knowledge base to inform swift, adaptive reactions to this event. Thus the individual is overwhelmed, leading to intrusive or omissive states of mind.

Because most traumatic events involve injury, loss, or threat of these to the point that the person feels overwhelmingly frightened about their possibility, such events tend to destabilize schemas of self as competent, efficacious, good, or strong. A person with poor-self schemas and attachment bonds will be more vulnerable to trauma with loss (Bowlby, 1969, 1973, 1980). Of course, any person might tend to activate latent schemas of the self as weak if he or she had been unable to prevent (or perhaps in some way caused) the stressful event. Yet persons with enduring and especially bad, degraded, incompetent, helpless, or worthless self-schemas will have particular difficulty in working through the memory of a traumatic event (Horowitz, 1990).

Thus, the emotional response that may occur with recollection of a traumatic event results from several factors: (a) the emotion activated during the event that is part of the memory and so tends to return again with its recollection due to activation of the memory's associated meaning network; (b) a mnemic repetition of the sensory imagery, evoking new kinds of emotional response as new implications are recognized during the here-and-now of recollection; and (c) alarm emotions due to recognition of schematic discord, such as the inability of the self to cope with expected situations.

The recollection of a traumatic memory will also incorporate the appraisal of the self's capacity to cope with the event were it to be repeated (as suggested by Lazarus, 1966, and Bandura, 1977). This estimation of self-efficacy will be affected by the type of schemas activated during the recollection process. Activation of weak self-schemas from a repertoire of multiple self-schemas would lead to more fear, shame, or despair on remembrance than would memory reconstruction and appraisal as organized by strong self-schemas.

In ordinary states of mind, conscious reflection and communication may be organized by relatively stable schemas, as by a single schema of self, and a single view of how the self relates to the environment. But traumatic events do not fit usual schemas (Bowlby, 1969, 1973, 1980; Horowitz, 1986). The person tends to respond unconsciously by relating the traumatic situation to many schemas by means of parallel processing. This, in turn, tends to lead to the activation of various preexisting self-concepts and views of relationships. The person processes the meaning of the event along several parallel streams. Consciousness may be derived from different elements of these parallel streams, leading to confusing shimmerings of different emotions related to different streams. The confusion leads to further anxieties about fragmentation, incoherence, chaos, loss of continuity, or depersonalization of the self.

A clinical example may illustrate how traumatic events can activate latent self-schemas or role–relationship models and set in motion a process in which new schemas are formed. The patient was a young woman who was doing well at work and in relationship at the time of the sudden and unexpected death of her father. Previously she had difficulties in terms of feeling that she might be too like her mother, a person who was seen as too impulsively emotional and disruptive to the family because of her rages and sobbing episodes over minor incidents. In the course of her young adulthood, the patient had mastered control over her own emotions and felt herself to be a poised and competent person in almost all situations.

After the death of her father she began to weep impulsively in social settings. She felt she was now like her mother. This was an activation of a latent self-schema that had been based on identification with her mother, one that had been relatively dormant because of the development of more competent and controlled self-schemas. Moreover, the death of the patient's father tended to activate a latent role–relationship model in which the father would be critical of her for being a "messy emoter," just as he had been very critical of her mother.

She tended to inhibit crying in thinking of her father, but the inclination to mourn meant that she tended to review all memories related to the father, and also to pine and yearn for him now that he had died. In the course of psychotherapy she learned to recognize the normal crying that may be a part of the mourning process, and to differentiate this from the view of herself as a messy emoter. The new experience was to be emotional in the context of the relationship with the therapist, and then with her friends, in a way that she had not previously experienced because she had made so many efforts at emotional containment.

The role–relationship model in which a person is criticized as a messy emoter, and then is forced to experience shame or anger in retaliation or response, was just one of many topics activated by the death of her father. Other themes having to do with the adult-to-adult relationship that had developed between them, previous arguments that made her feel remorse now that he was dead, and more child-like longings for dependency were all reviewed in therapy. Each of these role–relationship models was based on person schemas that contained emotional qualities; as these schemas were reviewed emotions were, for a time, re-experienced during conscious contemplation or in dreams related to memories of her father and to his death.

Control Processes

In the face of trauma, certain basic questions commonly focus mental activity. One such focus is "who is to blame." It is important to arrive at an answer to such a question in order to integrate a traumatic memory into personal meaning systems of value, identity, and self-esteem. On the other hand, incipient thoughts about such topics may activate so much emotion (e.g., guilt, shame, self-disgust) that control processes intercede to dampen feelings and prevent entry into overwhelmed states of mind. Control processes may affect not only taxonomic or semantic memory codings but also the different modes of representation of ideas and emotions and the repertoire of schemas. Excessive inhibitions, ones that are too extensive or prolonged, could interrupt a working through process.

The experience just mentioned, of a person in a denial phase reporting a traumatic memory without emotion, may be due to the person activating person schemas, such as role–relationship models, in which the current self-schema is dissociated from activity in the traumatic memory. The self-concept derived from such role–relationship models may be that of a storyteller, an outsider—not the same person who experienced and acted during the event. Such dissociations are common during very intense ongoing traumas, wherein the individual feels helpless, and have even been implicated in the multiple personality disorders (see Braun & Frischholz, this volume). Indeed, the literature on experimentally induced "learned helplessness" suggests that behavioral dissociation is a characteristic response to helplessness in humans and many other species (Abramson, Seligman, & Teasdale, 1978).

In control process theory, ego defense mechanisms such as undoing and projection are not seen as "mechanisms" but rather as labels for certain outcomes of control processes. The control processes involve the "mechanisms" or functions of inhibition, facilitation, disinhibition, or dysregulation of separable systems of mental activity, and separable modules of brain activity (Horowitz, et al., 1990).

The experience of trauma is often followed by a tendency to repeat the memory. Active important memories are reviewed in order to bring them into accord with enduring schemas, but intense negative emotions occur due to a discord between these memories and schemas, leading to a sense of loss of control over mental contents. Anticipation of undermodulated and dreaded states of mind motivates efforts to institute control processes. The operation of the control processes may be nonconscious, and the anticipation of the dreaded states of mind may also be outside of consciousness. Thus, the purpose and the processes of control may operate unconsciously, producing as an outcome various states of mind such as those that occur in phasic responses to stressful life events. Phases of denial, most especially, are ones in which there is a high activity of inhibitory control processes. As an aspect of these control processes, the person may even facilitate activities and memories other than those associated with traumatic event.

Control processes can also operate relatively selectively. Instead of globally denying the implications and emotions of a traumatic memory, the person may recollect aspects of the memory of the traumatic event while specifically dampening associated emotions. This can be done, for example, by facilitating lexical representational modes while inhibiting imagistic representational modes. Interdiction of imagery tends to reduce immediate emotional response. In addition, control processes may inhibit self-schemas as the agent of experience. The traumatic memory may be recollected as if it were the experience of someone else. Thus the person may relate the experience in a way that activates emotion in the listener, whereas the speaker remains unnaturally calm.

Control processes may inhibit conscious representation but allow the activation of unconscious schemas, especially in the presence of perceptual reminders. The person may see a date on a newspaper that activates schemas of a relationship that ended by death on such a date. The person may not consciously realize that this is the anniversary of the death of the loved one, but the activation of unconscious memories and the activation of schemas about what the self has lost may lead to a mood that is consciously felt. The person may not consciously have an explanation of this mood because of the operation of inhibitions of associations that might otherwise be represented and available to awareness.

CONCLUSION

Many studies of emotion have dealt with the outflow pattern: brain activity leading to peripheral nervous system activity, in turn leading to the expression of basic emotions such as anger, joy, surprise, and disgust. Such emotional outflow is well characterized, for example, in the studies of facial expression by Ekman (1982, 1984), Ekman and Friesen (1975), and Izard (1977). The kind of emotion theory addressed here is more proximal and relates to mental activities, to the distributed meaning systems of the mind. Here emotions are not regarded as distinct from meaning systems; there is no cleavage between cognition and emotion. Our proposed relational theory of emotionality involves views of self, other, and transactional scripts. The advantage of this relational theory, which adds schemas to ideas of cognitive processing and associative networks, is that it allows one to address the complexity of emotions in states such as revengeful rumination, bitter resignation, shimmering shame and rage, poignant sorrow, or terror-stricken grief. These complex emotional states are explained by describing the schematic meaning structure, a form of generalized memory, that organizes each particular state and gives it a quality of sameness when it recurs.

ACKNOWLEDGMENTS

This chapter is based on research supported by the Program on Conscious and Unconscious Mental Processes of the John D. and Catherine T. MacArthur Foundation. Earlier research on stress response syndromes and the delineation of post-traumatic stress disorders was supported by the National Institute of Mental Health, and the Center for the Study of Neuroses, UCSF.

REFERENCES

Abramson, L. Y., Seligman, M. E. P., & Teasdale, J. D. (1978). Learned helplessness in humans—critique and reformulation. *Journal of Abnormal Psychology*, 87(1), 49–74.

American Psychiatric Association. (1986). Diagnostic and statistical manual of mental disorders (DSM-IIIR). Washington, DC.

Bandura, A. (1977). Self-efficacy: Toward a unified theory of behavioral change. *Psychological Review*, 84, 191–215.

Bowlby, J. (1969). *Attachment and loss, Vol. 1: Attachment*. New York: Basic Books.

Bowlby, J. (1973). *Attachment and loss, Vol. 2: Separation, anxiety and mourning.* New York: Basic Books.
Bowlby, J. (1980). *Attachment and loss, Vol. 3: Loss, sadness and depression.* New York: Basic Books.
Ekman, P. 1982. *Emotion in the human face* (2nd ed.). New York: Cambridge University Press.
Ekman, P. (1984). Expression and the nature of emotion. In P. Ekman & K. Sherer (Eds.), *Approaches to emotion.* New York: Lawrence Erlbaum Associates.
Ekman, P., & Friesen, W. (1975). *Unmasking the face.* Englewood Cliffs, NJ: Prentice-Hall.
Horowitz, M. J. (1975). Intrusive and repetitive thoughts after experimental stress. *Archives of General Psychiatry, 32,* 1457–1463.
Horowitz, M. J. (1986). *Stress response syndromes* (2nd ed.). Northvale, NJ: Jason Aronson.
Horowitz, M. J. (1988a). *Introduction to Psychodynamics.* New York: Basic Books.
Horowitz, M. J. (Ed.). (1988b). *Psychodynamics and cognition.* Chicago: University of Chicago Press.
Horowitz, M. J. (1990). A model of mourning: Change in schemas of self and other. *Journal of American Psychoanalytic Association, 38,* 297–324.
Horowitz, M. J. (Ed.). (1991). *Person schemas and maladaptive interpersonal patterns.* Chicago: University of Chicago Press.
Horowitz, M. J., Fridhandler, B., & Stinson, C.H. (in press). Person schemas and emotion. *Journal of American Psychoanalytic Association.*
Horowitz, M. J., Markman, H. C., Stinson, C. H., Ghannam, J. H., & Fridhandler, B. (1990). A classification theory of defense. In J. Singer (Ed), *Repression and dissociation: Implications for personality theory, psychopathology, and health.* Chicago: University of Chicago Press.
Horowitz, M. J., Merluzzi, T. V., Ewert, M., Ghannam, J., Hartley, D., & Stinson, C.H. (1991). Role-Relationship Models Configuration (RRMC). In M. J. Horowitz (Ed.), *Person schemas and maladaptive interpersonal patterns.* Chicago: University of Chicago Press.
Horowitz, M. J., Wilner, N., & Alvarez, W. (1979). The impact of event scale: A measure of subjective stress. *Psychosomatic Medicine, 41*(3), 209–218.
Horowitz, M. J., Wilner, N., Kaltreider, N., & Alvarez, W. (1980). Signs and symptoms of post-traumatic stress disorder. *Archives of General Psychiatry, 37,* 85–92.
Izard, C. (1977). *Human emotions.* New York: Plenum Press.
Lazarus, R. S. (1966). *Psychological stress and the coping process.* New York: McGraw-Hill.
Lindemann E. (1944). Symptomatology and management of acute grief. *American Journal of Psychiatry, 101,* 141–148.
Mandler, G. (1988). Problems and directions in the study of consciousness. In M. J. Horowitz (Ed.), *Psychodynamics and cognition* (pp. 21–45). Chicago: University of Chicago Press.
Zilberg, N., Weiss, D., & Horowitz, M. J. (1982). Impact of event scale: A cross-validation study and some empirical evidence. *Journal of Consulting and Clinical Psychology, 50,* 407–414.

15

Overcoming Traumatic Memories

Kent D. Harber
Stanford University

James W. Pennebaker
Southern Methodist University

Recovery from traumatic events is typically a painful and lengthy process. Beyond the insult and injury experienced when the traumatic episode occurs, there are tremendous feelings of uncertainty, anxiety, and self-doubt following in the trauma's wake. Traumas cause victims to question fundamental assumptions about their own merit, and about the orderliness of the world. This upheaval of emotional bedrock leaves victims yearning to regain a sense of stability and meaning about themselves and the world around them.

Despite their wishes for peace of mind, trauma victims frequently experience repeated, unbidden memories of the traumatic event. Variously designated as intrusive thinking, rumination, or compulsive thinking, these spontaneously arising memories are virtually the signature of post-traumatic stress (American Psychiatric Association, 1980). For most people, intrusive thoughts are an ongoing and enduring aspect of loss. The intrusions, which are typically vivid and absorbing, occur with moderate to extreme frequency for most survivors of tragic events (Tait & Silver, 1989).

The role these memories play in traumatic recovery is a complicated one. On the one hand, they can inflame post-traumatic scars by causing victims to mentally relive traumatic events (see Horowitz, this volume), by dousing victims with negative emotions such as sorrow and anguish (Tait & Silver, 1989), and by coaxing victims into sometimes futile searches for meaning in tragedy (Silver, Boon, &

Stones, 1983). Additionally, many traumas can be a source of social ostracism when shared with others (Coates, Wortman, & Abbey, 1979). For these reasons, it is understandable that trauma victims would try to suppress thinking or speaking about trauma-related memories, as well as the feelings associated with these recollections.

Rather than alleviating post-traumatic distress, active inhibition of traumatic memories may compound victims' difficulties by inducing physical illness. As is discussed in greater detail later, inhibitory or suppressive responses to traumatic thoughts and feelings elevate levels of autonomic activity, deplete immune functioning, and increase incidence of physical illness (see Pennebaker, 1989, Pennebaker, Colder and Sharp, 1990, for reviews). Traumatic ruminations, then, can corner recovering victims into a cruel paradox; although visitations of these unbidden reminders are psychologically disrupting, chronic suppression of them is physically debilitating.

The intrusions of traumatic thoughts and memories are best understood within a general context of emotional assimilation. In this perspective, traumatic events represent significant challenges to fundamental beliefs. As long as basic beliefs and traumatic realities are at odds, the psyche will be compelled to work toward their accommodation (cf. Epstein, in press; Horowitz, 1986). As is seen later, in order to achieve the task of traumatic assimilation, and the insight fostering such assimilation, victims must consciously confront the memories and emotions associated with their traumatic ordeals. This confrontation is best accomplished by translating the chaotic swirl of traumatic ideation and feelings into coherent language.

In this chapter, we explore the psychological and social factors associated with the unwanted thoughts and memories of traumatic experiences. In particular, we point to the problems inherent in attempts to inhibit the expression of thoughts and emotions of significant personal experiences. Based on findings that reveal the benefits of translating traumatic memories into language, we argue that language brings about the organization and assimilation of traumatic memories and emotions.

THE EXPRESSION OF EMOTIONS
AND BELIEFS WITHIN A SOCIAL CONTEXT

Victims face two distinct dilemmas in their efforts to overcome recurring thoughts and emotions surrounding upsetting experiences. One of these involves an intrapsychic conflict between basic beliefs and traumatic realities that challenge them (Epstein, in press;

Horowitz, 1986). The other dilemma, which is interpersonal, surrounds victims' natural urge to talk about traumas and listeners' disinclination to hear about the victims' experiences. Both of these dilemmas suspend victims between countervaling tendencies to reveal their private thoughts and feelings, and to inhibit emotional expression that may lead to personally disturbing, and socially costly, disclosures. It is in this ambivalent middle ground that thought intrusions flourish and that the health-debilitating stress of inhibition is most intense.

The Emotional Correlates
of Traumatic Memories

Asked his opinion of a nimble-footed opponent, the boxer Joe Louis made the now famous comment that "he can run, but he can't hide." Louis's quip describes the relationship between trauma victims and their intrusive memories. Whereas unwanted thoughts can be avoided temporarily, they relentlessly return (Martin & Tesser, 1989). Why can't trauma victims simply banish distressing memories to some gulag in long-term storage and thereby be rid of them? Wegner's work on thought suppression supplies some answers to this question (Wegner, 1989; Wegner, Shortt, Blake, & Page, 1990). In his research on intentional efforts to control unwanted thoughts, Wegner found that subjects told to not think of a white bear were subsequently inundated with white bear thoughts. Indeed, they had more frequent intrusive thoughts than did subjects instructed *to try to think* of a white bear. Wegner's explanation for this phenomenon is that people try to avoid unwanted thoughts by haphazardly employing proximal stimuli as distractors. Over time, these objects (e.g., ceiling tiles, carpeting) become associated with the unwanted thought, so that eventually the would-be suppressor is surrounded by reminders of it. The abundance of cues for the unwanted thought make it that much more difficult to suppress, and as a result suppressors attend more to "forbidden" material than do nonsuppressors.

Of particular importance is that the boomerang of suppressed thoughts back into consciousness occurs with much more force for emotionally tagged thoughts. Wegner et al. (1990) demonstrated the greater intrusive potency of emotional content in an experiment where subjects were told to suppress either exciting thoughts (e.g., about sex) or unexciting thoughts (e.g., the dean of students). Results showed that, for the emotionally charged topic only, suppression led to more frequent unbidden thoughts of the topic, longer fixation upon the topic, and elevated bodily arousal (as measured by skin conductance) when intrusions occurred. The conclusion Wegner et al. drew from these results is that intrusive thoughts get much of their propulsive force from unexpressed emotions. This, in turn, suggests that the problems of post-traumatic thought intrusions lie not so much with the memories themselves, as with the unassimilated emotions that drive these memories to the surface of consciousness (see Leventhal, 1980, for a similar argument).

Reviewing the cognitive functions that emotions serve may help clarify their role in post-traumatic rumination. There is a fairly established theoretical tradition that views emotions as a sensitive mental radar, alerting people to the occurrence, significance, and nature of subjectively significant events (Easterbrook, 1959; Plutchik, 1980; Simon, 1967). Advances in the development of schema theory (e.g., Neisser, 1976; Rumelhart & Ortony, 1977) have allowed emotion theorists to refine our understanding of emotion's attentional advantages. As used here, schemas are implicit theories people maintain to understand, and operate in, their environments. Schemas include goals, beliefs, and expectations (Fiske & Taylor, 1984). By providing a context against which they can evaluate the concordance between new information and past learning, schemas help people recognize and make sense of novel events.

A number of theorists contend that emotions arise when schemas are disrupted and/or when current conditions conflict with established expectations or beliefs (Higgins, 1987; Mandler, 1964). According to these discrepancy theorists, when we encounter something inconsistent with pre-existing schemas, an emotional impulse is generated that draws our attention to the source of this disparity, permitting schemas to update themselves by accommodating this new information. Once schemas and situations have been realigned (e.g., by taking action that conforms situations to schemas, or by amending schemas to better fit situations), the emotion is deactivated (Horowitz, 1986). The adaptive value of this affect–schema correspondence is fairly clear: it directs our attention to novel or unanticipated features of our surroundings and permits continual correction of our schema-based navigation system.

Once activated by significant disparities between expectations and events, emotions tend to be quite dogged about completing their cognitive agendas. According to Horowitz (1986), emotions remain active as long as the disparities that evoked them go unresolved. This insistence of emotions to meet their schema-directed agendas has been likened to the Zeigarnik effect. Classic demonstrations of the

Zeigarnik phenomenon show that when subjectively valued goals are interrupted, they remain active in memory (Martin & Tesser, 1989). Tension surrounding these uncompleted goals motivate their resolution, which—when achieved—deactivates the goal-related memories. According to Mandler (1964) the tension created and sustained by disrupted plans is distressing and serves as impetus to goal completion. Summarizing this perspective, Horowitz (1986) noted that "the organism thus favors completion to end distress." (p. 93).

Martin and Tesser (1989) supplied a theory of ruminative thought that fits closely with this model. According to these authors, ruminative thoughts arise when valued goals are blocked. The ruminations serve to direct attention toward uncompleted goals that can then spur problem solving. Although Martin and Tesser do not directly relate their theory to post-traumatic ruminations, their key points are consistent with hypotheses presented by trauma researchers (i.e., that disparities between expectations and events require resolution, and that intrusive thoughts keep these disparities under the limelight of consciousness). Further, the characterization of emotions as goal directed (e.g., Baumeister & Tice, 1987) links goal-compeltion models of rumination with Horowitz's emotional completion-tendency explanation.

We should point out that in some cases ruminative cycles can be broken without addressing underlying emotions. Morrow and Nolen-Hoeksema (1990), for example, show that moderately sad people can circumvent bothersome ruminations by engaging in activities that evoke positive emotions. Apparently, the positive associations created by pleasant distractors override the negative thinking sadness promotes. It is not clear, however, that emotions of traumatic magnitude are as amenable to distraction as are the much less intense negative states evoked in laboratory settings. Martin and Tesser, speaking in the language of goals rather than emotions, per se, address this point. In concordance with Morrow and Nolen-Hoeksema, Martin and Tesser observe that intrusive thoughts can be terminated by identifying a substitute goal of equal or greater value. However, Martin and Tesser also point out that a major problem with these substitution solutions is that some cardinal goals defy replacement. The completion goals evoked by traumatic events—entailing reformation of fundamental beliefs—seem to be unlikely candidates for easy substitution. In fact, experimental studies and clinical reports suggest that neither emotional distraction nor goal substitution are effective antidotes for unresolved traumatic distress (Silver et al., 1983; Tait & Silver, 1989).

The Intransigence of Trauma-Implicated Beliefs

One of the reasons that traumatic emotions remain unresolved is that the goals they seek to accomplish are, in themselves, psychologically threatening. Consider some of the experiences that cause trauma: deaths of loved ones, sexual assaults, disabling accidents, torture, and natural disasters. Beyond injury and loss, upheavals such as these shake fundamental beliefs about the orderliness of the world, and challenge one's own credentials as an efficacious participant in society (Horowitz, 1986; Pennebaker, 1989; Wortman & Silver, 1987). According to both Epstein (in press) and Janoff-Bulman (1989), psychological health rests on three implicit beliefs about the world: that it is basically benevolent, meaningful, and that the self is worthy. According to Epstein, traumas challenge one or more of these basic assumptions so severely that the entire triadic scaffolding of psychological functioning is destabilized. Consequently, traumas can undermine victims' confidence in the world or in their ability to participate in it satisfactorily.

Because disruption of basic beliefs is so destabilizing, people are—by nature—averse to information that contradicts fundamental assumptions. Marris (1986) has termed this inherent scepticism a "conservative impulse" and considers it most energetic in the defense of constructs that have demonstrated validity in the past. There is considerable evidence that the beliefs that traumas challenge (i.e., in one's own worthiness, and in the meaningfulness of the world) are those most resistant to change. For example, researchers have found that once a self-relevant belief has been instantiated, it will persevere even in the face of incontestable countervailing evidence (Lord, Lepper, & Preston, 1984; Ross, Lepper, & Hubbard, 1975). In fact, only by engaging in the cognitively energetic task of "considering the opposite" can people discard personal beliefs based on performance feedback that they knew was false (Lord et al., 1984). The robustness of self-aggrandizing memory biases (Greenwald, 1980) and of ego-protective attributional biases (Snyder, Stephan, & Rosenfield, 1978) further indicate the resilience of belief in one's own worthiness.

Persistence of beliefs in a just, well-ordered world are also well documented. Lerner (1980), for example, has found that people will derogate innocent victims in order to sustain beliefs in a just world. Similarly, recent research in "Terror Management Theory" shows that people become highly punitive to those who even indirectly challenge their feelings of personal invulnerability, moral correctness, or spiritual certainty (Greenberg, Pyszczynski, Solomon, Rosenblatt,

Veeder, Kirkland, & Lyon, 1990; Rosenblatt, Greenberg, Solomon, Pyszczynski, & Lyon, 1989).

Traumatic amnesias, and dissociative episodes, supply some of the more striking examples of how the psyche can defend self-concept from traumatic insult (Christianson & Nilsson, 1984, 1989; Horowitz, 1986; Spiegel, 1988). In traumatic amnesias, victims temporarily forget not only the traumatic event but their own identities as well. Christianson and Nilsson (1989) suggested that this self-forgetting is a victim's refuge of last resort, a psychic trap door through which his or her sense of self can avoid the pain of catastrophic insult. Commenting on the traumatic amnesia suffered by a rape victim, these researchers (Christianson & Nilsson, 1989) wrote: "The rape implied such an unbearable insult to her identity and assault upon her self image that a temporary loss of identity perhaps became necessary in order to handle the immediate post-traumatic distress" (p. 305).

A less extreme, although still dramatic, form of traumatic defense of one's self-image is found in profound emotional dissociation. Spiegel (1988) reported that trauma victims can undergo such complete emotional detachment during the time of their ordeals that they experience themselves as impassive observers of their own assaults. Like Christianson and Nilsson, Spiegel interprets this defense as an adaptive isolation of an overwhelmingly threatened sense of self.

Horowitz describes self-protective defenses against traumatic insult as "controls" and says that the intrusive cycling most trauma victims experience is a display of these protective devices. According to Horowitz, control processes staunch the flow of post-traumatic ideation when they threaten to flood the victims' already shaken self-beliefs. However, as fear recedes the controls relax, releasing the memories anew until feelings of distress cause controls to again isolate sense of self from traumatic memories. Especially relevant to our thesis is Horowitz's contention that this cycling ceases when accord is achieved between the traumatic events and the basic beliefs that they threaten.

Social Obstacles to Trauma Assimilation

Despite the apprehension associated with confronting traumas, many victims do, in fact, seek to confide in others. In some cases, desires to disclose are thwarted by an absence of confidants. However, it is not only the socially stranded who may lack adequate disclosure opportunities. To a surprising degree, victims find that their urge to confide is not matched by confidants' willingness to listen. Coates et al. (1979) explored the receptivity of victims' supporters to victims' disclosure needs. These researchers reported that, as bearers of disturbing thoughts and negative emotions, victims themselves become the objects of suppression. Would-be listeners disrupt victims' disclosure attempts by switching the topic of conversation away from the trauma, by attempting to press their own perspective of the trauma upon the victim, or by simply avoiding contact with trauma victims altogether.

In situations of widespread catastrophe, where many people find themselves in both the victim and listener roles, the opposing disclosure goals of victims and listeners can create interesting social dilemmas. For example, we found that in the months following the 1989 Loma Prieta earthquake many people reported a desire to share their personal experiences with others (Pennebaker & Harber, 1990). However, a significantly smaller percentage of the people we surveyed reported wanting to hear about other people's earthquake stories. The attitude of many Bay Area residents may have been reflected in printed T-shirts appearing in the area that said "Thank you for not sharing your earthquake experience."

Indeed, listening to traumatic stories can be stressful in and of itself. In a recent study, for example, college students viewed one of several 1–2-hour videotaped interviews of Holocaust survivors recounting their often tragic and horrifying experiences in Europe during World War II. Autonomic nervous system activity such as skin conductance level (SCL) of the survivors had been continuously monitored during the videotape session (Pennebaker, Barger, & Tiebout, 1989). Similarly, continuous SCL readings were collected from the students who viewed the videotapes. A comparison of the SCL of the Holocaust survivors and the student listeners indicated a negative relationship; that is, when the survivors disinhibited and talked about particularly horrible events (as rated by independent judges), the SCL levels of the listeners increased. Talking about horrible experiences may be healthy for speakers but unhealthy for listeners (Shortt & Pennebaker, 1990). [1]

---

[1] An intriguing question stemming from the Shortt and Pennebaker (1990) study is whether listeners risk intrusive thoughts as a result of hearing victims' traumatic disclosures. We know of no research on the contagion of ruminative reactions, though under certain conditions this spread of unwanted thought seems likely to occur. For example, people are less willing to sympathetically listen to victims' stories when they, the listeners, see themselves as incapable of positively altering the victim's situation (Smith, under review). This finding makes us suspect that the more helpless listeners feel as audience to traumatic disclosures, the more subject they themselves may be to intrusive thoughts regarding victims' travails.

As might be expected, listeners' reluctance to hear victims' disclosures is motivated by the same defenses that inhibit victims' trauma assimilation efforts. Hearing about victims' suffering can threaten listeners' assumptive worlds, creating in listeners levels of distress antagonistic to empathic attention. According to Coates et al., listeners' just-world beliefs are frequently threatened by the random hazard and wanton cruelty that characterize victims' travails. To bolster their own world views, listeners often impose upon victims interpretations of the trauma that exaggerate victims' personal responsibility.

Interactions with victims can also challenge listeners' beliefs about their own self-worth. For example, listeners may feel inadequately skilled, or insufficiently caring, to help victims recover. These feelings of social gracelessness are often compounded by the tenacity and depth of victims' distress (see also Locke & Horowitz, 1990, for an experimental demonstration of the social friction arising between distressed and nondistressed acquaintances).

And finally, the feelings victims can display, in their seemingly relentless intensity and negativity, can disturb even the most empathic listeners' repose. Victims are typically well aware of the social censure they risk by freely disclosing their traumatic memories and emotions. In fact, the more urgent are victims' needs to confide, the more apparent to victims are others' resistances to hearing (Silver, Worton, & Crofton, 1990). Wishing to avoid social isolation and stigma, victims will respond to inhibitory social cues by suppressing their own pressing expressive needs. Their situation is concisely summarized by Coates et al., (1979) who wrote: "Victims may be trapped in a complicated dilemma, in which they can maximize their social acceptance only at the expense of their personal adjustment" (p. 28).

To recap, then, trauma victims face two major obstacles in their efforts to express their trauma-related emotions: their own reluctances to revise fundamental world assumptions, and other peoples' resistance to hearing about traumatic events. Yet completion tendencies of traumatic emotions continue unabated and generate intrusive memories that continue drawing victims back to the traumatic experience. Consequently, trauma victims can be caught between incessant demands to amend challenged schemas, and resistances—internal and external—to the modification of fundamental beliefs. It is within this standoff between implacable emotions and resistant beliefs that victims become subject to the suppressive cycle, and its associated health risks.

THE EFFECTS OF INHIBITING VERSUS
CONFRONTING TRAUMATIC MEMORIES

Researchers have long recognized a connection between the inhibition or constraint of emotional expression and health risks. Studies of individual differences in the tendency to avoid the disclosure of emotion are associated with cancer (Cox & McCay, 1982; Jensen, 1987; Kissen, 1966), coronary ailments (Davies, 1970; Friedman, Hall, & Harris, 1985; Weinberger, Schwartz, & Davidson, 1979), and other types of illness (Blackburn, 1965; Pelletier, 1985). It has also been shown that the proclivity to disclose potent emotions improves the prognosis for sufferers of serious illness. For example, breast cancer patients who most freely expressed anger and depression regarding their conditions lived longest, following diagnosis (Derogatis, Abeloff, & Melisaratos 1979). Particularly impressive is a recent study by Spiegel, Bloom, Kraemer, and Gottheil (1989), wherein half of 86 patients with advanced breast cancer were randomly assigned to weekly therapy sessions where the expression of emotion was encouraged. Overall, those in the therapy condition lived, on average, 1½ years longer than controls.

Links have also been reported between personal disclosure and recovery from traumatic events. Pennebaker and O'Heeron (1984), for example, identified such a correspondence in a survey of recently-bereaved widows and widowers. The study found that these individuals were significantly healthier if they talked with others about the deaths than if they did not talk. In addition, the more frequently survivors talked about their spouses' demise, the less they ruminated about it in the year following the death. These findings square with those in a large national sample in Germany (Stroebe & Stroebe, 1988).

Inhibition and Confrontation
of Traumatic Memories

There is little doubt that traumatic experiences can result in a variety of physical and psychological health problems in the months or years following their occurrence (e.g., Holmes & Rahe, 1967). Less clear, however, are the long-term mechanisms mediating trauma and disease. One important candidate to explain the long-term trauma/illness relationship concerns inhibition. Over the last several years, the second author has been developing and testing a general theory of psychosomatics based on the following premises:

1. Inhibiting ongoing thoughts, feelings, or behaviors is associated with physiological work.

a. Short-term inhibition is manifested by increased autonomic nervous system activity, such as electrodermal activity (Fowles, 1980), and selective central nervous system action traditionally associated with behavioral inhibition, such as the hippocampus (Gray, 1975) and frontal lobes (Luria, 1981).

b. Long-term inhibition serves as a low-level cumulative and general biological stressor (e.g., Selye, 1976). The long-term stress of inhibition can cause or exacerbate a variety of health problems ranging from minor difficulties (e.g., colds, flu) to major ones (cardiovascular problems, cancer; Pennebaker & Susman, 1988).

2. Active inhibition is also associated with potentially deleterious changes in information processing. In holding back significant thoughts and feelings associated with an event, individuals typically do not process the event fully. By not talking about an inhibited event, for example, people usually do not translate the experience into language that aids in the understanding and assimilation of the event (Pennebaker, 1989). Consequently, traumas that are inhibited are likely to surface in the forms of ruminations, dreams, and associated cognitive symptoms.

3. The opposite pole of inhibition is confrontation, which refers to individuals actively thinking and/or talking about a trauma as well as acknowledging relevant emotions. Confronting traumatic memories can help negate the effects of inhibition both physiologically and cognitively (Pennebaker, 1989).

a. The act of confronting the memories of a trauma reduces the physiological work of inhibition in both the short run (e.g., as measured by drops in electrodermal activity) and long term (e.g., improvements in health).

b. Actively confronting traumatic memories helps individuals to understand and ultimately assimilate the event.

The core of the inhibition and health program has been built around studies that use autonomic nervous system changes or actual illness rates as outcome measures. Although we have typically not focused on memory per se, many of our findings are relevant to an understanding of traditional memory-related topics, such as retrieval, storage, reconstruction, etc. Before discussing our approach to memory, it is important to briefly summarize the major results from our research. (For a more detailed discussion of this research program, see Pennebaker 1989, Pennebaker, Colder, & Sharp, 1990).

Correlational Studies. Consistent with research discussed earlier, several surveys that we have conducted indicate that not talking about significant personal upheavals with others is correlated with a variety of health problems. Across studies, self-reports of the failure to disclose traumatic experiences surrounding sexuality, death, divorce, and so forth, has consistently been associated with both self-reported and actual physician visits for illness, major and minor health complaints, in both retrospective (e.g., Pennebaker & Susman, 1988) and prospective (Pennebaker, 1989) studies. These effects have emerged with a variety of samples including individuals who have suffered the sudden death of their spouses (Pennebaker & O'Heeron, 1984), corporate employees (Pennebaker & Susman, 1988), a large national sample of magazine readers (Pennebaker, 1985), and, of course, college students (Pennebaker, 1989). These effects hold when statistically controlling for the effects of social class, sex, nature of trauma, education, and social support indicators (e.g., Pennebaker & Susman, 1988).

Trauma Confession Studies. A more persuasive test of the inhibition model has surrounded a series of experiments wherein subjects have been brought to the laboratory and have been randomly assigned to write (or talk) about either deeply traumatic experiences or superficial topics. Depending on the study, subjects write for 15 or 20 minutes each day for 3 to 4 consecutive days. Other studies that examine the psychophysiology of ongoing disclosure require students to talk about both traumatic and superficial topics for 3 to 7 minutes each on the same day.

In the standard writing experiments, the experimental manipulation consists of having subjects write, extemporaneously, without regard for spelling, grammar, or punctuation. Experimental subjects are requested to write, with as much candor as possible, about their deepest thoughts and feelings surrounding a past trauma. An example of the writing instructions given experimental subjects indicates how disclosures were invited (from Pennebaker, Kiecolt-Glaser, & Glaser, 1988):

> During each of the four writing days, I want you to write about the most traumatic and upsetting experience of your entire life. You can write on different topics each day, or on the same topic for all four days. The important thing is that you write about your deepest thoughts and feelings. Ideally, whatever you write should deal with an event or experience that you have not talked with others about in detail.

Control subjects are requested to write in a nonemotional way about mundane and trivial topics, such as detailed descriptions of their shoes, or a microscopic outline of their daily schedule. All subjects write (or speak) in private rooms or in cubicles. The writing settings are dimly lit in order to increase subjects' feelings of privacy, and to create novel situations free of inhibiting associations to subjects' daily lives.

From all our studies, it is clear that the disclosure process is remarkably powerful. In the experiments wherein subjects talk about traumas for only a few minutes, a quarter cry. In the writing studies, subjects in the experimental conditions routinely report feeling extremely distraught after writing. Indeed, their writing samples portray horror and tragedy. In each study that we have conducted, one or more students have written about incidents of sexual assault or incest, family violence, suicide attempts, divorce, etc. Although participants report that writing about upsetting experiences is painful, follow-up questionnaires 6 weeks to 6 months after the study indicate that they are as happy or happier than controls.

Most impressive about all the writing studies are the improvements in health among the experimental subjects. In our own studies, health center visits for illness (gleaned from health center records) are significantly lower after writing traumatic thoughts and feelings. Averaging across our three recent writing studies, the mean illness visits per month for experimental and control subjects are as follows: Experimental before writing = 0.19; experimental after writing = 0.12; Control before writing = 0.14; Control after writing = 0.24.[2] These numbers are based on over 200 subjects who have participated in the writing studies (Pennebaker & Beall, 1986; Pennebaker, Colder, & Sharp, 1990; Pennebaker, Kiecolt-Glaser, & Glaser, 1988). It should be pointed out that the health improvements are not permanent. Close inspection of our recent studies suggest that the health gains from writing about traumatic experiences appear to last from 2 to 4 months after writing.

Finally, similar studies in other labs have replicated the same basic patterns of effects. Murray, Lamnin, and Carver (1989), using self-reported physician visits, found a marginally significant effect that indicated that subjects who wrote about traumas on two occasions separated a week apart remained healthier than controls. In a

---

[2]The drop in controls' health reflects the general pattern of increased illness among college students as the Fall term—when most of these studies were conducted—progresses.

reanalysis of an apparent failure to replicate (Greenberg & Stone, 1990a), researchers at SUNY at Stony Brook reported that individuals who wrote about deeply traumatic experiences showed health improvements compared to trauma subjects who wrote about relatively minor traumas and to control subjects (Greenberg & Stone, 1990b).

THE BENEFITS OF WRITING

Clearly one of the most robust findings of the inhibition and health research program is that confronting traumas reverses inhibitory stresses. Yet the basic paradigm for demonstrating the value of trauma confrontation involves a very simple manipulation—translating traumatic experiences into prose. Why should language, and perhaps writing in particular, provide such a potent antidote to traumatic inhibition? In this section we discuss both the behavioral and intrapsychic benefits that come from putting traumas into language. First we describe the self-perceptual and morale-enhancing benefits that the *act* of writing supplies. We then consider how narrative renderings of traumas make these events more comprehensible and review attributes of subjects' writing that support this analysis. Finally, we speculate on structural changes in the coding of traumas that occur as a result of writing, and how through these changes traumatic distress is dissipated.

Writing as Active Coping

To some degree, writing may advance recovery by recasting victims' relations to their traumas. According to Moos, when people face crises directly, they gain confidence in their coping strengths, feel greater personal coherence, enjoy heightened self-esteem, and experience increased optimism (Holahan & Moos, 1990). In a similar vein, Folkman and Lazarus (1988) reported that people feel better when they turn to the sources of their distress, and that planful responses to fearful emotions make these emotions less distressing. By allowing victims to intentionally confront traumatic memories, rather than being ambushed by them, writing may promote the "active coping" that Moos and Lazarus advocate. Additionally, writing can also supply self-perceptual benefits. Because it is a constructive, energetic activity that yields tangible products (i.e., completed essays), writing can help victims see themselves as problem solvers, and their traumatic recoveries as tractable tasks, rather than as ordeals to be passively borne.

Clearly, the environment subjects encounter in the writing studies is conducive to approaching previously avoided trauma. The writing occurs under psychologically safe conditions, in which experimenters emphasize that essays will not be judged, and that confidentiality has been protected. Also, the time constraint placed on writing (i.e., 20 minutes) sets a tolerable limit on subjects' outlay of cognitive effort and duration of emotional exposure. Perhaps most importantly, writing permits subjects to engage their traumas to a degree, and at a rate, at which they feel comfortable. By governing the flow and direction of traumatic memories, writers can experience a heightened sense of control over events that have so fundamentally dominated them.

We see these allied benefits of active coping—the heightened confidence, subjective safety, greater perceived control—as advancing people to the arena of traumatic assimilation. However, it is important not to confuse benefits that promote the process of traumatic assimilation with assimilation itself. If recovery were just facing the facts of past trauma, or of braving troubling emotions, then subjects in Pennebaker's "facts-only" or "emotions-only" writing conditions should have realized the same benefits as did subjects who wrote emotionally about their trauma-related thoughts and feelings. Yet in most cases, subjects relating only facts or only emotions appeared no healthier, and in some cases marginally less healthy, than did the trivia-writing controls. Thus, we believe that the self-perceptual and morale-boosting properties of active coping facilitate, but do not constitute, the essential benefit of writing. Instead, we see writing, and language generally, as uniquely suited to the essential task of traumatic recovery—assimilating the traumatic event into the network of beliefs that traumas challenge. It is to these particular mental benefits of language that we now turn.

Writing as the Construction of Narrative

Social psychologists have become increasingly interested in the ways that people use narrative structures to make sense of their lives (Sarbin, 1986; Vitz, 1990). Paul Vitz (1990) provided a helpful overview of this perspective. He explained that by engaging in narrative thought, people translate their lives into coherent stories. Turning their lives into literature helps people frame events within the goals, social relationships, and other themes that organize experience.

Trauma victims, who struggle so tenaciously to find meaning in their ordeals, might be particularly well served by the organizing benefits of narrative expression. Indeed, translating life experiences into biographical sketches can have therapeutic advantages. According to psychoanalytic theorist Donald Spence (in Vitz, 1990), psychoanalysis's chief benefit lies in giving patients the opportunity to construct stories and to thereby make narrative sense of their lives.

The notion that the formal characteristics of narrative prose can advance coping is supported by Pennebaker's trauma and writing studies. Analyses of subjects' essays reveal that the more their writing succeeds as narrative—by being organized, emotionally compelling, vivid, and fluid—the more subjects benefitted from the writing task. We review the narrative features of subjects' writing, and the relation of these to disinhibition, next.

The Topics That People Choose to Write About. In the writing studies, people disclose remarkably intimate aspects of their lives. They freely admit embarrassing experiences and deeply felt emotions. Averaging across four experiments wherein students wrote or talked about traumas, a breakdown of the percentage of the primary topics within the essays or tapes were as follows: death of family member or friend (18.0%), interpersonal conflicts with lovers or friends (17.9%), family conflict including divorce (15.7%), academic issues such as coming to college (14.8%), illness or injury experiences (13.6%), psychological or behavioral problems (7.6%), sexual traumas (5.3%), and other issues (5.0%). See Pennebaker (1989) for a more detailed breakdown of topics.

In carefully debriefing hundreds of people who have undergone this paradigm, we have suspected that a person was fabricating a traumatic experience only once. The profound changes in facial expression, posture, and overall affect convince us that the disclosures are real and deeply felt. These impressions have been corroborated by researchers in all other laboratories that have used the paradigm.

Writing Speed. In disclosing traumatic experiences, participants write and talk at a much higher rate than individuals asked to describe what they have done since arising in the morning or other control topics. Averaging across the writing trauma studies, for example, subjects in the trauma conditions wrote 27% more words than those in the control conditions (Pennebaker & Beall, 1986; Pennebaker, Kiecolt-Glaser, & Glaser, 1988). In the talking study wherein subjects talked about both traumatic and trivial topics for 3.3 minutes each in a counterbalanced order, participants spoke 7% faster when conveying traumatic topics. All the preceding effects were highly significant.

Subjects had, by and large, not discussed their traumatic events with others nor had they rehearsed them prior to coming to the experiment. Additionally, in those studies wherein subjects wrote on traumas day after day, their actual speed was as fast or faster on the first day. The retrievability of traumatic material, therefore, seems to reflect emotional salience, rather than intentional priming.[3]

Vividness and Fluidity. As a university teacher who routinely assigns research papers and essay exams, the second author has been struck by the quality of writing that the students exhibit when disclosing traumas. Grammar, sentence structure, and general writing style are remarkably good. Indeed, participants are far better writers when conveying traumatic experiences for the first time than when expounding on reinforcement theory on their first or even third draft.

Structure. In writing, the majority of people who tell about a trauma convey it in a story format—with a clear beginning, middle, and end. There are clearly some large situational and individual differences. Based on a recent analysis of the Pennebaker, Kiecolt-Glaser, and Glaser (1988) essays by seven independent judges, the story structure is typically better on the last day of writing than on the first. Of particular importance is that improvement in immune function from before to 6 weeks after writing (as measured by heightened blastogenic responses using PHA as the mitogen; i.e., t-lymphocyte response) among trauma subjects was marginally related to both overall good story structure ($r = .35$, $p = .13$) and improvement in story structure from the first to the fourth day of writing ($r = .35$, $p = .13$).

The Centrality of Emotion in Describing Trauma. Across several studies, we have directly and indirectly examined the value of expressing emotion during the disclosure process. In the Pennebaker

---

[3]These results fit with Horowitz's contention that, until assimilated, traumatic material hovers near consciousness in an "active memory" state. Active memory is much the same as short-term storage, differing only in the assimilative pressure that active-memory material possesses. According to Horowitz, when defensive controls over active memory relax, the traumatic content automatically flows from it into the attentional spotlight.

and Beall (1986) writing study, for example, students were randomly assigned to one of four conditions. In addition to controls who wrote about superficial topics for the four days, some subjects were asked to write about their emotions and thoughts surrounding traumas (trauma-combination group). Two additional trauma groups were told to restrict their writing to either the facts without reference to their emotions (trauma-fact condition) or their emotions without reference to the facts (trauma-emotion group) surrounding the trauma. On all major health and self-report dependent measures, the trauma fact and controls were identical. Although the trauma-emotion subjects were as physically ill as controls, their self-reports of health and well-being were more similar to those in the trauma-combination condition. Writing only about the cold facts of a traumatic experience, then, does not appear to be psychologically or physically beneficial.

More recent studies have examined the emotionality of speakers who are disclosing personal traumas. Those who convey the greatest emotion in their voices (as rated by judges), exhibit the greatest skin conductance reductions during their disclosure (Pennebaker, Hughes, & O'Heeron, 1987). Similarly, Holocaust survivors who exhibit the greatest skin conductance drops during the times that they are talking about particularly traumatic experiences are significantly healthier a year after the interview (Pennebaker, Barger, & Tiebout, 1989).

Subjects' Comments on the Efficacy of Writing. When asked what effect writing had on them, the vast majority of subjects reported that it had helped them put their traumatic experiences into manageable perspective. As one subject reported at the end of his participation (Pennebaker, Colder, & Sharp, 1990): "(The writing) helped me to look at myself from the outside" (p. 534). This is particularly significant in light of Spiegel's contention that placing traumas in perspective is the most appropriate goal for PTSD treatment (Spiegel, 1988). By giving their traumas clear beginnings, middles, and ends, writers may circumscribe the boundaries of bad events and thereby get past them. As a result, the traumas no longer intrude upon consciousness, terminating the stress and attendant health deficits of inhibition.

General Applicablity of Writing. Prose writing is certainly a skill, and the variability in its mastery ranges from the crudest graffiti to Shakespeare. Does this mean that only the most literate can use narrative as a coping device? We think not. Whereas few of us achieve poetry, we are nearly all trained narrativists. Exposure to stories, and to the storytelling form, is something we generally receive in early childhood (see Nell, 1988). By age 10, most American children can compose narratives with plots recognizable throughout the western world (Sutton-Smith, 1986). Eventually narrative thinking becomes so fundamental to our ordering of experience that it operates as a basic causal heuristic (Robinson & Hawpe, 1986). In sum, nearly all people are able to organize and express their experience through narrative channels. What we intend to show in the remainder of this chapter is that the constraints of narrative supply cognitive tools particularly well suited to the emotional work of traumatic assimilation.

Writing and the Mechanisms
of Trauma Assimilation

Recall that trauma assimilation involves accommodating particular experiences into extant schematic structures. Tulving's distinction between episodic and semantic memory sheds light on what this accommodation may entail, and how the assimilative process may be advanced by writing. According to Tulving's (1983) model, episodic memory consists of "the recording and subsequent retrieval of memories of personal happenings and doings" (p. 9). Episodic memory is chronologically organized and self-focused—it contains stories that feature the self. Semantic memory, on the other hand, is concerned with abstract knowledge about the world, independent of the person's memory or past. It is conceptually organized and contains facts and propositions. Further, only episodic memory is believed to have emotional content; semantic memory is seen as affectless. Because traumas so centrally involve the self, exist as life events, and are saturated with emotion, we reason that they are encoded in episodic memory. We further suppose that fundamental beliefs, built on propositions and organized conceptually, reside in semantic memory.

Tulving's model suggests that traumatic assimilation involves accommodating key features of the semantic code (i.e., beliefs) to massive changes in episodic representation (i.e., trauma); that is, it involves extracting from the trauma facts that amend premises upon which semantically maintained world assumptions are constructed.[4] However, properties of traumas may hinder this tranference between an event "that happened" to principles "one knows." As episodic memories, traumas are temporally organized around the

---

[4]See McClelland and Rumelhart (1985, pp. 184–185) regarding the contribution of episodic material to semantic structures.

chain of events that constitute them. Thus, all the emotions, images, and thoughts attending a trauma are held together solely by the traumatic incident itself. This integrated structure may complicate the winnowing of assumptive morals from traumatic dramas. At the same time, the distress that traumas evoke when encountered in toto discourages efforts at making this translation.

The act of writing may help dismantle the phenomenal wholes that traumas constitute, and in a way that moderates traumatic distress. The grammatical constraints of language are such that only a restricted number of details can be fit into any sentence. Sentences, in turn, must be organized into meaningful sequences in order to convey more sophisticated concepts. In sum, we cannot "say" the traumatic experience all at once, but only over time, and in conceptual bits. Suppose I were to describe the experience of being in a major earthquake. If I were to make the event understood, I would need to supply a setting ("I was in the psychology department, conducting a discussion section") and a time ("It was in the early evening"). A description of my mental states before, during, and after the jolt hit, the sequence of events preceding the quake, as well as the students' reactions—all these components, and more, I would need to reveal to my listener. By spinning out my tale into a coherent narrative string, I begin to unravel the traumatic knot. And, the more detailed I get in describing any facet of my experience, the more completely I extract it as a conceptual entity separate from the trauma as a whole. As a result, I will break the event down into smaller conceptual bits, each of which should be subjectively less threatening, and at the same time much more easily parsed than the memory as a whole.

However, as evidenced by Pennebaker's "facts only" subjects, the health debilitating stress of inhibition is not alleviated solely by objectively recounting a traumatic event. Writers must allow themselves to emotionally re-engage the trauma, in order for writing to promote assimilation. Research on mood and memory (Bower, 1981) indicates why emotionally involved writing is so necessary to the process of assimilation. According to Bower, emotional states can serve as potent organizers of experience. Additionally, by reviving a particular affective state, one is better able to recall the circumstances (under which that state was generated). Writing *emotionally* about one's deepest thoughts and feelings should produce these state-dependent memory effects. Because emotionally charged writing more fully activates traumatic memory, more of the trauma is arrayed in consciousness, where its verbal rendering can occur.

Indeed, in the trauma-writing studies, experimental instructions were designed to engage subjects with their trauma-induced emotions. Subjects were told "let go and dig down to your very deepest emotions and thoughts, and explore them in your writing" (Pennebaker et al., 1990). Together, "letting go" and "exploring" may be the keys to post-traumatic recovery. By entering the emotional depths of a past trauma, disclosers gain vastly greater access to the facts and details associated with their ordeals. By searching the traumatic landscape that their emotions reveal, and preserving it in language, disclosers are better able to map out the dimensions and facets of their experiences and thereby make traumas more comprehensible.

Writing Creates Bonds Between Traumas and Other Experiences

Emotional writing can also promote assimilation by associating traumatic recollections to nontraumatic memories. When writers re-engage traumatic emotions, memories that are not directly related to the trauma—but that are associated with the traumatic emotion—should be activated. This collateral activation of nontraumatic memories may help writers articulate their traumatic experiences by supplying a vocabulary of related images, events, and concepts. Describing the trauma in terms of these emotionally related concepts and events should, in turn, strengthen ties between the trauma and other experiences. As a result, the trauma becomes more fully integrated within the person's network of memories and beliefs.

The emotional intensity of trauma should be moderated by the bridges that language constructs between traumatic and non-traumatic memories. Before this integration occurs, the activation of traumatic memory is likely to evoke only traumatic emotions. However, the exclusive arousal of traumatic distress is less likely to occur when traumas are richly related to memories that are themselves linked to less aversive emotions. Consequently, the collateral activation of these nontraumatic memories should buffer the impact of traumatic recall. For example, if remembering my earthquake experience was also to evoke memories of hazards I have averted or mastered, or if it reminded me of other people who had suffered experiences similar to my own, then feelings of competence and solidarity supplied by these other associations should mute the traumatic memory's emotional impact.

Recent research on the emotional architecture of repression (Hansen & Hansen, 1988) corresponds to this formulation. Hansen and Hansen found that for repressors fearful memories have relatively few associative links to other memories. This isolation of fearful material reduces repressors' experience of fear as supplemental to other negative emotions. Because repressors have fewer afferent links joining fearful material to sad or angry memories (for example), the excitation of these other emotions is less likely to subsequently trigger fear. However, there is a cost to this emotional segregation; on those occasions where fear is the primary emotion evoked, there are few efferent channels by which this distress can be dissipated. Hansen and Hansen (1988) suggested that "Because repressors' fearful memories are associated with fear, anxiety, and little else, a . . . (fearful memory) . . . is more likely to elicit escape or behavioral paralysis from a repressor than from a non-repressor" (p. 817).

Individual differences in cognitive architectures may predict how well people respond to traumas. If coping involves the cognitive integration of traumas, then people with relatively rich stories of memories, and more flexible beliefs and attitudes should be those most resilient to negative events. The hardiness of these more "cognitively complex" (cf. Tetlock, 1983) individuals would, according to our perspective, derive in part from their having a more plentiful array of mental constructs over which a trauma could be dispersed. Linville's self-complexity theory and related research is consistent with this line of reasoning (Linville, 1987). According to Linville, people who possess more complex self-images—self-images comprised of various attributes and proclivities—have more options for organizing negative experience and are therefore better able to cope with adversity.

EVIDENCE THAT LANGUAGE PROMOTES TRAUMATIC RECOVERY

If language plays such a central role in trauma assimilation, then victims' abilities to articulate their experiences should predict beneficial outcomes of disclosure. In this final section, we briefly summarize results from the inhibition research indicating that emotional lucidity corresponds to post-traumatic coping. We also review work on "Referential Activity," an allied area of investigation that explores the links between expressivity and psychological adjustment.

Evidence from Inhibition Research

Earlier, we identified two attributes of language characterizing disclosures that promote assimilation. Effective disclosures should be *organized* in order to promote the semantic parsing of episodically coded, private experience. Disclosures should also be *emotional* in order to activate traumatic memories, and to facilitate the integration of these memories into pre-existing networks. Analyses of subjects' writings and writing-related behavior confirm the importance of both these conditions. As we have mentioned, there is a moderate correspondence between essays' degree of organization and improved immune functioning. Subjects whose essays showed more coherent narrative structures tended to be those showing heightened blastogenic responses. There was a more robust association between emotional expressiveness and improved health. Again recapping previously detailed findings, subjects who realized the greatest health benefits were those who physiologically and behaviorally displayed the most intense emotional disclosure, and whose essays contained the greatest number of emotional words.

Referential Activity

A particularly intriguing explanation for the role of language in distress coping comes from recent research on Referential Activity (Bucci, in press; Ellenhorn, 1989). Referential Activity (RA) explores stylistics of language that permit people to put their feelings into words, and to make their private experiences understood by others.

RA theorists draw heavily on Paivio's (1971, 1986) dual code mode of mental representations. This model identifies three modalities by which knowledge is represented: verbal, visual, and referential. The verbal mode is much like Tulving's semantic memory. It is comprised of words, connected according to the sequencing rules of grammar, and organized in terms of hierarchical category systems. Visual representations, like Tulving's episodic memory, are experientially-based. The visual modality stores imagery in all its forms, and is organized around emotions.

Referential links are the medium through which the analogic—and often private and ideosyncratic—contents of the nonverbal mode are connected with the logically ordered, shared communicative code that is the verbal mode. It is through these referential links that personal experiences, and emotional reactions, get articulated.

RA researchers focus on the nature of these referential links, and on how their employment shapes the course of psychotherapy.

According to Bucci (in press), referential links enlist linguistic elements and structures for the communication of emotions and other
subjective experience. These links are most successful at giving
public voice to private experience when they possess sensory concreteness (e.g., "hot", "rough"), specificity (degree of detail), clarity
(sharpness of linguistic focus), and imagery (ability to sympathetically evoke pictures and sensations in listeners).

RA is not a variant of verbal intelligence. For example, highly
abstract and complicated discourse can represent low RA. However,
RA is an attribute upon which people systematically differ. Bucci has
developed and validated a system for scoring RA and uses it to
measure personality difference and to monitor the course of psychotherapy sessions. In studies using this scale, she has found that RA
scores rise as people reveal more private and emotionally arousing
facts about their lives. Additionally, RA measures taken when a
person enters psychotherapy indicates how much he or she will
benefit from this treatment. For example, RA measures were employed in a recent study designed to identify individuals most likely
to be helped by brief dynamic psychotherapy (Horowitz, Rosenberg,
& Kalehzan, under review). RA dimensions of clarity and specificity
proved to be effective at discriminating between patients whose
problems were more interpersonally oriented (and therefore better
suited for dynamic treatment) from patients with less interpersonally based difficulties.[5]

There are some interesting conceptual and empirical parallels
between investigations of the RA model and trauma-writing paradigm.
Both RA and the inhibition research predict that psychologically
beneficial insights occur when private, emotionally distressing
memories are clearly articulated in language. Additionally, both
perspectives contend that emotional release is required in order to
bring undisclosed material to consciousness, and to thereby promote
the mental reorganization that constitutes insight.

Empirical support for these models also overlap. For example, two
of the dimensions on which RA is determined—specificity and

---

[5]According to Bucci, a measure of successful disclosure is how powerfully
listeners are affected by it. If lucidity and compellingness are criteria for successful
disclosure, then perhaps interchanges between victims and listeners are mutually
beneficial. The victim serves as newscaster, whose compulsion to disclose harrow-
ing events serves as forewarning to his or her community. For example, if I relay my
earthquake story with clarity and feeling, my listeners will have the knowledge and
motive to prepare for similar events. Additionally, if I need to relate my story
repeatedly, the number of people who can profit from my experience will be
multiplied. One can easily imagine how such a social psychodynamic would be of
adaptive value.

clarity of speech—are comparable to the dimension of "organization" that Pennebaker relates to positive outcomes in his research (Pennebaker et al., 1988). Additionally, RA levels increase when individuals emotionally "let go." Bucci cites sample cases where referentially rich speech is accompanied by crying, and other displays of emotional distress, whereas referentially pallid speech corresponds to signs of emotional detachment. The concordances between RA research, and Pennebaker's inhibition studies, suggests that direct links between these lines of investigation be tested.

CONCLUSION

The British novelist E.M. Forster wrote that it is by the forming of connections—between past and present, ideals and reality, self and others—that people achieve serenity in a difficult and disruptive world (Forster, 1910). For trauma victims, the business of connection seems to be of vital importance. As we have seen in this chapter, traumas are, by nature, events that sever ties between personal experience and basic assumptions. They threaten the matrix of beliefs through which daily experience is made meaningful, by contradicting the premises that hold this network together. Other dislocations follow this basic rift. One is the effortful segregation of traumatic memory, leading to health-debilitating physiological stress; another is the social isolation brought on by victims' negative moods and morbid preoccupations.

However, by putting their experiences into language, trauma victims can begin the reconstructive process of trauma assimilation. The capacity of speech and writing to represent emotion—through metaphor, inflection, imagery, and other devices—permits articulation of traumas' private and seemingly ineffable qualities. At the same time, the linear structure of language restricts emotional flow to channels banked by the organizational rules of grammar. By evoking memories that carry emotional content, yet in a controlled and structured way, language gives victims stewardship over the course of traumatic assimilation. As a result, victims can experience themselves as authors, rather than as objects, of past traumas.

ACKNOWLEDGMENTS

The preparation of this chapter was made possible by National Science Foundation grant BNS 9001615. We thank Sven-Åke Christianson, Steve Cole, Albert Hastorf, Mardi Horowitz, Stephen

Reidbord, and Roxane Cohen Silver for their helpful advice and comments on an earlier draft of this chapter.

REFERENCES

American Psychriatric Association (1980). *Diagnostic and statistical manual of mental disorders* (3rd. ed.). Washington, DC: American Psychological Society.
Baumeister, R., & Tice, C. (1987). Emotion and self presentation. In R. Hogan & W. H. Jones (Eds.), *Perspectives in personality*. Greenwich, CT: JAI Press.
Blackburn, R. (1965). Emotionality, repressive sensitivity and maladjustment. *British Journal of Psychology, III*, 399–400.
Bower, G. (1981). Mood and memory. *American Psychologist, 36*, 129–148.
Bucci, W. (in press). Referential Activity measures and the Dual Code Model. In N. Miller, L. Luborsky, & J. Docherty (Eds.), *Dynamic psychotherapies: A clinicians' guide to doing treatment research*.
Christianson, S.-Å., & Nilsson, L.-G. (1984). Functional amnesia as induced by a psychological trauma. *Memory and Cognition, 12*, 142–155.
Christianson, S.-Å., & Nilsson, L.-G. (1989). Hysterical amnesia: A case of aversively motivated isolation in memory. In T. Archer & L.-G. Nilsson (Eds.), *Aversion, avoidance and anxiety* (pp. 289–310). Hillsdale, NJ: Lawrence Erlbaum Associates.
Coates, D., Wortman, C. B., & Abbey, A. (1979). Reactions to victims. In I. H. Frieze, D. Bar-Tal, & J. S. Carroll (Eds.), *New approaches to social problems*. San Francisco: Jossey-Bass.
Cox, T., & McCay, C. (1982). Psychosocial factors and psychophysiological mechanisms in the aetiology and development of cancers. *Social Science and Medicine, 16*, 381–396.
Davies, M. (1970). Blood pressure and personality. *Journal of Psychosomatic Research, 14*, 89–104.
Derogatis, L. R., Abeloff, M. D., & Melisaratos, N. (1979). Psychological coping mechanisms and survival time in metastatic breast cancer. *Journal of the American Medical Association, 242*, 1504–1508.
Easterbrook, J. A. (1959). The effect of emotion on cue utilization and the organization of behavior. *Psychological Review, 66*, 183–201.
Ellenhorn, T. (1989). *The symbolic transformation of subjective experience in discourse*. Unpublished doctoral dissertation. Adelphi University, Garden City, NY.
Epstein, S. (in press). The self-concept, the traumatic neurosis, and the structure of personality. In D. Ozer, J. M. Healy, Jr., & A. J. Steward (Eds.), *Perspectives in personality* (Vol. 3). Greenwich, CT: JAI Press.
Fiske, S., & Taylor, S. (1984). *Social cognition*. New York: Random House.
Folkman, S., & Lazarus, R. (1988). Coping as a mediator of emotion. *Journal of Personality and Social Psychology, 54*, 466–475.
Forster, E. M. (1910). *Howards end*. Cambridge: The Provost and Scholars of King's College.
Fowles, D. (1980). The three-arousal model: Implications of Gray's Two-Factor Theory for heart rate, electrodermal activity and psychotherapy. *Psychophysiology, 17*, 87–104.
Friedman, H. S., Hall, J. A., & Harris, M. J. (1985). Type A behavior, non-verbal expressive style and health. *Journal of Personality and Social Psychology, 48*, 1299–1315.
Gray, J. (1975). *Elements of a two-factor theory in learning*. New York: Academic Press.

Greenberg, J., Pyszczynski, T., Solomon, S., Rosenblatt, A., Veeder, M., Kirkland, S., & Lyon, D. (1990). Evidence for Terror Management Theory II: The effects of mortality salience on reactions to those who threaten or boltster cultural worldview. *Journal of Personality and Social Psychology, 58,* 308–318.

Greenberg, M. A., & Stone, D. A. (1990a). Writing about disclosed versus undisclosed trauma: Health and mood effects [Abstract]. *Health Psychology, 9,* 114–115.

Greenberg, M. A., & Stone, D. A. (1990b). *Writing about disclosed versus undisclosed trauma II.* Unpublished manuscript.

Greenwald, A. G. (1980). The totalitarian ego: Fabrication and revision of personal history. *The American Psychologist, 35,* 603–618.

Hansen, R., & Hansen, C. (1988). Repression of emotionally tagged memories: The architecture of less complex emotions. *Journal of Personality and Social Psychology, 55,* 811–818.

Hastie, R. (1981). Schematic priniciples in human memory. In E. T. Higgins, C. P. Herman, & M. P. Zanna (Eds.), *Social Cognition: The Ontario Symposium Vol. 1* (pp. 39–88). Hillsdale, NJ: Lawrence Erlbaum Associates.

Higgins, E. T. (1987). Self-discrepancy theory: A theory relating self and affect. *Psychological Review, 94,* 319–340.

Holahan, C., & Moos, R. (1990). Life stressors, resistance factors and improved psychological functioning: An extension of the stress resistance paradigm. *Journal of Personality and Social Psychology, 58,* 909–917.

Holmes, T. H., & Rahe, R. H. (1967). The Social Readjustment Rating Scale. *Journal of Psychosomatic Research, 52,* 946–955.

Horowitz, L. M., Rosenberg, S. E., & Kalehzan, B. M. (1990). *The capacity to describe other people clearly: A predictor of interpersonal problems and outcome in brief dynamic psychotherapy.* Submitted for review, Stanford University, Stanford, CA.

Horowitz, M. J. (1986). In *Stress response syndromes* (2nd Ed.). Northvale, NJ: Jason Aronson.

Janoff-Bulman, R. (1989). Assumptive worlds and the stress of traumatic events: Applications of the schema construct. *Social Cognition, 7,* 113–136.

Jensen, M. R. (1987). Psychobiological factors predicting the course of breast cancer. *Journal of Personality, 55,* 317–342.

Kissen, D. M. (1966). The significance of personality in lung cancer among men. *Annals of the New York Academy of Science, 125,* 820–826.

Lerner, M. J. (1980). *The belief in a just world.* New York: Plenum Press.

Leventhal, H. (1980). Toward a comprehensive theory of emotion. In L. Berkowitz (Ed.), *Advances in experimental social psychology* (pp. 139–207). New York: Academic Press.

Linville, P. (1987). Self complexity as a buffer against stress-related illness and depression. *Journal of Personality and Social Psychology, 52,* 663–676.

Locke, K., & Horowitz, L. (1990). Satisfaction in interpersonal interactions as a function of similarity in level of dysphoria. *Journal of Personality and Social Psychology, 58,* 823–831.

Lord, C. G., Lepper, M. R., & Preston, E. (1984). Considering the opposite: A corrective strategy for social judgment. *Journal of Personality and Social Psychology, 47,* 1231–1243.

Luria, A. R. (1981). *Language and cognition.* New York: Wiley.

Mandler, G. (1964). The interruption of behavior. *Nebraska symposium on motivation* (pp. 163–220).

Marris, P. (1986). *Loss and change* (rev. ed.). London: Routledge & Kegan Paul.

Martin, L., & Tesser, A. (1989). Toward a motivational and structural theory of ruminative thought. In J. S. Uleman & J. A. Bargh (Eds.), *Unintended thought* (pp. 306–326). New York: Guilford.

McClelland, J., & Rumelhart, D. (1985). Distributed memory and the representation of general and specific information. *Journal of Experimental Psychology: General, 114*, 159–188.

Morrow, J., & Nolen-Hoeksema, S. (1990). Effect of responses to depression on the remediation of depressive affect. *Journal of Personality and Social Psychology, 58*, 519–527.

Murray, E., Lamnin, A., & Carver, C. (in press). Psychotherapy versus written confession: A study of cathartic phenomenon. *Journal of Social Issues.*

Neisser, U. (1976). *Cognition and reality.* San Francisco: W. H. Freeman.

Nell, V. (1988). In *Lost in a book: The psychology of reading for pleasure.* New Haven, CT: Yale University Press.

Paivio, A. (1971). *Imagery and verbal processes.* New York: Holt, Rinehart, & Winston.

Paivio, A. (1986). *Mental representations: A dual coding approach.* New York: Oxford University Press.

Pelletier, K. R., (1985). *Mind as healer, mind as slayer.* New York: Delacorte Press.

Pennebaker, J. W. (1985). Traumatic experience and psychosomatic disease: Exploring the roles of behavioral inhibition, obsession, and confiding. *Canadian Psychology, 26*, 82–95.

Pennebaker, J. W. (1989). Confession, inhibition and disease. In L. Berkowitz (Ed.), *Advances in experimental social psychology* (Vol. 22, pp. 211–244). New York: Academic Press.

Pennebaker, J. W., Barger, S., & Tiebout, J. (1989). Disclosure of traumas and health among Holocaust survivors. *Psychosomatic Medicine, 51*, 577–589.

Pennebaker, J. W., & Beall, S. K. (1986). Confronting a traumatic event: Toward an understanding of inhibition and disease. *Journal of Abnormal Psychology, 95*, 274–281.

Pennebaker, J. W., & Harber, K. D. (1990). *The psychological and health effects of the Loma Prieta earthquake.* Unpublished manuscript.

Pennebaker, J. W., Hughes, C., & O'Heeron, R. (1987). The psychophysiology of confession: Linking inhibitory and psychosomatic processes. *Journal of Personality and Social Psychology, 52*, 781–793.

Pennebaker, J. W., & Susman, J. (1988). Disclosure of trauma and psychosomatic processes. *Social Science and Medicine, 26*, 327–332.

Pennebaker, J. W., Colder, M., & Sharp, L. (1990). Accelerating the coping process. *Journal of Personality and Social Psychology, 58*, 528–537.

Pennebaker, J. W., Kiecolt-Glaser, J., & Glaser, R. (1988). Disclosure of traumas and immune function: Health implications for psychotherapy. *Journal of Consulting and Clinical Psychology, 56*, 239–245.

Pennebaker, J. W., & O'Heeron, R. (1984). Confiding in others and illness rate among spouses of suicide and accidental-death victims. *Journal of Abnormal Psychology, 93*, 473–476.

Plutchik, R. (1980). *Emotions: A psychoevolutionary synthesis.* New York: Harper & Row.

Robinson, J. A., & Hawpe, L. (1986). Narrative thinking as a heuristic process. In T. Sarbin (Ed.), *Narrative psychology: The storied nature of human conduct* (pp. 67-90). New York: Praeger.

Rosenblatt, A., Greenberg, J., Solomon, S., Pyszczynski, T., & Lyon, D. (1989). Evidence for Terror Management Theory I: The effects of mortality salience on reactions to those who violate or uphold cultural values. *Journal of Personality and Social Psychology, 57,* 681–690.

Ross, L., Lepper, M. R., & Hubbard, M. (1975). Perseverance in self-perception and social perception: Biased attributional processes in the debriefing paradigm. *Journal of Personality and Social Psychology, 32,* 880–892.

Rumelhart, D. A., & Ortony, A. (1977). The representation of knowledge in memory. In R. C. Anderson, R. J. Spiro, & W. E. Montague (Eds.), *Schooling and the acquisition of knowledge.* Hillsdale, NJ: Lawrence Erlbaum Associates.

Sarbin, T. R. (1986). The narrative as root metaphor for psychology. In T. R. Sarbin (Ed.), *Narrative psychology: The storied nature of human conduct* (pp. 3–21). New York: Praeger.

Selye, H. (1976). *The stress of life.* New York: McGraw-Hill.

Shortt, J., & Pennebaker, J. W. (1990). *Talking versus hearing about the Holocaust experiences.* Unpublished manuscript.

Silver, R., Boon, C., & Stones, M. (1983). Searching for meaning in misfortune: Making sense of incest. *Journal of Social Issues, 39,* 81–102.

Silver, R. K., Wortman, C. B., & Crofton, C. V. (1990). Social support: An international view. In B. R. Sarason, & G. Pierce (Eds.), (p. 52). New York: Wiley & Sons.

Simon, H. (1967). Motivational and emotional controls of cognition. *Psychological Review, 74,* 29–39.

Smith, K. D. (under review). *Do the dispositionally sympathetic seek out or avoid sympathy-arousing situations?* University of Washington.

Snyder, M. L., Stephan, W., & Rosenfield,. D. (1978). Attributional egotism. In J. H. Harvey, W. Ickes, & R. Kidd (Eds.), *New directions in attribution research (Vol. 2)* pp. 91–117. Hillsdale, NJ: Lawrence Erlbaum Associates.

Spiegel, D. (1988). Dissociation and hypnosis in post-traumatic stress disorders. *Journal of Traumatic Stress, 1,* 17–33.

Spiegel, D., Bloom, J. H., Kraemer, H. C., & Gottheil, E. (1989). Effects of psychosocial treatment of patients with metastatic breast cancer. *Lancet, 2,* 888–891.

Stroebe, W., & Stroebe, M. S. (1988). *Bereavement and health: The psychological and physical consequences of partner loss.* New York: Cambridge University Press.

Sutton-Smith, B. (1986). Children's fiction making. In T. Sarbin (Ed.), *Narrative psychology: The storied nature of human conduct* (pp. 67–90). New York: Praeger.

Tait, R., & Silver, R. C. (1989). Coming to terms with major negative life events. In J. S. Uleman & J. A. Bargh (Eds.), *Unintended thought* (pp. 351–382). New York: Guilford.

Tetlock, P. (1983). Cognitive style and political ideology. *Journal of Personality and Social Psychology, 45,* 118–126.

Tulving, E. (1983). *Elements of episodic memory.* New York: Oxford University Pres.

Vitz, P. (1990). The use of stories in moral development: New psychological reasons for an old educational method. *American Psychologist, 45,* 709–720.

Wegner, D. M. (1989). *White bears and other unwanted thoughts.* New York: Viking Press.

Wegner, D., Shortt, J. W., Blake, A. W., & Page, M. S. (1990). The suppression of exciting thoughts. *Journal of Personality and Social Psychology, 58,* 409–418.

Weinberger, D. A., Schwartz, G. E., & Davidson, R. J. (1979). Low anxious, high anxious and repressive coping styles: Psychometric patterns and behavioral and physiological responses to stress. *Journal of Abnormal Psychology, 88,* 369–380.

Wortman, C. B., & Silver, R. C. (1987). Coping with irrevocable loss. In G. R. Vanden-Bos & B. K. Bryant (Eds.), *Cataclysms, crises and catastrophes: Psychology in action (Master Lecture Series),* (Vol. 6, pp. 189-235). Washington, DC: American Psychological Association.

16

Landmark Life Events and the Organization of Memory: Evidence from Functional Retrograde Amnesia

Molly Treadway
Michael McCloskey
Barry Gordon
Johns Hopkins University

Neal J. Cohen
University of Illinois

INTRODUCTION

As the present volume amply illustrates, many different approaches may be taken to the study of relationships between emotion and memory. The approach we adopt in this chapter involves the study of patients who exhibit psychogenic retrograde amnesia, or amnesia that is apparently motivated by a psychological need to "block out" from memory certain highly emotional events. We present case studies of two patients (K and F) who exhibit persisting amnesia for all forms of memory acquired during a 39-year (K) or 16-year (F) time period apparently framed or punctuated by emotionally unpleasant events. These amnesias bring into sharp focus questions concerning the role of major life events in the organization of memory, and questions about the emotional factors underlying functional impairments of memory.

Although the amnesias exhibited by K and F are presumed to be of psychogenic origin, they differ from the usually reported cases of psychogenic amnesia. In typical cases of psychogenic amnesia the memory impairment is informationally specific, affecting only memory for autobiographical events (e.g., Christianson & Nilsson, 1989), and temporally general, often involving the loss of all autobiographical memories, regardless of when they were acquired (see Schacter & Kihlstrom, 1989, for a review). The amnesias reported here, however, have the opposite pattern: Loss of memory is temporally specific and informationally general. These retrograde amnesias encompass not only memory for facts and personal events, but also world knowledge, skills, and the sense of personal identity derived from, and shaped by, experience. K's and F's amnesias are apparently defined by the *time* at which memories were acquired, rather than by the content of the memories or any other organizing principle.

How could such amnesias come about? What must we assume about the organization of normal memory such that disruption of the memory system could lead to this kind of impairment? And, what role do emotional life events play in determining the occurrence and form of the amnesia? In attempting to address these questions, we have tested both patients extensively and (with the patients' permission) have also conducted far-reaching investigations of their lives prior to the onset of amnesia. These investigations included examination of school, medical, and employment records; interviews with friends, employers, and family members; and observation of available public records relating to K's and F's personal histories. Initially, this information was gathered toward the end of developing materials to test the nature and extent of the patients' amnesias. As the study proceeded, however, it became apparent that both patients had experienced significant life events near both boundaries of the periods for which they are now amnesic.

In the following sections we first present case histories of these patients, noting major life events near the boundaries of their amnesias. We then consider possible interpretations, suggesting that memory may be organized around important life contexts demarcated by landmark events. From this perspective, we suggest that significant changes in life context occurring for both K and F allowed functional dissociations among memories acquired during different time periods.

Patient K

In December, 1984, K, a 53-year-old man, was discovered by his wife and children lying on the kitchen floor of their home, clutching the heating element from the electric oven (which he had been attempting to repair). He was unresponsive to attempts by his family and by the paramedics called to the scene to rouse him, and his right hand was twitching. Taken to a local hospital, he remained unresponsive until the following day. When he then became able to communicate, his comments and questions indicated that he thought the year was 1945, that he was 14 years old, and that he was in his hometown, a place from which he had moved many years earlier. He did not recognize his wife and two teenage children and repeatedly asked why his mother and father were not there to visit him. In fact, his father had died 11 years earlier, and his mother still lived in K's hometown, which was thousands of miles away.

The last memory K reported was of being hit in the head with a baseball bat while playing ball with several of his friends, an incident he dates as having occurred in early August, 1945. He thought that this was the cause of his hospitalization and repeatedly rubbed his forehead as if expecting to feel a bump from the injury. He felt that only a few moments had passed between the time he was hit with the bat and the time when he "came to" in the hospital. (K was in fact hit in the head by a bat as a child, but the date of this incident has not been independently verified, and it does not seem to have been serious enough to warrant hospitalization at the time.)

He was astonished by the television in his hospital room and K spent most of his time watching it. When his wife drove him home from the hospital, the family car looked to him like a "space car." Once he arrived at home, K failed to recognize his house, the neighborhood, or the family dog. In addition, he was fascinated by the various appliances and technological equipment in the house, such as his children's stereo systems (which he had recently purchased for them), the television, and the VCR, and he was mystified about how these devices were operated. K's profound retrograde amnesia has remained unchanged since the time of his accident.

In contrast to the retrograde amnesia, K has no significant anterograde amnesia. Since his accident in 1984 he has been able to learn much about the forgotten 1945–1984 time period. However, his newly acquired knowledge about this period has a book-learning quality that is quite different from the richly detailed and integrated character of his knowledge about the period prior to August, 1945 (see following).

As one might imagine from the absence of significant anterograde amnesia, K is aware that it is no longer 1945, and that he is no longer 14. However, having—in his experience—been one moment 14 years old in the world of 1945, and the next moment 53 years old in the world of 1984, K has found his situation quite difficult to assimilate.

He reports that for a long time after his accident he thought that he was caught in a dream, or that someone was playing an extremely elaborate trick on him. Further, he occasionally slips back into thinking of himself as a child in the year 1945, referring to an adolescent boy as "about my age," and dating events occurring in the early 1940s as "4 or 5 years ago."

Neurological Status. K's profound and persistent retrograde amnesia occurs in the absence of any observable neurological damage. Neurological testing at the time of K's accident in 1984, and subsequently at Johns Hopkins Hospital in 1986, revealed no evidence of neurological impairment. K appeared completely intact on electroencephalography (EEG), computerized tomography (CT), and magnetic resonance imaging (MRI). Visual fields and reflexes were normal, as was the remainder of the neurological exam.

Nature and Extent of the Retrograde Amnesia. Both informal observations and formal testing suggest that K has intact memory from early childhood through roughly August or September of 1945. In stark contrast he apparently has no memory for events occurring between this time and his accident in December, 1984. For example, K can remember his teachers, classmates, and specific personal episodes up through the seventh grade (which he completed in 1945). As far as world events, K can remember information about World War II, including the Allied victory in Europe, and the conventional bombing of Japan in the continuing Pacific war. Yet he does not remember the dropping of the atomic bomb on Hiroshima (August 6, 1945), the beginning of his next school year, or any other personal or public events that occurred after August or September of 1945. Thus he does not remember the places in which he has lived or visited, the friends and colleagues with whom he has had relationships, or the training and jobs he has had since 1945. He does not remember his marriage, the birth of his children, or the death of his father; and he does not remember the assassination of John F. Kennedy, or the Korean and Vietnam wars.

His hometown appears to be frozen in his memory just as it was in 1945, in terms of the location of shops and other landmarks, despite the fact that K had lived in or near this town through 1952 and had visited many times in more recent years, including several times in the 1980s. The following is an excerpt from a tape-recorded narrative that K made at our request when his mother drove him through his hometown for the first time since the onset of his amnesia:

We're just driving up North Main Street, and we're heading for F. Turnpike,[1] where I live, I used to live . . . . This is Main Street, but . . . that stuff right there is different. I don't recognize that part. And this is new. L.L. wasn't there, it was over there . . . . Now over here on the left is our house, you went by. There's the Post Office. Our house is not there! And the hotel is gone! See? Over there's changed. That building's new. All that's gone . . . And this is where Daddy's [store] used to be, but it's different now. I don't recognize any of that at all. That's all new. This street's one way coming up now, and it used to be you could come either way . . . . Turn right, right here. This is where the school is. See right here is the school. [pause] And it's not here anymore. Used to get my hair cut right here, and that's not there. Sears!? Sears is here now? (Note the present-tense "where I live" early in the quotation.)

When we asked him to describe the stores and businesses that could be found on Main Street as he remembered it, K described the street as it was in 1945. He included only those stores and businesses that were present in 1945, and none that moved there after that time, despite the fact that nearly half (48%) the stores and businesses present in 1945 had moved away by the early 1950s and fully 89% of them had changed by 1984. Nor did K confuse the town layout of 1945 with the layout of earlier years. For example, a sporting goods store described by K as being in a particular location had moved to that location from another address on the same street in 1943. We were able to verify the temporal specificity of K's descriptions through the use of city directories for the relevant years.

K's memory for all information, including the layout of the town, appears to be remarkably clear for the period prior to 1945. For example, K told us that in late July and early August of 1945 he was with his family on a trip to Chicago. When asked to describe what he remembered of the trip, K reported (among other things) that he remembered seeing a front-page newspaper article about an airplane crashing into the Empire State Building in New York City. This incident did in fact occur: On July 29, 1945, a bomber hit the Empire State Building, killing 13 people and injuring many others. The date of this event corresponds with K's description of when he heard about it. Further, K correctly described the type of airplane (B-25) and the foggy weather that contributed to the crash.

Similarly, K's memory for everyday information appears to specifically reflect the 1945 time period. For example, K was accurate in describing the color of license plates in his home state during the year

---

[1]We have introduced abbreviations for some specifically named locations, to eliminate potential identifying information.

1945. Although at first this may not seem remarkable, the colors described by K and verified by us were in fact used in this state for only a brief period of time. He also remembers having seen the Broadway plays *Hellzapoppin* and *Sons O' Fun* on trips to New York City with his father. We were able to verify that both of these plays ran in the late 1930s and early 1940s.

We have attempted to clarify just how sharp the boundary is between the period K remembers and the period he has forgotten. His memory may not be cut off at exactly the same time for all events at the beginning of the forgotten period. For example, although he does not remember Hiroshima (August 6), he has, on at least one occasion, spoken of going to his grandmother's funeral, which took place in early September of that year. However, dozens of hours of taped interviews with K have revealed only two events subsequent to September, 1945, for which K may have some memory. For example, K thought that he may have listened to a famous football game in which the powerful Notre Dame and Army teams played to a 0–0 tie. However, an account of this game, which was played in 1946, appears in a book that K's family gave him in an attempt to jog his memory, and K himself is unsure whether he actually heard the game or only read about it.

His memory also appears to be sharply bounded at the more recent end of the forgotten period. For example, when in 1986 K was shown photographs from *Life* magazine's "The Year in Pictures" for 1984 and 1985, he failed to recognize individuals who were widely publicized in 1984, such as Walter Mondale, Geraldine Ferraro, and Olympic star Mary Lou Retton. In contrast, he had no trouble identifying individuals who appeared prominently in 1985, such as Dr. Ruth Westheimer, William "the Refrigerator" Perry of the Chicago Bears football team, and Sylvester Stallone's movie character "Rambo." This temporal specificity has been corroborated by K's family members, who lived with him for several years after the onset of amnesia.

Formal testing with K confirms the initial clinical impression of a 4-decades-long retrograde amnesia. On a 4-choice recognition test of public events (Cohen & Squire, 1981), K scored 75% correct for events occurring between 1940 and 1945, but at chance (24% correct) for events from the period from 1946 through 1979 (the latest year for which events were included on the test). Similarly, when shown photographs of famous public events (Sagar, Cohen, Corkin, & Growdon, 1985), K had no difficulty identifying events from 1945 and earlier, such as Wendell Wilkie campaigning for president in 1940. However, he could not identify famous post- 1945 photographs, such as that of Jack Ruby shooting Lee Harvey Oswald (1963); and he failed to recognize former President Carter in two separate news photographs.

Personal Identity. K's retrograde amnesia extends beyond the domains of memory for public and personal events to include personal identity and personality. K feels himself to be a 14-year-old in an adult's body, startling himself each day when he looks into the mirror to shave. In a test requiring the reporting and dating of memories for personally experienced events (Crovitz & Schiffman, 1974; Zola-Morgan, Cohen, & Squire, 1983), he occasionally dated grade school events as having occurred only several years ago, instead of over 40 years ago. Furthermore, he acts much like an adolescent: He frequently skips or runs, giggles, and exhibits the posture and facial expressions of a young boy, says "sir" or "ma'am" to people 20 and 30 years younger than he is, is terribly embarrassed by sex and "girls," and talks of having "no one to play with." K also feels that his children, who were 15 and 17 at the onset of his amnesia, are older than he is.

Skills. K's retrograde amnesia appears to extend to skills. His family noted immediately following the 1984 incident that he no longer knew how to shave, drive a car, or operate the electronic devices in his house. Furthermore, there was a marked change in his handwriting and in his accent, both becoming more like those he exhibited when he was young. In 1984 K was a competent amateur photographer; but when tested in 1986 he could not operate his or our cameras, did not understand the use of lenses and filters, and took very poor photographs with his Polaroid autofocus camera.

Life Events. A persistent question in our study of K involved why his memory loss extended back to a specific time period in 1945. Our investigation of K's history revealed that many significant changes had taken place in his life within a short time after August, 1945. First, and most obvious, World War II ended in August, 1945. Further, K's paternal grandmother, to whom he had been very close, died in September, 1945. Also, in June, 1945, K had completed the highest grade (seventh) at a school where he was part of a small and apparently closely knit class; in September, 1945, he began attending a much larger school where he was evidently much less happy. In 1946 K's parents invested a large amount of money in a farm about 15 miles from where K had grown up, and K moved there with them in 1947, changing to a different school system for the remainder of his high school years. In the late 1940s, the uninsured farmhouse in which the family was living burned down. This loss caused considerable family hardship and forced major and lasting changes in the family's life style. Thus, a variety of changes, most of them negative, occurred in K's life shortly after the beginning of the forgotten period.

According to reports from K's family members, and as documented in his employment records, K was also experiencing a great deal of stress just prior to the onset of his amnesia in 1984. First, K was beginning to receive negative performance evaluations at his place of employment. This had also happened to him in several previous positions. An investigation of his employment records indicates that, when applying for these jobs, he had exaggerated his credentials, and that his lack of training and experience had soon been realized by previous employers as a result of his disappointing work performance.

Second, K had been working for several months on a business venture that was to have been finalized around the time of the onset of his amnesia. According to his wife, K was "extremely excited" about this venture; however, it is also likely that he was experiencing some trepidation about it, as he had failed in previous business ventures. Finally, K and his wife were apparently experiencing some marital problems prior to the onset of amnesia.

The stress evidently resulting from these factors manifested itself in a nervous condition involving restricted breathing, chest pains, and speech difficulties. Indeed, at the time of the accident precipitating his amnesia, K was on disability leave from work as a result of this apparently psychogenic problem. The accident occurred shortly before the date K was scheduled to return to work.

Patient F

The second patient we consider, F, displays a pattern of retrograde impairment that is similar to K's in many respects. In 1976, at the age of 39, F was in the bank one day when she suddenly "felt as though [her] head was going to explode." She remembers leaving the bank, driving home as quickly as she could, arriving home and telling her children she could not take them to the swimming pool that day, and then going up to her room. When her husband arrived shortly after this, he found her confused and incoherent, and took her to a local hospital. She remained drowsy and incoherent, and 5 days later she transferred to another hospital, where she subsequently underwent surgery for a double carotid artery aneurysm with a large left infratemporal hematoma.

When F regained consciousness in the hospital after her surgery, she thought that the year was 1960, and that she was 23 years old. Her most recent family oriented memory involved moving into a new house with her husband and three children, whom she remembered as being between the ages of about 2 and 5 years old. In fact, at the time of her stroke, F had four children, the youngest of whom was 14 years old, and she had lived in the home that she remembered as being new for 16 years.

When F's children came to the hospital to visit her, she recognized the older three children, although they looked much older than she remembered; however, her youngest child did not look at all familiar to F. She found it very difficult to even accept the fact that she had a fourth child and did not believe this until she saw her name listed as mother on the child's birth certificate.

As is the case with K, F's amnesia extends to world knowledge as well. Despite the fact that she now has had almost 15 years to learn about events that happened between 1960 (the early boundary of the amnesic period) and 1976 (the time of onset of amnesia), and despite the absence of a clinically significant anterograde amnesia, her knowledge of world events from this time period is impoverished compared to her knowledge of events that occurred both before and after the amnesic period. This is seen clearly, for example, on a test in which she was shown slides of famous scenes from various time periods and asked to describe the scene and the event with which it was associated in as much detail as possible (Sagar et al., 1985). She was scored according to whether she recognized the event, and on the basis of the level of detail of description she could give about the event. The detail of description was rated by two judges on a scale of 0 to 3, with 0 meaning the least amount of detail, and 3 meaning the richest detail.

As shown in Fig. 16.1a, F correctly recognized 62% of events from pre-1960, 23% of events from between 1960 and 1976, and 60% of events from post-1976. Thus, she recognized the planting of the flag by Marines at Iwo-Jima (1944), the incorrect newspaper headline stating that Dewey had defeated Truman (1948), the assassination attempt on Sadat (1980), and the royal wedding of Prince Charles and Lady Diana (1981). However, she did not recognize pictures of Jack Ruby shooting Lee Harvey Oswald (1963), Martin Luther King, Jr.'s assassination (1968), or Patty Hearst dressed in her Symbionese Liberation Army (SLA) uniform (1974).

Figure 16.1b shows the level of detail of the descriptions given by F for events from the three relevant time periods. The bars depict the percentage of scene descriptions from each time period that received

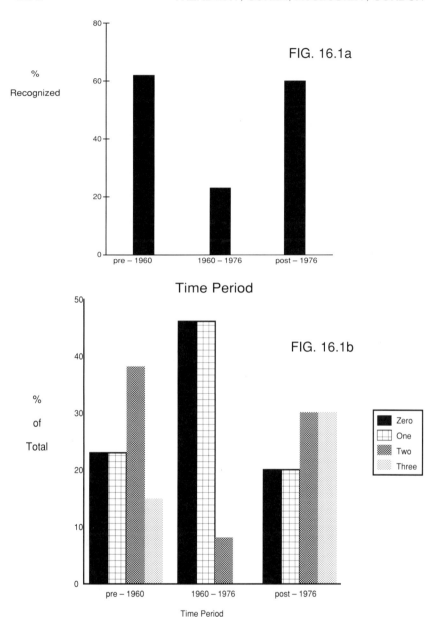

FIG. 16.1. F's performance on a test involving recognition and description of scenes associated with famous public events from various time periods. (a) Percentage recognized for scenes from pre-1960, 1960–1976 (the period for which F is amnesic), and post-1976. (b) Level of detail in descriptions of scenes from the three time periods (0 = low level of detail; 3 = high level of detail).

ratings of 0, 1, 2, or 3. As this figure shows, the distributions of ratings for the pre-1960 and post-1976 periods are relatively even. In contrast, 92% of the scores for events between 1960 and 1976 are either 0 or 1, and there are no event descriptions from this time period that received a rating of 3.

Consider, for example, one of the event descriptions from the affected time period. The following is an excerpt from F's description of a newsphoto related to the Watergate scandal. The picture used as a stimulus for the description of this event showed a Marine holding a portrait of Richard Nixon under his arm, walking in front of a wall on which hangs a portrait of Gerald Ford. This is a description for which F earned a score of 1.

F: There's Ford, the klutz. And a picture of Richard Nixon.

MT: Okay, so what do you think this is all about? What's going on here?

F: Um, that means Nixon's no longer president, and Ford is.

MT: Why is Nixon no longer president?

F: I know that one. Uh, he did something. Oh, what did he do? He did, oh, the tapes, tapes.

MT: What was the name of that?

F: Oh God, this was just on TV not too long ago. Um, Nixon and the, um, um, he bleeped the tapes...

MT: Do you remember the names of any of the other people who were involved?

F: Agnew. How's that? Agnew. He used to be governor of Maryland...

MT: Okay, and under what conditions did Nixon leave office? Was he impeached, or--

F: You know, everything that I've seen on TV, I can't understand that either. . .the only thing that they had on TV was that somebody else did something -- I don't know who it was -- but, other people did something, they broke into a building. And he had nothing to do with it.

In addition to her lack of memory for personal and world events, F also did not remember new products or technological advances that had occurred since 1960. The last car she remembered owning, for example, was a 1956 Ford. The car that she actually owned at the time of her stroke, a 1976 Grand Prix, looked to her like "one of *Life* magazine's 'Cars of the Future.'" As another example, she did not know how to operate the dishwasher that her family had acquired sometime after 1960.

Our research revealed that, as with K, a salient emotional event had occurred in F's life shortly after the beginning of the period for which she is now amnesic. Specifically, we were informed by what we consider to be reliable sources that F had an affair of uncertain duration with a neighbor, and that her fourth child (whom she did not remember after the onset of her amnesia) resulted from this affair. Although no genetic tests have been conducted to determine with certainty the paternity of the fourth child, the available information suggests that F believed the neighbor to be the father of this child. Both F and the neighbor were married at the time of this affair.

As with K, a stressful situation appears to have arisen shortly before the onset of F's amnesia, as well. Several months before the onset of amnesia in 1976, F had discovered that one of her daughters, who was then an unmarried teenager, had just had an abortion. F was extremely shocked and upset by this information and refused to speak to the daughter for a long period of time. After the onset of amnesia, F remembered nothing about this incident.

Is F's amnesia psychogenic, as we have assumed thus far? Unlike K, F suffered a definite neurological incident and sustained brain damage (to the left temporal region). However, F's amnesia is unlike any previously reported amnesia of clearly organic origin (although see Andrews, Poser, & Kessler, 1982, for a somewhat similar case with a possibly, but not definitely, organic basis). Further, F's amnesia is very similar to that of K, both in the nature of the memory impairment, and in the presence of unpleasant emotional events at the beginning and end of the forgotten time period. Given that K's amnesia is almost certainly psychogenic, this similarity suggests that F's deficit may also be psychogenic. Thus, in the following discussion we assume that F's amnesia, like K's, is functional, although we cannot entirely rule out the possibility that her memory impairment resulted from brain damage. It may be noted that the question of whether F's amnesia is functional or organic is not of central import for the first issue we discuss (i.e., the implications of the amnesias for views of memory organization), although it is clearly relevant to the second matter we consider (the psychopathological factors underlying the amnesias).

IMPLICATIONS

The remarkable memory impairments evidenced by K and F raise two related questions: (1) What must the human memory system be like, such that this type of temporally specific, informationally general amnesia could occur?; and (2) why was it psychologically necessary for K and F to forget the specific time periods for which they became amnesic? Given that we are cognitive scientists with no expertise in the area of psychopathology, we feel much more comfortable with the first question than with the second and hence focus in the following discussion on issues of memory organization. Nevertheless, we also endeavor to offer a few speculations concerning the psychopathological basis for the form taken by the amnesias.

Memory Organization

At least three hypotheses are potentially capable of accommodating the memory impairments exhibited by K and F. We discuss these hypotheses in order of what we consider to be increasing plausibility.

Dissociated Memory Systems. The first hypothesis holds that the human memory system can be "split" by a neurological or psychological event, such that information acquired after that event is stored separately from information acquired before the event. Applying this account to K, we might assume that some incident in August, 1945 (perhaps the presumed blow from the baseball bat), altered K's memory system in such a way that information acquired thereafter was stored separately from information acquired earlier. The observed amnesia could then have been created by rendering inaccessible this second set of memories (i.e., the memories from August, 1945, through December, 1984). Similarly, in the case of F we might assume that some incident in 1960 split her memory system, and that the subsequently stored memories were rendered inaccessible at the time of her hospitalization in 1976.

A possible instantiation of the dissociated-systems hypothesis is to be found in multiple personality disorder. Some patterns of memory impairment reported in the multiple personality literature are consistent with the idea of memory systems that can be dissociated from one another (e.g., Ludwig, Brandsma, Wilbur, Bendfeldt, & Jameson, 1972; Sidis & Goodhart, 1905; see Schacter & Kihlstrom, 1989, for a review); that is, it has been argued that information acquired in one personality state may be at least partially inaccessible when the individual is in some other personality state.

Although intriguing, the dissociated-systems hypothesis suffers from several difficulties, at least as applied to K and F. The most serious problem is that this hypothesis requires the assumption that the splitting of the memory system was sufficiently profound to explain the observed impairments (which involve apparently total amnesia for the affected time period, and apparently normal memory for other periods) yet nevertheless allowed apparently normal learning and memory between the time of the initial split and the onset of amnesia 39 years (for K) or 16 years (for F) later. Note in this context that no cases reported in the multiple personality literature show a dissociation as complete and extensive as that exhibited by K and F.

Temporal Coding of Stored Information. The second, and somewhat simpler, hypothesis asserts that normal memory maintains information about the time at which information was stored. For example, one might assume that each item stored in memory is associated with a time-of-acquisition tag. On this account, a temporally specified functional retrograde amnesia might occur if all memories with temporal tags within a particular range were rendered inaccessible.

Although not entirely unreasonable, this hypothesis encounters two significant difficulties. First, to explain the scope of K's and F's amnesias, it must be assumed that storage of temporal information extends not only to autobiographical episodes but also to skills, world knowledge, and the aspects of experience that shape personality and personal identity. This assumption conflicts with current views of memory, which almost universally stress an organization based on explicitly nontemporal dimensions, especially for world knowledge and skills (e.g., Anderson, 1983; Tulving, 1983).

Further, even for autobiographical events, the available data concerning temporal information in normal memory (e.g., Brown, Shevell, & Rips, 1986) certainly do not suggest that stored temporal coding is sufficiently complete or precise to provide a basis for the sharply bounded amnesias exhibited by K and F; that is, the available data do not provide any basis for supposing that temporal coding of stored information would be adequate to discriminate time intervals as small as a few months for information stored decades ago (which would appear to be necessary, at least in the case of K).

Landmark Events in Memory. The third hypothesis, and the one we prefer, posits a contextual organization of memory. This view holds that memory may be organized around "life contexts" bounded by salient landmark events. Instead of viewing memory as one large, fully integrated set of associations, this hypothesis envisions coalitions or constellations of memories. Such constellations would be composed of memories that are tied more strongly to other memories sharing the same life context than to memories that share some other life context. On this view landmark life events (e.g., moves from one city to another, job changes, marriage) may significantly alter life contexts and so may demarcate constellations of associated memories. (See Schacter, Wang, Tulving, & Freedman, 1982, for an application of similar ideas to a case of functional amnesia.)

For example, for people whose lives were directly affected by World War II—by having served in battle, having lost friends or family members in the conflict, having suffered through rationing of food and materials, and so forth—the war would be an obvious life context, and the beginning and end of the war would constitute landmark events associated with a contextual change. Memories of events occurring during the war years (whether or not they had anything to do with the war itself), as well as memories of subsequent events shaped by the outcome of the war, would likely be tied together and less loosely tied to memories organized around other life contexts.

That memories seem to be organized into constellations of this kind is suggested by the commonplace experience we have when we hear a song that we have neither heard nor thought about for many years. What we often experience is that not only can we retrieve many of the words of the song, but we also gain access to all kinds of seemingly long-forgotten memories of what we were doing and what our lives were like at the time when that song was popular. It seems that our memory for that song is tied to memories of people, places, and events within a particular life context, particularly such emotion-laden ones as the summer we had our first romance, or our senior year of high school, or the year our team won the championship, or so forth. What we would add to such a notion is that truly important changes in life context might be expected to produce distinct constellations of memories, each organized around a distinct life context.

To apply this idea to K and F, we would need to posit for each patient significant landmark events that ushered in a change in life context near the beginning of the forgotten period (1945 for K, 1960 for F). This would serve to produce distinct constellations of memories for the periods before and after the landmark events. On this account, K's post-1945 memories were organized separately from his pre-1945 memories, and F's post-1960 memories were organized separately from her pre-1960 memories. As noted earlier, it is indeed the case for both K and F that major events occurred in their lives near the beginning of the forgotten time period, events that significantly altered the nature and quality of their subsequent lives. For example, for K the end of World War II, the death of his grandmother, and the change of schools may have constituted a cluster of landmarks marking the beginning of a life context that shortly thereafter came to include the burning of his house and consequent life-style changes. Similarly, for F the move to a new house and the subsequent affair with the neighbor were significant life changes that occurred within a short span of time. Thus, the temporally specific retrograde amnesias evidenced by K and F might have involved a rendering inaccessible of all memories acquired subsequent to the change in life context.

In contrast to the temporal coding hypothesis, the landmark hypothesis does not require the assumption that information in memory is temporally marked in any way; that is, the amnesias evidenced by K and F may be interpreted without postulating any explicit temporal tagging of stored information, by assuming in the manner just discussed that organization of memory according to contexts demarcated by (nondated) landmark events allows incidents occurring before a landmark event to be distinguished from those occurring subsequent to the landmark.

On the other hand, the landmark hypothesis, as well as the available normal memory data, are consistent with the assumption that at least some events (often landmarks) are associated with specific temporal information. Research with normal subjects suggests that people can often use memories of salient events, stored with specific temporal information, to derive temporal order and dating information about other, less important events (e.g., Loftus & Marburger, 1983). Most of the evidence supporting the use of landmark events as recall cues in dating other events comes from introspective reports made by subjects as they attempt to estimate the date of a given event. For example, Thompson (1982) describes a subject who, having broken up with her boyfriend, indicated that she thought of events according to whether they were "before Jeff" or "after Jeff." This is consistent with the suggestion made by Brown et al. (1986) that autobiographical contexts may encompass large periods of time bounded by landmark events that alter social, educational, geographical, or occupational situations. For example, people who move often may be able to date events by remembering where they lived at the time the event occurred.

Whether or not we incorporate assumptions about temporal marking of some events into the landmark hypothesis, this hypothesis differs in a very significant way from the hypothesis considered earlier that all information in memory is temporally coded. On the hypothesis that all memories are temporally coded, a temporally specific amnesia could occur for any arbitrary time period. For example, the period forgotten by K could just as well have begun in early 1944, or late 1950, as in mid-1945. In contrast, the landmark hypothesis asserts that stored information is sufficient to distinguish memories from before and after a particular point in time only if that point in time corresponds to one or more landmark events in the individual's life, events that cause or are at least associated with a significant change in life context. Thus, the landmark hypothesis predicts that for any patient presenting with a temporally specific amnesia of the type evidenced by K and F, the forgotten period should be found to be delimited by landmark events. We have already noted that such events were present for both K and F. It may further be noted that in the most similar case in the amnesia literature (Andrews et al., 1982) the patient's 40-year forgotten period began in the winter of 1941–1942, the time at which the United States entered World War II. Indeed, Andrews et al. (1982) reported that the patient (an American) remembered the United States declaring war on Japan on December 8, 1941, but "could not remember anything more about the war or how it ended" (p. 444).

One issue that must be considered in regard to the landmark hypothesis concerns the role of life contexts in memory for nonautobiographical information. To account for the fact that K's and F's amnesias extended to world knowledge and skills, the hypothesis must assume that these kinds of information, as well as information about personal events, can be related to particular life contexts; that is, whatever process renders inaccessible stored information from a to-be-forgotten time period must be able to determine for nonautobiographical as well as autobiographical knowledge whether the knowledge was acquired in the critical period. One might assume that nonautobiographical as well as autobiographical memories are organized around life contexts. Perhaps a more plausible possibility, however, is that world knowledge and skills, although not organized around life contexts, are sufficiently linked to stored autobiographical knowledge to allow them to be related directly or indirectly to particular life contexts. For example, knowledge of public events may be stored in memory as a "narrative" that is largely distinct from the personal narrative of autobiographical events (e.g., Brown et al., 1986; Neisser, 1982). However, occasional links between the public and personal narratives in memory may help to maintain an alignment between the two. For example, a person who remembers where she was living at the time of a presidential election can thereby place this public event in a personal life context. Further, if she remembers that a particular political scandal erupted shortly before the election, she may thereby be able to relate the scandal indirectly to a life context, even in the absence of direct links between memories of the scandal and autobiographical memories.

A related argument may be developed with respect to skills. Although the stored knowledge underlying skilled performance may be separate from autobiographical memories, autobiographical knowledge may well be sufficient to place the acquisition and exercise of skill in a particular life period. For example, although in 1984 K may not have remembered any of the specific episodes in which he learned to use a camera and became increasingly skilled at photography, he almost certainly had available in memory sufficient information to indicate over what period in his life the skill had been acquired and refined.

From this perspective, temporally defined functional amnesias that extend to world knowledge and skills are possible because the world knowledge and skills have sufficient direct or indirect links to autobiographical memories to allow them to be related to particular life contexts. Note that this account does not require the assumption that precise circumstances-of-learning information is stored with world knowledge and skills, but only that sufficient information is available in memory to place the nonautobiographical knowledge within a general life context.

One phenomenon that may appear to pose problems for a hypothesis that does not posit a temporal organization of memory is the pattern of recovery frequently observed in patients with certain forms of amnesia. Several classes of patients, including those who have sustained severe head injury, and those undergoing bilateral ECT for treatment of depression, exhibit a temporally limited retrograde amnesia that extends back for up to several years prior to the onset of amnesia (Squire & Cohen, 1984). The resolution of these amnesias often involves a gradual recovery of memories from the affected time period, with more remote memories being recovered before more recent ones (Benson & Geschwind, 1967; Levin, Benton, & Grossman, 1982; Russell & Nathan, 1946).

This temporally ordered recovery may perhaps reflect some degree of temporal organization in the memory system. On the other hand, the recovery pattern (as well as the form of the amnesia itself) may reflect consolidation processes occurring over a substantial period of time following the creation of a memory trace. On a consolidation account, newer memories are more severely disrupted and later to recover than older memories because the former are less fully consolidated than the latter (Squire, Cohen, & Nadel, 1984). This view, which does not require any assumptions about temporal organization of stored information, is consistent with the fact that the *most* recent memories (i.e., those acquired just prior to the onset of a retrograde amnesia) are often permanently disrupted (e.g., Benson & Geschwind, 1967).

Note that although a consolidation account may perhaps be invoked to explain retrograde amnesias covering periods of up to a few years, the much more extensive amnesias exhibited by K and F cannot be adequately explained by the notion of consolidation (Cohen, 1987). The idea that memories could be continuously consolidating over time, such that even memories 40 years old could be selectively subject to disruption, is not palatable, particularly when the boundaries of such extensive amnesias are so clearly demarcated.

Psychopathological Bases for the Amnesias

We turn now to the psychopathological factors that may have led to the (presumably) functional amnesias in K and F. It seems likely that, as for other functional amnesias, the memory loss represented a means of coping with severe life stresses; that is, although in both cases the amnesias may have been triggered by physically traumatic events (a presumed electric shock for K, and a ruptured aneurysm for F), the underlying causal factor was very likely the unpleasantly stressful and emotional circumstances present in the lives of both patients at the time of onset of amnesia. Indeed, researchers who have studied functional amnesia often cite family problems and business worries as the most common precursors of functional amnesia (e.g., Abeles & Schilder, 1935; Parfitt & Gall, 1944).

Why, though, did the amnesias extend back to 1945 (for K) and 1960 (for F), as opposed to some other points in time? We have already addressed this question in part. According to the landmark hypothesis, the forgotten period in temporally specific amnesias will always be bounded by landmark events. However, this is only a partial answer to the present question, because K and F surely experienced many landmark events in their lives (e.g., getting married, the birth of children, changes of residence, and so forth). Thus, the question that arises is why the amnesias extended back to the specific landmark events of mid-1945 for K, and 1960 for F, and not to some other landmarks.

Two related possibilities may be mentioned. First, for both K and F the amnesia may in some sense have represented an attempt to return to the last time in their lives when they were relatively happy. In both cases there is ample reason to suspect that life was never quite as good after the landmark events occurring at the beginning of the forgotten period.

A second, more specific, possibility is that the boundaries of the amnesic period are related in both cases to the significant parallels between the events that precipitated the amnesias (in 1984 for K, and 1976 for F), and the events occurring in the patients' lives at the beginning of the forgotten time period (1945 for K, and 1960 for F). This interpretation is perhaps most compelling in the case of F. The pregnancy of F's unmarried daughter shortly before the onset of her amnesia parallels in obvious ways the events in F's life shortly after the beginning of the period she has forgotten. For K the parallels are less striking but nevertheless potentially significant. His difficulties at home and work, and his anticipation of an impending business deal, may have triggered memories of the emotions he experienced when his parents spent a great deal of money purchasing and renovating their farm property, only to have it destroyed a short time later in a fire. Thus, for both patients the events occurring shortly before the onset of amnesia may have rearoused the unpleasant memories from the earlier time period. The motivated forgetting of all memories from the earlier events forward may therefore have served to protect against remembering either of the painful situations. The suppression of memories for the earlier events may even have been necessary to maintain amnesia for the more recent events; due to the parallels between the earlier and later events, the two sets of memories may have been sufficiently interconnected in memory that retrieval of memories about the earlier events would have strongly activated the more recent memories (and therefore made them difficult to suppress).

What remains mysterious on any account of normal memory organization, and any hypotheses about underlying psychopathological factors in the amnesias, is what type of psychological mechanism could produce a functional amnesia; that is, what kind of process, operating below the level of awareness, could prevent a specific subset of memories from coming to consciousness?

Obviously, we are far from having a complete understanding of K's and F's impairments and the lessons they hold for theories of memory and psychopathology. As we have attempted to point out, however, these intriguing cases raise some important questions and suggest some interesting answers about the role of major life events in the organization of memory, and about the emotional factors underlying functional amnesias.

ACKNOWLEDGMENTS

We are grateful to K's family for sharing so much information with us, to several of K's friends and former teachers and employers for providing further information, and to the library staff in K's home town for help in obtaining historical records. F's family was also extremely helpful and cooperative in all phases of this research. Our theorizing and research was aided enormously by Robert Kaye, Scott Sokol, Lisa Tabor, and members of the cognitive group at Johns Hopkins. Several research assistants also helped in many ways, including David Bernstein, Laura Smith, and Mary Beth Wade. Finally, we thank John Hart, Joan Sobkov, and Carol Miller for assistance in testing.

REFERENCES

Abeles, M., & Schilder, P. (1935). Psychogenic loss of personal identity. *Archives of Neurology and Psychiatry, 34*, 587–604.

Anderson, J. R. (1983). *The architecture of cognition.* Cambridge, MA: Harvard University Press.

Andrews, E., Poser, C. M., & Kessler, M. (1982). Retrograde amnesia for forty years. *Cortex, 18*, 441–458.

Benson, D. F., & Geschwind, N. (1967). Shrinking retrograde amnesia. *Journal of Neurology, Neurosurgery, and Psychiatry, 30*, 539–544.

Brown, N. R., Shevell, S. K., & Rips, L. J. (1986). Public memories and their personal context. In D.C. Rubin (Ed.), *Autobiographical memory.* Cambridge: Cambridge University Press.

Christianson, S.-Å., & Nilsson, L.-G. (1989). Hysterical amnesia: A case of aversively motivated isolation of memory. In T. Archer & L.-G. Nilsson (Eds.), *Aversion, avoidance, and anxiety* (pp. 289–310). Hillsdale, NJ: Lawrence Erlbaum Associates.

Cohen, N. J. (1987, November). *Re-evaluation of the consolidation hypothesis of amnesia: Assessment of the evidence.* Paper presented at the annual meeting of the Society for Neuroscience, New Orleans.

Cohen, N. J., & Squire, L. R. (1981). Retrograde amnesia and remote memory impairment. *Neuropsychologia, 19*, 337–356.

Crovitz, H. F., & Schiffman, H. (1974). Frequency of episodic memories as a function of their age. *Bulletin of the Psychonomic Society, 4*, 517–518.

Levin, H. S., Benton, A. L., & Grossman, R. G. (1982). *Neurobehavioral consequences of closed head injury.* New York: Oxford University Press.

Loftus, E. F., & Marburger, W. (1983). Since the eruption of Mt. St. Helens, has anyone beaten you up? Improving the accuracy of retrospective reports with landmark events. *Memory and Cognition, 11*, 114–120.

Ludwig, A. M., Brandsma, J. M., Wilbur, C. B., Bendfeldt, F., & Jameson, D. H. (1972). The objective study of a multiple personality. *Archives of General Psychiatry, 26*, 298–310.

Neisser, U. (1982). *Memory observed: Remembering in natural contexts.* San Francisco: W. H. Freeman.

Parfitt D. N., & Gall, C. M. C. (1944). Psychogenic amnesia: The refusal to remember. *The Journal of Mental Science, 90*, 511–531.

Russell, W. R., & Nathan, P. W. (1946). Traumatic amnesia. *Brain, 69*, 280–300.

Sagar, H. J., Cohen, N. J., Corkin, S., & Growdon, J. (1985). Dissociations among processes in remote memory. *Annuals of the New York Academy of Sciences, 444*, 533–535.

Schacter, D. L., & Kihlstrom, J. F. (1989). Functional amnesia. In F. Boller & J. Grafman (Eds.), *Handbook of Neuropsychology,* (Vol. 3, pp. 209–231). New York: Elsevier Science Publishers B. V.

Schacter, D. L., Wang, P. L., Tulving, E., & Freedman, M. (1982). Functional retrograde amnesia: A quantitative case study. *Neuropsychologia, 20*, 523–532.

Sidis, B., & Goodhart, S. P. (1905). *Multiple personality.* New York: D. Appleton.

Squire, L. R., & Cohen, N. J. (1984). Human memory and amnesia. In G. Lynch, J. L. McGaugh, & N. M. Weinberger (Eds.), *Neurobiology of learning and memory* (pp. 3–64). New York: The Guilford Press

Squire, L. R., Cohen, N. J., & Nadel, L. (1985). The medial temporal region and memory consolidation: A new hypothesis. In H. Weingartner & E. Parker (Eds.), *Memory consolidation* (pp. 185–209). Hillsdale, NJ: Lawrence Erlbaum Associates.

Thompson, C. P. (1982). Memory for unique personal events: The roommate study. *Memory and Cognition, 10*, 324–332.

Tulving, E. (1983). *Elements of episodic memory.* Oxford: Oxford University Press.

Zola-Morgan, S., Cohen, N. J., & Squire, L. R. (1983). Recall of remote episodic memory in amnesia. *Neuropsychologia, 21*, 487–500.

17

Remembering and Forgetting in Patients Suffering From Multiple Personality Disorder

Bennett G. Braun
Edward J. Frischholz
Rush-Presbyterian-St. Luke's Medical Center
University of Illinois at Chicago

Although we are all able to remember some of the events that occurred in our past, the accuracy of these recollections are typically less than perfect (e.g., Adams, 1967; Frischholz, 1990; Klatsky, 1980; Loftus, 1979). For example, sometimes we are unable to remember anything about a past event. At other times, what we do recall may not reflect what actually transpired despite a strong sense of subjective confidence in the veracity of our recollection (Deffenbacher, 1980). In other words, there are two types of potential decrements in memory performance: inaccurate recollections and complete recall failures. Unfortunately, the majority of research on human memory processes carried out in the last century focused on identifying those variables that moderate our ability to remember correctly the events of our past (Ebbinghaus, 1885; Frischholz, 1990; Klatsky, 1980; Loftus, 1979; McGeoch, 1932; Thorndike, 1913). By contrast, much fewer studies have explored those factors that determine incorrect recollections or a failure to recall anything at all (Frischholz, 1990).

A number of clinicians and investigators have consistently reported that some psychiatric disorders/syndromes are associated with performance decrements on a variety of memory tasks. For example, by definition, patients suffering from dissociative disorders (e.g., Multiple Personality Disorder, Psychogenic Amnesia, Psychogenic Fugue & Depersonalization Disorder) display many different forms of amnesia. Likewise, patients with degenerative neurological conditions (e.g., Alzheimer's disease, Korsakoff 's syndrome) or various medical problems (e.g., gunshot wounds, brain tumors) also typically manifest a variety of memory deficits. The type of memory deficit observed often appears to be influenced by: (a) the type of material to be remembered (e.g., traumatic vs. nontraumatic; see Christianson & Loftus, 1987; Christianson & Nilsson, 1984) and (b) the type of clinical group being studied (e.g., dissociative disorder patients vs. patients suffering from organic brain syndromes; see APA, 1980, 1987).

The purpose of this chapter is to identify and describe some memory deficits that have been observed in patients suffering from Multiple Personality Disorder (MPD). We go on to suggest that studying the factors that influence memory performance in dissociative disorder patients can also have heuristic value for understanding the variables that affect memory performance in "normals" and other clinical groups. We begin by briefly reviewing some recent findings on memory for traumatic and nontraumatic events in "normal" populations. Next, we consider what MPD is and how it differs from other medical and psychiatric conditions. In this regard, we specifically focus on the difference between structural and functional memory deficits and how they are related to encoding, storage, and retrieval processes.

MEMORY FOR TRAUMATIC AND NONTRAUMATIC EVENTS

Some critical events in our lives are particularly well remembered whereas others are not. For example, most people over age 35 can recollect where they were and what they were doing on November 22, 1963, when they heard that President Kennedy had been assassinated. Although most would consider such an event as extremely important, it was not necessarily traumatizing because the majority of Americans did not personally witness or were not personally endangered by what happened. Rather, for an event to be considered traumatic, it should have some type of energizing negative affect that an individual experiences as being extremely unpleasant. Personal exposure to such an event (in contrast to viewing a film of a traumatic event) may increase the probability that such negative affect will be aroused.

Many clinicians and researchers alike have observed that memory for self-witnessed traumatic events appears to be worse than that for nontraumatic events (e.g, Braun, 1986; Christianson & Nilsson, 1984; Nemiah, 1969, 1979; Terr, 1988). For example, a number of empirical studies have consistently shown that a witness' recollection is poorer for details of violent events than for details of nonviolent occurrences (e.g., Clifford & Hollin, 1981; Clifford & Scott, 1978). Sometimes memory for details that occurred immediately before or after a traumatic event are also adversely effected (i.e., retrograde and anterograde amnesia; Christianson & Nilsson, 1984; Loftus & Burns, 1982; Nemiah, 1969, 1979). Furthermore, recent research has suggested that memories for traumatic events are poorer than memories for nontraumatic events because recollection of peripheral information, rather than central details, is what is impaired (Christianson & Loftus, 1987; Christianson & Nilsson, 1984).

A number of explanations have been offered to account for why memories for traumatic occurrences and the events immediately preceding and following them are poorer than recollections for details of nontraumatic events. For example, Easterbrook (1959) proposed that the number of details or environmental cues that are utilized or attended to decreases as a function of the increased emotional arousal associated with exposure to a traumatic event. According to this explanation, people are inhibited from attending to the same number of details than they would if the event were nontraumatic. Because the capacity of conscious awareness is limited (Miller, 1956), this suggests that people exposed to a traumatic event should pay more attention to central rather than peripheral details. Mandler (1975) has agreed with Easterbrook's contention and suggested a mechanism that accounts for the "attention-demanding characteristics of autonomic nervous system arousal." Traumatic arousal is presumed to adversely affect memory performance because a more limited proportion of conscious attentional capacity is available for immediate task processing (Eysenck, 1982). This suggests that self-witnessed traumatic events stimulate the use of nonoptimal encoding processes. This, in turn, is the source of poorer memory performance associated with remembering a traumatic event.

Other investigators have proposed that poorer memory for self-witnessed traumatic events occurs because of a failure to store this information in long-term memory (e.g., Glickman, 1961; Milner 1965, 1966). In this case, the traumatic event somehow interferes with normal consolidation processes, which, in turn, inhibits its integration with other long-term memories. Thus, short-term learning and memory is preserved, but it cannot be transferred (i. e., stored) into the long-term memory store.

Finally, many psychodynamically oriented clinicians and researchers (e.g., Erdelyi, 1985; Fenichel, 1945; Freud, 1915; Rapaport, 1942) have suggested that we are motivated to not remember unpleasant events and consequently do not utilize optimal retrieval strategies to improve our recollection of these episodes. Likewise, Warrington and Weiskrantz (1968, 1970) and Weiskrantz and Warrington (1970a, 1970b) have demonstrated that amnesic patients who learned a word list evidenced a significant decrement in their later ability to freely recall these words when compared to normals. However, when these amnesic patients had their recollection for this word list stimulated by exposure to various cues (e.g., priming), their performance significantly improved, although it was still somewhat below that of normals. Hence, utilization of better retrieval strategies (e.g., cuing) improved the memory of amnesic patients. Collectively, these findings suggest that exposure to self-experienced traumatic events may interfere with the utilization of optimal retrieval processes, and that changing to a more effective retrieval strategy can overcome this deficit.

In a systematic program of research, Christianson and his colleagues (e.g., Christianson, 1984, 1986, 1987; Christianson & Loftus, 1987; Christianson & Nilsson, 1984, 1989) examined the role of encoding, storage, and retrieval factors on the accuracy of memories for a self-witnessed traumatic event in an experimental context. Collectively, they observed that memory for peripheral information relating to a traumatic event was poorer than that for nontraumatic versions of this same event. They concluded that both encoding and retrieval factors, but not storage factors, were responsible for this effect. Later, we disagree with their conclusion and argue that all three factors can be related to different types of memory deficits observed in MPD patients, "normals," or other clinical groups.

A BRIEF DESCRIPTION OF
MULTIPLE PERSONALITY DISORDER

MPD is a dissociative syndrome in which one or more different personalities seem to occupy the same physical body (APA, 1980, 1987). Each of these personalities reports its own life history, and range of cognitions and emotions. Generally, at least one or more of these personalities is usually unaware of the existence of one or more of the others. Hence, one personality may be completely unaware of information that was obtained when another personality had executive control of the body. For a more detailed discussion of MPD, the interested reader is referred to other sources (e.g., Braun, 1984; Braun & Sachs, 1985; Kluft, 1984; Putnam, 1989; Sackeim & Vingiano, 1984).

One feature of MPD that distinguishes it from other psychiatric syndromes is its relation to a long history of exposure to repeated traumatic events. For example, a number of clinicians and researchers have found that the self-reported incidence of physical, sexual, and/or psychological abuse is much higher in MPD patients compared to that observed in "normals" or in other psychiatric disorders (e.g., Braun & Sachs, 1985; Coons & Milstein, 1986; Putnam, Guroff, Silberman, Barban, & Post, 1986; Schultz, Braun, & Kluft, 1989). Collectively, these studies observed that more than 90% of the MPD patients in the combined study samples claimed to have been repeatedly exposed to numerous abusive, traumatic events from early childhood through adolescence. This observation has led some to characterize MPD as one specific type of "post-traumatic stress disorder" (Putnam, 1985; Spiegel, 1984).

Most clinicians who have treated a large number of these patients have suggested that the reason they developed MPD was due to the interactive influence of a chronically abusive environment with their innate capacity to dissociate (e.g., Braun, 1984; Braun & Sachs, 1985; Frischholz, 1985; Kluft, 1982). This inborn ability protects their ego from being overwhelmed by both the immediate exposure to a traumatic event and later recollections of this event. Persons without this innate dissociative ability who were also exposed to an abusive environment during their early history will probably develop some other type of psychiatric disorder (e.g., schizophrenia, antisocial personality disorder, borderline personality disorder; Braun & Sachs, 1985). This is because they were unable to dissociate when exposed to such traumatic events and also are less likely to develop an amnesia for these events.

Multiple Personality Disorder patients and other victims of traumatic events (e.g., child-abuse victims, post-traumatic stress disorder patients) have been observed to be significantly more hypnotizable than "normals" and other clinical groups (Bliss, 1984; Frischholz, Lipman, & Braun, 1984; Frischholz, Spiegel, Lipman, Spiegel, Bark, & Tryon, 1989; Frischholz, Spiegel, Spiegel, Balma, & Markell, 1982; Lipman, Braun, & Frischholz, 1984; Pettinati, Kogan, Evans, Wade, Horne, & Staats, 1990; D. Spiegel, Detrick, & Frischholz, 1982; D. Spiegel, Hunt, & Dondershine, 1988; H. Spiegel & Spiegel, 1978). Likewise, MPD patients show significantly higher levels of instructed posthypnotic amnesia than college students or other psychiatric patient samples (Frischholz, Braun, Lipman, & Sachs, 1990). Many have postulated a relationship between high hypnotic responsivity, the tendency to manifest amnesias, and dissociative psychopathology (e.g., Bliss, 1984; Braun & Sachs, 1985; Frischholz, 1985; Hilgard, 1977; H. Spiegel, 1963; H. Spiegel & Spiegel, 1978).

The "host" personality (i.e., the personality that has executive control of the body the greatest percentage of time during any given period; Braun, 1986) is usually unable to remember any of the traumatic events that occurred in his/her life. This observation seems paradoxical when one considers one of the oldest laws of memory: The more exposure one has to a stimulus event, the better one should be able to remember that event. Yet, just the opposite seems to occur in victims of repeated traumatic abuse. For example, several authors have noted that both children and adults who are exposed to a single traumatic event may initially display some amnesia for this episode that usually remits over time. However, Terr (1988) reported that children exposed to repeated traumatic events are less able to recall them and that their amnesia usually remits less over time when compared to children who were exposed to only a single traumatic event. In other words, repeated traumatic exposures seem to produce greater memory deficits.

One of the central features of MPD is the variety of amnesias that can be manifested by patients suffering from this syndrome. For example, an MPD patient may not only forget a particular detail; he/she may also not know that it was forgotten. This observation is based on findings concerning the "feeling of knowing" phenomenon (e.g., Nelson, 1984) that has been observed in "normals." This phenomenon occurs when a subject is unable to remember a particular detail but insists that he/she "knows" what it is although he/she cannot currently articulate what it is. For example, consider a student taking an examination who encounters a test question where he/she cannot generate the answer in spite of a strong feeling that he/she should know what it is. This experience stands in sharp contrast to when one cannot generate an answer to a test question and has no accompanying subjective "feeling of knowing" what the answer is. In both cases, similar behavioral responses (i.e., being unable to generate an answer) are associated with different cognitive states (a "feeling of knowing" vs. "not knowing"). In this regard, one MPD patient described her amnesia for information obtained by another personality as lacking this "feeling of knowing" quality. Thus, some information may be potentially available in an MPD patient's overall system of personality states. However, different personality states may not be aware of all the information that is potentially available.

Other types of amnesias/dissociations have also been described and reported (e.g., one-way vs. two-way amnesias between personalities; double dissociations; for a more thorough discussion of this issue see Braun, 1988a, 1988b; Hilgard, 1977; Sackeim & Vingiano, 1984; Taylor & Martin, 1944).

The types of amnesia observed in MPD and other dissociative disorder patients are assumed to be different from those seen in other neurological or medical conditions. For example, MPD amnesia is considered to be functional rather than structural. Structural amnesias are ones where the to-be-remembered material cannot be accessed because of an injury to the physiological hardware of the memory system. For example, a gunshot wound to the head may structurally damage the physiological mechanisms that underlie encoding, storage, or retrieval. In MPD, the physiological hardware of the memory system is assumed to be structurally intact, although dysfunctional. This suggests that memories affected by dissociative amnesia are available (i.e., potentially retrievable), but not presently accessible. In contrast, some amnesias associated with a structural injury are not assumed to be reversible; that is, they may no longer be available unless the physiological hardware can somehow be repaired (however, see the reports by Warrington & Weiskrantz, 1970, and Weiskrantz and Warrington, 1970a, 1970b). Next, we consider the potential role of encoding, storage, and retrieval factors and how they may affect memories for traumatic events in MPD patients, "normals", and other types of psychiatric and medical conditions.

Encoding Factors

Many factors seem to determine how details about a traumatic event are initially perceived or encoded. For example, Frischholz (1990) empirically demonstrated that not all details associated with a traumatic event (in this case a film of a bank robbery that resulted in two suspects and one police officer being shot) are encoded equally well. Using an immediate multiple choice recognition test to assess type of initial encoding status for various details in the event, Frischholz (1990) found that some were encoded correctly, some incorrectly, and some were not encoded at all (that is, subjects were encouraged to endorse an "I don't know/I don't remember" option if they could not immediately remember the correct detail). This suggests that exposure to a single traumatic event does not insure that all the details associated with it are encoded correctly. Consequently, future decrements on memory tests about this event may be due to the fact that a particular target detail was never encoded in the first place or was initially encoded incorrectly. Thus, both MPD patients and/or normals are unlikely to correctly encode every detail associated with a traumatic event.

Second, most MPD patients were initially abused when they were young children. Hence, their cognitive schema were not very well developed at this time and may not have been particularly sensitive to encoding specific kinds of details (e.g., discriminating sexual touching from washing). Furthermore, chronic exposure to repeated, but random, abuses by the same perpetrator undoubtedly influences the development of their cognitive schemas. This is because the abused children often come to view the perpetrator as both "good" and "bad" (e.g., a person who behaves differently over time in similar circumstances). This suggests that selective encoding processes come to operate in these individuals that were initially based on the nonoptimal cognitive schemas of young children who were trying to make sense out of an abusive, but sometimes loving, environment.

Third, the abuses that many MPD patients suffered as children were often unpredictable. For example, Braun and his colleagues (Braun & Sachs, 1985; Kluft, Braun, & Sachs, 1984; Sachs & Braun, 1989) reported that MPD patients were often randomly praised or punished by their abusers for the same kinds of behaviors. This suggested that MPD patients had no way of predicting when they would be rewarded or abused for behaving in a certain way. In fact, this factor is probably what facilitated the development of different personalities. For instance, consider a little boy who is sometimes affectionately embraced for not finishing his dinner and other times brutally beaten for wasting the food. The child has no way of predicting what type of response his behavior will elicit from a random abuser. Hence, he begins to develop two ways of viewing himself and his abuser. On days when he is praised and rewarded, he views himself and the abuser as good. Conversely, when he is abused, he may come to view both himself and the abuser as bad. It is very difficult for the child to integrate these two polemic views of himself and the abuser. However, if he has an innate dissociative ability, it may be possible for him to separate these two incompatible perceptions in different memory stores that over time begin to operate independently of each other.

Storage Factors

Two storage factors that are presumed to affect the recollection of MPD patients are considered here: (a) the assumption that encoded information is transferred into independently operating long-term memory stores; and (b) the assumption that information present in one long-term memory store interacts unusually with information in another store or that it does not appear to interact at all. The notion that information about past events is transferred into different long-term memory stores among MPD patients is based on clinical observation of the phenomenology of this syndrome. The very existence of different personalities, each with their own life history and range of cognitions and emotions, seems axiomatic proof that different long-term memory stores do appear to develop in these individuals. However, making this observation is not the same as explaining how these different long-term memories stores come to exist. Both Braun (1986; 1988a, 1988b; Braun & Sachs, 1985) and Putnam (1989) have presented intriguing speculations about this issue that are not considered here.

The assumption that information in the long-term memory stores of different personalities shows an unusual form or lack of reciprocal influence is often used to justify the existence of unique memory systems. However, it is a separate issue with two component parts: unusual interactions between different memory stores, and lack of interaction between different memory stores. One of the most obvious examples of different long-term memory stores is based on clinical observations of passive influence phenomena and auditory hallucinations in MPD patients (Kluft, 1987). For example, an MPD patient may say something and then deny knowing why he/she said it. Later, another personality will claim responsibility for this remark. This phenomenon is different from memory interference observed in normal subjects; that is, MPD patients do not seem to know the source of the interference, whereas "normals" can usually identify it readily.

Historically, both passive influence phenomena and auditory hallucinations are both Schneiderian First Rank symptoms associated with schizophrenia (Mellor, 1970). However, Kluft (1987) observed that MPD patients appear to manifest significantly more Schneiderian symptoms than schizophrenics. In addition, Kluft (1987) noted qualitative differences between the auditory hallucinations of MPD patients and schizophrenics. For example, schizophrenics typically experience auditory hallucinations as coming from outside their heads, whereas MPD patients report hearing voices inside their heads. Collectively, these observations demonstrate that unusual interactions between the long-term memory stores of different personalities do exist (e.g., the feeling that another personality is commenting on or influencing another personality' s behavior). These unusual interactions cannot be simply explained as "normal" memory interference or the same type of deficit as that observed in schizophrenia.

Three studies have investigated whether the information contained in the long-term memory store of one personality affects the cognitive performance of a different personality. For example, Livingston (1981) used a method to investigate this phenomenon that was originally developed by Luchins (1942). In the original Luchins' (1942) paradigm, "normal" subjects learned how to solve a number of water jar problems that could only be done by a "long" computational method. This constituted what Luchins called the "set" (i.e., the "long" computational method). Later, the same subjects were asked to solve a number of similar water jar problems, some of which could be solved by both a "long" or a "short" computational method. Interestingly, these subjects did not seem to notice that some of the problems could be solved by a "short" method and continued to use the "long" method. In contrast, subjects who had never been exposed to the "long" method solved the "short" water jar problems with the "short" method. Luchins (1942) hypothesized that learning the "long" problem-solving algorithm interfered with a subject's ability to detect when a similar problem could be solved by a "short" method (referred to as the "Einstellung effect").

In the dissertation study carried out by Livingston (1981), different personality states (hereinafter collectively referred to as Personality A) who purportedly had a one-way amnesia for information contained in another personality (hereinafter collectively referred to as Personality B) were identified in MPD patients. Personality states A each learned how to solve a number of water jar problems by the "long" method. Then the B personality states were asked to solve a number of new water jar problems, some of which could be solved by either the "long" or "short" method. Then, personality A states were asked to solve the same water jar problems that had just been attempted by the B personality states. Half of the B personality states demonstrated no interference effect and were able to solve the easy problems by the "short" method whenever this was possible. However, all A personality states attempted to solve the same water jar problems by the "long" method despite the fact that some of them had B personality states that correctly identified the "short" solution. In contrast, normal subjects exposed to this same paradigm, almost always show this interference effect (Frischholz & Sachs, unpublished data; Huesmann, Gruder, & Dorst, 1987).

Whereas half of the sample in the Livingston (1981) study did not show a storage interference effect, the other half did. Ludwig, Brandsma, Wilbur, Bendfeldt, and Jameson (1972) observed that material stored in one personality state influenced the learning of a similar word list in another personality in one MPD patient. However, Ludwig et al. (1972) also observed that alternate personalities processed emotionally laden words differently than the same personality state tested twice. No such difference was observed for emotionally neutral words, suggesting that emotionally laden to-be-remembered material moderated the magnitude of the interference effect. Likewise, Silberman, Putnam, Weingartner, Braun, and Post (1985) also did not observe quantitative memory differences between alternate MPD personalities and simulating controls using an emotionally neutral set of words. However, Silberman et al. (1985) observed qualitative memory differences between MPD patients and controls that were not predicted a priori. For example, the memory performance of real MPD patients actually improved over test sessions (perhaps showing a slight facilitation effect), whereas the performance of subjects simulating MPD on the same tasks actually declined (perhaps due to a memory overload effect). Collectively, empirical support for the notion that information learned in one personality unusually interacts or fails to interact with the cognitive processing of another personality is mixed. Future research needs to be undertaken to identify the discrepancies observed for this effect when using different experimental paradigms.

Retrieval Factors

Retrieval factors undoubtedly underlie many of the memory deficits observed in MPD. This is because much of the to-be remembered information ultimately proves to be retrievable under different conditions. Hence, this information must have been encoded and stored. Therefore, it is informative to examine some of the conditions that appear to selectively influence the retrieval of this material.

One recent study (Frischholz, Braun, Lipman, & Sachs, 1990) examined potential differences among MPD patients, "normals," and other psychiatric groups (schizophrenic, mood, and anxiety-disorder patients) in the ability to experience instructed posthypnotic amnesia as it is assessed on the Stanford Hypnotic Susceptibility Scale, Form C (Weitzenhoffer & Hilgard, 1962). This scale contains 12 test suggestions, the last of which contains an instruction to forget the previous 11 items posthypnotically until the experimenter cancels the amnesia with a prearranged verbal cue. Both MPD patients and schizophrenics showed significantly more amnesia than normals or other clinical groups while the amnesia suggestion was in effect. In addition, MPD patients evidenced significantly more amnesia than schizophrenics. A different pattern of results emerged between groups, however, when the amnesia suggestion was canceled. This time the schizophrenics showed less reversible amnesia than normals and other clinical groups. In contrast, MPD patients showed significantly greater reversibility of the amnesia than normals and all other clinical groups. Collectively, the findings suggest that reliable differences between the ability to posthypnotically forget and remember are observed between normals and different abnormal groups. Yet, the findings tell us little about the nature of these differences. Is it due to the deleterious effects of different kinds of psychopathology or is it due to the fact that different groups use different kinds of retrieval strategies?

Braun (1984) has suggested that memory differences between personalities in MPD patients may be a state-dependent learning effect (e.g., Bower, Gilligan, & Monteiro, 1981). This means that material learned in one state (or personality) is more likely to be recollected whenever that state is reinstated. However, both Blaney (1986) and Putnam (1988) have argued that a mood congruence effect (i.e., the affective valence of the to-be-remembered material is more likely to be recalled when one is in a similar affective state) can also explain memory differences between personalities.

The possibility that different personalities may actively suppress their recollection of material through the use of distraction or selective inhibition must also be considered. These types of active response strategies are likely to be employed by subjects who are simulating MPD. However, this explanation seems unlikely in light of the findings of Silberman et al. (1985), who found qualitative differences between alternate personalities in MPD patients and sham alternates in simulating controls. In other words, the memory deficits observed in MPD patients do not appear to be similar to those manifested by role-playing subjects. Collectively, the evidence suggests that a number of retrieval factors may explain differences in the memory performance of alternate personalities in MPD patients.

CONCLUSION

Human recollection is fallible. Some things we remember correctly, incorrectly, or not at all. One factor that appears to systematically moderate particular kinds of memory deficits is the presence/absence of some medical or psychiatric conditions. For example, structural amnesias are often associated with traumatic brain injuries in which the physiological hardware of the memory system may have become damaged. In contrast, functional amnesias such as those observed in MPD do not necessarily involve damage to the memory system because the to-be-remembered material is available but differentially accessible. In this chapter we have noted how some encoding, storage, and retrieval factors may influence the differential accessibility of the to-be-remembered material in MPD. These factors have also been implicated in studying other kinds of memory problems in both normals and other clinical groups. Hopefully, future research will provide us with new insights into the factors that influence remembering and forgetting in dissociative syndromes.

ACKNOWLEDGMENTS

The authors would like to acknowledge the advice and comments made by Sven-Åke Christianson, Ph.D., Philip Freedman, Ph.D., Laura Hopkins, B.A., Jennifer Lewis, James N. Pasquotto, M.A., James W. Pennebaker, Ph.D. and Denise Shaeffer, which helped to improve the quality of this chapter.

REFERENCES

Adams, J. A. (1967) *Human memory.* New York: McGraw–Hill.
American Psychiatric Association (1980). *Diagnostic and statistical manual of mental disorders* (3rd ed.). Washington, DC.: American Psychiatric Association.
American Psychiatric Association (1987). *Diagnostic and statistical manual of mental disorders* (rev. 3rd ed.). Washington, DC: American Psychiatric Association.
Blaney, P. H. (1986). Affect and memory: A review. *Psychological Bulletin, 99*, 229–246.
Bliss, E. L. (1984) Spontaneous self-hypnosis in multiple personality disorder. In B.G. Braun (Ed.), Symposium on Multiple Personality, *Psychiatric Clinics of North America, 7*, 135–148.
Bower, G. H., Gilligan, S. G., & Monteiro, K. P. (1981). Selectivity of learning caused by affective states. *Journal of Experimental Psychology: General, 110*, 451–473.
Braun, B. G. (1984). Towards a theory of multiple personality disorder and other dissociative phenomena. In B. G. Braun (Ed.), Symposium on Multiple Personality, *Psychiatric Clinics of North America, 7*, 171–194.
Braun, B. G. (1986). Issues in the treatment of multiple personality disorder. In B. G. Braun (Ed.), *Treatment of multiple personality disorder* (pp. 3–28). Washington, DC: American Psychiatric Association.
Braun, B. G. (1988a). The BASK (behavior, affect, sensation, knowledge) model of dissociation. *Dissociation, 1*, 4–23.
Braun, B. G. (1988b). The BASK model of dissociation: Clinical applications. *Dissociation, 1*, 16–23.
Braun, B. G., & Sachs, R. G. (1985). The development of multiple personality disorder: Predisposing, precipitating, & perpetuating factors. In R. P. Kluft (Ed.),

Childhood antecedents of multiple personality, (pp. 37–64). Washington, DC: American Psychiatric Press.

Christianson, S.-Å. (1984). The relationship between induced emotional arousal and amnesia. *Scandinavian Journal of Psychology, 25,* 147–160.

Christianson, S.-Å. (1986). Effects of positive emotional events on memory. *Scandinavian Journal of Psychology, 27,* 287–299.

Christianson, S.-Å. (1987). Emotional and autonomic responses to visual traumatic stimuli. *Scandinavian Journal of Psychology, 28,* 83–87.

Christianson, S.-Å., & Loftus, E.F. (1987). Memory for traumatic events. *Applied Cognitive Psychology, 1,* 225–239.

Christianson, S.-Å., & Nilsson, L.-G. (1984). Functional amnesia as induced by a psychological trauma. *Memory and Cognition , 12,* 142–155.

Christianson, S.-Å., & Nilsson, L.-G. (1989). Hysterical amnesia: A case of aversively motivated isolation of memory. In T. Archer & L.-G. Nilsson (Eds.), *Aversion, avoidance, and anxiety: Perspectives on aversively motivated behavior* (pp. 289–310). Hillsdale, NJ: Lawrence Erlbaum Associates.

Clifford, B. R., & Hollin, C. (1981). Effects of type of incident and the number of perpetrators on eyewitness memory. *Journal of Applied Psychology, 66,* 364–370.

Clifford, B. R., & Scott, J. (1978). Individual and situational factors in eyewitness testimony. *Journal of Applied Psychology, 63,* 352–359.

Coons, P. M., & Milstein, V. (1986). Psychiatric problems associated with child abuse. In J. Jacobsen (Ed.), *Psychiatric sequelae of child abuse* (pp. 169–200). Springfield, IL: Charles C. Thomas.

Deffenbacher, K. (1980). Eyewitness accuracy and confidence: Can we infer anything about their relationship. *Law and Human Behavior, 4,* 243–260.

Easterbrook, J. A. (1959) The effect of emotion on cue utilization and the organization of behavior. *Psychological Review, 66,* 183–201.

Ebbinghaus, H. (1885). *Uber das gedachtnis.* Leipzig: Duncker & Humbolt.

Erdelyi, M. H. (1985). *Psychoanalysis: Freud's cognitive psychology.* New York: W. H. Freeman.

Eysenck, M. W. (1982). *Attention and arousal: Cognition and performance.* Berlin: Springer–Verlag.

Fenichel, O. (1945). *The psychoanalytic theory of neurosis.* New York: Norton.

Freud, S. (1915). Repression. (Tran. by C. M. Baines & J. Strachey). In J. Strachey (Ed. and Trans.), *The standard edition of the complete psychological works of Sigmund Freud* (Vol. 14). London: Hogarth Press.

Frischholz, E. J. (1985). The relationship between dissociation, hypnosis, and child abuse in the development of multiple personality disorder. In R. P. Kluft (Ed.), *Childhood antecedents of multiple personality* (pp. 99–126). Washington, DC: American Psychiatric Press.

Frischholz, E. J. (1990). *Understanding the Postevent Information Contamination Effect.* Unpublished doctoral dissertation, University of Illinois, Chicago.

Frischholz, E. J., Braun, B. G., Lipman, L. S., & Sachs, R. G. (1990). Suggested posthypnotic amnesia in psychiatric patients and normals: A replication and reinterpretation of the findings. *American Journal of Clinical Hypnosis.* Manuscript submitted for publication.

Frischholz, E. J., Lipman, L. S., & Braun, B. G. (1984). Hypnotizability and multiple personality disorder: Part II. Special hypnotic phenomena. In B. G. Braun (Ed.), *Dissociative disorders 1984: Proceedings of the first international conference on multiple personality/dissociative states* (pp. 101). Chicago: Rush-Presbyterian-St. Luke's Medical Center.

Frischholz, E. J., Spiegel, D., Lipman, L. S., Spiegel, H., Bark, N., & Tryon, W. W. (1989). *The hypnotic induction profile and psychopathology.* Manuscript submitted for publication.

Frischholz, E. J., Spiegel, D., Spiegel, H., Balma, D. L., & Markell, C. S. (1982). Differential hypnotic responsivity of smokers, phobics, and chronic pain control patients: A failure to confirm. *Journal of Abnormal Psychology, 91,* 269–272.

Glickman, S. E. (1961). Perseverative neural processes and consolidation of the memory trace. *Psychological Bulletin, 58,* 218–233.

Hilgard, E. R. (1977). *Divided consciousness: Multiple controls in human thought and action.* New York: Wiley.

Huesmann, L. R., Gruder, C. L., & Dorst, G. (1987). Process models of "posthypnotic amnesia." *Cognitive Psychology, 19,* 33–62.

Klatsky, R. L. (1980). *Human memory: Structures and processes.* San Francisco: W. H. Freeman.

Kluft, R. P. (1982). Varieties of hypnotic interventions in the treatment of multiple personality. *American Journal of Clinical Hypnosis, 24,* 230–240.

Kluft, R. P. (1984). An introduction to multiple personality disorder. *Psychiatric Annals, 14,* 21–24.

Kluft, R. P. (1987). First-rank symptoms as a diagnostic clue to multiple personality disorder. *American Journal of Psychiatry, 144,* 293–298.

Kluft, R. P., Braun, B. G., & Sachs, R. G. (1984). Multiple personality, intrafamilial abuse, and family psychiatry. *International Journal of Family Psychiatry, 5,* 283–302.

Lipman, L. S., Braun, B. G., & Frischholz, E. J. (1984). Hypnotizability and multiple personality disorder: Part I. Overall hypnotic responsivity. In B.G. Braun (Ed.), *Dissociative disorders 1984: Proceedings of the First International Conference on Multiple Personality/Dissociative States* (pp. 100). Chicago: Rush-Presbyterian-St. Luke's Medical Center.

Livingston, J. D. (1981). *The dissociative process in multiple personality disorder—An empirical study.* Unpublished doctoral dissertation, University of Illinois, Chicago.

Loftus, E. F. (1979). *Eyewitness testimony.* Cambridge: Harvard University Press.

Loftus, E. F., & Burns, T. (1982). Mental shock can produce retrograde amnesia. *Memory and Cognition, 10,* 318–323.

Luchins, A. S. (1942). Mechanization of problem solving. *Psychological Monographs, 54* (whole no. 54).

Ludwig, A. M., Brandsma, J., Wilbur, C., Bendfeldt, F., & Jameson, D. M. (1972). The objective study of a multiple personality: Or, are four heads better than one? *Archives of General Psychiatry, 25,* 248.

Mandler, G. (1975). *Mind and emotion.* New York: Wiley.

McGeoch, J. A. (1932) Forgetting and the law of disuse. *Psychological Review, 39,* 352–370.

Mellor, C. S. (1970). First rank symptoms in schizophrenia. *British Journal of Psychiatry, 117,* 15–23.

Miller, G. A. (1956). The magical number seven, plus or minus two: Some limits of our capacity for processing information. *Psychological Review, 63,* 81–97.

Milner, B. (1965). Memory disturbance after bilateral hippocampal lesions. In P. Milner & S. Glickman (Eds.), *Cognitive processes and the brain.* New York: Van Nostrand.

Milner, B. (1966). Amnesia following operation on the temporal lobes. In C. W. Whitty & O. L. Zangwill (Eds.), *Amnesia.* London: Butterworth.

Nelson, T. (1984). A comparison of current measures of the accuracy of feeling-of-knowing predictions. *Psychological Bulletin, 95,* 109–134.

Nemiah, J. C. (1969). Hysterical amnesia. In G. A. Talland & N. C. Waugh (Eds.), *The pathology of memory*. New York: Academic Press.

Nemiah, J. C. (1979). Dissociative amnesia: A clinical and theoretical reconsideration. In J. F. Kihlstrom & F. J. Evans (Eds.), *Functional disorders of memory* (pp. 303–323). Hillsdale: Lawrence Erlbaum Associates.

Pettinati, H. M., Kogan, L. G., Evans, F. J., Wade, J. L., Horne, R. L., & Staats, J. M. (1990). Hypnotizability of psychiatric inpatients according to two different scales. *American Journal of Psychiatry, 147*, 69–75.

Putnam, F. W. (1985). Dissociation as a response to extreme trauma. In R. P. Kluft (Ed.), *Childhood antecedents of multiple personality* (pp. 65–98). Washington, DC: American Psychiatric Press.

Putnam, F. W. (1988). The switch process in multiple personality disorder and other state-change disorders. *Dissociation, 1*, 24–32.

Putnam, F. W. (1989). *The diagnosis and treatment of multiple personality disorder.* New York: Guilford Press.

Putnam, F. W., Guroff, J. J., Silberman, E. K., Barban, L., & Post, R. M. (1986). The clinical phenomenology of multiple personality disorder: A review of 100 recent cases. *Journal of Clinical Psychiatry, 47*, 172– 175.

Rapaport, D. (1942). *Emotions and memory.* New York: International Universities Press.

Sachs, R. G., & Braun, B. G. (1989). *Parallels between the symptom manifestations of multiple personality disorder (MPD) and the patient's family of origin.* Manuscript submitted for publication.

Sackeim, H. A., & Vingiano, W. A. (1984). Dissociative disorders. In S. M. Turner & M. Hersen (Eds.), *Adult psychopathology and diagnosis.* New York: Wiley.

Schultz, R. G., Braun, B. G., & Kluft, R. P. (1989). Multiple personality disorder: Phenomenology of selected variables in comparison to major depression. *Dissociation, 2*, 45–51.

Silberman, E. K., Putnam, F. W., Weingartner, H. Braun, B. G., & Post, R. M. (1985). Dissociative states in multiple personality disorder: A quantitative study. *Psychiatry Research, 15*, 253–260.

Spiegel, D. (1984). Multiple personality as a post-traumatic stress disorder. In B. G. Braun (Ed.), *Symposium on Multiple Personality, Psychiatric Clinics of North America, 7*, 101–110.

Spiegel, D., Detrick, D., & Frischholz, E. J. (1982). Hypnotizability and psychopathology. *American Journal of Psychiatry, 139*, 431–437.

Spiegel, D., Hunt, T., & Dondershine, H. E. (1988). Dissociation and hypnotizability in posttraumatic stress disorder. *American Journal of Psychiatry, 145*, 301–305.

Spiegel, H. (1963). The dissociation–association continuum. *Journal of Nervous and Mental Disease, 136*, 374–378.

Spiegel, H., & Spiegel, D. (1978). *Trance and treatment: Clinical uses of hypnosis.* New York: Basic Books.

Taylor, W. S., & Martin, M. F. (1944). Multiple personality. *Journal of Abnormal and Social Psychology, 39*, 281–300.

Terr, L. (1988). What happens to early memories of trauma? A study of twenty children under age five at the time of documented traumatic events. *Journal of the American Academy of Child and Adolescent Psychiatry, 27*, 96–104.

Thorndike, E. L. (1913). *Educational psychology.* New York: Teachers College Press.

Warrington, E. K., & Weiskrantz, L. (1968). A new method of testing long term retention with special reference to amnesic patients. *Nature, 217*, 972–974.

Warrinton, E. K., & Weiskrantz, L. (1970). Amnesic syndrome: Consolidation or retrieval? *Nature, 228,* 628–630.

Weiskrantz, L., & Warrington, E. K. (1970a). A study of forgetting in amnesic patients. *Neuropsychologia, 8,* 281–288.

Weiskrantz, L. & Warrington, E. K. (1970b). Verbal learning and retention by amnesic patients using partial information. *Psychonomic Science 20,* 210–211.

Weitzenhoffer, A. M., & Hilgard, E. R. (1962). *Stanford Hypnotic Susceptibility Scale, Form C.* Palo Alto, CA: Consulting Psychologists Press.

18

Clinical Anxiety, Trait Anxiety, and Memory Bias

Michael W. Eysenck
Royal Holloway and Bedford New College
University of London

Karin Mogg
St. George's Hospital Medical School
University of London

INTRODUCTION

There has been a considerable increase in interest in cognitive approaches to clinical anxiety in recent years. Much of this interest has stemmed from the theoretical work of Beck (e.g., Beck & Clark, 1988; Beck & Emery, 1985). In essence, Beck has argued that individuals who become clinically anxious are characterized by certain schemas (e.g., organized collections of knowledge) relating to personal vulnerability and danger. It is assumed that these schemas remain latent until triggered or activated by appropriate environmental events (e.g., stressful life events). When these schemas are activated, they influence the processing of threat-related information in several ways: The processes affected include those involved in attention, comprehension, and retrieval.

Beck has consistently focused on the importance of structural or trait-like aspects of emotion with his emphasis on the role played by schemas. However, the fact that he argues that the danger and vulnerability schemas possessed by anxious patients only become active in stressful conditions means that state anxiety (the anxiety actually experienced in a situation) is also relevant in the production of affect-congruent effects.

A very different theoretical framework that nevertheless generates many of the same predictions as stem from the theory of Beck and Emery (1985) has been proposed by Bower (1981, 1987). In essence, he put forward a semantic network model designed to account for the effects of mood on memory. According to this model, information in long-term memory is stored as nodes in a network, and nodes that are related to each other are connected together. Information is accessed within the network by activation of the appropriate node. When a given node is activated, activation spreads from that node to other nodes connected to it, making them more available to the cognitive system. A key assumption is that each emotional state is represented by a node within the semantic network. When an emotional state is experienced, this produces activation of the corresponding emotion node. This then leads to activation of related nodes, most of which contain affect-congruent information.

It follows from Bower's (1981, 1987) theory that the processing of information that is congruent with a currently experienced mood state will be facilitated because such information is already partially activated. As a consequence, someone in an anxious mood state should show superior processing of anxiety-relevant stimuli to nonrelevant stimuli across a wide range of perceptual, attention, and memorial tasks. Whereas Bower (1981, 1987) focused on mood effects, his general theoretical approach could be extended to accommodate the effects of, for example, trait anxiety defined by Spielberger, Gorsuch, & Lushene (1970) as "relatively stable individual differences in anxiety processes"(p. 3). There are presumably more, and stronger, associations between the anxiety node and other anxiety-congruent nodes in those high in trait anxiety than in those low in trait anxiety. As a consequence, affect-congruent effects should be more pronounced in high trait anxious individuals.

Beck and Bower differ considerably in terms of the precise processes involved in producing affect-congruent effects. According to Beck, these effects stem primarily from top-down processes initiated by relevant schemas, whereas Bower emphasizes bottom-up processes based on priming of nodes. In spite of these differences, both theorists predict the existence of extensive affect-congruent effects throughout the cognitive system. So far as memory is concerned, the expectation from both theories is that anxious individuals should exhibit superior long-term memory than nonanxious individuals for information that is relevant to anxiety. The remainder of this chapter is concerned with the empirical evidence that has accumulated on this issue.

Two rather different kinds of anxious groups are discussed in this chapter. Firstly, there are normal individuals high in trait anxiety. Secondly, there are clinically anxious patients, and in particular patients suffering from generalized anxiety disorder. These patients typically have much higher levels in trait anxiety than normals. There are various reasons why it is of interest to compare functioning in clinical and normal anxious groups. The most important single reason is that there may be major links between trait anxiety and clinical anxiety, with trait anxiety predisposing to clinical anxiety. Support for this viewpoint was obtained by McKeon, Roa, and Mann (1984). They discovered that obsessive–compulsive patients who had had a highly anxious premorbid personality experienced only half as many life events on average as did those with low premorbid anxiety. The implication is that high trait anxious individuals are more vulnerable to stress and so need fewer life events to precipitate a disorder. In any comparison between clinical and normal anxious groups, it is important to consider memorial functioning.

Comparisons between the memory performance of high trait anxious normals and clinically anxious groups can also help to elucidate the reasons why clinically anxious patients differ from normal controls. Suppose that high trait anxious normals were found to differ from low trait anxious normals in the same way. This would suggest that a semipermanent predisposition to experience anxiety is responsible for the performance of the anxious patients rather than clinically anxious mood state per se. If memory performance were unaffected by trait anxiety level in normals, then the implication would be that clinically anxious mood state played a part in producing the memory performance of the anxious patients.

Anxious individuals might differ from nonanxious individuals in their memory for threat-related stimulus material in at least two rather different kinds of experimental paradigm. The first involves comparing the retention of unequivocally threatening and nonthreatening information in the two groups. The second involves the presentation of ambiguous stimuli that can be interpreted in either a threatening or a nonthreatening fashion. If anxious and nonanxious individuals differ in their retention of such ambiguous stimuli, it may well reflect the operation of an interpretative bias at the time of comprehension. Although the two experimental paradigms are clearly related, it does seem important to discuss the findings from the paradigms separately. This separation has not always been adhered to in the literature.

INTERPRETATION OF AMBIGUITY

Memory is often divided into encoding, storage, and retrieval stages, all of which need to be considered if memory performance is to be understood. Thus, for example, the nature of the original encoding determines what is stored and what can subsequently be retrieved. In this section of the chapter we consider the effects of anxiety on the encoding of ambiguous stimuli.

There are theoretical reasons for assuming that anxious groups would be more likely than nonanxious groups to interpret ambiguous stimuli in a threatening fashion. For example, Byrne (1964) argued that repression–sensitization is an important personality dimension. According to him, sensitizers typically approach threatening stimuli, whereas repressors tend to avoid such stimuli. One of the implications of this theoretical position is that sensitizers should be more likely than repressors to provide threatening interpretations of ambiguous stimuli.

This theory is of relevance here because repression–sensitization, as assessed by Byrne's Repression–Sensitization Scale, is essentially the same personality dimension as trait anxiety. This has been shown by Watson and Clark (1984), who reported that scores on the Repression–Sensitization Scale typically correlate at least +.80 with those on tests of trait anxiety. Thus, Byrne's (1964) hypothesis effectively states that those high in trait anxiety have a greater probability than those low in trait anxiety of interpreting ambiguous stimuli in a threatening way.

Beck and Emery (1985) have argued that the same is true of clinically anxious patients. According to them, "The range of stimuli that can evoke anxiety in generalized anxiety disorder may increase until almost any stimulus is perceived as a danger" (p.32). In spite of the intuitive reasonableness of this statement, there was very little relevant empirical evidence until quite recently.

Bower's (1981) network theory also predicts that the interpretation of ambiguous stimuli should tend to be resolved in favor of the more affect-congruent interpretation. In the case of those in an anxious mood state, anxiety-relevant information should be partially activated before the presentation of any stimuli. This should increase the probability of the interpretative process favoring any of these anxiety-relevant activated nodes.

Studies by Blaylock (1963) and by Haney (1973) investigated the interpretation of ambiguity in repressors and sensitizers. Blaylock (1963) asked her subjects to provide associations to homographs having aggressive and neutral interpretations. Sensitizers provided more threatening associations than repressors in one study, but this interpretative bias was not replicated in a further experiment. Haney (1973) presented ambiguous sentences. After each sentence had been presented, subjects had to decide which of two further sentences was closer in meaning to the ambiguous sentence. Sensitizers were significantly more likely than repressors to select the sentence containing the more threatening meaning of the ambiguous sentence.

Trait anxiety was investigated by Eysenck, MacLeod, and Mathews (1987). They presented a list of words auditorily, some of the words being homophones having both a threat-related and a neutral interpretation (e.g., die, dye; groan, grown). Subjects were instructed simply to write down the spelling of each word as it was presented. Trait anxiety correlated +.60 with the number of threatening homophone interpretations written down. A limitation with this study is that it is possible that response bias may have played a part in these findings.

Trait anxiety and clinical anxiety were both considered by Mathews, Richards, and Eysenck (1989). They used the homophone task with currently anxious patients, recovered anxious patients, and normal controls. Skin conductance responses to the homophones were recorded. The reasons for this is that it was assumed that a greater skin conductance response would be produced if a homophone were interpreted in a threatening fashion than if it were interpreted in a nonthreatening fashion. Response bias could be assessed, because subjects who interpreted homophones in a threatening way but wrote down the neutral spelling would have unexpectedly large skin conductance responses. In fact, the skin conductance responses provided no evidence of group differences in response bias.

Mathews et al. (1989) confirmed the importance of trait anxiety in the interpretation of ambiguous stimuli. There was a highly significant correlation of +.49 between trait anxiety and the number of threatening interpretations across all subjects, but the correlation was .00 in the recovered anxious group. The currently anxious group produced significantly more threatening homophone spellings than the controls, and the recovered anxious group was intermediate and nonsignificantly different from either of the other two groups. Because the recovered anxious group did not differ from the controls, there was no convincing evidence that the interpretative bias shown by the current anxious patients was part of a cognitive vulnerability factor.

Simpson (1984) discussed theoretical accounts of the processes involved in the resolution of ambiguity. There is much support for the exhaustive access model, according to which all the meanings of ambiguous words are activated automatically. The particular mean-

ing of an ambiguous word that reaches conscious awareness may
well be determined in part by selective biases that either facilitate or
inhibit the additional processing of the threatening interpretations
of ambiguous words. Normals high in trait anxiety may differ from
those low in trait anxiety in terms of such selective biases, and the
same may be true of current anxious patients compared to normal
controls.

Long-term memory for ambiguous stimuli was investigated by
Eysenck, Mogg, May, Richards, and Mathews (in press). In Experiment 1 they presented numerous sentences to currently anxious
patients, recovered anxious patients, and normal controls. Some of
the sentences were ambiguous and could be interpreted in either a
threatening or a nonthreatening fashion (e.g., "The two men watched
as the chest was opened"). On a subsequent unexpected
recognition-memory test, subjects had to decide whether each sentence corresponded in meaning to one of the sentences presented
previously. Reworded versions of the ambiguous sentences were
used and were written to capture the meaning of either the threatening or the nonthreatening interpretation of those sentences.

The analysis of the data provided evidence of an interpretative
bias in the currently anxious patients. They recognized more of the
threatening interpretations and fewer of the neutral interpretations
than did members of the other two groups. There was very little
difference in the memory performance of the recovered anxious
group and the normal controls, suggesting that the interpretative
bias shown by the currently anxious patients was attributable to
their clinically anxious mood state.

An interpretative problem with all the studies considered so far is
that group differences in performance may simply reflect *response
bias*. In other words, anxious individuals may be more likely than
nonanxious individuals to produce or to endorse threatening responses in spite of not differing in their encoding processes. This
possibility was examined systematically by Eysenck et al. (in press;
Experiment 2). They applied signal-detection analyses to the recognition of ambiguous, threatening, and neutral sentences, and
discovered that anxious patients did not differ from normal controls
in response bias. However, they did differ as predicted in sensitivity,
suggesting that anxious patients have a genuine interpretative bias
in the encoding of ambiguous material.

The fact that anxious patients differ from normal controls in terms
of an *interpretative bias* applied to ambiguous stimuli may be of
relevance to an understanding of the findings reported by Nunn,
Stevenson, and Whalan (1984). They found that agoraphobic patients

recalled more phobia-related material than neutral material, whereas normal controls did not. An inspection of the stimulus material used by Nunn et al. (1984) suggested that the two groups of subjects probably interpreted some of the presented words in very different ways. Words such as "street," "cinema," and "travel" may be threatening for agoraphobics but certainly not for ordinary individuals. This interpretative difference could have played a part in producing the observed group differences in recall. Because Pickles and van den Broek (1988) failed to replicate these findings, it is probably not worth devoting more attention to accounting for the findings of Nunn et al. (1984).

In sum, there is strong evidence that anxious groups differ from nonanxious groups in terms of an interpretative bias with ambiguous stimuli. As yet, the relative contributions of state and trait anxiety to that bias remain unclear. However, the evidence from studies of clinical anxiety is that the interpretative bias depends on a current state of clinical anxiety, because no good evidence of an interpretative bias has been found in recovered anxious patients. It may well be that the tendency of anxious patients to interpret ambiguous stimuli in a threatening fashion plays a part in the maintenance of the clinically anxious mood state.

NEGATIVE MEMORY BIAS: NONCLINICAL STUDIES

Research on individual differences in retention of threatening information in anxious groups has been much influenced by a study reported by Rogers, Kuiper, and Kirker (1977). They instructed their subjects to make judgments about words. The judgment tasks were as follows: self-referent judgments (i.e., describes you?); semantic judgments (i.e., means the same as?); and structural judgments (i.e., capital letters?). Their most striking finding was that the subjects who made self-referent judgments recalled many more words on a subsequent unexpected recall test than did any of the other groups of subjects. According to Rogers et al. (1977), everyone possesses an extensive self-schema that is activated by the task of making self-referent judgments, especially when the judgments are affirmative. Such a self-schema may provide a network containing numerous associations that assist the retrieval process.

It has been argued by several researchers that anxious individuals might differ from nonanxious ones on a modified version of the self-referent task used by Rogers et al. (1977). In essence, anxious individuals allegedly possess schemas relating to vulnerability and danger, whereas nonanxious individuals do not (cf. Beck & Emery, 1985). As a consequence, threat words related to their negative self-schemas should be relatively better recalled by anxious than by nonanxious groups, but the groups should not differ in their recall of positive or neutral words. This predicted pattern of results for anxious groups is generally termed negative memory bias.

Precisely the same logic has been applied in the case of depression, where it is assumed (e.g., by Beck, 1976) that depressed individuals have schemas based on worthlessness, guilt, rejection, personal deficiency, and deprivation. It has been found in studies using the self-referent task that depressed groups show a negative memory bias for negative words relevant to these self-schemas. This is a reasonably robust finding that has been obtained several times with both nonclinical depressed groups (see Blaney, 1986, for a review).

There have been a number of attempts to demonstrate the existence of a negative memory bias in nonclinical anxious groups. O'Banion and Arkowitz (1977) presented a series of positive and negative trait adjectives to their subjects and gave them all the same misleading information about which of the adjectives accurately described them. On a subsequent unexpected test of recognition memory, those subjects who were high in social anxiety recognized more of the negative trait adjectives than did those subjects who were low in social anxiety. However, the interaction between social anxiety and the emotional valence of the trait adjectives was not statistically significant, and so the findings do not provide support for a negative memory bias in the anxious group.

There is a major methodological problem with the study by O'Banion and Arkowitz (1977), which is that it is improbable that the subjects believed that all the trait adjectives that allegedly described them actually did so. Breck and Smith (1983) presented the same adjectives to their subjects and instructed some of them to decide whether each adjective was self-descriptive. On average, only approximately half the adjectives were rated as self-descriptive.

The study by Breck and Smith (1983) used subjects high and low in social anxiety. The subjects were informed that the experiment would be followed by social interaction or that it would not. An important finding on the unexpected test of free recall that followed the decision task was that there was a highly significant interaction between social anxiety and trait adjective valence. In this interaction, a higher proportion of negative self-descriptive adjectives was recalled by the anxious than by the nonanxious subjects, whereas the opposite was the case for recall of the positive self-descriptive adjectives. However, this interaction was significant only when the subjects anticipated a subsequent social interaction. Breck and Smith (1983) drew the following conclusions: "The results of the current investigation suggest that socially anxious subjects do have a more negative self-schema than do nonanxious subjects and that the self-schema may be activated when anticipating social interactions" (p. 75).

Kent (1985) divided his subjects into high and low anxious groups on the basis of the Dental Anxiety Scale. He investigated their memory for pain by comparing their experienced pain reported at the end of a dental appointment with the amount of pain they recalled having experienced when they were questioned 3 months later. The low anxious group of subjects had reasonably accurate memory for experienced pain, whereas the high anxious group recalled much higher levels of pain than had actually been experienced. This finding is consistent with the notion that those high in dental anxiety have a bias in their memory for negative events. However, Kent (1985) did not investigate memory bias for positive events, so it is not possible to be sure that the memory bias was specific to negative stimuli.

Norton, Schaefer, Cox, Dorward, and Wozney (1988) presented a list of neutral, anxiety-related, and anger-related words for learning on four trials. Each trial was followed by a test of free recall. Before the list was presented on the first trial, the subjects were given a paragraph describing someone having a panic attack, becoming very angry, or becoming hungry. The subjects themselves were either nonclinical panickers or nonpanickers. The panickers recalled significantly more anxiety-relevant words than the nonpanickers on the first two trials only, and only when they had been given the paragraph about someone having a panic attack. Thus, there was some evidence of a negative memory bias, but priming and/or induction of anxious mood state was required in order to obtain it.

Kennedy and Craighead (1988) carried out two experiments in which they asked various groups of subjects to estimate the number of times they had received positive and negative feedback during a learning task. Nonclinical anxious subjects did not differ from nonanxious subjects in their estimates for positive feedback. For negative feedback, however, anxious subjects gave higher estimates than nonanxious subjects, and this difference was statistically significant in the first experiment. A noteworthy feature is that these results were obtained with the level of depression equated between the two groups. Thus, there is evidence here of a negative memory bias in anxious subjects unconfounded by depression levels.

Mayo (1983) investigated the retrieval of real-life personal experiences in response to a series of words. Neuroticism (which correlates approximately +.7 with trait anxiety) predicted the number of unpleasant memories retrieved, even after controlling for the effect of mood state at the time of testing. Mayo (1989) carried out a very similar study and found that normals high in neuroticism tended to recall fewer happy memories. The effects of trait anxiety were stronger, with those high in trait anxiety retrieving fewer happy and more unhappy memories than those low in trait anxiety. As in the study by Mayo (1983), the associations between personality and types of memory retrieved were scarcely affected by mood at test.

It is not possible to provide an unequivocal interpretation of the findings reported by Mayo (1983, 1989). In essence, it is not clear whether individual differences in memorial processes were responsible, or whether it was simply that individuals varying in personality differ in the nature of the information they have stored in long-term memory. It should also be noted that the personality dimension of neuroticism is not precisely the same as that of trait anxiety, and so any effects of neuroticism on memory may not necessarily be attributable to anxiety per se.

Young and Martin (1981) used a self-referent task and discovered that normals high in neuroticism showed a negative recall bias. However, it is possible that individual differences in familiarity with the negative trait words was at least partially responsible for this bias effect. However, this interpretation cannot account for the findings obtained by Martin, Ward, and Clark (1983). They replicated the negative recall bias of Young and Martin (1981) among those high in neuroticism but found no evidence for selective bias when the encoding task involved the presentation of trait words descriptive of "a typical undergraduate from your college."

Because neuroticism correlates with depression scores, and because depression has been found to be associated with a negative memory bias, it could be argued that the findings of Young and Martin (1981) and of Martin et al. (1983) are due to the influence of depression rather than neuroticism or anxiety. However, it is important to note that Martin et al. (1983) assessed depression and discovered that it was neuroticism rather than depression that was responsible for the negative recall bias.

Evidence Against a Memory Bias

As Eysenck, MacLeod, and Mathews (1987) pointed out, anxious individuals show more evidence of a processing bias in favor of threat-related stimuli when the environment requires selection between a threatening and a neutral stimulus. If there is a selective processing bias, then it would seem reasonable to assume that a negative memory bias could be demonstrated more readily when the learning conditions permit the selective processing bias to operate. MacLeod (1990) investigated this issue by presenting pairs of words differing in their affective valence either sequentially or concurrently, with each word being presented to a different location. Presentation was followed by a cue indicating that the word previously presented at that location was to be recalled. Normals high and low in trait anxiety did not differ in their recall latencies for either threat-related or neutral words with sequential presentation. With concurrent presentation, high trait anxious subjects had longer latencies to recall threatening rather than neutral words, whereas low trait anxious subjects showed the opposite pattern. These results are totally inconsistent with the notion of an affect-congruent memory bias.

Further findings diametrically opposed to a negative memory bias in anxious individuals were reported by Watts, Trezise, and Sharrock (1986). They presented spider phobics and controls with a series of freeze-dried spiders mounted on cards. Recognition memory for the large spiders was worse for the spider phobics than for the controls. With small spiders, there was either no difference between the two groups, or a nonsignificant recognition superiority for the spider phobics.

One of the surprising characteristics of research on schemata in nonclinical anxious groups is the high level of reliance that has been placed on a high level of memory performance for schema-relevant information as an indication of an activated schema. This reliance may well be misplaced. Friedman (1979) found that objects that were inconsistent with the schema or frame that was activated were attended to more than those objects that were consistent. Subsequent recognition memory performance was much better for schema-inconsistent objects than for those that were consistent. Thus information that is consistent with a currently activated schema is sometimes not attended to or remembered.

Bartlett (1932), who was the first psychologist to make systematic use of the "schema" construct in explaining the phenomena of human memory, argued that the presence of schemas or schemata can be inferred from schema-relevant distortions and intrusions on a memory test. Such errors provide a rather different way of establishing the existence of an underlying schema. Calvo (1986) investigated errors made in recalling a text about a hypothetical student who was placed in an evaluation situation. The text was read after the subjects had been exposed to failure or success feedback, or no feedback, on a task. High trait anxious subjects made more negative intrusion errors in recall than low trait anxious subjects when they had previously experienced failure feedback, but not when they had received success feedback or no feedback. Calvo (1986) concluded that a negative schema was activated in high trait anxious subjects receiving failure feedback, and it was for this reason that schema-relevant intrusions were observed in recall. However, it is also possible that the intrusions simply reflect response bias rather than a genuine memorial phenomenon.

It is difficult to provide an assessment of the studies have been discussed in this section of the chapter. Several studies are less clear in their implications than would be desirable because of a failure to demonstrate that any group differences depend on anxiety rather than on depression. This is an important deficiency because measures of anxiety generally correlate quite highly with measures of depression (Watson & Clark, 1984).

Another problem is that some cases of negative memory bias in anxious individuals may have occurred simply because threat-related words are more familiar to anxious individuals than to nonanxious ones. It has often been found that common words are better recalled than rare words (see Eysenck, 1977). However, Breck and Smith (1983), Norton et al. (1988), and Martin et al. (1983) all discovered that a negative recall bias in anxious individuals was obtained in some conditions but not in others. If word familiarity were impor- tant, then there should have been a recall bias in all conditions.

In spite of the rather inconsistent nature of the findings, there is accumulating evidence for the existence of a negative memory bias in nonclinical anxious groups. Most of this evidence stems from experiments using the self-referent judgment task, and memory bias is more prevalent when there is priming of the relevant schema and/ or induction of an anxious mood state. This suggests that schemas need to be activated in order to produce a negative memory bias.

Supportive evidence was reported recently by Richards and Whittaker (1990). They discovered that state anxiety was positively related to the speed with which specific personal memories were retrieved to anxiety-related cue words. However, the contradictory nature of the evidence is shown by the findings of another recent study by Foa, McNally, and Murdock (1989). Their subjects were instructed to rate the self-descriptiveness of anxiety-related and positive adjectives, and this was followed by free recall. State anxiety was manipulated at both encoding and at recall but had no effect on the relative recall of anxiety-related words. However, anxiety-related words were recalled least often by subjects whose heart rate increased from encoding to recall.

How strongly does the available evidence support the theoretical position of Beck and Emery (1985), with its emphasis on negative self-schemas in anxious individuals? A problem with interpretations of data from the self-referment task has been identified by Klein and Kihlstrom (1986). They discovered that self-referent judgments do not lead to better recall than other kinds of semantic processing provided that the encoding task necessitates the organization of the stimulus material into categories. In other words, self-referent encoding has typically been confounded with categorical organization, and the latter factor appears to be more important than the former. It may thus not be necessary to assume that there are individual differences in self-schemas in order to account for the data.

IMPLICIT MEMORY BIAS:
NONCLINICAL STUDIES

We have focused so far on studies involving explicit memory rather than implicit memory. These terms were defined by Graf and Schacter (1985): "Implicit memory is revealed when performance on a task is facilitated in the absence of conscious recollection; explicit memory is revealed when performance on a task requires conscious recollection of previous experiences" (p. 501). All the studies considered so far used explicit memory, because the subjects were instructed to recall or to recognize the stimulus material that had been presented previously.

There is powerful evidence that different processes are involved in explicit and implicit memory. Most amnesic patients are substantially impaired in their ability to remember information acquired after the onset of amnesia when a test of explicit memory is used. In contrast, their performance is often at approximately the same level as that of normals when a test of implicit memory is used (see Eysenck & Keane, 1990).

Why is it of interest to investigate implicit memory for threatening materials in anxious individuals? Firstly, implicit memory appears to be less affected than explicit memory by the various strategies that subjects use at the time of encoding, and the fact that subjects are unaware that their memory is being tested presumably reduces the strategic complexity of the processes used at the time of test. As a consequence, implicit memory may possess certain advantages over explicit memory as a way of studying memory that is relatively uncontaminated by strategic factors. Secondly, because implicit memory differs qualitatively from explicit memory, it is by no means clear that the effects of anxiety on explicit memory will be duplicated in tests of implicit memory. If there are any differences in the effects obtained, then this could be very informative about the memorial processes influenced by anxiety.

Anne Richards (personal communication, 23rd April, 1991) has recently completed a study in which normals high and low in trait anxiety were presented with a set of words. They were then given a word-fragment completion task on which they were simply asked to write down any word they thought of that fitted the presented fragment (e.g., -SS–SS--). What was of interest was the tendency to complete the word fragments with list words. The high trait anxious subjects provided evidence of a negative memory bias on this test of implicit memory. However, when a test of explicit memory was used, there was no memory bias. The possible theoretical significance of a negative implicit memory bias in high trait anxious subjects is discussed later.

NEGATIVE EXPICIT MEMORY BIAS:
CLINICAL ANXIETY

We have already seen that there are various reasons for supposing that clinically anxious patients should exhibit a negative memory bias. It is certainly predicted by the theory proposed by Beck and Emery (1985), and by the theoretical position adopted by Bower (1981). In addition, there is evidence that anxious patients selectively attend to threat-related stimuli (e.g., MacLeod, Mathews, & Tata, 1986), and it might be expected that this selective bias would be associated with elevated levels of recall for threatening material by anxious patients.

If we exclude the methodologically suspect studies of Nunn et al. (1984) and of Pickles and van den Broek (1988) that have already been discussed, then the major relevant research in this area has been reported by Mogg, Mathews, and Weinman (1987), Mathews, Mogg, May, and Eysenck (1989), Mogg (1988), and McNally, Foa, and Donnell (1989). In all of the first three studies, the threatening negative stimuli used consisted of a mixture of social threat (e.g., stupid) and physical threat (e.g., mutilated) words.

Striking disconfirmation of the predicted negative memory bias was reported by Mogg et al. (1987) in a study using patients with generalized anxiety disorder and normal controls. The standard self-referent task was used with a mixture of positive threatening negative, and nonthreatening negative adjectives, or the subjects were asked to decide whether each adjective described a well-known television performer. There were subsequent unexpected tests of recall and recognition, and the anxious patients had relatively poorer memory for the threatening material than did the normal controls.

Mogg (1988) carried out several experiments in which generalized anxiety disorder patients were tested for their long-term retention of threat-related and neutral words. The patients showed no evidence of a negative memory bias in four experiments in which a recall test was used. In a fifth experiment, both intentional recall and recognition tests were utilized. The patients did not show a negative memory bias on the recognition-memory test, but they did exhibit a significant negative memory bias on the recall test. Overall, then, the results were by no means favorable to the prediction based on the theoretical positions of Beck and Emery (1985) and Bower (1981).

Further negative findings were reported by Mathews et al. (1989). They presented current generalized disorder patients, recovered generalized disorder patients, and normal controls with a series of threat-related words and nonthreatening words (positive or neutral in emotional tone), and instructed their subjects to imagine themselves in a scene involving themselves and the referent of each word. The three groups did not differ in their performance on a subsequent test of cued recall.

Mogg and Mathews (1990) used a self-referent and an other-referent task with generally anxious patients and with normal controls. On a subsequent test of free recall, the anxious patients showed some evidence of an affect-congruent recall (i.e., relative to controls, they tended to recall more threat-related words). However, there were indications in the data that this finding might simply be due to response bias. For example, the anxious patients produced relatively more threat-related intrusion errors, and the recall bias was observed regardless of whether the encoding task has involved self-reference or other-reference.

Apparently more positive findings were obtained by Greenberg and Beck (1989). They presented a list of positive and negative depression-relevant and anxiety-relevant adjectives, and each adjective had to be judged with respect to one of the following questions: "Describes you?"; "Describes the world?"; or "Describes the future?" This task was followed by free recall, with the scores of interest being the numbers of words recalled that had received "yes" judgments previously. Anxious patients did not differ from normal controls in their recall of "yes" rated depression-relevant adjectives; with "yes", rated anxiety-relevant adjectives, however, anxious patients recalled considerably more negative than positive adjectives, whereas the control subjects did not differ in their recall of the two types of adjectives. This finding appears to indicate the existence of a negative memory bias for anxiety-relevant adjectives by anxious patients. However, the anxious patients responded "yes" to far more negative anxiety-relevant adjectives than did the controls on the initial encoding task, and Greenberg and Beck (1989) only reported recall performance in terms of raw scores. Thus, the results almost certainly reflect the fact that anxious patients had many more negative anxiety-relevant adjectives than controls that they could potentially have recalled, and so it is not appropriate to claim that a negative memory bias has been found.

More convincing evidence was obtained by McNally et al. (1989). They presented panic-disordered patients and normal controls with a self-referent task or threat-related and nonthreat-related words. On a subsequent test of free recall, there was a significant interaction between group and word valence: panic-disordered patients recalled more threat-related than nonthreat-related words, whereas the normal controls showed the opposite tendency. However, the patients were significantly more depressed (as well as anxious) than the controls, and so it is possible that their memory bias was mediated by depression rather than anxiety.

In sum, it must be concluded that there is very little empirical support for the existence of a negative memory bias in anxious patients, at least when explicit memory is tested. This is rather striking in view of the numerous reports of a negative memory bias in depressed patients. One obvious implication is that at least some of the cognitive processes involved in anxiety are different from those involved in depression, in spite of the fact that anxiety and depression are related mood disorders. A further implication is that the notion that there is affect-congruent processing throughout the cognitive system (e.g., Beck & Emery, 1985; Bower, 1981) is incorrect. Other implications of the failure to detect a negative memory bias in anxious patients with episodic memory are discussed later in the chapter.

IMPLICIT MEMORY BIAS: CLINICAL ANXIETY

The failure of Mathews et al. (1989) to obtain a negative memory bias in anxious patients on a cued recall test has already been discussed. However, they also made use of an implicit memory test requiring word completion. Subjects were simply instructed to complete a word stem with the first word that came to mind, and the extent to which the previous presentation of list words increased the tendency to produce list words as completions was the measure of implicit memory. The currently anxious patients produced more word completions than the normal control that corresponded to threat-related list words, but fewer word completions corresponding to nonthreatening list words. In other words, the currently anxious patients exhibited a negative memory bias in implicit memory.

Mathews et al. (1989) included a group of recovered anxious patients. The performance of these patients on the word-completion task was closer to that of the normal controls than that of the currently anxious patients. This suggests that a clinically anxious mood state is required in order to obtain a negative memory bias in implicit memory, and that, therefore, this memory bias does not form part of a cognitive vulnerability factor.

MacLeod (1990) recently carried out a study in which both explicit and implicit memory were tested with anxious patients and normal controls. In the first part of the experiment, threat-related and neutral words were presented in a modified Stroop paradigm in which the colors in which the words were printed had to be named. Explicit memory was tested by means of a recognition-memory test, and implicit memory was tested by assessing perceptual thresholds for words that had and had not been presented on the modified Stroop. The extent to which perceptual thresholds were lower for previously presented words was the measure of implicit memory. The anxious patients had a significant negative memory bias on the test of implicit memory, but there was no evidence of a memory bias in explicit memory.

Whereas it would be very useful to have additional empirical evidence, it appears that anxious patients have a negative memory bias on tests of implicit memory, but not on tests of explicit memory. In order to make sense of these findings, it is obviously necessary to have a good theoretical understanding of the processes involved in explicit and implicit memory. Unfortunately, there are various different theoretical views here. Graf, Squire, and Mandler (1984) argued that implicit memory depends on automatic activation of the internal representations of the words presented to a subject; this activation can persist for hours. In contrast, explicit memory depends on elaboration, which involves the generation of links with other words. Roediger and Blaxton (1987) claimed persuasively that there is typically a confounding between whether explicit or implicit memory is tested and whether data-driven processes (i.e., those initiated directly be external stimuli) or conceptually driven processes (i.e., those initiated by subject) are involved. In other words, explicit memory usually involves conceptually driven processes, whereas implicit memory typically involves data-driven processes, and the distinction between data-driven and conceptually driven processes may be more important than the one between explicit and implicit memory.

THEORETICAL ANALYSIS

The findings on negative memory bias in anxious groups have been more complicated than was originally expected. In essence, high trait anxious normals sometimes exhibit an explicit memory negative memory bias (especially if the underlying schemas have been activated by priming or by induced mood) and they may also display an implicit memory negative memory bias. In contrast, anxious patients do not appear to have an explicit memory negative memory bias, but there are indications that they possess an implicit memory negative memory bias.

The theoretical positions of Bower (1981) and Beck and Emery (1985) led to the expectation that anxious groups (clinical or normal) should exhibit both an implicit and and explicit negative memory bias. The reason is that both network theory and schema theory imply that there should be affect-congruent processing throughout the cognitive system. It is clear, therefore, that these theories are oversimplified and cannot provide a satisfactory account of the findings. What is needed (although difficult to supply at present) is a much more detailed description of those cognitive processes and structures involved in memory that are affected by anxiety than is provided by either Bower (1981) or by Beck and Emery (1985).

The most puzzling finding from a theoretical perspective is the failure to demonstrate an explicit negative memory bias in anxious patients. This is especially so in view of the fact that such a bias has been shown several times with depressed patients (see Blaney, 1986). One possible way of accounting for the data is to argue that depressed patients possess negative schemas but anxious patients do not. However, one problem with that argument is the evidence that high trait anxious normals provide evidence consistent with the notion that they have negative schemas. If, as is assumed in this chapter, such individuals are more vulnerable than others to clinical anxiety, it would follow that at least a significant proportion of clinically anxious patients would also have negative schemas.

We favor an alternative approach that resembles that proposed by Williams, Watts, MacLeod, and Mathews (1988). This approach assumes that the encoding of threat-related and neutral information involves at least two major processes: relatively automatic or basic processes occurring at a preattentive level, and more controlled processes involving elaborate encoding of the presented stimulus. Threat-related stimuli may receive more relatively automatic processing among anxious than nonanxious groups. However, clinically anxious patients may have developed avoidance strategies that restrict the elaboration of processing; this is done because of the highly aversive effects of continued processing of threatening material. These avoidance strategies can sometimes counteract the greater automatic processing of threatening stimuli by anxious patients to such an extent that such patients will sometimes recall proportionately less threat-related material than controls (Mogg et al., 1987).

Why is that high trait anxious normals sometimes exhibit a negative memory bias in explicit memory? Presumably the reason is that they find elaborative processing of threat-related material to be less aversive than do clinically anxious patients. As a consequence, they do not restrict elaborative processing of such material, and so their performance on tests of explicit memory is not necessarily the same as that of high trait anxious normals.

It was mentioned earlier in the chapter that the precise mechanisms involved in implicit memory are not known. However, it seems probable that implicit memory depends primarily, or exclusively, on relatively automatic and basic processes. Because these processes are more active among anxious than nonanxious groups in the encoding of threat-related materials, it follows that there should be a negative memory bias in implicit memory for anxious groups.

Although we have attempted to provide an overall theoretical interpretation, there are many inconsistencies in the available data. If progress is to be made in the future, it will be necessary to address various issues. For example, the apparently discrepant findings in nonclinical studies may depend in part on the use of paradigms differing in encoding tasks, stimulus materials, retention measures, and so on. Another issue is that explicit memory strategies are likely to be influenced by instructions and other experimental demands. It may be "natural" for clinically anxious patients to avoid elaborate encoding of threat, but this may be reversed or obscured by forced encoding or intentional recall. Finally, it is necessary to attempt to disentangle the effects of anxiety and depression, but this is often not done.

In summary, it seems likely that anxious individuals have a disproportionate number of threatening events represented in their memory due to a bias in interpreting ambiguous events in a threatening way. As a consequence, an anxious individual's cognitive representation of the world may be as an unduly dangerous place, and this could serve to intensify their anxious mood state. However, anxious individuals sometimes are no better than nonanxious individuals at remembering unambiguously threatening information. Indeed, anxious patients sometimes have greater difficulty in retrieving such information, possibly due to avoidance of elaborate processing. This would appear to be consistent with the function of anxiety, which is to detect threat in the environment in order to take immediate appropriate action (e.g., if one is just about to be run over by a bus, it is not adaptive to engage in elaborate processing of its number).

Although representations of threat in memory are not necessarily more retrievable (i.e., no explicit memory bias in anxiety), such representations do seem to be more accessible (i.e., an implicit memory bias). Once activated (in a study phase), threat information is subsequently more likely to come to mind in anxious individuals. This increased accessibility of threat information in memory may explain the presence of persistent and recurrent anxiety-related thoughts (i.e., worry), which are not only a defining feature of generalized anxiety disorder, but which may also serve to maintain anxious mood state. Whereas this formulation is speculative, it seems clear that anxiety does not have a uniform effect on all aspects of processing of anxiety-related stimuli as assumed by Bower (1981) and by Beck and Emery (1985). Thus, in order to develop a comprehensive theory of anxiety, it is essential to establish the precise loci of anxiety-related biases within memorial processes.

ACKNOWLEDGMENT

Much of the research discussed in this chapter was funded by the Wellcome Foundation, London, England.

REFERENCES

Bartlett, F. C. (1932). *Remembering: A study in experimental and social psychology.* Cambridge: Cambridge University Press.
Beck, A. T. (1976). *Cognitive therapy and the emotional disorders.* New York: International Universities Press.

Beck, A. T., & Clark, D. A. (1988). Anxiety and depression: An information processing perspective. *Anxiety Research, 1,* 23–36.

Beck, A. T., & Emery, G. (1985). *Anxiety disorders and phobias: A cognitive perspective.* New York: Wiley.

Blaney, P. H. (1986). Affect and memory: A review. *Psychological Bulletin, 99,* 229–246.

Blaylock, B. A. H. (1963). *Repression sensitization, word asssociation responses, and incidental recall.* Unpublished master's thesis, University of Texas, Austin.

Bower, G. H. (1981). Mood and memory. *American Psychologist, 36,* 129–148.

Bower, G. H. (1987). Commentary on mood and memory. *Behaviour Research and Therapy, 25,* 443–456.

Breck, B. E., & Smith, S. H. (1983). Selective recall of self-descriptive traits by socially anxious and nonanxious females. *Social Behaviour and Personality, 11,* 71-76.

Byrne, D. (1964). Repression–sensitization as a dimension of personality. In B. A. Maher (Ed.), *Progress in experimental personality research* (Vol. 1, pp. 87–128). New York: Academic Press.

Calvo, M. G. (1986). Influencia de las condiciones evaluativas sobre la accessbilidad de representaciones aversivas. *Revista de Psicologia General y Applicada, 41,* 565–583.

Eysenck, M. W. (1977). *Human memory: Theory, research and individual differences.* Oxford: Pergamon.

Eysenck, M. W., & Keane, M. T. (1990). *Cognitive Psychology: A student's handbook.* London: Lawrence Erlbaum Associates.

Eysenck, M. W., & MacLeod, C., & Mathews, A. (1987). Cognitive functioning and anxiety. *Psychological Research, 49,* 189–195.

Eysenck, M. W., Mogg, K., May, J., Richards, A., & Mathews, A. (in press). Bias in interpretation of ambiguous sentences related to threat in anxiety. *Journal of Abnormal Psychology.*

Foa, E. B., McNally, R., & Murdock, T. B. (1989). Anxious mood and memory. *Behaviour Research and Therapy, 27,* 141–147.

Friedman, A. (1979). Framing pictures: The role of knowledge in automatised encoding and memory for gist. *Journal of Experimental Psychology: General, 108,* 316–355.

Graf, P., & Schacter, D. L. (1985). Implicit and explicit memory for new associations in normal and amnesic subjects. *Journal of Experimental Psychology: Learning, Memory and Cognition, 11,* 501–518.

Graf, P., Squire, L. R., & Mandler, G. (1984). The information that amnesic patients do not forget. *Journal of Experimental Psychology: Learning, Memory and Cognition, 10,* 164–178.

Greenberg, M. S., & Beck, A. T. (1989). Depression versus anxiety: A test of the content-specificity hypothesis. *Journal of Abnormal Psychology, 98,* 9–13.

Haney, J. N. (1973). Approach–avoidance reactions by repressors and sensitizers to ambiguity in a structured free-association task. *Psychological Reports, 33,* 97–98.

Kennedy, R. E., & Craighead, W. E. (1988). Differential effects of depression and anxiety on recall of feedback in a learning task. *Behavior Therapy, 19,* 437–454.

Kent, G. (1985). Memory of dental pain. *Pain, 21,* 187–194.

Klein, F. B., & Kihlstrom, J. F. (1986). Elaboration organisation and self-reference effect in memory. *Journal of Experimental Psychology: General, 115,* 26–38.

MacLeod, C. (1990). Mood disorders and cognition. In M. W. Eysenck (Ed.), *International review of cognitive psychology* (pp. 9–56). Chichester: Wiley.

MacLeod, C., Mathews, A., & Tata, P. (1986). Attentional bias in emotional disorders. *Journal of Abnormal Psychology, 95,* 15–20.

Martin, M., Ward, J. C., & Clark, D. M. (1983). Neuroticism and the recall of positive and negative personality information. *Behaviour Research and Therapy, 21,* 495–503.

Mathews, A., Mogg, K., May, J., & Eysenck, M. W. (1989). Implicit and explicit memory biases in anxiety. *Journal of Abnormal Psychology, 98,* 236–240.

Mathews, A., Richards, A., & Eysenck, M. W. (1989). Interpretation of homophones related to threat in anxiety states. *Journal of Abnormal Psychology, 98,* 31–34.

Mayo, P. R. (1983). Personality traits and the retrieval of positive and negative memories. *Personality and Individual Differences, 4,* 465–472.

Mayo, P. R. (1989). A further study of the personality-congruent recall effect. *Personality and Individual Differences, 10,* 247-252.

McKeon, J., Roa, B., & Mann, A. (1984). Life events and personality trait in obsessive–compulsive neurosis. *British Journal of Psychiatry, 144,* 185-189.

McNally, R. J., Foa, E. B., & Donnell, C. D. (1989). Memory bias for anxiety information in patients with panic disorder. *Cognition and Emotion, 3,* 27–44.

Mogg, K. (1988). *Processing of emotional information in clinical anxiety states.* Unpublished doctoral thesis, University of London.

Mogg, K. & Mathews, A. (1990) Is there a self-referent mood-congruent recall bias in anxiety? *Behaviour Research and Therapy, 28,* 91–92.

Mogg, K., Mathews, A., & Weinman, J. (1987). Memory bias in clinical anxiety. *Journal of Abnormal Psychology, 96,* 94–98.

Norton, G. R., Schaefer, E., Cox, B. J., Doneasd, J., & Wozney, K. (1988). Selective memory effects in non-clinical panickers. *Journal of Anxiety Disorders, 2,* 169–177.

Nunn, J. D., Stevenson, R. J., & Whalan, G. (1984). Selective memory effects in agoraphobic patients. *British Journal of Clinical Psychology, 23,* 195–201.

O'Banion, K. & Arkowitz, H. (1977). Social anxiety and selective memory for affective information about the self. *Social Behavior and Personality, 5,* 321–328.

Pickles, A. J., & van den Broek, M. D.(1988). Failure to replicate evidence for phobic schemata in agoraphobic patients. *British Journal of Clinical Psychology, 27,* 271–272.

Richards, A., & Whittaker, T. M. (1990). Effects of anxiety and mood manipulation in autobiographical memory. *British Journal of Clinical Psychology, 29,* 145–153.

Roediger, H. L., III., & Blaxton, T. A. (1987). Retrieval modes produce dissociations in memory for surface information. In D. S. Gorfein & R. R. Hoffman (Eds.) *Memory and cognitive processes: The Ebbinghaus Centennial Conference* (pp. 249–269). Hillsdale, NJ: Lawrence Erlbaum Associates.

Rogers, T. B., Kuiper, N. & Kirker, W. (1977). Self-reference and the encoding of personal information. *Journal of Personality and Social Psychology, 35,* 677–688.

Simpson, G. B. (1984). Lexical ambiguity and its role in models of word recognition. *Psychological Bulletin, 96,* 316–340.

Spielberger, C. D., Gorsuch, R., & Lushene, R. (1970). *The State Trait Anxiety Inventory (STAI) Test Manual.* Palo Alto, CA: Consulting Psychologists Press.

Watson, D., & Clark, L. A. (1989). Negative affectivity: The disposition to experience emotional states. *Psychological Bullet*in, 96, 465–490.

Watts, F. N., Trezise, L., & Sharrock, R. (1986). Processing of phobic stimuli. *British Journal of Clinical Psychology, 26,* 113–126.

Williams, J. M. G., Watts, F. N., McLeod, C., & Mathews, A. (1988). *Cognitive psychology and emotional disorders.* Chichester: Wiley.

Young, G. C. D., & Martin, M. (1981). Processing of information about self by neurotics. *British Journal of Clinical Psychology, 20,* 205–212.

19

Autobiographical Memory and Emotional Disorders

J. Mark G. Williams
University College of North Wales,
Bangor, Unitied Kingdom

INTRODUCTION

> I wake up in the morning and the depression hits me. I think "Oh God,
> I'm still here." My mind is flooded with all the things I've failed at—in
> the job I used to have, in looking after my children, in my marriage. Yes,
> there were some good times, but they'll never come back. I end up
> thinking "What's the point in carrying on?"

In psychotherapy with depressed people, such as the person who
spoke these words, it is not long before the person's past becomes an
important issue in therapy. Many research studies confirm that
emotionally disturbed people have experienced more losses and life
events in the remote as well as the recent past, in addition to many
chronic difficulties (Brown & Harris, 1978; see Brown, 1989, for a
recent review). For this patient, her job, her children, and her
marriage had been significant sources of stress for her.

In addition to these external sources of stress, however, the
cognitive theory of emotion (Beck, Rush, Shaw, & Emery, 1979;
Scott, Williams, & Beck, 1989) suggests that people who are prone to
emotional disorders are biased in the way they attend to and remember
their world, especially as it relates to the self. This theory would
suggest that the aforementioned patient's hopeless conclusion "What's
the point in carrying on?" comes from the interaction of real-life

451

stressors and an internal bias in the way information relating to the self is processed. Of all information-processing biases, a bias in memory for events in one's life is potentially one of the most disabling. Such a bias exacerbates the effect of negative life events, reduces self-esteem, and ultimately undermines attempts to cope with current problems. The aim of the research reported in this chapter is to investigate such memory biases associated with emotional disorders. Understanding more about the causes and mechanisms underlying such biases will allow clinicians to develop better techniques for reversing them. Early studies in this field were concerned with whether a bias existed and how it should best be measured. Although the initial impetus for this research came from observation of clinical patients, much of this early work necessarily involved laboratory studies using mood induction to analogize emotional disturbance. However, in reviewing the more recent studies, I focus on understanding memory processes in emotionally disturbed patients.

Mood and Autobiographical Memory

Lloyd and Lishman (1975) used a list of neutral words as stimuli to cue memories in clinically depressed patients attending the Maudsley Hospital in London. Patients were instructed to recall either a pleasant or an unpleasant memory, and to signal to the experimenter by tapping on the table when a suitable memory came to mind. The time taken to retrieve memories to each cue word was recorded by stopwatch. They found that the more severe the depression, measured by the Beck Depression Inventory, the quicker the patient was to retrieve an unpleasant memory.

There were two major problems in interpreting these results however. First, the more severely depressed patients may have had more genuinely depressing experiences, so they may have found it easier to retrieve any one of them. Secondly, the more severely depressed may simply have been evaluating more of their neutral or ambiguous experiences as more unpleasant, thus spuriously inflating the number of memories from which to choose. Both of these were taken into account in later research by John Teasdale and co-workers at Oxford. The first used nondepressed volunteers whose moods had been experimentally manipulated using Velten's (1968) negative and positive self-statements (Teasdale & Fogarty, 1979). In this case, subjects were randomly allocated to "elation" or "depression" conditions so that the amount of actual depressive experiences could be assumed to be equal prior to mood induction. Despite this,

.they found that latencies to remember positive or negative personal events were biased. Both this and later experiments showed that the memories recalled were actually pleasant or unpleasant (when rated in neutral mood), and so the bias could not simply be explained in terms of the overinclusive effects of depressed mood (Teasdale, Taylor, & Fogarty, 1980).

Further research used clinically depressed individuals selected for the presence of diurnal variation of mood (Clark & Teasdale, 1982). Patients were given words as cues and asked to respond with the first personal memory that came to mind. These memories were later rated for pleasantness/happiness. Two independent effects were observed. First, happy memories were less probable and depressing memories more probable when patients were more depressed. When the same patients were at the less depressed point in their cycle, this picture was reversed—patients were now more likely to respond to the cues with happy memories than unhappy memories. These within-subject results clearly cannot be explained with reference to different frequencies of actual depressive experiences. Second, ratings of the experiences were also mood dependent, the events being rated more negatively the more depressive the current mood. This effect was not by itself sufficient to explain the memory biasing, however. Similar results have been found by Fogarty and Hemsley (1983). They conducted a longitudinal study of depressed patients, testing them when depressed, and again when the depression had reduced. They found that reduction in depression was associated with an increase in probability of happy memories and a decrease in probability of sad memories.

Results consistent with those of Teasdale have been found using mood induction procedures other than the Velten technique (e.g., hypnosis, Gilligan & Bower, 1984; Autobiographical Recollections Method, Salavoy & Singer, 1985). Gilligan and Bower (1984) asked subjects to keep diaries for 1 week, noting any positive or negative events (time, place, gist) and giving an intensity rating. One week after handing in the diary, subjects were randomly allocated to two groups. Subjects were hypnotized and either a happy or depressed mood suggested. Percentage recall of happy incidents averaged 32% for both types of recall mood. However, this proportion fell to 23% for those subjects recalling negative events in happy mood and rose to 38% for those subjects recalling negative events in sad mood. In another study, subjects spent 10 minutes generating memories from childhood, giving details of the gist, time, and place, while either in hypnotically induced happy or sad mood. Next day they returned and rated the memories (in neutral mood) for how positive or negative they were. Ninety-two percent of memories recalled by "happy" subjects were positive, compared with 45% for the "sad" subjects.

These findings imply that the biases in autobiographical memory found in emotionally disturbed patients were not artefactual. Bias induced by mood induction parallels that which occurs in clinical depression. Methods of cueing personal memory have also been varied without affecting the nature of the results. Lloyd and Lishman (1975) and Teasdale and Fogarty (1979) used neutral words and told subjects to retrieve a pleasant or an unpleasant memory to each cue. Teasdale et al., (1980) and Clark and Teasdale (1982) used neutral words but allowed subjects to retrieve any personal memory that was later rated for its hedonic valence. Gilligan and Bower (1984) did not use any specific cues, allowing subjects to recall anything that came to mind from their diary or their childhood.

These studies have been helpful in establishing the reliable association between memory and current mood state, but they are not without problems. First, they have focused on depression, and although recent evidence suggests that anxious mood in normal subjects has a similar priming effect on their memories for threatening situations (Richards & Whittaker, 1990), this has yet to be reliably demonstrated in anxious patients. We need to know whether mood-memory biasing phenomena occur in other clinical conditions and is associated with a wider range of moods.

Second, despite the fact that the early work by Lloyd and Lishman (1975) and by Teasdale and Fogarty (1979) were carried out without reference to network models, most recent work has adopted the network model as its framework. The problems with this framework, including many nonreplications of the original findings that supported its heuristic value (see Bower & Mayer, 1985; Hasher, et al., 1985), are now widely recognized (see Blaney 1986; Williams, Watts, MacLeod, & Mathews, 1988, pp. 82–90 for fuller discussion).

One of the problems is that network models of memory have developed independently of recent research on autobiographical memory. In particular, experiments within the network framework have confined attention to the *probability* or *latency* with which positive or negative items are retrieved, given congruent or incongruent moods at encoding or retrieval. These effects are then simply taken to reflect either the structure of the network or the levels of activation of particular emotion nodes and their associates within the network. This emphasis neglects other concerns that have been more central to autobiographical memory theorists: the search strategies involved in retrieval from autobiographical memory; the relation of memories for public events to those for private events; the time course of acquisition and decay of autobiographical memory, etc. (see Neisser & Winograd, 1988; Rubin, 1986 for reviews).

In our research on autobiographical memory associated with emotional disturbance, our data forced us to confront these issues. I therefore describe our findings and what alternative models we have adopted to make sense of them. I then describe our attempts to narrow the causes and mechanisms of the memory phenomena we observed, and to draw out clinical and theoretical implications from the work.

Emotional Disturbance: Suicidal Behavior as a Paradigm Case

Parasuicide (or "deliberate self-harm"—over 90% by overdose of drugs) remains one of the most common reasons for acute emergency admission to medical wards in the United Kingdom. Rates vary between 2.5 to 3.0 per thousand, per year. There is still no physical or psychological intervention that reliably reduces the risk of repetition of parasuicide (though Dialectical Behaviour Therapy, Linehan, 1988, and Problem Solving Therapy, Salkovskis, Atha, & Storer, 1990, may, if replicated, offer hope). Many parasuicide episodes are impulsive. Over half these patients have thought about harming themselves only for 1 hour or less before the event occurs. Even those who have more suicidal intent and have been thinking about it for longer know what resources are available to help them but do not use them. For example, most patients know of the existence of, or even the telephone number of, Crisis Intervention Centers and Suicide Prevention Centers in their locality, but they do not make use of them during the crisis. Our original aim was to understand more about the state of mind of such people prior to such episodes that change stress into a suicidal crisis. However, the research has broadened to apply to any situation in which negative events are responded to in catastrophic ways, a phenomenon that is commonly seen in depressed as well as suicidal patients. We started with the assumption that, immediately prior to a crisis, the person does not use available resources and is not amenable to persuasion, partly because he or she can remember nothing but a string of failures, arguments, and disappointments. If this were the case, one might expect this bias to still be present in many patients immediately after the attempt.

Williams and Broadbent (1986) studied patients within a few days of admission following deliberate self-poisoning, after the psychopharmacalogical effects of the overdose were no longer apparent. Patients' latencies to retrieve specific autobiographical memories to positive or negative cue words (e.g., happy, angry) were compared with nondepressed patients from the same hospital and volunteer subjects, matched for age, sex, and educational level. As one might expect, overdose patients were more depressed, anxious, confused, hostile, fatigued, and less vigorous than the two control groups that did not differ from each other. (The Profile of Mood Scales was used as our mood measure; McNair, Lorr, & Droppleman, 1981). The overdose patients were also significantly more hopeless on the Beck Hopelessness Scale (Beck, Weissman, Lester, & Trexler, 1974). Results of the autobiographical memory cueing task showed that the overdose patients took longer than controls to retrieve a memory when given a positive cue word (see Fig. 19.1), but were comparable to controls when given a negative cue word, confirming that a bias against memories that were incongruent with current mood was present in these patients.

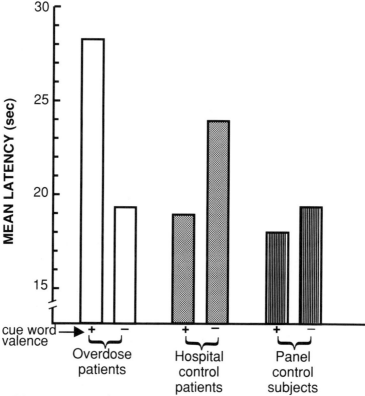

FIG. 19.1. Mean latencies to retrieve specific autobiographical memories in response to positive or negative cue-words (Williams & Broadbent, 1986).

Level of Specificity in Retrieval. In addition to these results there was one feature of the results that particularly interested us. Despite the fact that we had asked subjects to retrieve specific memories, the overdose patients tended, as a first response to the cues, to retrieve inappropriately general memories: memories referring to people, places, activities, or objects, where a time period was not referred to)[1] Table 19.1 gives some examples from the protocols of control and overdose subjects. Control patients' first responses tend to focus on

TABLE 19.1
Examples of Controls' and Overdose Patients'
Autobiographical Memory Responses
(cumulative latencies to first word of response given in parentheses)

	Control	*Patient*
HAPPY	(10) The day we left to go on holiday	(8) When I'm playing squash (18) When I beat my policeman friend 3 weeks ago*
SORRY	(6) When I dropped something and my flatmates got annoyed	(3) When I've had to do something (12) When I lie to my mum
SAFE	(13) Down in London last week-end getting off the bus at 4am	(6) When I'm at home in my house (15) When Stuart's around
ANGRY	(6) With my supervisor on Monday	(6) When I've had a row (16) A month ago I stormed off in a car*
CLUMSY	(1) I spilt some milk on holiday	(1) I fall down the stairs (20) It happens so often (35) A month ago when the Jehovah's witnesses came to the door*
SUCCESSFUL	(1) When I passed my driving test	(2) In my job until the company went bankrupt (15) Building up the sales force (25) One of the reps. sent me a letter*

Note: These items are specific memories retrieved following prompting.

[1]Reliability of the allocation of memories to general/specific categories was checked after completion of the experiment by having two independent judges categorize a random 10% sample of the 750 responses obtained. This yielded 87% and 93% agreement with the experimenter's categories.

particular days and times. By contrast, overdose patients' memories were over general and often needed to be prompted before they retrieved a specific memory, and it was this extra prompting and the request for additional responses that was largely responsible for the longer latency to retrieve positive memories.

When we looked at the proportion of first responses that were over general, our initial impressions were confirmed statistically (see Fig. 19.2). There were two significant effects. There was a main effect $[F(2, 67) = 11.73; p < .001]$ due to the overdose group being more overgeneral for both positive and negative memories. Second, there was a significant Group by Cue Valence interaction, $(F(2, 67) = 4.24;$

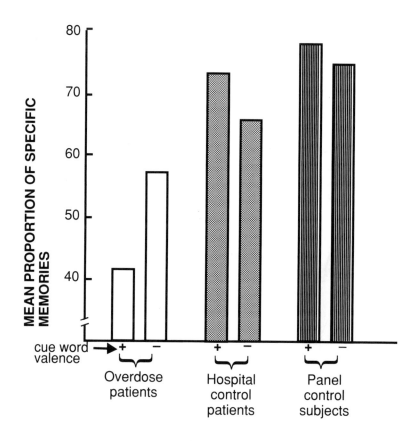

FIG. 19.2.   Mean proportion of responses that were specific memories (Williams & Broadbent, 1986).

$p < .025$) due to overdose patients finding it especially difficult to be specific in response to positive cue words.

Could this phenomenon be due to the effects of drugs? We had given patients and controls in this study a semantic processing task that was known to be sensitive to the effects of drugs (Baddeley, 1981). In this task the person says whether sentences are true or false (e.g., "pork chops are meat," "doctors are sold in pairs"). Patients make 50 true/false decisions, as quickly as they can, making as few errors as possible. The times taken to make decisions on 50 sentences were 116, 112, and 77 seconds for the overdose, hospital, and nonhospital controls, respectively, ($F(2, 69) = 7.52$, $p < .005$). The nonhospital control group was faster than the two hospital groups (Duncan's test, $p < .005$ in each case), but the overdose and hospital control group did not differ from each other. Note how this pattern is different from the autobiographical memory results in which the overdose group differed from both the control groups that did not themselves differ from each other. These data strongly suggest that the tendency to give overgeneral memories is not simply due to the effect of the drugs.

The alternative possibility is that the overdose group was sampling memories from a more distant time period in their lives. Recent work by Pillemer, Goldsmith, Panter, and White, (1988) has shown that older memories tend to be more generalized. However, we had asked all subjects and patients for details of the age of the memories. We found no differences between the groups in the time interval from which their memories were taken.

We were interested in pursuing this phenomenon further because of its relevance to therapy with emotionally disturbed patients. Such patients can often retrieve general classes of information about themselves or their families but find it difficult to retrieve specific examples (Truax & Carkhuff, 1967; Wahler & Afton, 1980; Williams, 1984, p.120). It appeared that although we had started out to investigate latency biases in autobiographical memory, our data was encouraging us to confront another important aspect of memory: the level of generality or specificity retrieval. The results raised questions that had not been addressed within network paradigms: How do people specify the level of detail in a memory? What processes exist to enable people to stop searching memory when they have reached their predefined criteria of specificity? How do emotional disturbances affect these processes?

We needed to find alternative models of memory that made more explicit reference to the processes by which information is encoded into and retrieved from memory and move away from models of memory that focused exclusively on the associative structures.

Alternatives to Network Models[2]

Examining the retrieval protocols of the suicidal patients in Table 19.1, it appears that as a minimum the following stages or aspects of cued retrieval of personal memories are involved: (a) elaborating/defining the cue word; (b) retrieving a plausible context (activity, place, etc.); (c) generating possible episodes as example of the chosen context; (d) checking appropriateness; (e) responding. This description is consistent with many previous accounts of retrieval processes but shares most in common with three statements by M. D. Williams and Hollan (1981), by Reiser, Black, and Abelson (1985), and by Kolodner (1985). For example, M. D. Williams and Hollan (1981) attempted to characterize retrieval from very long-term memory (trying to remember the names of high school classmates). They view retrieval as "a process in which some information about a target item is used to construct a description of the item and this description is used in attempts to recover new fragments of information" (p.87). They start from the assumption that a person encodes only a limited amount of possible information (an incomplete list of features or properties or a partial image); and that to encode or retrieve any packet of information, a partial description is formed that provides an initial entry point in to the memory (Norman & Bobrow, 1979); that is, the description acts as an index for the memory packet. Clearly, there may be some aspects of their model that are determined by the specific nature of their task, but their subprocesses of retrieval, "find a context," "search," and "verify," appear to map closely onto the retrieval stages apparent in our patients' protocols.

Similarly, Reiser et al., (1985) summarized their principle processing claims for autobiographical memory search as follows: First, experiences are retrieved by accessing the knowledge structure used to encode the event and then by specifying features that discriminate

---

[2]Note that I am not saying that the network model is "wrong." There is no contradiction between the network and processing accounts of memory. Network models are concerned with interconnections within the structure of the memory trace, whereas processing accounts deal with how the trace is encoded and retrieved. My point is that the memory data we were seeing in our patients were best accommodated by looking elsewhere than toward interconnections within a network, and at trying to understand aspects of the memories not accessible by the probability or latency of negative/positive responses.

an event with the target features from others indexed within that context. Second, the retrieval query is elaborated using general information contained in the knowledge structures to predict additional features of the target event, thus directing search to paths likely to lead to that event (Reiser et al., 1985, p. 95).

Although the notion that personal memories are organized in semantic categories has been criticized (Conway & Bekerian, 1987), there is a general agreement that there are "organizing contexts" or "descriptions" that are important both for encoding and retrieval of personal memories. The indices that link the contexts to specific episodes are defined as those aspects of episodes that distinguish them from other similar situations or activities (Schank & Abelson, 1977). Although the experimental findings of Williams and Broadbent (1986) were made independently of the preceding models, the advantage of viewing the results in terms of these descriptions frameworks (Norman & Bobrow, 1979) is clear, because they have implications for how the system might be affected and in turn might affect emotional disturbance. We assume that our patients were accessing an "intermediate description" but stopping short of a specific example. If this is the case (see Fig. 19.3), then perhaps overdose patients need particular help in forming appropriate descriptions.

Process:	Elaborate the Cue →	Retrieve Approximate→ Context	Use Indices to Retrieve Candidate Episodes	Check → Appropriateness → of Candidate	Respond
		↑	↑		
Two Possible "blocks":		(a) context inappropriate or incomplete	(b) cannot use indices to search for episodes (search may be effortful or indices inappropriately specified)		
Remedial strategy:	↑ Give appropriate context (e.g., Activity)				

FIG. 19.3. Possible ways in which retrieval process may be blocked in emotionally disturbed patients.

Providing "Descriptions" to Aid Specific Retrieval

Williams and Dritschel, (1988) added activity cues to emotional words (e.g., "going for a walk" was added to the cue "fatigue") to see if these cues would provide a more adequate description to increase the specificity of overdose patients' memory. If this failed to help, we might conclude that patients are able to generate appropriate descriptions but cannot, or do not, use them to search the indices appropriately.

Once again, patients admitted to medical wards at Addenbrooke's Hospital following self-poisoning were interviewed after recovering from the overdose (range 12 hours to 10 days following admission). Subjects from the Applied Psychology Unit Subject Panel matched for age and educational level with the patient group were used as control group. All completed the Profile of Mood Scale (Short Form), Hopelessness Scale, and the Autobiographical Memory Test in which half the 10 positive and 10 negative words were paired with an additional activity cue (e.g., sickness—travelling by train). For the trials where no activity cue was presented, the emotion words were accompanied by the phrase "any event at all." The time taken to make any response to the cue was recorded using a stopwatch. If the first response was overgeneral, further prompting was given, and latency to the first word of the subsequent responses was recorded cumulatively.

Results on the Autobiographical Memory Test showed that the latency to recall a specific memory (after prompting by the experimenter if necessary) was significantly longer for the Overdose (17.4 secs) than Controls (13.3 secs); ($p < .005$). However, the fact that this difference was once again due to the greater need to prompt overdose patients is suggested by the fact that the time taken to make a first response did not differ between the groups (Overdose, $M = 11.3$ secs, $S.D.$ 5.7; Controls, $M = 10.9$ secs, $S.D.$ 5.4). This suggests that the overdose patients were not generally more sluggish to respond. However, as in the previous study, the memories of the overdose subjects were more likely to be overgeneral [$F(1, 46) = 23.1; p < .001$] (see Fig19.4). Furthermore, the tendency to be overgeneral was again more evident for overdose subjects when they attempted to retrieve positive memories (Group × Valence Interaction: $F(1, 46) = 5.95$; $p < .025$).

Figure 19.5 shows the effect of adding activity cues to emotion word cues on response specificity. There was no evidence that activity cues helped people to retrieve more specific memories. It made no difference to the suicidal patients, and the slight difference for control subjects was not statistically reliable. This suggests that, even when contexts are provided, the clinical group remains unable to use these to retrieve specific episodes. If there is a retrieval deficit, it appears to occur after the generation of the intermediate description. Perhaps then they cannot use these descriptions to derive adequate cues for recollection.

UNDERSTANDING OVERGENERAL MEMORIES:
POSSIBLE CAUSES

In attempting to understand this phenomenon of overgeneral recall, it is helpful to distinguish between causation and mechanism. "Causes" include those factors internal or external to the person (e.g.,

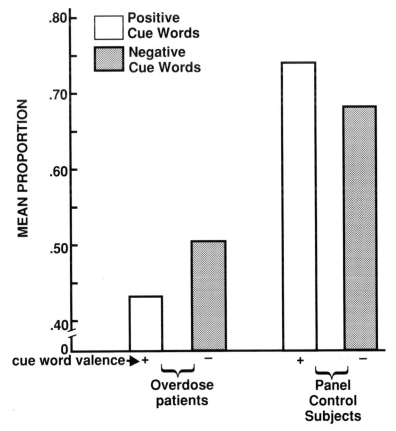

FIG. 19.4.   Mean proportion of responses that were specific memories (Williams & Dritschel, 1988).

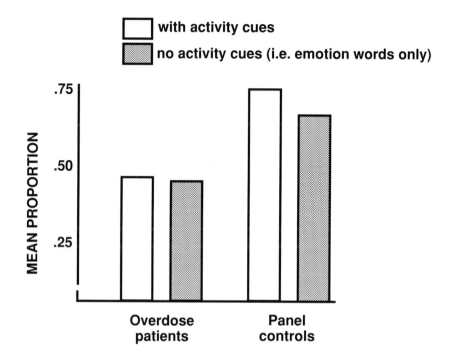

FIG. 19.5. Mean proportion of specific memories in response to emotion words with or without additional activity cues.

mood, cognitive style, recent life events) that contribute to the effects in question. "Mechanisms" include those individual, or combination, of cognitive processes, that are being affected by the causes. Let us look first at the possible causes.

First, it is possible that there is something peculiar about suicidal people or suicidal crises that brings about overgeneral memory. It would be helpful to study a group of patients who were depressed but not suicidal. Second, we need to ask whether such a phenomenon is caused by short-term factors brought about by the crisis, or long-term, more stable aspects of the person's cognitive style. To address this, it is helpful to study patients who have recovered from their crises. Third, if there are short-term factors involved, how much can the transient mood disturbance generated by an event be blamed, and how much may the event itself be disrupting memory quite apart from mood.

Is Overgeneral Recall Peculiar
to Suicidal Patients?

We have done two studies that suggest that the phenomenon of overgeneral recall is not confined to these patients. Williams and Scott (1988) gave positive and negative cue words to 20 depressed in-patients. They had not recently attempted suicide and were not currently suicidal. They were matched with normal subjects on age, sex, educational level, and performance on Baddeley's (1981) Semantic Processing Task. Figure 19.6 shows the probability that the first response would be a *specific* memory.

It is clear that the depressed patients show a pattern of response similar to overdose subjects. The depressed patients as compared to the controls are much less likely to give specific memories as their first response to the cue words, $(F(1, 38) = 32.0, p < .001)$, and they show the same differential pattern of specificity in response to pleasant and unpleasant cue words (Group × Cue Valence interaction, $F(1, 38) = 13.4, p < .001$); that is, there is a significantly greater tendency to be specific in response to negative (50%) than positive (30%) cue words, $t(19) = 2.97, p < .01$). In summary, both suicidal

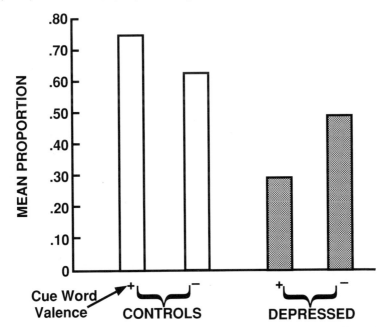

FIG. 19.6.   Mean proportion of specific memories in controls and depressed patients in response to positive and negative cue-words (Williams & Scott, 1988).

patients and major depressives tend to be inappropriately general and especially in response to positive cue words.

Another study of depressives allowed us to extend our findings by examining whether the phenomenon generalizes to a situation using different kinds of cueing procedures. As part of the research on depressed patients' perceptions of how much social support they receive, Moore, Watts, and Williams (1988) presented eight positive and eight negative scenarios to depressed patients and matched controls. In each case, subjects were asked to have a particular person in mind (e.g., "a neighbor helped me with some practical problem"; "my partner criticized me"). The subject's task was to recall specific instances in response to these cues. The percentage of first responses that were inappropriately general was 40% for depressives and 19% for controls, $F(1, 32) = 11.07, p < .01$). The fact that these patients were overgeneral in their memories is consistent with our own findings using different methods of cueing.

The Effect of Transient Mood and Circumstances Versus Cognitive Style

The fact that overgeneral recall can be found in depressed patients shows that a recent suicide attempt is not a necessary precondition for this form of memory deficit. But it remains unclear whether overgeneral recall is caused by transient factors at time of recall. First, both suicidal patients and depressed patients were disturbed in their mood at time of testing. Second, recent events and circumstances (e.g., the stress of hospitalization) could affect memorial processes quite apart from current affective disturbance.

Alternatively, individuals who are prone to give up under stress, take an overdose, or become depressed may have either a different cognitive style or a genuinely disrupted personal history in which positive events have been rare. These relatively permanent characteristics may contribute both to lack of specificity in memory retrieval and to more widespread vulnerability to react to stress maladaptively. Either transient or trait factors may operate independently or interactively to determine either overall levels of recall specificity or the relatively greater difficulty these patients have with positive memories.

To help determine the extent to which state or trait factors are responsible for overgeneral recall, a group of subjects were recruited who had taken an overdose some time before. Williams and Dritschel (1988) interviewed 16 recovered patients who had taken an overdose between 3–14 months prior to the interview. They were given 10 positive and 10 negative cue words. Results (shown in Fig. 19.7 that include the previous data from *current* overdose patients and controls for comparison) showed that the recovered patients had become more specific in response to positive cues, but their negative memories remained overgeneral. The proportion of responses to positive and negative cues that were specific memories was .61 and .46, respectively, $t(15) = 3.15$, $p < .01$). The overall effect was that recovered patients remained more overgeneral than normal but showed the more normal pattern of being more specific for positive events in their life.

But the question could be raised whether these people really were recovered in their *mood*? In fact, both our clinical evaluations and the results of the Profile of Mood Scale suggested that, whereas eight of the patients were truly recovered, the other eight remained very disturbed in their mood, despite the absence of a recent suicidal crisis.

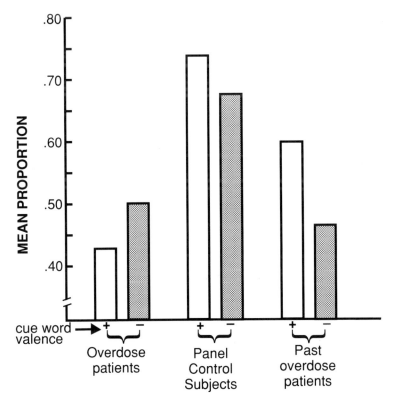

FIG. 19.7.   Proportion of specific memories in people who have taken an overdose in the past (overdose and panel groups for comparison).

To examine the effect of mood on memory, we divided the recovered patients into two subgroups. The "nondisturbed" recovered patients (N = 8) had a level of disturbance that was comparable with the control group from the previous study. The "disturbed" group's mood was as disturbed as that of the overdose patients in the previous study. The mean scores of hopelessness for these two subgroups were 3.1 (*SD* 3.7) and 14.5 (*SD* 4.2) for the nondisturbed and disturbed groups, respectively.

Figure 19.8 shows the number of first responses that were specific autobiographical memories for each recovered patient in these two subgroups. Only 3 out of the 16 patients gave more specific memories in response to negative cue words (2 in the disturbed group and 1 in the nondisturbed group). It is clear from these series of patients that

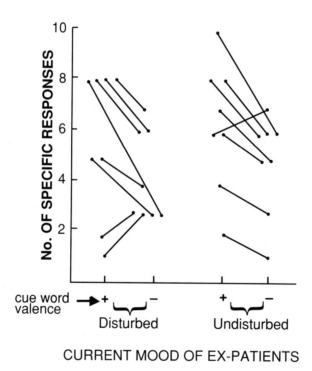

FIG. 19.8. Number of specific responses given in response to 10 positive and negative cue-words by each expatient.

one cannot discriminate between the memory performance of people who have very high from those who have very low levels of current mood disturbance. Transient affective disturbance does not account either for the general tendency to give overgeneral memories, or for the interaction with cue valence.

Conclusions about Causes

The pattern of results we have obtained suggests the following conclusions. First, we need to move beyond studying whether positive or negative events are more accessible to studying the way in which they are encoded or retrieved and learn how this affects the quality of the memory (how specific or general). Second, we need to distinguish between the *overall* tendency to be overgeneral (the "main effect" in these experiments) from the *relative* tendency to be more overgeneral in response to positive or negative cues (the interaction with cue valence). The main effect appears a relatively stable aspect of emotionally disturbed individuals. It is not dependent on transient mood disturbance, and not a function of being in the midst of a current crisis or having recently suffered hospitalization.

By contrast, the extent to which overgeneral memories are given in response to positive or negative cue words (the interaction) appears to depend on more transient factors. At the outset there were two main candidates for what these transient factors may be: (a) current mood disturbance, or (b) the disruption of context due to recent crises including hospitalization. The data presented in Fig. 19.8 argue strongly against mood disturbance as a mediator of cue-valence effects on specificity. Both disturbed and nondisturbed groups showed the more "normal" pattern of greater specificity for positive than negative memories. The alternative explanation is thus more likely to be correct: that occurrence or nonoccurrence of a recent stressful event will determine whether positive or negative events will be the most difficult to retrieve specifically.

In summary, the current data suggest that two components to overgeneral recall may be distinguished: a stable tendency to be nonspecific whatever the valence of the memory that is being retrieved; and a tendency for this to be more evident for positive or negative memories, which depends on whether recent negative events dominate the retrieval context. Neither component of overgeneral recall appears to be mood dependent. Let us now examine in more detail the encoding and retrieval problems these patients may have.

UNDERSTANDING OVERGENERAL MEMORY:
POSSIBLE MECHANISMS

The Encoding Dysfunction

We suggest that intermediate levels of description are used by subjects both at encoding and at retrieval, and that overgeneral recall in suicidal and depressed patients is a function of both encoding and retrieval processes. Overgeneral encoding may be illustrated by the following example. Suppose you are in a supermarket looking for a certain brand of breakfast cereal. After searching for some time, you realize that it was in front of you all the while. That might be encoded as an episode of failure to find that particular cereal, or as a failure to find one way around that shop, or as one instance amongst many recent failures to find what one is looking for. The important point to note is that affective significance is more likely to attach to the more general encoding context. Of all the multiple levels at which an episode can be encoded, the levels that carry most affect are the more general, because they evaluate behaviors according to longer term criteria. If one is feeling upset for any reason, one will tend to preferentially encode the affectively significant aspect of the situation. By the nature of what this aspect is likely to be—the more general aspects—the episode will be encoded as one instance of a long series (for example, a depressive person may link such episodes together so that each is seen as further evidence of impending dementia). The trace that is laid down may vary in its discriminability from other traces, mnemonic cues that are associated with the to-be-encoded material may differ in their specificity, or the to-be-encoded episode may be absorbed into a schematic representation of like instances without many individual tags or indices. Whichever precise mechanism is involved, a consequence of such preferential encoding at a more general level would be that subsequent recollection of a specific episode might be relatively poor, but access to the general class of memories would be favored. In sum, emotionally disturbed individuals tend to focus on and therefore encode the affective aspects of situations. These aspects tend to be those encoding features that link the specific episode to a generic class of events. The preferential encoding of hedonically valent (and thus generic) features explains why recall may be overgeneral even when retrieval mood is normal. These patients have developed, over time, intermediate descriptions that contain more information that is both generic and emotionally self-relevant.

The Retrieval Dysfunction

Such overgeneral encoding of hedonic memories may render the person vulnerable to particular difficulties when they attempt to retrieve such memories. Their overall difficulty in being specific will be compounded if there are insufficient retrieval cues to help the recollection process. When someone has suffered a recent life event or been recently hospitalized, there are few positive stimuli, and many more negative stimuli, which are available as contextual cues to help search for specific memories. The relative ease or difficulty of being specific in search for a positive or negative memory is thus explicable in terms of the availability of positive or negative contextual cues to help the recollection process at retrieval.

I do not mean to assert that this account is the only way of describing the mechanisms underlying overgeneral recall in our patients. For example, it is possible that patients are overgeneral because it is more effortful to be specific, either at encoding or retrieval or both. This is an attractive notion, especially in the way it would account for the retrieval phenomena. The use of contextual description to generate mnemonic cues, and the use of such cues in searching for specific episodes, may demand more effort than these patients are able or willing to expend. If they take longer to reach even the first (general) level, they may then abort the search prematurely. The result would be to respond with the currently available output, a general memory. However, despite being attractive, cognitive effort models leave unspecified which aspect of the encoding or retrieval process is most effortful. Furthermore, without independent measures of effort, such models tend to lead to circular arguments, where any deficit is explained in terms of its effortfulness and any facilitation is explained by assuming the task required less effort!

A question that this research does not address is how much emotionally disturbed patients are nonspecific in their memory as a deliberate strategy. It is possible that they stop short of the recall of specific episodes as a strategy to avoid the pain of talking about details of incidents, or because they do not want to disclose specifics to an experimenter.

However, the fact that patients show similar recall failures during therapy sessions after a great deal of trust has been established and many painful areas already discussed argues against the phenomenon being a consciously deliberate strategy. This does not preclude the possibility that these patients' encoding and retrieval processes are automatically censoring the input and output of specific information, and this possibility deserves further enquiry.

Clinical Implications: Autobiographical
Memory and Problem Solving

Cognitive theories of emotional disorder link the maintenance,
incubation of, and speed of recovery from emotional disturbance to
the tendency some people have to overgeneralize from one event to
another. When such overgeneralization takes place, any stressful
situation appears to be more catastrophic than is, in reality, the case.
Measures of such tendencies to give global negative self-descriptions
have been found to predict the course of depression (Dent & Teasdale,
1988). We believe that such overgeneralization arises from underlying
deficits in the way memories relating to the self are encoded and
retrieved. Access to specific positive events is impaired in a crisis, at
the moment when specific recall would be most useful in suggesting
antidepressive strategies. Even outside the crisis, both positive and
negative memories are linked together in a summary form. Under
these circumstances, problem solving is likely to suffer. Both the
definition of a problem and the generation of alternative solutions
demands an ability to adequately address the memory "database."

For example, let us imagine a case in which a person is unhappy
and trying to think of things that would help his or her mood. He/she
tries to remember things that have helped in the past. If he or she can
only retrieve the generic memory "When I have been with Bill," this
memory will not itself suggest many alternative ways out of the
unhappy situation (especially if Bill's leaving is the cause of the
misery). Contrast the situation for the person who is not prone to
emotional disorders but is unhappy at the moment and tries to
remember what has made him or her happy. For this person, a more
specific memory such as "When I was with Marsha, Zindel, and
friends in the pub at Grantchester last June" may be retrieved. This
more specific memory provides a richer database from which one
can generate alternative strategies for one's current problems (each
individual friend, the pub, Grantchester, last June), and each of these
may cue other alternatives. My colleagues and I are currently in the
process of collecting data to address these links more explicitly. For
example, a colleague, Julie Evans, has been assessing both overgeneral
memory and problem solving, using the Means–End Problem Solving Task (Platt & Spivack, 1975). She has found that suicidal patients
who are most overgeneral in their memory generate the least effective alternative ways of solving the problems.

These findings are reminiscent of two older studies that have
focused on specificity of processing. Truax and Carkhuff (1967)
studied verbal interaction in group psychotherapy. They found that

independent ratings of specificity were correlated with a patient's score on a Process Scale designed to measure depth of self-exploration, and on an Insight Scale designed to measure occurrence of new perceptions of relations between old experiences or feelings. This suggests that generic memories are not helpful for therapeutic process. It is consistent with the clinical impression that greater benefit is obtained in cognitive therapy if depressed patients are able to go beyond the general statement "I've always been a failure" or "I used to be so happy" to describe the details of particular instances when they feel they have failed, or been happy.

Second, a study by Wahler and Afton (1980) showed how change in memory strategies that takes place within a psychotherapy session is unlikely to have lasting benefits unless it changes the strategy that a patient uses outside a therapeutic situation. They found that disturbed mothers who had relationship problems with their children were often unable to give detailed accounts of their childrens' behavior. They assumed that these mothers, on seeing their children misbehave, ignore the elements that are specific to that particular situation and quickly classify their child's behavior as naughty or malicious. Wahler and Afton (1980) monitored this tendency to be overgeneral as treatment progressed. There was a significant association between overall outcome (assessed independently on several clinical variables) and the degree to which mothers had become more specific in the descriptions of stress situations. Of course, no claims about cause or effect can be made on the basis of these treatment data, but it is consistent with the notion that a cognitive style that tends to produce overgeneral memories is intimately linked to real-world problems in living. It also makes clear that, at least in some patients, this style may be changed by treatment.

I have suggested in this chapter that overgeneral recall of autobiographical material is not mood dependent. If this is true of the phenomena observed by Wahler and Afton (1980), it suggests that it is insufficient for psychological treatments merely to reduce the amount of mood disturbance. Lasting therapeutic progress will be made only if change is brought about in underlying cognitive processes that cause the preferential encoding or retrieval of overgeneral aspects of episodes.

Anamnestic Therapy

Anamnesis is the term given to the deliberate recollection of events from one's past. I suggest that training in anamnestic strategies should be explicitly built into structured psychotherapies with depressed and suicidal patients. First, patients should be encouraged to be vigilant for any occurrence of overgeneral memories (e.g., "I've always hated parties"; "Mary is never on time"; "We used to enjoy going out"). When patients are practiced at noticing such memories, training in how to search for a particular event should be given within treatment sessions. For example, cues such as activities, places, people, or time periods might be systematically tried, until the particular combination of cues that is most helpful for that individual is found. Clearly, using these techniques with positive memories holds the greatest hope for affecting current mood and problem solving and could be recommended for use between therapy sessions. However, a systematic approach to learning to recall specific negative experiences within therapy sessions using similar cues may be helpful. That is because they will encourage patients to go beyond the generic labelling of such negative events. The result is that additional aspects of the individual events will be recalled. Noticing such new information will assist in the reinterpretation of the events.

The data and theories that I have discussed suggest that where such anamnesis is already part of therapy, it is effective because it allows the person to gain access to specific event records independently of the generic category into which the event has been encoded. It will have beneficial effects on problem solving when it results in a more elaborate database of specific past events that can be used to generate effective solutions to current problems. Already in more structured psychotherapies (e.g., cognitive therapy, Beck et al., 1979; self-control therapy, Rehm, Fuchs, Roth, Kornblith, & Romano, 1979), diaries are used extensively to record activities, moods, and thoughts. I suggest that these are important not just because they record significant processes, but because they encourage such specific encoding and retrieval. I would predict that a patient's ability to use (or be easily taught to use) such diaries would be a good prognostic indicator for predicting the eventual outcome of psychotherapy. This is because such ability is a marker for individual difference in ability to retrieve specific memories.

CONCLUDING REMARKS

This line of research has built upon the very useful foundation laid by Bower, Teasdale, and others in their experiments on mood–memory biasing. Our data forced us to look beyond their frameworks, however, towards those that had been investigating the encoding and retrieval processes in autobiographical memory.

In doing so, we were able to move beyond the quantitative aspects of memory (how much more probable negative memories are relative to positive memories; or how much faster one type is accessed relative to the other). Instead we focused on the qualitative features of memory responses—how specific or generic they are. We found that negative events are more easily accessible than pleasant events in emotionally disturbed patients, but a more salient feature was the difficulty in being specific in recalling events, particularly positive events. This tendency differs from person to person. Our data suggest that some people have a cognitive style of encoding and retrieving events at a generic level, a style that is easily assessed by simple cue-word methods. It appears that this memory phenomenon becomes especially prominent following stressful life events. Our preliminary conclusions about how memory is affected by and, in turn, contributes to the maintenance of emotional disorder has implications for structured psychotherapies such as cognitive therapy. These will need to include strategies that will make patients more aware of their biases in memory and particularly to help them encode and retrieve events more specifically. Only if this is done effectively will we be able to help patients prevent these memory biases feeding through to problem-solving deficits and into hopelessness for the future.

ACKNOWLEDGMENTS

I am grateful to my colleagues Keith Broadbent and Barbara Dritschel for help with the studies reported here; to Alan Baddeley, Debra Bekerian, Donald Broadbent, Don Norman, and David Rubin for helpful discussions about the theoretical issues involved; and to Sven-Åke Christianson and John Kihlstrom for helpful comments on the text of this chapter.

REFERENCES

Baddeley, A. D. (1981). The cognitive psychology of everyday life. *British Journal of Psychology, 72*, 257–269.

Beck, A. T., Rush, B. F., Shaw, A. J., & Emery, G. (1979). *Cognitive therapy of depression.* New York & Chichester: Wiley.

Beck, A. T., Weissman, A., Lester, D., & Trexler, L. (1974). The measurement of pessimism: The hopelessness scale. *Journal of Consulting & Clinical Psychology, 42*, 861–865.

Blaney, P. H. (1986). Affect and memory: A review. *Psychological Bulletin, 99,* 229–246.

Bower, G. H., & Mayer, J. D. (1985). Failure to replicate mood-dependent retrieval. *Bulletin of the Psychonomics Society, 23,* 39–42.

Brown, G. W. (1989). Depression: A radical social perspective. In K. R. Herbst & E. S. Paykel (Eds.), *Depression: An integrative approach.* Oxford: Heinemann Medical Books.

Brown, G. W., & Harris, T. O. (1978). *Social origins of depression: A study of psychiatric disorder in women.* London: Tavistock Publications, New York: Free Press.

Clark, D. M., & Teasdale, J. D. (1982). Diurnal variation in clinical depression and accessibility of positive and negative experiences. *Journal of Abnormal Psychology, 91,* 87–95.

Conway, M. A., & Bekerian, D.A. (1987). Organisation in autobiographical memory. *Memory & Cognition, 15,* 119–132.

Dent, J., & Teasdale, J. D. (1988). Negative cognition and the persistence of depression. *Journal of Abnormal Psychology, 97,* 29–34.

Fogarty, S. J., & Hemsley, D. R. (1983). Depression and the accessibility of memories—a longitudinal study. *British Journal of Psychiatry, 142,* 232–237.

Gilligan, S. G., & Bower, G. H. (1984). Cognitive consequences of emotional arousal. In C. Izard, J. Kagen, & R. Zajonc (Eds.), *Emotions, cognitions & behaviour* pp. 547–588. New York: Cambridge University Press.

Hasher, L., Rose, K. C., Zacks, R. T., Sanft, H., & Doren, B. (1985). Mood, recall and selectivity effects in normal college students. *Journal of Experimental Psychology: General, 114,* 104–118.

Kolodner, J. (1985). Memory for experience. In G. Bower (Ed.), *The psychology of learning & motivation* (Vol. 19, pp. 1–57). New York: Academic Press.

Linehan, M. (1988). Dialectical behaviour therapy for borderline personality disorder: Theory and method. *The Bulletin of the Menninger Clinic, 51,* 261–276.

Lloyd, G. G., & Lishman, W. A. (1975). Effect of depression on the speed of recall of pleasant and unpleasant experiences. *Psychological Medicine, 5,* 173–180.

McNair, D. M., Lorr, M., & Droppleman, L. F. (1981). *Manual for the profile of mood states* (2nd ed.). San Diego: Edets.

Moore, Watts, F. N., & Williams, J. M. G. (1988). The specificity of personal memories in depression. *British Journal of Clinical Psychology, 27,* 275–276.

Neisser, U., & Winograd, E. (1988). *Remembering reconsidered: Ecological and traditional approaches to the study of memory.* Cambridge, New York: Cambridge University Press.

Norman, D. A., & Bobrow, D. G. (1979). Descriptions: An intermediate stage in memory retrieval. *Cognitive Psychology, 11,* 107–123.

Pillemer, D. B., Goldsmith, L. R., Panter, A. T., & White, S. H. (1988). Very long-term memories of the first year in college. *Journal of Experimental Psychology: Learning, Memory, & Cogition, 14,* 709–715.

Platt, J. J., & Spivack, G. (1975). Manual for the Mean–Ends Problem Solving Test (MEPS): A measure of intepersonal problem solving skill. Philadelphia: Hahnemann Medical College and Hospital.

Rehm, L. P., Fuchs, C. Z., Roth, D. M., Kornblith, S. J., & Romano, J. M. (1979). A comparison of self-control and assertion skills treatment of depression. *Behaviour Therapy, 10,* 429–442.

Reiser, B. J., Black, J. B., & Abelson, R. P. (1985). Knowledge structures in the organization and retrieval of autobiographical memories. *Cognitive Psychology, 17,* 89–137.

Richards, A., & Whittaker, T. M. (1990). Effects of anxiety and mood manipulation in autobiographical memory. *The British Journal of Clinical Psychology, 29,* 145–154.

Rubin, D. C. (Ed.) (1986). *Autobiographical memory.* New York: Cambridge University Press.

Salavoy, P., & Singer, J. A. (1985, August). *Mood and recall of autobiographical memories.* Paper given at APA, Los Angeles.

Salkovskis, P. M., Atha, C., & Storer, D. (1990). Cognitive behavioural problem solving in the treatment of patients who repeatedly attempt suicide: A controlled trial. *British Journal of Psychiatry, 157,* 871–876.

Schank, R. C., & Abelson, R. P. (1977). *Script plans goals and understanding.* Hillsdale, NJ: Lawrence Erlbaum Associates.

Scott, J., Williams, J. M. G., & Beck, A. T. (1989). *Cognitive therapy in clinical practice: An illustrative casebook.* London: Routledge.

Teasdale, J. D., & Fogarty, S. J. (1979). Differential effects of induced mood on retrieval of pleasant and unpleasant memories from episodic memory. *Journal of Abnormal Psychology, 88,* 248–257.

Teasdale, J. D., Taylor, R., & Fogarty, S. J. (1980). Effects of induced elation-depression on the accessibility of memories of happy and unhappy experiences. *Behaviour Research & Therapy, 18,* 339–340.

Truax, C. B., & Carkhuff, R. R. (1967). *Concreteness: A neglected variable in research in psychotherapy.* Unpublished manuscript, Psychotherapy Research Program, Universities of Kentucky and Wisconsin.

Velten, E. (1968). A laboratory task for induction of mood states. *Behaviour Research & Therapy, 6,* 473–482.

Wahler, R. G., & Afton, A. D. (1980). Attentional processes in insular and non-insular mothers: Some differences in their summary reports about child problem behaviours. *Child Behaviour Therapy, 2,* 25–41.

Williams, J. M. G. (1984). *The psychological treatment of depression: A guide to the theory and practice of cognitive behaviour therapy.* Beckenham: Croom Helm, UK, and New York: Free Press.

Williams, J. M. G., & Broadbent, K. (1986). Autobiographical memory in attempted suicide patients. *Journal of Abnormal Psychology, 95,* 144–149.

Williams, J. M. G., & Dritschel, B. (1988). Emotional disturbance and the specificity of autobiographical memory. *Cognition & Emotion, 2,* 221–234.

Williams, J. M. G., & Scott, J. (1988). Autobiographical memory in depression. *Psychological Medicine, 18,* 689–695.

Williams, J. M. G., Watts, F. N., MacLeod, C, & Matthews, A. (1988). *Cognitive psychology and emotional disorders.* Chichester: Wiley.

Williams, M. D., & Hollan, J. D. (1981). Process of retrieval from very long term memory. *Cognitive Science, 5,* 87–119.

Author Index

Subject Index